MARK

This volume provides a comprehensive, accessible introduction to the Gospel of Mark, now widely considered the first recorded treatment of Jesus. Darrell Bock explains how this text, once the least-used Gospel, came to be regarded as the starting point for understanding Jesus. Drawing together previous arguments and discussion in a constructive summary, he traces the significance of Mark and addresses key features such as its cultural and historical background, its narrative flow, and the role of Greek in supplying meaning. This commentary highlights the issues Mark's Gospel raises and develops Mark's message surrounding Jesus' claims of kingdom authority and salvation, the call to disciples to follow him, and the preparation of those disciples to face suffering in light of their choice. *Mark* will be a valuable resource for students, teachers, and pastors alike.

Darrell Bock is Executive Director of Cultural Engagement and Senior Research Professor of New Testament Studies at Dallas Theological Seminary. He is the author or editor of more than thirty books, and his recent publications include *Truth in a Culture of Doubt: Engaging Skeptical Challenges to the Bible* (with Andreas J. Köstenberger and Josh D. Chatraw) and *Parables of Enoch: A Paradigm Shift* (with James H. Charlesworth).

NEW CAMBRIDGE BIBLE COMMENTARY

GENERAL EDITOR: Ben Witherington III

HEBREW BIBLE/OLD TESTAMENT EDITOR: Bill T. Arnold

The *New Cambridge Bible Commentary* (NCBC) aims to elucidate the Hebrew and Christian Scriptures for a wide range of intellectually curious individuals. While building on the work and reputation of the *Cambridge Bible Commentary* popular in the 1960s and 1970s, the NCBC takes advantage of many of the rewards provided by scholarly research over the last four decades. Volumes utilize recent gains in rhetorical criticism, social scientific study of the Scriptures, narrative criticism, and other developing disciplines to exploit the growing advances in biblical studies. Accessible jargon-free commentary, an annotated "Suggested Readings" list, and the entire New Revised Standard Version (NRSV) text under discussion are the hallmarks of all volumes in the series.

PUBLISHED VOLUMES IN THE SERIES
Psalms, Walter Brueggemann and William H. Bellinger, Jr.
Matthew, Craig A. Evans
Genesis, Bill T. Arnold
Exodus, Carol Meyers
Judges and Ruth, Victor H. Matthews
1–2 Corinthians, Craig S. Keener
The Gospel of John, Jerome H. Neyrey
James and Jude, William F. Brosend II
Revelation, Ben Witherington III

FORTHCOMING VOLUMES
Deuteronomy, Brent Strawn
Joshua, Douglas A. Knight
1–2 Chronicles, William M. Schniedewind
Isaiah 1–39, Jacob Stromberg
Jeremiah, Baruch Halpern
Hosea, Joel, and Amos, J. J. M. Roberts
The Gospel of Luke, Amy-Jill Levine and Ben Witherington III
The Letters of John, Duane F. Watson

Mark

Darrell Bock
Dallas Theological Seminary

CAMBRIDGE
UNIVERSITY PRESS

32 Avenue of the Americas, New York, NY 10013–2473, USA

Cambridge University Press is part of the University of Cambridge.

It furthers the University's mission by disseminating knowledge in the pursuit of education, learning, and research at the highest international levels of excellence.

www.cambridge.org
Information on this title: www.cambridge.org/9781107677678

First published 2015

Printed in the United States of America

A catalog record for this publication is available from the British Library.

Library of Congress Cataloging in Publication Data
Bock, Darrell.
Mark / Darrell Bock.
   pages cm. – (New Cambridge Bible commentary)
Includes bibliographical references and index.
ISBN 978-1-107-03421-1 (alk. paper)
1. Bible. Mark – Commentaries.   2. Jesus Christ – Person and offices.
3. Jesus Christ – Historicity.   I. Title.
BS2585.53.B63   2015
226.3′07–dc23   2015020957

ISBN 978-1-107-03421-1 Hardback
ISBN 978-1-107-67767-8 Paperback

Contents

Preface

This commentary on Mark is designed for anyone interested in the meaning, background, and discussion of this Gospel. It is designed to lead the reader into the text as well as guide one into further study if that is desired. References throughout are designed to tell the reader where useful additional discussion can be found. The introduction is purposefully selective, dealing with core issues of how Mark became important to Gospel study as well as issues of author, date, and setting. The list of suggested readings is organized by passage unit, so that study in a given passage is facilitated by the presence of its support materials. Not all the passages listed in the suggested readings are cited in the discussion in the text, so these lists truly supplement the passage discussion by pointing to a wider array of resources.

I worked through Mark with a collection of major commentaries at hand. They were my discussion partners for the book. You will see them referred to regularly, as one of my goals was to reflect the discussion they raise about the book. Issues of meaning and historical background are my focus in the commentary. The goal was to allow the reader quick access to the major issues that a passage raises.

I want to thank Cambridge University Press for the invitation to contribute to the *New Cambridge Bible Commentary* series. Ben Witherington was kind enough to ask me to write on Mark and was an encouragement along the way. I also need to thank my intern, Heather Zimmermann, who worked diligently in running down references as well as carefully and thoughtfully reading the draft. Her ability to ask good questions and think through what I was saying has enhanced what I have said. Her contribution mirrors what I have experienced during more than three decades of teaching – that excellent students make teaching a joy and stimulate learning. So I dedicate the commentary to my students who have taught me so much. I hope many of them will find this commentary useful and see it as an expression of appreciation for their own dedicated commitment to learn more about Mark.

Abbreviations

This list contains only works and periodicals cited in the commentary. Standard abbreviations have been used for ancient works as well as for works noted in the suggested readings.

ABD	*Anchor Bible Dictionary*
ABRL	Anchor Bible Reference Library
ANRW	*Aufstieg und Niedergang der römischen Welt*
ATR	*Anglican Theological Review*
BAR	*Biblical Archaeology Review*
BDAG	Bauer, Danker, Arndt, Gingrich, *A Greek-English Lexicon of the New Testament*
BDF	Blass, Debrunner, Funk, *A Greek Grammar of the New Testament*
BECNT	*Baker Exegetical Commentary on the New Testament*
BEThL	*Bibliotheca ephemeridum theologicarum lovaniensium*
Bib	*Biblica*
BRev	*Bible Review*
CBQ	*Catholic Biblical Quarterly*
CBR	*Currents in Biblical Research*
CM	*Christianity in the Making*
EKKNT	*Evangelisch-katholischer Kommentar zum Neuen Testament*
ET	English translation
GfC	*Geschichte des frühens Christentums*
HTR	*Harvard Theological Review*
Int	*Interpretation*
IRT	*Issues in Religion and Theology*
JBL	*Journal of Biblical Literature*
JETS	*Journal of the Evangelical Theological Society*

JJS	*Journal of Jewish Studies*
JQR	*Jewish Quarterly Review*
JR	*Journal of Religion*
JSNT	*Journal for the Study of the New Testament*
JSNTSup	*Journal for the Study of the New Testament Supplement Series*
JTS	*Journal of Theological Studies*
KTU	*Keilalphabetische Texte aus Ugarit*
LSJ	Liddell, Scott, Jones, *A Greek-English Lexicon*
NIGTC	*New International Greek Testament Commentaries*
NLT	New Testament Library
NovT	*Novum Testamentum*
NTS	*New Testament Studies*
PRR	Princeton Readings in Religion
ResQ	*Restoration Quarterly*
SBLSymS	Society of Biblical Literature Symposium Series
TDNT	*Theological Dictionary of the New Testament*
TLZ	*Theologische Literaturzeitung*
WBC	*Word Biblical Commentary*
WUNT	*Wissenschafliche Untersuchungen zum Neuen Testament*
ZDPV	*Zeitschrift für des deutschen Palästina-Vereins*
ZNThG	*Zeitschrift für Neuere Theologiegeschichte*
ZNW	*Zeitschrift für die Neutestamentliche Wissenschaft*

I. Introduction to Mark

INTRODUCTION

This introduction will focus on two issues as it summarizes the commentary discussion of the setting of Mark. Initially we give consideration to issues of authorship, setting, and date, not discussing each category separately, but rather looking at how commentators have handled the combination. The key questions here revolve around whether we can identify the Mark tied to the Gospel, whether he had connections to Peter, and whether Mark was written before or after the destruction of Jerusalem. This forms the backdrop for my own discussion of where I place the setting of the Gospel, its themes, and other key issues tied to it.[1]

COMMENTARY DISCUSSION OF AUTHOR, DATE, AND SETTING

The common scholarly position that Mark is the earliest Gospel means that there has been an intensification of attention paid to this Gospel. This attention has resulted in several excellent commentaries, some of which I will discuss in groups for reasons of space. Because there are so many valuable treatments, our survey of commentaries on Mark will not review Synoptic Gospel issues, but will focus on questions tied to Mark's setting, date, and authorship.

---

[1] This introductory discussion combines two previous pieces I have done elsewhere. "Commentaries on the Synoptic Gospels: Traditional Issues of Introduction," in *On the Writing of New Testament Commentaries: Festschrift for Grant R. Osborne on the Occasion of His 70th Birthday,* eds. Stanley E. Porter and Eckhard J. Schnabel (Leiden: Brill, 2012), 339–63, and "The Gospel of Mark and the Historical Jesus," in *Jesus Research: New Methodologies and Perceptions. The Second Princeton-Prague Symposium on Jesus Research,* ed. James Charlesworth with Bryan Rhea (Grand Rapids: Eerdmans, 2014), 551–76.

Vincent Taylor's classic commentary works faithfully through the Greek text.[2] It does not have a plethora of background discussion, since key Second Temple finds came after the bulk of his work. Still, the commentary is a useful treatment of Mark with a full introduction of 149 pages. This introduction covers the history of the Gospel in the early church and in modern criticism; it provides a careful look at the manuscripts behind the text, vocabulary syntax and style, the Semitic background of the Gospel, his sources, the Markan materials, and its forms, literary structure, arrangement, theology, and historical value. On authorship, Taylor argues there can be no doubt the author was Mark, Peter's attendant. He argues that the external testimony to Mark is unanimous and that Mark is not a likely candidate to surface as author unless there was a reason to make the connection. He says the Gospel shows local knowledge of the region (places like Bethphage, Bethany, Gethsemene, and Golgotha). The Gospel dates to the decade of the sixties, with AD 65–67 likely, given things like the emphasis on persecution and suffering as well as Gentile freedom from the law. It was probably written for Rome as the anti-Marcionite prologue, Irenaeus, and Clement of Alexandria testify.

Another major commentary from a past generation is from C. E. B. Cranfield.[3] It also is focused on the Greek text and treats historicity questions unit by unit. The introduction is a crisp twenty-six pages. Like Taylor, Cranfield argues the authorship is not open to serious doubt. He responds to claims about uncertainty from Jerome and the lack of mention of many writers before him as assuming the identity as known. He challenges the idea that Mark has got the reference to the timing of Passover wrong as evidence against Markan authorship. Mark is to be dated between 65 and 70 CE. Mark writes for Gentiles, since he explains Jewish customs (Mark 7:3–4; 15:42). Rome is the likely locale, and its quick wide dissemination, as evidenced by its use in the other Gospels, also suggests the support of a key church. He sees Mark as an "extremely honest and conscientious compiler."[4] Mark had contact with Peter and used oral tradition. The fact that witnesses, both hostile and believing, were alive when he wrote limits the possibility of embellishment. Mark's willingness to publish embarrassing material also speaks to his general reliability.

---

2   *The Gospel According to St Mark: The Greek Text with Introduction, Notes and Indexes.* 2nd ed. (London: Macmillan 1966). The first edition was published in 1952.
3   *The Gospel According to St Mark.* The Cambridge Greek Commentary (Cambridge: Cambridge University Press, 1959). Supplemental notes were last added in 1977.
4   Cranfield, *St Mark*, 16.

Two more modest commentaries from the United Kingdom by Hurtado and Hooker express uncertainty about the exact setting of Mark.[5] Both regard the only case for Mark being John Mark as the claims of tradition. They do not so much argue against Mark as argue there is no compelling evidence for him as the author. Hooker argues the identification may come from a deduction by Papias working with 1 Peter 5:13. Of course, Papias' claim, as reported in Eusebius, is that his knowledge of this link is from conversation in the context of his relationships, not from reading or hearing a text (through John the Elder, see Eusebius, *Ecclesiastical History* 3.39.7). The author writes to Gentiles explaining Semitic terms and Jewish customs. Hurtado argues the Gospel was written in a window from 50–75 CE, whereas Hooker opts for a date right around (probably after) 70 CE, somewhere between 65 and 75 CE. Dating is related to two issues: how the Olivet discourse is seen (give evidence of a post-destruction setting or not?) and how early to place it in light of dating of the other Synoptics. The setting might be Rome, but neither commentator stakes much in the possibility. What both commentators do is discuss the debate that goes on about Mark between historical roots and adaptation to the setting. Hooker argues that there is not creation of material *ex nihilo*, but there is adaptation of materials in arrangement, wording, and presentation. Both commentators stress the writing of the Gospel to present and defend the suffering of Jesus and the mystery of his messiahship as roots for a call to followers to be prepared to suffer in the journey of discipleship.

Two very full commentaries going different ways on the setting are by Rudolf Pesch and Robert Gundry.[6] Pesch's sixty-nine-page introduction makes a case against accepting the traditional ascription of authorship to John Mark. As Hooker does, Pesch sees the connection as informed by an awareness of the 1 Peter link of Mark and Peter and uncertainty that John the Elder (noted by Eusebius of Papias) knew of a relationship between Peter and Mark. A desire for apologetic strengthening of the Gospel has forged the link. The author may have been named Mark, but cannot be tied to John Mark and to Peter. The locale is likely not Rome, but a Gentile-oriented community in the East (Galilee, Syria, or the Decapolis). The date,

---

[5] Larry W. Hurtado, *Mark*. New International Biblical Commentary (Peabody, MA: Hendrickson, 1989); Morna D. Hooker, *The Gospel According to Saint Mark*. Black's New Testament Commentaries (Peabody, MA: Hendrickson, 1991).

[6] Pesch, *Das Markusevanglium*. Herders theologisicher Kommentar zum Neuen Testament. New ed. (Freiburg: Herder, 1984); Gundry, *Mark: A Commentary on His Apology for the Cross* (Grand Rapids: Eerdmans, 1993).

because of the Olivet discourse and the dates of the Gospels that used Mark, is post-70 CE. Gundry saves his introduction for the end of his commentary. It runs twenty-nine detailed pages. He argues that the traditional ascription to Mark is old, reaching back to circa 100 CE, not 130 as many claim, and the conversation being passed on seems to belong to the late first century and involves only three steps (apostles, those who heard the apostles, Papias). The chronological order of discussion in Eusebius' *Chronicon* is for this conclusion. John the Elder and John the Apostle are not distinct figures as some argue, nor is Mark distinct from John Mark. This tradition is "as early and authoritative as one could wish."[7] Details against this Markan connection to authorship on claims of community forming (versus a singular author background), supposed errors in Palestinian and Syrian geography (especially as it relates to issues in the north), ignorance of Jewish customs, the Gospel's handling of Peter, and appeals to 1 Peter 5:13 are not substantive objections, as Gundry works through each category one at a time. His responses are to the point with perhaps the one exception tied to issues of geography, which if they were to have come through Peter would not involve someone unconnected to the north, as Gundry claims for Mark by seeing the evangelist as a Jerusalemite responsible for these discrepancies. Gundry dates the Gospel pre-70 CE, likely before Peter died in the early sixties. He also contends for Rome as the locale, as extensive Latinisms in the book suggest. Mark is an apologetic, defending the cross and Jesus' suffering as part of God's plan where the cross is a cause of glory. Such a theme would be very appropriate for this locale where Christians were facing rising persecution.

The Word Biblical Commentary for Mark has been shared by two authors, Robert Guelich and Craig Evans, with the latter currently engaged in revising work on Mark 1:1–8:26 so his treatment of the Gospel can be full.[8] This commentary is a very full treatment of issues and exegesis tied to Mark and follows the Word commentary format. Guelich's introduction is a mere twenty-four pages, but covers the key issues well. He defends the age of the authorship tradition and its roots. He argues there is no hard evidence for making a distinction between Mark and John Mark, calling it "special pleading." He notes that Papias' explanation of Petrine roots for

---

7   Gundry, *Mark*, 1034.
8   Robert A. Guelich, *Mark 1:1–8:26*. Word Biblical Commentary (Dallas: Word, 1989); Craig Evans, *Mark 8:27–16:20*. Word Biblical Commentary (Nashville: Thomas Nelson, 2001). Evans hopes to have the volume out in a few more years.

the material is oversimplified, given the evidence of the tradition in Mark being similar in form to what we see about Jesus elsewhere in the tradition. A question remaining for Guelich is the influence of someone like Peter on the traditions about Jesus that circulated broadly in the church. Guelich sees the remarks of Papias about Mark's lack of order as having less to do with chronology and more to do with rhetoric as fits a Greco-Roman context. He responds to geographical issues as Gundry did, noting the references are not as improbable as some claim. The locale of the Gospel is uncertain, with Latinisms slightly favoring the traditional locale of Rome. He sees it as more likely the Gospel was written at the beginning of Rome's War with the Jews than after Jerusalem's fall, so 67–69 CE. What this commentary on Mark shares between its two authors is full references to potential background from the Second Temple context, something Evans especially brings to his treatment of Mark.

Similar in approach to the setting is the work by Ben Witherington and his sixty-two-page introduction.[9] For him, the Latinisms are the key evidence the work is rooted in Rome and not from a setting farther east. Order is about rhetoric, not chronology, as the remarks of Papais are full of rhetorical technical terminology that Witherington traces in some detail. It is hard to imagine someone making up a connection to Mark. Rather the tradition shows signs of being quite old and early. He also notes that Mark's themes on suffering and servanthood suggest a Pauline connection as well. Rome as the setting makes sense. The Gospel fits a post-Neronian persecution context in which Mark is defending the need to persevere through persecution. A date in the latter period from AD 66–70 is likely.

A classic evangelical commentary on Mark comes from William Lane.[10] He sees Mark's task as "the projection of Christian faith in a context of suffering and martyrdom."[11] Twenty-eight pages of introduction overview Gospel criticism as well as the background for the Gospel. The rise of persecution meant Roman Christians needed to see the parallel between their situation and that of Jesus. He places the Gospel in the aftermath of the Neronian persecution in the second half of the sixties, agreeing with the testimony from the anti-Marcionite prologue and Irenaeus. The author is John Mark. Lane notes that Papias both sees a key role for Peter and yet

---

[9]   Witherington, *The Gospel of Mark: A Socio-Rhetorical Commentary* (Grand Rapids: Eerdmans, 2001).

[10] Lane, *The Gospel According to Mark*. The New International Commentary on the New Testament (Grand Rapids: Eerdmans, 1974).

[11] Lane, *Mark*, 15.

recognizes the initiative and independence of Mark. The Roman setting fits the Latinisms and the use of a four-watch method of reckoning time.

On the other hand, Eugene Boring produces a commentary that emphasizes Mark's theological creativity as an evangelist.[12] He argues in a consistent and thorough way for some distance between the Jesus of history and the Christ of faith. In fact, if one desires a handy source for how the argument can be made for Mark presenting an apocalyptic take on Jesus that incorporates the Messianic secret as well as the abiding tension between what he calls "Kenosis Christology" and "Epiphany Christology," then this commentary is an excellent guide. The key statement that drives the commentary is that

Whatever the first readers knew of the life-story of Jesus of Nazareth was subverted by the Markan story. They were not familiar with this plot: Jesus' presence in Galilee, his single journey to Jerusalem to be rejected, tried and crucified, the resurrection, and the surprising silence of the women. It saw the light of day for the first time when Mark invented it.[13]

What Boring later calls a two-level story with the contemporary needs of Mark's audience almost always trumping any historical concerns is a consistent theme of Boring's treatment of Mark. Twenty-five pages of introduction introduce the setting. The Gospel was written somewhere between 65 and 75 CE. The author is "a Christian teacher who writes not as a charismatic individual but as a member of the community."[14] He seeks to curb the "irresponsible excesses" of the Christian prophets. Mark's tie to Peter is part of a later theological legitimization by the second-century church, given that the tradition is not consistent and is aimed at theological validity. The claim in defense of the tradition that the church would not make such a connection, given Mark's otherwise obscure role, is met with Boring's reply that such an argument is not used for non-canonical Gospels where apostolic names appear. However, the issue here involves both claimed authorship and reception, as well as a date that makes such an association even plausible. Mark has that combination, while the other Gospels Boring names (*Thomas, Judas, Matthias, Bartholomew*) do not, in part because there was doubt about the source of these other Gospels' materials. For Boring, the author may have been named Mark, but the material comes to him through community tradition versus contact with

[12]   Boring, *Mark: A Commentary*. The New Testament Library (Louisville: Westminster John Knox Press, 2006).
[13]   Boring, *Mark*, 9.
[14]   Boring, *Mark*, 20.

eyewitnesses such as Peter. The Gospel lacks accuracy about Palestine or Palestinian Judaism in references we will note and discuss later in our evaluation of Mark and the ancient testimony about his potential association with Peter. Mark likely wrote for Syria or Galilee. The message encourages discipleship in a threatening, confused, and conflicted situation. It is a work designed to edify his readers in faith.

Another full presentation of the Gospel comes from Joel Marcus.[15] His introduction is sixty-two pages. Someone named Mark is the likely author, since the adoption of this name as a pseudonym is unlikely. More than that, the obscurity of this figure makes it likely that the name was attached for a reason. Against such a connection are the Gentile orientation of the Gospel and supposed issues tied to Jewish customs and Palestinian geography. Marcus argues the Gentile orientation does not make the author a non-Jew (e.g., Paul) but does see issues in the way what is said about handwashing in Mark 7 is treated, how the beginning of the day is reckoned in 14:12, and how the Law is handled in a kind of yes in terms of observing the thrust of the law (go to the temple, show mercy) but not the details (1:40–45; 2:23–28; 7:1–23). In the end, Marcus has responses to each of these concerns. For example, he notes the tension in how the law is seen is paralleled by the very Jewish Paul. He argues that positive evidence for John Mark is not overwhelming, since Marcus regards the strong apologetic tone in Papias as rendering that testimony suspect. So, in the end, Marcus argues we are likely dealing with a Mark, but not one with Petrine connections, although that connection cannot be entirely excluded. The case is "not proven."[16]

My own view stands in contrast to Marcus here. It seems difficult to accept the initial reception of this Gospel, if the Mark in question is an unknown or random Mark. Surely something that ended up circulating early in the church's distribution of accounts about Jesus would have had roots known to the early leaders who circulated it. After all, most Gospel scholars see Mark as a source used by the other Gospel writers.

Marcus argues that the setting more likely supposes a Syrian community and the Jewish War over a Roman context, even though there is no direct evidence of persecution of Christians in that war. Marcus argues such evidence does exist for the 132–35 CE war and that the same might have taken place earlier. The Gospel is written in the shadow of the Temple's destruction, between 69 and 74 CE.

---

[15] Marcus, *Mark 1–8*. The Anchor Bible (New York: Doubleday, 1999); *Mark 8–16*. The Anchor Yale Bible (New Haven: Yale University Press, 2009).
[16] Marcus, *Mark*, 24.

Adele Collins has produced a full commentary that carefully examines the social background to Mark's Gospel and is especially rich in Hellenistic sources.[17] Also full is her introduction, which comprises 125 pages. Mark is an eschatological sacred history written with an eye on Hellenistic historiography and biography. It is most like the didactic type of ancient biography as well as the historical type of ancient biography. It also has parallels with how Jews related history about key leaders like Moses, Elijah, Elisha, and David, but with an eschatological focus that serves as a counterpoint to these biblical foundational histories. She notes the importance of giving titles to works when they go public in the ancient world on the model of Galen's testimony in *De libris propriis liber*. This is a way to argue that the tradition tying the Gospel to Mark would likely have been old once it circulated. Papias is critical of Mark's lack of order, but has come to terms with it in the end. Collins argues that had 1 Peter 5 driven the identification, Silvanus would have likely been named as the Gospel's author. She sees the author as Jewish, not a Gentile, challenging claims in this direction that argue that the handling of Passover, handwashing, and the reckoning of the day by sunrise cannot come from a Jewish author. In the end, she appears to hold to the author as John Mark but never says so explicitly. Although the external evidence favors Rome as the setting, the internal evidence points to Syria. She notes that the geographical description of the Decapolis region, often challenged, has parallels in Pliny the Younger's work in that the area of Damascus is included (*Natural History* 5.16.74). The way coins are referenced also points to this setting.[18] She makes a plausible case for this setting, although Rome remains a possibility as well. A careful walk through Mark 13 leads her to conclude the Gospel is written in a window from 66 to 74 CE. The slight differences between what is said and what took place in 70 CE cause her to prefer a date in 68–69 CE. The Gospel is a historical work on the ancient model, articulated by Aristotle (*Rhetoric* 1.4.13 = 1360A), Quintilian (*Institutio Oratorio* 2.4.2), and Polybius (39.1.4 and 1.2.8) where memorable deeds are recorded. Collins also traces how the Messiah for Mark is tied to the revelation of the hidden Son of Man at the end of Jesus' ministry, a theme that has conceptual parallels in the *Similitudes* of *1 Enoch*. This suffering is a model for the discipleship Mark also highlights.

---

17   Collins, *Mark*. Hermeneia (Minneapolis: Fortress, 2007).
18   Collins follows the work of Gerd Theissen, *Gospels in Context: Social and Political History in the Synoptic Tradition* (Minneapolis: Fortress, 1991), for this position.

Two commentaries focused on application are by David Garland and myself.[19] Both accept John Mark as the author. Garland prefers a date that is pre-70 CE during the period of the war, an option Bock also regards as quite possible, while noting that an earlier date in the late fifties to early sixties is possible if one accepts a strand of tradition from Clement of Alexandria that argues Mark wrote before Peter died. Both accept a Roman setting for the Gospel. Garland's treatment spends much time in the movement toward application, as do all the NIV Application commentaries. Bock's treatment of Mark is more concise, moving quickly between notes on key points in the Gospel and commentary that summarizes the unit's argument in a brief space.

Robert Stein treats this Gospel for the Baker series.[20] His introduction is thirty-five pages. He also notes how the tradition surrounding Mark as the author is early. Stein notes how inventing a name for a Gospel involving a non-apostle would be unusual. He cites all the major witnesses to authorship from the tradition up to Jerome, thereby showing the early and widespread affirmation that Mark is the author. Stein argues for a Roman setting, as he notes that the author knew Jewish practice and Aramaic, but his audience did not, a point more likely for Rome than the Decapolis or Syria. He also deals with claims about supposed geographical, chronological, and customs discrepancies along the lines noted previously. He argues that traces of perspective from within Syria and Palestine point to the roots of the Gospel tradition Mark works with rather than being an indication of Mark's setting. The reference to a "Syrophoenician" makes more sense for a Roman audience than a Syrian one, where Phoenician would have sufficed. Latinisms and the right of women to divorce also fit here. Stein rejects the attempt to date Mark early (in the fifties or early sixties) by appealing to what he sees as the open ending of Acts as setting a limit to where Mark must fit. He argues that Luke ignores the Pauline prison outcome not because he writes before its resolution, but because it rounds out the goal of Acts, namely, to show how the message got to Rome. So a date before 62 CE is not required for Mark. Stein traces the lack of evidence for a post-70 CE perspective in Mark 13 and prefers a date of

---

[19] David Garland, *Mark*. The NIV Application Commentary (Grand Rapids: Zondervan, 1996); Darrell Bock, "The Gospel of Mark," in *Cornerstone Biblical Commentary: The Gospel of Matthew, The Gospel of Mark*. Vol. 11 (Carol Stream, IL: Tyndale House Publishers, 2005).

[20] Stein, *Mark*. Baker Exegetical Commentary on the New Testament (Grand Rapids: Baker Academic, 2008).

68–69 CE. Mark's Christology points to a "more-than-human" status for Jesus. He challenges the idea that the motif of the messianic secret is a Markan theological construction by noting its presence in primitive materials and the fact that a resurrection would not push one to make someone a messiah who was not already regarded as such. The secret makes historical sense because it averts direct challenge of Rome and was required to prevent misunderstanding about the type of suffering Jesus foresaw the Messiah possessing that the crowds did not anticipate. Stein also challenges the idea that Mark writes against the Twelve when he depicts them as so slow to respond to Jesus. He notes especially how positively they are portrayed at the start and the end of the Gospel, where they are even commissioned to take the message out (16:7). I might add that Peter gives the key confession of the book at Caesarea Philippi, a point that hardly shows the apostles as rejected figures. In the end, Mark wrote to encourage disciples in the face of persecution, appealing to the example of Jesus' own suffering.

R. T. France has written a forty-five-page introduction that spends more time setting up his commentary than engaging in detailed introductory discussion.[21] France says his commentary is about the exegesis of Mark and not a commentary on commentaries that gets lost in discussing theories of textual or tradition origin. Mark is modeled on Greco-Roman biography. France defends the external tradition about Mark, relying heavily on the work by Martin Hengel on the second Gospel.[22] Hengel argues the Gospels would not have circulated anonymously once there was more than one circulating in the church. This would make authorship identification a very early activity for the church. A setting in Rome also seems to fit far better than a Syrian context. Translation of Aramaic, the explanation of terms like *two lepta* and the *aulē,* and the naming of the Syrophoenician woman point in this direction. France never explicitly discusses the date but questions the tradition that argues Mark wrote after Peter's death while also noting Hengel's preference for a date in 69 CE. He argues that because these Gospels were intended to circulate widely, determining a specific setting is not so important. For this emphasis, he appeals to work by Richard Bauckham who argues the Gospels were composed for a broad audience.[23]

21 France, *The Gospel of Mark.* The New International Greek Testament Commentary (Grand Rapids: Eerdmans, 2002).

22 Martin Hengel, *Studies in the Gospel of Mark.* ET (London: SCM, 1985).

23 Bauckham, ed. *The Gospel for All Christians: Rethinking the Gospel Audiences* (Edinburgh: T & T Clark, 1998).

HISTORICAL SETTING OF MARK AND EMERGENCE OF THE GOSPEL'S CENTRAL ROLE IN HISTORICAL JESUS DISCUSSION

For centuries the Gospel of Mark was the lost orphan among the Gospels. It was little used and mostly incorporated in the more widely circulated Matthew. All this changed in the nineteenth century when Jesus research undertook a new direction. The result was the rediscovery of the role of Mark within the Jesus tradition. Today Mark is the "most widely translated book in the world."[24] By the 1980s it had been rendered into more than 800 languages and dialects, a number that is surely even higher three decades later, given that many Bible translators now start with this Gospel once they codify a new language. In contrast, no major father of the church in the first five centuries wrote a commentary on Mark.[25]

In Jesus research today, Mark is a starting point or a key source for most serious historical treatments of Jesus. A few examples will suffice.

E. P. Sanders does not begin his *Jesus and Judaism* giving any benefit of the doubt to any particular Gospel source. He works one piece of material at a time, pointing out how events, and not just sayings, matter in discussing Jesus. But he questions whether the use of the criterion of authenticity can do the job. Finding a context for Jesus is a key element in the equation.[26] Sanders prefers to work with the context of Jesus' ministry and then see whether texts credibly fit into that context. For Sanders a key beginning point is that Jesus study "should situate Jesus believably in Judaism and yet explain why the movement initiated by him eventually broke with Judaism."[27] Although somewhat an artificial gauge, if we look at Sanders's index of scriptural passages, we see a study dominated by discussion rooted in Matthew and

---

[24] Seán P. Kealy, *Mark's Gospel: A History of Its Interpretation* (New York: Paulist Press, 1982), 1.

[25] Victor of Antioch in the fifth century complained about the lack of a commentary on Mark (Kealy, *Mark's Gospel*, 28). He produced a collection of allusions to Mark compiled from commentaries on other Gospels by past luminaries like Origen, Titus of Bostra, Theodore of Mopsuestia, John Chrysostom, and Cyril of Alexandria. Slightly later Gregory the Great finally composed a commentary on Mark. By contrast, for Augustine, Mark was but a slavish summarizer of Matthew (*Cons.* 1.2.4).

[26] Sanders, *Jesus and Judaism* (Philadelphia: Fortress, 1985), 1–58. More recently, Dale Allison has raised similar questions in "The Historians' Jesus and the Church," in *Seeking the Identity of Jesus: A Pilgrimage*, ed. B.R. Gaventa and R. B. Hays (Grand Rapids: Eerdmans, 2008), 79–95, here 79–83. The key criteria most often used are dissimilarity, multiple attestation, and coherence.

[27] Sanders, *Jesus and Judaism*, 18. He is working with Joseph Klausner's starting point here from his book, *Jesus of Nazareth: His Life, Times, and Teachings*. Trans. Herbert Danby (New York: Macmillan, 1957).

Mark. Matthew occupies seven and one-half columns, whereas Mark has five and one-half columns though it is only 60 percent as long as Matthew. By contrast, Luke is two columns long, despite being the longest Gospel, whereas John has only three-quarters of a column.

John P. Meier describes the canonical Gospels as "the major problem" in sorting out who Jesus was.[28] That these works are influenced by the faith of the writers is seen as a key difficulty, as is the fact that they do not claim or set themselves up to be a complete narrative of Jesus' life. Meier begins his treatment, following form critics of the 1920s, by noting how Mark offers remnants of oral and written traditions tied together by common words, themes, and forms. He lists the Galilean controversy stories of Mk 2:1–3:6, Jerusalem controversy stories of 11:27–12:34, miracle stories linked by the word *bread* in 6:6b–8:21, and the parables collection of 4:1–34. Meier notes we do not necessarily have chronological order in these texts. Nonetheless, we do have evidence of traditionally rooted "rosary beads" present in these texts. Their roots stretch back into the oral phase of the tradition. He sees Mark, with Q and John, as major sources for Jesus, with M and L also of potential significance.[29]

James D. G. Dunn has reintroduced in a serious way the role of oral tradition, while challenging a strictly literary model in his presentation of Jesus.[30] After surveying the topic of external sources and the earliest references to Jesus in Paul (1 Cor 15:3; Gal 1:18–20; 1 Cor 9:5), he begins his treatment of full sources with Mark, referring to it as a "primary source used by both Matthew and Luke."[31] He considers the overlap of material with Matthew especially to be a key argument, noting that 95 percent of Mark is found in either Matthew or Luke and 90 percent of Mark's subject matter reappears in Matthew. Combine this with the fact that where the texts overlap Mark is the longer version, it becomes likely that Mark is first in the sequence.[32] Some have questioned whether this was Mark as we have it now or some earlier version, commonly called *Ur-Markus*. At the least, most see the use of a source very much like our canonical Mark. These possible variations with Mark and the prehistory of such texts through oral

[28]   Meier, *A Marginal Jew: Rethinking the Historical Jesus.* Vol. 1: *The Roots of the Problem and the Person.* ABRL (New York: Doubleday, 1991), 41.

[29]   Ibid., 44.

[30]   Dunn, *Jesus Remembered.* CM 1 (Grand Rapids: Eerdmans, 2003).

[31]   Ibid., 144–46.

[32]   I shall return to such arguments and give more detail for Markan priority in the next section.

tradition lead Dunn to suggest the likelihood that things are more complicated than a strict literary dependence model. Nonetheless, Dunn gives
Mark a key role as one of our extant sources. In fact, despite the distinct
approaches of Sanders, Meier, and Dunn, all our examples recognize that
Mark serves as a key source about Jesus.

So we see the reasons for Mark's importance, even central role, in most
Jesus research. After reviewing what brought this original reassessment, we
will examine why Mark is seen to possess such a key role today.

Move to the Priority of Mark

What led to this repositioning of the Second Evangelist in Jesus studies? The
short answer is that the nineteenth century's focus on the Synoptic problem
led the way to this reassessment. This transition began with H. J. Holtzmann
in 1863 as he made the argument that Mark was the first written Gospel
among the canonical sources.[33] Although this discussion moved into the
twentieth century and solidified with B. H. Streeter's work in 1924, the tide
was already well turned by the end of the nineteenth century.[34]

Eight arguments have been set forth as evidence of Mark's priority
among the four Gospels.[35] Not all of these are equally persuasive, but as a
group they have led to something of a consensus that Mark is our earliest
available written source about Jesus.[36]

1. The first argument comes from Mark's length. Mark has 661 verses
   compared to Matthew's 1,068 and Luke's 1,149. (The rough count of
   words, depending on various textual decisions, is 11,025 in Mark versus
   Matthew's 18,293 and Luke's 19,376).[37] Such numbers have been crunched
   in a variety of ways, but (a) almost all of Mark is found in either Matthew

---

[33] Holtzmann, *Die synoptischen Evangelien: Ihr Ursprung und geschichtlicher Charakter* (Leipzig: Engelmann, 1863).

[34] Streeter, *The Four Gospels* (London: Macmillan, 1924).

[35] Robert Stein, *Studying the Synoptic Gospels: Origin and Interpretation.* 2nd ed. (Grand Rapids: Baker, 2001), 49–96.

[36] Various competing theories have been put forward, including the Augustinian hypothesis arguing that Matthew was first and Mark second, and the two-Gospel hypothesis arguing that Matthew was first and Mark third among the Synoptics. The vigorous defense of this latter view by William Farmer, *The Synoptic Problem: A Critical Analysis* (New York: Macmillan, 1964), has made this the second most popular approach to the question of the order of the Gospels. In the early church, Matthew was seen as the first account written, but no reason was given beyond the assertion in Clement of Alexandria's *Hypotyposes* that the Gospels with genealogies were written first (as Eusebius reports, *Hist. eccl.* 6.14.5).

[37] Stein, *Studying the Synoptic Gospels*, 50.

and/or Luke (on the order of 93 percent), and (b) when Mark parallels the other Gospels, his accounts are often more detailed, making unlikely the idea Mark is a summarizer of the other Gospels.[38] This last observation works against what has been called the Griesbach hypothesis (also called the two-Gospel hypothesis), which sees the Synoptic Gospel order as Matthew, Luke, and Mark.

The study of distinctive vocabulary in Matthew and Luke also indicates that Mark is unlikely to have used either of the other Gospels. Mark has 11,025 words, of which Matthew uses 10,072 and Luke 9,743. This is 97.2 percent of Mark's terms present in Matthew and 88.4 percent in Luke. Yet of Matthew's 18,239 words, 7,392 are missing from Mark, and 10,259 from Luke's 19,376 – 40.4 percent and 52.9 percent, respectively. Now, if Mark is based on either of these Gospels, why would Mark lack so much of their vocabulary? With such figures, it is hard to conceive of Mark following the other Gospels.

2. The second argument for Mark's priority is Mark's poorer expression, often improved by the other Gospels. This includes the reduction of redundancies (cf. Mt 9:14 = Mk 2:18 = Lk 5:33; Mt 12:3–4 = Mk 2:25–26 = Lk 6:3–4), as well as the fixing of grammatical details. Examples include Mark's use of an aorist middle in Mk 10:20 to express the rich man's observation of the law from his youth; Mt 19:20 and Lk 18:21 use the more grammatically correct aorist active here. The slang term *pallet* (*krabatton*) in Mk 2:4 is altered to "bed" in Matthew and Luke, but with different variations of the term (Matthew, *kilnēs*; Luke, *klinidiō*).

3. The next argument involves Mark's harder readings, which disappear in the other Gospels. For instance, Mk 6:5–6 records Jesus' inability to heal because of unbelief; this is softened in the parallels. There is the removal of criticism of the disciples; for instance, Mk 6:52 records their lack of understanding, which Matthew and Luke omit. Mark records that Abiathar, not his father Ahimelech, was high priest when David ate from the holy bread (Mk 2:25; 1 Sam 21:1–9; 22:20–23); Matthew and Luke remove this detail (Mt 12: 3–4; Lk 6:3–4). Mark 13:32 has the Son not knowing the time of the return of the Son of Man (cf. Mt 24:36; Acts 1:7–8).[39]

---

38 Stein (ibid., 53–55) has a table detailing this phenomenon. In 51 overlapping pericope, Mark is longer in 21, Matthew in 11, and Luke in 10, whereas in 10 pericope, two of the Gospels are of similar length.

39 Mt 24:36 is textually uncertain about whether the Son expresses his ignorance, but may indicate a smoothing out of this harder reading. Similar in point, but lacking any expression of ignorance, is Acts 1:7–8.

4. The fourth argument involves the number of combinations involving Markan agreements with other Gospels versus those excluding him. The force of this argument is debated. The claim is that the number of Matthew-Luke agreements against Mark is far fewer than options including Mark. This is true. However, as many as 500 cases of Matthean-Lukan agreements exist. Such a large number of non-Markan agreements has proven one of the more troublesome arguments used against Markan priority.

5. The argument from order made famous by Holtzmann has proven to be an important element in the case for Mark's priority. Matthew and Luke very often agree in order when Markan material is also present (and apparently being used). When the material is shared by only Matthew and Luke, they often disagree in order. In addition, Matthew and Luke are said to never agree in order against Mark, whereas Matthew and Mark do agree against Luke or Mark and Luke agrees against Matthew. Most see this as evidence that Mark is either first or last in the sequencing. However, the case against Mark being last seems to be precluded by its length and the strong impression that Mark does not look like a summarizer in how he handles specifics overlapping units.[40] This leaves Mark in first place.

The remaining arguments contend that when it comes to literary comparison (argument 6), the test of redaction (argument 7), and Mark's more primitive theology (argument 8), the second Gospel looks most often to be the earliest of the sequence. In argument 6, Matthew is often seen to reword or summarize Mark. For argument 8, the use of *kyrios* is the key example, being far more common in Matthew and Luke, including appearances in Matthew that are hard to explain if Mark and Luke agree (Mt 17:4 = Mk 9:5–6 = Lk 9:33). These details are more complex to assess, needing to be examined on a case-by-case basis, but a kind of cumulative weight has convinced most scholars that there is some merit to these arguments even if they are not as persuasive on their own as other arguments.

In sum, a careful look at comparisons between the Gospels has led many Jesus scholars over the last few centuries to give Mark first place among the written Gospels. Most of this detailed internal analysis of the Gospels took place in the nineteenth century and produced a shift in appreciation for Mark. The resultant position of Mark as the first of recorded witnesses

---

[40] The "summarizer" argument was noted earlier.

among the canonical sources catapulted it into a key position in Jesus research.

Ancient Testimony on Mark's Sources and the Roots of His Treatment of Jesus' Life

The ancient testimony about Mark connects him in an interesting way to Peter but also indicates that Mark was not an eyewitness to Jesus. Whether we think of Irenaeus or Papias' testimony about Mark through Eusebius, they both connect the second Gospel's Evangelist to Peter.[41] Here are the words of Irenaeus:

Matthew also issued a written Gospel among the Hebrews in their own dialect, while Peter and Paul were preaching at Rome, and laying the foundations of the Church. After their departure, Mark, the disciple and interpreter of Peter, did also hand down to us in writing what had been preached by Peter. (*Adv. haer.* 3.1.1)

The testimony of Papias comes to us through Eusebius. What makes these remarks significant is that Papias wrote in about 130 CE and had contact with some who had contact with the apostolic circle. Here is what Eusebius reports him as saying:

This also [John] the presbyter said: Mark having become the interpreter of Peter, wrote down accurately, though not in order, whatsoever he remembered of the things said or done by Christ. For he neither heard the Lord nor followed him, but afterward, as I said, he followed Peter, who adapted his teaching to the needs of his hearers, but with no intention of giving a connected account of the Lord's discourses, so that Mark committed no error while he thus wrote some things as he remembered them. For he was careful of one thing, not to omit any

---

[41]   Other early testimonies include, from the second century: the anti-Marcionite Prologues and Clement of Alexandria as cited by Eusebius, *Hist. eccl.* 2.15.2; 6.14.6-7; from the third century: Tertullian, *Marc.* 4.5.3 (also in *Hist. eccl.* 6.25.5); and from the fourth century, Jerome, *Vir. ill.* on Simon Peter 1.1 and *Comm. Matt.* preface 6 (also in *Hist. eccl.* 2.16.24). See also M. Eugene Boring, *Mark.* NTL (Louisville: Westminster John Knox, 2006), 10. For this section, also see Joel Marcus, *Mark 1-8: A New Translation with Introduction and Commentary.* AB 27 (New York: Doubleday, 2000), 17-24. Marcus's claim that some manuscripts circulating in the fourth century lack the superscription may be misreading the remarks of Adamantius, who spoke of no name of Mark being found in the Gospel. This may refer only to the Gospel proper, not to any additions or notes attached to it. See *The Dialogue on the Orthodox Faith,* a fourth-century work often known as Adamantius'. For the relevant portion of the text, see C. Clifton Black, *Mark: Images of an Apostolic Interpreter* (Studies on Personalities of the New Testament, 1994; repr., Minneapolis: Fortress, 2001), 150.

of the things which he had heard, and not to state any of them falsely." These things are related by Papias concerning Mark. (*Hist. eccl.* 3.39.15)[42]

The connection to John the Presbyter is Papias' claim that this information goes back to one who had access to the apostolic circle. According to tradition, Papias writes circa 130 CE, but Papias' research is older and the traditional date for Papias' remarks as coming from 130 CE can also be seen as being too late. These are points Richard Bauckham has argued.[43] Furthermore, Bauckham makes a full case that Mark does give evidence of a Petrine perspective. It should be recalled that Justin Martyr referred to the Gospel of Mark as Peter's memoirs (*Dial.* 106.3). Finally, it is very hard to see how the name Mark became so stubbornly applied unless *a* Mark wrote it. Joel Marcus makes the point well:

The relative insignificance of this person is one reason for thinking that the Gospel was actually written by a Mark; if, lacking a sure tradition of

[42] The entire citation on the Gospels, including the portion cited on Mark, is in Eusebius, *Hist. eccl.* 3.39.14–16. I will not get into the discussion of whether John the Elder equals John the Apostle, although that is possible. I will assume he is another person for this discussion. For the option that identifies them as the same person, see Robert H. Gundry, *Mark: A Commentary on His Apology for the Cross* (Grand Rapids: Eerdmans, 1993), 1029–34, who believes that Eusebius misunderstood Papias about a distinction between the two Johns.

[43] Richard Bauckham, *Jesus and the Eyewitnesses: The Gospels as Eyewitness Testimony* (Grand Rapids: Eerdmans, 2006), 12–21 for Papias, 155–82 for Mark and Peter. Bauckham has summarized his points about Papias in chapter 22 of this volume, "Gospel Traditions: Anonymous Community Traditions or Eyewitness Testimony?" Bauckham argues for the failure of the form-critical model and the need to take Papias' testimony seriously. We will evaluate the other arguments brought against Mark and the accuracy of the tradition later. As Bauckham notes, "There is no reason at all to regard Papias' claims in this passage as apologetic exaggeration, for they are strikingly modest" (*Jesus and the Eyewitnesses*, 20). Papias does not fabricate a claim that he heard any of the Twelve directly, but only secondhand. I shall return to the "apologetic" argument from another angle shortly. Note also Philip of Side, frg. 16 in J. Kürzinger, *Papias von Hieropolis und die Evangelien des Neuen Testaments* (Regensburg: Pustet, 1983), 116–17 = frg. 5 in *The Apostolic Fathers*, 2nd ed., ed. J. B. Lightfoot, J. R. Harmer, and M. W. Holmes (Grand Rapids: Baker, 1989), 317–18. Philip claimed that some of those who were raised from the dead by Jesus lived into the reign of Hadrian (117–138 CE). Since Papias comes in Eusebius' account at a time when association with Clement of Rome and Ignatius are in view, his involvement looks to date back to a time before Ignatius' martyrdom in 107 CE; so also Gundry, *Mark*, 1027–34; see *Hist. eccl.* 3.36.1–2; 3.39.1. The discrediting of Papias in general by Eusebius when it comes to millennial views also speaks to the credibility of Eusebius using him for such points. Papias is actually considering a period a few decades earlier than this 130 CE traditional date. Papias' locale in Hieropolis is significant. This is the site of a major early Christian community and the meeting point of a road from Syrian Antioch to Ephesus. This locale means that the tradition he has access to is located at a main transmission point and economic crossroads in the empire. Gundry's entire discussion of Papias' credibility is worth study (1027–44).

authorship, a scribe had wished to ascribe an anonymous Gospel fictionally to a church hero, he would have chosen a more illustrious name, probably that of one of Jesus' twelve disciples.[44]

If this patristic claim about one of Mark's sources is accurate, then one important source is Peter. It would hardly be possible to get deeper into the apostolic circle. Moreover, in the last several decades, Mark's key position as a source has not been premised on accepting this traditional view of Mark's roots, as many scholars have not accepted Papias' claim. So if this claim is correct, the already well-received and established position of Mark becomes enhanced. This issue of Markan authorship and a possible Petrine connection is worth exploring in a little more detail.

The view of Petrine involvement and Markan authorship has been challenged directly by claims made about the internal evidence.[45] The basis for such a challenge includes issues like (1) Mark's handling of topography in Mk 7:31; (2) his remarks about Jewish views, including a woman's right to divorce in 10:11–12; (3) his assertion that the practice of handwashing is all-pervasive; (4) the controversial claim for a person with Jewish roots that Jesus canceled the distinction between prohibited and kosher food (Mk 7:19b); (5) the lack of ties between Peter and Mark in the New Testament or in other available evidence (an issue dependent in part on views of 1 Peter's authorship); and (6) the claim that little in Mark looks Petrine in origin. These objections form the core of what C. Clifton Black has called the "minimalist" take on Mark.[46]

---

[44] Marcus (*Mark 1–8*, 18) cites Streeter as making this argument in his *Four Gospels*, 560–62.

[45] Probably the most complete challenge comes from Kurt Niederwimmer, "Johannes Markus und die Frage nach dem Verfasser des zweiten Evangeliums," *ZNW* 58 (1967): 172–88. Also important is a series of essays by D. E. Nineham, "Eyewitness Testimony and the Gospel Tradition, I, II, III," *JTS* 9 (1958): 13–25, 243–52; and 11 (1960): 253–64. Arguing for a more positive reading is Robert Yarbrough, "The Date of Papias: A Reassessment," *JETS* 26 (1983): 181–91.

[46] Black, *Mark*, 4–7. Black revisits these arguments in detail on pages 195–250. Boring (*Mark*, 10–12) raises numerous questions about the Peter-Mark connection, arguing that it emerged over the second and third centuries. He argues that an apologetic and theological legitimization of Mark is the point, not a belief in Mark's accuracy. He also claims that the evidence shows that the materials "bear the marks of having been mediated to the author not by an individual, but by a generation of community teaching, preaching, and worship" (12). This final point is asserted, not really defended, except by appeal to the results of form criticism; Bauckham's essay in that volume challenges whether such results are demonstrated to the degree Boring uses them. More than that, the likely possibility that this Gospel is in touch both with individual sources and community tradition is not even entertained. Marcus (*Mark 1–8*, 18–24) also raises the question of whether Mark knew Peter.

I cannot deal with these claims in detail here. However, a few key questions about the minimalist take are worth raising, especially about the claim that an apologetically rooted theological legitimization can explain all our testimony. For example, why work so hard to defend Mark in this manner if Matthew and John are already held up as "apostolic" witnesses and receiving a wider reception than Mark in this period?[47] Is this type of non-apostolic legitimization really the first step in reception? Why does the name Mark remain tied to the collection of four Gospels so consistently and stubbornly across these three centuries, appearing with other witnesses who also were seen as having been well established by that church? In fact, on the legitimization hypothesis, some of these others texts are far better established with direct apostolic claims than Mark, and yet Mark still remains. The testimony is that Peter was involved in this Gospel *without being its author.* Why did the church not just call it the "Gospel According to Peter," if creating a legitimizing association was the point in naming an author? That Peter's association is so carefully made distinct speaks for the tradition and against a legitimization motive. Another question is: Can or should one distinguish between theological legitimization and accuracy, as M. Eugene Boring does? Is not the point of raising Peter to make an affirmation about accuracy? How can we really tell that one motive is in play *at the expense of* the other? This may well be a both-and, not an either-or, situation.

These questions mean that a simple appeal to theological legitimization as a means of dismissing a Markan-Petrine connection is not persuasive. The tradition is too stubborn, and the logic of the proposal has too many holes to require theological legitimization be embraced as explaining how we get both Mark and Peter in this tradition.

But what about the eight specific arguments for Mark's priority among the four Gospels discussed earlier? We need to re-examine some of them here.

1. When it comes to Mark's sense of topography in 7:31, it is clear on a surface reading that one does not get from Tyre to the Decapolis region to the west by way of Sidon to the north. The question is whether the description reflects a more conscious kind of itinerary, like a circuit of ministry.[48]

---

[47] Remember, the claim here is that the authorship has been supplied later by the community, probably sometime in the second century.

[48] This has been argued by F. G. Lang, "'Über Sidon mitten ins Gebiet der Dekapolis': Geographie und Theologie in Markus 7,31," *ZDPV* 94 (1978): 145–60, a view defended by Robert Guelich, *Mark 1–8:26.* WBC 34A (Dallas: Word, 1989), 391–93.

F. G. Lang argues for a trip north and east through Gentile lands before the events that follow in Mark. Robert Guelich argues that having 8:1–10 at the Sea of Galilee means a trip north through the Gentile regions of Tyre, Sidon, and Decapolis and then to the sea, utilizing a few isolated traditions where Jesus engaged Gentiles (7:24–30; 7:32–37).

2. Mark 10:12 appears more complicated, but really is not. Jews generally did not allow women to divorce their husbands (Josephus, *Ant.* 15.259260; 18.136; *m. Yebam.* 14:1), although there were exceptions (Sir 23:22–23).[49] There also was the well-known exceptional situation of Herodias leaving her husband to marry Herod Antipas.[50] Further, when Salome sent her husband Costobarus a document dissolving their marriage, Josephus noted this was against Jewish law (*Ant.* 15.259; *kata tous Ioudaiōs nomous*).[51] Beyond this, we know that Jesus involved women openly in his work (Lk 8:1–3; 10:38–42). So it is not impossible Jesus would have been comfortable with a gender-balanced statement in this regard.[52] The claim, then, that the second Gospel gives evidence of a Gentile perspective and sloppiness on Jewish views is not as strong as it initially appears. The later section on archaeology and evidence of cultural sensitivity to Jewish practice will argue the opposite for this author.

3. In the case of 7:3 and the extensive nature of handwashing, we may be dealing only with a hyperbole that speaks of how many Jews kept such practices. After all, this is how practicing pious Jews differed from the Gentiles in Mark's audience. Mark uses *pantes* this way in other texts (Mk 1:5, 32–33; 6:33; 11:11).[53]

4. Mark 7:19, with its claim that Jesus canceled the food distinctions between clean and unclean foods, is a reflective statement that could well have been made by any follower of Jesus committed to the Gentile mission. It is a statement that any Paulinist could have made, as the table fellowship incident in Gal 2 attests. Because Mark is said to have worked with Paul, it is not beyond his later view of the significance of what Jesus taught. The verse is a later parenthetical remark made in reflection, especially on what Mk 7:15b says. As such, it can fit into the supposed

---

[49] David Instone-Brewer, "Jewish Women Divorcing Their Husbands in Early Judaism: The Background to Papyrus Sie'elim 13," *HTR* 92 (1999): 349–57.

[50] Robert Stein, *Mark*. BECNT (Grand Rapids: Baker, 2008), 458.

[51] R. T. France, *The Gospel of Mark*. NIGTC (Grand Rapids: Eerdmans, 2002), 394.

[52] Of course, in a Roman context women had this right, which is why many see evidence of a Gentile perspective here.

[53] Guelich, *Mark 1–8:26*, 364.

setting of the Gospel, since the point is an implication of what Jesus said that was realized later.

5 and 6. In many ways, these two challenges are similar. How can we be sure the connection between Mark and Peter existed? Is there evidence for it? How one views the authorship of 1 Peter is clearly important here, since 1 Pet 5:13 sends greetings from Mark as a "son" in the context of a greeting sent from "Babylon," a term often used as a code word for the world's power (i.e., Rome).[54] John Mark is consistently seen as the same person in the New Testament materials (Acts 12:12–17, 25; 13:5, 13; 15:36–41; Col 4:10; Phlm 24). Although the belief that 1 Peter is a pseudonymous letter is quite common, Karen Jobes has made a strong case that this is not so.[55] She notes that the vast territory encompassed in the book's address reflects a possible response to Rome's recent colonization of these five same areas under Claudius (1:1, Pontus, Cappadocia, Galatia, Asia, Bithynia, a region slightly smaller than the state of California in size). She suggests that the language of foreigners and aliens in a strange land fits this kind of colonization effort, which would have used deported people. Further, no evangelists' names are associated with establishing Christianity in the region, so it is possible the Christians present came as part of those who resettled the area, possibly as the result of Claudius' edict that removed Jews from Rome (Suetonius, *Claudius* 25.4). Jobes opts for a date when Silvanus, Mark, and Peter were together as either the early 50s in Jerusalem and Antioch (Acts 15:22, 36–40) or an occasion in the mid-60s in Rome. The latter option is more likely in my view. The overlap in concerns about how to live in the midst of potential persecution, reflected in both the Gospel and 1 Peter, points to a time of growing danger for Christians in the empire, such as the 60s.

Boring's challenge to such a connection is that there is no "primary evidence" that the Mark who was Paul's coworker "was a Jerusalem or Judean Christian."[56] To make this claim, Boring has to treat Acts as useless for accurate information about people's whereabouts, because

---

[54] On this identification in early Christian literature, see Eusebius, *Hist. eccl.* 2.15.2; minuscule 2138 reads "Rome" at 1 Pet 5:13. Goppelt defends the traditional connections made here. For a contrastive view that sees a pseudonymous reference, see Norbert Brox, *Der erste Petrusbrief.* EKKNT 21 (Zurich: Benzinger, 1979), 246–48.

[55] Jobes, *1 Peter.* BECNT (Grand Rapids: Baker, 2005), 5–41. For a case that the early church association of Peter with Mark is strictly an apologetic move, see Boring, *Mark*, 10–12.

[56] Boring, *Mark*, 10–11.

Acts 12 locates Mark in Jerusalem in the 40s. Mark hardly has a polemical or apologetic role in Acts. He is strictly a minor character who consistently looks less than worthy as an exemplary disciple. Boring's consistent and wholesale rejection of disparate traditions from early Christianity reflects an excessive skepticism about our earliest sources. Instead, Boring constructs a hypothesis about how Silvanus and Mark came to be associated with Peter and Paul as two martyred apostles by the end of the first century. But the one question this scenario cannot answer is why one would choose to create such an association with an otherwise obscure apostolic contact. More than that, Mark is a figure whose reputation is seriously tainted by the second century, when the link is supposedly created. After all, Luke tells us Mark was far from a stellar follower. According to Acts, what we know about him is that he failed to make it through the first missionary journey and caused a rift between Paul and Barnabas. This is hardly a résumé that suggests this person should be chosen from a pool of many possible figures to elevate the status of an otherwise anonymous Gospel that needs a public relations boost. Finally, if it was so easy to supply authorship to elevate a Gospel's status in this part of the new Jesus community, why not simply call it Peter's Gospel, since this apostle supposedly had a point of contact with the "to-be-supplied" author of the second Gospel? That this was not done in this case points to a restraining factor at work in the tradition when it comes to authorship.

Thus I find it more compelling to trust the traditional associations of Mark and Peter with this Gospel. Both the variety of ancient references consistently appealing to this connection and the lack of clear qualifications Mark brings – selected out of a hat, as it were, and named out of the blue – support both the authorship and sourcing associations. If these associations are accurate, there are reasons for Mark being significant as a source for Jesus research other than its relatively early date. It reflects a Gospel in touch, in part, with the apostolic circle. Mark's sources, then, would have involved a combination of access to apostolic memory through Peter, as well as likely use of other circulating (mostly oral) tradition. Luke alludes to such tradition in Lk 1:2. The passion material is often held to be one of the earliest such sources to be assembled. But what would have motivated Mark to record a new kind of work that tries to tell the story of Jesus?

Need for the Gospels by about 65–80 CE

Two key things are happening around the Jesus Movement as we come into the 60s: (1) increased tension for Jewish and Christian communities, as well as (2) the aging of the original generation of Jesus followers. Both factors contribute to the move to record, and not merely to pass on orally, Jesus' story and teachings.

Acts portrays the increased tension between Jews and the newly emerging movement as ongoing from the initial decade of the movement. However, the tension became so great at certain points that we see it spill over into reports we have from outside sources about the new movement. For example, in Rome the tension, possibly between the two groups, appears to have caused Claudius to issue an edict expelling Jews, as the travels of Priscilla and Aquila apparently corroborate (Suetonius, *Claudius* 25.4). Interestingly, as members of the new movement, they still had to depart Rome, being considered Jews (Acts 18:2). In the early 60s in Jerusalem, Annas II slays James, the brother of Jesus, as the family feud between the Annas I– Caiaphas–Annas II clan and the family of Jesus extends into a fourth decade (*Ant.* 18.197–203). In the mid-60s, tensions arise between the Jews and Romans leading to the failed revolt at the end of the decade. So we have a period of social and political uncertainty that may have led a new movement to ask where it stood in light of the heightened tensions. That Mark spends so much time dealing with the likelihood of suffering and presenting Jesus as a model for suffering leads us to assume the book was composed in such a tension-filled context, a context that remained well into the decade of the 70s.

In addition to the political tension, the original generation of followers was aging. The oral tradition, which likely centered in key communities such as Jerusalem, Antioch, Rome, and the Ephesian region, was originally rooted in this generation that experienced Jesus and that could tell about him through the respected "living voice" ancients often preferred. However, as the decades moved on, access to such living voices waned. What could possibly preserve their experience? Part of what the citation from Papias indicates to us is that these written memoirs, which is how Justin Martyr described these works, served to preserve and pass on to succeeding generations this original voice of the new community. Here is how Justin says it in his First Apology:

For the apostles, in the memoirs composed by them, which are called Gospels, have thus delivered to us what was enjoined upon them. . . . And on the day called Sunday, all who live in cities or in the country gather together to one place, and the memoirs of the apostles or the writings of the prophets are read, as long as time permits; then, when the reader has ceased, the president verbally instructs, and exhorts to the imitation of these good things. (1 Apol. 1:66–67)

Justin uses this term *memoir* fifteen times in his writings when he refers to the Gospels. It is important to point out that this expression is present in a period before the more formal appeals to the Gospels' teaching authority we hear in Ireneaus and his declaration that there are only four Gospels (*Adv. haer.* 3.1.1; 3.11.8). With this name, Justin emphasizes the contact this material has with the earliest generation of followers through the remains of their memory passed on to following generations.[57] Elsewhere Justin speaks of works composed by Jesus' apostles and those who accompanied them (*Dial.* 103.8). This seems parallel to the statement from Papias.[58] This desire to preserve this early memory was enhanced by the increasing pressure on the new community and its changing identity within the Roman and Jewish worlds. These two key factors led to the emergence of the Gospels, with Mark, for the reasons already noted, likely being the first of the group. Thus the most reasonable range for dating this Gospel fits in the sixties and extends into the early eighties. The lack of explicit mention of Jerusalem's destruction favors a date earlier in this range versus later, as does the way Matthew and Luke, which used Mark, also treats the destruction by not explicitly mentioning a fulfilment. However, it needs to be noted that the key issue for Mark and its handling of the Jesus tradition is not whether its date is earlier or later in this range, but the quality of the tradition that it used and how deep its roots ran.

Reliability of Mark with Regard to Jewish Matters

One of the ways to test the reliability of Mark's traditions is to examine them in light of the Jewish context that was Jesus' setting. The numerous points of contact here show that the material Mark draws from fits that

---

[57] Martin Hengel, *Studies in the Gospel of Mark.* Trans. John Bowden (Philadelphia: Fortress, 1985), 68–69.

[58] Cf. Justin, *Dial.* 106.3, on Mark's Gospel as being Peter's recollections. Bauckham (*Jesus and the Eyewitnesses,* 213) notes how the idea of relating from memory is shared between Papias and Justin (*apomnēmoneumata*). Hengel also sees these remarks as rooted in an oral tradition we can take back into the late first century and ties the names of the Gospels to the same early period (*Studies,* 72–84).

world. Its scope suggests one who came from this world and appreciated the concerns Jewish matters raised for the new community.

Apocalyptic Worldview

Whether one considers John the Baptist, the "two-age" view of Jesus, the Olivet discourse, or the hope of vindication, the Jesus of Mark's Gospel is immersed in a perspective that reflects Second Temple apocalyptic hope. The kind of innovative baptism over which John presided, and with which Jesus identified in being baptized by John, is rooted in a worldview that says God will one day vindicate his people and restore righteousness.[59] Such hope we also see vividly in the expectant yet separatist lifestyle at Qumran. When Jesus went to the desert and shared in this baptism, he was identifying with and affirming what John was preaching. The parallel appeals to Isa 40 found in the associations of John the Baptist and Qumran reflect these shared perspectives (Mk 1:3; 1QS VIII, 13–14). Yet Jesus was also distinct from the Essenes in refusing to live a life of separation from the people he sought to persuade by his preaching.[60]

Also rooted in Jewish apocalyptic is the hope expressed within Jesus' kingdom preaching. Jesus speaks with an apocalyptic backdrop through his appeal to the Son of Man and his expectation of a comprehensive presence through the kingdom of God.[61] The Son of Man will judge the world and the kingdom will spread to cover the earth, so that this hope covers the bringing of righteousness and justice to the world. Throughout this Gospel, Jesus' key self-designation is "the Son of Man." This title clearly reflects this apocalyptic milieu, with its roots in works like Daniel and *1 Enoch*.[62] Here

---

[59] For a full study of John the Baptist and his affirmation of an apocalyptic worldview, see Robert Webb, *John the Baptizer and Prophet: A Socio-Historical Study.* JSNTSup 62 (Sheffield: Sheffield Academic Press, 1991).

[60] For how Jesus is distinct from the Essenes, see James Charlesworth, "The Dead Sea Scrolls and the Historical Jesus," in *Jesus and the Dead Sea Scrolls,* ed. Charlesworth (ABRL; New York: Doubleday, 1992), 22–30.

[61] According to Adela Yarbo Collins, Mark is "an eschatological historical monograph" (*Mark.* Hermeneia [Minneapolis: Fortress, 2007], 42–44, also 11–14). She argues that a historical monograph focused on an individual reflects a Hellenistic context, while the apocalyptic and eschatological dimensions are Jewish.

[62] The availability of this title to Jesus in his Galilean context is explored in a volume edited by James Charlesworth and myself. There we and others contend for the point that the Son of Man title was very much a topic for reflection in first-century Galilee. This monograph is entitled *Parables of Enoch: A Paradigm Shift* (New York: Bloomsbury, 2013), and my essay is a *Forschungsbericht* on the *Similitudes* section of *1 Enoch*.

the unfolding of a divine plan also is important, as Mk13 shows. Other touches include the "must" of divine program and the way in which God breaks into creation, whether in language where the heavens split so the Spirit can alight on Jesus or the appearance of a cloud (Mk 1:10; 9:7). This reflects the apocalyptic perspective of Judaism.

Finally, the way the Gospel concludes points to an eschatological hope. In 16:1–8, faith is to be invoked through the story of an empty tomb and the declaration of a hope of vindication and resurrection. This vindication serves as attestation for the kingdom claims Jesus made. These themes also point to a Jewish apocalyptic hope that includes a physical dimension to resurrection and the expectation of a life to come. The very open-ended nature of this short conclusion to the Gospel in 16:1–8 lacks the level of polemics of the other Gospels. It simply calls for faith that God is vindicating Jesus. As a result of these events, those tied to him are called to faith, moving beyond the fear that initially existed in the women.[63]

Such traditions reflect an apocalyptic perspective that is at the core of themes running throughout Mark's Gospel. This perspective fits tightly a Second Temple Jewish context.[64]

Pictorial Language, Use of Scripture, and Telling of Parables

There is a Jewish flavor to the way Mark tells stories. Unlike the other three Gospels, Mark is more into action and story versus long blocks of discourse, such as we see in Matthew and John, or several units of shorter teaching, as we see in Luke. This use of parable and story is like units we see in the writings of Second Temple Judaism, where action and parable also are prevalent, such as 1 *Maccabees* telling the story of the emergence of the Maccabean family or the importance of parables to present God's program in 1 *Enoch*.[65] Consider how the story and teaching mix in parable in the

---

[63]   For a full discussion on issues tied to the ending of Mark, see D. A. Black, ed., *Perspectives on the Ending of Mark: Four Views* (Nashville: Broadman & Holman Academic, 2008), esp. my essay, "The Ending of Mark: A Response to the Essays," 124–42. I defend the original presence of the shorter ending, while interacting with the other options. In the narrative logic, the women themselves moved beyond the fear or otherwise no one would have known the story Mark tells in chapter 16.

[64]   This presentation of Mark as apocalyptic runs counter to claims made in the widely circulated PBS documentary *From Jesus to Christ: The First Christians* (M. Mellowes and W. Cran; Burbank, CA: Warner Home Video, 1998) that Mark's Gospel contains only wisdom themes and is not apocalyptic in orientation. The very fact Mark has the Olivet discourse is against such claims.

[65]   In fact, an entire section of 1 *Enoch* is called the *Similitudes* (chs. 37–71).

examples of Nathan confronting David (2 Sam 12:1–14) and the parable of the vineyard (Isa 5:1–7). The use of parable to challenge and bring reflection is very Jewish, even if one cannot call it exclusively Jewish.[66] The Hebrew *mashal* refers to a gamut of genres: from Balaam's oracles (Num 23:7) to the extended discourses of Job (Job 27:1; 29:1) to riddles (Ezek 17:2). It points to a rich tradition of picturing reality through imagery. Jesus' comparing his presence to that of a wedding celebration and a bridegroom reflects the imagery of celebration at God's presence (Mk 2:19–20), a comparison the story of Hosea exploits in a more emotive way (Hos 1–3).[67]

Alongside this use is the appeal to Scripture, especially in controversy. Here numerous points of contact with Jewish story and reading exist: David serves as an example in a surprising way (Mk 2:25–26); the creation of the Sabbath for humanity alludes to Genesis (Mk 2:27–28; Gen 2:1–3); and the telling of the calming of the sea (Mk 4:35–41) hovers around Ps 107:25–32 (cf. Ps 89:25). There are the numerous halakic debates of the Gospels: Mk 7 over purity, 10:2–9 over divorce, 12:18–27 over resurrection, and 12:35–37 over Ps 110:1. There also are the prophetic-like appeals to the second part of the Ten Words in Mk 10:19 and to the Great Commandment in 12:24–27. We have the use of prophetic rebukes from Isa 56:7 and Jer 7:11 to describe the state of the temple in Mk 11:17. In addition, there are the pictures of the withered fig tree in 11:20–25 (also 13:28–29) and of the vineyard in 12:1–11, the image of the desolating sacrilege in 13:14, the recasting of Passover in 14:12–25, the appeal to Ps 110:1 and Dan 7:13–14 in Mk 14:62, and the cry of Ps 22:1 in Mk 15:34. This is a writer who uses traditions that breathe of Jewish life and reflection. His portrayal shows why Jesus could well be thought of as acting out of the great prophetic tradition of Judaism. The portrait shows a figure who thinks and acts out of the breadth of Jewish expression: out of Judaism's wisdom tradition, utilizing its prophetic critique, and appealing to an apocalyptic hope that God has a plan that will resolve itself on behalf of the righteous.

---

[66] We must recall that parables are not unique to Judaism, being used in an array of cultural contexts; see Klyne Snodgrass, *Stories of Intent: A Comprehensive Guide to the Parables of Jesus* (Grand Rapids: Eerdmans, 2008), 37–39. On pages 42–46, Snodgrass traces the extent to which parables appear in late Second Temple literature. He notes that in Greco-Roman contexts, parables are most common from philosophers and those who confront people for their failures (46).

[67] The *Story of Ahiqar* also belongs in this discussion as an example of the use of story.

Debate over Purity

Perhaps no section of Mark reflects its Jewish roots – and the debate over
that background – as much as the dispute with Jesus described in 7:1–23.
The controversy revolved around his failure to observe ritual purity and
wash his hands before a meal. This text was once seen as a sloppy rendering
of a Jewish custom by a confused evangelist intent on a polemic against
legalism,[68] but recent reflection over new evidence of Jewish practice has
brought the scene into line with its supposed setting, pointing to a tradition
with solid roots. That such a scene would appear at all and require an
explanation to make its cultural context clear shows that Mark was interested in discussing things Jesus did that were no longer directly relevant to
his audience.[69] The details that required explanation also suggest that the
Gospel of Mark's audience was predominantly Gentile.

Jonathan Klawans, in an important summary essay, has detailed the
distinctions and differences that existed between moral and ritual purity
within Second Temple Judaism.[70] He notes three errors commonly made in
discussing purity in Judaism: (1) identifying sin with impurity, (2) assuming
this label applies to social status (such as to women or Gentiles) beyond sin,
and (3) arguing that purity was a means the Pharisees used to exercise power
over those they wished to dominate. Rather, purity was related to issues of
religious loyalty and identity that fed sincere debates about walking faithfully
with God. The roots of such concerns are a reflection of seriously engaging
texts like Lev 11–15 and Num 19. Ritual impurity did not involve sin but was
seen as something contracted in the midst of the natural result of the activity
of life. It was temporary but potentially contagious, which is why it was an
issue. Washing was a common way to remove the possibility of impurity
spreading. Respect for the sacred led to concern about purity and approaching God with respect for his uniqueness. All this stands in contrast to moral
purity, which was concerned with sin.

This is the backdrop that fuels the discussion in Mk 7. Jesus had failed to
wash his hands before a meal. This failure raised ritual purity concerns for
the more scrupulous of Jesus' observers, the Pharisees. The key saying in

---

[68]   Edward Schweizer (*The Good News According to Mark*. Trans. D. H. Madvig [Atlanta:
       John Knox, 1970], 145–47) sees the passage as largely a church perspective against
       legalism, with verse 15 as a kernel going back to Jesus.
[69]   Gundry, *Mark*, 348.
[70]   Klawans, "Moral and Ritual Purity," in *The Historical Jesus in Context*, ed. Amy-Jill
       Levine, Dale C. Allison Jr., and John Dominic Crossan (PRR; Princeton: Princeton
       University Press, 2006), 266–84.

the passage is 7:15, "there is nothing outside a person that by going in can defile, but things that come out of a person are what defile."[71] Defilement is not contagious in the sense the Pharisees are arguing. As Klawans says, "We cannot say the statement is too radically anti-Jewish to be considered historically authentic: as we recognize the statement's ambiguity, so too we must recognize its possible historicity."[72] Jesus' statement points to a priority of moral concerns over those of ritual purity, remarks that have parallels in the prophetic tradition (e.g., Hos 6:6). It is also important to observe that the later narrative remark about Jesus declaring all food clean is a comment by the Evangelist (Mk 7:19c), a redaction on the tradition, that likely refers to an implication drawn from the remarks of the tradition itself. As such it does not impact the assessment of the tradition. The tradition indicates that Jesus did not compartmentalize issues of purity and sin to the degree that rabbis did; rather, he prioritized them, a perfectly understandable matter of debate in first-century Judaism. What the Pharisees saw as distinct discussions, both of which needed careful attention, Jesus saw as more closely related. This spectrum fits Jewish concerns and sensitivities. The detail shows the quality of the Markan tradition at this point concerning an event that did not directly involve Mark's audience. The dispute here is purely halakic.[73] A concern for how food is eaten could be raised (and was) from reflection on texts such as Lev 11:40 and 17:15. This kind of implication was behind the debate over second-degree impurity (*m. Zabim* 5:1; *t. Zabim* 4:3).[74]

Yet, there is another feature to this passage that is important. The evidence of the widespread use of stone vessels and/or *miqvaot* points to the presence of widespread concerns about ritual purity in the culture at large.[75] More

---

[71] See also Mt 15:11, 23:25–26; *Gos. Thom.* 14; P.Oxy. 840.

[72] Klawans, "Moral and Ritual Purity," 281. We see this kind of inherent ambiguity in several places in Mark. I argued that ambiguity was present in the resurrection scene and will argue it is present in how Jesus handles the title of Messiah. It shows an absence of polemical design and so points to an old tradition.

[73] Clinton Wahlen, *Jesus and the Impurity of Spirits in the Synoptic Gospels*. WUNT 2/185 (Tübingen: Mohr Siebeck, 2004), 75.

[74] Thomas Kazen, *Jesus and Purity Halakhah: Was Jesus Indifferent to Impurity?* ConBNT 38 (Stockholm: Almqvist & Wiksell, 2002), 161–64. Kazen summarizes the Mk 7 issues on pages 86–88. He stresses how the issue of handwashing would imply issues of bodily impurity quite naturally.

[75] Roland Deines (*Jüdische Steingefässe und pharisäische Frömmigkeit: Ein archäologisch-historischer Beitrag zum Verständnis vom Joh 2,6 und der jüdischen Reinheitshalacha zur Zeit Jesu*. WUNT 2/52 [Tübingen: Mohr Siebeck, 1993]) discusses these issues in detail and argues for concerns developing from the end of the first century BCE.

than 300 stepped pools have been found in places as far apart as Jericho, Sepphoris, Gamla (Gamala), and Qumran. Such immersions allowed one to become clean before sunset, a practice called *tebul yom* (4QMMT B15). Kazan refers to an "expansionist purity practice" in Second Temple Judaism as being in evidence through these finds.[76] Such concerns moved the discussion beyond concerns for purity in the temple to a focus on purity in everyday life. The example here is concern for corpse purity, which need not be connected to whether one was headed to the temple (Josephus, *Ag. Ap.* 2.205; Philo, *Spec.* 3.205–206).[77] So when Mark says, somewhat hyperbolically, "For the Pharisees, and all the Jews, do not eat unless they wash their hands observing the tradition of the elders" (Mk 7:3), the Evangelist is explaining a common and growing custom, the development of which had become an issue of more concern over the past few decades before the time of Jesus.

Such detail not only indicates some evidence of Markan redaction in a passage (i.e., Mk 7:19c), but also points to the quality of the circulating tradition Mark is using: the details of these events are included, although they are not the direct concern of the audience. That Mark had access to such quality tradition helps to speak to the importance of his Gospel for Jesus research. It also indicates how important it is for those working in Jesus research and New Testament studies to keep an eye on developments both in Second Temple Jewish studies and the field of archaeology.

Calendar

This topic and the next one (pilgrimage) are examples not so much of what Mark says as how Mark relates to other information in the Jesus tradition. Mark provides one of two time lines for how to date the events in Jesus' last week of ministry. Mark 14:12, 16–18 leave a clear impression that Jesus celebrated a Passover meal with his disciples just before he was arrested at Gethsemane.[78] In contrast, Jn 18:28 with 19:14 appear to place that same meal a day later. Sorting out the origin and relationship between these two time lines has been a long-standing, and mostly unresolved, issue in New Testament scholarship.

[76]   Kazen, *Jesus and Purity Halakhah*, 72–78.
[77]   Kazen (ibid., 73–74) notes how restrictionist and expansionist traditions appear side by side in the Mishnah and Tosefta.
[78]   For the details about the chronological discussion, see Raymond E. Brown, *The Death of the Messiah*. 2 vols. ABRL (New York: Doubleday, 1994), 2:1350–78.

The issues tied to this dispute are multiple and complex. Did the Evangelists and their traditions consistently render the hours of the day from 6:00 AM or from midnight? Most scholars opt for a 6:00 AM starting point. Did the day start at sunset, as was common in Judaism, or at midnight, or at sunrise? This detail also seems resolvable, as the haste to get Jesus buried shows a concern for the day ending at sunset. But how do we count Passover? Is it the Passover feast, or can it refer to any point in the eight-day Passover–Unleavened Bread feast period, feasts that Josephus also combines (*Ant.* 9.271; *J.W.* 5.99)? The possibility of speaking, by these expressions, of something like the Passover season cannot be ruled out, complicating the determination of exact timing. Does the reference to Passover (Heb. *Pesaḥ*; Gk. *pascha*) refer to the day, the meal, or its preparation? The usage of the term requires asking this question on a case-by-case basis.

Another issue here is the amount of activity taking place in the midst of such high holy days. For some historians, there is too much taking place on what is normally a day of rest for the account to be credible. Joachim Jeremias has defended the scene by arguing that each of the events described can be shown as having taken place on a feast day.[79] There is still, however, debate about whether so much unusual activity could take place on one day. One explanation often put forward is that the leadership was in a hurry to resolve the case while Pilate was present and could give a response; thus exceptional circumstances led to exceptional practices. The point in raising this category is not to resolve what may not even be resolvable, but simply to note that Mark is the source for one of two time lines that are important in Jesus research, even in the midst of uncertainty about how to relate Mark's timing to John's chronology.

Pilgrimage

A similar discussion ensues when one compares Mark to John. The question here involves how many trips Jesus took to Jerusalem. John refers to at least three Passovers, possibly four (Jn 2:13; 6:4; 11:15 with 12:1; 13:1; 18:28, 39; and 19:14; possibly also 5:1). In contrast, the events of the last week are Jesus' only trip to Jerusalem in Mark. Many have suggested that in Mark, Jesus'

---

[79] Jeremias, *The Eucharistic Words of Jesus*. Trans. Norman Perrin (Philadelphia: Fortress, 1977), 74–79. One issue here involves the late dates of the sources to which Jeremias appeals.

entire ministry takes place within a year. This may be reading too much
into the text. When Jesus sends the disciples to prepare the Last Supper, he
appears to have prearranged the locale before coming down for this final
time (Mk 14:12–16). Was this his standard locale for the meal, or was it
arranged just a few days earlier? Either is possible, but the scene would
seem to include some previous contact with the owner and host before the
time of the meal. So the difference in trips may be only an apparent one.
What is clear is that Mark, in telling Jesus' story, was not concerned with
giving us a detailed chronology (which Papias told us centuries ago).

Archaeology

Archaeology usually cannot prove the details of a passage, but often it can
shed light on the background for a text and whether it fits nicely into the
context in which it appears.[80]

Several points from archaeology tied to Mark may show the quality of
Mark's traditions. The role of synagogues, including the presence of an old
synagogue in Capernaum, sheds light on Capernaum as a headquarters for
Jesus.[81] Although some debate whether such synagogues were present in
the first century, the synagogue at Gamla is clearly first century, and most
take the foundation of the synagogue at Capernaum as the remains of such
a building from the first century. The related find of Peter's house in
Capernaum not far from the synagogue adds to this background. The
association of this domicile with early Byzantine pilgrim activity and the
placement of a basilica over it in the sixth century speak for the likelihood
of the identification.[82]

---

[80]   For a thorough survey of issues tied to archaeology and the NT, including a careful
        statement of the relationship of archaeology to ancient texts, see James H. Charlesworth,
        ed., *Jesus and Archaeology* (Grand Rapids: Eerdmans, 2006), esp. Charlesworth's open-
        ing essay, "Jesus Research and Archaeology: A New Perspective," 11–63. There he
        discusses what archaeology can achieve and why NT scholars should pay attention to
        realia (26–27).

[81]   Charlesworth, "Jesus Research and Archaeology," 29–30; Paul Anderson, "Aspects of
        Historicity in the Gospel of John: Implications for Investigations of Jesus and
        Archeology," in *Jesus and Archaeology*, ed. Charlesworth, 587–618, here 591.

[82]   Charlesworth, "Jesus Research and Archaeology," 49–50; idem, *Jesus within Judaism:
        New Light from Exciting Archaeological Discoveries*. ABRL (New York: Doubleday, 1988),
        109–12. Charlesworth notes that this house has a central room with special plaster
        reserved for special rooms. Cf. J. Murphy-O'Connor, *The Holy Land: An Oxford
        Archaeological Guide from Earliest Times to 1700*. 4th ed. (Oxford: Oxford University
        Press, 1998), 220.

The likely site of the crucifixion as having exposed rock, as the name Golgotha suggests, also makes for a nice cultural fit. The association of this detail with the locale of the Holy Sepulcher is probable, given the sepulcher's age as a holy site.[83] This locale is all the more plausible given the recent discovery that Herod's third wall was built after Jesus' death; the locale, at the time, was outside the city.[84]

The role of *mikvaot* and stone vessels tied to issues of purity were noted previously. All these links serve as another indication that traditions like those in Mark may well have ancient roots.

Messianic Ambiguity

Perhaps one of the most debated features of Mark's Gospel is how he presents Jesus in relationship to being "the Christ." Two issues are mixed together here. The first is the ambiguity of this title in Judaism itself during the time of Jesus.[85] There are a plethora of messianic options in the period, although the most common one appears to have involved a political leader who would deliver Israel from Rome. What these various portraits all shared was a desire to deliver Israel to shalom, the promised peace of God with a cleansing of evil, the establishment of justice, and the vindication of the righteous. Thus, whether we think of *PssSol* 17–18 with its political cleansing figure, *1En* 37–71 with its transcendent Son of Man, or the two messiahs of Qumran, political victory and the establishment of justice is the point of the hope. Thus, any intimation of a messianic hope likely would draw Roman attention, as the survey of Josephus (*Ant.* 18) also indicates.

The second issue is the clarity with which the earliest Jesus followers made such a declaration after the crucifixion. Here, all we need to consider is how tightly connected the title "Christ" became to Jesus' name, even to the point of almost looking like a family name.[86] The evidence for how

---

[83]   Shimon Gibson reaches a similar conclusion in *The Final Days of Jesus: The Archaeological Evidence* (New York: HarperCollins, 2009), 116–22.

[84]   Anderson, "Aspects of Historicity," 591, 594. Anderson ties the detail to John, but Mark also attests to such a site (Mk 15:22).

[85]   Three key studies are J. Neusner, W. S. Green, and E. S. Frerichs, eds., *Judaisms and Their Messiahs at the Turn of the Christian Era* (Cambridge: Cambridge University Press, 2008); John J. Collins, *The Scepter and the Star*. ABRL (New York: Doubleday, 1995); and Adela Yarbro Collins and John J. Collins, *King and Messiah as Son of God: Divine, Human, and Angelic Messianic Figures in Biblical and Related Literature* (Grand Rapids: Eerdmans, 2008).

[86]   Martin Hengel, "Jesus, the Messiah of Israel," in *Studies in Early Christology*. Trans. Paul Cathey (Edinburgh: T&T Clark, 1995), 1–72, esp. 1–19.

early and pervasive such an identification was in the early community indicates at least that this title was connected to Jesus early in the post-crucifixion phase of the new movement.

This is where Mark's Gospel comes in. From the time of William Wrede, a common explanation for this phenomenon and the lack of explicit messianic confession in the Synoptic tradition was the claim that Mark had theologized the retrojection of a later messianic confession onto Jesus with the "messianic secret."[87] Mark created Jesus' calls for silence, runs the argument, as a cover for the fact that Jesus did not present himself as a messiah in any sense during his ministry. Anything messianic tied to Jesus, Wrede argued, reflected the early church's theology, not that of Jesus. However, two phenomena in our historical information make this a difficult position to hold: (1) the depth of the early evidence for such a confession in our material (as was just noted), and (2) the fact that the *titulus* on the cross presents Jesus as a king and fits culturally with what crime got someone crucified in Rome, namely, sedition. Apparently Wrede himself eventually realized the difficulty with this interpretation of Mark. Most people are unaware that before Wrede died, he renounced his own view of the secret in a private letter to Adolf Harnack.[88]

Recognizing the complexity of first-century Jewish messianic expectation helps us appreciate the ambiguity of such a title in Jesus' time and the issues such an association would have raised for Jesus. The very ambiguity of the Caesarea Philippi scene in Mk 8:27–30 makes cultural sense for Jesus. It gives another indication of a solid tradition related to him. Here is not the open affirmation of Peter's confession that we see in Mt 16, but instead a call not to speak to anyone. This kind of ambiguity around the title points far less to a church creation, where the title was openly embraced, than to a careful recognition that this declaration, unexplained, could be not only dangerous but also misleading, given how Jesus saw himself operating in the program of God. The next Markan scene has Jesus introduce suffering

---

[87] Wrede's work *Das Messiasgeheimnis in den Evangelium* created quite a stir upon its release in 1901 (ET: *The Messianic Secret*. Trans. J. C. G. Greig [London: James Clarke, 1971]). A study of the discussion surrounding this work, which impacted Markan studies as almost a precursor to redaction criticism, is found in Christopher Tuckett, ed., *The Messianic Secret*. IRT (London: SPCK, 1983).

[88] Martin Hengel and Anna Maria Schwemer, *Jesus und das Judentum*. GfC 1 (Tübingen: Mohr Siebeck, 2007), 507–10; also H. Rollmann and W. Zager, "Unveröffentliche Briefe William Wredes zur Problematisierung des messianischen Selbtverständnis Jesu," *ZNThG* 8 (2001): 274–322, esp. 317; Andrew Chester, *Messiah and Exaltation*. WUNT 207 (Tübingen: Mohr Siebeck, 2007), 309.

into this role, with Peter denying the possibility. Peter's challenge led to Jesus' rebuking Peter as Satan for taking that stance. This second scene assumes the contrast to the first confession and points to the likelihood that this tradition sequence is rooted in real memory, not early church creation. The criterion of embarrassment applies here. Would the early church have created such a Christological sequence where one of its most prominent leaders is called Satan for rejecting something the Savior and Lord said?[89] It seems more likely that the ambiguity Mark places around the term *Messiah* reflects the care with which Jesus approached this title, a dangerous category he was working to recast, not simply accept. Part of the reason for Jesus' care in using the term was that the term could become a cause to incite people in a politically revolutionary manner against Rome, as the Bar Kokhba revolt of the next century subsequently demonstrated. However, another reason for proceeding carefully was that Jesus saw his messianic activity as more complex than most of the varieties of messianic Jewish expectation of the Second Temple period.[90]

Thus, a scene like this one, stated with much less bravado than the early church normally gave to Jesus but so central to Mark's understanding of Jesus, has a good likelihood of being authentic and, therefore, showing the value of Mark's Gospel for Jesus research.

Conclusion on the Roots of Mark's Gospel

I have traced a variety of reasons why Mark is important, even central, for Jesus studies.

First, the internal evidence of the Gospel indicates it was the first of the Synoptics to be written. Compared to Matthew and Luke, Mark's inclusion of narrative details and lengthy descriptions and his exclusion of discourse and parabolic material make more sense if Mark came first than if it were later.

Second, ancient references such as Papias suggest Mark's sources have apostolic roots, placing the material early, especially when compared to many sources for other ancient works.

Third, a need for written Gospels emerged as the apostles died, persecution increased, and Jesus' anticipated return seemed to be delayed; the

---

[89]   It is important to remember who Jesus was seen to be in the early church frame if one is going to argue for creation of this scene.

[90]   The possibility that Qumran had a suffering role for any eschatological figure is uncertain. With this exception, Jesus' emphasis here is unique in a Jewish context.

Gospel tradition moved from a strictly oral dimension to one including written Gospels. The "living voice" of the earliest generation was thus preserved – what Justin called the "memoirs of the apostles."

Fourth, Mark demonstrates accuracy in several matters related to Jewish practice, such as his apocalyptic worldview and issues tied to purity.

Fifth, archeological details appear to fit the Markan tradition, such as the importance of ritual cleansing, synagogues, and Peter's house in Capernaum.

Finally, what we might call "less developed theological reflection" points to Mark's age and importance. Here we see traces of a less direct way to say things, something that makes it more likely that Mark's traditional roots are old versus reflecting the theology of his own time.

Given this list, some might appeal to the evidence of Markan redaction. I have not made much of this category. With Mark likely being the first Gospel, we lack direct access to the content of Mark's sources. So it is hard to be confident of his redactional moves. We can only do a kind of redaction "in reverse" by comparing what he has or lacks with what is contained in the later Gospels. In some areas, I have noted this, such as in the case of messianic ambiguity, but have not sought to treat it as a distinct category. Such considerations, usually resulting in a perception that Mark expresses himself more primitively than the other Gospels do, also point to the age of Mark's traditions.

These are some of the key reasons Mark went from being on the edge of Gospel reflection on Jesus in the ancient period to being virtually indispensable as a source for Jesus study today. It explains why those who study Jesus cannot and do not ignore Mark.

Structure of Mark's Gospel

The highest-level outline of Mark according to our commentary is as follows:

1:1-15 Introduction to the Gospel: John the Baptist and Jesus
1:16–3:6 Jesus in Galilee: Ministry and Controversy
3:7–6:6 Jesus in Galilee: Jesus Teaches and Shows His Power
6:7–8:26 Jesus in Galilee: Jesus' Acts Yield a Confession
8:27–10:52 After a Key Confession, Jesus Heads to Jerusalem and Prepares His Disciples for the Suffering That Is to Come
11:1–16:8 In Jerusalem, Jesus Meets Controversy and Rejection, Leading to His Death and Resurrection, as He Also Teaches of Suffering, Judgment, and Vindication

The genre of Mark is ancient *bios*.[91] This means that Mark focuses on the acts and sayings of Jesus. This Gospel is unlike modern biography in that it is neither discusses the physical attributes of the person described nor delves into an analysis of the influences that drove a person to say and do what he or she did. Rather, it reflects a style that presents Jesus as a hero whose life is worthy of reflection and emulation. It seeks both to describe what Jesus said and did, and to address how those events impact the way the community is to live now. In other words, Mark focuses on the historical concern of the genre in looking at who Jesus is and was, along with what he did and why that matters. One need not choose between history and theology or application. For Mark, the two work together, as one is at the roots of the other. Mark does reflect a perspective of what the disciples had come to appreciate about Jesus by looking back and reflecting on what he did, but the purpose of that is to bring to surface what was believed to be inherent in what Jesus did and said. So, Mark's Gospel is not to be compared to a novel in which an evangelist creates a heroic figure based on what he or she wishes Jesus to be.

A second influence of Mark's genre comes from the historiography of the Hebrew Scripture. This element gives God a prominent place and presents him as a key to the events. It embraces a view that sees God as active in the world of people, revealing himself to them in acts and promises that also look back to a hope Israel had possessed for a long time. So Mark's Gospel has diverse roots, with a background in ancient Hellenistic biography, while also reflecting a Jewish perspective about God's activity in relationship to his promises made long ago.

The structure basic to Mark helps us to see the Gospel's core themes. The first major unit simply introduces the Gospel by focusing on how John and Jesus both announced the kingdom of God (1:1–15). This kingdom language evokes the hope of something promised and longed for that now is arriving.

There are three sections covering Jesus' ministry in Galilee (1:16–8:26: 1:16–3:6 Controversy; 3:7–6:6 Power; 6:7–8:26 To Confession) in which we

---

[91] Richard Burridge, *What Are the Gospels? A Comparison with Greco-Roman Biography* (Grand Rapids: Eerdmans, 2004). See the previous discussion of Adele Yarbo Collins's views of Mark's genre and Hellenistic parallels. Burridge's detailed study compares Mark to other ancient biographies and looks at how the main character is described even in the way sentences are structured in the various samples. The way Jesus is presented parallels how the main figures in other *bios* accounts are handled. So details in how *bios* works are found here.

see Jesus minister and the effects of his ministry. Early in Mark, in 2:1–3:6, we are introduced to a series of five controversies treating four topics that show us what made Jesus controversial. Those topics are: (1) a claim to forgive sins as the Son of Man, (2) the association of Jesus with tax collectors and sinners, (3) questions about Jesus' style of piety in terms of fasting, and (4) two Sabbath controversies where Jesus claims the Son of Man is Lord of the Sabbath. There is a literary bracket in this controversy section involving the title Son of Man. It lays Christological groundwork for the rest of the book by pointing to a figure with unprecedented authority who forgives sin and controls the Sabbath. These activities reflect traits normally reserved for God.

Second, this is followed by kingdom teaching using parables in Mark 4. Third and finally, alongside Jesus' teachings on the arrival of hope comes a variety of miracles that serve as power points, what are called "powers" (*dunamis*), about God's presence with him and the authority he possesses. Though Jesus ministers in the Decapolis and does perform a miracle for a Syro-Phoenician woman, the bulk of the activity in the first half of the Gospel is in Galilee and to the nation of Israel. He meets with rejection in Nazareth, a fact Mark notes as he also tells of the execution of John the Baptist, foreshadowing the note of rejection and suffering that will dominate the second half of Mark. Seeing the Gospel's structure in this way, as an extended three-part discussion of ministry in Galilee, followed by confession of Jesus as Messiah and then teaching about suffering as the entourage heads to Jerusalem, shows how everything turns once Peter confesses Jesus to be the Messiah in the villages of Caesarea Philippi. The question becomes, "What kind of Messiah?" The description of Jesus' powerful ministry in the three-part presentation of Galilean ministry indicates what motivated Peter to confess Jesus as more than a mere prophet – as one who is, in fact, the promised central figure of deliverance according to divine promise.

The emphasis on suffering that follows in Mark 8:27 serves as an initial surprise for one called Messiah. That figure of hoped-for deliverance had been expected only to display victorious power. This teaching on suffering sets a model for following in his path. Yet the Transfiguration previews a greater glory to come. Predictions of what Jesus will face in Jerusalem follow, but the disciples are slow to get the point. Healings continue to underscore that God is still with Jesus, despite the talk about suffering.

The events in Jerusalem take an interesting turn in light of the emphasis on suffering. From the entry amid praise about the coming kingdom of

David to the cleansing of the temple, Jesus acts out a regal claim on the nation. He also takes up the expected call to purge the nation's worship in a messianic act that evokes the need for the nation to be cleansed and to embrace the opportunity to share in promise. A series of controversies keeps the issue of Jesus' authority front and center. These climactic events turn the reader's attention to Jesus' authority as the journey to the cross shows Jesus anticipating a vindication from God that underscores his right to teach about the kingdom and to make the claims that he does about himself. The parable of the wicked tenants and the exchange before the Jewish leadership about a cloud-riding Son of Man seated at the right hand of God predict this vindication, as does the hope that the Son of Man will return to gather the elect. The teaching about the return shows that the program of the Messiah goes from suffering to exaltation, with the deliverance being completed in the return. The career of Messiah does not come all at once, as had been anticipated; rather, it comes in two distinct stages.

The abrupt description of resurrection at the end of the Gospel says crisply and simply that God has delivered on this hope of vindication. Jesus may have suffered, but the sequel to his death shows the way to the hope of fulfilment of promise. The Son of Man is now seated with God. In the women's fear that the empty tomb generated is the need for a decision about what one will do with the Jesus whose life and ministry Mark has just presented. The Gospel possesses an ending that should lead into reflection on the good news story just told. What will one do with what God has done for Jesus and what this Jesus asks of those who hear about him?

II. Suggested Readings on the Gospel of Mark

This list of suggested readings is divided into two parts. The first covers commentaries consulted. The second offers supportive articles, listed by passage unit, and concluding with a bibliography on the various endings of Mark. Standard abbreviations are used; therefore, abbreviations in this section are not included in the abbreviations list, which lists only works cited in the commentary proper.

COMMENTARIES

D. Bock, "The Gospel of Mark," in *Cornerstone Biblical Commentary: The Gospel of Matthew, The Gospel of Mark*. Vol. 11 (Carol Stream, IL: Tyndale House Publishers, 2005).

E. Boring, *Mark: A Commentary*. The New Testament Library (Louisville: Westminster John Knox Press, 2006).

A. Collins, *Mark*. Hermeneia (Minneapolis: Fortress, 2007).

C. Cranfield, *The Gospel According to St Mark*. The Cambridge Greek Commentary (Cambridge: Cambridge University Press, 1959, 1977).

J. Donahue and D. Harrington, *The Gospel of Mark* (Collegeville, MN: Michael Glazier Press, 2002).

J. Edwards, *The Gospel According to Mark* (Grand Rapids: Eerdmans, 2002).

C. Evans, *Mark 8:27–16:20*. Word Biblical Commentary (Nashville: Thomas Nelson, 2001).

C. Focant, *The Gospel According to Mark: A Commentary* (Eugene, OR: Pickwick Press, 2012).

R. T. France, *The Gospel of Mark*. The New International Greek Testament Commentary (Grand Rapids: Eerdmans, 2002).

D. Garland, *Mark*. The NIV Application Commentary (Grand Rapids: Zondervan, 1996).

R. Guelich, *Mark 1:1–8:26*. Word Biblical Commentary (Dallas: Word, 1989).

R. Gundry, *Mark: A Commentary on His Apology for the Cross* (Grand Rapids: Eerdmans, 1993).

M. Hooker, *The Gospel According to Saint Mark*. Black's New Testament Commentaries (Peabody, MA: Hendrickson, 1991).

L. Hurtado, *Mark*. New International Biblical Commentary (Peabody, MA: Hendrickson, 1989).

A. Kuruvilla, *Mark: A Theological Commentary for Preachers* (Eugene, OR: Cascade Books, 2012).

W. Lane, *The Gospel According to Mark*. The New International Commentary on the New Testament (Grand Rapids: Eerdmans, 1974).

J. Marcus, *Mark 1–8*. The Anchor Bible (New York: Doubleday, 1999).

J. Marcus, *Mark 8–16*. The Anchor Yale Bible (New Haven: Yale University Press, 2009).

R. Pesch, *Das Markusevanglium*. Herders theologisicher Kommentar zum Neuen Testament. New ed. (Freiburg: Herder, 1984).

E. Schweizer, *The Good News According to Mark*. Trans. D. H. Madvig (Atlanta: John Knox, 1970).

R. Stein, *Mark*. Baker Exegetical Commentary on the New Testament (Grand Rapids: Baker Academic, 2008).

V. Taylor, *The Gospel According to St Mark: The Greek Text with Introduction, Notes and Indexes*. 2nd ed. (London: Macmillan, 1966).

B. Witherington, *The Gospel of Mark: A Socio-Rhetorical Commentary* (Grand Rapids: Eerdmans, 2001).

ARTICLES BY PASSAGE UNIT

Mark 1:1–14

E.-M. Becker, "Die markinschen Summarien – ein literarischer und theologischer Schlussel zu Markus 1–6," *NTS* 56 (2010): 452–74.

R. Bultmann, *The History of the Synoptic Tradition*. 2nd ed. Trans. John Marsh (New York: Harper & Row, 1968), 247–53.

A. B. Caneday, "Mark's Provocative Use of Scripture in Narration 'He Was with the Wild Animals and Angels Ministered to Him,'" *BBR* 9 (1999): 10–36.

M. A. Chancey, "How Jewish Was Jesus' Galilee?" *BAR* 33 (2007): 42–50, 76.

B. Chilton, *Jesus' Baptism and Jesus' Healing* (Harrisburg, PA: Trinity Press, 1998), 1–29.

A. Y. Collins, "Establishing the Text: Mark 1:1," in *Texts and Contexts: Biblical Texts in the Textual and Situational Contexts Essays in Honor of Lars Hartman*, ed. T. Fronberg and D. Hellholm (Oslo: Scandinavian University Press, 1995), 111–27.

N. C. Croy, "Where the Gospel Text Begins: A Non-Theological Interpretation of Mark 1:1," *NovT* 43 (2001): 105–127.

R. E. DeMaris, "Possession, Good and Bad – Ritual, Effects and Side-Effects: The Baptism of Jesus and Mark 1.9–11 from a Cross-Cultural Perspective," *JSNT* 80 (2000): 3–30.

R. J. Dillon, "Mark 1:1–15: A 'New Evangelization,'" *CBQ* 76 (2014): 1–18.

E. P. Dixon, "Descending Spirit and Descending Gods: A 'Greek' Interpretation of the Spirit's 'Descent as a Dove' in Mark 1:10," *JBL* 128 (2009): 759–80.

R. Dormandy, "Jesus' Temptations in Mark's Gospel: Mark 1:12–13," *ExpTim* 114 (2003): 183–87.

D. Dormeyer, "Die Kompositionsmetapher 'Evangelium Jesu Christi, des Sohnes Gottes' Mark 1.1: Ihre theologische und literarische Aufgabe in der Jesus-Biographie des Markus," *NTS* 33 (1987): 452–68.

B. Ehrman, *The Orthodox Corruption of Scripture: The Effect of Early Christological Controversies on the Text of the New Testament* (Oxford: Oxford University Press, 1993), 72–75.

J. K. Elliot, "Mark 1.1–3 – A Later Addition to the Gospel?" *NTS* 46 (2000): 585–88.

C. Evans, "Mark's Incipit and the Priene Calendar Inscription: From Jewish Gospel to Greco-Roman Gospel," *Journal of Greco-Roman Christianity and Judaism* 1 (2000): 67–81.

H. T. Fleddermann, *Mark and Q: A Study of the Overlap Texts* (BEThL 122; Leuven: Leuven University Press/Peeters, 1995), 31–39.

P. Head, "A Text Critical Study of Mark 1.1: The Beginning of the Gospel of Jesus Christ," *NTS* 37 (1991): 621–29.

J. P. Heil, "Jesus with the Wild Animals in Mark 1:13," *CBQ* 68 (2006): 63–78.

J. C. Hutchinson, "Was John the Baptist an Essene from Qumran?" *BibSac* 159 (2002): 187–200.

C. E. Joynes, "The Returned Elijah? John the Baptist's Angelic Identity in the Gospel of Mark," *SJT* 58 (2005): 455–67.

L. Keck, "The Introduction to Mark's Gospel," *NTS* 12 (1966): 352–70.

J. A. Kelhoffer, "Did John the Baptist Eat Like a Former Essene? Locust-Eating in the Ancient Near East and at Qumran," *DSD* 11/3 (2004): 293–314.

"'Locusts and Wild Honey' (Mk 1.6 c and Mt 3.4 c): The Status Quaestionis concerning the Diet of John the Baptist," *CBR* 2 (2003): 104–127.

H. Moxnes, "The Construction of Galilee as a Place for the Historical Jesus – Part I," *BTB* 31 (2001): 26–37.
"The Construction of Galilee as a Place for the Historical Jesus – Part II," *BTB* 31 (2001): 64–77.

S. Moyise, "Scripture in the New Testament: Literary and Theological Perspectives," *Neot* 42 (2008): 305–326.

R. S. Notley, "The Sea of Galilee: Development of an Early Christian Toponym," *JBL* 128 (2009): 183–88.

M. Öhler, "The Expectation of Elijah and the Presence of the Kingdom of God," *JBL* 118 (1999): 461–76.

M. Patella, "The Sites of Jesus' Baptism," *TBT* 40 (2002): 375–79.

M. Peppard, "The Eagle and the Dove: Roman Imperial Sonship and the Baptism of Jesus (Mark 1.9–11)," *NTS* 56 (2010): 431–51.

D. Rudman, "The Crucifixion as Chaoskamf: A New Reading of the Passion Narrative in the Synoptic Gospels," *Bib* 84 (2003): 102–107.

S. Samuel, "The Beginning of Mark: A Colonial/Postcolonial Conundrum," *BibInt* 10 (2002): 405–419.

L. Schiavo, "The Temptation of Jesus: The Eschatological Battle and the New Ethic of the First Followers of Jesus in Q," *JSNT* 25 (2002): 141–64.

D. C. Smith, "Jewish Proselyte Baptism and the Baptism of John," *ResQ* 25 (1982): 13–32.

K. Snodgrass, "Streams of Tradition Emerging from Isaiah 40:1–5 and Their Adaptation in the New Testament," *JSNT* 8 (1980): 24–45.

C. H. Turner, "'ὁ υἱός μου ὁ ἀγαπητός,'" *JTS* 27 (1926): 113–29.

T. Wasserman, "The 'Son of God' Was in the Beginning (Mark 1:1)," *JTS* 62 (2011): 20–50.

R. L. Webb, "Jesus' Baptism: Its Historicity and Implications," *BBR* 10 (2000): 261–309.

Mark 1:16–29

P. Achtemeier, "'He Taught Them Many Things': Reflections on Marcan Christology," *CBQ* 42 (1980): 465–81.

A. W. Argyle, "The Meaning of Exousia in Mark 1:22, 27," *ExpTim* 80 (1969): 343.

O. Bächli, "Was habe ich mit Dir zu schaffen?" *TZ* 33 (1977): 69–80.

O. Bauernfeind, *Die Worte der Dämonen im Markusevangelium* (Stuttgart: Kohlhammer, 1927), 3–10, 14–15, 28–31, 68–69.

D. Daube, "Ἐξουσία in Mark 1:22 and 27," *JTS* 39 (1938): 45–59.

E. Eve, *The Jewish Context of Jesus' Miracles* (Edinburgh: T & T Clark, 2002), 13–15.

M. Hengel, *The Charismatic Leader and His Followers*. 1st English ed. (New York: Crossroad, 1981), 42–50.

H. C. Kee, "The Changing Meaning of Synagogue: A Response to Richard Oster," *NTS* 40 (1994): 281–83.

"The Terminology of Mark's Exorcism Stories," *NTS* 14 (1967–68): 232–46.

"The Transformation of the Synagogue after 70 C.E.: Its Import for Early Christianity," *NTS* 36 (1990): 117–23, 191–99.

L. I. Levine, "The Nature and Origin of the Palestinian Synagogue Reconsidered," *JBL* 115 (1996): 425–48.

"The Second Temple Synagogue: The Formative Years," in *The Synagogue in Late Antiquity*, ed. L. Levine (Philadelphia: American School of Oriental Research, 1987), 201–222.

D. Luhrmann, "Die Pharisaer und die Schriftgelehrten im Markusevangelium," *ZNW* 78 (1987): 169–85.

R. E. K. Mchami, "Demon Possession and Exorcism in Mark 1:21–28," *AfricanTheoJ* 24 (2001): 17–37.

J. Murphy-O'Connor, "Fishers of Fish, Fishers of Men: What We Know of the First Disciples from Their Profession," *BRev* 15/3 (1999): 22–28.

Holy Land. 5th ed. (Oxford: Oxford University Press, 2008), 188–93.

M. Nun, "Ports of Galilee," *BARev* 25/4 (1999): 18–31.

R. Oster, "Supposed Anachronism in Luke-Acts' Use of Sunagoge: A Rejoinder to H. C. Kee," *NTS* 39 (1993): 178–208.

P. Richardson, *Building Jewish in the Roman East* (JSJSup 92; Waco, TX: Baylor University Press; Leiden: Brill, 2004), 111–33.

D. Rudman, "The Significance of the Phrase 'Fishers of Men' in the Synoptic Gospels," *IBS* 26 (2005): 106–118.

C. W. F. Smith, "Fishers of Men: Footnotes on a Gospel Figure," *HTR* 52 (1959): 187–203.

F. S. Spencer, "'Follow Me.' The Imperious Call of Jesus in the Synoptic Gospels," *Int* 59 (2005): 142–53.

J. Starr, "The Meaning of 'Authority' in Mark 1,22," *HTR* 23 (1930): 302–305.

R. H. Stein, "The 'Redaktionsgeschichtliche' Investigation of a Markan Seam (Mc 1:21f.)," *ZNW* 61 (1970): 70–94.

W. H. Wuellner, *The Meaning of the Fishers of Men* (Philadelphia: Westminster Press, 1967), 10–17, 67–75, 109–114.

Mark 1:30–45

C. Bonner, "Traces of Thaumaturgic Technique in the Miracles," *HTR* 20 (1927): 171–81.

H. C Cave, "The Leper: Mark 1.40–45," *NTS* 25 (1978–79): 245–50.

J. D. G. Dunn, "Jesus and Purity: An Ongoing Debate," *NTS* 48 (2002): 449–67.

J. K. Elliott, "The Conclusion of the Pericope of the Healing of the Leper and Mark 1,45," *JTS* 22 (1971): 153–57.

W. C. Kannaday, "'Are Your Intentions Honorable?': Apologetic Interests and the Scribal Revision of Jesus in the Canonical Gospels," *TC* 11 (2006): pars. 1–30.

G. D. Kilpatrick, "Mark i 45 and the Meaning of λόγος," *JTS* 40 (1939): 389–90.

K. Lake, "Ἐμβριμησάμενος and Ὀργισθείς (Mark 1:40–43)," *HTR* 16 (1923): 197–98.

C. H. Turner, "Marcan Usage: Notes, Critical and Exegetical, on the Second Gospel," *JTS* 26 (1925): 145–56.

P. J. Williams, "An Examination of Ehrman's Case for οργισθεις in Mark 1:41," *NovT* 54 (2012): 1–12.

Mark 2:1–12

M. Albertz, *Die synoptischen Streitgespräche: Ein Beitrag zur Formengeschichte des Urchristentums* (Berlin: Trowitzsch & Sohn, 1921), 5–16, 57–117.

G. H. Boobyer, "Mark II. 10a and the Interpretation of the Healing of the Paralytic," *HTR* 47 (1954): 115–20.

H. Branscomb, "Mark 2:5, 'Son Thy Sins Are Forgiven,'" *JBL* 53 (1934): 53–60.

C. P. Ceroke, "Is Mark 2:10 a Saying of Jesus?" *CBQ* 22 (1960): 369–90.

J. Dewey, *Markan Public Debate: Literary Technique, Concentric Structure, and Theology in Mark 2:1–3:6* (Chico, CA: California Scholars Press, 1980), 28–29, 43–52.

L. S. Hay, "The Son of Man in Mark 2:10, and 2:28," *JBL* 89 (1970): 69–75.

H.-J. Klauck, "Die Frage der Sündenvergebung in der Perikope von der Heilung des Gelähmten," *BZ* 15 (1981): 223–48.

H.-W. Kuhn, *Ältere Sammlungen im Markusevangelium* (StUNT 8; Göttingen: Vandenhoeck & Ruprecht, 1971), 18–24, 58–61, 75–98, 232–34.

D. Lührmann, "Die Pharisäer und die Schriftgelehrten im Markusevangelium," *ZNW* 78 (1987): 169–85.

R. T. Mead, "The Healing of the Paralytic a Unit?" *JBL* 80 (1961): 348–54.

N. Perrin, *A Modern Pilgrimage in New Testament Christology*. (Philadelphia: Fortress, 1974), 84–93.

D. N. Peterson, "Translating παραλυτικος in Mark 2:1–12: A Proposal," *BBR* 16 (2006): 261–272.

C. Tuckett, "The Present Son of Man," *JSNT* 14 (1982): 58–81.

B. M. F. van Iersel, "Concentric Structures in Mark 1:14–3:35 (4:1) with Some Observations on Method," *BibInt* 3 (1995): 75–98.

W. Weiß, *"Eine Neue Lehre in Vollmacht": Die Streit – und Schulgespräche des Markus – Evangeliums* (BZNW 52; Berlin: de Gruyter, 1989), 20–23.

M. Wolter, " 'Ihr sollt aber wissen . . . ,' Das Anakoluth nach ινα δε ειδητε in Mk 2, 10–11 parr," *ZNW* 95 (2004): 269–75.

W. Wrede, "Zur Heilung des Gelähmten (Mc 2,1 ff.)," *ZNW* 5 (1904): 354–58.

Mark 2:13–17

A. I. Baumgarten, "The Name of the Pharisees," *JBL* 102 (1983): 411–28.

E. Best, "Mark's Use of the Twelve," *ZNW* 69 (1978): 11–3.

F. C. Burkitt, "Levi Son of Alphaeus," *JThS* 28 (1927): 273–74.

J. R. Donahue, "Tax Collectors and Sinners: An Attempt at Identification," *CBQ* 33 (1971): 39–61.

J. D. G. Dunn, "Mark 2.1–3.6: A Bridge between Jesus and Paul on the Question of the Law," *NTS* 30 (1984): 395–415.

J. Jeremias, "Zöllner und Sünder," *ZNW* 30 (1931): 293–300.

B. Lindars, "Matthew, Levi, *Lebbaeus and the Value of the Western Text*," *NTS* 4 (1958): 220–222.

D. Lührmann, "Die Pharisäer und die Schriftgelehrten im Markusevangelium," *ZNW* 78 (1987): 169–85.

E. S. Malbon, "Τῇ οἰκίᾳ ἁτοῦ: Mark 2:15 in Context," *NTS* 31 (1985): 282–92.

R. Pesch, "Levi-Matthäus (Mc 2, 14 / Mt 9, 9; 10, 3) ein Beitrag zur Lösung eines alten Problems," *ZNW* 59 (1968): 40–56.

Mark 2:18–22

B. W. Bacon, "Pharisees and Herodians in Mark," *JBL* 39 (1920): 102–12.

H. J. Ebeling, "Die Fastenfrage (Mark 2.18–22)," *TSK* 108 (1937–38): 382–96.

D. Flusser, "Do You Prefer New Wine?" *Immanuel* 9 (1979): 26–31.

F. Hahn, "Die Bildworte vom neuen Flicken und vom jungen Wein," *ET* 31 (1971): 357–75.

A. Kee, "The Old Coat and the New Wine: A Parable of Repentance," *NovT* 11 (1969): 13–21.

"The Question about Fasting," *NovT* 12 (1970): 161–73.

K. T. Schäfer, "'. . . und dann werden sie fasten, an jenem Tage' (Mk 2,20 und Parallelen)," in *Synoptische Studien*, FS A. Wikenhauser (Munich: Karl Zink, 1953), 124–47.

J. A. Ziesler, "The Removal of the Bridegroom: A Note on Mark II, 18–22 and Parallels," *NTS* 19 (1972–73): 190–94.

Mark 2:23–28

F. W. Beare, "The Sabbath Was Made for Man," *JBL* 79 (1960): 130–36.

M. Casey, *Aramaic Sources of Mark's Gospel.* (Cambridge: Cambridge University Press, 1998), 145–53.

D. M. Cohn-Sherbok, "An Analysis of Jesus' Arguments Concerning the Plucking of Grain on the Sabbath," *JSNT* 2 (1979): 31–41.

S. S. Cohon, "The Place of Jesus in the Religious Life of His Day," *JBL* 48 (1929): 82–106.

D. Daube, "Responsibilities of Master and Disciples in the Gospels," *NTS* 19 (1972–73): 1–15.

J. D. M. Derrett, "Judaica in St. Mark," in *Studies in the New Testament* (Leiden: Brill, 1977), 1.85–100.

L. S. Hay, "The Son of Man in Mark 2:10 and 2:28," *JBL* 89 (1970): 69–75.

A. J. Hultgren, "The Formation of the Sabbath Pericope in Mark 2:23–28," *JBL* 91 (1972): 38–43.

J. Jeremias, "Die älteste Schicht der Menschensohn-Logien," *ZNW* 58 (1967): 159–72.

T. W. Manson, "Mark II.27 f," *ConNT* 11 (1947): 138–46.

J. P. Meier, "The Historical Jesus and the Plucking of the Grain on the Sabbath," *CBQ* 66 (2004): 561–81.

C. S. Morgan, "When Abiathar Was High Priest," *JBL* 98 (1979): 409–410.

F. Neirynck, "Jesus and the Sabbath: Some Observations on Mark ii,27," in *Jésus aux origines de la christologie*, ed. J. Dupont (BETL 40; Gembloux: J. Duculot, 1974), 227–70.

K. Queller, "'Stretch Out Your Hand' Echo and Metalepsis in Mark's Sabbath Healing Controversy," *JBL* 129 (2010): 737–58.

A. D. Rogers, "Mark 2.26," *JTS* 2 (1951): 44–45.

J. W. Wenham, "Mark 2.26," *JTS* 1 (1950): 156.

Mark 3:1–6

W. J. Bennet, "The Herodians of Mark's Gospel," *NovT* 17 (1975): 281–98.

A. Cane, "Contested Meanings of the Name 'Judas Iscariot,'" *ExpTim* 112 (2000): 44–45.

E. Lohse, "Jesu Worte über den Sabbat," in *Judentum, Urchristentum und Kirche*, FS J. Jeremias, ed. W. Eltester (BZNW 26; Berlin: Töpelmann, 1960), 79–89.

E. Ottenheijm, "Impurity between Intention and Deed: Purity Disputes in First Century Judaism and in the New Testament," in *Purity and Holiness: The Heritage of Leviticus*, ed. M. J. H. M. Poorthuis and J. Schwartz (JCPS 2; Leiden/Boston/Cologne: Brill, 2000), 135–43.

H. H. Rowley, "The Herodians in the Gospels," *JTS* 41 (1940): 14–27.

C. W. Skinner, "'Whom He Also Named Apostles': A Textual Problem in Mark 3:14," *BibSac* 161 (2004): 322–29.

Mark 3:7–12

O. Betz, "The Concept of the So-called 'Divine Man,'" in *Studies in New Testament and Early Christian Literature*, FS A. P. Wikgren, ed. D. Aune (Leiden: Brill, 1972), 229–40.

B. Blackburn, *Theios Aner and the Markan Miracle Traditions: A Critique of the Theios Aner Concept as an Interpretative Background of the Miracle Tradition* (Tübingen: Mohr/Siebeck, 1990).

T. A. Burkill, "Mark 3,7–12 and the Alleged Dualism in the Evangelist's Miracle Material," *JBL* 87 (1968): 409–417.

C. W. Hedrick, "The Role of 'Summary Statements' in the Composition of the Gospel of Mark: A Dialogue with Karl Schmidt and Norman Perrin," *NovT* 26 (1984): 289–311.

L. Keck, "Mk 3,7–12 and Mark's Christology," *JBL* 84 (1965): 341–58.

J. Kingsbury, "The 'Divine Man' as the Key to Mark's Christology – The End of an Era?" *Int* 35 (1981): 243–57.

U. Luz, "Die Geheimnismotiv und die markinische Christologie," *ZNW* 56 (1965): 9–30.

Mark 3:13–19

E. Best, "Mark's Use of the Twelve," *ZNW* 69 (1978): 11–35.

"The Role of the Disciples in Mark," *NTS* 23 (1976–77): 377–401.

O. Betz, "Donnersöhne, Menschenfischer und der davidische Messias," *RevQ* 3 (1961): 41–70.

R Buth, "Mark 3:17 ΒΟΝΕΡΓΕΣ and Popular Etymology," *JSNT* 10 (1981): 29–33.

J. Fitzmyer, "Aramaic *Kepha* and Peter's Name in the New Testament," in *To Advance the Gospel: New Testament Studies* (New York: Crossroad, 1981), 112–24.

J. Fitzmyer, "The Name Simon," in *Essays in the Semitic Background of the New Testament* (London: Chapman, 1971), 105–112.

P. Lampe, "Das Spiel mit dem Petrus-Namen – Matt. xvi. 18," *NTS* 25 (1978–79): 227–45.

S. McKnight, "Jesus and the Twelve," in *Key Events in the Life of the Historical Jesus: A Collaborative Exploration of Context and Coherence*, ed. Darrell L. Bock and Robert L. Webb (Tübingen: Mohr/Siebeck, 2009), 181–214.

B. Rigaux, "Die 'Zwölf' in Geschichte und Kerygma," in *Der historische Jesus und der kerygmatische Christus*, ed. H. Ristow and K. Matthiae (Berlin: Evangelische Verlaganstalt, 1964), 468–86.

J. T. Rook, "'Boanerges, Sons of Thunder' (Mk 3:17)," *JBL* 100 (1981): 94–95.

C. C. Torrey, "The Name 'Iscariot,'" *HTR* 36 (1943): 52–56.

Mark 3:20–35

E. Best, "Mark iii. 20, 21, 31–35," *NTS* 22 (1975–76): 309–319.

L. Briskin, "Tanakh Sources of Judas Iscariot," *JBQ* 32 (2004): 189–197.

R. Jordan, "The Significance of Mark 3:20-end for Understanding the Message of Mark's Gospel," *ExpTim* 124 (2013): 227–33.

A. Busch, "Questioning and Conviction: Double-Voiced Discourse in Mark 3:22–30," *JBL* 125 (2006): 477–505.

M. E. Boring, "The Unforgivable Sin Logion, Mark iii 28–29/Matt xii 31–32/ Luke xii 10: Formal Analysis and History of the Tradition," *NovT* 18 (1976): 258–79.

C. Colpe, "Der Spruch von der Lästerung des Geistes," in *Der Ruf Jesu und die Antwort der Gemeinde*, FS J. Jeremias, ed. E. Lohse (Göttingen: Vandenhoeck & Ruprecht, 1970), 65–79.

O. E. Evans, "The Unforgivable Sin," *ExpTim* 68 (1956–57): 240–44.

L. Gaston, "Beelzebul," *TZ* 18 (1962): 247–55.

J. Lambrecht, "The Relatives of Jesus in Mark," *NovT* 16 (1974): 241–58.

V. K. Robbins, "Beelzebul Controversy in Mark and Luke: Rhetorical and Social Analysis," *Forum* 7 (1991): 261–77.

H. Wansbrough, "Mark 3, 21 – Was Jesus out of His Mind?" *NTS* 18 (1972): 233–35.

D. Wenham, "The Meaning of Mark iii.21," *NTS* 21 (1974–75): 295–300.

J. G. Williams, "A Note on the 'Unforgivable Sin' Logion," *NTS* 12 (1965–66): 75–77.

Mark 4:1-34

M. A. Beavis, "The Power of Jesus' Parables: Were they Polemical or Irenic?" *JSNT* 82 (2001): 3–30.

B. C. Crisler, "The Acoustics and Crowd Capacity of Natural Theaters in Palestine," *BA* 39 (1976): 137.

J. D. Crossan "The Seed Parables of Jesus," *JBL* 92 (1973): 244–66.

N. A Dahl, "The Parables of Growth," *ST* 5 (1951): 132–66 = *Jesus in the Memory of the Early Church* (Minneapolis: Augsburg, 1976), 141–66.

J. D. M. Derrett, "Preaching to the Coast (Mark 4:1)," *EvQ* 73 (2001): 195–203.

C. Dietzfelbinger, "Das Gleichnis vom ausgestreuten Samen," in *Der Ruf Jesu und die Antwort der Gemeinde*, ed. E. Lohse (Göttingen: Vandenhoeck & Ruprecht, 1970), 80–93.

C. A. Evans, *To See and Not Perceive: Isaiah 6.9–10 in Early Jewish and Christian Interpretation* (JSNTSup 64; Sheffield: JSOT Press, 1989), esp. 53–80.

H. Frankemölle, "Hat Jesus sich selbst verkündigt? Christologische Implikationen in den vormarkinischen Parabelen," *BibLeb* 13 (1972): 184–207.

B. Gerhardsson, "The Parable of the Sower and Its Interpretation," *NTS* 14 (1967–68): 165–93.

M. Hengel, *Studies in the Gospel of Mark*. Trans. J. Bowden (London: SCM Press, 1985), 95–96.

J. Jeremias, "Palästinakundliches zum Gleichnis vom Sämann," *NTS* 13 (1966–67): 48–53.

V. J. John, "Ecology in the Parables: The Use of Nature Language in the Parables of the Synoptic Gospels." *AsiaJourTheo* 14.2 (2000): 304–327.

D. H. Juel, "Encountering the Sower (Mark 4:1–20)," *Int* 56 (2002): 273–83.

E. Kellenberger, "Heil und Verstockung. Zu Jes 6, 9f. bei Jesaja und im Neuen Testament," *TZ* 48 (1992): 268–75.

M. P. Knowles, "Abram and the Birds in Jubilees 11: A Subtext for the Parable of the Sower?" *NTS* 41 (1995): 145–51.

M. Lau, "Entlang des Weges gesat – doch nicht vergebens! Ein Notiz zu Mk 4, 4 im Licht von Mk 10,46," *BN* 142 (2009): 99–103.

R. K. McIver, "One Hundredfold Yield – Miraculous or Mundane? Matthew 13:8, 23; Mark 4:8, 20; Luke 8:8." *NTS* 40 (1994): 606–608.

J. Marcus, "Mark 4:10–12 and Markan Epistemology," *JBL* 103 (1984): 557–74.

S. Nelavala, "Smart Syrophoenician Woman: A Dalit Feminist Reading of Mark 7:24–31," *ExpTim* 118 (2006): 64–69.

R. North, "How Loud Was Jesus's Voice? Mark 4:1," *ExpTim* 112 (2001): 117–20.

D. C. Parker, *The Living Text of the Gospels* (Cambridge: Cambridge University Press), 104–18, 183.

P. B. Payne, "The Order of Sowing and Ploughing in the Parable of the Sower," *NTS* 25 (1978–79): 123–29.

B. Pixner, *With Jesus Through Galilee* (Corazin Press, 1992), 41–42.

R. S. Schellenberg, "Kingdom as Contaminant? The Role of Repertoire in the Parables of the Mustard Seed and the Leaven," *CBQ* 71 (2009): 527–43.

P. Sellew, "Oral and Written Sources in Mark 4.1–34," *NTS* 36 (1990): 234–67.

K. Snodgrass, "A Hermeneutics of Hearing Informed by the Parables with Special Reference to Mark 4," *BBR* 14 (2004): 59–79.

G. E. M. Suess, "Enemies of the Harvest," *Jerusalem Persp* 53 (1997): 18–23.

G. Theissen, "Der Bauer und die von selbst Frucht bringende Erde," *ZNW* 85 (1994): 167–82.

J. J. Vincent, "Outworkings: Urban Mission in Mark 4," *ExpTim* 122 (2011): 531–38.

K. W. White, "The Parable of the Sower," *JTS* n.s. 15 (1964): 300–307.

A. N. Wilder, The Parable of the Sower: Naiveté and Method in Interpretation," *Semeia* 2 (1974): 134–51.

Mark 4:35–41

P. Achtemeier, "Gospel Tradition and the Divine Man," *Int* 26 (1972): 174–97. "The Origin and Function of the Pre-Markan Miracle Catenae," *JBL* 91 (1972): 198–221.

"Person and Deed. Jesus and the Storm-Tossed Sea," *Int* 16 (1962): 169–76.

"Toward the Isolation of Pre-Markan Miracle Catenae," *JBL* 89 (1970): 265–91.

B. Batto, "The Sleeping God: An Ancient Near Eastern Motif of Divine Sovereignty," *Bib* 68 (1987): 153–77.

E. Best, "The Miracles in Mark," *RevExp* 75 (1978): 539–54.

O. Betz, "The Concept of the So-called 'Divine Man' in Mark's Christology," in *Studies in New Testament and Early Christian Literature*, FS A. P. Wikgren, ed. D. E. Aune (*NTS* 33; Leiden: Brill, 1972), 229–40.

K. M. Fisher and V. C. von Wahlde, "The Miracles of Mark 4:35–5:43: Their Meaning and Function in the Gospel Framework," *BTB* 11 (1981): 13–16.

J. D. Kingsbury, "The 'Divine Man' as the Key to Mark's Christology – The End of an Era?" *Int* 35 (1981): 243–57.

K. W. Larsen, "Matthew 8:27 and Mark 4:36: Relics of a Prior Source?" *ResQ* 54 (2012): 186–90.

W. L. Liefeld, "The Hellenistic 'Divine Man' and the Figure of Jesus in the Gospels," *JETS* 16 (1973): 195–205.

R. Meye, "Psalm 107 as 'Horizon' for Interpreting the Miracle Stories of Mark 4:35– 8:26," in *Unity and Diversity in New Testament Theology*, FS G. E. Ladd, ed. R. A. Guelich (Grand Rapids: Eerdmans, 1978), 1–13.

G. Petzke, "Die historische Frage nach den Wundertaten Jesu," *NTS* 22 (1975–76): 180–204.

A. Reichert, "Zwischen Exeges und Didaktik. Die markinische Erzahlung von der Sturmstillung (Mk 4:35–41)," *ZTK* 101 (2004): 489–505.

V. K. Robbins, "Dynameis and Semeia in Mark," *BR* 18 (1973): 5–20.

M. Smith "Prolegomena to a Discussion of Aretalogies, Divine Men, the Gospels and Jesus," *JBL* 90 (1971): 174–99.

R. Strelan, "A Greater than Caesar: Storm Stories in Lucan and Mark," *ZNW* 91 (2000): 166–79.

V. Tzaferis, "A Pilgrimage to the Site of the Swine Miracle," *BARev* 15/2 (1989): 45–51.

I. Wallis, "Relating Mark's 'Stilling of the Storm' Pericope (Mark 4, 35–41) to Discipleship Today. An Experiment in Resurrection Faith," *Theology* 111 (2008): 346–51.

Mark 5:1–20

C. E. Arnold, "Exorcism 101. What Can We Learn from the Way Jesus Cast out Demons?" *CT* 45 (2001): 58.

C. Bonner, "The Technique of Exorcism," *HTR* 36 (1943): 39–49.

T. Burda, "Gadarenes, Gerasenes, Gergesenes and the 'Diatesseron' Tradition," in *Neotestamentica et Semitica*, FS M. Black, ed. E. Ellis and M. Wilcox (Edinburgh: T. & T. Clark, 1969), 181–97.

C. Burdon, "'To the Other Side': Construction of Evil and Fear of Liberation in Mark 5.1–20," *JSNT* 27 (2004): 149–67.

T. Calpino, "The Gerasene Demoniac (Mark 5:1–12): The Pre-Markan Function of the Pericope," *BR* 53 (2008): 15–23.

C. H. Cave, "The Obedience of the Unclean Spirits," *NTS* 11 (1964): 93–97.

J. F. Craghan, "The Gerasene Demoniac," *CBQ* 30 (1968): 522–36.

J. D. M. Derrett, "Contributions to the Study of the Gerasene Demoniac," *JSNT* 3 (1979): 2–17.

R. Dormandy, "The Expulsion of Legion. A Political Reading of Mark 5:1–20," *ExpTim* 111 (2000): 335–37.

J. Frey, "Zu Test Und Sinn des Freer-Logion," *ZNW* 93 (2002): 13–34.

J. Garroway, "The Invasion of a Mustard Seed: A Reading of Mark 5.1–20," *JSNT* 32 (2009): 57–75.

M. J. Geller, "Jesus' Theurgic Powers: Parallels in the Talmud and Incantation Bowls," *JJS* 28 (1977): 141–55.

M. Lau, "Die Leigio X Fretensis und der Besessene von Gerasa Anmerkungen zur Zahlenangabe 'ungefahr Zweitausend,'" *Bib* 88 (2007): 351–64.

M. Klinghardt, "Legionsschweine in Gerasa. Lokalkolorit und historischer Hintergrund von Mk 5, 1–20," *ZNW* 98 (2007): 28–48.

S. T. Parker, "The Decapolis Reviewed," *JBL* 94 (1975): 437–41.

R. Pesch, "The Markan Version of the Healing of the Gerasene Demoniac," *ER* 23 (1971): 349–76.

P. J. R. Rajkumar, "A Dalithos Reading of a Markan Exorcism: Mark 5:1–20," *ExpTim* 118 (2007): 428–35.

N. J. Torchia, "Eschatological Elements in Jesus' Healing of the Gerasene Demoniac: An Exegesis of Mk. 5:1–20," *IBS* 23 (2001): 2–27.

Mark 5:21–43

P. Achtemeier, "Toward the Isolation of Pre-Markan Miracle Catenae," *JBL* 89 (1970): 265–91.

M. R. D'Angelo, "Gender and Power in the Gospel of Mark: The Daughter of Jairus and the Woman with the Flow of Blood," in *Miracles in Jewish and Christian Antiquity: Imagining Truth*, ed. J. C. Cavadini (Notre Dame: Notre Dame University Press, 1999), 83–109.

S. J. D. Cohen, "Menstruants and the Sacred in Judaism and Christianity," in *Women's History and Ancient History*, ed. S. B. Pomeroy (Chapel Hill/London: University of North Carolina Press, 1991), 273–99, esp. 278–79.

J. M. D. Derrett, "Mark's Technique: The Hemorrhaging Woman and Jairus' Daughter," *Bib* 63 (1982): 474–505.

J. Dewey, "Jesus' Healing of Women: Conformity and Non-Conformity to Dominant Cultural Values as Clues for Historical Reconstruction," *BTB* 24 (1995): 122–31.

S. Haber, "A Woman's Touch: Feminist Encounters with the Hemorrhaging Woman in Mark 5.24–34," *JSNT* 26 (2003): 171–92.

C. Hedrick, "Miracle Stories as Literary Compositions: The Case of Jairus' Daughter," *Perspectives in Religious Studies* 20 (1993): 217–33.

A.-J. Levine, "Discharging Responsibility: Matthean Jesus, Biblical Law, and Hemorrhaging Woman," in *Treasures New and Old: Recent Contributions to Matthean Studies*, ed. D. R. Bauer and M. A. Powell (SBLSymS 1; Atlanta: Scholars Press, 1996), 379–97.

U. Luz, "The Secrecy Motif and Marcan Theology," in *The Messianic Secret*, trans. R. Morgan, ed. C. Tuckett (London/Philadelphia: SPCK/Fortress, 1983), 75–96.

C. R. Moss, "The Man with the Flow of Power: Porous Bodies in Mark 5:25–34," *JBL* 129 (2010): 507–519.

J. Neusner, "The Idea of Purity in Ancient Judaism," *JAAR* 43 (1975): 15–26.

R. Pesch, "Jairus (Mk 5,22/Lk 8,41)," *BZ* 14 (1970): 252–56.

V. K. Robbins, "Dynameis and Semeia in Mark," *BR* 18 (1973): 5–20.

"The Woman who Touched Jesus' Garment: Socio-Rhetorical Analysis of he Synoptic Accounts," *NTS* 33 (1987): 502–515.

M. J. Selvidge, "Mark 5:25–34 and Leviticus 15:19–20: A Reaction to Restrictive Purity Regulations," *JBL* 103 (1984): 619–23.

Mark 6:1–6

O. Betz, "Jesus in Nazareth," in *Israel hat dennoch Gott zum Trost*, FS Schalom Ben-Chorin, ed. G. Müller (Trier: Paulinus, 1978), 44–60.

K. M. Campbell, "What Was Jesus' Occupation?" *JETS* 48 (2005): 501–519.

J. D. Crossan, "Mark and the Relatives of Jesus," *NovT* 15 (1973): 81–113.

E. Grässer, "Jesus in Nazareth (Mark VI.1–6a): Notes on the Redaction and Theology of St. Mark," *NTS* 16 (1969–70): 1–23.

L. Hartman, "Mk 6,3a im Lichte einiger griechisher Texte," *ZNW* 95 (2004): 276–79.

W. C. Kannaday, "'Are Your Intentions Honorable?': Apologetic Interests and the Scribal Revision of Jesus in the Canonical Gospels," *TC* 11 (2006): pars. 1–30.

H. K. McArthur, "Son of Mary," *NovT* 15 (1973): 38–58.

G. D. Miller, "An Intercalation Revisited: Christology, Discipleship, and Dramatic Irony in Mark 6.6b–30," *JSNT* 35 (2012): 176–95.

C. E. Powell, "The 'Passivity' of Jesus in Mark 5:25–34," *BibSac* 162 (2005): 66–75.

V. K. Robbins, "Dynameis and Semeia in Mark," *BR* 18 (1973): 5–20.

R. L. Sturch, "The 'ΠΑΤΡΙΣ' of Jesus," *JTS* 28 (1977): 94–96.

Mark 6:7–13

B. Ahern, "'Staff or No Staff,'" *CBQ* 5 (1943): 332–37.

H. D. Betz, "Jesus and the Cynics: Survey and Analysis of a Hypothesis," *JR* 74 (1994): 453–75.

G. B. Caird, "Uncomfortable Words 11: Shake off the Dust from Your Feet," *ExpTim* 81 (1969): 40–47.

J. Jeremias, "Paarweise Sendung im Neuen Testament," in *Abba: Studien zur neutestamentlichen Theologie und Zeitgeschichte* (Göttingen: Vandenhoeck und Ruprecht, 1966).

F. J. Moloney, "Mark 6:6b–30: Mission, the Baptist, and Failure," *CBQ* 63 (2001): 647–63.

J. Neusner, "'First Cleanse the Inside,'" *NTS* 22 (1976): 486–95.

E. Power, "The Staff of the Apostles, A Problem in Gospel Harmony," *Biblica* 4 (1923), 241–66.

T. J. Rogers, "Shaking the Dust off the Markan Mission Discourse," *JSNT* 27 (2004): 169–92.

G. Theissen, "Wanderradikalismus: Literatursoziologische Aspekte der Ueberlieferung vom Worten Jesu im Urchristentum," *ZTK* 70 (1973): 245–71.

Mark 6:14–29

C. Focant, "La tete du prophete sur un plat, ou, L'anti-repas d'allianc (Mc 6.12–29)," *NTS* 47 (2001): 334–53.

D. M. Hoffeditz and G. E. Yates, "Femme Fatale Redux: Intertextual Connection to the Elijah/Jezebel Narratives in Mark 6:14–29," *BBR* 15 (2005): 199–221.

R. Janes, "Why the Daughter of Herodias Must Dance (Mark 6.14–29)," *JSNT* 28 (2006): 443–67.

C. Karakolis, "Narrative Funktion und christologische Bedeutung der markinischen Erzahlung vom Tod Johannes des Taufers (Mk 6:14–29)," *NovT* 52 (2010): 134–55.

M. McVann, "The 'Passion' of John the Baptist and Jesus before Pilate: Mark's Warnings about Kings and Governors," *BTB* 38 (2008): 152–57.

R. Pesch, "Zur Entstehung des Glaubens der Auferstehung Jesu," *TQ* 153 (1973): 201–228.

W. Schenk, "Gegenschaft und Tod des Täufers: Erwägungen zur Christologie und ihre Konsequenzen," *NTS* 29 (1983): 453–83.

A. Smith, "Tyranny Exposed: Mark's Typological Characterization of Herod Antipas (Mark 6:14–29)," *BibInt* 14 (2006): 259–293.

P.-B. Smit, "Eine Neutestamentliche Geburtstagsfeier und die Charakterisierung des 'Konigs' Herodes Antipas (Mk 6, 21–29)," *BZ* 53 (2009): 29–46.

C. Wolff, "Zur Bedeutung Johannes des Täufers im Markusevangeliums," *TLZ* 102 (1977): 857–65.

Mark 6:30–44

P. Achtemeier, "Toward the Isolation of Pre-Markan Miracle Catenae," *JBL* 89 (1970): 265–91.

"The Origin and Function of the Pre-Markan Miracle Catenae," *JBL* 91 (1972): 198–221.

G. H. Boobyer, "The Eucharistic Interpretation of the Miracles of the Loaves in St. Mark's Gospel," *JTS* 3 (1952): 161–71.

"The Miracles of the Loaves and the Gentiles in St. Mark's Gospel," *SJT* 6 (1953): 77–87.

K. P. Donfried, "The Feeding Narratives and the Marcan Community," in *Kirche*, FS G. Bornkamm, ed. D. Lührmann and G. Strecker (Tübingen: Mohr, 1980), 95–103.

G. Friedrich, "Die beiden Erzählungen von der Speisung in Mark 6, 31–44, 8,1–9," *TZ* 20 (1964): 10–22.

A. Heising, "Exegese und Theologie der Alt – und Neutestamentlichen Speisewunder," *ZTK* 86 (1964): 80–96.

B. W. van Iersel, "Die wunderbare Speisung und das Abendmahl in der synoptischen Tradition (Mk VI. 35–44 par VIII. 1–20 par)," *NovT* 7 (1964): 167–94.

L. H. Jenkins, "A Marcan Doublet," in *Studies in History and Religion*, FS H. W. Robinson, ed. E. A. Payne (London: Lutterworth, 1942), 87–111.

L. E. Keck, "Mark 3:7–12 and Mark's Christology," *JBL* 84 (1965): 341–58.

S. Masuda, "The Good News of the Miracle of the Bread. The Tradition and Its Markan Redaction," *NTS* 28 (1982): 191–219.

H. Montefiore, "Revolt in the Desert? (Mark vi. 30ff.)," *NTS* 8 (1961–62): 135–41.

F. Neugebauer, "Die wunderbare Speisung (Mk 6,30–44 parr.) und Jesu Identität," *KD* 32 (1986): 254–77.

H. Patsch, "Abendmahlterminologie ausserhalb der Einsetzungsberichte: Erwägungen zur Traditionsgeschichte der Abendmahlsworte," *ZNW* 62 (1971): 210–31.

A. Standhartinger, "'Und alle assen und wurden satt' (Mk 6,42 par.). Die Speisungserzahlungen im Kontext romisch-hellenistischer Festkulturen," *BZ* 57 (2013): 60–81.

B. E. Thiering, "'Breaking of Bread' and 'Harvest' in Mark's Gospel," *NovT* 12 (1970): 1–12.

G. Ziener, "Die Brotwunder im Markusevangelium," *BZ* 4 (1960): 282–85.

Mark 6:45–52

A. Y. Collins, "Rulers, Divine Men, and Walking on the Water (6:45–52)," in *Religious Propaganda and Missionary Competition in the Greco-Roman World*, ed. L. Bormann, K. del Tredici, and A. Standhartinger (D. Georgi Festschrift; NTS 74; Leiden: Brill, 1994), 207–227.

J. R. Combs, "A Ghost on the Water? Understanding an Absurdity in Mark 6:49–50," *JBL* 127 (2008): 345–58.

J. D. M. Derrett, "Why and How Jesus Walked on the Sea," *NovT* 23 (1981): 330–48.

H. Fleddermann, "And He Wanted to Pass by Them (Mark 6:48c)," *CBQ* 45 (1983): 389–95.

S. W. Henderson, "'Concerning the Loaves': Comprehending Incomprehension in Mark 6:45–52," *JSNT* 83 (2001): 3–26.

J. Kremer, "Jesu Wandel auf dem See nach Mk 6,45–52," *BibLeb* 10 (1969): 221–32.

D. Ortlund, "The Old Testament Background and Eschatological Significance of Jesus Walking on the Sea (Mark 6:45–52)," *Neot* 46 (2012): 319–37.

H. Ritt, "Der 'Seewandel Jesu' (Mk 6, 45–52 par): Literarische und theologische Aspekte," *BZ* 23 (1979): 71–84.

S. H. Smith, "Bethsaida via Gennesaret: The Enigma of a Sea-Crossing in Mark 6:45–53," *Bib* 77 (1996): 349–74.

Mark 6:53–56

J. Verheyden, "Mark 1:32–34 and 6:53–53: Tradition or Redaction?" *ETL* 64 (1988): 415–32.

Mark 7:1–23

C. E. Carlston, "The Things That Defile (Mark vii. 14) and the Law in Matthew and Mark," *NTS* 15 (1968–69): 57–69.

J. G. Crossley, "Halakah and Mark 7.4: '. . . and beds,' " *JSNT* 25 (2003): 433–47.

"Halakah and Mark 7.3: 'With the Hand in the Shape of a Fist,'" *NTS* 58 (2012): 57–68.

D. J. M. Derrett, "ΚΟΠΒΑΝ, Ο ΕΣΤΙΝ ΔΩΠΟΝ," *NTS* 16 (1969–70): 364–68.

E. Regev, "Pure Individualism: The Idea of Non-Priestly Purity in Ancient Judaism," *JSJ* 31 (2000): 176–202.

"Moral Impurity and the Temple in Early Christianity in Light of Ancient Greek Practice and Qumranic Ideology," *HTR* 97 (2004): 383–411.

Z. W. Falk, "On Talmudic Vows," *HTR* 59 (1966): 309–12.

J. Fitzmyer, "The Aramaic Qorban Inscription from Jebel Hallet Et-turi and Mk 7:11/Mt 15:5," *JBL* 78 (1959): 60–65 = *Essays in the Semitic Background of the New Testament* (London: Geoffrey Chapman, 1971), 93–100.

Y. Furstenberg, "Defilement Penetrating the Body: A New Understanding of Contamination in Mark 7.15," *NTS* 54 (2008): 176–200.

T. R. Hatina, "Did Jesus Quote Isaiah 29:13 against the Pharisees? An Unpopular Appraisal," *BBR* 16 (2006): 79–94.

M. Hengel, "Mk 7,3 πυγμῇ: Die Geschichte einer exegetischen Aporie und der Versuch ihrer Lösung," *ZNW* 60 (1969): 182–98.

H. Hubner, *Das Gesetz in der synoptischen Tradition* (Witten: Luther, 1973).

"Mark vii. 1–23 und das 'jüdisch-hellenistische' Gesetzes Verständnis," *NTS* 22 (1976): 319–45.

W. G. Kümmel, "Äussere und innere Reinheit bei Jesus," in *Das Wort und die Wörter*, FS G. Friedrich, ed. H. Balz and S. Schulz (Stuttgart: Kohlhammer, 1973), 35–46.

"Jesus und der jüdische Traditionsgedanke," *ZNW* 33 (1934): 105–130.

J. Lambrecht, "Jesus and the Law: An Investigation of Mk 7, 1–23," *ETL* 53 (1977): 24–82.

D. Lührmann, "Die Pharisäer und die Schriftgelehrten im Markusevangelium," *ZNW* 78 (1987): 169–85.

"... Womit er alle Speisen für rein erklärten (Mk 7,19)," *WD* 16 (1981): 71–92.

N. J. McEleney, "Authenticating Criteria and Mark 7, 1–23," *CBQ* 34 (1972): 431–60.

W. D. McHardy, "Mark 7, 3 – A Reference to the Old Testament?" *ExpTim* 87 (1976): 119.

H. Merkel, "Mk 7,14 – das Jesuswort über die innere Verunreinigung," *ZRGG* 20 (1968): 340–63.

J. Neusner, "'First Cleanse the Inside,'" *NTS* 22 (1975–76): 486–95.

"The Idea of Purity in Ancient Judaism," *JAAR* 43 (1975): 15–26.

J. C. Poirier, "The Interioirty of True Religion in Mark 7,6–8. With a Note on Pap.Egerton 2," *ZNW* 91 (2000): 180–91.

J. C. Poirier, "Purity beyond the Temple in the Second Temple Era," *JBL* 122 (2003): 247–65.

S. M. Reynolds, "Πυγῇ (Mark 7, 3) as 'Cupped Hand,'" *JBL* 85 (1966): 87–88.

"A Note on Dr. Hengel's Interpretation of Πυγμῇ in Mark 7, 3," *ZNW* 62 (1971): 295–96.

J. M. Ross, "With the Fist," *ExpTim* 87 (1976): 374–75.

D. J. Rudolph, "Jesus and the Food Laws: A Reassessment of Mark 7:19b," *EvQ* 74 (2002): 291–311.

C. Settler, "Purity of Heart in Jesus' Teaching: Mark 7:14–23 par. as an Expression of Jesus' Bawsileia Ethics," *JTS* 55 (2004): 467–502.

P. R. Weis, "A Note on ΠΤΓΜΗΙ," *NTS* 3 (1956–57): 233–36.

S. Zeitlin, "Korban," *JQR* (1962): 160–63.

"Korban: A Gift," *JQR* 59 (1968): 133–35.

Mark 7:24–30

T. A. Burkill, "Historical Development of the Story of the Syro-Phoenician Woman," *NovT* 9 (1967): 161–77.

"The Syrophoenician Woman, the Congruence of Mk 7, 24–31," *ZNW* 57 (1966): 22–37.

J. D. M. Derrett, "Law in the New Testament: The Syro-Phoenician Woman and the Centurion of Capernaum," *NovT* 15 (1973): 161–86.

L. D. Hart, "The Canaanite Woman: Meeting Jesus as Sage and Lord: Matthew 15:21–28 & Mark 7:24–30," *ExpTim* 122 (2010): 20–25.

M. D. Nanos, "Paul's Reversal of Jews Calling Gentiles 'Dogs' (Philippians 3:2): 1600 Years of an Ideological Tale Wagging an Exegetical Dog?" *BibInt* 17 (2009): 448–82.

J. Perkinson, "A Canaanite Word in the Logos of Christ, or, The *Difference the Syro-Phoenician Woman Makes to Jesus,"* *Semeia* 75 (1996): 61–85.

N. R. Petersen, "The Composition of Mark 4:1– 8:26," *HTR* 73 (1980): 185–217.

P. Pokorny, "From a Puppy to a Child: Some Problems of Contemporary Biblical Exegesis Demonstrated from Mark 7:24–30/Ma 15:21–28," *NTS* 41 (1995): 321–27.

D. Rhodes, "Jesus and the Syrophoenician Woman in Mark: A Narrative Critical Study," *JAAR* 62 (1994): 343–75.

J. C. H. Smith, "The Construction of Identity in Mark 7:24–30: The Syrophoenician Woman and the Problem of Ethnicity." *BibInt* 20 (2012): 458–81.

W. Storch, "Zur Perikope von der Syrophönizierin. Mk 7,28 und Ri 1,7," *BZ* 14 (1970): 256–57.

G. Theissen, "Lokal – und Socialkolorit in der Geschichte von der syrophönikischen Frau (Mk 7:24–30," *ZNW* 74 (1984): 202–225.

Mark 7:31–37

T. Baird, "Translating Orthos at Mark 7:35," *ExpTim* 92 (1981): 337–38.

C. Bonner, "Traces of Thaumaturgic in Miracles," *HTR* 20 (1927): 171–81.

J. Emerton, "ΜΑΡΑΝΑΘΑ and ΕΦΦΑΘΑ," *JTS* 18 (1967): 427–31.

F. G. Lang, "'Über Sidon mitten ins Gebiet der Dekapolis': Geographie und Theologie in Markus 7,31," *ZDPV* 94 (1978): 145–60.

U. Luz, "Das Geheimnismotiv und die markinische Christologie," *ZNW* 56 (1965): 9–30.

S. Morag, "Εφφαθά (Mark vii. 34): Certainly Hebrew, Not Aramaic?" *JSS* 17 (1972): 198–202.

S. T. Parker, "The Decapolis Reviewed," *JBL* 94 (1975): 437–41.

I. Rabinowitz, "'Be Opened' = Ἐφφαθά (Mark 7,34): Did Jesus Speak Hebrew?" *ZNW* 53 (1962): 229–38.

"ΕΦΦΑΘΑ (Mark VII. 34): Certainly Hebrew, Not Aramaic," *JSS* 16 (1971): 151–56.

Mark 8:1–9

F. W. Danker, "Mark 8,7," *JBL* 82 (1963): 215.

K. P. Donfried, "The Feeding Narratives and the Marcan Community," in *Kirche*, FS G. Bornkamm, ed. D. Lührmann and G. Strecker (Tübingen: Mohr, 1980), 95–103.

A. Farrer, "Loaves and Thousands," *JTS* 4 (1953): 1–14.

A. Heising, "Exegese und Theologie der Alt – und Neutestamentlichen Speisewunder," *ZTK* 86 (1964): 80–96.

B. W. van Iersel, "Die wunderbare Speisung und das Abendmahl in der synoptischen Tradition (Mk VI. 35–44 par VIII. 1–20 par)," *NovT* 7 (1964): 167–94.

S. Masuda, "The Good News of the Miracle of the Bread: The Tradition and Its Markan Redaction," *NTS* 28 (1982): 191–219.

F. Neugebauer, "Die wunderbare Speisung (Mk 6,30–44 parr.) und Jesu Identität," *KD* 32 (1986): 254–77.

H. Patsch, "Abendmahlsterminologie ausserhalb der Einsetzungsberichte," *ZNW* 62 (1971): 210–231.

L. Perkins, "The Markan Narrative's Use of the Old Greek Text of Jeremiah to Explain Israel's Obduracy," *TynBul* 60 (2009): 217–38.

B. E. Thiering, "'Breaking of Bread' and 'Harvest' in Mark's Gospel," *NovT* 12 (1970): 1–12.

G. Ziener, "Die Brotwunder im Markusevangelium," *BZ* 4 (1960): 282–85.

Mark 8:10–13

G. W. Buchanan, "Some Vow and Oath Formulas in the New Testament," *HTR* 58 (1965): 319–24.

J. B. Gibson, "Jesus' Refusal to Produce a Sign," *JSNT* 38 (1990): 37–66.

K. R. Iverson, "Incongruity, Humor, and Mark: Performance and the Use of Laughter in the Second Gospel (Mark 8:14–21)," *NTS* 59 (2013): 2–19.

O. Linton, "The Demand for a Sign from Heaven (Mk 8, 11–12 and Parallels)," *ST* 19 (1965): 112–29.

V. K. Robbins, "Dunameis and Semeia in Mark," *BR* 18 (1973): 5–20.

K. Seybold, "Dalmanutha (8:10)," *ZDPV* 116 (2000): 420–48.

W. Schenk, "Der Einfluss der Logienquelle auf das Markusevangelium," *ZNW* 70 (1979): 141–65.

G. Schmitt, "Das Zeichen des Jona," *ZNW* 68 (1978): 123–29.

J. Swetnam, "No Sign of Jonah," *Bib* 66 (1985): 126–30.

A. Vögtle, "Der Spruch vom Jonazeichen," in *Das Evangelium und die Evangelien: Beiträge zur Evangelienforschung* (Düsseldorf: Patmos, 1971), 103–136.

Mark 8:14–21

N. A. Beck, "Reclaiming a Biblical Text: The Mark 8:14–21Discussion about the Bread in the Boat," *CBQ* 43 (1981): 49–56.

G. H. Boobyer, "The Miracles of the Loaves and the Gentiles in St. Mark's Gospel," *SJT* 6 (1953): 77–87.

W. Countryman, "How Many Baskets Full? Mark 8:14–21 and the Value of the Miracles in Mark," *CBQ* 47 (1985): 643–55.

J. B. Gibson, "The Rebuke of the Disciples in Mark 8:14–21," *JSNT* 27 (1986): 31–47.

D. J. Hawkin, "The Incomprehension of the Disciples in the Marcan Redaction," *JBL* 91 (1972): 491–500.

K. R. Iverson, "Incongruity, Humor, and Mark: Performance and the Use of Laughter in the Second Gospel (Mark 8:14–21)," *NTS* 59 (2013): 2–19.

E. E. Lemcio, "External Evidence for the Structure and Function of Mark iv. 1–20, vii. 14–23 and viii. 14–21," *JTS* 29 (1978): 323–38.

J. Manek, "Mark viii. 14–21," *NovT* 7 (1964): 10–14.

C. L. Mitton, "Leaven," *ExpTim* 84 (1972–73): 339–43.

P. Sellew, "Composition of Didactic Scenes in Mark's Gospel," *JBL* 108 (1989): 613–34.

G. Ziener, "Das Bildwort vom Sauerteig, Mk 8, 15," *TTZ* 67 (1958): 247–48.

Mark 8:22–26

E. Best, "Discipleship in Mark: Mark 8:22–10:52," *SJT* 23 (1970): 223–37 = *Disciples and Discipleship: Studies in the Gospel According to Mark* (Edinburgh: T. & T. Clark, 1986), 1–16.

J. D. M. Derrett, "Trees Walking, Prophecy and Christology," *ST* 35 (1981): 33–54.

E. Eve, "Spit in Your Eyes: The Blind Man of Bethsaida and the Blind Man of Alexandria," *NTS* 54 (2008): 1–17.

H. Hegermann, "Bethsaida und Gennesar: Eine traditions – und redaktionsgeschichtliche Studie zu Mc 4–8," in *Judentum, Urchristentum,*

Kirche, FS J. Jeremias, ed. W. Eltester (BZNW 26; Berlin: Töpelmann, 1960), 130–40.

J. K. Howard, "Men and Trees, Walking: Mark 8:22–26," *SJT* 37 (1984): 163–70.

E. S. Johnson, "Mark VIII. 22–26: The Blind Man from Bethsaida," *NTS* 25 (1979): 370–84.

A. Kuby, "Zur Konzeption des Markus-Evangeliums," *ZNW* 49 (1958): 52–64.

K. W. Larsen, "A Focused Christological Reading of Mark 8:22– 9:13," *Trinity Journal* 26 (2005): 33–46.

J. Marcus, "A Note on Marcan Optics," *NTS* 45 (1999): 250–56.

J. I. Miller, "Was Tischendorf Really Wrong? Mark 8:26b Revisited," *NovT* 28 (1986): 97–103.

J. M. Ross, "Another Look at Mark 8:26b," *NovT* 29 (1987): 97–99.

J. Ruis-Camp, "El Ciego de Betsaida/Betania (Mc 8,22–26)," *EstBibi* 58 (2000): 289–308.

R. S. Sugirtharajah, "Men, Trees, Walking: A Conceptual Solution to Mk 8:24," *ExpTim* 103 (1992): 172–74.

Mark 8:27–30

A. M. Berlin, "Debate: Where Was Herod's Temple to Augustus? Banias Is Still the Best Candidate," *BAR* 29.5 (2003): 22–24.

O. Betz, "Die Frage nach dem messianischen Bewusstsein Jesu," *Nov Test* 6 (1963): 20–48.

E. Dinkler, "Petrusbekenntnis und Satanswort" Das Problem der Messianität Jesus," in *Zeit und Geschichte*, ed. Dinkler (R. Bultmann Festschrift; Tübingen: Mohr, 1964), 127–53.

J. Ernst, "Petrusbekenntnis – Leidensnakindigung – Satanswort (8:27–33)," *Catholica* 32 (1978): 46–73.

W. Horbury, "The Cult of Christ and the Cult of the Saints," *NTS* 44 (1998): 444–69.

M. de Jonge, "The Use of the Word 'Anointed' in the Time of Jesus," *Nov Test* 8 (1966): 132–48.

E. Netzer, "A Third Candidate: Another Building at Banias," *BAR* 29.5 (2003): 25.

G. W. E. Nickelsburg, "Enoch, Levi and Peter: Recipients of Revelation in Upper Galilee," *JBL* 100 (1981): 575–600.

J. Andrew Overman, Jack Olive, Michael Nelson, "Discovering Herod's Shrine to Augustus: Mystery Temple Found at Omrit," *BAR* 29.2 (2003): 40–49, 67–68.

R. Pesch, "Das Messiasbekenntniss des Petrus (8:27–30)," *BZ* 17 (1973): 178–95.

"Das Messiasbekenntniss des Petrus (8:27–30)," *BZ* 18 (1974): 20–31.

W. S. Vorster, "Characterization of Peter in the Gospel of Mark." *Neot* 21 (1987): 57–76.

Mark 8:31–9:1

G. Aichele, "Jesus Frankness," *Semeia* 69–70 (1995): 261–80.

W. A. Beardslee, "Saving One's Life by Losing It," *JAAR* 47 (1979): 57–72.

W. J. Bennett "The Son of Man Must . . .," *NovT* 17 (1975): 113–29.

M. Bird, "The Crucifixion of Jesus as the Fulfillment of Mark 9:1," *Trinity Journal* 24 (2003): 23–36.

T. R. Hatina, "Who Will See 'The Kingdom of God Coming with Power' in Mark 9,1 –Protagonists or Antagonists?" *Bib* 86 (2005): 20–34.

J. Lambrecht, "A Note on Mark 8.38 and Q 12.8–9," *JSNT* 85 (2002): 117–25.

B. J. Malina, " 'Let Him Deny Himself' (Mark 8:34 & Par): A Socio Psychological Model of Self Denial," *BTB* 24 (1994): 106–119.

E. Nardoni, "A Redactional Interpretation of Mark 9:1," *CBQ* 43 (1981): 365–84.

B. A. E. Osborne, "Peter: Stumbling Block and Satan," *NovT* 15 (1973): 187–90.

N. Perrin, "The Composition of Mark ix.1," *NovT* 11 (1969): 67–70.

W. Rebell, " 'Sein Leben verlieren' (Mark 8,35 parr.) als Strukturmoment vor – und nachösterlichen Glaubens." *NTS* 35 (1989): 202–218.

D Rhoads, "Losing Life for Others: Mark's Standard of Judgment," *Int* 47 (1993): 358–69.

N. F. Santos, "Jesus' Paradoxical Teaching in Mark 8:35; 9:35 and 10: 43–44," *BibSac* 157 (2000): 15–25.

U. Schmidt, "Zum Paradox vom 'Verlieren' und 'Finden' des Lebens," *Bib* 89 (2008): 329–51.

G. Turner, "Jesus' Prophecies of His Death and Resurrection: An Exercise in Hermeneutics," *Scripture Bulletin* 30 (2000): 15–22.

Mark 9:2–8

G. Aichele and R. Walsh, "Metamorphosis, Transfiguration, and the Body," *BibInt* 19 (2011): 253–75.

A. del Aqua-Perez, "The Narrative of the Transfiguration as a Derashic Scienification of a Faith Confession," *NTS* 39 (1993): 340–54.

S. Barton, "The Transfiguration of Christ According to Mark and Matthew: Christology and Anthropology," in *Auferstehung-Resurrection*, ed. A. Avemarie and H. Lichtenberger (Tübingen: Mohr/Siebeck, 2001), 231–46.

C. Begg, "Josephus' Portrayal of the Disappearances of Enoch, Elijah and Moses: Some Observations," *JBL* 109 (1990): 691–93.

J. P. Heil, "A Note on 'Elijah with Moses' in Mark 9:4." *Bib* 80 (1999): 115.

M. Hooker, " 'What Doest Thou Here, Elijah?': A Look at St. Mark's Account of the Transfiguration," in *The Glory of Christ in the New Testament*, ed. L. D. Hurst (Oxford: Clarendon, 1987), 59–70.

C. R. Moss, "The Transfiguration: An Exercise in Markan Accommodation," *BibInt* 12 (2004): 69–89.

U. B. Müller, Die Christologische Absicht des Markusevangeliums und die Verklarungsgeschichte," *ZNW* 64 (1973): 159–93.

J. Murphy-O'Conner, "What Really Happened at the Transfiguration?" *Bible Review* 3 (1987): 8–21.

A. Standhartinger, "Jesu, Elia und Mose auf dem Berg," *BZ* 47 (2003): 66–85.

R. Stein, "Is the Transfiguration (Mark 9:2–8) a Misplaced Resurrection Account?" *JBL* 95 (1976): 76–96.

A. Puig I Tarrech, "The Glory on the Mountain: The Episode of the Transfiguration of Jesus," *NTS* 58 (2012): 151–72.

B. Viviano, "Rabbouni and Mark 9:5," *RB* 95 (1990): 207–218.

Mark 9:9–13

J. K. Aitken, "The Proposed Aramaic Background to Mark 9:11," *JTS* 53 (2002): 75–80.

D. Allison, "Elijah Must Come," *JBL* 103 (1984): 256–58.

M. Casey, "The Aramaic Background of Mark 9:11: A Response to J. K. Aitken," *JTS* 55 (2004): 92–102.

M. Faierstein, "Why Do the Scribes Say Elijah Must Come First?" *JBL* 100 (1981): 75–86.

J. A. Fitzmyer, "More about Elijah Coming First," *JBL* 104 (1985): 295–96.

J. Marcus, "Mark 9, 11–13: 'As It Has Been Written,'" *ZNW* 80 (1989): 42–63.

J. A. T. Robinson, "Elijah, John, and Jesus: An Essay in Detection," *NTS* 4 (1958): 263–81.

J. Taylor, "The Coming of Elijah, Mt. 17:10–13 and MK 9:11–13: The Development of the Texts," *RB* 98 (1991): 107–119.

Mark 9:14–29

P. J. Achtemeier, "Miracles and the Historical Jesus; A Study of Mark 9:14–29," *CBQ* 37 (1975): 471–91.

J. D. Derrett, "Responding to Unreliability (Mark 9:14–29)," *Downside Review* 121 (2003): 119–34.

T. Nicklas, "Formkritik und Leserrezeption: Ein Beitrag zur Methodendiskussion am Beispiel Mk 9,14–29," *Bib* 82 (2001): 496–514.

G. Petzke, "Die historische Frage nach den Wundertaten Jesu dargestellt am Beispiel des Exorcismus Mark, ix.14–29 par," *NTS* 22 (1975–76): 180–204.

W. Schenk, "Tradition und Redaktion in der Epileptiker-Perkope Mk 9,14–29," *ZNW* 63 (1972): 76–94.

G. E. Sterling, "Jesus as Exorcist: An Analysis of Matthew 17:14–20; Mark 9:14–29; Luke 9:37–43a," *CBQ* 55 (1993): 467–93.

Mark 9:30–32

P. J. Achtemeier, "'He Taught Them Many Things': Reflections on Marcan Christology," *CBQ* 42 (1980): 465–81.

G. Strecker, "Die Leidens – und Auferstehungsvoraussagen im Markusevangelium (Mk 8,31; 9, 31; 10,32–34," *ZTK* 64 (1967): 16–39.

Mark 9:33–50

P. J. Achtemeier, "An Exposition of Mark 9:37–50," *Int* 30 (1976): 178–82.

C. B. Bridges, "Jesus and Paul on Tolerance: The Strange Exorcist and the Strange Concession," *Stone Campbell Journal* 1 (1998): 59–66.

D. J. Clark, "Some Misunderstanding in Mark," *The Bible Translator* 44 (1993): 245–46.

W. Deming, "Mark 9.42–10.12, Matthew 5:27–32, and B. Nid. 13b: A First-Century Discussion of Male Sexuality," *NTS* 36 (1990): 130–41.

J. D. M. Derrett, "Mylos onikos (Mk 9.42 par.)," *ZNW* 76 (1985): 284.

J. D. M. Derrett, "Salted with Fire (Mk 9:42 par.)," *Theology* 76 (1973): 364–68.

H. Fleddermann, "The Discipleship Discourse (Mark 9:33–50)," *CBQ* 43 (1981): 57–75.

I. H. Henderson, "'Salted with Fire' (Mark 9:42–50): Style, Oracles, and (Socio-) Rhetorical Gospel Criticism," *JSNT* 80 (2000): 44–65.

P. V. Kea, "Salting with Salt: Q 14:34–35 and Mark 9:49," *Forum* 6 (1990): 239–44.

H. Koester, "Mark 9:43–48 and Quintilian 8.3.75," *HTR* 71 (1978): 151–53.
M. Lattke, "Salz der Freundschaft in Mk 9.50c," *ZNW* 75 (1984): 44–59.
C. Milikowsky, "Which Gehenna? Retribution and Eschatology in the Synoptic Gospels and Early Jewish Texts," *NTS* 34 (1988): 238–49.
W. Nestle, "Wer nicht mit mir ist, ist wider mich," *ZNW* 13 (1912): 84–87.
U. C. von Wahdle, "Mark 9,33–50: Discipleship, the Authority That Serves," *BZ* 29 (1985): 49–67.

Mark 10:1–12

E. Bammel, "Markus 10,11f und das jüdische Eherecht," *ZNW* 61 (1970): 95–101.
"Nomological Exegesis in Qumran 'Divorce' Texts," *RQ* 18 (1998): 561–79.
B. Brooten, "Konnten Frauen im alten Judentum dis Scheidung betreiben: Überlegungen zu Mk 10,11–12 und 1 Kor 7,10–11," *EvT* 42 (1982): 65–80.
D. R. Catchpole, "The Synoptic Divorce Material as a Traditio-Historical Problem," *BJRL* 57 (1974–75): 92–127.
H. G. Coiner, "Those 'Divorce and Remarriage' Passages (Matt. 5:32; 19:9; 1 Cor. 7:10–16), with Brief Reference to the Mark and Luke Passages," *CTM* 39 (1968): 367–84.
C. E. B. Cranfield, "The Church and Divorce and the Re-Marriage of Divorced Persons in the Light of Mark 10.1–12," in *The Bible and Christian Life: A Collection of Essays* (Edinburgh: T. & T. Clark, 1985), 229–34.
J. D. M. Derrett, "The Teaching of Jesus on Marriage and Divorce," in *Law in the New Testament* (London: Darton, Longman & Todd, 1970), 363–88.
J. A. Fitzmyer, "The Matthean Divorce texts and Some New Palestinian Evidence," *TS* 37 (1976): 197–226.
D. E. Garland, "A Biblical View of Divorce," *RevExp* 84 (1987): 419–32.
B. Green, "Jesus' Teaching on Divorce in the Gospel of Mark," *JSNT* 38 (1990): 67–75.
W. J. Harrington, "Jesus' Attitude toward Divorce," *ITQ* 37 (1970): 199–209.
D. Instone-Brewer, "Jewish Women Divorcing Their Husbands in Early Judaism: The Background of Papyrus Ṣeʾelim 13," *HTR* 92 (1999): 349–57.
J. Jensen, "Does Porneia Mean Fornication? A Critique of Bruce Malina," *NovT* 20 (1978): 161–84.
B. N. Kaye, "'One Flesh' and Marriage," *Colloquium* 22 (1990): 46–57.

B. J. Malina, "Does Porneia Mean Fornication?" *NovT* 14 (1972): 10–17.

J. Nolland, "The Gospel Prohibition of Divorce: Tradition History and Meaning," *JSNT* 58 (1995): 19–35.

G. Schneider, "Jesu Wort über die Ehescheidung in der Überlieferung des Neuen Testaments," *TTZ* 80 (1971): 65–87.

B. Vawter, "Divorce and the New Testament," *CBQ* 39 (1977): 528–42.

A. Warren, "Did Moses Permit Divorce?: Modal Weqatal as Key to New Testament Readings of Deuteronomy 24:1–4," *Tyndale Bulletin* 49 (1998): 39–56.

Mark 10:13–16

J. L. Bailey, "Experiencing the Kingdom as a Little Child: A Rereading of Mark 10:13–16," *Word and World* 15 (1995): 58–67.

A. D. Clarke, "Do Not Judge Who Is Worthy and Unworthy': Clement's Warning Not to Speculate about the Rich Young Man's Response (Mark 10.17–31)," *JSNT* 31 (2009): 447–68.

J. G. Crossley, "The Damned Rich (Mark 10:17–31)," *ExpTim* 116 (2005): 397–401.

L. L. Eubanks, "Mark 10:13–16," *RevExp* 91 (1994): 401–405.

R. Hicks, "Markan Discipleship According to Malachi: The Significance of μη αποστερησης in the Story of the Rich Man (Mark 10:17–22)," *JBL* 132 (2013): 179–99.

V. K. Robbins, "Pronouncement Stories and Jesus' Blessing of Children: A Rhetorical Approach," *Semeia* 29 (1983): 43–74.

P. Spitaler, "Welcoming a Child as a Metaphor for Welcoming God's Kingdom: A Close Reading of Mark 10.13–16," *JSNT* 31 (2009): 423–46.

A. P. Stanley, "The Rich Young Ruler and Salvation," *BibSac* 163 (2006): 46–62.

Mark 10:17–31

E. Best, "Uncomfortable Words: VII. The Camel and the Needle's Eye (Mark 10:25)," *ExpTim* 82 (1970–71): 83–89.

J. D. Derrett, "A Camel through the Eye of a Needle," *NTS* 32 (1986): 465–70.

R. Gundry, "Mark 10:29: Order in the List," *CBQ* 59 (1997): 465–75.

J. H. Hellermann, "Wealth and Sacrifice in Early Christianity: Revisiting Mark's Presentation of Jesus' Encounter with the Rich Young Ruler." *Trinity Journal* 21 (2000): 143–64.

D. Malone, "Riches and Discipleship: Mark 10:23–31," *BTB* 9 (1979): 78–87.

D. M. May, "Leaving and Receiving: A Socio-Scientific Exegesis of Mark 10:29–31," *Perspectives in Religious Studies* 17 (1990): 141–51, 154.

W. D. MacHardy, "Mark 10:19: A Reference to the Old Testament?" *ExpTim* 107 (1996): 143.

J.-C. Okoye, "With Persecutions – Mark 10:30," *New Theology Review* 10 (1997): 31–38.

J. C. O'Neill, "'Good Master' and the 'Good' Sayings in the Teaching of Jesus," *Irish Biblical Studies* 15 (1993): 167–78.

D. Sänger, "Recht und Gerechtigkeit in der Verkündigung Jesu: Erwägungen zu Mk 10,17–22 und 12,28–34," *BZ* 36 (1992): 179–94.

T. E. Schmidt, "Mark 10.29–30; Matthew 19.29: 'Leave Houses ... and Region?" *NTS* 38 (1992): 617–20.

Mark 10:32–34

R. McKinnis, "An Analysis of Mark X 32–34," *NovT* 18 (1976): 81–100.

M. J. Selvidge, "'And Those Who Followed Feared' (Mark 10:32)," *CBQ* 45 (1983): 396–400.

Mark 10:35–45

A. Y. Collins, "The Signification of Mark 10:45 among Gentile Christians," *HTR* 90 (1997): 371–82.

B. Lindars, "Salvation Proclaimed: VII. Mark 10,45: A Ransom for Many," *ExpTim* 93 (1981–82): 292–95.

W. J. Moulder, "The Old Testament Background and the Interpretation of Mark 10:45," *NTS* 24 (1977–78): 120–27.

M. Oberweis, "Das Martyrium der Zebedaiden in Mk 10.35–45 (Mt 20.20–3) und Offb 11.3–13," *NTS* 44 (1998): 74–92.

D. Seeley, "Rulership and Service in Mark 10:41–45," *NovT* 35 (1993): 234–50.

C. F. Stone, "Allusion to Isa 11.10 LXX in Mark 10:42b," *NTS* 48 (2002): 71–83.

P. Stuhlmacher, *Versöhnung, Gesetz und Gerechtigkeit: Aufsätze zur biblischen Theologie* (Göttingen: Vandenhoeck & Ruprecht, 1981), 27–42; ET *Reconciliation, Law and Righteousness* (Philadelphia: Fortress, 1986), 16–29.

R. E. Watts, "Jesus and the Suffering Servant," in *Jesus and the Suffering Servant: Isaiah 53 and Christian Origins*, ed. W. Bellinger, Jr., and W. R. Farmer (Harrisburg, PA: Trinity Press International, 1998), 125–52.

M. Weinfeld, "The King as the Servant of the People: The Source of the Idea," *JJS* 33 (1982): 189–94.

O. Wischmeyer, "Herrschen als Dienen–Mk 10,41–45," *ZNW* 90 (1999): 28–44.

Mark 10:46–52

P. J. Achtemeier, "'And He Followed Him': Miracles and Discipleship in Mark 10:46–52," *Semeia* 11 (1978): 115–45.

S. J. D. Cohen, "Epigraphical Rabbis," *JQR* 72 (1981–82):1–17.

A. Culpepper, "Mark 10:50: Why Mention the Garment?" *JBL* 101 (1982): 131–32.

D. Duling, "Solomon, Exorcism and the Son of David," *HTR* 68 (1975): 237–52.

H.-J. Eckstein, "Markus 10,46–52 als Schlüsseltext des Markusevangeliums," *ZNW* 87 (1996): 33–50.

S. Guijarro-Oporto, "Healing Stories and Medical Anthropology: A Reading of Mark 10:46–52," *BTB* 30 (2000): 102–112.

R. Hanig, "Christus als 'wahrer Salomo' in der Früher Kirche," *ZNW* 84 (1993): 111–34.

E. S. Johnson, "Mark 10:46–52: Blind Bartimaeus," *CBQ* 40 (1978): 191–204.

M. N. Keller, "Opening Blind Eyes: A Revisioning of Mark 8:22–10:52," *BTB* 31 (2001): 151–67.

J. C. Ossandon, "Bartimaeus' Faith: Plot and Point of View in Mark 10,46–52," *Bib* 93 (2012): 377–402.

V. K. Robbins, "The Healing of Blind Bartimaeus (10,46–52) in Marcan Theology," *JBL* 92 (1973): 224–43.

M. G. Steinhauser, "The Form of the Bartimaeus Narrative (Mark 10,46–52)," *NTS* 32 (1986): 583–95.

Mark 11:1–11

W. Bauer, "The 'Colt' of Palm Sunday," *JBL* 72 (1953): 220–29.

E. F. F. Bishop, "Hosanna: The Word of the Joyful Jerusalem Crowds," *ExpTim* 53 (1941–42): 212–14.

J. Blenkinsopp, "The Oracle of Judah and the Messianic Entry," *JBL* 80 (1961): 55–64.

J. Blenkinsopp, "The Hidden Messiah and His Entry into Jerusalem," *Scr* 13 (1961): 51–56, 81–88.

R. G. Bratcher, "A Note on Mark xi.3 ὁ Κύριος αὐτοῦ χρείαν ἔχει," *ExpTim* 64 (1952–53): 93.

T. Bromboszcz, "Der Einzug Jesu in Jerusalem bei Mondschein? Ein Beitrag zur Chronologie der Leidensgeschichte," *BZ* 9 (1911): 164–70.

S. G. Brown, "Mark 11:1–12:12: A Triple Intercalation?" *CBQ* 64 (2002): 78–89.

F. F. Bruce, "The Book of Zechariah and the Passion Narrative," *BJRL* 43 (1960–61): 336–53.

T. A. Burkill, "Strain on the Secret: An Examination of Mark 11:1–13:37," *ZNW* 51 (1960): 31–46.

D. R. Catchpole, "The 'Triumphal' Entry," in *Jesus and the Politics of His Day*, ed. E. Bammel and C. F. D. Moule (Cambridge: Cambridge University Press, 1984), 319–35.

J. D. Derrett, "Law in the New Testament: The Palm Sunday Colt," *NovT* 13 (1971): 241–58.

P. B. Duff, "The March of the Divine Warrior and the Advent of the Greco-Roman King: Mark's Account of Jesus' Entry into Jerusalem," *JBL* 111 (1992): 53–71.

V. Eppstein, "The Historicity of the Gospel Account of the Cleansing of the Temple," *ZNW* 55 (1964): 42–58.

C. F. Evans, " 'I Will Go before You into Galilee,' " *JTS* n.s. 5 (1954): 3–18.

H. St. J. Hart, "Hosanna in the Highest," *SJT* 45 (1992): 283–301.

B. Kinman, "Jesus' Royal Entry into Jerusalem," *BBR* 15 (2005): 223–60.

J.R.D. Kirk, "Time for Figs, Temple Destruction, and Houses of Prayer in Mark 11:2–25," *CBQ* 74 (2012): 509–527.

H. W. Kuhn, "Das Reittier Jesu in der Einzugsgeschichte des Markusevangeliums," *ZNW* 50 (1959): 82–91.

H. Leander, "With Homi Bhabha at the Jerusalem City Gates: A Postcolonial Reading of the 'Triumphant' Entry (Mark 11:1–11)," *JSNT* 32 (2010): 309–335.

E. Lohse, "Hosianna," *NovT* 6 (1963): 113–19.

B. A. Mastin, "The Date of the Triumphal Entry," *NTS* 16 (1969): 76–82.

H. Patsch, "Der Einzug Jesu in Jerusalem: Ein historischer Versuch," *ZTK* 68 (1971): 1–26.

M. Pope, "Hosanna – What It Really Means," *BR* 4 (1988): 16–25.

E. R. Richards, "An Honor/Shame Argument for Two Temple Clearings," *Trinity Journal* 29 (2008): 19–43.

J. M. Ross, "Names of God: A Comment on Mark 11:3 and Parallels," *BT* 35 (1984): 443.

K. Stock, "Gliederung und Zusammenhang in Mk 11–12," *Bib* 59 (1978): 481–515.

K. J. Wenell, "Contested Temple Space and Visionary Kingdom Space in Mark 11–12," *BibInt* 13 (2007): 323–37.

E. Werner, "'Hosanna' in the Gospels," *SJT* 38 (1985): 491–504.

Mark 11:12–21

J. Ådna, "The Attitude of Jesus to the Temple," *Mishkan* 17–18 (1992–93): 65–80.

H.-W. Bartsch, "Die Verfluchung des Feigenbaumes," *ZNW* 53 (1962): 256–60.

J. N. Birdsall, "The Withering of the Fig-Tree (Mark xi.12–14, 20–22)," *ExpTim* 73 (1962): 191.

M. Broshi, "The Role of the Temple in the Herodian Economy," *JJS* 38 (1987): 31–37.

G. W. Buchanan, "An Additional Note to 'Mark 11.15–19: Brigands in the Temple,'" *HUCA* 31 (1960): 103–105.

"Mark 11.15–19: Brigands in the Temple," *HUCA* 30 (1959): 169–77.

"Symbolic Money-Changers in the Temple?" *NTS* 37 (1991): 280–90.

F. C. Burkitt, "The Cleansing of the Temple," *JTS* o.s. 25 (1924): 386–90.

I. Buse, "The Cleansing of the Temple in the Synoptics and in John," *ExpTim* 70 (1958–59): 22–24.

A. Caldecott, "The Significance of the 'Cleansing of the Temple,'" *JTS* o.s. 24 (1923): 382–86.

J. Carmignac, "Studies in the Hebrew Background of the Synoptic Gospels," *ASTI* 7 (1970): 64–93.

F. A. Cooke, "The Cleansing of the Temple," *ExpTim* 63 (1951–52): 321–22.

W. J. Cotter, "'For It Was Not the Season for Figs,'" *CBQ* 48 (1986): 62–66.

J. D. Crossan, "Redaction and Citation in Mark 11:9–10 and 11:17," *BR* 17 (1972): 33–50.

R. A. Culpepper, "Mark 11:15–19," *Int* 34 (1980): 176–81.

J. D. M. Derrett, "Figtrees in the New Testament," *HeyJ* 14 (1973): 249–65.

"The Zeal of Thy House and the Cleansing of the Temple," *DRev* 95 (1977): 79–94.

R. Dormandy, "Jesus' Cutting Irony: Further Understanding of Mark 11:17," *ExpTim* 114 (2003): 333–34.

I. B. Driggers, "The Politics of Divine Presence: Temple as Locus of Conflict in the Gospel of Mark," *BibInt* 15 (2007): 227–47.

J. R. Edwards, "Markan Sandwiches: The Significance of Interpolations in Markan Narratives," *NovT* 31 (1989): 193–216.

V. Eppstein, "The Historicity of the Gospel Account of the Cleansing of the Temple," *ZNW* 55 (1964): 42–58.

P. F. Esler, "The Incident of the Withered Fig Tree in Mark 11: A New Source and Redactional Explanation," *JSNT* 28 (2005): 41–67.

C. A. Evans, "Jesus' Action in the Temple: Cleansing or Portent of Destruction?" *CBQ* 51 (1989): 237–70.

"Jesus and the 'Cave of Robbers': Toward a Jewish Context for the Temple Action," *BBR* 3 (1993): 93–110.

H. Giesen, "Der verdorrte Feigenbaum: Eine symbolische Aussage? Mk 11,12–14.20 f.," *BZ* 20 (1976): 95–111.

N. Q. Hamilton, "Temple Cleansing and Temple Bank," *JBL* 83 (1964): 365–72.

R. H. Hiers, "Not the Season for Figs," *JBL* 87 (1968): 394–400.

"Purification of the Temple: Preparation for the Kingdom of God," *JBL* 90 (1971): 82–90.

P. Hollenbach, "Liberating Jesus for Social Involvement," *BTB* 15 (1985): 151–56.

M. D. Hooker, "Traditions about the Temple in the Sayings of Jesus," *BJRL* 70 (1988): 7–19.

J. Jeremias, "Zwei Miszellen: 1. Antik-jüdische Münzdeutungen; 2. Zur Geschichtlichkeit der Tempelreinigung," *NTS* 23 (1977): 177–80.

E. Lohmeyer, "Die Reinigung des Tempels," *TBl* 10 (1941): 257–64.

T. W. Manson, "The Cleansing of the Temple," *BJRL* 33 (1950–51): 271–82.

J. Massyngberd Ford, "Money 'Bags' in the Temple (Mk 11,16)," *Bib* 57 (1976): 249–53.

F. J. Matera, "The Trial of Jesus," *Int* 45 (1991): 12–14.

S. Mendner, "Die Tempelreinigung," *ZNW* 47 (1956): 93–111.

J. Neusner, "The Absoluteness of Christianity and the Uniqueness of Judaism," *Int* 43 (1989): 18–31.

"Money-Changers in the Temple: The Mishnah's Explanation," *NTS* 35 (1989): 287–90.

D. E. Oakman, "Cursing Fig Trees and Robbers' Dens," *Semeia* 64 (1993): 253–72.

R. Pesch, "Der Anspruch Jesu," *Orientierung* 35 (1971): 53–56.

C. Roth, "The Cleansing of the Temple and Zechariah xiv 21," *NovT* 4 (1960): 174–81.

R. Schnackenburg, "The Primitive Church and Its Traditions of Jesus," *Perspective* 10 (1969): 103–124.

E. L. Schnellbächer, "The Temple as Focus of Mark's Theology," *HBT* 5 (1983): 95–112.

E. Schwartz, "Der verfluchte Feigenbaum," *ZNW* 5 (1904): 80–84.

G. Schwarz, "'ἀπὸ μακρόθεν / ἐπὶ τῆς ὁδοῦ," *BN* 20 (1983): 56–57.

D. Seeley, "Jesus' Temple Act," *CBQ* 55 (1993): 263–83.

C. W. F. Smith, "No Time for Figs," *JBL* 79 (1960): 315–27.

T. Söding, "Die Tempelaktion Jesu: Redaktionskritik–Überlieferungs-geschichte–historische Rückfrage," *TTZ* 101 (1992): 36–64.

E. Spiegel, "War Jesus gewalttätig? Bemerkungen zur Tempelreinigung," *TGl* 75 (1985): 239–47.

G. Theissen, "Jesus' Temple Prophecy: Prophecy in the Tension between Town and Country," in *Social Reality and the Early Christians: Theology, Ethics, and the World of the New Testament* (Minneapolis: Fortress, 1992), 94–114.

M. Tilly, "Kanaanäer, Handler und der Tempel in Jerusalem," *BN* 57 (1991): 30–36.

R. E. Watts, "The Lord's House and David's Lord: The Psalms and Mark's Perspective of Jesus and the Temple," *BibInt* 15 (2007): 307–322.

W. W. Watty, "Jesus and the Temple: Cleansing or Cursing?" *ExpTim* 93 (1981–82): 235–39.

A. J. M. Wedderburn, "Jesus' Action in the Temple: A Key or a Puzzle?" *ZNW* 97 (2006): 1–22.

R. E. Winkle, "The Jeremiah Model for Jesus in the Temple," *AUSS* 24 (1986): 155–62.

Mark 11: 22–25 [26 not likely original to Mark]

D. C. Arichea, Jr., "'Faith' in the Gospels of Matthew, Mark, and Luke," *BT* 29 (1978): 420–24.

E. Best, "Peter in the Gospel According to Mark," *CBQ* 40 (1978): 547–58.

E. K. Broadhead, "Which Mountain Is 'This Mountain'? A Critical Note on Mark 11,22–25," *Paradigms* 2 (1986): 33–38.

D. J. Clark, "Our Father in Heaven," *BT* 30 (1979): 210–13.

B. R. Crockett, "The Function of Mathetological Prayer in Mark," *IBS* 10 (1988): 123–39.

J. D. M. Derrett, "Moving Mountains and Uprooting Trees (Mk 11.22; Mt 17.20; 21.21; Lk 17.6)," *BO* 30 (1988): 231–44.

F. Hahn, "Jesu Wort vom bergversetzenden Glauben," *ZNW* 76 (1985): 149–69.

B. von Kienle, "Mk. 11:12–14, 20–25: Der verdorrte Feigenbaum," *BN* 57 (1991): 17–25.

S. H. Kio, "A Prayer Framework in Mark 11," *BT* 37 (1986): 323–28.

L. A. Losie, "The Cursing of the Fig Tree: Tradition Criticism of a Marcan Pericope: Mk 11:12–14, 20–25," *Studia Biblica et Theologica* 7 (1977): 3–18.

A. De Q. Robin, "The Cursing of the Fig Tree in Mark xi: A Hypothesis," *NTS* 8 (1962): 276–81.

G. Schwarz, "πίστιν ὡς κόκκον σινάπεως," *BN* 25 (1984): 27–35.

Mark 11:27–33

E. F. F. Bishop, "Jesus Walking or Teaching in the Temple (Mk xi.27, Jn x.23)," *ExpTim* 63 (1952): 226–27.

F. H. Colson, "Mark xi 27 and Parallels," *JTS* o.s. 25 (1925): 71–72.

J. H. Hellermann, "Challenging the Authority of Jesus: Mark 11:27–33 and Mediterranean Notions of Honor and Shame," *JETS* 43 (2000): 213–28.

S. Kim, "Jesus – The Son of God, the Stone, the Son of Man, and the Servant: The Role of Zechariah in the Self-Identification of Jesus," in *Tradition and Interpretation in the New Testament*, FS E. E. Ellis, ed. G. F. Hawthorne and O. Betz (Grand Rapids, MI: Eerdmans, 1987), 134–48.

J. Kremer, "Jesu Antwort auf die Frage nach seiner Vollmacht: Eine Auslegung von Mk 11,27–33," *BibLeb* 9 (1968): 128–36.

C. Marucci, "Die implizite Christologie in der sogenannten Vollmachtsfrage (Mk 11,27–33)," *ZTK* 108 (1986): 292–300.

R. Schnackenburg, "Die Vollmacht Jesu: Zu Mk 11,27–33," *Katholische Gedanke* 27 (1971): 105–109.

G. S. Shae, "The Question on the Authority of Jesus," *NovT* 16 (1974): 1–29.

Mark 12:1–12

T. Baarda, "'The Cornerstone': An Aramaism in the Diatessaron and the Gospel of Thomas?" *NovT* 37 (1995): 285–300.

E. Bammel, "Das Gleichnis von den bösen Winzern (Mc 12,1–9) und das jüdische Erbrecht," *RIDA* 3.6 (1959): 11–17.

L. W. Barnard, "The Testimonium concerning the Stone in the New Testament and in the Epistle of Barnabas," *SE* 3 [= *TU* 88] (1964): 306–313.

J. M. Baumgarten, "4Q500 and the Ancient Conception of the Lord's Vineyard," *JJS* 40 (1989): 1–6.

M. Black, "The Christological Use of the Old Testament in the New Testament," *NTS* 18 (1971–72): 1–14.

"The Parable as Allegory," *BJRL* 42 (1959–60): 273–87.

J. Blank, "Die Sendung des Sohnes: Zur christologischen Bedeutung des Gleichnisses von den bösen Winzern Mk 12,1–12," in *Neues Testament und Kirche*, FS R. Schnackenburg, ed. J. Gnilka (Freiburg: Herder, 1974), 11–41.

G. J. Brooke, "4Q500 1 and the Use of Scripture in the Parable of the Vineyard," *DSD* 2 (1995): 268–94.

R. E. Brown, "Parable and Allegory Reconsidered," *NovT* 5 (1962): 36–45.

F. F. Bruce, "New Wine in Old Wine Skins: III. The Corner Stone," *ExpTim* 84 (1972–73): 231–35.

M. Cahill, "Not a Cornerstone! Translating Ps 118,22 in the Jewish and Christian Scriptures," *RB* 106 (1999): 345–57.

J. D. Crossan, "Parable, Allegory, and Paradox," in *Semiology and the Parables*, ed. D. Patte (Pittsburgh: Pickwick, 1976), 247–81.

"The Parable of the Wicked Husbandmen," *JBL* 90 (1971): 451–65.

"The Servant Parables of Jesus," *Semeia* 1 (1974): 17–62.

J. D. M. Derrett, "Allegory and the Wicked Vinedresser," *JTS* n.s. 25 (1974): 426–32.

"Fresh Light on the Wicked Vinedressers," in *Law in the New Testament* (London: Darton, Longman & Todd, 1970), 286–312.

"The Stone That the Builders Rejected," *SE* 4 [= *TU* 102] (1968): 180–86.

H. Dombois, "Juristische Bemerkungen zum Gleichnis von den bösen Weingärtnern (Mk. 12.1–12)," *Neue Zeitschrift für systematische Theologie und Religionsphilosophie* 8 (1966): 361–73.

R. Dormandy, "Hebrews 1:1–2 and the Parable of the Wicked Husbandmen," *ExpTim* 100 (1988–89): 371–75.

J. Drury, "The Sower, the Vineyard, and the Place of Allegory in the Interpretation of Mark's Parables," *JTS* n.s. 24 (1973): 367–79.

E. van Eck and A. G. van Aarde, "A Narratological Analysis of Mark 12:1–12: The Plot of the Gospel of Mark in a Nutshell," *HTS* 45 (1989): 778–800.

C. Evans, "How Septuagintal Is Isa. 5:1–7 in Mark 12:1–9?" *NovT* 45 (2003): 105–110.

"Jesus' Parable of the Tenant Farmers in Light of Lease Agreements in Antiquity," *JSP* 14 (1996): 65–83.

"On the Vineyard Parables of Isaiah 5 and Mark 12," *BZ* 28 (1984): 82–86.

R. Feldmeier, "Heil im Unheil: Das Bild Gottes nach der Parabel von den bösen Winzern (Mk. 12,1–12 par.)," *TBei* 25 (1994): 5–22.

H. Frankemölle, "Hat Jesus sich selbst verkündet? Christologische Implikationen in den vormarkinische Parabeln," *BibLeb* 13 (1972): 184–207.

A. Graffy, "The Literary Genre of Isaiah 5,1–7," *Bib* 60 (1979): 400–409.

A. Gray, "The Parable of the Wicked Husbandmen (Matthew xxi. 33–41; Mark xii. 1–9; Luke xx. 9–16)," *HibJ* 19 (1920–21): 42–52.

M. Hengel, "Das Gleichnis von den Weingärtnern Mc 12,1–12 im Lichte der Zenonpapyri und der rabbinischen Gleichnisse," *ZNW* 59 (1968): 1–39.

J. D. Hester, "Socio-Rhetorical Criticism and the Parable of the Tenants," *JSNT* 45 (1992): 27–57.

E. H. Horne, "The Parable of the Tenants as Indictment," *JSNT* 71 (1998): 111–16.

J. Jeremias, "Eckstein-Schußstein," *ZNW* 36 (1937): 154–57.

"Κεφαλὴ γωνίας – Ἀκρογωνιαῖος," *ZNW* 29 (1930): 264–80.

S. Kim, "Jesus – The Son of God, the Stone, the Son of Man, and the Servant: The Role of Zechariah in the Self-Identification of Jesus," in *Tradition and Interpretation in the New Testament*, FS E. E. Ellis, ed. G. F. Hawthorne and O. Betz (Grand Rapids, MI: Eerdmans, 1987), 134–48.

C. A. Kimball, "Jesus' Exposition of Scripture in Luke (20: 9–19): An Inquiry in Light of Jewish Hermeneutics," *BBR* 3 (1993): 77–92.

H.-J. Klauck, "Das Gleichnis vom Mord im Weinberg (Mk 12,1–12; Mt 21,33–46; Lk 20,9–19)," *BibLeb* 11 (1970): 118–45.

J. S. Kloppenborg Verbin, "Egyptian Viticultural Practices and the Citation of Isa 5:1–7 in Mark 12:1–9," *NovT* 44 (2002): 134–59.

"Isa 5:1–7 LXX and Mark 12:1–9 Again," *NovT* 46 (2004): 12–19.

"Self-Help or Deus ex Machina in Mark 12.9?" *NTS* 50 (2004): 495–518.

W. G. Kümmel, "Das Gleichnis von den bösen Weingärtnern (Mk. 12. 1–9)," in *Aux sources de la tradition Chrétienne*, FS M. Goguel, ed. O. Cullmann and P. H. Menoud (Bibliothèque Théologique; Neuchâtel; Paris: Delachaux et Niestlé, 1950), 120–31.

S. R. Llewelyn, "Business Transactions §13: Self-Help and Legal Redress: The Parable of the Wicked Tenants," *NewDocs* 6 (1992): 86–105.

E. Lohmeyer, "Das Gleichnis von den bösen Weingärtnern (Mark. 12,1–12)," *ZST* 18 (1941): 242–59.

M. Lowe, "From the Parable of the Vineyard to a Pre-Synoptic Source," *NTS* 28 (1982): 257–63.

J. D. McGaughey, "Two Synoptic Parables in the Gospel of Thomas," *ABR* 8 (1960): 24–28.

A. Milavec, "The Identity of 'The Son' and 'The Others': Mark's Parable of the Wicked Husbandmen Reconsiderd," *BTB* 20 (1990): 30–37.

"Mark's Parable of the Wicked Husbandmen as Reaffirming God's Predilection for Israel," *JES* 26 (1989): 289–312.

H. W. Montefiore, "A Comparison of the Parables of the Gospel According to Thomas and of the Synoptic Gospels," *NTS* 7 (1960–61): 220–48.

J. C. de Moor, "The Targumic Background of Mark 12:1–12: The Parable of the Wicked Tenants," *JSJ* 19 (1998): 63–80.

J. E. Newell and R. R. Newell, "The Parable of the Wicked Tenants," *NovT* 14 (1972): 226–37.

J. C. O'Neill, "The Source of the Parables of the Bridegroom and the Wicked Husbandmen," *JTS* n.s. 39 (1988): 485–89.

S. Pedersen, "Zum Problem der vaticinia ex eventu: Eine Analyse von Mt. 21,33–46 par.; 22, 1–10 par," *ST* 19 (1965): 167–88.

J. A. T. Robinson, "The Parable of the Wicked Husbandmen: A Test of Synoptic Relationships," *NTS* 21 (1974–75): 443–61.

W. R. Schoedel, "Parables in the Gospel of Thomas: Oral Tradition or Gnostic Exegesis?" *CTM* 43 (1972): 548–60.

G. T. Sheppard, "More on Isaiah 5:1–7 as a Juridical Parable," *CBQ* 44 (1982): 45–47.

K. R. Snodgrass, "The Gospel of Thomas: A Secondary Gospel," *SecCent* 7 (1989): 19–38.

"The Parable of the Wicked Husbandmen: Is the Gospel of Thomas Version the Original?" *NTS* 21 (1974–75): 142–44.

"Recent Research on the Parable of the Wicked Tenants: An Assessment," *BBR* 8 (1998): 187–215.

D. Stern, "Jesus' Parables from the Perspective of Rabbinic Literature: The Example of the Wicked Husbandmen," in *Parable and Story in Judaism and Christianity*, ed. C. Thoma and M. Wyschogrod (SJC; New York: Paulist, 1989), 42–80.

J. J. Vincent, "The Parables of Jesus as Self-Revelation," *SE* 1 [= *TU* 73] (1959): 79–99.

W. J. C. Weren, "The Use of Isaiah 5,1–7 in the Parable of the Tenants (Mark 12,1–12; Matthew 21,33–46)," *Bib* 79 (1998): 1–26.

J. T. Willis, "The Genre of Isaiah 5:1–7," *JBL* 96 (1977): 337–62.

G. A. Yee, "The Form-Critical Study of Isaiah 5:1–7 as a Song and a Juridical Parable," *CBQ* 43 (1981): 30–40.

Mark 12:13–17

W. J. Bennett, Jr., "The Herodians of Mark's Gospel," *NovT* 17 (1975): 9–14.

F. F. Bruce, "Render to Caesar," in *Jesus and the Politics of His Day*, ed. E. Bammel and C. F. D. Moule (Cambridge: Cambridge University Press, 1984), 249–63.

M. Bünker, "Gebt dem Kaiser, was des Kaisers ist!" *Kairos* 29 (1987): 85–98.

J. D. Crossan, "Mark 12:13–17," *Int* 37 (1983): 397–401.

J. D. M. Derrett, "Render to Caesar," in *Law in the New Testament* (London: Darton, Longman & Todd, 1970), 313–38.

P. C. Finney, "The Rabbi and the Coin Portrait (Mark 12:15b, 16)," *JBL* 112 (1993): 629–44.

C. H. Giblin, "'The Things of God' in the Question concerning Tribute to Caesar (Lk 20:25; Mk 12:17; Mt 22:21)," *CBQ* 33 (1971): 510–27.

K. Haacker, "Kaisertribut und Gottesdienst (Eine Auslegung von Markus 12,13–17)," *TBei* 17 (1986): 285–92.

H. St J. Hart, "The Coin of 'Render unto Caesar...' (A Note on Some Aspects of Mark 12:13–17; Matt. 22:15–22; Luke 20:20–26)," in *Jesus and the Politics of His Day*, ed. E. Bammel and C. F. D. Moule (Cambridge: Cambridge University Press, 1984), 241–48.

H. G. Klemm, "De censu Caesaris: Beobachtungen zu J. Duncan M. Derretts Interpretation der Perikope Mk. 12:13–17 par," *NovT* 24 (1982): 234–54.

D. Lührmann, "Die Pharisäer und die Schriftgelehrten im Markusevangelium," *ZNW* 78 (1987): 169–85.

J. P. Meier, "The Historical Jesus and Historical Herodians," *JBL* 119 (2000): 740–46.

A. B. Ogle, "What Is Left for Caesar? A Look at Mark 12:13–17 and Romans 13:1–7," *TToday* 35 (1978–79): 254–64.

R. Oster, "Numismatic Windows into the Social World of Early Christianity: A Methodological Inquiry," *JBL* 101 (1981): 195–223.

D. T. Owen-Ball, "Rabbinic Rhetoric and the Tribute Passage," *NovT* 35 (1993): 1–14.

P. Perkins, "Taxes in the New Testament," *JRE* 12 (1984): 182–200.

G. Petzke, "Die historische Jesus in der sozialethischen Diskussion: Mk 12,13–17 par," in *Jesus Christus in Historie und Theologie*, FS H. Conzelmann, ed. G. Strecker (Tübingen: Mohr-Siebeck, 1975), 223–36.

M. Rist, "Caesar or God (Mark 12:13–17)? A Study in Formgeschichte," *JR* 16 (1936): 317–31.

E. A. Russell, "Church and State in the New Testament," *ITQ* 44 (1977): 192–207.

K.-G. Sandelin, "The Jesus-Tradition and Idolatry," *NTS* 42 (1996): 412–20.

S. Schreiber, "Caesar oder Gott (Mk 12, 17)? Zur Theoriebildung im Umgang mit politischen Texten des Neuen Testaments," *BZ* 48 (2004): 65–85.

A. Stock, "Jesus, Hypocrites, and Herodians," *BTB* 16 (1986): 3–7.

"'Render to Caesar,'" *TBT* 62 (1972): 929–34.

D. F. Taylor, "The Monetary Crisis in Revelation 13:17 and the Provenance of the Book of Revelation," *CBQ* 71 (2009): 580–96 [Mark treated in Appendix].

B. T. Viviano, "Render unto Caesar," *TBT* 26 (1988): 272–76.

Mark 12:18–27

B. J. Bamberger, "The Sadducees and the Belief in Angels," *JBL* 82 (1963): 433–35.

G. Baumbach, "The Sadducees in Josephus," in *Josephus, the Bible, and History*, ed. L. H. Feldman and G. Hata (Detroit: Wayne State University Press, 1989), 173–95.

S. Belkin, "Levirate and Agnate Marriage in Rabbinic and Cognate Literature," *JQR* 60 (1970): 275–329.

A. H. Cadwallader, "In Go(l)d We Trust: Literary and Economic Currency Exchange in the Debate over Caesar's Coin (Mark 12:13–17)," *BibInt* 14 (2006): 486–507.

D. Daube, "On Acts 23: Sadducees and Angels," *JBL* 109 (1990): 492–97.

P. B. Decock, "Holy Ones, Sons of God, and the Transcendent Future of the Righteous in 1 Enoch and the New Testament," *Neot* 17 (1983): 70–82.

F. G. Downing, "The Resurrection of the Dead: Jesus and Philo," *JSNT* 15 (1982): 42–50.

E. E. Ellis, "Jesus, the Sadducees and Qumran," *NTS* 10 (1963–64): 274–79.

J. G. Janzen, "Resurrection and Hermeneutics: On Exodus 3.6 in Mark 12.26," *JSNT* 23 (1985): 43–58.

T. W. Manson, "Sadducee and Pharisee: The Origin and Significance of the Names," *BJRL* 22 (1938): 144–59.

J. L. Mays, "Is This Not Why You Are Wrong?' Exegetical Reflections on Mark 12:18–27," *Int* 60 (2006): 32–46.

J. P. Meier, "The Debate on the Resurrection of the Dead: An Incident from the Ministry of the Historical Jesus?" *JSNT* 77 (2000): 3–24.

F. Mussner, "Jesu Lehre über das kommende Leben nach den Synoptiker," *Concilium* 6 (1970): 692–95.

M. Reiser, "Das Leben nach dem Tod in der Verkündigung Jesu," *Erbe und Auftrag* 66 (1990): 381–90.

K. Schubert, "Die Entwicklung der Auferstehungslehre von der nachexilischen bis zur frührabbinischen Zeit," *BZ* 6 (1962): 177–214.

D. M. Sherbok, "Jesus' Defense of the Resurrection of the Dead," *JSNT* 11 (1981): 64–73.

B. R. Trick, "Death, Covenants, and the Proof of Resurrection in Mark 12:18–27," *NovT* 49 (2007): 232–56.

W. E. Weir, "Would Viagra Have Helped? A Discussion of Mark 12:18–27 from a Liberationist Standpoint," *ExpTim* 114 (2003): 187–92.

S. Zeitlin, "The Sadducees and the Belief in Angels," *JBL* 83 (1964): 67–71.

Mark 12:28–34

D. C. Allison, "Mark 12.28–31 and the Decalogue," in *The Gospels and the Scriptures of Israel*, ed. C. A. Evans and W. R. Stegner (JSNTSup 104, SSEJC 3; Sheffield: Sheffield Academic, 1994), 270–78.

L. Berg, "Das neutestamentliche Liebesgebot: Prinzip der Sittlichkeit," *TTZ* 83 (1974): 129–45.

G. Bornkamm, "Das Doppelgebot der Liebe," in *Neutestamentliche Studien*, FS R. Bultmann, ed. W. Eltester (BZNW 21; Berlin: Töpelmann, 1954), 85–93.

W. Diezinger, "Zum Liebesgebot Mk xii,28–34 und Parr," *NovT* 20 (1978): 81–83.

J. R. Donahue, "A Neglected Factor in the Theology of Mark," *JBL* 101 (1982): 563–94.

J. Ernst, "Die Einheit von Gottes – und Nächstenliebe in der Verkündigung Jesu," *TGl* 60 (1970): 3–14.

V. P. Furnish, "Love of Neighbor in the New Testament," *JRE* 10 (1982): 327–34.

G. W. Hoyer, "Mark 12:28–34," *Int* 33 (1979): 293–98.

K, Kertelge, "Das Doppelgebot der Liebe im Markusevangelium," in *À Cause de l'évangile: Études sur les Synoptiques et les Actes*, FS J. Dupont, ed. F. Refoulé (LD 123; Paris: Cerf, 1985), 303–322.

J. Marcus, "The Authority to Forgive Sins upon the Earth: The Shema in the Gospel of Mark," in *The Gospels and the Scriptures of Israel*, ed. C. A. Evans and W. R. Stegner (*JSNTSup* 104, SSEJC 3; Sheffield: JSOT Press, 1994), 196–211.

J. S. Miller, "The Neighbour," *ExpTim* 96 (1984–85): 337–39.

H. W. Montefiore, "Thou Shalt Love Thy Neighbor as Thyself," *NovT* 5 (1962): 157–70.

R. Pesch, "Jesus und das Hauptgebot," in *Neues Testament und Ethik*, FS R. Schnackenburg, ed. H. Merklein (Freiburg: Herder, 1989), 99–109.

G. Schneider, "Die Neuheit der christlichen Nächstenliebe," *TTZ* 82 (1973): 257–75.

J. B. Stern, "Jesus' Citation of Dt 6,5 and Lv 19,18 in the Light of Jewish Tradition," *CBQ* 28 (1966): 312–16.

J. van Vurst, "The Scribe's Insight," *TBT* 25 (1987): 37–41.

O. Wischmeyer, "Das Gebot der Nächstenliebe bei Paulus: Eine traditions-geschichtliche Untersuchung," *BZ* 30 (1986): 161–87.

W. Wolpert, "Die Liebe zum Nächsten, zum Feind und zum Sünder," *TGl* 74 (1984): 262–82.

Mark 12:35–37

K. Berger, "Die königlichen Messiastraditionen des Neuen Testaments," *NTS* 20 (1973–74): 1–44.

O. Betz, "Donnersöhne, Menschenfischer und der davidische Messias," *RevQ* 3 (1961): 41–70:20–48.

G. H. Boobyer, "Mark XII. 35–37 and the Preexistence of Jesus in Mark," *ExpTim* 51 (1939–40): 393–94.

J. H. Charlesworth, "Solomon and Jesus: The Son of David in Ante-Markan Traditions (Mk 10:47)," in *Biblical and Humane*, FS J. F. Priest, ed. L. B. Elder et al. (Homage 20; Atlanta: Scholars Press, 1996), 125–51.

"The Son of David: Solomon and Jesus (Mark 10.47)," in *The New Testament and Hellenistic Judaism*, ed. P. Borgen and S. Giversen (Aarhus: Aarhus University Press, 1995), 72–87.

B. Chilton, "Jesus ben David: Reflections on the Davidssohnfrage," *JSNT* 14 (1982): 88–112.

J. A. Fitzmyer, "Der semitische Hintergrund des neutestamentlichen Kyriostitels," in *Jesus Christus in Historie und Theologie*, FS H. Conzelmann, ed. G. Strecker (Tübingen: Mohr-Siebeck, 1975), 267–98.

"The Son of David Tradition and Mt 22:41–46 and Parallels," *Concilium* 10.2 (1966): 40–46.

D. Flusser, "Familien vom 'Haus Davids' in der Zeit Jesu," in *Jesus – Qumran – Urchristentum. Vol. 2 of Entdeckungen im Neuen Testament* (Neukirchen-Vluyn: Neukirchener Verlag, 1999), 1579–84.

G. Friedrich, "Messianische Hohepriesterwartung in den Synoptikern," *ZTK* 53 (1956): 265–311.

R. P. Gagg, "Jesus und die Davidssohnfrage: Zur Exegese von Markus 12,35–37," *TZ* 7 (1951): 18–30.

S. E. Johnson, "The David-Royal Motif in the Gospels," *JBL* 87 (1968): 136–50.

M. de Jonge, "Jesus, Son of David and Son of God," in *Intertextuality in Biblical Writings*, FS B. M. F. van Iersel, ed. S. Draisma (Kampen: Kok, 1989), 95–104.

W. R. G. Loader, "Christ at the Right Hand – Ps. CX. 1 in the *NT*," *NTS* 24 (1978–79): 199–217.

E. Lövestam, "Die Davidssohnfrage," *SEÅ* 27 (1962): 72–82.

F. J. Moloney, "The Re-Interpretation of Psalm VIII and the Son of Man Debate," *NTS* 27 (1980–81): 656–72.

F. Neugebauer, "Die Davidssohnfrage (Mark xii. 35–7 Parr.) und der Menschensohn," *NTS* 21 (1974–75): 81–108.

G. Schneider, "Zur Vorgeschichte des christologischen Prädikats 'Sohn Davids,'" *TTZ* 80 (1971): 247–53.

"Der Davidssohnfrage (Mk 12,35–37)," *Bib* 53 (1972): 65–90.

A. Suhl, "Der Davidssohn im Matthäus-Evangelium," *ZNW* 59 (1968): 57–81.

W. O. Walker, "The Origin of the Son of Man Concept as Applied to Jesus," *JBL* 91 (1972): 482–90.

Mark 12:38–40

J. D. M. Derrett, "'Eating Up the Houses of Widows': Jesus's Comment on Lawyers?" *NovT* 14 (1972): 1–9.

H. T. Fleddermann, "A Warning about the Scribes (Mark 12.37b–40)," *CBQ* 44 (1982): 52–67.

K. H. Rengstorf, "Die στολαί der Schriftgelehrten: Eine Erläuterung zu Mark. 12,13," in *Abraham unser Vater: Juden und Christen im Gespräch über die Bibel*, FS O. Michel, ed. O. Betz et al. (AGSU 5; Leiden: Brill, 1963), 383–404.

G. Schmitt, "Das Zeichen des Jona," *ZNW* 69 (1978): 123–29.

Mark 12:41–44

M. A. Beavis, "Women as Models of Faith in Mark," *BTB* 18 (1988): 3–9.

A. I. Berglund, "The Treasury in God's Temple (Mk. 12:41–44)," *Credo* 5 (1959): 2–4.

J. Jeremias, "Zwei Miszellen: 1. Antik-jüdische Münzdeutungen. 2. Zur Geschichtlichkeit der Tempelreinigung," *NTS* 23 (1976–77): 177–80.

E. S. Malbon, "The Poor Widow in Mark and Her Poor Rich Readers," *CBQ* 53 (1991): 589–604.

R. S. Sugirtharajah, "The Widow's Mite Revalued," *ExpTim* 103 (1991–92): 42–43.

A. G. Wright, "The Widow's Mites: Praise or Lament? – A Matter of Context," *CBQ* 44 (1982): 256–65.

Mark 13:1–37

E. Adams, "Historical Crisis and Cosmic Crisis in Mark 13 and Lucan's Civil War," *TynBul* 48 (1997): 329–44.

B. W. Bacon, "The Apocalyptic Chapter of the Synoptic Gospels," *JBL* 28 (1909): 1–25.

R. Bauckham, "Synoptic Parousia Parables and the Apocalypse," *NTS* 23 (1976–77): 162–76.

"Synoptic Parousia Parables Again," *NTS* 29 (1983): 129–34.

G. K. Beale, "The Use of Daniel in the Synoptic Eschatological Discourse and in the Book of Revelation," in *The Jesus Tradition Outside the Gospels*, ed. D. Wenham (Gospel Perspectives 5; Sheffield: JSOT Press, 1985), 129–53.

G. R. Beasley-Murray, "The Eschatological Discourse of Jesus," *RevExp* 57 (1960): 153–66.

"The Rise and Fall of the Little Apocalypse Theory," *ExpTim* 64 (1952–53): 346–49.

"Second Thoughts on the Composition of Mark 13," *NTS* 29 (1983): 414–20.

E. Best, "The Gospel of Mark: Who Was the Reader?" *IBS* 11 (1989): 124–32.

M. Bird, "Mission as an Apocalyptic Event: Reflections on Luke 10:18 and Mark 13:10," *EvQ* 76 (2004): 117–34.

C. C. Black, "An Oration at Olivet: Some Rhetorical Dimensions of Mark 13," in *Persuasive Artistry: Studies in New Testament Rhetoric*, FS G. A. Kennedy, ed. D. F. Watson (*JSNTSup* 50; Sheffield: JSOT Press, 1991), 66–92.

P. T. Coke, "The Angels of the Son of Man," *SNTSU* 3 (1978): 91–98.

H. Conzelmann, "Geschichte und Eschaton nach Mc 13," *ZNW* 50 (1959): 210–21.

A. C. Cotter, "The Eschatological Discourse," *CBQ* 1 (1939): 125–32, 204–213.

C. B. Cousar, "Eschatology and Mark's Theologia Crucis: A Critical Analysis of Mark 13," *Int* 24 (1970): 321–35.

C. E. B. Cranfield, "St. Mark 13," *SJT* 6 (1953): 189–96, 287–303.
"St. Mark 13," *SJT* 7 (1954): 284–303.
"Thoughts on New Testament Eschatology," *SJT* 35 (1982): 497–512.

B. S. Crawford, "Near Expectation in the Sayings of Jesus," *JBL* 101 (1982): 225–44.

D. Daube, "The Abomination of Desolation," in *The New Testament and Rabbinic Judaism* (London: Athlone, 1956), 418–37.

L. A. DeBruyn, "Preterism and 'This Generation,'" *BibSac* 167 (2010): 180–200.

W. D. Dennison, "Miracles as 'Signs,'" *BTB* 6 (1976): 190–202.

F. Dewar, "Chapter 13 and the Passion Narrative in St Mark," *Theology* 64 (1961): 99–107.

C. H. Dodd, "The Fall of Jerusalem and the 'Abomination of Desolation,'" *JRS* 37 (1947): 47–54.

J. A. Draper, "The Development of the 'Sign of the Son of Man' in the Jesus Tradition," *NTS* 39 (1993): 1–21.

C. A. Evans, "Predictions of the Destruction of the Herodian Temple in the Pseudepigrapha, Qumran Scrolls, and Related Texts," *JSP* 10 (1992): 89–147.

A. M. Farrer, "An Examination of Mark XIII.10," *JTS* n.s. 7 (1956): 75–79.

C. H. T. Fletcher-Louis, "The Destruction of the Temple and the Relativization of the Old Covenant: Mark 13:31 and Matthew 5:18," in *'The Reader Must Understand': Eschatology in Bible and Theology*, ed. K. E. Brower and M. W. Elliott (Leicester: Inter-Varsity Press, 1997), 145–69.

F. Flückiger, "Die Redaktion der Zukunftsrede in Markus. 13," *TZ* 26 (1970): 395–409.

D. Flusser, "Prophetische Aussagen Jesu über Jerusalem," in *Jesus – Qumran – Urchristentum*. Vol. 2 of *Entdeckungen im Neuen Testament* (Neukirchen-Vluyn: Neukirchener Verlag, 1999), 152–78.

G. C. Fuller, "The Olivet Discourse: An Apocalyptic Timetable," *WTJ* 28 (1966): 157–63.

H. Giesen, "Christliche Existenz in der Welt und der Menschensohn: Versuch einer Neuinterpretation des Terminwortes Mk 13,30," *SNTSU* 8 (1983): 18–69.

K. Grayston, "The Study of Mark XIII," *BJRL* 56 (1973–74): 371–87.

H. R. Graham, "A Markan Theme: Endurance in Time of Persecution," *TBT* 23 (1985): 297–304.

"A Passion Prediction for Mark's Community: Mark 13:9–13," *BTB* 16 (1986): 18–22.

F. X. Gumerlock, "Mark 13:32 and Christ's Supposed Ignorance: Four Patristic Solutions," *Trinity Journal* 28 (2007): 205–213.

J. J. Gunther, "The Fate of the Jerusalem Church: The Flight to Pella," *TZ* 29 (1973): 81–84.

F. Hahn, "Die Rede von der Parusie des Menschensohnes Markus 13," in *Jesus der Menschensohn*, FS A. Vögtle, ed. R. Pesch and R. Schnackenburg (Freiburg: Herder, 1975), 240–66.

T. R. Hatina, "The Focus of Mark 13:24–27 – The Parousia, or the Destruction of the Temple?" *BBR* 6 (1996): 43–66.

I. Hermann, "Die Gefährdung der Welt und ihre Erneuerung: Auslegung von Mk 13,1–37," *BibLeb* 7 (1966): 305–309.

M. D. Hooker, "Trial and Tribulation in Mark XIII," *BJRL* 65 (1982): 78–99.

J. K. Howard, "Our Lord's Teaching concerning His Parousia: A Study in the Gospel of Mark," *EvQ* 38 (1966): 52–58, 68–75, 150–57.

M. F. van Iersel, "Failed Followers in Mark: Mark 13:12 as a Key for the Identification of the Intended Readers," *CBQ* 58 (1996): 244–63.

M. de Jonge, "The Earliest Christian Use of Christos: Some Suggestions," *NTS* 32 (1986): 321–43.

M. Karnetzki, "Die galiläische Redaktion im Markusevangelium," *ZNW* 52 (1961): 238–72.

G. D. Kilpatrick, "The Gentile Mission in Mark and Mark xiii.9–11," in *Studies in the Gospels*, FS R. H. Lightfoot, ed. D. E. Nineham (Oxford: Blackwell, 1955), 145–58.

C. Koester, "The Origin and Significance of the Flight to Pella Tradition," *CBQ* 51 (1989): 90–106.

H. Kosmala, "The Time of the Cock-Crow," *ASTI* 2 (1963): 118–20.

W. G. Kümmel, "Eschatological Expectation in the Proclamation of Jesus," in *The Future of Our Religious Past*, FS. R. Bultmann, ed. J. M. Robinson (London: SCM Press; New York: Harper & Row, 1971), 29–48.

J. Lambrecht, "Die Logia-Quellen von Markus 13," *Bib* 47 (1966): 321–60.

"Die 'Midrasch-Quelle' von Mk 13," *Bib* 49 (1968): 254–70.

E. Lohse, "Apokalyptik und Christologie," *ZNW* 62 (1971): 48–67.

E. Lövestam, "The ἡγενεὰ αὕτη Eschatology in Mk 13,30 parr.," in *L'Apocalypse johannique et l'apocalyptique dans le Nouveau Testament*, ed. J. Lambrecht (Gembloux: Duculot, 1980), 403–413.

G. Lüdemann, "The Successors of Pre-70 Jerusalem Christianity: A Critical Evaluation of the Pella-Tradition," in *The Shaping of Christianity in the Second and Third Centuries*. Vol. 1 of *Jewish and Christian Self-Definition*, ed. E. P. Sanders (Philadelphia: Fortress, 1990), 161–73, 245–54.

W. Manson, "The Son of Man and History," *SJT* 5 (1952): 113–22.

G. Martin, "Procedural Register in the Olivet Discourse: A Functional Linguistic Approach to Mark 13," *Bib* 90 (2009): 457–83.

T. W. Martin, "Watch during the Watches (Mark 13:35)," *JBL* 120 (2001): 685–701.

M. Meinertz, "Dieses Geschlecht," *BZ* 1 (1957): 283–89.

F. Mussner, "Die Wiederkunft des Menschensohnes nach Markus 13,24–27 und 14,61–62," *BK* 16 (1961): 105–107.

"Wer ist 'dieses Geschlecht' in Mk 13,30 parr.?" *Kairos* 29 (1987): 23–28.

B. M. Nolan, "Some Observations on the Parousia and New Testament Eschatology," *ITQ* 36 (1969): 283–314.

L. Perkins, "'Let the Reader Understand': A Contextual Interpretation of Mark 13:14," *BBR* 16 (2006): 95–104.

R. Pesch, "Markus 13," in *L'Apocalypse johannique et l'apocalyptique dans le Nouveau Testament*, ed. J. Lambrecht (BETL 53; Gembloux: Duculot; Leuven: Peeters, 1980), 355–68.

T. Radcliffe, "'The Coming of the Son of Man': Mark's Gospel and the Subversion of the Apocalyptic Imagination," in *Language, Meaning and God*, FS H. McCabe, ed. B. Davies (London: Chapman, 1987), 167–89.

B. Reicke, "Synoptic Prophecies on the Destruction of Jerusalem," in *Studies in New Testament and Early Christian Literature*, FS A. P. Wikgren, ed. D. E. Aune (NovTSup 33; Leiden: Brill, 1972), 121–34.

B. Rigaux, "βδέλυγμα τῆς ἐρημώσεως (Mc 13,14; Mt 24,15)," *Bib* 40 (1959): 675–83.

D. M. Roarck, "The Great Eschatological Discourse," *NovT* 7 (1964–65): 122–27.

L. Sauborin, "The Biblical Cloud: Terminology and Traditions," *BTB* 4 (1974): 290–311.

R. Schnackenburg, "Kirche und Parusie," in *Gott in Welt*, FS K. Rahner, ed. J. B. Metz et al., 2 vols. (Freiburg: Herder, 1964), 1:551–78.

S. G. Sowers, "The Circumstances and Recollection of the Pella Flight," *TZ* 26 (1970): 305–320.

O. F. J. Seitz, "The Future Coming of the Son of Man: Three Midrashic Formulations in the Gospel of Mark," *SE* 6 [= *TU* 112] (1973): 478–94.

R. S. Snow, "Let the Reader Understand: Mark's Use of Jeremiah 7 in Mark 13:14," *BBR* 21 (2011): 467–77.

W. A. Such, "The Significance of τὸ σημεῖον in Mark 13:4," *IBS* 13 (1991): 134–54.

V. Taylor, "The 'Son of Man' Sayings Relating to the Parousia," *ExpTim* 58 (1946–47): 12–15.

"Unsolved New Testament Problems – The Apocalyptic Discourse of Mark 13," *ExpTim* 60 (1948–49): 94–98.

J. W. Thompson, "The Gentile Mission as an Eschatological Necessity," *ResQ* 14 (1971): 18–27.

W. S. Vorster, "Literary Reflections on Mark 13:5–37: A Narrated Speech of Jesus," *Neot* 21 (1987): 203–224.

N. Walter, "Tempelzerstörung und Synoptische Apokalypse," *ZNW* 57 (1966): 38–49.

T. J. Weeden, "The Heresy That Necessitated Mark's Gospel," *ZNW* 59 (1968): 145–58.

D. Wenham, " 'This Generation Will Not Pass . . .': A Study of Jesus' Future Expectation in Mark 13," in *Christ the Lord: Studies in Christology*, FS D. Guthrie, ed. H. H. Rowdon (Leicester: Inter-Varsity Press, 1982), 127–50.

Mark 14:1–11

Y. Arbeitman, "The Suffix of Iscariot," *JBL* 99 (1980): 122–24.

S. C. Barton, "Mark as Narrative: The Story of the Anointing Woman (Mk 14:3–9)," *ExpTim* 102 (1991): 230–34.

F. W. Danker, "The Literary Unity of Mark 14:1–25," *JBL* 85 (1966): 467–72.

D. Daube, "The Anointing at Bethany and Jesus' Burial," *ATR* 32 (1950): 186–99.

J. D. M. Derrett, "The Anointing at Bethany," *SE* 2 [= *TU* 87] (1964): 174–82.

J. K. Elliott, "The Anointing of Jesus," *ExpTim* 85 (1974): 105–107.

S. Guijarro and A. Rodriguez, "The 'Messianic' Anointing of Jesus (Mark 14:3–9)," *BTB* 41 (2011): 132–143.

J. R. Harris, "Did Judas Really Commit Suicide?" *AJT* 4 (1900): 490–513.

K. Hein, "Judas Iscariot: Key to the Last-Supper Narratives?" *NTS* 17 (1970–71): 227–32.

J. Jeremias, "Markus 14,9," *ZNW* 44 (1952–53): 103–107.

"Die Salbungsgeschichte Mc 14,3–9," *ZNW* 35 (1936): 77–82.

R. Park, "The Coronation of the Christ: Mark's Characterization of the Christ in Light of 14:1–11," *ExpTim* 124 (2012): 112–118.

H. Preisker, "Der Verrat des Judas und das Abendmahl," *ZNW* 41 (1942): 151–55.

C. C. Torrey, "The Name 'Iscarioth,'" *HTR* 36 (1943): 51–62.

N. Walker, "Concerning the Jaubertian Chronology of the Passion," *NovT* 3 (1959): 317–20.

J. Ynag, "'One of the Twelve' and Mark's Narrative Strategy," *ExpTim* 115 (2004): 253–257.

Mark 14:12–31

S. Aalen, "Das Abendmahl als Opfermahl im Neuen Testament," *NovT* 6 (1963): 128–52.

W. C. Allen, "The Last Supper Not a Passover Meal," *ExpTim* 20 (1908): 377.

A. G. Arnott, "'The First Day of Unleavened . . . ,' Mt 26.17, Mk 14.12, Lk 22.7," *BT* 35 (1984): 235–38.

G. J. Bahr, "The Seder of the Passover and the Eucharistic Words," *NovT* 12 (1970): 181–202.

M. Black, "The Arrest and Trial of Jesus and the Date of the Last Supper," in *New Testament Essays*, FS T. W. Manson, ed. A. J. B. Higgins (Manchester: Manchester University Press, 1959), 19–33.

B. M. Bokser, "Was the Last Supper a Passover Seder?" *BR* 3.2 (1987): 24–33.

L. C. Boughton, "'Being Shed for You/Many': Time-Sense and Consequences in the Synoptic Cup Citations," *TynBul* 48 (1997): 249–70.

D. Brady, "The Alarm to Peter in Mark's Gospel," *JSNT* 4 (1979): 42–57.

M. J. Cahill, "Drinking Blood at a Kosher Eucharist? The Sound of Scholarly Silence," *BTB* 32 (2002): 168–81.

D. B. Carmichael, "David Daube on the Eucharist and the Passover Seder," *JSNT* 42 (1991): 45–67.

M. Casey, "The Date of the Passover Sacrifices and Mark 14:12," *TynBul* 48 (1997): 245–47.

"The Original Aramaic Form of Jesus' Interpretation of the Cup," *JTS* 41 (1990): 1–12.

B. Cooke, "Synoptic Presentation of the Eucharist as Covenant Sacrifice," *TS* 21 (1960): 1–44.

R. Daly, "The Eucharist and Redemption: The Last Supper and Jesus' Understanding of His Death," *BTB* 11 (1981): 21–27.

A. Gilmore, "The Date and Significance of the Last Supper," *SJT* 14 (1961): 256–69.

F. Hahn, "Die alttestamentlichen Motive in der urchristlichen Abendmahlsüberlieferung," *EvT* 27 (1967): 337–74.

P. J. Heawood, "The Time of the Last Supper," *JQR* 42 (1951–52): 37–44.

D. Instone-Brewer, "Jesus's Last Passover: The Synoptics and John," *ExpTim* 112 (2001): 122–23.

J. Jeremias, "This is My Body," *ExpTim* 83 (1971–72): 196–203.

E. J. Kilmartin, "The Last Supper and the Earliest Eucharists of the Church," *Concilium* 40 (1969): 35–47.

J. Klawans, "Interpreting the Last Supper: Sacrifice, Spiritualization, and Anti-Sacrifice," *NTS* 48 (2002): 1–17.

H. Kosmala, "The Time of the Cock-Crow," *ASTI* 2 (1963): 118–20.

"The Time of the Cock-Crow," *ASTI* 6 (1968): 132–34.

J. A. O'Flynn, "The Date of the Last Supper," *ITQ* 25 (1958): 58–63.

G. Ogg, "Review of *La Date de la Cène*, by A. Jaubert," *NovT* 3 (1959): 149–60.

R. Pesch, "Die Verleugnung des Petrus: Eine Studie zu Mk 14,54.66–72 (und Mk 14,26–31)," in *Neues Testament und Kirche*, FS R. Schnackenburg, ed. J. Gnilka (Freiburg: Herder, 1974), 42–62.

"The Gospel in Jerusalem: Mark 14:12–26 as the Oldest Tradition of the Early Church," in *The Gospel and the Gospels*, ed. P. Stuhlmacher (Grand Rapids, MI: Eerdmans, 1991), 106–48.

D. P. Senior, "The Eucharist in Mark: Mission, Reconciliation Hope," *BTB* 12 (1982): 67–72.

P. W. Skehan, "The Date of the Last Supper," *CBQ* 20 (1958): 192–99.

B. D. Smith, "The Chronology of the Last Supper," *WTJ* 53 (1991): 29–45.

P. Stuhlmacher, "The New Testament Witness concerning the Lord's Supper," in *Jesus of Nazareth - Christ of Faith* (Peabody, MA: Hendrickson, 1993), 58–102.

J. W. Wenham, "How Many Cock-Crowings? The Problem of Harmonistic Text-Variants," *NTS* 25 (1978–79): 523–25.

J. L. White, "Beware of Leavened Bread: Markan Imagery in the Last Supper," *Forum* 3.4 (1987): 49–63.

M. Wilcox, "The Denial-Sequence in Mark xiv. 26–31, 66–72," *NTS* 17 (1970–71): 426–36.

S. Zeitlin, "The Time of the Passover Meal," *JQR* 42 (1951–52): 45–50.

Mark 14:32–42

R. S. Barbour, "Gethsemane in the Tradition of the Passion," *NTS* 16 (1969–70): 231–51.

J. Barr, "'Abba, Father' and the Familiarity of Jesus' Speech," *Theology* 91 (1988): 173–79.

"Abba Isn't Daddy," *JTS* n.s. 39 (1988): 28–47.

E. F. F. Bishop, "A Stone's Throw," *ExpTim* 53 (1941–42): 270–71.

M. Black, "The Cup Metaphor in Mark xiv. 36," *ExpTim* 59 (1947–48): 195.

T. Boman, "Der Gebetskampf Jesu," *NTS* 10 (1963–64): 261–73.

C. E. B. Cranfield, "The Cup Metaphor in Mark xiv. 36 and Parallels," *ExpTim* 59 (1947–48): 137–38.

M. M. Culy, "Would Jesus Exaggerate? Rethinking Matthew 26.38// Mark 14.34," *BT* 57 (2006): 105–109.

J. B. Green, "Jesus on the Mount of Olives (Lk. 22.39–46)," *JSNT* 26 (1986): 29–48.

W. Kelber, "Passion Christology and Discipleship Failure," *ZNW* 63 (1972): 166–87.

M. Kiley, "Lord, Save My Life (Ps 116:4) as Generative Text for Jesus' Gethsemane Prayer (Mark 14:36a)," *CBQ* 48 (1986): 655–59.

M. Latke, "Eine bemerkenswerte syrische Lesart in Mark 14,25," *ZNW* 104 (2013): 146.

B. Saunderson, "Gethsemane: The Missing Witness," *Bib* 70 (1989): 224–33.

T. Söding, "Gebet und Gebetsmahnung Jesu in Getsemani: Eine redaktionskritische Auslegung von Mk 14,32–42," *BZ* 31 (1987): 76–100.

Mark 14:43–52

R. Allen, "Mark 14, 51–52 and Coptic Hagiography," *Bib* 89 (2008): 265–68.

A. W. Argyle, "The Meaning of καθ᾽ ἡμέραν in Mark xiv.49," *ExpTim* 63 (1951–52): 354.

F. W. Belcher, "A Comment on Mark xiv.45," *ExpTim* 64 (1952–53): 240.

H. Fleddermann, "The Flight of a Naked Young Man (Mark 14:51–52)," *CBQ* 41 (1979): 412–18.

M. J. Haren, "The Naked Young Man: A Historian's Hypothesis on Mark 14,51–52," *Bib* 79 (1998): 525–31.

R. A. Horseley, "Popular Messianic Movements around the Time of Jesus," *CBQ* 46 (1981): 409–432.

     "Popular Prophetic Movements at the Time of Jesus: Their Principal Features and Social Origins," *JSNT* 26 (1986): 3–27.

H. M. Jackson, "Why the Youth Shed His Cloak and Fled Naked: The Meaning and Purpose of Mark 14:51–52," *JBL* 116 (1997): 273–89.

N. Kreiger, "Der Knecht des Hohenpriesters," *NovT* 2 (1957): 73–74.

A. Kuruvilla, "The Naked Runaway and the Enrobed Reporter of Mark 14 and 16: What Is the Author Doing with What He Is Saying?" *JETS* 54 (2011): 527–45.

E. Nestle, "Zum Judaskuss," *ZNW* 15 (1914): 92–93.

J. M. Ross, "The Young Man Who Fled Naked," *IBS* 13 (1991): 170–74.

G. Schneider, "Die Verhaftung Jesu: Traditionsgeschichte von Mk 14,43–52," *ZNW* 63 (1972): 188–209.

E. L. Schnellbächer, "Das Rätsel des νεανίσκος bei Markus," *ZNW* 73 (1982): 127–35.

L. P. Trudiger, "Davidic Links with the Betrayal of Jesus: Some Further Observations," *ExpTim* 86 (1974–75): 278–79.

B. T. Viviano, "The High Priest's Servant's Ear: Mark 14:47," *RB* 96 (1989): 71–80.

Mark 14:53–65

H. W. Bartsch, "Historische Erwägungen zur Leidensgeschichte," *EvT* 22 (1962): 449–59.

     "Wer verurteilte Jesus zum Tode? Zu der Rezension des Buches von Paul Winter On the Trial of Jesus, durch Ethelbert Stauffer," *NovT* 7 (1964–65): 210–16.

M. A Beavis, "The Trial before the Sanhedrin (Mark 14:53–65): Reader Response and Greco-Roman Readers," *CBQ* 49 (1987): 581–96.

L. L. Ber, "The Illegalities of Jesus' Religious and Civil Trials," *BibSac* 161 (2004): 330–42.

O. Betz, "Probleme des Prozesses Jesu," in *ANRW* II.25.1 (Berlin: Walter de Gruyter, 1982), 613–44.

J. Blinzler, "Das Synedrium von Jerusalem und die Strafprozessordnung der Mischna," *ZNW* 52 (1961): 54–65.

"The Trial of Jesus in the Light of History," *Judaism* 20 (1971): 49–55.

D. L. Bock, *Blasphemy and Exaltation in Judaism and the Jewish Examination of Jesus: A Philological-Historical Study of the Key Jewish Themes Impacting Mark 14:61–64* (Tübingen: Mohr/Siebeck, 1998).

"Blasphemy and the Jewish Examination of Jesus," *BBR* 17 (2007): 53–114.

H. K. Bond, "Caiaphas: Reflections on a High Priest." *ExpTim* 113 (2002): 183–87.

J. W Bowker, "The Offence and Trial of Jesus," in *Jesus and the Pharisees* (New York: Cambridge University Press, 1973), 42–52.

W. S. Campbell, "Engagement, Disengagement and Obstruction: Jesus' Defense Strategies in Mark's Trial and Execution Scenes (14. 53–64; 15:1–39)," *JSNT* 26 (2004): 283–300.

D. R. Catchpole, "The Answer of Jesus to Caiaphas (Matt. XXVI.64)," *NTS* 17 (1970–71): 213–26.

"The Problem of the Historicity of the Sanhedrin Trial," in *The Trial of Jesus: Cambridge Studies*, FS C. F. D. Moule, ed. E. Bammel (*SBT* 13; London: SCM; Naperville, IL: Allenson, 1970), 47–65.

A. Y. Collins, "The Charge of Blasphemy in Mark 14.64," *JSNT* 26 (2004): 379–401.

J. R. Donahue, "Temple, Trial, and Royal Christology (Mark 14:53–65)," in *The Passion in Mark: Studies on Mark 14–16*, ed. W. Kelber (Philadelphia: Fortress, 1976), 61–79.

C. A. Evans, "'Peter Warming Himself': The Problem of an Editorial 'Seam,' " *JBL* 101 (1982): 245–49.

D. Flusser, "A Literary Approach to the Trial of Jesus," *Judaism* 20 (1971): 32–36.

D. Flusser, "'At the Right Hand of Power,'" *Immanuel* 14 (1982): 42–46.

R. H. Gundry, "Jesus' Supposed Blasphemy (Mark 14:61b–64)," *BBR* 18 (2008): 131–33.

D. Hill, "Jesus before the Sanhedrin – On What Charge?" *IBS* 7 (1985): 174–86.

W. Horbury, "The Trial of Jesus in Jewish Tradition," in *The Trial of Jesus: Cambridge Studies*, FS C. F. D. Moule, ed. E. Bammel (*SBT* 13; London: SCM Press; Naperville, IL: Allenson, 1970), 103–21.

L. A. Huizenga, "The Confession of Jesus and the Curses of Peter. A Narrative-Christological Approach to the Text-Critical Problem of Mark 14:62," *NovT* 53 (2011): 244–66.

J. Jeremias, "Zur Geschichtlichkeit des Verhörs Jesu vor dem hohen Rat," *ZNW* 43 (1950–51): 145–50.

M. de Jonge, "The Use of Ο ΧΡΙΣΤΟΣ in the Passion Narrative," in *Jésus aux origines de la christologie*, ed. J. Dupont et al. (BETL 40; Gembloux: Duculot, 1975), 169–92.

D. Lührmann, "Markus 14.55–64: Christologie und Zerstörung des Tempels im Markusevangelium," *NTS* 27 (1980–81): 457–74.

F. J. Matera, "The Trial of Jesus: Problems and Proposals," *Int* 45 (1991): 5–16.

F. E. Meyer, "Einige Bemerkungen zur Bedeutungen des Terminus 'Synhedrion' in den Schriften des Neuen Testaments," *NTS* 14 (1967–68): 545–51.

F. Millar, "Reflections on the Trials of Jesus," in *A Tribute to Geza Vermes: Essays on Jewish and Christian Literature and History*, ed. P. R. Davies and R. T. White (*JSOTSup* 100; Sheffield: JSOT Press, 1990), 355–81.

N. Perrin, "Mark xiv.62: The End Product of a Christian Pesher Tradition?" *NTS* 12 (1965–66): 150–55.

W. Reinbold, *Der älteste Bericht über den Tod Jesu: Literarische Analyse und historische Kritik der Passionsdarstellungen der Evangelisten* (Berlin: Walter de Gruyter, 1994).

H. Ritt, "Wer war Schuld am Jesu Tod? Zeitgeschichte, Recht und theologische Deutung," *BZ* 31 (1987): 165–75.

S. Rosenblatt, "The Crucifixion of Jesus from the Standpoint of the Pharisaic Law," *JBL* 75 (1956): 315–21.

S. Sandmel, "The Trial of Jesus: Reservations," *Judaism* 20 (1971): 69–74.

G. Schneider, "Gab es eine vorsynoptische Szene 'Jesus vor dem Synedrium'?" *NovT* 12 (1970): 22–39.

"Jesus vor dem Sanhedrin," *BibLeb* 11 (1970): 1–15.

K. Schubert, "Biblical Criticism Criticised: With Reference to the Markan Report of Jesus' Examination before the Sanhedrin," in *Jesus and the Politics of His Day*, ed. E. Bammel and C. F. D. Moule (Cambridge: Cambridge University Press, 1984), 385–402.

A. N. Sherwin-White, "The Trial of Christ," in *Historicity and Chronology in the New Testament*, ed. D. E. Nineham et al. (Theological Collections 6; London: S. P. C. K., 1965), 97–116.

E. M. Smallwood, "High Priests and Politics in Roman Palestine," *JTS* n.s. 13 (1962): 14–34.

R. A. Stewart, "Judicial Procedure in New Testament Times," *EvQ* 47 (1975): 94–109.

W. Trilling, "Der 'Prozess Jesu,' " in *Fragen zur Geschichtlichkeit Jesu* (Düsseldorf: Patmos, 1966), 130–41.

W. C. van Unnik, "Jesus the Christ," *NTS* 8 (1961–62): 101–116.

F. Watson, "Why Was Jesus Crucified?" *Theology* 88 (1985): 105–112.

Mark 14:66–72

R. Fox, "Peter's Denial in Mark's Gospel," *TBT* 25 (1987): 298–303.

G. H. Guyot, "Peter Denies His Lord," *CBQ* 4 (1942): 111–18.

G. Klein, "Die Verleugnung des Petrus: Eine traditionsgeschichtliche Untersuchung," *ZTK* 58 (1961): 285–328.

G. W. H. Lange, "St. Peter's Denial," *BJRL* 55 (1972–73): 346–68.

N. J. McEleney, "Peter's Denials – How Many? To Whom?" *CBQ* 52 (1990): 467–72.

Mark 15:1–15

A. Bajsic, "Pilatus, Jesus und Barabbas," *Bib* 48 (1967): 7–28.

E. Bammel, "Pilatus' und Kaiphas' Absetzung," in *Judaica: Kleine Schriften I* (WUNT 37; Tübingen: Mohr-Siebeck, 1986), 51–58.

"The Trial before Pilate," in *Jesus and the Politics of His Day*, ed. E. Bammel and C. F. D. Moule (Cambridge: Cambridge University Press, 1984), 415–51.

O. Betz, "The Temple Scroll and the Trial of Jesus," *SWJT* 30 (1988): 5–8.

K. Berger, "Zum Problem der Messianität Jesu," *ZTK* 71 (1974): 1–30.

H. Bond, "The Coins of Pontius Pilate: Part of an Attempt to Provoke the People or to Integrate them into the Empire?" *JSJ* 27 (1996): 241–62.

G. Braumann, "Markus 15,2–5 und Markus 14,55–64," *ZNW* 52 (1961): 273–78.

T. A. Burkhill, "The Condemnation of Jesus: A Critique of Sherwin-White's Thesis," *NovT* 12 (1970): 321–42.

C. B. Chaval, "The Releasing of a Prisoner on the Eve of Passover in Ancient Jerusalem," *JBL* 60 (1941): 273–78.

S. L. Davies, "Who Is Called Bar Abbas?" *NTS* 27 (1980–81): 260–62.

P. S. Davies, "The Meaning of Philo's Text about the Gilded Shields," *JTS* n.s. 37 (1986): 109–114.

A. D. Doyle, "Pilate's Career and the Date of the Crucifixion," *JTS* o.s. 42 (1941): 190–93.

J. A. Fitzmyer, "Crucifixion in Ancient Palestine, Qumran Literature, and the New Testament," *CBQ* 40 (1978): 493–513.

G. Fuks, "Again on the Episode of the Gilded Shields at Jerusalem," *HTR* 75 (1982): 503–507.

P. Geurnsey, "The Criminal Jurisdiction of Governors," *JRS* 58 (1968): 51–59.

K. Haacker, "Wer war Schuld am Tode Jesu?" *TBei* 25 (1994): 23–36.

A. C. Hagedorn and J. H. Neyrey, "'It Was Out of Envy That They Handed Jesus Over' (Mark 15.10): The Anatomy of Envy and the Gospel of Mark," *JSNT* 69 (1998): 15–56.

E. F. Harrison, "Jesus and Pilate," *BSac* 105 (1948): 307–319.

D. Hill, "Jesus and Josephus' 'Messianic Prophets,'" in *Text and Interpretation*, FS M. Black, ed. E. Best and R. McL. Wilson (Cambridge: Cambridge University Press, 1979), 143–54.

W. Horbury, "Christ as a Brigand in Ancient Anti-Christian Polemic," in *Jesus and the Politics of His Day*, ed. E. Bammel and C. F. D. Moule (Cambridge: Cambridge University Press, 1984), 197–209.

R. W. Husband, "The Pardoning of Prisoners by Pilate," *AJT* 21 (1917): 110–16.

J. Irmscher, "Σὺ λέγεις (Mk 15,2; Mt 27,1; Lc 23,3)," *Studii Clasice* 2 (1960): 151–58.

B. R. Kinman, "Pilate's Assize and the Timing of Jesus' Trial," *TynBul* 42 (1991): 282–95.

K.-S. Kieger, "Pontius Pilatus – Ein Judenfeind? Zur Problematik einer Pilatusbiographie," *BN* 78 (1995): 63–83.

"Die Problematik chronologischer Rekonstruktionen zur Amtszeit des Pilatus," *BN* 61 (1992): 27–32.

G. M. Lee, "Mark xv 8," *NovT* 20 (1978): 74.

H. Z. Maccoby, "Jesus and Barabbas," *NTS* 16 (1969–70): 55–60.

P. L. Maier, "The Episode of the Golden Shields at Jerusalem," *HTR* 62 (1969): 109–121.

"Sejanus, Pilate, and the Date of the Crucifixion," *CH* 37 (1968): 3–13.

R. L. Merritt, "Jesus Barabbas and the Paschal Parson," *JBL* 104 (1985): 57–68.

R. L. Overstreet, "Roman Law and the Trial of Christ," *BSac* 135 (1978): 323–32.

R. Riesner, "Das Prätorium des Pilatus," *BK* 41 (1986): 34–37.

G. Schneider, "The Political Charge against Jesus (Luke 23:2)," in *Jesus and the Politics of His Day*, ed. E. Bammel and C. F. D. Moule. Cambridge: Cambridge University Press, 1984), 403–414.

A. N. Sherwin-White, *Roman Society and Roman Law in the New Testament* (Oxford: Oxford University Press, 1963), 12–47.

A. Simmonds, "Mark's and Matthew's Sub Rosa Message in the Scene of Pilate and the Crowd," *JBL* 131 (2012): 733–54.

E. M. Smallwood, "The Date of the Dismissal of Pontius Pilate from Judaea," *JJS* 5 (1954): 12–21.

R. Staats, "Pontius Pilatus im Bekenntnis der frühen Kirche," *ZTK* 84 (1987): 493–513.

J. Vardaman, "A New Inscription Which Mentions Pilate as 'Prefect,'" *JBL* 81 (1962): 70–71.

Mark 15:16–20a

K. E. Bailey, "The Fall of Jerusalem and Mark's Account of the Cross," *ExpTim* 102 (1991): 102–105.

C. Bonner, "The Crown of Thorns," *HTR* 46 (1953): 47–48.

B. Pixner, "Noch einmal das Prätorium: Versuch einer neuen Lösung," *ZDPV* 95 (1979): 56–86.

T. E. Schmidt, "Mark 15.16–32: The Crucifixion Narrative and the Roman Triumphal Procession," *NTS* 41 (1995): 1–18.

Mark 15:20b–41

R. A. Ayton, "'Himself He Cannot Save' (Ps xxii, 29 and Mark xv, 31)," *JTS* o.s. 21 (1919–20): 245–48.

E. Bammel, "Crucifixion as a Punishment in Palestine," in *The Trial of Jesus: Cambridge Studies*, FS C. F. D. Moule, ed. E. Bammel (SBT 13; London: SCM Press, 1970), 162–65.

"The *Titulus*," in *Jesus and the Politics of His Day*, ed. E. Bammel and C. F. D. Moule (Cambridge: Cambridge University Press, 1984), 353–64.

N. B. Baker, "The Cry of Dereliction," *ExpTim* 70 (1958–59): 54–55.

R. Bauckham, "Salome the Sister of Jesus, Salome the Disciple of Jesus, and the Secret Gospel of Mark," *NovT* 33 (1991): 245–75.

P. H. Bligh, "Christ's Death Cry," *HeyJ* 1 (1960): 142–46.

"A Note on Huios Theou in Mark 15:39," *ExpTim* 80 (1968): 51–53.

T. Boman, "Das letzte Wort Jesu," *ST* 17 (1963): 103–119.

K. E. Brower, "Elijah in the Markan Passion Narrative," *JSNT* 18 (1983): 85–101.

C. Burchard, "Markus 15,34," *ZNW* 74 (1983): 1–11.

J. B. Chance, "The Cursing of the Temple and the Tearing of the Veil in the Gospel of Mark," *BibInt* 15 (2007): 268–91.

J. A. Charlesworth and J. Zias, "Crucifixion: Archaeology, Jesus, and the Dead Sea Scrolls," in *Jesus and the Dead Sea Scrolls*, ed. J. H. Charlesworth (ABRL; New York: Doubleday, 1992), 273–89.

H. L. Chronis, "The Thorn Veil: Cultus and Christology in Mark 15:37–39," *JBL* 101 (1982): 97–114.

D. Cohn-Sherbok, "Jesus' Cry on the Cross: An Alternative View," *ExpTim* 93 (1981–82): 215–17.

A. Y. Collins, "Mark's Interpretation of the Death of Jesus," *JBL* 128 (2009): 545–54.

J. G. Cook, "Crucifixion as Spectacle in Roman Campania," *NovT* 54 (2012): 68–100.

"Envisioning Crucifixion: Light from Several Inscriptions and the Palatine Graffito," *NovT* 50 (2008): 262–85.

J. D. Crossan, "Mark and the Relatives of Jesus," *NovT* 15 (1973): 81–113.

F. W. Danker, "The Demonic Secret in Mark: A Reexamination of the Cry of Dereliction (15:34)," *ZNW* 61 (1970): 48–69.

D. Daube, "The Veil of the Temple," in *The New Testament and Rabbinic Judaism* (London: Athlone, 1956), 23–26.

P. G. Davis, "Mark's Christological Paradox," *JSNT* 35 (1989): 3–18.

S. Dowd and E.S. Malbon, "The Significance of Jesus' Death in Mark: Narrative Context and Authorial Audience," *JBL* 125 (2006): 271–97.

T. Elgvin, "The Messiah Who Was Cursed on the Tree," *Them* 22.3 (1997): 14–21.

A. T. Georgia, "Translating the Triumph: Reading Mark's Crucifixion Narrative against a Roman Ritual of Power," *JSNT* 36 (2013): 17–38.

H. Gese, "Psalm 22 und das Neue Testament," *ZTK* 65 (1968): 1–22.

T. F. Glasson, "Mark xv. 39: The Son of God," *ExpTim* 80 (1969): 286.

J. Gnilka, "Mein Gott, mein Gott, warum hast du mich verlassen? (Mk 15,34 Par.)," *BZ* 3 (1959): 294–97.

D. M. Gurtner, "The Rending of the Veil and Markan Christology: 'Unveiling' The υιος θεου (Mark 15:38–39)," *BibInt* 15 (2007): 292–306.

"The Veil of the Temple in History and Legend," *JETS* 49 (2006): 97–114.

H. A. Guy, "Son of God in Mk 15:39," *ExpTim* 81 (1969–70): 151.

M. Hengel, "Maria Magdalena und die Frauen als Zeugen," in *Abraham unser Vater: Juden und Christen im Gespräch über die Bibel*, ed. O. Betz et al. (AGSU 5; Leiden: Brill, 1963), 243–56.

L. Hurtado, "Jesus' Death as Paradigmatic in the NT," *SJT* 57 (2004): 413–33.

H. M. Jackson, "The Death of Jesus in Mark and the Miracle from the Cross," *NTS* 33 (1987): 16–37.

E. S. Johnson, "Is Mark 15:39 the Key to Mark's Christology?" *JSNT* 31 (1987): 3–22.

"Mark 15:39 and the So-Called Confession of the Roman Centurion," *Bib* 81 (2000): 406–413.

M. de Jonge, "The Earliest Christian Use of Christos: Some Suggestions," *NTS* 32 (1986): 321–43.

C. Keith, "The Role of the Cross in the Composition of the Markan Crucifixion Narrative," *Stone Campbell Journal* 9 (2006): 61–75.

T. H. Kim, "The Anarthrous υἱὸς θεοῦ in Mark 15,39 and the Roman Imperial Cult," *Bib* 79 (1998): 221–41.

E. Koskenniemi, K. Nisula, and J. Toppari, "Wine Mixed with Myrrh (Mark 15.23) and Crurifragium (John 19.31–32): Two Details of the Passion Narratives," *JSNT* 27 (2005): 379–91.

R. S. Kraemer, "Implicating Herodias and Her Daughter in the Death of John the Baptizer: A (Christian) Theological Strategy?" *JBL* 125 (2006): 321–49.

G. M. Lee, "Mark xv 21, 'The Father of Alexander and Rufus,' " *NovT* 17 (1975): 303.

A. Mahoney, "A New Look at 'The Third Hour' of Mark 15,25," *CBQ* 28 (1966): 292–99.

J. R. Michaels, "The Centurion's Confession and the Spear Thrust," *CBQ* 29 (1967): 102–109.

J. V. Miller, "The Time of the Crucifixion," *JETS* 26 (1983): 157–66.

H. W. Montefiore, "Josephus and the New Testament," *NovT* 4 (1960): 139–60.

S. Motyer, "The Rending of the Veil: A Markan Pentecost?" *NTS* 33 (1987): 155–57.

R. L. Plummer, "Something Awry in the Temple? The Rending of the Temple Veil and Early Jewish Sources That Report Unusual Phenomena in the Temple around AD 30," *JETS* 48 (2005): 301–316.

J. Pobee, "The Cry of the Centurion – A Cry of Defeat," in *The Trial of Jesus*, FS C. F. D. Moule, ed. E. Bammel (*SBT* 13; London: SCM Press, 1970), 91–102.

J. E. Powell, " 'Father, into Thy Hands . . .,' " *JTS* n.s. 40 (1989): 95–96.

R. Riesner, "Golgota und die Archäologie," *BK* 40 (1985): 21–26.

M. S. Rindge, "Reconfiguring the Akedah and Recasting God: Lament and Divine Abandonment in Mark," *JBL* 131 (2012): 755–74.

P. Rodgers, "Mark 15:28," *EvQ* 61 (1989): 81–84.

G. Rojas-Flores, "From John 2.19 to Mark 15.29: The History of Misunderstanding," *NTS* 56 (2009): 22–43.

T. E. Schmidt, "Cry of Dereliction or Cry of Judgment? Mark 15:34 in Context," *BBR* 4 (1994): 145–53.

"Mark 15.16–32: The Crucifixion Narrative and the Roman Triumphal Procession," *NTS* 41 (1995): 1–18.

G. Schneider, "The Political Charge against Jesus (Luke 23:2)," in *Jesus and the Politics of His Day*, ed. E. Bammel and C. F. D. Moule (Cambridge: Cambridge University Press, 1984), 403–414.

W. T. Shiner, "The Ambiguous Pronouncement of the Centurion and the Shrouding of Meaning in Mark," *JSNT* 78 (2000): 3–22.

W. Stegner, "Bemerkungen zum Begriff "Räuber" im Neuen Testament und bei Flavius Josephus," *BK* 37 (1982): 89–97.

A. Stock, "Hinge Transitions in Mark's Gospel," *BTB* 15 (1985): 27–31.

K. Stock, "Das Bekenntnis des Centurio: Mk 15,39 im Rahmen des Markusevangeliums," *ZKT* 100 (1978): 289–301.

S. K. Stockklausner and C. A. Hale, "Mark 15:39 and 16:6–7: A Second Look," *McMaster Journal of Theology* 1 (1990): 34–44.

J. P. Sweeny, "The Death of Jesus in Contemporary Life-of-Jesus Research," *Trinity Journal* 24 (2003): 221–41.

V. Taylor, "The Narrative of the Crucifixion," *NTS* 8 (1961–62): 333–34.

C. B. Tkacz, "ανεβοησεν φωνη μεγαλη. Susanna and the Synoptic Passion Narratives," *Gregorianum* 87 (2006): 449–86.

L. P. Trudinger, "'Eli, Eli, Lama Sabachthani?' A Cry of Dereliction? or Victory?" *JETS* 17 (1974): 235–38.

V. Tzaferis, "Crucifixion: The Archaeological Evidence," *BAR* 11 (1985): 44–53.

D. Ulansey, "The Heavenly Veil Torn: Mark's Cosmic Inclusio," *JBL* 110 (1991): 123–25.

J. W. van Henten, "Martyrdom, Jesus' Passion and Barbarism," *BibInt* 17 (2009): 239–64.

T. J. Weeden, "The Cross as Power in Weakness (Mark 15:20b–41)," in *The Passion in Mark: Studies on Mark 14–16*, ed. W. Kelber (Philadelphia: Fortress, 1976), 115–34.

R. E. O. White, "That 'Cry of Dereliction' …?" *ExpTim* 113 (2002): 188–89.

M. F. Whitters, "Why Did the Bystanders Think Jesus Called upon Elijah before He Died (Mark 15:34–36)? The Markan Position," *HTR* 95 (2002): 119–24.

M. Wilcox, "'Upon the Tree' – Deut 21:22–23 in the New Testament," *JBL* 96 (1977): 85–99.

J. Wilkinson, "The Physical Cause of the Death of Christ," *ExpTim* 4 (1972): 105–107.

"The Seven Words from the Cross," *SJT* 17 (1964): 69–82.

J. F. Williams, "Foreshadowing, Echoes, and the Blasphemy at the Cross (Mark 15:29)," *JBL* 132 (2013): 913–33.

"Is Mark's Gospel an Apology for the Cross?" *BBR* 12 (2002): 97–122.

A. Wypadlo, "Wahrhaftig, dieser Mensch war Gottes Sohn' (Mk 15,39). Überlegungen zur Funktion des Centuriobekenntnisses im christologischen Entwurf des Markusevangeliums," *BZ* 55 (2011): 179–208.

F. Zugibe, "Two Questions about Crucifixion: Does the Victim Die of Asphyxiation? Would Nails in the Hands Hold the Weight of the Body?" *BRev* 5 (1989): 35–43.

Mark 15:42–47

W. B. Barrick, "The Rich Man from Arimathea (Matt 27:57–60) and 1QIsaᵃ," *JBL* 96 (1977): 235–39.

R. E. Brown, "The Burial of Jesus (Mark 15:42–47)," *CBQ* 50 (1988): 233–45.

L. E. Evans, "The Holy Sepulchre," *PEQ* 100 (1968): 112–36.

R. Hachlili, "Burials: Ancient Jewish," *ABD* 1:789–94.

A. Killebrew, "Jewish Funerary Customs during the Second Temple Period in Light of the Excavations at the Jericho Necropolis," *PEQ* 115 (1983): 109–139.

J. Magness, "What Did Jesus' Tomb Look Like?" *BAR* 32 (2006): 38–40, 70.

E. M. Meyers, "Secondary Burials in Palestine," *BA* 33 (1970): 2–29.

J. Schreiber, "Die Bestattung Jesu: Redaktionsgeschichtliche Beobachtungen zu Mk 15,42–47 par," *ZNW* 72 (1981): 141–77.

R. H. Smith, "The Tomb of Jesus," *BA* 30 (1967): 74–90.

Mark 16:1–8

W. C. Allen, "St. Mark xvi.8. 'They Were Afraid.' Why?" *JTS* o.s. 47 (1946): 46–49.

J. E. Alsup, "Resurrection and Historicity," *ASB* 103 (1988): 5–18.

K. Backhaus, "'Dort werdet ihr Ihn sehen' (Mk 16:7): Die redaktionelle Schlussnotiz des zweiten Evangeliums als dessen christologische Summe," *TGl* 76 (1986): 277–94.

H.-W. Bartsch, "Der Schluss des Markus-Evangeliums," *TZ* 27 (1971): 241–54.

"Der Ursprung des Osterglaubens," *TZ* 31 (1975): 16–31.

W. Bindemann, "Geht nach Galiläa! Vom Kult zum Gottesdienst im Alltag der Welt," *Texte und Kontexte* 11 (1981): 23–39.

P. G. Bolt, "Mark 16:1–8:The Empty Tomb of a Hero?" *TynBul* 47 (1996): 27–37.

T. E. Boomershine, "Mark 16:8 and the Apostolic Commission," *JBL* 100 (1981): 225–39.

G. L. Bartholomew, "The Narrative Technique of Mark 16:8," *JBL* 100 (1981): 213–23.

P. J. J. Botha, "οὐκ ἔστιν ὧδε . . .: Mark's Stories of Jesus' Tomb and History," *Neot* 23 (1989): 195–218.

D. J. Bowman, "The Resurrection in Mark," *TBT* 11 (1964): 709–713.

H. J. Cadbury, "Mark 16:8," *JBL* 46 (1927): 344–50.

D. R. Catchpole, "The Fearful Silence of the Women at the Tomb," *JTSA* 18 (1977): 3–10.

W. L. Craig, "The Bodily Resurrection of Jesus," in *Studies of History and Tradition in the Four Gospels*, ed. R. T. France and D. Wenham (Gospel Perspectives 1; Sheffield: JSOT Press, 1980), 47–74.

"The Empty Tomb of Jesus," in *Studies of History and Tradition in the Four Gospels*, ed. R. T. France and D. Wenham (Gospel Perspectives 2; Sheffield: JSOT, 1981), 173–200.

"The Empty Tomb of Jesus," in *Studies of History and Tradition in the Four Gospels*, ed. R. T. France, "The Historicity of the Empty Tomb of Jesus," *NTS* 31 (1985): 39–67.

"The Empty Tomb of Jesus," in *Studies of History and Tradition in the Four Gospels*, ed. R. T. France, "On Doubts about the Resurrection," *Modern Theology* 6 (1989): 53–75.

C. E. B. Cranfield, "St. Mark 16.1–8," *SJT* 5 (1952): 282–98, 398–414.

J. M. Creed, "The Conclusion of the Gospel According to Saint Mark," *JTS* o.s. 31 (1930): 175–80.

J. G. Davies, "Factors Leading to the Emergence of Belief in the Resurrection of the Flesh," *JTS* n.s. 23 (1972): 448–55.

N. Denyer, "Mark 16:8 and Plato, Protagoras 328d," *TynBul* 57 (2006): 149–50.

J. W. Drane, "Some Ideas of Resurrection in the New Testament Period," *TynBul* 24 (1973): 99–110.

R. Dudrey, "What the Writers Should Have Done Better: A Case for the Resurrection of Jesus Based on Ancient Criticisms of the Resurrection Reports," *Stone Campbell Journal* 3 (2000): 55–78.

C. A. Evans, "Mark's Use of the Empty Tomb Tradition," *SBT* 8.2 (1978): 50–55.

D. Flusser, *Jesus* (Jerusalem: Magnes, 2001).
Judaism and the Origins of Christianity (Jerusalem: Magnes, 1988), 588–92.

R. H. Fuller, "The Resurrection of Jesus and the Historical Method," *JBR* 34 (1966): 18–24.

M. D. Goulder, "The Empty Tomb," *Theology* 79 (1976): 206–14.
"Mark xvi. 1–8 and Parallels," *NTS* 24 (1977–78): 235–40.

N. Q. Hamilton, "Resurrection Tradition and the Composition of Mark," *JBL* 84 (1965): 415–21.

G. Hebert, "The Resurrection-Narrative in St. Mark's Gospel," *SJT* 15 (1962): 66–73.

M. Hengel, *Crucifixion in the Ancient Word and the Folly of the Message of the Cross.* Philadelphia: Fortress, 1977.
"Ist der Osterglaube noch zu retten?" *TQ* 153 (1973): 252–69.
Studies in Early Christology (Edinburgh: T & T Clark 1995), 12–14.

J. D. Hester, "Dramatic Inconclusion: Irony and the Narrative Rhetoric of the Ending of Mark," *JSNT* 57 (1995): 61–86.

P. W. Horst, "Can a Book End with γάρ? A Note on Mark xvi.8," *JTS* n.s. 23 (1972): 121–24.

B. M. F. van Iersel, "'To Galilee' or 'in Galilee' in Mark 14,28 and 16,7?" *ETL* 58 (1982): 365–70.

K. Iverson, "A Further Word on Final Γάρ (Mark 16:8)," *CBQ* (2006): 79–94.

A. K. Jenkins, "Young Man or Angel?" *ExpTim* 94 (1983): 237–40.

C. E. Joynes, "The Sound of Silence: Interpreting Mark 16:1–8 through the Centuries," *Int* 65 (2011): 18–29.

W. Kasper, "Der Glaube an die Auferstehung Jesu vor dem Forum historischer Kritik," *TQ* 153 (1973): 229–41.

D. Kendall and G. O'Collins, "The Uniqueness of the Resurrection Appearances," *CBQ* 54 (1992): 287–307.

A. Kloner, "Did a Rolling Stone Close Jesus' Tomb?" *BAR* 25.5 (1999): 22–29, 76.

W. Lillie, "The Empty Tomb and the Resurrection," in *Historicity and Chronology in the New Testament*, ed. D. E. Nineham et al. (Theological Collections 6; London: S. P. C. K., 1965), 117–34.

A. T. Lincoln, "The Promise and the Failure: Mark 16:7, 8," *JBL* 108 (1989): 283–300.

E. Linnemann, "Der (wiedergefundene) Markusschluss," *ZTK* 66 (1969): 255–87.

G. Lohfink, "The Resurrection of Jesus and Historical Criticism," *TD* 17 (1969): 110–14.

J. Mánek, "The Apostle Paul and the Empty Tomb," *NovT* 2 (1958): 276–80.

J. I. H. McDonald, "Resurrection Narratives in Pastoral Perspective," *ExpTim* 113 (2002): 219–23.

H. Merklein, "Mk 16,1–8 als Epilog des Markusevangelium," in *The Synoptic Gospels*, ed. C. Focant (BETL 110; Leuven: Peeters and Leuven University Press, 1993), 209–38.

R. P. Meye, "Mark 16:8 – The Ending of Mark's Gospel," *BR* 14 (1969): 33–43.

F. Mildenberger, "Auferstanden am dritten Tage nach den Schriften," *EvT* 23 (1963): 265–80.

R. C. Miller, "Mark's Empty Tomb and Other Translation Fables in Classical Antiquity," *JBL* 129 (2010): 759–76.

C. F. D. Moule, "St. Mark xvi.8 Once More," *NTS* 2 (1955–56): 58–59.

F. Neirynck, "John and the Synoptics: The Empty Tomb Stories," *NTS* 30 (1984): 161–87.

F. Niemann, "Die Erzählung vom leerer Grab bei Markus," *ZKT* 101 (1979): 188–99.

P. Oakeshott, "How Unlike an Angel. The Youth in Mark 16," *Theology* 111 (2008): 362–69.

L. Oberlinner, "Die Verkündigung der Auferweckung Jesu im geöffneten und leeren Grab," *ZNW* 73 (1982): 159–82.

G. O'Collins, "The Fearful Silence of Three Women (Mark 16:8c)," *Greg* 69 (1988): 489–503.

    and D. Kendall, "Mary Magdalene as Major Witness to Jesus' Resurrection," *TS* 48 (1987): 631–46.

H. Paulsen, "Mk xvi 1–8," *NovT* 22 (1980): 138–75.

P. Perkins, "The Resurrection of Jesus of Nazareth," in *Studying the Historical Jesus: Evaluations of the State of Current Research*, ed. B. D. Chilton and C. A. Evans. (NTTS 19; Leiden: Brill, 1994), 423–42.

R. Pesch, "Zur Entstehung des Glaubens an die Auferstehung Jesu," *TQ* 153 (1973): 201–228.

N. R. Petersen, "When Is the End Not the End? Literary Reflections on the Ending of Mark's Narrative," *Int* 34 (1980): 151–66.

R. Schwindt, "Erschutterung statt Freude. Zum Schluss des Markusevangeliums (Mk 16, 8)," *TTZ* 117 (2008): 56–79.

J. A. Sint, "Die Auferstehung Jesu in der Verkündigung der Urgemeinde," *ZKT* 84 (1962): 129–51.

D. A. Smith, "Revisiting the Empty Tomb: The Post-Mortem Vindication of Jesus in Mark and Q," *NovT* 45 (2003): 123–37.

R. H. Smith, "New and Old in Mark 16:1–8," *CTM* 43 (1972): 518–27.

A. B. Spencer, "The Denial of the Good News and the Ending of Mark," *BBR* 17 (2007): 269–83.

A. Standhartinger, "'What Women Were Accustomed to Do for the Dead Beloved by Them' (Gospel of Peter 12.50): Traces of Laments and Mourning Rituals in Early Easter, Passion, and Lord's Supper Traditions," *JBL* 129 (2010): 559–74.

H. Staudinger, "The Resurrection of Jesus Christ as Saving Event and as 'Object' of Historical Research," *SJT* 36 (1983): 309–326.

R. H. Stein, "A Short Note on Mark. XIV. 28 and XVI. 7," *NTS* 20 (1973–74): 445–52.

"The Ending of Mark," *BBR* 18 (2008): 79–98.

J. C. Thomas, "A Reconsideration of the Ending of Mark," *JETS* 26 (1983): 407–419.

B. B. Thurston, "Faith and Fear in Mark's Gospel," *TBT* 23 (1985): 305–310.

G. W. Trompf, "The First Resurrection Appearance and the Ending of Mark's Gospel," *NTS* 18 (1971–72): 308–330.

W. S. Vorster, "The Religio-Historical Context of the Resurrection of Jesus and Resurrection Faith in the New Testament," *Neot* 23 (1989): 159–75.

F. Watson, "'Historical Evidence' and the Resurrection of Jesus," *Theology* 90 (1987): 365–72.

G. J. Williams, "Narrative Space, Angelic Revelation, and the End of Mark's Gospel," *JSNT* 35 (2013): 263–84.

N. T. Wright, *The Resurrection of the Son of God* (Minneapolis: Fortress, 2003), esp. 210–11, 372–74, 685–718.

Other Endings

K. Aland, "Bemerkungen zum Schluss des Markusevangeliums," in *Neotestamentica et Semitica*, FS M. Black, ed. E. E. Ellis and M. Wilcox (Edinburgh: T. & T. Clark, 1969), 157–80.

"Der Schluss des Markusevangeliums," in *L'Évangile selon Marc: tradition et redaction*, ed. M. Sabbe (2nd rev. ed., Leuven: Leuven University Press/Peeters, 1988; 1st ed., 1974), 435–70.

D. A. Black, ed. *Perspectives on the Ending of Mark: 4 Views* (Nashville: Broadman and Holman, 2008).

T. E. Boomershine and G. L. Bartholomew, "The Narrative Technique of Mark 16:8," *JBL* 100 (1981): 213–23.

S. G. Brown, "On the Composition History of the Longer ('Secret') Gospel of Mark," *JBL* 122 (2003): 89–110.

F. F. Bruce, "The End of the Second Gospel," *EvQ* 17 (1945): 169–81.

S. L. Cox, *A History and Critique of Scholarship concerning the Markan Endings* (Lewiston, NY: Mellen, 1993), 223–27.

J. K. Elliott, "The Text and Language of the Endings to Mark's Gospel," *TZ* 27 (1971): 255–62.

P. W. van der Horst, "Can a Book End with a ΓΑΡ? A Note on Mark XVI.8," *Journal of Theological Studies* 23 (1972): 121–24.

J. A. Kelhoffer, *Miracle and Mission: The Authentication of Missionaries and Their Message in the Longer Ending of Mark* (WUNT 2.112; Tübingen: Mohr/Siebeck, 2000), 48–156.

F. G. Kenyon, "Papyrus Rolls and the Ending of St. Mark," *JTS* n.s. 40 (1939): 56–57.

J. L. Magnus, *Marking the End: Sense and Absence in the Gospel of Mark* (Eugene, OR: Wipf and Stock, 2002).

T. R. Shepherd, "Narrative Analysis as a Text Critical Tool: Mark 16 in Codex Was a Test Case," *JSNT* 32 (2009): 77–98.

A. B. Spencer, "The Denial of the Good News and the Ending of Mark," *BBR* 17 (2007): 269–83.

R. Stein, "The Ending of Mark," *BBR* 18 (2008): 79–98.

J. F. Williams, "Literary Approaches to the End of Mark's Gospel," *JETS* 42 (1999): 21–35.

III. Commentary on Mark

1:1 Introduction

1:1 Beginning of the gospel of Jesus Christ [Son of God]

The incipit, or opening words of the text, introduces the theme of this literary work. The life of Jesus Christ is good news, Gospel. We think of "the gospel" as a genre of literature, but here Mark is referring to the opening of an account of events that God has pointed to through Scripture. That is why the next verses cite texts of the Hebrew Scripture. However, the reference to the beginning of the story shows the verse is not a title for the whole Gospel. The person the beginning introduces is the subject of the entire Gospel in the roles the verse introduces. In pointing to the start of this key story, the verse introduces the topic of the entire work, the Gospel and Jesus as Christ and Son of God.

How much of the opening of the Gospel does this initial verse cover? If we allow the opening word link to be a clue, then verses 14–15 are a candidate.[1] Mark 1:14–15 is a call to repent and believe the Gospel. That call invokes the Gospel message for the first time, with multiple mentions in the body of the Gospel (Mark 8:35; 10:29; 13:10; 14:9). John the Baptist is the key figure in this introduction until verse 9. Verses 9–11 have Jesus and John overlap. Then Jesus becomes the center of the story. Jesus' first utterance comes in verse 15. The call to the kingdom and its drawing near initiate the Gospel story in Jesus' ministry.

---

[1] Joel Marcus, *Mark 1–8: A New Translation with Introduction and Commentary.* Yale Anchor Bible 27 (New Haven: Yale University Press, 2008), 137–38, makes the case for 1:14–15 as the end and a transition in the Gospel.

There is an important cultural allusion in the term *Gospel*. "Good news" is what emperors claimed to bring to Roman culture.[2] Mark is noting those rulers have nothing on Jesus. In terms of significance to the world, Mark is making the amazing claim that this Jewish Galilean teacher has something to offer that the rulers of Rome do not: access to God's rule. God's good news is distinct from what Rome celebrates.

Good news also has Jewish background in the eschatological hopes of deliverance from Isaiah (Isa 40:9; 41:27; 52:7; 60:6; 61:1). It is no accident that a text from Isaiah 40 follows. Here God is coming in victory and the establishment of his rule.[3] The Qumranian community also expressed its hope by appealing to this text (1QS 8.12–16).[4]

The good news here can be from Jesus (subjective genitive) or about Jesus (objective genitive) or simply tied to Jesus (taking the genitive as plenary, working in both directions). The latter sense reflects the entirety of Mark's message. Jesus as the Messiah (Christ) is the topic.

The phrase "Son of God" is in brackets because the presence of these words in Mark's text is rightly debated.[5] The original hand of א plus a few other manuscripts lack the phrase.[6] It is quite possible that an error of reading led to the omission, as uncial abbreviations would have led to a series of upsilons in the manuscript over which eyes could easily skip (ΙῩΧΥΥΘῩ). It may have simply been accidentally omitted as well. Mark

2   Leander Keck, "The Introduction to Mark's Gospel," *NTS* 12 (1966): 352–70. A good news inscription has been found at Priene about the birthday of Octavian being the beginning of good news. It reads, "The birthday of the god was for the world *the beginning of joyful tidings* which have been proclaimed on his account" (*Inscr. Priene*, 105, 40). Also see Craig Evans, "Mark's Incipit and the Priene Calendar Inscription: From Jewish Gospel to Greco-Roman Gospel," *Journal of Greco-Roman Christianity and Judaism* 1 (2000): 67–81.

3   Adam Winn, *The Purpose of Mark's Gospel* (Tübingen: Mohr/Siebeck, 2008), 96–99, sees both the Jewish and Greco-Roman backgrounds in play for Mark.

4   Klyne Snodgrass, "Streams of Tradition Emerging from Isaiah 40:1–5 and Their Adaptation in the New Testament," *JSNT* 8 (1980): 24–45.

5   Bruce Metzger, *A Textual Commentary on the Greek New Testament*. 2nd ed. (New York: United Bible Society, 1994), 62. For exclusion of the phrase, Adela Y. Collins, "Establishing the Text: Mark 1:1," in *Texts and Contexts: Biblical Texts in the Textual and Situational Contexts Essays in Honor of Lars Hartman*, ed. Tord Fronberg and David Hellholm (Oslo: Scandinavian University Press, 1995), 111–27; Bart Ehrman, *The Orthodox Corruption of Scripture: The Effect of Early Christological Controversies on the Text of the New Testament* (Oxford: Oxford University Press, 1993), 72–75; and Peter Head, "A Text Critical Study of Mark 1.1: The Beginning of the Gospel of Jesus Christ," *NTS* 37 (1991): 621–29. Collins, Ehrman, and Head agree the omission is the harder reading and that the evidence of the Fathers is significant. Head adds we have no text critical evidence of "Son of God" being omitted from another text where it appears.

6   Those other manuscripts are: Θ, 28^c, 1555, syr^p, arm, geo, and Origen.

15:39 possesses a climactic confession involving the Son of God, making an *inclusio* with this start if it is original.[7] If the manuscript evidence for omission were more widespread, a claim of a scribal addition for theological reasons might make more sense, given that its absence is the harder reading. Still, the evidence for omission *is* weighty, although thin. If it was added, it had to have been fairly early, since the external evidence for inclusion is so widespread. If added, it makes a point about all of who Jesus is. If original, it sets a theme of Jesus not only as the Christ but also as the Son of God. This is the story Mark tells, whether the phrase is original or not. If it was added, then the copyist certainly read Mark well, as it is clear this is part of the point of his Gospel as a whole, to show how special Jesus is to God's program. All in all, its exclusion is slightly more likely than its inclusion, since it is hard to see how the shorter reading emerged and why only the Latin Fathers have the longer reading. Thus, our uncertainty has been expressed by putting the phrase in brackets.

1:2–8 John the Baptist Fulfills Scripture in Preparing the People and Tells of the One to Come

1:2 Even as it is written in Isaiah the prophet,
"Behold I am sending my messenger before you
who will prepare your way,
1:3 *a voice crying*
in the wilderness prepare the way of the Lord,
Make straight his paths."
1:4 John came [the one][8] baptizing in the wilderness and preaching a baptism of repentance for the forgiveness of sins.

---

7   Camille Focant, *The Gospel According to Mark: A Commentary* (Eugene, OR: Pickwick Press, 2012), 26, argues for inclusion on the basis of the external evidence of strong manuscript attestation.

8   There is real doubt about whether the definite article is original. Although Mark can express himself this way (Mark 6:14, 24), the pair of participles in parallelism look more like examples of periphrasis, which would lack the article and which Mark uses regularly (Mark 1:6; 2:6; 5:5; 9:7; and 14:54 are but a few of the twenty-five times in Mark). ℵ and B are among the manuscripts that have the article. Robert Stein, *Mark* (Grand Rapids: Baker, 2008), 52–53. If the article is read, then the reference is to "John the one who baptizes came. . . ." The participle becomes a title. A copyist familiar with the title may well have added the article. It is hard to know what the harder reading would have been in this case, as the title had become common by the time scribes were copying the text. Metzger, *Textual Commentary* (1994), 62, argues the lack of an article is the harder reading and is original.

1:5 And all of the region of Judea and all of Jerusalem came out to him and they were baptized by him in the Jordan River, confessing their sins.

1:6 John was clothed in camel hair and a leather belt around his waist, eating locusts and wild honey.

1:7 And he preached saying, "One stronger than me comes after me, I am not worthy of bending down to untie the strap of his sandals.

1:8 I baptize you with water, but he will baptize you with the Holy Spirit."

Mark opens with the ministry of John the Baptist. The story proper begins with Scripture and points to fulfilment (vv 2–3). It is a mixed citation with an introductory formula that only mentions Isaiah. The text, however, is from Exodus 23:20a and Malachi 3:1 ("my messenger"), with a second portion from Isaiah 40:3 ("a voice crying"). Some argue Mark is sloppy here with the introductory formula and does not know where his citation comes from, since it is a mixed citation, not just from Isaiah. However, a check of the following exposition shows Mark only develops the portion of the citation dealing with the wilderness, which is the portion from the major prophet. The introductory formula then either simply presents the author of the most prominent part of the citation or names the part that is developed by *gezera shewa* ("an equivalent regulation" – the linking of words between citations or between a citation and its application). The point is to argue that John the Baptist's coming to prepare the people is something Isaiah declared.

Two points are made in the citation. John is a messenger calling the people to clear a path for the Lord. Second, that path is to be straight. The implication is to take a life and national direction of the people as a whole that has been crooked and straighten it out. The allusion is to the baptism of repentance for the forgiveness of sins noted in verse 4. John readies the people for the program of God. A responsive heart is what shows a people ready for God's deliverance to come. A mass response of many shows the nation is ready. One is not to make a choice between the individual and the nation here. This is a national call met one person at a time.

All of this takes place in the wilderness (v 4), which is often a gathering place for events that precede the delivery of promise. It is in the call made in the wilderness that this preparation takes place. Paths are made straight for God starting there, where one will respond to John who preaches in the wilderness. Participation in John's baptism is the call John issues (v 4). In other words, get your heart right and be ready for what God is about to do.

The wilderness is an important place in Israel's history. Israel entered into the promise in the wilderness (Josh 1:11), and it was a destination for a person fleeing from sin (2 Macc 5:27; *Martyrdom of Isaiah* 2:7–11; 1QS 8:12–16). Some anticipated that God would launch his great assault on evil from the wilderness (Isa 40:1–11, a "new exodus" deliverance; 1QM 1:2–3). So this locale evokes hope and deliverance themes.

To have this call take place apart from the temple while focusing on the heart alone is significant. God is doing something fresh as a new era is dawning.

So how does Mark view John's ministry? John's call involved an eschatological rite of spiritual cleansing. Baptism refers to cleaning or immersing something, like a piece of cloth into dye.[9] Judaism had *mikvaot* (cleansing baths) into which a person walked to immerse themselves in water to picture purification. John's washing is similar but placed in a new sphere. This is an eschatological washing looking to the arrival of a time of fulfilment and deliverance versus mere moral or ritual correction.

John's baptism was for the forgiveness of sins. Many from Judea and Jerusalem came to John (v 5). The "alls," tied to the recipients from Judea and Jerusalem, reflect rhetorical hyperbole. John did draw a significant number out to him to be baptized. They were baptized in the desert region of the Jordan River, a description that fits better for the southern region of the river before it reaches the Dead Sea versus the more northern site at Yardenit, often said to be the site for modern tourists of Israel. Also fitting this location is the fact he drew people from Judea and Jerusalem versus Galilee. The description is laid out in a chiasm (all/Judea/Jerusalem/all).

The rite was the focus of John's preaching. In seeking forgiveness, they were acknowledging and confessing their sins. Repentance, forgiveness of sins, and confession of sins show the attitude that accompanied the washing baptism pictures. It was not the rite that brought the cleansing but the attitude it pictured. Repentance means a change of mind, so this was a new way of thinking about how they lived, a turning back to God. The Hebrew equivalent idea describes a "turning." In the Old Testament, the Hebrew word meaning "to turn" was often used to signify repentance (Jer 8:8; Jonah 3:9–10; TDNT 4:989–92). Making straight paths for God before his program comes involved a change of heart about one's way of life. The expression "in the desert" connects us back to the citation in Mark 1:2–3. The cleansing may well allude to Ezekiel 36:25–28, a washing that anticipates the coming of the Spirit in the new era and being prepared for

---

[9]   LSJ, 305–306.

his arrival, as verses 7–8 look to the coming of the Spirit from the one to come.[10]

Although Judaism had washings associated with cleansing (Lev 13–17; Num 19), baptisms tied to proselytes becoming members of the community, and Qumran had washings tied to joining and being a part of their community (1QS 3.4–5.9; 5:13–14), this baptism appears to be a special kind of eschatological cleansing that said, "I am ready for God to come." The fact it took place apart from the temple was significant. It showed John operating independently of common Jewish priestly structures. The other Jewish rites suggested as possible background are not strictly parallel. Proselyte baptism involved only Gentiles and is of uncertain origin in terms of dating.[11] It also was likely self-administered, as were other cleansings in Judaism. Qumranian washings were continual.[12] John's baptism was aimed at Jews and appears to have been a one-time-only washing. So although the Jewish background pictures cleansing, John's baptism appears to have been unique in its thrust, pointing to a preparation of the new era, an era involving the stronger one to come, as verses 7–8 make clear.

Josephus also describes this ministry (*Antiquities* 18.5.2 §§ 116–19). Josephus summarizes John's work as follows: [he] "commanded the Jews to exercise virtue, both as to righteousness towards one another, and piety towards God, and so to come to baptism; for that the washing would be acceptable to him, if they made use of it, not in order to put away some sins, but for the purification of the body; supposing still that the soul was thoroughly purified beforehand by righteousness." Josephus describes John's action in Greek terms for his audience in speaking about virtue and piety. Souls "purified by righteousness" is another way to speak of dealing with sin as a whole (not just individual acts).[13]

John's lifestyle is Mark's next topic. John lives a modest, aesthetic life. His home is in the desert. His cloths are a simple covering of camel's hair with a belt (**v 6**). The allusion here is to Elijah (2 Kings 1:8; Mark 9:9–13;

---

10   Adela Y. Collins, *Mark: A Commentary of the Gospel of Mark* (Minneapolis: Fortress, 2007), 139.
11   In fact, it may post-date our period. Derwood C. Smith, "Jewish Proselyte Baptism and the Baptism of John," *ResQ* 25 (1982): 13–32.
12   B. Chilton, *Jesus' Baptism and Jesus' Healing* (Harrisburg, PA: Trinity Press, 1998), 1–29.
13   For a discussion of John the Baptist and Josephus, as well as the historical cultural context of John's work, see Robert Webb, "Jesus' Baptism by John: Its Historicity and Significance," in *Key Events in the Life of the Historical Jesus*, ed. Darrell L. Bock and Robert L. Webb (Tübingen: Mohr/Siebeck, 2009), 95–150, esp. 116–17, 119–20, 127–28.

Luke 1:17; John 1:21, 25). His diet is locusts and wild honey, simply what he can pick up along the way. Because these foodstuffs would not be touched by anyone, it may point to a diet guaranteed to be ritually clean (Lev 11:22).[14] It is a life lived in full dependence on God and looks like it was designed to mirror Elijah, with the exception that John is not associated with miracles as Elijah was.[15]

John's message was about more than a baptism. He pointed the way to one to come after him. He called him "the stronger one to come" (v 7; Isa 11:2; *Pss Sol* 17:37; *1 Enoch* 49:3). The way in which Jesus is strong will be Mark's burden in his Gospel. In this context, the allusion is vague, to a figure of deliverance in the eschaton, so a messianic figure is likely intended. Luke 3:15–17 is explicit in this regard. The key opponent is less Rome than it is spiritual forces (Mark 3:22–27; 9:14–29). The greatness of the person to come points toward the greatness of the era to come. The image of the stronger one points to someone who can engage in battle and may suggest a regal figure. Another chiasm takes place here (stronger one/I/I/he).

Although John is a prophet (v 7b), he is not worthy to be the coming one's slave and perform the most menial of tasks for him. John describes himself as not worthy to untie the strap of the sandal of this one. This depicts preparing to wash a master's feet. This was something seen as so menial that later Jewish tradition said it was something a Jewish slave should not do (*Mekilta Exodus* 21.2; *b. Ketubbot* 96a – "all service that a slave must render to his master a student must render to his teacher, except untying his shoe"). The humility this represents is like what we see in John 3:27–30. If John can say this as a prophet, it suggests that the category of the one to come puts him in a class far greater than a prophet.

John contrasts his preparatory water baptism with the baptism of the Spirit the stronger one will bring (v 8). Mark is very brief here. Luke 3:16 and Matthew 3:11 mention the baptism as one of Spirit and fire with imagery like Isaiah 4:4. The evoking of the Spirit points back to the New Covenant of Jeremiah 31:31–33 (also Isa 32:15; 44:3; 63:10–14; Ezek 36:26–27; 39:29; Joel 2:28–32). With people who are cleansed, the Spirit is now able to fill that vessel (2 Cor 1:22; 5:5; Eph 1:14). Luke-Acts makes much more of this

---

[14] For how this diet has been viewed by interpreters, see James A. Kelhoffer, " 'Locusts and Wild Honey' (Mk 1.6c and Mt 3.4c): The *Status Quaestionis* concerning the Diet of John the Baptist," *CBR* 2 (2003): 104–127.

[15] M. Öhler, "The Expectation of Elijah and the Presence of the Kingdom of God," *JBL* 118 (1999): 461–76.

theme (Luke 24:49; Acts 1:4–5; 2:16–36). The offer of the new life in the Spirit is at the core of the new age, so John highlights the fact that this is the distinctive gift the one to come brings. Mark does not have any other examples of John's preaching like Matthew 3:7–9 and Luke 3:7–14 do.

The idea that an original form of this saying spoke only about fire ignores the fact that the eschaton is about the vindication of the righteous, so that their righteous status would be important to affirm.[16] The eschaton is not primarily a negative idea of judgment, but one of the establishment of shalom.

More difficult to decide is whether the reference is to being baptized with the Spirit or in the Spirit, as the preposition can carry either sense. "In" sees the person being placed in a Spirit-led community, immersed in the Spirit. "With" looks more to an indwelling presence. The analogy with Jesus' own baptism points to the latter. It is appropriate to see Jesus' baptism as the precursor and model for those who follow him.

1:9–15 Jesus Is Baptized, Tempted, and Preaches the Kingdom

1:9 And it came about in those days Jesus came from Nazareth of Galilee and was baptized in the Jordan by John.

1:10 And immediately coming up out of the water, he beheld the heavens ripping open and the Spirit like a dove coming down upon him.

1:11 And a voice came from the heavens, "You are my Beloved son, in whom I am well pleased."

1:12 And immediately the Spirit cast him out into the wilderness.

1:13 And he was in the wilderness forty days being tested by Satan, and he was with the wild animals, and the angels were ministering to him.

1:14 After John was arrested Jesus came into Galilee, preaching the gospel of God

1:15 and saying, "The time is fulfilled and the kingdom of God is near. Repent and believe the gospel."

With John's ministry introduced, Mark turns his attention to Jesus (**v 9**). During the time of John's ministry, Jesus came from Nazareth of Galilee to be baptized in the Jordan by John. Geography matters. The remark reflects intentionality from Jesus that indicates Jesus' embrace of John's message and practice. He came down from the north into Judea and the Jordan area.

---

[16] Collins, *Mark*, 146, cites positively the views of Fleddermann here. Harry T. Fleddermann, *Mark and Q: A Study of the Overlap Texts*. BEThL 122 (Leuven: Leuven University Press/Peeters, 1995), 31–39.

Whereas those baptized by John had been tied to Judea and Jerusalem in verse 5, Jesus came from Nazareth. By coming to be baptized, he shared in the affirmation of the eschatological program John proclaimed. He shared in the call to Israel to repent. John was not the only one to make an affirmation about Jesus. With the forerunner and the one to come now together, heaven would now speak.

As Jesus comes up from the water and the baptism (**v 10**), the shift from an era of water to one of the Spirit begins. Jesus sees the heavens rip open and the Spirit coming upon him like a dove. The only other splitting Mark describes in his Gospel is of the veil at the temple as Jesus is crucified (Mark 15:38). Marcus speaks of a ripping open that is not to be reversed.[17] God's program is here to stay.

The divine voice evokes the direct engagement of heaven with the earth (**v 11**). Such descriptions of divine voices are often called legend at a literary or form critical level.[18] The significance of calling this account a legend raises worldview questions about God's presence and engagement in and with the world. For Mark, there is no doubt he was describing a real event. Mark sees this moment as a key one in Jesus' life that showed him to be the "anointed," a call-vision experience.[19] More neutrally than the suggestive category of legend, the account portrays an experience of a divine encounter.

This event also is one of the most secure elements of Jesus' life that can be historically corroborated. The early church with its post-Easter theology would not have created this event. Why would Jesus need to be baptized by John? It gives an appearance of Jesus being inferior to him. For the early church, of what would Jesus need to repent? Jesus was perfectly qualified to be the Savior according to that theology. These incongruities mean that the church is very unlikely to have fabricated this event. The reality of Jesus being baptized by John was too well established to either ignore or reframe.

This call experience is the sign from God that it is time for Jesus to begin his ministry. Mark presents it as a private event between Jesus and God. His

---

[17] Marcus, *Mark 1–8*, 165.
[18] Collins, *Mark*, 146–47, citing Bultmann, *The History of the Synoptic Tradition*. 2nd ed. Trans. John Marsh (New York: Harper & Row, 1968), 247–48. Her comparison to Aesop as a literary parallel ignores the time and tradition differential between the Aesop material and the Jesus tradition. The theme is analogous, but the perspective of the account and genre is very distinct.
[19] Robert Webb, in Bock and Webb, *Key Events*, 94–144, esp. 108–112, 141–44. This classification seems better than the designation as legend, which can suggest a lack of reality to the experience Mark portrays as present.

readers get to share in this heavenly moment. Only John 1:29–34 indicates
that John also saw the Spirit descending like a dove as a witness to Jesus, but
John's Gospel does not indicate that John heard anything. It will be in the
power of the Spirit that Jesus' ministry takes place. Heaven has opened the
door and entered into the life of the world in a fresh way. The description
may well be history's reply to the plea of Isaiah 64:1 where God is asked to
come down from heaven by tearing open the sky (also *Apoc Bar* 22.1; *T. Levi*
2:6; 5:1; 18:6; *T. Jud* 24.2; Rev 4:1; 11:19; 19:11).

In verse 10, the association of the Spirit with the eschatological period
parallels a theme of many Jewish texts (Isa 11:2; 42:1; 61:1; 63:11; also *Pss Sol*
17:37). Though many options for what the dove symbolizes have been
proposed, no explanation seems clear.[20] The best one may be Genesis 1:2
where the Spirit is tied to creation. Here we have reclamation of the
creation, so the Spirit might be tied to that fresh creative work to bring
new, restored life. If there is no intended symbolism, then the Spirit is
simply compared to a dove in its arrival to mark out Jesus. What is not clear
is whether the description is of the shape of what was seen or the manner of
descent. More important than how the Spirit comes, is that he comes.[21]
This points to the new era.

After the Spirit's descent, there came a confirming voice declaring Jesus
to be the beloved Son (Ps 2:7) and the one with whom God is pleased (Isa
42:1). Matthew 12:17–21 cites Isaiah 42 directly. Jesus is commissioned as a
Son-Servant, a Messiah and herald. He is a king with a message and
eschatological task. To the extent the Spirit evokes the Servant, Isaiah
61:1–2 may be seen to describe his mission.[22] The terms also parallel how
Israel often was described, so he is a representative of theirs (Exod 4:22–23;
Deut 1:31; Hos 11:1). 4Q174 shows that the idea of the Son of God as a
messianic designation existed in that time for Judaism. This *Florilegium*
passage is a collection of Hebrew Scripture texts that were seen as prophetic
of the one to come. 2 Samuel 7:14 also appears there.

Sonship is important to Mark (1:1; 3:11; 5:7; 9:7; 12:6; 13:32; 14:61; 15:39). To
be pleased with someone often was directed to an only son (Gen 22:2, 12,
16 – of Isaac as Abraham's only son).[23] The reference to beloved is the
language of affection and family. The description as a whole points to Jesus'

[20]   Stein, *Mark*, 57.
[21]   Robert Guelich, *Mark 1:1–8:26* (Dallas: Word, 1998), 35.
[22]   Collins, *Mark*, 149. Luke 4:18–19 cites this text in another context where Jesus' mission
       and commission are being described.
[23]   C. H. Turner, " 'ὁ υἱός μου ὁ ἀγαπητός,' "*JTS* 27 (1926): 113–29; Guelich, *Mark 1–8:26*, 34.

uniqueness and the unique role he will have in God's program. He is the Son as regal king and as one with a unique relationship to the one who speaks from heaven.

With Luke 3:22, but unlike Matthew 3:17, the address is cast as a direct word to Jesus speaking to "you," a second-person singular. Noting the overall significance of the utterance, Matthew has the feel of a presentation to his readers and says, "This is my beloved Son. . . ." For him the baptism is especially Jesus' active entrance onto the stage of history. Jesus has already been presented as the stronger one to come to whom John will point, so this is not an adoption.[24] In that text (Mark 1:7), Jesus is described as the one who is stronger than John, so appointment to a new role is not so much the point here as a heavenly confession marking out who Jesus is and that his ministry is now equipped to begin the era that will be marked by the work of the Spirit. God confirms here this is "the one," and it is time to begin the program of deliverance. The familial association is not one Jesus steps into but a relationship he has that is affirmed here as he begins his calling.

Jesus represents Israel as Son and Servant (**v 12**), but he represents humanity when the Spirit casts him out into the wilderness to face temptation. The place of wild beasts is seen as a threatening place (Isa 13:19–22; 34:13–14; Ezek 34:5, 25; *T. Naph* 8.4; *T. Iss* 7.7 – "every spirit of Beliar shall flee you; and no deed of wicked men shall rule over you; and every wild beast you will subdue"; *T. Benj* 5.2). Although some speak of a restoration of paradise with wild animals subdued, there is really nothing to indicate a positive sense. It is a test Jesus faces here.

Mark uses a historical present for cast out, the first of many he writes to give vividness to the account. It is a violent term for Mark, used often with exorcisms (Mark 1:34, 39; in other settings, usually of intense physical displacement: 1:43; 5:40; 9:47; 11:15; 12:8). Matthew 4:1 and Luke 4:1 speak only of Jesus being led into the wilderness. Although Mark's version of the temptations is much shorter than Matthew's or Luke's, the point of being qualified to represent both God and humanity is still made as Jesus survives the temptations.

Jesus is thrown into a hostile environment for forty days and emerges on the other side intact (**v 13**). "Forty" days appears at key moments in Israel's history: the wilderness wanderings (Num 14:34), Elijah's fast (1 Kings 19:8), and Moses' time on Sinai (Exod 34:28). In one sense, for Mark this is more

---

[24]   Hooker, *Mark*, 48.

an encounter with Satan than with specific temptations, but the point
emerging from the result is the same. Satan means "the accuser or adver-
sary" (1 Kings 11:14) and is portrayed in Scripture as the archenemy of God
(Job 1–2). Interestingly, Satan is not a major foe in Mark, although exorcism and the challenge of demons are shown by the exorcisms Jesus performs. So it is the entire realm of evil forces that Jesus battles. Satan is
mentioned only when some claim Jesus heals by him (Mark 3:23, 26), in the
parable of the sowing of the seed (4:15), and in Jesus' rebuke to Peter when
the disciple challenges the idea that Jesus will suffer (8:33). Satan and wild
animals have a shot at derailing him, and they do not (Ps 91:9–14). At
Qumran, Psalm 91 is tied to texts about exorcism (11QapPs^a = 11Q11).[25] So
there maybe irony in Satan depicted as citing a text that would be applied to
the protection from demons. As the test is being completed, heaven also
supports Jesus as the angels minister to him through the test.

Mark focuses on the ministry of Jesus as it emerged following the arrest
of John the Baptist by Herod (**v 14**). The expression used here is the passive
"delivered over." It is an expression that can point to arrest or even to
something allowed to take place in God's plan (Mark 9:31; 10:33; 14:21, 41).
Because no one arranged to have John "handed over," the expression may
well relate to what God has permitted. Mark will pick up the story of John's
demise in Mark 6:14–29. Luke structures his Gospel similarly, since he tells
John's story in Luke 3 and then has the baton of promise passed on to Jesus.

For Mark and Luke, John is a transitional figure bridging the old era with
the new as he points to the arrival of the one who brings the promise. John's
Gospel shows more overlap in the ministries of the two, as John 3:22–4:2
presents an earlier Perean phase to Jesus' ministry that the Synoptics do not
have. So Mark has Jesus coming to Galilee for what all the Gospels see as
the main locale for his teaching and work. Mark moves from Galilee and
the area around it (Mark 1:14–9:50) to Judea (10:1–16:8). This is a selective
presentation of Jesus' activity.

These final verses (**vv 14–15**) of Mark's introduction present several key
terms: *Gospel, the time, the kingdom of God, repent,* and *believe.* Each is
important to Mark's overall narrative. Jesus' message of repentance echoes
that of John (Mark 1:4; also the disciples in 6:12). The time, the kingdom,
repentance, and belief are at the core of what the Gospel is.

The "time" is a reference to the promised time of salvation, the arrival of
the eschaton. It is fulfilled. The perfect tense points to it being and

---

[25]   Collins, *Mark,* 152.

remaining fulfilled. The eschatological calendar has decisively turned a page for all time. This frames the entire Gospel. God had made certain commitments in the Hebrew Scripture of a time of ultimate salvation, as texts like Isaiah 40–66, Ezekiel 34–37, and Jeremiah 30–33 argue. Jesus' arrival brings that time. That is what the Gospel or good news is all about. Although people today think of the last days as yet to come, for earliest Christians, Jesus' coming to earth began that new era.

The good news is that this time of promise and deliverance has now drawn near. The Gospel of God is both from him and about him, reflecting a broad or plenary use of the genitive case. The double use of the term *Gospel* in these verses connects back to Mark 1:1 and forms an *inclusio* that brackets the entire introduction. Hope is becoming reality.

The structure at the center of this arriving reality of the new time is the kingdom of God, the promised rule of God that brings with it life and hope (Matt 4:17; Luke 4:42–43).[26] This expression appears thirteen times in Mark (4:11, 26, 30; 9:1, 47; 10:14, 15, 23, 24, 25; 12:34; 14:25; 15:43) and appears in sixty-one distinct Synoptic sayings.[27] The term has been variously defined: (1) a strictly Davidic kingdom in Jerusalem, (2) a spiritual kingdom of the heart, (3) an imminent end-of-history rule with the final judgment, (4) the promised rule of God now fully arrived, and (5) an arrival now in fulfilment of promises tied to the Spirit with a consummation to come.

So what is one to make of these options? Nowhere does Jesus speak of the kingdom as being in the heart, so view 2 is not persuasive. The idea of a future consummation of the kingdom with complete peace when it comes

---

[26] A more complete look at the kingdom, its roots, and the debates tied to its use can be found in Darrell Bock, *Jesus According to Scripture* (Grand Rapids: Baker, 2002), 556–93. Is the *kingdom* a realm over which God rules or a dynamic pointing to his effective presence? Is the term static (fixed) in its meaning or tensive (flexible in its use, depending on context)? Is it apocalyptic or a part of this world's history? Is it present, future, or both? The discussion argues that these choices are not mutually exclusive. The core hope tied to the kingdom is that it is a realm where deliverance takes place and the righteous are vindicated into a place where God's rule and presence is active.

[27] Stein, *Mark*, 72. He gives the five categories that follow. He opts for a dynamic meaning versus realm, but this understates where the kingdom is and is headed. It functions among the people of God now and will encompass the realm of the earth in the future, even as it is sown in the world now to make a claim on all and establish accountability over all humanity now, with an accountability to be applied in judgment later (Matt 13:38). So, although most uses are dynamic, the issue of God's rule claiming or even creating a realm ultimately is also in view in the term. Witherington, *The Gospel of Mark*, 78, expresses this idea this way: "When it refers to something in the future, it appears to also have additional connotation – namely, a place or a realm where such a divine reign is manifest. When Jesus speaks of entering, obtaining, or inheriting the dominion in the future (cf. Mark 9:47; 10:15b; 14:25), not merely a condition but a place seems entailed."

is against a completely realized kingdom in the present (view 4). View 3 has a flaw in specifying the timing as soon and looking only to the consummation. There is room for view 1 in what lies ahead in the kingdom program, as the consummation is expressed in terms that look back to the hope as it was expressed in the Hebrew Scripture, but it is too narrow a meaning because it excludes an already realized dimension to some aspects of the promise tied to forgiveness and the Spirit's coming. This already realized dimension emerges in how Jesus will appeal to the blood of the New Covenant as bringing the promise through his death at Mark's discussion of the Last Supper, something the church picks up and celebrates in the Lord's Supper (1 Cor 11:23–26). Mark 2:21–22 also makes a point that what comes with Jesus brings new realities, those are tied to what he is doing, not just what comes at the end. John had already said the sign of the one to come and the program tied to him are the baptism by the Spirit. That is a key point of Acts 2 as well. For the early church, forgiveness and the provision of the indwelling Spirit are the presupposition for the kingdom's presence and provision that one enters by faith.

There are only two things to do, given the kingdom's approach, namely, to repent and to believe. These two responses are actually related to each other. Repent is to change one's mind, so it looks at where one is and says I need to be different. It is the change of direction that John's baptism had pictured. It means one is open to what God will do and is ready for it. Out of that change of mind is to come belief in the Gospel. That is where one is to land, in a faith that trusts God to do what he promises and that rests in what God will provide. So these terms introduce the themes of his ministry and set the tone for all that follows.

There is an interesting juxtaposition in what is said here. The time is fulfilled, but the kingdom is only near. The language is of arrival but of something less than completion. This is likely because the kingdom program is a process coming in phases and is introduced by the previous remark that the time has come.[28] So the kingdom is arriving and the time is here to remain, but the fullness of what lies ahead for the kingdom has not yet come.[29] One other point is important to note. Although the Psalms and other OT texts speak of the kingdom of God in present and comprehensive

---

[28] R. T. France, *The Gospel of Mark: A Commentary on the Greek Text* (Grand Rapids: Eerdmans, 2002), 92.

[29] C. E. B. Cranfield, *The Gospel According to Saint Mark: An Introduction and Commentary* (Cambridge: Cambridge University Press, 1959), 63–68; Guelich, *Mark 1:1–8:26*, 44.

terms, that is not what this language is describing. God has the right to rule because he is Creator. It is this inherent right to rule that the OT texts describe. Here we have the arrival of an awaited and promised kingdom, a kingdom where restoration of the Creator's claims take place. To say the kingdom is near is to proclaim the approach of this new, restorative aspect of God's rule, a rule he had called Israel to expect. Mark is saying that this hoped-for promise is being inaugurated with Jesus' coming, but consummation still awaits.

1:16–3:6 JESUS IN GALILEE: MINISTRY AND CONTROVERSY

1:16–20 Calling of the Four

1:16 And passing by the Sea of Galilee, he saw Simon and Andrew, the brother of Simon, casting a net into the sea; for they were fishermen.
1:17 And Jesus said to them, "Come after me, and I will make you fishers of people."
1:18 And immediately, leaving their nets, they followed him.
1:19 And going on a little, he saw James, a son of Zebedee and John, his brother, and they were in the boat mending the nets.
1:20 And immediately he called them. And leaving their father Zebedee in the boat with the laborers, they came out after him.

The work in Galilee continues as Jesus passes by the Sea of Galilee (Mark 1:14, 16). The Sea is about 13 by 7 miles in size. It is more like a lake. Near the fount of the Jordan River, it lies 700 feet below sea level. Josephus speaks of the region with pride for its bountiful provision (*War* 3.516–21). There were no fewer than sixteen ports on the lake. It had a high volume of fishing traffic, so much that, years later in CE 68, Josephus could use 230 such boats as part of his military operation (*War* 2.635).[30]

The scene picks up on this setting and a key vocation that was a part of life in the region. Two fishermen are doing their work, casting their nets into the sea. Fishing was a key occupation in the region, part of an international export to Alexandria in Egypt and Antioch in Syria.[31] Such

---

[30] J. R. Edwards, *The Gospel According to Mark* (Grand Rapids: Eerdmans, 2002), 49.
[31] Details on the background to this passage can be found in Wuellner, *The Meaning of "Fishers of Men"* (Philadelphia: Westminster, 1967); Edwards, *Mark*, 49; J. Murphy-O'Connor, "Fishers of Fish, Fishers of Men: What We Know of the First Disciples from Their Profession," *BRev* 15/3 (1999): 22ff.; and Nun, "Ports of Galilee," *BAR* 25/4 (1999): 18–31.

businesses may well have included people who knew Greek to conduct such business.

Peter and Andrew are at work (**v 16**). John 1:44 tells us they originally were from Bethsaida, although Andrew was associated with a figure, John the Baptist (John 1:35, 40–42), as much as with this locale. The fact that they own a boat and have a livelihood means they are not socially at a mere subsistence level. Tradition has Peter residing in Capernaum during Jesus' ministry. The nets such fishermen used were about 20 feet in diameter and had weights that pulled them down into the water to help catch the fish when they were drawn in.

Jesus calls to them to come after him. The two callings of verses 16–20 have the same four-part core structure: situation (vv 16, 19), calling (vv 17, 20a), response of leaving what they were doing (vv 18a, 20b), and departure with Jesus (vv 18b, 20c). His promise is that they will be catching people for God (**v 17**). The call is to follow in the path of the one who is bringing people back to God. Although the image of catching fish in the OT is negative (Jer. 16:16; Ezek. 29:4–5; 38:4; Amos 4:2; Hab. 1:14–17) as it is at Qumran (1QH 13:8), Jesus' remark is positive in force. Often nets are used at Qumran to describe what Beliar [Satan] or scoundrels do (CD 4:15–16; 1QH 3:26), catching people in their nets and snares. So at Qumran people fish and hunt for those who are evil or to bring them to evil, but Jesus and those he calls to follow him catch people for God, rescuing them from the threat of judgment. The idea of a teacher being a fisher of people is not unusual in either the Greek or Jewish context (Plato, *Sophist* 218d–222d; *'Abot R. Nat* (A) 40).[32]

This calling presupposes that Jesus is about forming a new community of the faithful, a point that fits the earlier call to repent and believe the Gospel in Mark 1:14–15, and now raised by the idea of following Jesus. The key verb "to follow" (**v 18**) refers to discipleship and is an important term in Mark (TDNT 2.210–216; Mark 1:18; 2:14–15; 8:34; 10:21, 28; 15:41). With one exception (Rev 14:4), the use of this term to refer to discipleship is limited to the Gospels. "Following" involves a commitment that makes all other

---

[32] Wuellner, *Fishers of Men*, 12–15, 111–12; Marcus, *Mark 1–8*, 184, has a survey of the uses of the imagery but reads Jer 16:16 too positively, for it is of a gathering for judgment, not a regathering of Israel. Collins, *Mark*, 159–60, also has Greco-Roman conceptual parallels. Her clearest example is from Diogenes Laertius, *Vita Philosophorum* 2.67, where, in order to win someone over to a philosophical point of view, the teacher is willing to be insulted, or to "take a carp." Collins notes *Joseph and Aseneth* 21:21, which has the righteous caught by God like a fish and brought to him as a bride.

ties secondary, which is why Jesus' followers often left other things behind (1:18, 20; 2:14; 10:21, 28; cf. Matt 8:22; Luke 9:61–62). Although Jesus' disciples are often compared to rabbinical students, this term is never used in regard to a rabbi's student[33], so the expression with this nuance appears to be of Christian origin. Another difference from the way the rabbis worked is that students picked the rabbis they followed. Here Jesus calls his disciples to himself. Hengel argues that this call is not like one by a rabbi, but more like one by a charismatic leader in the Elijah-Elisha mode (1 Kings 19:20).

Here is radical discipleship. Jesus is put first, so family and vocation become secondary (Mark 8:33–34). There is a parallel with how that text is laid out as well (disciple/Jesus says/Me/Follow after).[34] Jesus calls regular vocational people to join him. He is not forming a school of elites. His work will be accomplished because people are motivated to share with their neighbors. There may be a distinction between the calling all have from Jesus to join a movement and the commission John the Baptist and Jesus have in leading the establishment of a movement to mark the change of era.

The account as a whole is a call narrative. Given Andrew's background and ties to John the Baptist, it is likely that these fishermen may have been aware of Jesus already. So they leave their nets and follow him, answering the call. This is not an absolute leaving, as later we see Peter with his mother-in-law, caring for her. We also see them fishing in John 21. What this pictures is a fresh set of priorities that does eventually lead to Peter traveling through Judea and other regions to oversee the progress of the Gospel. Of course, the rest of the Gospel makes clear what lies ahead: if they follow Jesus' path, it will not be easy. Though there will be a battle with some who reject Jesus' invitation into the kingdom, others will be gathered.

The same process is repeated with James and John, the sons of Zebedee (vv 19–20). Calling them the "sons of Zebedee" distinguishes them from other figures named John and James in the narrative, people such as John the Baptist; James, son of Alphaeus (Mark 3:18), and James, the Lord's brother (Mark 6:3). These brothers also were fishermen. Jesus calls them as they were mending the nets, either fixing them or preparing them for

---

[33]   Martin Hengel, *The Charismatic Leader and His Followers* (Edinbrugh: T & T Clark, 1981), 50–57.

[34]   Abe Kuruvilla, *Mark: A Theological Commentary for Preachers* (Eugene, OR: Cascade Books, 2012), 26–27. He also notes this is the third call we have had in Mark so far: John (sent according to Scripture), Jesus (a sent Spirit and divine voice), and disciples (Jesus issues a calling to go and be fishers of people).

future use. Normally this would happen in the evening, after fishing was done.

When Jesus issued his call, James and John left their father in the boat with his workers and came after Jesus. The fact that this family business had laborers points to a business of modest means. The picture of followers of Jesus as rural peasants may be oversimplified.[35]

The move pictures the allegiance to Jesus that becomes primary (Mark 10:28–29), which was significant given that honoring one's family was a priority in Judaism (Exod 20:12; Deut 5:16; Prov 23:22–25; Tob 5:1; Sir 3:1– 16). The language of "following" forms an *inclusio* with verse 17 and Jesus' call to Simon and Andrew to come after him. So also the sons of Zebedee came after Jesus. Simon and Andrew left their boat, but James and John also left their father. Jesus is a priority over both business and family. To demand and receive such a commitment shows the importance of who Jesus is and the calling his ministry represents.[36] In the Greco-Roman world, such a move was not unusual for someone called to a philosophical school or for a religious commitment.

That this is the first act of Jesus in Mark also is important. He is gathering an array of followers who will help carry the message and share the burden of the ministry Jesus brings. They become the core of the new community the Jesus Movement will form. Their early, constant, and thorough involvement with Jesus formed the foundation for overseeing the development of the church and its message.

1:21–39 Jesus' Time in Capernaum

1:21–28 A Summary and an Exorcism

1:21 They went into Capernaum. And immediately on the Sabbath entering the synagogue, he was teaching.

1:22 And they were amazed at his teaching, for he was teaching them as one having authority and not like the scribes.

1:23 And then there was a man in the synagogue with an unclean spirit and he cried out,

1:24 saying, "What have you to do with us, Jesus of Nazareth? Have you come to destroy us? I know who you are, the Holy One of God."

---

[35] Marcus, *Mark 1–8*, 181, speaks of a middle-class status; Collins, *Mark*, 159, not of "Palestine's lowest social stratum."

[36] Hengel, *Charismatic Leader*, 18–21, compares this to the dedication of one who entered into the holy war of defending Judaism during the Maccabean War.

1:25 But Jesus rebuked him, saying, "Be silent, and come out of him."

1:26 And the unclean spirit, convulsing him and crying out with a loud voice came out of him.

1:27 And all were amazed so that they discussed with one another, "What is this? A new teaching with authority, and he commands the unclean spirits and they obey him."

1:28 And the report about him immediately went out everywhere in the whole of the entire region of Galilee.

Mark 1:21–22 presents a summary account about Jesus' teaching and authority. It is followed by an exorcism that underscores that power. This word and deed combination is a theme in the Synoptic Gospels. Mark actually presents less explicit teaching than the other Synoptics. He highlights action, beginning with this exorcism, the first of three other exorcisms to follow (Mark 5:1–20; 7:24–30; 9:14–29). Mark also has nine healing miracles and five nature miracles.[37] By comparison in terms of healings, Matthew adds only the healing of the centurion's son (Matt 8:5–13). Matthew also hints at a nature miracle in the provision of the temple tax from the fish (Matt 17:24–27). Luke has this additional centurion son's healing plus four more acts of power in his journey to Jerusalem section (dumb, demon-possessed man, Luke 11:14; crippled woman, Luke 13:10–17; dropsy, Luke 14:1–6; the ten lepers, Luke 17:11–19) and the ear of the slave of the high priest (Luke 22:50–51). The core of Jesus' work showing his acts of connection to God comes from Mark.[38] Mark does highlight Jesus as a teacher, as he uses the term "teaching" five times, "teacher" twelve times, and the verb "to teach" fifteen times with reference to Jesus.[39]

Jesus enters Capernaum (**v 21**). The name means "village of Nahum" and had a population of around 1,500 people. The events stay here through Mark 1:38 and cover more than one day. This small fishing town becomes his headquarters. Its remains, which are visible still today, cover about a mile located on the northwest part of the Sea of Galilee, 2.5 miles west from where the Jordan enters the lake. It was part of an east-west trade route and included a toll station (Matt 9:9–13). It had a synagogue that can be seen

---

[37] Stein, *Mark*, 83.

[38] The term *miracle* is more a reflection of a modern worldview that sees such acts as extreme exceptions, outside the normal "rules" of nature. In the NT, the terms used to summarize such acts are references to acts of power, as here where the act is an act of commanding unclean spirits (v. 27), or signs (John 2:11). On how these healings pointed to an eschatological end, see Eric Eve, *The Healer from Nazareth: Jesus' Miracles in Historical Context* (London: SPCK, 2009), 129–44.

[39] Guelich, *Mark 1:18:26*, 55.

today, although most of the visible synagogue is from a later period, around the fourth century. Most think the basalt base is old, stretching back to Jesus' time. Some have challenged whether synagogues extend back this far, but the synagogue at Gamla is evidence of a first-century synagogue in the region, as that city was destroyed and never rebuilt.[40] The remains of a synagogue and the breach in the city wall can still be seen today. Masada and the Herodium also point to the presence of synagogues. A more recent find is at Migdal. Synagogues are where the Law was read and studied, as well as being a place of prayer, education, and community events (TDNT 7:821–28). Any competent male could comment on Scripture.

Jesus' piety is indicated by his heading to this synagogue (Mark 1:39; 6:2). On the sacred day, he goes to the sacred place.[41] There he teaches, but it is instruction with a difference. The crowds notice that his teaching carries an authority unlike that of the scribes. This is teaching with a power that senses an authority is present (v 22). The arguments point to an innate versus derived authority. So those in the crowds were amazed (Mark 6:2; 7:37; 11:18). If later instruction is an example, the way the scribes taught was through text and tradition, citing the views of other rabbis (EDNT 1:259–60). They worked their way to a conclusion. Jesus' teaching involves direct declaration and, more importantly, comes with actions to support the claims. He reasons and does not cite the views of others. His appeal is to Scripture or to reflection over what he is doing. So he supports that teaching with action, as the next scene shows with an exorcism and a return to the mention of authority in Mark 1:27.[42] Jesus' teaching about the kingdom comes with a power others noticed.

The amazement could be positive or point to some discomfort at the difference. What is clear is that Jesus' style received attention and was not what people were used to. Mark often contrasts Jesus' teaching with that of the scribes (Mark 1:21–27; 2:5–12; 11:27–33). The scribes also are presented as

---

[40]   For this debate, see H. C. Kee, "The Transformation of the Synagogue after 70 CE: Its Import for Early Christianity," *NTS* 36 (1990): 117–23, 191–99; R. Oster, "Supposed Anachronism in Luke-Acts' Use of *Sunagoge*: A Rejoinder to H. C. Kee," *NTS* 39 (1993): 178–208; and Kee, "The Changing Meaning of Synagogue: A Response to Richard Oster," *NTS* 40 (1994): 281–83. For discussion, Witherington, *Mark*, 88–89; L. Levine, "The Second Temple Synagogue: The Formative Years," in *The Synagogue in Late Antiquity*, ed. L. Levine (Philadelphia: American School of Oriental Research, 1987), 201–222.

[41]   C. Myers, *Binding the Strong Man* (Maryknoll, NY: Orbis, 1988), 141. Textually the participle saying Jesus taught "coming" to the synagogue is likely to be original based on superior external evidence, Metzger, *A Textual Commentary on the Greek New Testament* (New York: United Bible Societies, 1971), 74–75.

[42]   By contrast, John's Gospel has no exorcisms.

Jesus' opponents (Mark 3:22; 7:1, 5; 8:31; 10:33; 14:1, 43, 53; 15:1, 31). Jesus' independence from this group of teachers is part of what produced tension with the leadership.

In Mark, Jesus' first act of healing is an exorcism. It takes place in a synagogue and involves an exchange revolving around naming and identifying, common in such settings (**v 23**). The reference to "their" synagogue probably shows that Mark was writing to a predominantly Gentile audience. Although a regional reference is possible, more likely is the point we are in a Jewish setting, as a regional reference would have meant little to Mark's audience. The demonic spirit cries out to Jesus of Nazareth and identifies him as the Holy One of God (**v 24**). Jesus as a Holy One contrasts with the uncleanness of the spirit. Purity faces off with impurity. As "the" Holy One, the demons confess the unique set-apart role Jesus has before God. The title could well be a synonym for "Son of God," although in a parallel setting Luke connects both titles to Jesus being the Christ (Luke 4:34, 41; also in John 6:69; Luke 1:35; Acts 2:27; 3:14; 4:27, 30; 13:35). Demoniacs will call Jesus "Son of God" (Mark 3:11) and Son of the Most High God (Mark 5:7).[43] In the OT, Aaron (Ps 106:16) and Elisha are seen as holy (1 Kings 4:9). At Qumran, a priestly Messiah is seen in such terms (1Q30). Jewish hope saw the eschatological High Priest as set apart in a similar way, including the defeat of Beliar [= Satan] (*T. Levi* 18:6–12).[44]

The reference to an unclean spirit in verse 23 reflects a Jewish way to say a demon is present, an evil malevolent transcendent force (*Jubilees* 10:1; *T. Benj* 5:2; 1QM 13:5 – associated with darkness). Such demons are seen as defiled beings (*1 Enoch* 15:3–4; *Jubilees* 7:21; 10:1). Zechariah 13:2 associates them with idols. Mark notes unclean spirits eleven times, with six of those mentions in two scenes (Mark 1:23, 26–27; 3:11, 30; 5:2, 8, 13; 6:7; 7:25; 9:25; also "demon," 1:34 [twice], 39; 3:15, 22 [twice]; 6:13; 7:26, 29, 30; 9:38). Demons are a threat to people and are described as destructive (Mark 5:2–13; 9:17–27). These battles with cosmic forces show where Jesus' key concerns lie, with those forces that attack the person from within.

Naming is seen as an effort to control the opponent in the battle that was an exorcism (*T. Solomon* 3:5–6; 5:2–3). The *Testament of Solomon*, in many places where the demons are present, shows the atmospherics of a text like this. The spirit also recognizes Jesus' authority, sensing that the teacher can destroy him. That declaration can be read as an exclamation or a question.

---

[43] William Lane, *The Gospel of Mark* (Grand Rapids: Eerdmans, 1974), 74.
[44] Marcus, *Mark 1–8*, 188.

With a question preceding, a question here is more likely. He tries to put Jesus off by these efforts as well as by suggesting they have nothing to do with him. "What do you want with us?" is an expression found in Judges 11:12 and 1 Kings 17:18 and queries why one would want to interfere in something.[45] Jesus is a threat to the spirit. The mood of the scene is one of spiritual combat. The mere presence of Jesus raises the tension for this unclean spirit. Part of Jesus' mission in bringing the kingdom is to defeat the influence of malevolent forces. The encounter, then, is a visual expression of what Jesus is about. His miracles in general are power points. This is part of what John the Baptist meant in referring to Jesus as the "stronger one." The scene makes sense in a context where Jesus' authority is the point. More than his ideas is meant in this authority. His person is what counts for Mark.

Jesus acts. He rebukes the spirit to silence and commands him to depart (v 25). The call to silence is not unusual for an exorcism. It was a common way to exert control in an exorcism (PGM IX.4, 9; PGM IV.1243, 1245, 3013).[46] PGM V.320-29 speaks of a spell against a person binding the speech and action, as we have here. The only difference is that here it is a demon who is muzzled by the exercise of power.[47] As such, appeals to any "messianic secret" for this scene are exaggerated and may ignore the cultural context.[48] Though there is a silencing here, it is not that Jesus is trying to not disclose something, as the demon has already spoken; it is that Jesus desires to stop the demon's activity, verbal and otherwise. Important to note is that there is no incantation or any other appeal that involves intermediary authority or magic. Jesus' word bears the authority. Evil is challenged by the presence of the kingdom and its hope.

The physical evidence for an exorcism is that the man the spirit possesses goes into convulsions and there is a loud cry on the spirit's departure from the body (v 26). The verb used for convulsions is used only of demonic activity in the NT (Mark 9:26; Luke 9:39). It describes a shaking that in other contexts might refer to animals or dogs shaking a victim. Guelich calls the loud cry a "death wail."[49] It may not be quite so extinguishing, but it is a sign that the demon has been defeated. Jesus has acted with power.

---

45   Guelich, *Mark 1:1–8:26*, 56–57. John 2:4 is similar in force.
46   Witherington, *Mark*, 91.
47   Collins, *Mark*, 173.
48   Lane, *Mark*, 75.
49   Guelich, *Mark 1:1–8:26*, 58.

The crowd reacts with amazement (**v 27**). This is one of two such words that will describe Jesus' ministry (*thambeomai*). In fact, a different term for astonishment was used in Mark 1:22 (*ekplesso*; also Mark 6:22; 10:26; 11:18). *Thambeomai* also appears in Mark 10:24 and 32. In Mark 10, as here, we get a juxtaposition of these two terms. *Thambeomai* points to a perplexity about what is taking place, a bewilderment combined with shock (BDAG 442; EDNT 2.128). These are but two of six such terms that point to amazement or wonder at what Jesus does in Mark (Mark 1:27; 2:12; 4:41; 5:15, 20, 33, 36, 42; 6:50, 51; 9:6, 15, 32; 10:24, 32 [twice]; 11:18; 12:17; 15:5, 44; 16:5-8).[50]

The result was a public discussion about who Jesus was (**vv 27-28**) and what exactly was going on (Mark 4:41; 9:10). These kind of reflective questions dot the narrative (Mark 4:41; 6:2; 8:27, 29; 11:28). Jesus had an authority that touched into the world of transcendent beings, not just in healings, but also in exorcisms. Mark characterizes it as a new teaching with authority, a power that extended beyond words to deeds, so that he could command the unclean spirits and they would obey him. In the grammar there is a debate about whether authority goes with the teaching or with the commanding of spirits.[51] The presence of *kai* where it is in the Greek appears to favor the former (reading it as "and," not "even"), but Mark's overall point is hardly impacted by this syntactical decision regardless of which option is chosen. The juxtaposition of teaching and action makes Mark's point here fresh, versus in Mark 1:22, and is something the unit of Mark 1:21-28 as a whole also does. Word and deed go together in Jesus' ministry, reinforcing each other and giving what he says credibility about the roots of his power.

Almost half of the first half of Mark covers Jesus' miraculous activity. What drew attention was not that Jesus did a miracle here and there, but rather the extent and scope of this activity.[52] The miracles were not automatic in bringing acceptance of Jesus, for opposition emerged. The counter opinion argued that although Jesus was doing amazing things, it was of the

---

[50] Witherington, *Mark*, 92.

[51] Textual variants are also tied to this issue, but tying the phrase about authority to new teaching seems the reading that best explains the other variants, Metzger, *Textual Commentary* (1994), 64.

[52] Eric Eve, *The Jewish Context of Jesus' Miracles* (Edinburgh: T & T Clark, 2002), 13-15, speaks of Jesus portrayed as a "bearer of numinous power" in his healing, not as a mediator or petitioner (Honi the Circle Drawer) of it, as in most other miracle accounts of the time. Apollonius is the exception to this observation, but his story is told centuries later in a context that may reflect a response to Jesus. By contrast, emperors such as Vespasian are credited with only a work or two to simply establish their credibility.

devil (Mark 3:6, 22). For Mark, this is the regal Servant-Son carrying out his calling and showing that the kingdom was designed to challenge evil and overthrow cosmic forces that sought to debilitate people. That could not be of the devil, as it is the reversal of the devil's activity that is taking place.

The report about him spread throughout Galilee.[53] The alternative of reading this as the whole region around Galilee is unlikely, given Mark's focus on Galilee in this portion of the Gospel. The spread of this report is said quite emphatically, as three terms are used to say all of Galilee was involved: everywhere, all, and whole region. The emphasis may express an explosion of discussion as a result of Jesus' time in Capernaum. Jesus' acts of power drew attention to him. This teaching involved more than words.

1:29–31 Healing Simon's Mother-in-Law

1:29 And immediately they[54] left the synagogue and entered the home of Simon and Andrew, with James and John.

1:30 Now Simon's mother-in-law lay ill with a fever, and immediately they spoke to him about her.

1:31 And he came and took her by the hand and lifted her up, and the fever left her, and she began to serve them.

The next miracle is a healing of Peter's mother-in-law. The detail clearly indicates Peter was married (1 Cor 9:5). The healing takes place later on the Sabbath day in private, a contrast to the very public exorcism. The remark that evening had come in Mark 1:32 makes it clear Jesus did not wait to perform the healing until after the Sabbath had passed. Luke 13:16–17 has Jesus explain at another healing that no day is more appropriate for a healing than another. The Sabbath was designed to allow people to contemplate God. What better way to do it than to heal.

The miracle takes places at Simon and Andrew's home (v 29). All we are told is that Jesus was told that she had a fever (v 30). In fact, this is among the shortest miracle accounts in the Gospels. All we have is the setting, the condition, the move to heal, and the evidence of recovery. We also have the four called in Mark 1:16–20 noted as present, multiple witnesses.

---

53 Reading *pantachou* as "in all directions," BDAG, 754.
54 The plural with the participle "going out" and verb "came" is more likely than the singular, despite the external evidence for the singular, because the plural is the harder reading, Metzger, *Textual Commentary* (1994), 64.

An ancient site in Capernaum was discovered in 1968 that has a claim to be Peter's home.[55] It is located only a few yards from the synagogue.

Jesus' touch heals her of the fever (**v 31**). All he does is lift her up and the fever is gone. Again there is no prayer, no incantation. Jesus' action is enough to care for her. The evidence of her being healed was her returning to serve them. The imperfect here is inceptive and probably points to the fixing of meals.

1:32–34 Healings in the Evening

1:32 When evening had come, when the sunset, they brought to him all those who were ill and the demon possessed.
1:33 And the entire city was gathered together at the door.
1:34 So he healed many who were sick with various diseases and cast out many demons. But he would not permit the demons to speak, because they knew him.

The discussion turns to a summary.[56] After evening came and the sun had gone down, people gathered at the door. Mark often has dual expressions of time (Mark 1:35; 2:20; 4:35; 10:30; 13:24; 14:12, 43; 15:42; 16:2). Now that the Sabbath had passed, others sought healing, both the sick and possessed. Mark consistently makes this distinction in this unit. Sickness was not always seen as demon possession.

Mark's use of "all" is hyperbolic, as he speaks later of many being healed (**v 32**). The word about Jesus clearly had spread. People now sought out the one who had been identified as a healer. We do not see Jesus out seeking to heal people. Those who need healing take the initiative and appeal to him.[57]

Mark makes nothing of Sabbath healing in the earlier events. That discussion is saved for later (Mark 2:23–3:6). What we see here is a pious community waiting for the Sabbath to pass before bringing people to Jesus and waiting in line for healing (**v 33**). CD 11:11 prohibits an infant from being carried on the Sabbath. In the Mishnah, *Shabbat* 14:3–4 looks to discuss what one can drink on the Sabbath and seems to imply that there is not to be healing on this day.[58]

---

[55] V. C. Corbo, *ABD* 1:867–68.
[56] For evidence this is a piece of tradition, and not a summary written by Mark, Guelich, *Mark 1:1–8:26*, 64, notes several expressions that are distinct here from the previous units in Mark, suggesting that a Markan summary would not be worded so distinctly.
[57] France, *Mark*, 109.
[58] Collins, *Mark*, 175.

The summary concludes by noting Jesus performing healings and exorcisms (**v 34**). Mark's own array of healing – fever, leprosy, paralysis, hemorrhage, deafness and blindness – shows the range of Jesus' healing work, which is distinguished from his exorcisms (Mark 1:30–31, 40–45; 2:1–12; 5:25–34; 7:31–37; 8:22–26; 10:46–52). Jesus' healing of "many" is to be taken inclusively of the all mentioned earlier. The rest of the Gospel shows he is healing all types of maladies. The crowd is drawn to him in part because of this. They risk not appreciating the real reason for his coming – not to heal physical needs, but to bring people closer to God's promise in the call to turn back to him.

The additional remark in verse 34b is that the demons were not allowed to speak because they knew him. This idea appears consistently in the Gospel (Mark 1:34, 44; 3:12; 5:43; 7:36; 8:26, 30; 9:9). This is said in the midst of exorcisms, to those healed of disease, and to the disciples. This note to be silent communicates Jesus' power and authority over such hostile forces. This is Mark's point – Jesus can control them.

Why does Jesus silence their knowledge of him? Given the variety in Jewish views about what the Messiah would do in the eschaton, Jesus prefers to choose the time to highlight this role. This awaits his entry into Jerusalem at the end of his ministry (Mark 11:1–10). In addition, demons validating one's authority is not exactly the best form of endorsement. So this remark is the first clear note of Jesus working not to publicize who he is, what has been called the "Messianic Secret."

For some, Mark has taken a non-messianic ministry and hidden it behind the secret, awaiting a claim by the early church that Jesus was not who he saw himself to be. The major issue with this theory is that there really was no reason to go to this claim unless it had some type of motivation from what Jesus directly did or said.[59] A messianic claim, where one was not necessary, put the community too far at risk with Rome to have been invented by the early church. Resurrection is no precedent for going there. Something must have been in place for the new community to so quickly and comprehensively preach Jesus as the Christ, even to the point of making the title the moniker of identification

---

[59]   J. R. Edwards, *The Gospel According to Mark* (Grand Rapids: Eerdmans, 2002), 64, says, "The only reasonable answer for their incurring the odium of fellow Jews in proclaiming the Gospel is that they believed Jesus to be God's Son and Messiah. Jesus could scarcely have been proclaimed as Messiah after the resurrection unless he had been recognized as such during his ministry."

for Jesus.[60] Demons know Jesus to be the "Holy One of God" (Mark 1:24) and "Son of [the Most High] God" (Mark 3:11; 5:7 has the longer title). It is not yet time for a full disclosure to become the focus of Jesus' work. Once the kingdom's message is in place and the disciples understand the program, then Jesus will disclose who he is and the type of messianic office he reflects.

1:35–39 Prayer and a Decision to Move On

1:35 **Very early in the morning, while it was still dark, Jesus went out and departed into a deserted place and prayed there.**
1:36 **Simon and those with him hunted him down.**
1:37 **And they found him and said to him, "Everyone is seeking you."**
1:38 **He replied, "Let's go elsewhere, into the surrounding villages, so I can preach there too. For that is what I came out here to do."**
1:39 **And he came[61] preaching in their synagogues in the whole of Galilee and casting out demons.**

This is yet another summary account about Jesus' sense of mission to the whole region. After another double time reference from Mark about the early morning (**v 35**), Jesus heads out to pray in a deserted place (not the wilderness we saw earlier, as we are in Capernaum). Despite the whirl of activity around him, Jesus takes time to commune with God. His program is not his alone. He is following the lead of God. So Mark frames these events with a continued look at a pious Jesus devoted to God and directed by him. This is the first of three such notes about prayer in Mark (Mark 6:46; 14:35–39). Each is an important time in the ministry. It also is the first of five references to solitude (Mark 1:35, 45; 6:31–32, 35).

The disciples search for Jesus and find him (**v 36**). The verb here (*katediōxen*) is quite vivid. It means "to hunt someone down" (Ps 17:38 LXX; BDAG 516). Their intense desire is for Jesus to return and minister some more in Capernaum. Everyone is seeking him (**v 37**). The verb "to

---

60 Some variants make an explicit reference to his being the Christ, but this looks like assimilation to Luke 4:41, since key manuscripts lack any such reference (א*, A, (D), K, Δ, it, vg, syr).

61 A variant here is "was" preaching. A few manuscripts add in the synagogues to the "was." The point is the same, but the construction with "came" is a more difficult reading and thus, likely original, since a scribe would more likely smooth out the construction and make it like Luke 4:44, Metzger, *Textual Commentary* (1994), 64–65. The earlier manuscripts have this harder reading.

seek" (*zēteō*) is consistently negative in Mark (Mark 1:32; 3:32; 8:11–12; 11:18; 12:12; 14:1, 11, 55). Even Mark 16:6 is somewhat negative, as they are seeking a Jesus who is no longer in the tomb. They were seeking Jesus where he was no longer to be found and should not have been sought, given that he had told them he would be raised.

The focus of the people looks to be on Jesus only as a healer-exorcist. It is a misdirected seeking. Jesus' intention is not to stay put in one place nor to be merely known for his miraculous work, but to cover the region and preach the kingdom. It is time to move on. In a short mission statement (**v 38**), Jesus declares that preaching to those in the region is what he has come to do. Mark 2:17 and 10:45 are other Markan mission statements. This ministry program involves an itinerant ministry. This is not so much a rejection of Capernaum as it is the recognition that to have impact, more than one location would be required.

The key to what Jesus is doing is his message, not his work of healing. So Jesus goes to the synagogues to preach. He came for this reason. The term *kērussō* points to missionary proclamation, either a call to repent and respond to the Gospel (Mark 1:4, 7, 14; 6:12; 13:10; 14:9) or to what Jesus has done (Mark 1:45; 5:20; 7:36), not to instruction, especially given the earlier reference to Mark 1:14–15.[62] Only these references in verses 38–39 and that in 3:14 do not reveal the content of what was preached. The term pictures a herald, an announcement (BDAG 543). Jesus will be described as teaching after this. He also continues his ministry of compassion, casting out demons. What he had done in Capernaum, he now does elsewhere. Word and deed remain together. It is exorcism that is the focus, as Mark has his eyes on the cosmic battle (also Mark 3:14–15; 6:7). Satan's defeat is being catalogued.

1:40–45 Into Galilee: The Healing of a Leper

> **1:40** And a leper came to him, calling him, and bowing to his knees, saying, "If you are willing, you are able to make me clean."
> **1:41** And being angry [or having compassion][63], he stretched out his hand, touched and said to him, "I am willing. Be clean."
> **1:42** The leprosy left him immediately, and he was clean.
> **1:43** And having warned him sternly, he sent him away immediately.

62　Guelich, *Mark 1:1–8:26*, 43.
63　The textual variants between anger and compassion are discussed in detail later.

1:44 And he said to him, "See that you don't say anything to anyone, but go show yourself to the priest and bring the offering that Moses commanded for cleansing as a testimony in relationship to them."

1:45 But as he went, he began to preach much and to spread the word, so that Jesus could no longer openly enter a town, but was in desolate places, and people were coming to him from every direction.

As Jesus travels in Galilee, an unclean leper approaches him with respect (v 40). The scene is a straightforward miracle healing account with a setting, exchange, healing, and evidence of healing.

Bowing before him, the leper asks to be cleaned.[64] Leprosy refers to an array of skin diseases that rendered a Jewish person unclean and required a life of isolation from society (Lev 13–14; *m. Nega'im*, esp 13:7–11; Josephus, *Ant.* 3.264). Leviticus 13:45–46 reads, "The person with such an infectious disease must wear torn clothes, let his hair be unkempt, cover the lower part of his face and cry out, 'Unclean! Unclean!' As long as he has the infection, he remains unclean. He must live alone; he must live outside the camp." Even chance encounters can render one unclean, as *m. Nega'im* 13:7 reads, "If an unclean man [afflicted with leprosy] stood under a tree and a clean man passed by, the latter becomes unclean. If a clean man stood under a tree and an unclean one passed by, the former remains clean. If the latter stood still, the former becomes unclean."[65] According to *m. Nega'im* 13:12, lepers could attend a synagogue provided there was a screen separating them from others. There was an awareness that this condition was contagious and could spread, leading to the isolation.

This condition involves more than what is known as Hansen's disease today. Lepers were to announce their presence and the danger of contamination by crying out, "Unclean, unclean!" (Lev 13:45–46). The leper's approach to Jesus violated this legal tradition, but it expressed the confidence that Jesus was capable of reversing his condition. Sometimes such diseases were regarded as divine judgments (2 Kings 5:7, where healing the disease is seen as restoring life). Other texts discussing the disease include Exodus 4:6–8; Numbers 12:9–15; 2 Kings 5:1–27; 2 Chronicles 26:16–21; Job 18:13; and 11QTemple[a] 45:17–18. This leprosy has caused him to be isolated

---

[64] There is uncertainty if the reference to kneeling is original, so the Greek text brackets it. ℵ, A, C, and L have it; but B, D, and W lack it. The parallels have something similar, suggesting that it was original, Metzger, *Textual Commentary*, (1994), 65.

[65] Lane, *Mark*, 85. Papyrus Egerton 2 has this scene in an embellished form, with a report in the first person by the leper, saying he contracted the leprosy while at an inn.

from society, so the request is not only to be healed, but also to be cleansed so that he can reenter life to the fullest. This is what the healing pictures.

The request in verse 40 indicates that Jesus is able to cleanse him if he wishes to do so. Jesus is not acting as a priest here in recognizing a healing; he is doing the healing. The request is a third-class condition, so it comes with no presumption. The choice is left completely in Jesus' hands by this portrayal. The leper's expectation and hope is shown by his willingness to approach Jesus without warning him he is a leper. The entire act is a statement of faith in Jesus' ability to heal. Love and authority trump ceremonial law here.

Jesus' reaction has three steps (v 41): (1) he has compassion on the man (or anger at the situation), a common Markan noting of Jesus' emotion (see the later discussion of the textual issue); (2) he touches the man, but rather than this touch rending Jesus unclean, it will be the touch of reversal, with uncleanness leading to healing; and (3) he tells the man he is willing and that the man is now clean. His command is a speech act in the most classic sense. Jesus' word resolves the situation and restores the man. Normally touching would have rendered Jesus unclean (Lev 13:45–46; Num 12:10–15; 2 Kings 7:3–4), but Jesus' sanctity is stronger than the uncleanness.

Some manuscripts, including D and some Old Latin renderings, read "moved with anger" (cf. NLT mg). Some argue that this is the harder reading, because it is more difficult to explain a copyist's move from compassion to anger. Matthew 8:3 and Luke 5:13 lack the remark entirely in their parallels, but not too much should be made of this, as they speak less of Jesus' emotions than Mark does, and Matthew often abbreviates the parallels he uses. On the other hand, they do sometimes make such a note about emotion (Matthew 9:36; Luke 7:13). If anger were original, then Jesus' anger would be set against the man's condition and the isolation and suffering it brings – life lived in a fallen world full of pain. In that sense it would have an element of compassion as well. John 11:33, 38 provided analogies to the sense here.[66] It is not the man's request that brings anger, given that Jesus healed regularly to show God's care for people, as his word and deed made a match that reinforced each other (Luke 13:16).[67] Neither should the anger be attributed to a demonic challenge or presence that leads Jesus to react. Nothing in the text points to a challenge. The reading of anger is quite possible, and a decision between the variants is

---

[66]   Guelich, *Mark 1:1–8:26*, 74.
[67]   Marcus, *Mark 1–8*, 206; Hooker, *Mark*, 79–80.

finely balanced. For reading compassion as original is the overwhelming external geographical and chronological spread of the MSS (א, B, W, and the great majority of MSS).[68] However, the difficulty of a move from anger to compassion means the original reading of anger is a harder reading and likely the original.

Mark loved to note Jesus' emotions. Jesus acted in reaction to the man's plight and his perceptive request that Jesus could do something about it. The healing would be extended with a symbolic touch, since Jesus' power to cleanse was greater than leprosy's power to stain (contrast 2 Kings 5:1–14; Num 12:9–15). The significance of this kind of act is clearer in other Gospel texts (Matt 11:5; Luke 7:22). Jesus' ability to cleanse typifies the Galilean ministry for which this is the lead-off event. For Jesus, the untouchable is touchable.

The man is healed in a moment (**v 42**). Jesus warns him and urges him to go to the temple to show himself to the priests in line with the requirements of the Law (**v 43**; see Lev 14:1–20). The verb for warn has an edge to it. The verb *embrimaomai* means "to snort" or "be indignant" (BDAG 322; Mark 14:5; John 11:33, 38; Lam 2:30; Dan 11:30). When a horse snorts, this is the verb used. It is a term of emotion. Jesus wanted to restrict the public announcement of what had taken place, at least for now (Mark 1:34; 3:12; 5:43; 7:36; 8:30, 9:9). This is an insistent warning. It may be aware of the disobedience to come (Mark 1:45). The instruction comes with a double negative, so the prohibition to say anything is expressed with emphasis.

The sacrifice is to be a testimony for/against them (**v 44**). The question is whether to take this positively or negatively. This is a close call. If it is positive, then it is to testify to God's grace for the man.[69] At the least, the sacrifice was to make this point, as that was the goal of such a declaration at the temple. If it is negative, then it is to challenge the priests to see what God is doing. The Greek allows for the interpretation, "a testimony against them." In other spots where this expression appears, France argues that it is

---

[68] Collins, *Mark*, 177; Metzger, *Textual Commentary* (1971), 76–77, also notes that Mark's use of anger is clearly attested in other verses (3:5; 10:14), so that scribes did not object to saying Jesus was angry. Still, anger in this Mark 1 context is less clear than in those other examples, so it is harder to see it being added here if compassion were original. Guelich, *Mark 1:1–8:26*, 72, correctly calls it "a genuine textual dilemma." I have changed my mind on this textual problem since writing about it earlier in the Cornerstone commentary on Mark, page 416. I have now decided an original compassion would not have led a scribe to produce a change to anger, while the reverse is quite likely.

[69] Stein, *Mark*, 108.

negative, meaning "against them" (Mark 6:11; 13:9; TDNT 4:502–503).[70] It may be that a more generic "as a testimony in relationship to them" is best as our translation suggests. Though he appears before one priest, the testimony extends to a group. In this case, the sacrifice serves as evidence of God's acting through Jesus *and* as a testimony against the priests when they come to reject the reality that God is working through Jesus. The action also may reflect a challenge to the claim that Jesus ignored the Law. Here he tells the healed leper to follow it. There has been nothing negative yet in Mark to point to this conflict, so the testimony is not so much immediate as it is ultimately shown. Jesus comes to do the work of God faithfully.

The man did not obey (**v 45**). He went around telling people what had taken place. News spread. Jesus gained fresh attention, so much so that he could not enter a town without drawing a crowd. So he ministered outside the towns. Still people came to him from everywhere. This healing ends with Jesus having garnered attention across the region. His healings were drawing crowds. As it was in Capernaum, so also in Galilee (Mark 1:35–39), except now the crowds pursued him in the desert versus just the disciples. That was not quite what Jesus had desired. For, as Mark had already indicated, Jesus was about more than healing. The next healing of the paralytic will also make that clear. The result helps to explain why Jesus sought to keep news of the healing as confined as he could.

The result of the event is that Jesus heals and cleanses apart from the temple. His authority continues to be powerfully demonstrated. God is working through one who is not located at the temple.[71]

2:1–3:6 Five Controversies: What Got Jesus into Trouble

2:1–12 Controversy 1 – Authority over Sin: Jesus and the Paralytic

2:1 And coming again into Capernaum after some days, it was reported that he was at home.

2:2 And many were gathered together, so that there was no longer room, even at the door. And he was speaking the word to them.

2:3 And they came, bearing to him a paralytic, being carried by four of them.

---

[70]   France, *Mark*, 120, but 13:9 is also debatable, with its parallel Matt 10:18. Matt 24:14 appears positive.

[71]   Marcus, *Mark 1–8*, 210–11.

2:4 And not being able to bring him in because of the crowd, they removed the roof where he was, and digging through, lowering the pallet where the paralytic lay.

2:5 And Jesus, seeing their faith, said to the paralytic, "Child, your sins are forgiven."

2:6 And there were some of the scribes there, seated and dialoging in their hearts,

2:7 "Who is this speaking this way? He blasphemes. Who is able to forgive sins but the one God?"

2:8 And Jesus, immediately knowing in his spirit that they were dialoging among themselves, said to them, "Why are you dialoging these things in your hearts?

2:9 Which is easier to say to the paralytic, 'Your sins are forgiven,' or to say, 'Take up your mat and walk?'

2:10 In order that you might know that the Son of Man has authority on earth to forgive sins," – he said to the paralytic –

2:11 "I say to you, 'Rise, take your mat, and go to your house.' "

2:12 And he was raised and immediately taking his mat, he went out before all, so that all were amazed and glorified God saying, "We have never seen anything like this."

This next account starts a series of five successive controversies. What Mark 2:1–3:6 and Luke 5:17–6:11 keep together as a likely topically oriented tradition, Matthew 8–12 splits up.[72]

This specific scene is a combination miracle account and pronouncement story. The miracle provides the context for the pronouncement, which serves as the commentary on the miracle's significance.

Jesus returns to his home and headquarters in Capernaum (v 1). This is likely Peter's home (Mark 1:29, 33, 35). A report gets out of his return, leading to a crowd again gathering at his home (v 2), just as in Mark 1:33. It is so full that people extend beyond the door. Jesus is drawing unending attention. The many in Mark 2:2 is a crowd in 2:6. In addition, scribes have gathered to take a look in Mark 2:7. He is speaking the word, a way to say he is sharing the Gospel (Mark 4:14–20, 33).

The crowd was so dense that four people bringing a paralytic to Jesus could not get into the house (vv 3–4). However, they were determined to place the man before Jesus. So they climbed up a ladder that led to the flat roof above, removed the covering, and dug through the roof to lower the man and his pallet before Jesus. This is not an unprecedented act, as Cicero

---

[72] Collins, *Mark*, 182, makes the case that this is extant tradition that Mark has passed on.

also describes such an event (*In M. Antonium oratio Philippica* II.18.45). The literal expression is they "unroofed the roof" (Josephus, *Ant.* 14.459). Any damage done likely came to be understood, given how the situation developed, and was repairable. Needless to say, the action would have been quite distracting. The pallet was made of wood and covered with cloth. Mud thatch and whatever other material, such as tree trunks, dried mud, and branches, were cleared away. Luke 5:19 also mentions tiles, suggesting a more well-to-do home. One could work or sleep on such roofs.

This is the only healing involving a paralyzed person in Mark and Luke. Matthew and Acts have other examples (Matt 4:24; 8:6; Acts 8:7; 9:33). Obstacles to healing are also noted in other Markan healings (Mark 5:21–24, 35–43; 10:46–52). Though some have tried to explain this as a way to prevent a demon of paralysis from gaining access through a door, there is nothing in this event pointing to an exorcism.[73] This is a healing account.

Jesus responds because of the faith of all of those participating in bringing the paralytic to him (**v 5**). Mark likes to use both the noun and the verb for faith (Mark 1:15; 4:40; 5:34–36; 9:19, 23–24, 42; 10:52; 11:22–24; other texts assume faith: 1:29–31, 40–45). Mark commends their faith as it was manifest in their action. In Mark, faith is expressed concretely as it overcomes obstacles placed in its way. The idea of one appealing for the healing of another is also common (Mark 5:21–43; 7:24–30; Matt 8:5–13; John 4:46–53). This group is confident Jesus can heal the man. Unlike other miracle accounts in the Greco-Roman world, faith precedes the healing versus being a result and response to it.[74]

Jesus does not move to heal the man yet, but instead forgives his sin. The present tense versus the perfect of Luke 5:20 fits Mark's style.[75] Sin and disease were often associated in the ancient world, something the discussion surrounding the blind man in John 9:2–3 assumes, but Jesus rejects as automatic (Ps 41:4; 103:3; James 5:15–16). Later in the Talmud, healing is not seen as possible without forgiveness (*B. Nedarim 41a*– "No one gets up from his sick-bed until all his sins are forgiven."). The surprise move to focus on sin and raise it directly drives this account. Surely the man who came to be healed also would have been surprised, but Jesus is again

---

[73]   This view is noted and properly rejected by Guelich, *Mark 1:1–8:26*, 85.

[74]   Theissen, *The Miracles Stories of the Early Christian Tradition* (Philadelphia: Fortress, 1983), 132.

[75]   The text-critical options here involve either a present or a perfect tense. Matthew 9:2 also has a present, which is unusual for him and points to a present in Mark, since Matthew likely follows Mark in this parallel, Metzger, *Textual Commentary* (1994), 66.

pointing to the fact that he is about more than mere healing. Healing is designed to picture deeper concerns.

Some commentators struggle to see why Jesus goes this direction here, even suggesting the theme is a later addition. However, if one sees that Jesus has already been fighting to show that he is about more than mere healing, the current focus on sin and dealing with it makes sense and shows an emerging Markan theme. The fact that table fellowship with sinners is the next controversy also shows this link to dealing with the topic of sin as part of the center of Jesus' ministry. His work pictures the "wholeness of the new age."[76]

This remark about forgiving sin got Jesus into trouble with the theologians present, as the scribes were shocked that Jesus would forgive sin and take up a divine prerogative (**vv 6-7**; Exod 34:6-7; Isa 43:25; Ps. 130:4; *Midrash Psalms* 17:3). Although it is expressed as a divine passive that could attribute forgiveness to God, they see Jesus as crossing a sacred line (see Lev 4:26, 31; 2 Sam 12:13 – Nathan announcing to David; or the debated Qumran's *Prayer of Nabonidus* [4Q242], where a diviner either points to God forgiving and announces it or in an exceptional text makes a direct declaration). Nothing Jesus does subsequently to the surfacing of this concern points to Jesus separating his declaration and responsibility for the utterance from God. This is a claim of shared authority. It is, as France calls it, a "performative utterance."[77] Jesus speaks directly for God. He is not interceding for God to act. He is not acting like a priest who simply declares what God has done through a rite. Jesus is making a declaration about sin, showing a shared responsibility for dealing with sin (Mark 2:10).

The scribes get it and complain to themselves. "This one" forgives sin. The scribes' fundamental task was to copy the sacred texts, not just to render judgment about them (TDNT 1:740-42). The great amount of time they spent with the sacred texts helped to qualify them for making judgments about the Law. The judgment they make appears to be theologically correct; only God has the power to forgive sin (Ps 51:1-3; 85:2). It introduces the tension of the scene. It also shows they are skeptical about Jesus; they are opponents from their opening appearance. These are private thoughts, but Jesus will sense them. It is common in the Gospels when one thinks

---

[76] Guelich, *Mark 1:1–8:26*, 86.

[77] France, *Mark*, 125. Stein, *Mark*, 119, notes nothing here or in Luke 5:17–26 or 7:36–50 goes in the direction of creating a distance for Jesus' claim that points only to God.

privately that Jesus will confront those thoughts (Mark 2:8; 8:16–1; 9:33; Luke 7:36–39). By speaking of the "one" God, they underline the uniqueness of God's authority as they make the complaint (Deut 6:4).

Something about the way Jesus expressed this forgiveness indicated that he was claiming to be more than a healer or prophet. In their view, Jesus was not honoring God, but slandering him by making such claims. Blasphemy is dishonoring or slandering someone, usually through arrogant or disrespectful speech against them (BDAG 178; Lev 24:10–16). It was an usurping of God's honor. In Jewish culture, blasphemy could also spill over into disrespectful acts.[78] Later Jesus traded charges of blasphemy with the teachers of religious law (Mark 3:22); he was convicted of blasphemy at his examination (Mark 14:63–64), and the people blasphemed Jesus while he was on the cross (Mark 5:29–30).

Jesus responds to the challenging reaction to his claim to forgive sins by asking why they are responding this way and dialoging in their hearts about what he has said (v 8). This insight into the internal response of the scribes points to the fact that Jesus has exceptional perception, adding to the portrait that here is someone most unusual. At the least, God is seen to have given him exceptional insight. However, more likely is an innate ability in Jesus, as the reference to his spirit points to his own insight. Other texts also point to such exceptional perception (John 2:25; 4:16–19; Mark 5:30; 12:15; 14:18–21; Luke 7:36–40).[79]

Jesus poses a question about what is easier to say when the issue is a problem of appearance versus verification (v 9). Is it easier to say your sins are forgiven or to tell the paralytic to take up his mat and walk? At the level of appearance, to say "take up your mat" is more difficult, for then the healing has to take place. Its success or failure is obvious. It is easy from appearance's sake to say your sins are forgiven because that cannot be seen or verified by the words alone. On the other hand, miracles are common, whereas human declarations of forgiveness are not. So the real issue is not one of appearance but of genuine authority. To have the authority to forgive sins is not extended to all. Only God has such authority. Jesus claims this prerogative is extended to the Son of Man (v 10). To show it, he will tell the paralytic to take up his mat (v 11). The observable healing linked to the unseeable claim will verify it as a sign, an indicator that God has

---

[78]   Darrell Bock, *Blasphemy and Exaltation in Judaism and the Final Examination of Jesus* (Tübingen: Mohr/Siebeck, 1998), 30–112.

[79]   Marcus, *Mark 1–8*, 217, calls this clairvoyant power.

given this authority to the Son of Man.[80] The question sets up a connection that Jesus makes in Mark 2:10. Jesus did not back off from the dispute; he wished to engage them on this controversial point and affirm his authority to do these things.

So Jesus tells the paralytic to take up his mat and walk. Some see a parenthesis in the entire verse here.[81] That reading is certainly possible, but the real break in thought is not in the "in order that" remark, but rather in the aside that has "he said" in it. The syntax here is clumsy; and if the remark is Mark's, all he would be doing is making explicit what is implicit in the event. However, the event can make sense as coming from Jesus, and the fact that the "Son of Man" is an expression elsewhere reserved for Jesus' own speech points to the utterance being his.[82] This is the first of fourteen Markan Son of Man sayings, and everywhere else it is Jesus who speaks. Mark may be alluding to these kinds of statements in Exodus (Exodus 8:22; 9:14).[83]

Mark 2:10 is the key pronouncement of the unit. It is what makes the scene a combination of a pronouncement account and a healing. The theology of the event is summarized here – God has given authority to the Son of Man to forgive sin. The new era has come.

This saying and Mark 2:28 are the only Son of Man passages that come before the confession at Caesarea Philippi. These two sayings are important, as both deal with divine authority (over sin and Sabbath). The *hina* clause could even be an imperative: "Know that. . . ." The "you may know" is expressed to the crowd, and then comes a shift of attention back to the scene and the paralytic. The paralytic gets what he came for, healing, plus the forgiveness of sins.

Healing can be seen, but forgiveness cannot be seen. Jesus said that his healing of the paralytic would make evident the truth of his claims about forgiveness. If God worked through him in healing, then these claims would be vindicated. Jesus' action also shows a total restoration as both

[80] Marcus, *Mark 1–8*, 217–18, seems to miss the point of contrast in arguing that the logic of the contrast is flawed. He makes it a lesser-to-greater argument, but it is really a seen-pointing-to-an-unseen argument.

[81] Witherington, *Mark*, 117, who notes parenthetical remarks in Mark 2:15, 28; 7:3–4, 19; 13:14; also Lane, *Mark*, 97.

[82] Guelich, *Mark 1:1–8:26*, 91. See also Stein *Mark*, 120, n. 9, who notes that if it were a parenthetical remark, it would have two breaks on top of each other, which he sees as unlikely, since "he says" is also a break.

[83] Marcus, *Mark 1–8*, 218.

healing and forgiveness take place. Again, Jesus came to do more than heal, a major opening Markan theme.

Beyond this text, the background to the Son of Man usage is important. The Son of Man is Jesus' favorite way to refer to himself. It is an idiom, meaning a human being, as well as a title in Daniel 7:13–14, picturing a human who rides on or with the clouds up to the Ancient of Days. So its usage here is ambiguous, as it can simply mean "I," and its OT connection might have become clear only later. Still, only transcendent beings ride the clouds in the OT and in the Ancient Near East (of God: Num 10:34; Deut 33:26; Ps 68:4, 33; 104:3; Isa 19:1).[84] So ultimately the term highlights humanity and transcendence in one expression. The use as a title is not clear as Jesus begins to use it, but his repeated use and later linkage to Daniel will show that is how he is using the term, along with the consistent rendering in the NT that this is "the" Son of Man (with the article present). By the time Mark's readers read it, the term would have had full force. The Son of Man has authority to forgive sin. Understanding who this figure is removes any objection one might raise. The suggestion that Jesus is claiming a general authority over people is certainly misguided. It is not a general ability that Jesus is demonstrating, but one particular to himself.[85] As Collins notes, Jesus is presented as a "fully authorized agent of God."[86]

So Jesus tells the paralytic to get up and go to his house. Jesus' word is enough. Nothing else intervenes. The man "was raised," indicating that the healing took place from outside himself (v 12). God had acted through Jesus. As the former paralytic departs with his mat in hand, everyone is

---

[84]   Baal was often characterized as a rider of the clouds. See Keilalphabetische Texte aus Ugarit, KTU 1.19: I: 38–46; KTU 1.2: IV:7–9; KTU 1.3: III:37–38.

[85]   Hooker, *Mark*, 87, surely has this correct, but her hesitation to connect this saying to Jesus rather than having it reside in the early church is not necessary. Something in Jesus' ministry likely precipitated the conviction that Jesus came to deal with sin. The arrival of the kingdom after a call to repent would push in this direction. All of it assumes a cleansing Jesus offers. Also, the early church normally tied the forgiveness of sins to Jesus' death, not as a category independent of it. See Guelich, *Mark 1:1–8:26*, 93, but he is wrong to say this is the only place where Jesus personally forgives sin in the Gospel tradition, as Luke 7:47–50 shows not only another text, but also one from another source (L), pointing to multiple attestation for the theme. It is the only place the Son of Man does this. Lane, *Mark*, 98, has expressed the uniqueness of sin and Son of Man correctly.

[86]   Collins, *Mark*, 187, but the idea that the saying is post-Easter because it is specific (188–89) is unlikely, as it is Jesus' usage of the title/idiom, even in Aramaic, that generates the specific use of "the" Son of Man. The church does not generate independent Son of Man sayings, as it never uses the title on its own. This peculiarity likely points to a particular practice in which Jesus' exclusivity of use is honored and preserved.

amazed, and they give glory to God, noting that they had not seen anything like this (Mark 1:27; 4:41; Isa 64:4). As the man walks, the declaration is not only of a healing, but also of the Son of Man's authority to forgive sin. Jesus' work is about more than healing. A new era is dawning (Isa 35:6; Jer 31:8). The open ending of the crowd's reaction invites the reader to contemplate what is taking place.

Unlike the act with the leper, this event is public, and all who see it are to contemplate what has just happened. The crowd is amazed and grateful. They glorify God. God does not work through sinners, so something must be going on. The theme of the controversy between Jesus as blasphemer or as divine agent with divine prerogatives will remain throughout Mark, as it will be the climactic issue in Mark 14 when the Jewish leadership decides Jesus is to be taken to Pilate. The first controversy in Mark will also be the last controversy. These are the two options about what to make of Jesus. Mark's choice is clear.

2:13–17 Controversy 2 – Associations: The Kingdom of God for Those in Need

2:13 **He went out again beside the sea, and an entire crowd came to him, and he was teaching them.**

2:14 **And as he was passing by he saw Levi, son of Alphaeus, seated at the tax booth, and he said to him, "Follow me." And arising, he followed him.**

2:15 **And as he reclined in his house, many tax collectors and sinners were reclining with Jesus and his disciples, for there were many who followed him.**

2:16 **And when the scribes of the Pharisees saw he was eating with sinners and tax collectors, they were saying to his disciples, "Why does he eat with tax collectors and sinners?"**

2:17 **When Jesus heard this, he said to them, "Those who are well do not have need of a physician, but those who are sick. I have not come to call the righteous but sinners."**

This scene is another call account tied to a pronouncement about Jesus' associations that might have made him appear impious. It opens with a summary. Mark notes that Jesus went out by the sea and the crowds were coming to Jesus to hear him teach (**v** 13). There is nothing symbolic in the mention of the sea because this is where he regularly ministered. As Jesus continued to move in (**v** 14), he passed a tax booth with Levi present. Herod Antipas would have controlled these sites. This booth was likely in

Capernaum. Jesus calls the tax collector to follow him, and Levi leaves the booth to follow Jesus. The calling of a tax collector is important, for they were seen very negatively in the culture. Later tradition compared them to murderers and robbers to whom one could lie without any sense of guilt (*m. Ned* 3:4). They were said to render a house unclean (*m. Teh* 7:6; *m. Hag* 3:6). Collecting taxes for Rome was not popular with Jews. Collecting these taxes would have been bid for by the collectors, who paid the state for the right to collect the taxes. A surcharge was added for the collector. These would have been usage taxes, more like tolls (sales, customs, and road taxes), but abuse was common in making the surcharges.[87] This was seen as supporting the foreign Gentiles in their land. Despite this, Jesus welcomes such a person to his entourage.

Levi may be the same person as Matthew, with Levi as his second name, as was common in Jewish contexts (Matt 9:9-13).[88] Levi is not mentioned anywhere else in the NT except in this list and Luke 5:27, the parallel to this account. There is a James, son of Alphaeus, in Mark 3:18; Matt 10:3; Luke 6:13; and Acts 1:13. Acts 1:13 is the list of the eleven and Matthew comes before James, son of Alphaeus, suggesting they may be brothers. Because Luke and Acts are part of the same author's listings, a Levi-Matthew identification is likely, although the naming of James tied to Alphaeus in lists of the Twelve without Levi complicates this explanation. Matthew 9 and Luke 5 lack references to Alphaeus. Levi follows Jesus immediately, just as Peter, Andrews, James, and John did in Mark 1:16-20. He leaves what he is doing behind to follow Jesus. Jesus is now the priority.

The scene switches to Levi's house where Jesus reclines to eat a formal meal with many followers present (**v 15**).[89] It introduces a controversy account that ends in a pronouncement that is the key to the passage.

Reclining is how one ate a formal meal in the ancient world, as one would lay back and lean forward on an arm and side to eat the meal, with pillows for support. Three times in two verses the phrase "tax collectors and sinners" appears, with sinners coming first only the second time. When a text was read out loud in the ancient world, as it usually was, this repetition

---

[87] This would have included fish; Lane, *Mark*, 102. For details on tax and toll collection, J. R. Donahue, "Tax Collectors and Sinners: An Attempt at Identification," *CBQ* 33 (1971): 39-61.

[88] Lane, *Mark*, 100-101. Some disagree; see Guelich, *Mark 1:1-8:26*, 99-100.

[89] The case for this being Levi's house is that Jesus did not seem to have his own home; Luke 5:29 appears to take it this way, and the likely fear of defilement is something that would have been a concern in Levi's home.

would stand out. Jesus' associations are the point. The combination is common in the NT (Matt 9:10–11; 11:19; Luke 5:30; 7:34; 15:1). Tax collectors were seen as sinners, as was already noted, but others with a reputation beyond the tax collectors likely were present (*m. Sanh* 3:3). Jesus had many followers from the group. Grace had drawn them, if Levi's call is a picture of what is taking place in the mention of many following him, an expression that is always positive in its eighteen uses in Mark (Mark 1:17–18; 3:7; 5:24; 6:1; 8:34; 9:38; 10:21, 28, 32, 52; 11:9; 15:41).[90] At the least, the group at the meal is open to his message. So Jesus is available to them.

However, the scribes of the Pharisees complain (**v 16**). This is the first mention of the Pharisees, but scribes have questioned Jesus in Mark 2:6 (also noted in Mark 1:22). A Pharisee was a "separated one," so the name is the issue here. Josephus discusses them in his section of the Jewish parties in *Antiquities* 18.12–15. These scribes copied, studied, and were concerned that the Law be kept properly. Scribes could be Sadducees or Pharisees, but here it is the Pharisees who are in view. Acts 23:9 looks to scribes of the Pharisees as well. Sadducean activity is mostly confined to Judea in the Gospels. These scribes ask his disciples why Jesus eats with tax collectors and sinners. In their view, the pious are to separate from sinners and not recline with them at table, an act that communicates intimacy and acceptance. Their objection could be that their food was not properly tithed (Deut 14:22; Matt 23:23) or prepared with proper attention to purity (Mark 7:1–8), or there may have been other issues related to cleanliness (*m. Hagigah* 2:7).[91] Or the term could be merely moral with no issues of defilement in view. NT scholars debate whether the term refers to the ritually impure (also called the "people of the land") or to the wicked.[92] Either way Jesus' action is seen as inappropriate for a man claiming to represent God and his new era (*m. Demai* 2:2–3). Of course, the forgiveness Jesus had already shown he could give in Mark 2:1–12 is also a factor in this scene.

Mark 2:17 is the pronouncement that drives the passage. It has two parts: a proverb and then a mission statement. Jesus responds to the challenge of his associations with a picture. The primary responsibility of a doctor

---

[90] Stein, *Mark*, 129.

[91] Hooker, *Mark*, 96; Marcus, *Mark 1–8*, 227.

[92] For the discussion, see E. P. Sanders, *Jesus and Judaism* (Philadelphia: Fortress, 1985), 174–211. Sanders argues for the wicked, but this may make too much of a technical term of the expression, just as people of the land may err in the other direction. Whether those present were unconcerned with the Law or notoriously wicked, the reaction to them would have been the same.

involves not treating those who are well, but rather those who are sick. This is a common proverb in the ancient world (Plutarch, *Apophthegmata Laconica* 230–31F – "The physicians he said are not to be found among the well but customarily spend their time among the sick"; Dio Chrysostom, *Orations*, 8.5 – speaks of a doctor going among the sick as a wise man must mix with fools; *Mekilta* to Exod 15:26 – "If they are not sick, why do they need a physician?").[93] In the OT, God is the healer when it comes to the soul and sin (Exod 15:26), so Jesus appears to take on another divine prerogative here (Philo, *Sacrifices of Abel and Cain* 70 calls God "the only doctor for sicknesses of the soul").[94]

Jesus' mission statement follows. He has come to call sinners, not the righteous. Those who sense their need to return to God are who he pursues. Jesus' kingdom message with the call to repent is the goal of the call (Mark 1:14–15).

The remark is rhetorical in the sense that he is not calling the Pharisees righteous, but he is speaking from the standpoint of awareness of need.[95] There is irony here that the "righteous" do not sense their need. There also is the likelihood we have a dialectical negation where the idea is that one gives more attention to one thing over the other. So sinners are a priority over the righteous. Jesus cites Hosea 6:6, which says God desires mercy not sacrifice. The point is that mercy comes first over sacrifice. This is another example of this rhetorical expression. The remark points back to Mark 2:7 and 10. Sinners who see their need come in repentance and faith. Mark 10:45 about offering his life as a ransom for many is the only other mission statement Mark has after this (Mark 1:38–39; "I came" sayings: Matt 5:17; 10:34–35; Luke 12:49; 19:10). How sin is dealt with awaits Mark 14:24.

Jesus' ministry takes the initiative with sinners. Luke 15 is a parallel from another source (L), pointing to the criteria of multiple attestation for this theme. Although many were grateful for sinners coming to God and this was sought by all those who sought to serve God, Jesus' taking the initiative in this regard brought an emphasis that clashed with the call to be completely separate. That extensive separation is what Jesus challenges here. One can live distinctly and righteously without completing isolating oneself from those who need to reconnect with God.

---

93 Collins, *Mark*, 195–96, has other examples from the Greco-Roman context.
94 Marcus, *Mark 1–8*, 228, 231.
95 Marcus, *Mark 1–8*, 228, speaks of those who think of themselves as righteous.

2:18–22 *Controversy 3 – A New Era Demands New Approaches*

2:18 Now the disciples of John and the Pharisees were fasting, and they came and said to him, "Why do the disciples of John and the disciples of the Pharisees fast, but your disciples do not fast?"

2:19 And Jesus said to them, "Can the wedding guests fast while the bridegroom is with them? As long as the bridegroom is with them, they cannot fast.

2:20 Days will come when the bridegroom is taken away from them. And then they will fast in that day.

2:21 No one sews a piece of unshrunk cloth on an old garment. If he does, the fullness of the new tears away from the old, and a worse tear comes.

2:22 And no one puts new wine into old wineskins. If he does, the wine bursts the skins, and the wine and wineskins are destroyed. But new wine is for fresh wineskins."

The third controversy scene also involves a pronouncement account. Here the issue is the distinct style of piety Jesus' disciples' display. Unlike John's disciples and the Pharisees who fasted regularly, Jesus' disciples do not (**v 18**). This is about voluntary fasting (Neh 9:1; Esth 9:31; Zech 7:5; 8:19 – later tradition tied the fourth-, fifth-, seventh-, and tenth-month fasts to the breaking of the tablets of the Law, destruction of the temple, murder of Gedaliah, and taking of Jerusalem by Babylon; *Pss Sol* 3:8). It is not about fasting tied to the Day of Atonement, the one required fast of the OT (Exod 20:10; Lev 16:1–34).[96] Some Pharisees fasted twice a week (Luke 18:12; *Didache* 8:1 notes this was on Monday and Thursday). These were dawn-to-sunset fasts and could be for a variety of things, such as mourning, repentance, illness, preparation for war, or other hard times. So the question comes from those concerned about why this is. They probably are not the Pharisees or John's disciples, as the third-person mention of those groups has the look of a question from outsiders. The question suggests Jesus is not pious enough.

A long pronouncement follows the query. The responses give a series of images that are the key to this text. Jesus explains that as long as the groom is present, it is a time for celebration, not mourning (**v 19**). The expression "sons of the wedding hall" can refer to the groom's attendants or all the guests, so either Jesus' key disciples or all who follow him. A broad reference is likely, as the issue is not just for those currently close to Jesus but for all associated with him, even though the question is about Jesus'

---

[96] Lane, *Mark*, 108, n. 57. Mishnah Ta'anith covers these fasts.

current disciples and their practice.[97] What Jesus says speaks to a general practice across the forming community. The same scope is present in the verses that follow, starting in Mark 2:21. When the groom is present, the wedding guests are not able to fast. The question here expects a negative reply. One does not fast at a wedding.

The wedding pictures the arrival of the new era (**v 20**). It also draws upon the picture of the people of God as married to him (Isa 54:4–8; 62:5; Ezek 16:7–14; Hos 2). John the Baptist is depicted using this image in John 3:29. Paul also uses this groomsman imagery in 2 Corinthians 11:2. There will be a time when the groom is removed; then they will fast. Jesus' presence was a special indication of divine presence and activity. Once again what is said of God is now applied to Jesus, although such expression was later tied to Messiah as God's representative (Isa 61:10; *Pesikta Rabbati* 149a; *Exodus Rabbah* 15 [79b] on Exod 12:2 speaks of a wedding taking place in the days of Messiah).[98] Of course, Jesus has yet to make messianic claims, so this is more a provocative claim about the time his presence represents in the arrival of the new era. This is a veiled remark in many ways. This situation meant it was a time for celebration and feasting, so that fasting was not appropriate. The point is that Jesus' ministry is a special time of joy. Later Jewish practice indicates that some religious obligations were not required of wedding celebrants (*b. Sukkah* 25b; living in booths was not required for celebrants of a wedding that took place during this feast).[99] Jesus' differentiation in practice differs from the fasting in Judaism and the early church for a limited time in the present. This hesitation to fast reflects a dissimilarity from both periods, which also points to the saying's authenticity based on a criterion of dissimilarity.

In terms of how the groom is removed, Jesus is not specific. Hooker argues this is a later addition on the premise that grooms are not taken away, but this is the common twist that often comes with Jesus' parables.[100] In addition, what has happened to John in being arrested (Mark 1:14) and the rise of opposition to him as these controversies show indicate that Jesus

---

97 France, *Mark*, 139, is right that the core point is the same no matter how narrow or broad the scope of the image is.

98 Lane, *Mark*, 110; Witherington, *Mark*, 124–25; Edwards, *Mark*, 90, n. 33.

99 Marcus, *Mark 1–8*, 233. No need to live in booths during a wedding is what *Sukkah* teaches.

100 Hooker, *Mark*, 99. Her appeal to *Thomas* 104 as lacking the problem with its remark that "when the bridegroom comes out of the bride-chamber" ignores the fact that that community, if it was Gnostic, had a rite known as the bridal chamber to which this may allude. She seems to defend the authenticity of Mark 2:19a.

is aware their message is not universally welcome.[101] The verb for removal can refer to violently being removed. Some see an allusion to Isaiah 53:8 here, but that is less than evident. Jesus' language points to rejection and removal but is not yet so clearly stated as to be a passion prediction per se.

At that time, when he is removed, things will change. They will fast then, a practice noted in Acts 13:2–3 and 14:23. The remark is cryptic and very indirect, another possible indication of authenticity.[102] It has an ambiguity the narrative resolves as being about Jesus' death, but it is very understated here. With Jesus departed, fasting will become appropriate again. The idea is not so much that Jesus is away in this period after his death as that all the groom came to bring is not yet realized, the world is still in need, and there is more to hope for in the future.[103] This is the first hint in the narrative that things will not go smoothly for Jesus. The apocalyptic backdrop to the remark may be indicated by a likely allusion to Amos 8:9–14.[104]

The answer also shows that Jesus is not against fasting. Context determines whether or not it is appropriate. There is a flexibility in how this is done that marks the "new way" Jesus brings. This final observation means that the supposed incongruity of what Jesus says here with what follows is more imagined than real.

Two pictures close the pronouncement. Each teaches one cannot mix the old and the new. The new era requires fresh packaging. Now that Jesus is here, fasting as an expression of repentance without the recognition of reasons for joy now that promise has come cannot work. However, this imagery looks to be broader in intent than merely treating fasting. The point is a general one, presenting the idea that a new era has different needs and style. Jesus is no add-on; he brings a new reality.

The two examples appeal to cloth and wine (**vv 21–22**). An old garment is not fixed with a new garment patch, and new wine needs new wineskins. The first example comes from the perspective of the need of the old garment, whereas the second points to the newness of the wine and its need for a proper container. New cloth is not to be tied to patch an old cloth. Nor is new wine to be placed in old wineskins. In both cases, if this is

---

[101] Edwards, *Mark*, 91.

[102] Lane, *Mark*, 111.

[103] Stein, *Mark*, 137–38, has a discussion about that day being only from death to resurrection, but that interpretation reads the remark too narrowly. Stein defends that interpretation by saying that the church did not believe Jesus was away, but although that is true, the issue is longing for and awaiting all that the Messiah came to bring, which has not yet taken place.

[104] Marcus, *Mark 1–8*, 234.

done, destruction results. The new cloth when it shrinks tears the worn old cloth. The old cloth is not helped. The new wine when it ferments rips the worn old wineskins. Everything, wine and wineskins, is lost. So Jesus states the new wine requires fresh wineskins. The end of the pronouncement is on the need of the new era. The point is that the new era leads to new realities and so to new practices, no matter how one looks at it.[105] A new era or dispensation is present.

Jesus' two illustrations (concerning the new patch and the new wine) show that one cannot simply fuse the message and person of Jesus to everything that Judaism had become. To do so would cause damage. Jesus asserted that something new also requires new ways.

2:23–28 Controversy 4 – *Plucking Grain and Authority over the Sabbath*

> 2:23 One Sabbath he was passing through the grain fields, and as they made their way, his disciples began to pluck heads of grain.
> 2:24 And the Pharisees were saying to him, "Look, why do they do what is not permitted on the Sabbath?"
> 2:25 And he said to them, "Have you never read what David did when he had need and hungered, he and those who were with him,
> 2:26 how they went into the house of God, in the period of Abiathar the high priest, and ate the bread of the Presence, which it is not lawful for anyone to eat except the priests, and he gave it also to those who were with him?"
> 2:27 And he was saying to them, "The Sabbath came for people, not people for the Sabbath.
> 2:28 So the Son of Man is Lord even of the Sabbath."

This controversy involves the Sabbath that again concludes with a key pronouncement. It is the first of two such Sabbath controversies in a row. The Sabbath ran from sunset Friday night to sunset Saturday night. This Jewish distinctive was important for Jewish identity, since it was a day of rest commanded by God that also was seen to mirror the creation (Gen 2:3; Exod 20:8–11 – the fourth commandment of the Ten Commandments; 34:21 – not to harvest; Lev 23:1–3; Deut 5:12–15; also the stricter CD 10:14–11:18 – could not assist a stranded animal or human or help an animal to give birth; *Jubilees* 2:17–33, verse 29 speaks of not preparing anything to be

---

[105]   *Thomas* 47 has the two illustrations in the reverse order.

eaten; 50:1–13). This was a more serious charge than the one in Mark 2:18, which dealt with voluntary fasting. Now the commandments were in view.

The Greek has Jesus and his disciples traveling and plucking grain (**v 23**), making a way, which likely has them passing through the fields as they pluck the grain. Certain areas of a field were reserved for travelers or foreigners (Deut 23:25), so taking the grain was not a problem. That grain was eatable means it likely is April or May, harvest season. It was the fact this was taking place on the Sabbath that was the issue. So the seeming violation was seen as a serious breach of piety. What constituted the violation was the plucking of grain on the Sabbath. This was perceived as a violation if *m. Shabbat* 7.2 is a guide. That text has the harvesting of grain as a violation, one of thirty-nine the passage notes. He who "sows, ploughs, reaps, binds sheaves, threshes or winnows" has violated the Sabbath according to this text. So when the Pharisees see or hear about the disciples plucking grain, they ask why the disciples do what the Law does not permit (**v 24**). We should not necessarily think the Pharisees are following the disciples around, so either this was a happenstance, as sometimes rabbis were in the fields on the Sabbath, or this is a response to something they knew the disciples had done.[106] Neither should we think the problem is how far the disciples walked on the Sabbath, as the key detail noted is the plucking of grain, which Jesus' reply also notes. Because Jesus as a teacher is responsible for his disciples' behavior, he is asked why they do this. As Marcus cites Seneca's remark from *Troades* 290, "He who forbids not sin when in control commands it."[107]

Given a question that challenges his disciples (**v 25**), Jesus responds with a question, just as he had in the previous controversy. The question then has a decisive pronouncement making two points following it.

Jesus appeals to the haggadic example of David and his men eating the bread of the presence (**v 26**; 1 Sam 21:1–6). David is explicitly said to eat in the 1 Samuel text, and that his men are included is likely implied from 1 Samuel 21:4–5, given that David asks for five loaves.[108] According to the strict reading of the law, neither David nor his men had right to this bread. This bread, consisting of twelve loaves a week, was reserved for the priests according to the Law (Lev 24:5–9; Exod 25:30). But Jesus also notes that

---

[106] Witherington, *Mark*, 129; especially, M. Casey, *Aramaic Sources of Mark's Gospel* (Cambridge: Cambridge University Press, 1998), 145–50.

[107] Marcus, *Mark 1–8*, 240.

[108] Marcus, *Mark 1–8*, 240–41, argues the men are not in view at all in 1 Samuel, calling the request for five loaves a trick by David.

David and his men had need and were hungry. So they ate. The assumption appears to be this need, and hunger meant that the Law need not be followed, but that is not explicitly said. The example also presumes that the lack of punishment to David and his men indicates God did not judge him for doing this. The key point is that what was done appeared to violate the Law and yet went unpunished by God. So when Jesus asks if they have not read this (Mark 12:10, 26), he is pointing to an example from Scripture that suggests the Law was not followed without exception, perhaps because another factor other than merely keeping the Law was more significant.[109] Jesus' mention of David's need and hunger suggests this additional feature of need to his argument, even though nothing similar is said of the disciples to explain their action. The question expects a positive reply, meaning Jesus knows they are aware of the event.

It may be implied that Jesus is one like or greater than David, but again this is left unstated and to be inferred at best. This connection is something, however, that is quite possible given how Jesus ends his pronouncement by pointing to the authority of the Son of Man over the Sabbath and the tie of David to the one who comes to ultimately deliver (Jer 23:5). What we clearly have here is a simple example from Scripture that shows a case where the Law is not followed to the letter, even if how this works exactly is left unexplained.

Now this Davidic event is not explicitly placed on the Sabbath according to Scripture, but was seen as such in Jewish tradition (*b. Menahot* 95b; *Yalqut Shim'oni* 2.130).[110] So it may be Jesus is citing a parallel kind of situation versus a Sabbath violation unless the tradition is old.

The remark in verse 26 that this took place when Abiathar was high priest has generated much discussion and a textual issue, since Abiathar is not the high priest during the time of this event. No clear resolution exists. The Samuel text has Ahimelech, Abiathar's father, as the high priest at this

---

[109] There is some discussion about how rabbinic Jesus' argument is. Some note that it does not follow rabbinic tradition in that haggadah (a scriptural event or example) cannot establish halakah (ruling of the Law). This method of argumentation is said to have irritated those who questioned Jesus. D. M. Cohn-Sherbok, "An Analysis of Jesus' Arguments Concerning the Plucking of Grain on the Sabbath," *JSNT* 2 (1979): 31–41. If this is the argument, it may also be Jesus' point to show that the Law never was intended to be extended so far. The parallel in Matthew 12:7 that has Jesus argue that God desires mercy and not sacrifice points more explicitly in this direction. Matthew's account has the most detailed response of the parallels to this event.

[110] Witherington, *Mark*, 130; Hooker, *Mark*, 103–104, who notes *Midrash Rabbah Lev* 32.3 has the bread being that which was being removed at the end of its week-long time to be consumed. That act would come on a Sabbath (Lev 24:8).

time (1 Sam 21:1, 2, 8). Abiathar is first mentioned in 1 Samuel 22:20, so his appearance does take place in a near context. Matthew 12:4 and Luke 6:4 omit the detail in their parallels, as do D, W, and other manuscripts. Other manuscripts insert *tou* before the reference to the high priest giving the force of in the time of Abiathar (A, C, Θ, family 13).[111] Another option is to see the reference as a general literary reference to the section in Scripture, a kind of literary shorthand locator. So either an idiom or a literary reference may be in view. A final possibility is simply that of choosing the better-known figure Abiathar, who would have been associated with the temple at the time and later became high priest, so the compression works in this direction.[112] Any of these three options might be at work here.

Jesus next makes a two-part pronouncement (v 27). The fact that a fresh remark is made about his speaking to them makes one wonder if this was said right at the time or somewhat later. The multiple use of such a break in ideas in an otherwise unified context tells us we are to closely associate what we have here with what was just said (Mark 4:2b, 11, 21, 24, 26 – in texts on the kingdom). Either way it makes two key points: one about the Sabbath and one about who has authority over it. It also shows the argument here is taking another track from the David example.

On the one hand, the Sabbath was made for people, not people for the Sabbath (note the A, B, B, A pattern: Sabbath, people, people, Sabbath). The point here is that the Sabbath was designed to be something that serves people for their good, not something that is to hinder them. Only Mark has this remark. Why Matthew and Luke lack it is not clear.[113] Removing it allows a focus only on Christology. Mark's point is that the way the Sabbath was being excessively restricted meant that people were now serving the Sabbath. Now *Jubilees* 2:17 said the Sabbath was a "great sign" and seen as a gift to be enjoyed. The later *Mekilta Exodus* [109b] on

---

[111] Casey, *Aramaic Sources*, 151–52, who sees a lack of precision in the bilingual move from Aramaic to Greek; Lane, *Mark*, 116, especially n. 86. Mark 12:26 is sometimes cited as a grammatical parallel for a Scripture location marker, though the reference is closer to the verb for reading in that parallel than it is here. Edwards, *Mark*, 95, n. 42, sees confusion surrounding the genealogy of Abiathar and Ahimelech contributing to the problem, as it is unclear whether Ahimelech is the father or son of Abiathar and whether there is more than one person with such a name (1 Sam 22:20; 2 Sam 8:17; 1 Chron 18:16; 24:6). This reference to Abiathar simplifies that potential confusion, while pointing to the more well-known figure.

[112] This is noted by France, *Mark*, 146; discussed by J. D. M. Derrett, "Judaica in St. Mark," in *Studies in the New Testament* (Leiden: Brill, 1977), 1.91–92.

[113] Western witnesses to Mark also lack it, but there is no reason to see that as original to Mark. Unless it is original to Mark, it is hard to know how it got here at all.

Exodus 31:13–14 said the Sabbath "was delivered to you, not you to the Sabbath."[114] It frames this remark in terms that Israel had a privilege of observing the Sabbath. So the point Jesus is making is known; the debate is over how to apply it.

As a result (in light of all that has been said in verses 23–27),[115] the Son of Man came to puts things right and is doing so in his role as Lord, even of the Sabbath (v 28).[116] This is part of the "new things" the new era is doing. It is showing where the Law should take people in terms of the heart and need. As the sent representative for humanity commissioned by God, Jesus has the right to determine what is proper on the Sabbath. This fits the other divine prerogative claims of Mark's controversy section – to forgive sin, to be the healer of sin, and to be the groom. This argument is at a completely different level than the previous example. The example from David showed that sometimes the Law is not followed, but this particular case provides the why. Jesus has the right to determine what takes place on the Sabbath. Here is a claim to control the sacred calendar and a day God established and commanded be observed, for God is Lord of the Sabbath (Gen 2:3; Exod 16:25; 20:10; 31:12–17; Lev 23:3; Deut 5:14). Jesus is not on the side of the creature who is under a command to observe the Sabbath, but rather, as the representative of humanity acting on their behalf, is over it. Jesus puts himself in the position of not being subject to that day but of being over it.[117] It is a strong claim and serves as the ultimate answer to the controversy he was asked to address.

This is another claim to unique authority that Jesus is making. Beyond forgiveness of sins made earlier in Mark 2, now we have an assertion of Jesus' authority over a day God commands. The challenge involving a day as serious and uniquely Jewish as the Sabbath was bound to engender a strong reaction from those who rejected what Jesus claimed. Hooker summarizes

114 Guelich, *Mark 1:1–8:26*, 124. See also *b. Yoma* 85b; 2 Bar 14.18.

115 Lane, *Mark*, 120; contra Guelich, *Mark 1:1–8:26*, 125. The wider context is implied, as representation of humanity is tied to kingship.

116 Witherington, *Mark*, 131, rightly alludes back to the previous controversy as a narrative frame for this one.

117 Perhaps the argument of the whole is: just as David had a right to do something unusual for his men and himself, so even more does the Son of Man have that right. Yet this still seems to say too little. Jesus is not making an analogy or a mere regal claim as *m. Sanh* 2.4 makes for the king ("the king's road has no prescribed measure"), but is making a sweeping claim of authority because the divinely established Sabbath is involved. Even kings are subject to God (contra Collins, *Mark*, 205). It is "the" Son of Man who is lord. Edwards, *Mark*, 96–97, rightly calls it a Promethean pronouncement and emphasizes the "the." This is Mark's first use of the term *Lord*. It will become a key term later.

well, "If Jesus allows his disciples to continue to be 'irreligious,' that demonstrates not carelessness in respect of the Torah, but the freedom of one who is confident that he is doing God's will; and the justification for their action, offered in v. 27, is not merely the opinion of one Jewish rabbi over against that of others but is the authoritative statement of the Son of man."[118]

Some see a mistranslation here with the point being that man is lord over the Sabbath, but that is not the point Jesus is making. He is not speaking of a generic authority but of one unique to him. His use of Son of Man just for himself shows this.

The Sabbath was designed to refresh (Exod 23:12; Deut 5:14), but if simply picking stalks was food preparation, then something had gone wrong. No food was being prepared. It was simply being consumed, with only basic needs being met. The one with authority over the Sabbath was making this point.

3:1–6 Controversy 5 – Healing and Doing Good on the Sabbath

3:1 **Then Jesus went into the synagogue again. And a man was there with a withered hand.**

3:2 **And they were keeping a close watch on him to see if he would heal on the Sabbath, so that they could accuse him.**

3:3 **So he said to the man having the withered hand, "Stand up in the middle."**

3:4 **Then he said to them, "Is it permitted to do good on the Sabbath or evil, to save a life or destroy it?" But they were silent.**

3:5 **After looking around at them with anger, grieving at their hardness of heart, he said to the man, "Stretch out your hand." He stretched it out and his hand was restored.**

3:6 **So coming out the Pharisees immediately with the Herodians made a plot against him so they might destroy him.**

The final controversy account in this sequence is another combination healing and pronouncement account. The healing of the man with the withered hand on the Sabbath leads to a commitment to deal decisively with Jesus, to kill him.

With so many controversies behind him, Jesus is now being watched very closely. So this time, as Jesus comes into the synagogue (**v** 1), those opposed to him are watching Jesus closely to see if he will heal a man with a

---

[118]   Hooker, *Mark*, 105.

withered hand on the Sabbath (v 2). The man's hand was withered (*exērammenēn*) like a plant desiccated by drought (BDAG 684; 1 Kings 13:4). The result was paralysis. They sensed that Jesus would heal, as he had in the past. Sabbath healings are multiply attested phenomena in the Jesus tradition (Luke 13:10–17; 14:1–6; John 5:1–18; 7:23–24; 9:13–16).

Just as a miracle opened the controversy section in Mark 2:1–12, so will one close the section in an *inclusio*. They want to point out Jesus' Sabbath violation. The expression "on the Sabbath" is thrown forward in Greek, making it emphatic. The term for Sabbath is plural. They are now watching to see whether Jesus will repeat his Sabbath offense. Did the earlier rebuke take with Jesus or not? Ironically, this term for watching is used to describe the keeping of days in accordance with the law in Galatians 4:10 (also seen in Luke 6:7; 14:1; 20:20; Acts 9:24).[119] The hostility level has been raised by all that has taken place. Protection of the Sabbath as a Jewish distinctive was important. We do not have an explicit indication that healing was not permitted on the Sabbath in Jewish materials, but such acts were so infrequent that it is unlikely a ruling was needed or even generated. Luke 13:14 and John 9 attest to such a protest, which was likely instinctive to a scrupulous Jew, and this attitude is also multiply attested in the tradition. In addition, *m. Yoma* 8:6 speaks of permission to place medicine in a man's throat because one does not know if the condition is life threatening (see also *m. Shab* 14:3–4, which also implies the same thing).[120] The assumption appears to be that if the situation is not life threatening, nothing should be done on the Sabbath.

Jesus will continue to be watched (Mark 12:13, 18). The opponents are not named, but their familiarity and expectation that Jesus would act points to opposition from scribes and/or Pharisees, something confirmed in Mark 3:6 as they go out and make the plot with Herodians. The addition of Herodians shows that now religious and political leaders are watching what Jesus is doing. Everything in the scene points to an escalation of concern. Sabbath violators were to be killed (Exod 31:14–17; Num 15:32–36; *Jubilees* 2:25–27; *m. Sanh* 7:4), though enforcement was not always applied (CD 12:3–6; *m. Shab* 7:1, 8). The goal is to catch Jesus doing wrong based on a certain definition of Sabbath observance. The debate is not whether the Sabbath should be kept, but how.[121] The synagogue is likely in Capernaum, since he enters "the" synagogue again, but it could be anywhere in Galilee.

---

119   Marcus, *Mark 1–8*, 248, notes how this term appears in Josephus for closely observing the Sabbath; *Ag. Ap* 2.282; *Ant* 3.91; 14:262.
120   Collins, *Mark*, 206–207.
121   Hooker, *Mark*, 106.

Jesus begins the healing by speaking to the man and having him stand in the midst of the people in the synagogue (**v** 3). Jesus will act intentionally and quite publicly. He is quite aware of what some in the crowd are thinking, as in Mark 2:8–9. He asks the crowd a question full of irony (**v** 4). Is it proper to do good or evil on the Sabbath, to save a life or destroy it? The verb for destroy (*apokteinai*) refers to political execution in other texts in Mark (Mark 6:19; 8:31; 12:5; 14:1). Jesus is being challenged for doing good and bringing life back to the man. Meanwhile, those watching Jesus are on the edge of doing evil and seeking to destroy a life. Jesus knows even that.

The Sabbath dispute is getting in the way of judgment about how people can be served. The question is Jesus' challenge to the claim of Sabbath violation. He is forcing the issue. He does not allow the option of doing nothing on the Sabbath to exist.[122] To give a word that does good on the Sabbath is not working on the Sabbath. It is being to people what God calls people to be. The issue is not whether the man's condition is a life-or-death one, so that one can act on the Sabbath; the issue is doing that which helps another. Rather than trying to detect someone doing wrong, Jesus is trying to bring a fresh depth to another's life. The healing Jesus will bring will permit the man to go back to the temple, if he wishes to go to Jerusalem and attend. It will allow him to more fully engage with God and labor in life (Lev 21:16–20). It will remove any social limits the man has experienced because of his condition. For Jesus the act will require only a word and take but a second. For Jesus, that is not labor, but doing what is good and right before God. It would be morally wrong, even unjust, to refuse to act.[123] God is honored, and one in the creation is blessed, by what he is about to do. Jesus puts all of this on the table before he acts. Saving a life is not just about a physical healing, but is about helping the person have the means to live fully again. That should not wait until after the Sabbath.[124] Two things are at stake here – the halakic challenge about what takes place on the Sabbath and Jesus' authority to heal and judge what is taking place. The remarks yield only silence.

---

[122] Witherington, *Mark*, 135, calls Jesus an agent provocateur here.
[123] Edwards, *Mark*, 99.
[124] Though posed too much as an either/or by Guelich, *Mark 1:1–8:26*, 135–36, in terms of the issue not being about Sabbath Law but about Jesus' authority, he is correct to note that the way Jesus argues does point to his authority to make a judgment about what is required. Guelich's rejection that doing evil does not hint at what the leaders are about to plan is nothing short of curious.

So Jesus, angry and grieving at the hardness or callousness of the leaders (*pōrōsei* – BDAG 900), tells the man to stretch out his hand (**v 5**). Mark often notes Jesus' emotions (Mark 1:41). A word to stretch out the hand was Jesus' laborious act of love. As France says, "If this was 'work,' it was of a very nonphysical variety."[125] The man could move his now restored hand (Mark 8:25; 9:12). Jesus had done well on the Sabbath. The narration is totally focused on Jesus. The man has done nothing but be there, stand up, and stretch out his hand in response to Jesus.

The act leads the Pharisees and Herodians to decide they must stop Jesus (**v 6**). The Herodians are not otherwise attested outside of the NT (Mark 8:15; 12:130), but they likely are those loyal to the Roman vassal family that ruled in Galilee and Judea.[126] Political and religious leadership is gathering against Jesus. They decide they must destroy him (Mark 11:18; Luke 13:33; 19:47).

And so, five controversies into Jesus' ministry, the die for his death have been cast with the leaders. Forgiving sin, associating with sinners, challenging rabbinic custom, and especially being loose about the Sabbath have been too much.[127] The response is not about stoning Jesus, but about stopping him.[128] The conclusion to this unit with its opposition to Jesus contrasts with Mark 1:45.

3:7–6:6 JESUS IN GALILEE: JESUS TEACHES AND SHOWS HIS POWER

3:7–35 As Jesus Gathers Disciples and Ministers, Discussion Emerges about Who He Is

3:7–12 *Jesus Ministers in Galilee but Urges the Disciples Not Yet to Make Him Known*

> **3:7 And Jesus withdrew with his disciples to the sea, and a great multitude from Galilee followed him,**

---

125 France, *Mark*, 151.
126 Herod's supporters are mentioned in Josephus, *War* 1.319; *Ant* 14.450. H. H. Rowley, "The Herodians in the Gospels," *JTS* XLI (1940): 14–27; W. J. Bennett, Jr., "The Herodians of Mark's Gospel," *NovT* 17 (1975): 9–14, who argues unpersuasively that the category is Mark's creation. A family as powerful as the Herods surely had their supporters.
127 Edwards, *Mark*, 101–102.
128 Contra Collins, *Mark*, 210, who says it is historically unlikely the Pharisees were seeking a death penalty against Jesus. This response was not about how to apply the Jewish law to blasphemy, but how to stop Jesus and the growing attention he was drawing. It also was not just a reaction to this one event but rather to the sequence of things Jesus was doing.

3:8 and from Judea, Jerusalem, Idumea, beyond the Jordan River, and around Tyre and Sidon a great multitude came to him to hear the things he had done.

3:9 And he said to his disciples to have a small boat prepared for him because of the crowd so that they would not press against him.

3:10 For he healed many, so that they pressed upon him that those with diseases might touch him.

3:11 And when the unclean spirits were seeing him, they were falling before him and crying out saying, "You are the Son of God."

3:12 And he sternly warned them not to make him known.

This summary section running through Mark 3:12 is one of the few sections unique to Mark in the Gospel. It is a ministry summary. Jesus withdrew to the sea. He was preparing to organize as the next passage on the calling of the Twelve shows. Jesus was drawing a great deal of attention, not just in Galilee. People were coming to him from the regions surrounding Galilee (vv 7–8) – north, south, east, and west. These included some regions that are outside Israel and Judaism, places like Tyre and Sidon, Idumea (= Edom, south of Judea, the Negev), and the area east of the Jordan (= Perea). Only Samaria and the Decapolis are not noted. Jesus' activity was drawing them (Mark 1:44).

The crowds were pressing against him to touch him for healing from an array of conditions (vv 9–10). The term *mastigas* (diseases) is vivid, referring to a whip or lash, and points to the torment of disease (BDAG 620). Their desire to touch him reflects cultural ideas tied to the ancient world and popular religion (Mark 5:27–31; 6:56; 7:37; Acts 5:15–16; 91:11–12). Healing was still a major reason people were drawn to him. The crush of people was great. The language here is vivid. People "were falling" to get to and touch Jesus. Touch is often tied to healing (Mark 1:40–45; 5:27–28; 6:56; 7:31–37; 8:22–26). The press is creating a mess. So Jesus asked for a boat to be ready to prevent the pressure (like Mark 1:45; 2:2–4).[129] From here on the edge of the sea, he could heal *and* teach (Mark 4:1–2). This is yet another indication from Mark, along with the description of the scene, that Jesus was about more than healing.

Some of this involved healing (v 10), and some of it involved exorcism (v 11). It is not clear that this scene involves only exorcisms. The term for torment in Mark 5:29 and 36 is of a condition of hemorrhaging and looks

---

[129] The diminutive for boat, normally meaning "little boat," is used. However, Mark uses the diminutive often enough (Mark 5:23, 39, 41; 6:9; 7:25, 27, 28; 8:7; 14:47) that one cannot be sure the boat's size is the point.

like a mere healing. Some appeal to a "divine man" perspective with reference to Jesus here. However, this conclusion has been challenged. Such a claim ignores the Jewish context of the event, and, even more problematically, there is a real question about whether the divine man construct is a genuine ancient category versus a modern composite portrait.[130] Jesus' healings involving touch have ample precedent in the depictions of prophets in the Old Testament, except there, in two of the examples, it is the prophet who takes the initiative to touch (2 Kings 13:21; 1 Kings 17:21; 2 Kings 4:34). So these miracles say more about how people approached Jesus than about what Jesus is seeking to communicate through his healing.

The unclean spirits that are exorcised are not silent as they fall before and confess him to be the Son of God (vv 11–12). The imperfect verbs point to the repetition of these acts, a series of such encounters. The naming is not about controlling Jesus by identifying him, since in this case they bow before him and recognize his authority.[131] This confession of sonship comes in the heading of the Gospel (Mark 1:1), the voice from heaven at the baptism and Transfiguration (Mark 1:11; 9:7), and the centurion at the cross (Mark 15:39). Jesus refers to himself as Son (Mark 13:32) and the High Priest will ask Jesus if he is the Son of the Most High (Mark 14:61). Demons confess him as the "Holy One of God" (Mark 1:24) and "Son of the Most High" (Mark 5:7) and know who he is (Mark 1:34). So this is an accurate description that is silenced.

Jesus sternly warns them to be silent. This is yet another Markan text where Jesus hesitates to have declared who he is until an appropriate time, in part because it could be misunderstood and cause more chaos than he is already facing in handling the crowds.[132] It repeats and intensifies Mark 1:32–34.[133] Jesus' actions and teaching are building a résumé to have people

---

[130]   Guelich, *Mark 1:1–8:26*, 147–48; Edwards, Mark, 105–109; O. Betz, "The Concept of the So-Called 'Divine Man,'" in *Studies in New Testament and Early Christian Literature*, FS A. P. Wikgren, ed. D. Aune (Leiden: Brill, 1972), 229–40; J. Kingsbury, "The 'Divine Man' as the Key to Mark's Christology – The End of an Era?" *Int* 35 (1981) 243–57; Barry Blackburn, *Theios Aner and the Markan Miracle Traditions: A Critique of the Theios Aner Concept as in Interpretative Background of the Miracle Tradition* (Tübingen: Mohr/Siebeck, 1990).

[131]   Edwards, *Mark*, 104, correctly calls this a "no contest" event. There is no hint of a power struggle here. He notes that Mark 3:27 with the house of evil being plundered is set up by this event.

[132]   Stein, *Mark*, 165, although his questioning that appropriate timing is not involved is curious, as Jesus will be public about who he is in the last week of his ministry.

[133]   Collins, *Mark*, 213.

consider who he is. He prefers it to emerge that way than from random declarations. There also is the risk of this all being misunderstood unless he is able to show in what sense he will be this figure. So there is a time to have such a confession, but it is not now. In addition, to have demons confess him is not the best kind of endorsement to receive, even though Mark does make use of it here. Mark does so because the reader knows more about Jesus now than those present would have known when the confessions were made. To them, without much context for Jesus, the confessions may have seemed bizarre.

The early disclosure does give Mark the opportunity to point to the awareness that transcendent forces have of who Jesus is. Humans want healing, but the demons know who Jesus is. That this naming of Jesus and his authority is the emphasis is clear because Mark does not even note that exorcisms actually took place here, although that surely is the case. It is Jesus' authority over them that is being highlighted. Demons will not thwart the program nor dictate the terms of how it is revealed. So they are not to make known who he is. Disclosure is to take place in other ways on Jesus' terms.

3:13–19 Jesus Calls the Twelve

> **3:13 Now Jesus went up to the mountain and called those he wanted, and they came out to him.**
> **3:14 And he made twelve, whom he named apostles,[134] so that they might be with him and he might send them to preach**
> **3:15 and to have authority to cast out demons.**
> **3:16 And he made the twelve[135]: He gave a name to Simon, Peter; to James and his brother John, the Sons of Zebedee, he gave the name Boanerges (that is, "sons of Thunder"); and Andrew, Philip, Bartholomew, Matthew, Thomas, James the son of Alphaeus, Thaddaeus, Simon the Canaanite, and Judas Iscariot, who betrayed him.**

This is a commissioning scene. Jesus now gathers followers to himself who will aid him in the task of preaching the kingdom. He calls or appoints

---

[134] A text-critical issue involves the word order of the Greek in this verse, but it does not impact the verses tying a reference of the Twelve to the role of apostle. Luke 6:13 might explain some of the phrase, but on the whole inclusion is more likely. Metzger, *Textual Commentary* (1994), 69.

[135] The presence of this phrase saying Jesus made the Twelve is textually disputed. Its inclusion, however, is widely attested. Metzger, *Textual Commentary* (1994), 69.

twelve to the mountain (**v 13**), a number that recalls the twelve tribes of Israel. Literally the text says he "made" twelve (**v 14**), but an idiom of appointment likely is present (1 Kgdms 12:6; 3 Kdgms 12:31; 13:33 LXX). Still, given what has been taking place, the idea is that Jesus is doing something fresh. As the nation's leaders are rejecting him, Jesus forms his own community and makes a fresh claim on the nation.[136] Within Israel, a picture of restoring Israel emerges (Matt 19:28; Luke 22:28–30; Isa. 49:6; Ezek. 45:8; Sir. 36:10; 48:10; *Pss. Sol.* 17:26–32; *Sib. Or.* 2.170–76; *T. Jos.* 19:1–7; Josephus, *Ant.* 11.133).[137] The mountain is likely more like a hillside in Israel, but the idea "he went up to a mountain" might allude to a place of revelation or disclosure, like Sinai (Exod 19:3; 24:1–4; Num 27:12; Deut 9:9).[138] He calls them apostles, which refers to ones sent. Some translations and the Greek text place this phrase on naming them apostles in brackets because it looks like Luke 6:13, but key mss (א, B) have it, making it look original.[139] These are commissioned messengers who really know him. They are to be with him and preach the message as those who really know what the message is because of the time spent with Jesus (Mark 1:14–15). They also are given authority to cast out demons (**v 15**). Jesus extends his power to others to underscore the credibility of his newly arrived message (Mark 1:39). The authority is not automatic, as the failure to heal in Mark 9:14–29 shows. The ability to do this points to the new age, especially if it is a bestowed ability, as that points to a hub figure for the eschaton (*T.* Levi 18:12). They also will heal (Mark 6:12–13).

Mark lists out the Twelve and likely repeats the reference as he resumes the list to underscore the number (**vv 16ff**).[140] These lists in the Gospels always start with Peter and end with Judas (Matt 10:2–4; Luke 6:14–16; Acts 1:13). The sons of Zebedee (James and John) always follow Peter. Most of

---

[136] Hooker, *Mark*, 111; Scot McKnight, "Jesus and the Twelve," in *Key Events in the Life of the Historical Jesus: A Collaborative Exploration of Context and Coherence*, ed. Darrell L. Bock and Robert L. Webb (Tübingen: Mohr/Siebeck, 2009), 181–214, has a full discussion of the Twelve in Jesus' ministry; Marcus, *Mark 1–8*, 262–63 defends their historicity as Judas' presence evokes the criterion of embarrassment and the consistent names, despite some of them not being mentioned later, points to the same likelihood.

[137] This is not a replacement for Israel in the sense that Israel falls out of God's plan. So, carefully, Guelich, *Mark 1:1–8:26*, 158. Witherington, *Mark*, 151, on eschatological restoration.

[138] Guelich, *Mark 1:1–8:26*, 156, challenges this, saying no revelation takes place, but a key salvation historical act is present.

[139] Metzger, *Textual Commentary* (1994), 69.

[140] External evidence favors inclusion. A sense it was repetitious likely led to its scribal excision.

the passage consists of the list of twelve names, given with little elaboration. This appears to assume the list is well known.

Simon is first. To show a new way and life, Simon gets a new name, Peter, which in Aramaic means "stone" or "rock." Simon was a most common name, whereas Peter was very rare, being unattested before Jesus' time.[141] John 1:42 and Matthew 16:17–18 detail this name change, one on an early scene, another later. Mark makes nothing of it except from here on Peter is the name Mark uses with one exception (Mark 14:37). Peter is seen to have a key role among the apostles.

John and James receive a second name (v 17), Boanerges or "sons of thunder." The fact that one name is shared with two brothers points to a nickname, and so is likely a word play of some type. No reason for the name is given, but it may reflect their temperament (Mark 9:38; 10:35–40; Luke 9:54). It is not a direct transliteration or translation. Nothing is made of it elsewhere, giving the detail a feel of authenticity, embedded in an old tradition.

There is very little said about the rest of the list (v 18). Andrew is Peter's brother (Mark 1:16–18; John 1:40–42, 44). Philip is mentioned in John 6:5, 12:21, and 14:8. Matthew the tax collector (Matt 10:3) and Simon the Cananean are likely on opposite sides of the spectrum in terms of their views, since a word play on Cananean means zealot.[142] One is collecting and working for Rome; the other is wanting them out. This shows the scope of Jesus' group. Bartholomew is a Greek form of an Aramiac surname, "son of Talmai." Thomas is unnamed outside of the lists and his presence in John's Gospel (John 11:16; 14:5; 20:24, 21:2; 26:29). James, son of Alphaeus, recalls Levi, son of Alphaeus, in Mark 2:14, but is a distinct person. In Luke's listing, Judas, son of James, is listed, whereas Thaddaeus is listed here (Luke 6:14–16; Acts 1:13). The difference may reflect two names for one person, as was common (e.g., Saul, Paul; Simon, Peter). The several different people named James requires some way to differentiate them all.

Judas is always noted last as the betrayer in these lists (v 19). Iscariot likely means "of Kerioth." The fact we know so little about so many of these figures suggests that this is a genuine tradition, since so little is made of so many of the names here elsewhere (Bartholomew; James, son of Alphaeus;

---

[141] Joseph, Fitzmyer, "Aramaic Kepha' and Peter's Name in the New Testament," in his *To Advance the Gospel* (Chestnut Ridge, NY: Crossroad, 1981), 112–24.
[142] On Matthew and Levi, see Mark 2:14 discussion. On Canaanite as a word play to zealot, not the later Jewish sect, Collins, *Mark*, 222–23.

Thaddaeus; Simon the Zealot). This is a known group, multiply attested in the tradition (1 Cor 15:5). It is a very diverse group of very common people. The Twelve Jesus trained came not from elites or religious professionals but from everyday life.

3:20–35 Debate over the Source of Jesus' Power and the Concerns of his Family

3:20 Jesus went into a home. And again the crowd gathered so he and the Twelve were not able to eat a meal.

3:21 When his people heard, they set out to seize him. For they said, "he was out of his mind."

3:22 And the scribes who came down from Jerusalem were saying, "He is possessed by Beelzebul and by the ruler of the demons he casts out demons."

3:23 So he called them and was saying in parables to them, "How is Satan able to cast out Satan?

3:24 If a kingdom is divided against itself, that kingdom is not able to stand.

3:25 And if a house is divided against itself, that house is not able to stand.

3:26 And if Satan rises up against himself, he is not able to stand but has come to an end.

3:27 But no one is able to enter a strong man's house and steal his property, if he does not first bind the strong man. Then he completely plunders his house.

3:28 Truly I say to you that every sin the sons of men commit will be forgiven, even whatever blasphemies they utter.

3:29 But whoever blasphemies against the Holy Spirit will never be forgiven, but are guilty of an eternal sin."

3:30 For they were saying, "he has an unclean spirit."

3:31 Then his mother and his brothers came. Standing outside, they sent word to him, to summon him.

3:32 And the crowd was sitting around him and was saying to him, "Look, your mother and your brothers and your sisters[143] are outside seeking you."

---

[143] This phrase including "sisters" is well enough attested, and its absence in verse 33 speaks for its presence here with a removal of the phrase by a scribe balancing the two verses. The inclusion of "sister" in verse 35 makes the call here more difficult, as one could harmonize this initial reference with that one. But an *inclusion* by Mark is also quite probable. Metzger, *Textual Commentary* (1994), 70.

3:33 And he answered them and said, "Who are my mother and my brothers?"

3:34 And looking at those sitting around him in a circle, he said, "Behold, my mother and brothers.

3:35 Whoever does the will of God, this one is my brother and sister and mother."

This longer scene has three parts, a classic Markan sandwich scene (A-B-A), so we have the family, then the dispute, and then back to the family.[144] The juxtaposition is not an accident. The issue that Jesus is beside himself (or possessed) leads into his strong defense that he is not acting under the power of Beelzebul. Strong opinions about Jesus are emerging in the face of his claims of authority, even from within his own family. He is not backing down from responding to them. This is another pronouncement scene that also reflects a controversy.

The setting comes in Mark 3:20–21, where the crowds and Jesus' response to them worries his family. This is the first appearance by Jesus' family. It is so unfavorable to Jesus that the scene fits the criterion of embarrassment and produced a host of textual variants.[145] Such an account is unlikely to have been a church creation, especially with Mary being highly regarded.

Two pronouncement accounts follow. In the first, the judgment of the Jewish leaders that Jesus casts out demons by Beelzebul's power leads to him speaking that that is not the answer and that blaspheming the Holy Spirit will not be forgiven (Mark 3:22–30). That is followed by a scene in which Jesus' family seeks to speak with him, which ends with a pronouncement from Jesus about who his real family is – those who hear and do God's will (Mark 3:31–35). Yet again Mark forcefully contends for the authority of Jesus, even in the face of concerns from the leaders and his own family.

Jesus returns to an unspecified home (**v 20**). The only house Mark has mentioned is Peter's (Mark 1:29). Many assume that it is his home that is noted here. This is possible but not clear. Again a large crowd gathers (Mark 3:7–9), preventing Jesus and the Twelve from functioning normally. They were unable to eat a meal. Jesus' family went to rescue him. Mark 3:31, as part of the sandwich structure, points to family members here. The

---

[144]   This is the first of six such Markan sandwich texts: Mark 5:2–43; 6:7–32; 11:12–25; 14:1–11; 14:53–72; Kuruvilla, *Mark*, 68–70.

[145]   Witherington, *Mark*, 154, notes variants that say Jesus escaped this situation. He sees the family's effort to protect family honor in light of the challenge of the leaders.

unspecified family members are simply called "those from him" (**v 21**; BDAG 756–57), which refers to some relatives and Mary. Seizing (*kratēsai*) almost suggests an arrest (Mark 6:17; 12:12; 14:1, 44, 46, 49, 51). They were concerned with all of this attention and the way Jesus accepted it. They thought he had lost his mind. He was doing and claiming too much. No other explanation is given other than this concern. It may be that his exorcisms make the family nervous, as that is implied in the context. John 7:5 notes that some in the family did not believe. Collins notes how, in some literature, a person who is close to God seems possessed to others (*Phaedrus* 249 C–D; Philo, *On Drunkenness* 36 §145–46).[146] Neither Luke nor Matthew have anything like this remark.

Not only is Jesus' family concerned about him, but scribes from Jerusalem also make two charges (**v 22**): (1) Jesus is possessed by Beelzebul and (2) by the power of the demons Jesus casts out demons. Jesus' attention has now reached the southern national leadership. There is no fact finding here, but instead a judgment against Jesus as the opposition to him escalates even more. *Epistle Aristeas* 32–39 shows such an authoritative delegation sent to Alexandria. Beelzeboul of the Greek is likely a variation of the rarely used Jewish term Beelzebub. It originally referred to a Canaanite or Syrian god Ekron (2 Kings 1:2) and could be associated with Baal.[147] It became an alternate way of referring to Satan as head of the demons, as it stands parallel to "prince of demons" in this verse. 1QS 3:20–21 and *T. Solomon* 2:9; 3:5; 6:1 refer to the hierarchy of demons, whereas 16:3 calls him "the master of spirits in the air, on the earth and under the earth." Jews had many names for Satan, including Beliar/Belial (*Jubilees* 1:20; 2 Cor 6:15), Asmodeus (Tobit 3:8), and Mastema (*Jubilees* 10:8; 11:5; 17:16). There is no doubt that Jesus was performing unusual and surprising works. Mark is unlike Matthew 12:22–23 and Luke 11:14, which have an exorcism before this discussion. Mark is simply looking at all Jesus has done. John 7:20, 8:48, 52, and 10:20 also present this charge, reflecting multiple attestation for this reaction against Jesus. The debate was the source of Jesus' power: from above or below? Later charges that Jesus was a magician or performed sorcery are similar (Justin Martyr, *Dial* 69; Origen, *Cel.* 1.6*b*. *b. Sanh* 43a; 107b). There is always room for a different reading of the same

---

[146] Collins, *Mark*, 227.
[147] Marcus, *Mark 1–8*, 271–72, though its exact derivation is disputed. It often is associated with the idea of the "Lord of the flies"; T. Lewis, "Beelzebul," *ABD* 1.638–40; Edwards, *Mark*, 120–21.

phenomenon. This was a serious charge, as it could bring a sentence of death (Lev 19:31; 20:27; CD 12:2–3; *m Sanh* 7:7).[148]

Jesus responds in verses 23–27 with a parable or maxim that if Jesus were casting out demons by malevolent powers, then Satan would be working against himself (**v 23**). That is neither likely nor logical.[149] The argument assumes that the hierarchy of evil spirits would not be in rebellion or else the long term of Satan's kingdom's well-being would be at risk. So a kingdom divided against itself in a type of civil war cannot stand, nor can a divided house stand (**vv 24–25**). These third-class conditional clauses actually expect a positive response and are statements expressed rhetorically (BDF § 372.1). The pictures may well look at Israel's own divided history and the divided Hasmonean family that allowed Rome to take over Israel in 63 BCE or Herod's own violent family history. There is precedent for what Jesus is saying. The reference to a divided house may imply a dynasty or rule and so a kingdom. The reference to Satan shows who Beelzebul is (**v 26**). Satan is not going to work to bring down his own kingdom, at least not intentionally. The assumption here is that Satan's house is under attack through Jesus' work. Satan is not at all responsible for that. Jesus is an opponent of Satan, as Mark 3:27 argues. Their conclusion could not be more incorrect.

A second image Jesus leaves is of the plundered house (**v 27**; Matt 12:29; Luke 11:21–22; *Thomas* 35). The image is multiply attested. It shows he opposes Satan and has overcome him. The image is that a strong man's house cannot be plundered unless he is first overrun and bound. Binding is a way of picturing Jesus' superior power, so that Satan is not able to counter what Jesus ultimately is doing. Restraining Satan, Jesus can release others from his grip. Having bound the strong one, Jesus controls the house. Mark 1:7–8 called Jesus the "stronger one" who brings the Spirit. To accuse the one who brings the Spirit of acting with Satanic power is blasphemy against the Spirit (**v 28**). Isaiah 49:24–26 is the likely conceptual background for taking ground from the captive.[150] It is God fighting for his people (also Ps 68:19). Again what the Old Testament has God do, Mark has Jesus do. Revelation 20:1–3 points to an ultimate binding of Satan still to come as part of the final eschatological victory, the normal way this imagery was used in Second Temple Judaism (*T. Levi* 18:12 – Beliar bound; *1 Enoch* 10:4 – Azazel

---

[148] Collins, *Mark*, 229.
[149] On the rhetoric involved in these verses, see V. K. Robbins, "Beelzebul Controversy in Mark and Luke: Rhetorical and Social Analysis," *Forum* 7 (1991): 261–77.
[150] France, *Mark*, 173.

bound; 54:3–5; 69:28; *Pss Sol* 5:3; *Jub* 5:6; 10:5–11 – Watchers bound). So these exorcisms and other acts show Jesus overtaking Satan's domain (*As Mos* 10:1). Jesus' battle with these forces was for the sake of reversing the pain of humanity. Jesus' actions represent an invasion of Satan's world, pointing to his defeat.

The judgment being made about what God is doing is important. In a saying introduced with the expression "truly I say," Jesus makes a signifi-cant application he wants all to get (Mark 8:12; 9:1, 41; 10:15, 29; 11:23; 12:43; 13:30; 14:9, 18, 25, 30). He describes the sins that the sons of men (= humanity) commits, as well as blasphemies. Blasphemy is slander against someone in word or deed.[151] He declares that all sins and even blasphemies are forgivable, but blasphemy against the Spirit is not (**v 29**; multiply attested: Luke 12:10; *Thomas* 44). That is an eternal and unforgi-vable sin. To miss what God is doing through Jesus now and to conclude it is by the power of Satan is to reject what the Spirit of God is doing. Their decision that Jesus had an unclean spirit missed what God was doing through him, placing the agency in the wrong place (**v 30**). This sin involves making a set decision about what the Spirit is doing through Jesus.[152] It is unpardonable to refuse to appreciate who Jesus is and that he comes from God to bring the kingdom and salvation. Ironically, those scribes seeking to defend God's honor in this scene are accused of risking blaspheming against him. What they see as an unclean spirit is the work of the Holy Spirit.

So the passage in Mark **3:31** returns to the concerns of the family,[153] and the sandwich structure comes full circle to resume discussion of the family. It opens another pronouncement scene, where Jesus' reply to his family's seeking him shows his priorities.

Jesus' mother and brothers stand outside the crowded house and wish to have him come to them (**v 31**). The detail makes it likely we are not in Jesus' family home. The reference to brothers would normally be a reference to siblings.[154] The absence of Joseph in any of the texts about Jesus' ministry

---

151 Bock, *Blasphemy and Exaltation.*

152 What many Christians worry about being the unpardonable sin does not involve this decided judgment about Jesus and so does not qualify.

153 The inclusion of "sisters" in some manuscripts, notably A and D, in Mark 3:32 is probably not original and seeks to create a parallelism with Mark 3:35; Metzger, *Textual Commentary* (1994), 70, opts for the shorter reading in our judgment correctly. It is unlikely that sisters culturally would take on such a role, but Jesus' response in Mark 3:35 has a reference to sisters, making it a likely addition here for balance.

154 Marcus, *Mark 1–8*, 276. The Catholic teaching of Mary's perpetual virginity leads some to see these as cousins, but this is unlikely, as a word for cousin (*anepsios*) exists in Greek (Col 4:10). The normal meaning of *adelphoi* is sibling when biological family is mentioned.

leads most to think he had died by that time. John 7:3–10 notes the unbelief of some in his family. The fact that some in his family did not believe is an embarrassing detail that points to the authenticity of the scene. The crowd around Jesus lets him know that they seek to call or summon Jesus (v 32). The verb *zētein* always points, in Mark's ten uses of it, to people trying to control or find Jesus.[155]

Jesus responds by simply asking who his mother and brothers are (v 33). The decisive pronouncement of the unit follows this rhetorical question. He has a new spiritual family that has priority (v 34). Doing the will of God trumps all (v 35). The picture is of those who sit and listen to his teaching as followers (Mark 10:29–30). To respond to Jesus, in contrast to the claim that he is from the devil or out of his mind, is to do the will of God. The concept of a spiritual family expressed in this saying is multiply attested, pointing to its authenticity (Matt 12:50; Luke 8:21; John 15:14; *Thomas* 99 but lacking any reference to sister and speaking of this group entering the kingdom; *Gospel of the Egyptians* 9:11).[156] The point is that relationship with God forms a new, extended family that has priority over biology. In a community meeting with a great deal of opposition, the point is important. The social role of such relationships is not unprecedented in the ancient world, as the Dead Sea Community was such a family (4Q502 frg. 9, lines 4, 9, 11) and the voluntary associations in the Greco-Roman world also functioned in this kind of a manner.[157]

So Jesus defends his activity as being from God, not Satan. He notes that he has a family that transcends biology. Those who do God's will belong to the divine family Jesus has come to affirm.

4:1–34 Jesus Teaches about the Kingdom through Parables

4:1–9 The Parable of the Soils

4:1 And again he began to teach by the sea. A great crowd gathered together to him, so that he got into a boat and sat in it on the sea and the entire crowd was on the ground by the sea.

---

[155] Edwards, *Mark*, 124; Mark 1:37; 8:11, 12; 11:18; 12:12; 14:1, 11, 55; 16:6.

[156] Stein, *Mark*, 188–89, who also notes how often Jesus uses the family metaphor in discipleship contexts, mostly in Q passages (Mark 10:29–30/Matt. 19:29/Luke 18:29–30; Matt. 10:35/Luke 12:53; Matt. 10:37/Luke 14:26; Matt. 8:21–22/Luke 9:59–60; Luke 11:27–28; also John 19:26–27).

[157] Collins, *Mark*, 236–37.

4:2 And he was teaching them in many parables, and in his teaching he said to them,

4:3 "Listen, a sower went out to sow.

4:4 And as he sowed some fell by the path, and the birds came and devoured it.

4:5 Other seed fell on rocky ground where it did not have much soil. It sprang up immediately because it did not have deep earth.

4:6 When the sun came up, it was scorched, and because it did not have root, it withered.

4:7 Other seed fell among the thorns, and they grew up and choked it, and it did not give produce.

4:8 But the other seed fell on good soil and had produce, sprouting and growing, some bearing thirty times, some sixty and some one hundred."

4:9 And he was saying to them, "The one who has ears, let him hear."

Once again Jesus teaches "on" the sea of Galilee from a boat (**v 1**), just as the crowd is on the shore making use of the natural acoustics of the region.[158] Jesus uses parables (note the plural) to picture the kingdom of God (**v 2**). These extended pictures each portray elements associated with the kingdom and are designed for hearers to ponder. They can be anything from simple metaphorical comparisons (*mashalim*) to complex stories. There is precedent in the Hebrew Scripture for this genre (2 Sam 12:1–14; Ezek 17:1–10). The term *parable* in the LXX renders a Hebrew *mashal*. There are around sixty such parables in the Gospels, with Matthew and Luke having the most, Mark a few, and John's Gospel having none.[159] The crowd is growing, with earlier references to it in Mark 2:13, and 3:9 and 20. It is now a large crowd (Mark 3:9 – also mentions teaching from a boat; boats in Mark 4:35–41; 6:45–52; 8:14–21). Such an ancient fishing boat was discovered at Ginnosar in Israel in 1986. It was 26.5 feet long, 7.5 feet wide, and 4.5 feet deep. The sea has been the locale for Jesus' acts in Mark 1:16; 2:13, and 3:7.

This discourse on the kingdom is one of two major speeches in Mark. The Olivet discourse of Mark 13 is the other. The distinctive feature in Mark 4 involves the use of parables that form the discourse. The lead-off parable is often called the Parable of the Sower or Seed, but a better name is the Parable of the Four Soils, because it is how the seed is received that is

---

[158] B. Cobbey Crisler, "The Acoustics and Crowd Capacity of Natural Theaters in Palestine," *The Biblical Archaeologist* 39 (1976): 128–41.

[159] Edwards, *Mark*, 127, who notes they are mostly for insiders and compares them to stained glass–dull on the outside but full of brilliant and radiant light on the inside.

the point.[160] It opens with a call to listen (**v 3**). The only other imperatival uses of the verb "to listen" in the Gospels are: Matt 15:10; 17:5; Mark 9:7; and Luke 9:35. Aside from Matt 15:10, God orders hearers to listen to Jesus during Transfiguration accounts. This verse is the only time it is used by the speaker in its own clause.

Jesus introduces the parable using the common agricultural picture of a farmer sowing seed by tossing it into the field. The season for sowing would be the autumn. Four landing spots are noted: the road, the rock, the thorns, and good soil. Four results emerge: birds devour the seed, the sun scorches the seed with no deep soil, thorns choke the seed, and the seed produces at various levels. The parable is not about six seed (three in poor conditions and three in good),[161] but involves a variety of seed cast into four types of soil and summarized in terms of kinds of yield.

The footpath that is the road is likely an area by the side of the field (**v 4**), where the repeated travel on foot would pack the soil, making penetration by the seed impossible so it would sit on or by the road as easy prey for hungry birds. Because we are discussing sowing in a field, a path is more likely than a road. The expression "by the road" reflects the idiom *para tēn hodon*, with Matt 20:30, Mark 10:46, and 18:35 looking to people standing by a road. There is debate whether in ancient Israel one sowed and then plowed[162] or the other way around.[163] It leads into a discussion of whether seed is scattered intentionally or unintentionally by the road. That may overinterpret the imagery.[164] The parable's point is the not detailed motive of the farmer but rather the result of his act. In addition, it really makes little difference. The area by the path is unlikely to have been plowed either way. So the parable is not merely about the arrival of seed as the word of the kingdom, but the differing reactions to it wherever it appears.

The middle two soils see a start of growth but no desired result because the seed never makes it to fruition as the sun and thin soil or the presence of

---

[160] *Thomas* 9 has a variation of this parable, which also leads the kingdom parable sequence in Matt 13 and Luke 8.

[161] Contra France, *Mark*, 188. Seed was not tossed one seed at a time but scattered in handfuls. Witherington, *Mark*, 165, is right to speak of three degrees of failure and success.

[162] So Lane *Mark*, 153, Marcus, *Mark 1–8*, 292, and France, *Mark*, 191. This is the most likely practice, but the point is not certain.

[163] Edwards, *Mark*, 128.

[164] So, correctly, Guelich, *Mark 1:1–8:26*, 193. Donahue and Harrington, *The Gospel of Mark* (Collegeville, MN: Michael Glazier Press, 2002), 138, point out the emphasis is on the result for the seed where it lands, rather than on the conditions of preparation for it as key to the result.

thorns prevent its coming to maturity (**vv 5–7**). In the end, the seed in these soils proves as unfruitful as the seed by the road. The parable assumes, in scattering a large amount of seed, that some of the seed will land in useless locations.

The fourth soil was good soil (**v 8**). Here the seed had a good place to be fruitful. So the seed sprouted and grew in various yields of thirty, sixty, and a hundredfold. Such yields are common in describing ancient crops, though they are higher than normal yields (Gen. 26:12 – a hundredfold; cf. Sib. Or. 3.263; Pliny, *Nat. Hist.* 18.21.95; Varro, *On Agriculture* 1.44.2).[165] In the good soil, the seed could do what it was planted to do.

Jesus closes the parable by urging the crowd to hear (**v 9**). The one with ears is to hear what the parable says. This is a common NT expression (Mark 4:23; Matt 11:15; 13:43; Luke 14:35; Rev 2:7, 11, 17, 29; 3:6, 13, 22; 13:9). They are to understand that the word requires good soil. The remark forms an *inclusio* with Mark 4:3, where there was also a call to hear. Open ears can give access to divine mysteries, as the next verses indicate (1QH 9:21). So the story pictures four types of landing spots that will correspond to four kinds of responses.

4:10–12 Jesus Explains the Mystery of Parables

> **4:10 When he was alone, those around him with the twelve were asking him about the parables.**
>
> **4:11 And he was saying to them, "To you is given the mystery of the kingdom of God, but to those outside all things come in parables,**
>
> **4:12 so that *seeing they may see but not behold, and hearing they hear but not understand, lest they repent and be forgiven.*"**

Mark places the explanation here, likely from a later time, to connect the private explanation of the parable to its presentation. We have another A-B-A sandwich construction (parable-explanation-parable). The question comes from disciples beyond the Twelve about Jesus' use of parables (**v 10**). The reference to Jesus being alone likely means he is away from the crowd in private (like Mark 4:34; 6:31–32; 7:14–17; 9:27–28; 10:2–12; 13:3). There are "those around him," an echo of Mark 3:31–35 and those who respond to Jesus. He explains that to those on the inside comes the mystery (in Aramaic, the *rāz*) of the kingdom (**v 11**). This is Mark's only use of the

---

[165] Guelich, *Mark 1:1–8:26*, 195. They are unlike the enormous yields in some eschatological texts, *1 Enoch* 10:19 (thousandfold); *2 Baruch* 29:5 (ten thousandfold); Stein, *Mark*, 200.

term that has roots in the book of Daniel (Dan 2:18–19; 27–30, 47). The "to you" in the verse is thrown forward in Greek for emphasis. This mystery involves access to the revelatory knowledge of God's plan and program, to know the "secret" of what God is doing. God has given this knowledge, which includes embracing the message, not just understanding its content. This equals the "good soil" of the parable. The "is given" is a divine passive. The kingdom has arrived; the seed is sown with more still to come. It has come without the complete eradication of the old era, small but penetrating.[166] They understand this and appreciate it. Those on the outside, those rejecting Jesus and not open to him, just hear the parables with no help as to how to comprehend them.[167] They have ears to hear, but do not (Ezek 12:1–2; Dan 12:8–10).[168] Those who hear in faith will appreciate the parable and become insiders.

Mark 4:12 is among the most complex and challenging in the Gospel. It is a shortened citation from Isa 6:9–10. The key differences are that third-person verbs (rather than second-person) open the first clause, and the concluding reference is to being forgiven rather than healed. These differences are like the targum of Isaiah.[169] The differences so strongly paralleled in the Aramaic setting may indicate that the age of the tradition reaches back into Jesus' time. Unlike the other texts, the Gospel of Mark reverses the order of perception to seeing/hearing. Marcus suggests that this is because Mark liked to highlight the role of vision (8:22–26; 10:46–52; numerous times in ch 13; 15:32, 36, 39).[170]

In its OT context, the statement explains that Isaiah's ministry was one of hardening. So is the role of parables today for outsiders who are closed to the message.[171] The historical context of Jesus' remarks is also important.[172] He has ministered and taught, with some saying he acts from Satan (Mark 3). Jesus' remark fits into a world where the kingdom has been openly offered up to this point and some have emphatically rejected it. The purpose of parables to those outsiders is a form of judgment. They see a parable but do not grasp its meaning. They hear it but do not understand it. For had they grasped it and understood it, they would have repented

---

[166] Marcus, *Mark 1–8*, 303.
[167] Hooker, *Mark*, 128.
[168] Witherington, *Mark*, 166.
[169] Marcus, *Mark 1–8*, 300.
[170] Marcus, *Mark 1–8*, 300.
[171] France, *Mark*, 199–200, explains the typology at work here in the appeal to Isaiah 6.
[172] Lane, *Mark*, 158, correctly stresses this.

(literally "turned") and received forgiveness. The soil the message lands on does not allow the bearing of fruit.

The debate about the passage in verse 12 centers on the term *hina*.[173] Is it the purpose of speaking in parables to have a non-response or is it a result of teaching in parables that there is no response?[174] The term usually carries a meaning of purpose. The likely point is that parables are a form of initial judgment to those closed to respond. The context of Mark 4 where the remarks appear is important to appreciating the force of what Jesus is saying. Only the person open to hearing what the parables say (Mark 4:3, 9) can benefit from what they teach. Failure to be open brings the risk of being closed off to gaining understanding of the word and, eventually, leads to judgment.

4:13–20 *Jesus Explains the Parable of the Soils*

4:13 He said to them, "Do you not understand this parable? And how will you know all the parables?

4:14 The sower sows the word.

4:15 These are the ones by the road, where the sower sows the word and when they hear, immediately Satan comes and takes the word that was sown in them.

4:16 These are the ones sown on the rocky ground. When they hear the word they immediately receive it with joy.

4:17 But having no root in themselves, they are temporary. When difficulty or persecution comes because of the word, immediately, they fall.

4:18 And others are sown among the thorns. These are the ones hearing the word

4:19 and the cares of the age, the love of riches, and the desire for the rest come in and choke the word, and it produces nothing.

---

[173] Stein, *Mark*, 209–10, notes no less than seven interpretive options that have been suggested for the expression plus three options for *mēpote* later in the verse. On the passage as a whole, C. A. Evans, *To See and Not Perceive: Isaiah 6.9–10 in Early Jewish and Christian Interpretation*. JSNTSup 64 (Sheffield: JSOT Press, 1989), 53–80, and esp. 92–99.

[174] Marcus, *Mark 1–8*, 299–300, opts for purpose, while Guelich, *Mark 1:1–8:26*, 211–12, prefers to see *hina* as epexegetical and *mēpote* as introducing an indirect question. Guelich's reading sees the verse as giving the effect of failing to understand. Matthew 13:10–17 and Luke 8:9–10 do render this part of the passage in a softer way than Mark. It may be best to retain the ambiguity of the language, sensing a mix of purpose and result.

4:10 But those that were sown on the good soil are the ones who hear the word and welcome it and bear fruit thirtyfold, sixtyfold and hundredfold."

Jesus now explains the parable of the sown word with its various reactions.[175] Such private teaching is common in Mark (Mark 7:17–23; 8:16–21; 9:28–29; 10:10–12; 11:21–25; 13:3–37). He asks if they understand the parable (v 13). The interrogative *ouk* assumes a positive reply. Jesus leans in the direction of assuming they will get it. He also notes in a rhetorical question that understanding it opens the way to understanding all the parables. So Jesus offers his insiders a way into understanding. The insider-outsider categories here are not static, but dynamic. The disciples have access to mysteries but still must pursue them with receptive ears. Openness to the word is the only way inside. The arrival of the kingdom does not come with automatic understanding and acceptance. In fact, many will not respond, but it has come nonetheless. The kingdom does not force itself upon people, but offers itself to them. Access is gained only through a welcoming heart.

Jesus interprets the parable (v 14), as he often does with other parables (Mark 13:29; Matt 13:36–43, 49–50; 18:14, 35; 20:16; 21:31–32, 43; 25:13; Luke 7:43–47; 10:36–37; 12:21; 15:7, 10; 16:8–13; 18:6–8, 14).[176] The sower sows the word (4 Ezra 8:41; 9:31). We are not told the subject of the word, but surely in the context of this Gospel it is the word concerning the message of the kingdom. We are not told who the sower is, but surely Jesus is meant as the messenger of the kingdom, along with any who share that message with others. The parable's focus is not on who brings the message but on what happens to it depending on where it lands. This fusion is part of what makes it hard to determine if the interpretation focuses on the seed or the differing groups in their response to it. It is the synergy between the two that is in view. So the "these" in these explanatory verses is primarily about the groups and their reaction to the word.

The first seed associated with the path never has a chance (v 15). Satan takes away that seed as soon as it lands. Demons were seen like birds in ancient texts (*1 En* 90:8–13; *Apoc Abr* 13:3–8; *Jub* 11:11–14 – Mastema,

---

[175] Stein, *Mark*, 213–15, defends the authenticity of the explanation, as does Philip Payne, "The Authenticity of the Parable of the Sower and Its Interpretation," in *Gospel Perspectives: Studies in the History and Tradition of the Four Gospels*, Vol. 1, ed. R. T. France and David Wenham (Sheffield: JSOT Press, 1980), 163–207.

[176] France, *Mark*, 202.

another name for Satan, sends cows to eat the planted seed).[177] Satan is active in opposing what Jesus is doing, as he has been throughout Mark up to here (Mark 1:13, 23–26, 32–33, 39; 3:11–12, 22–27). Here an active outside force prevents fruitfulness. Although Jesus as the stronger man has overcome him (Mark 3:27), Satan is still at work.[178] This is surely one of the mysteries of the kingdom.

The second seed on rocky ground has no root (**v 16**). These are the people who are open to the word, receive it with joy initially, but when tribulation or persecution arrives let go of their initial response. In Judaism, the wicked are commonly identified as rootless (Sir 23:25; 40:15; Wis 4:3).[179] Their temporary faith exposes them as lacking the genuine faith that brings forth fruit. Those with genuine faith do not let it go and walk away.

Related terms help us interpret the verb for offense here (**v 17**). The noun *skandalon* (offense) refers to someone who views the message of the cross as an offense, a barrier to belief (1 Cor 1:23). The verbal idea we have in Mark 4 means "to fall away out of offense" (noun: Mark 6:3; verb: 9:42–47; 14:27–29). It is to trip over an obstacle. Jesus' point is that in these cases, the shame of persecution is greater than a person's embrace of the message, so they stumble over the message in times of trouble. They let go of faith rather than facing rejection. This term denotes apostasy, or lack of real faith (TDNT 7:349). In the end, they leave their initial, now fleeting response and return to where they were before hearing the word. This is not a momentary lapse of faith, but a turning away from it.[180] The opposite, positive exhortation is to take up one's cross (Mark 8:34).

The third seed is sown among the thorns (**vv 18–19**). Here it is life that chokes growth: the cares of this world, the love of riches, and the desire for all that life offers are said to get in the way. The result is no fruit. The later Jewish text *Ecclesiastes Rabbah* in 4:14 refers to the evil inclination as "entangling people as if among thorns."[181] The seed among thorns pictures those who get so encumbered with the basic enticements of this world that they produce no fruit. The seed again fails to accomplish its purpose. The terms used here do not appear frequently in the Synoptics. "Worries" is used elsewhere only in Luke 21:34; "lure" appears only here and in its

---

177   Donahue and Harrington, *Mark*, 141–42.
178   Hooker, *Mark*, 131.
179   Marcus, *Mark 1–8*, 309.
180   France, *Mark*, 206.
181   Marcus, *Mark 1–8*, 309.

parallel, Matt 13:22; and "desire" has no parallel akin to its use here, although it is used positively in Luke 22:15. The theme of riches and the problems of the rich are a concern (Matt 6:24–25; 19:23–24; Mark 10:25; Luke 1:53; 12:21). Riches are said to be deceitful because what they promise, they cannot deliver in terms of real life. It is not the wealth that is the problem but what one expects from it and so how one uses it. The reference to "the rest" points to anything else in life that also chokes discipleship. With the group represented by this soil, the failure lies with the distractions that prevent a person from benefiting from the word. The one thing all three fruitless soils share is that none of them are fruitful. In the terms of the parable, they are all failures in terms of why someone sows seed.

Another key point these soils together show is that we are not dealing with an assessment that looks at an existential moment in life, but a "career" response to the word over a period of time across one's life. The passing of events and the effect of life choices are in view. Satan, persecution, and the lure of the world can get in the way of fruitfulness for God and a productive kingdom life.

The fourth soil hears and welcomes the word so fruit in various yields emerges: thirty, sixty and hundredfold (**v 20**). This is the good heart. It welcomes the word of God about the kingdom. The various yields point to a range of productiveness. After all, the goal of sowing seed is bearing fruit. So the word is to have a product that emerges from faith. Finally the seed bears the fruit for which it was intended. This is the only commended soil. The hope is that the hearts of hearers will be this type of soil, but the fact that Jesus spends so much time on the other soils means that the threat of a lack of response is real and varied.

4:21–25 The Light Comes to Expose and the Measure Shows the Heart

4:21 And he said to them, "Is a lamp brought in to be put under a basket, or under a bed, and not on a stand?

4:22 For nothing is secret except it be made manifest, nothing is hidden that is not become clear.

4:23 If anyone has ears, let him hear."

4:24 And he said to them, "Pay attention to what you hear. The measure by which you measure will be the measure you receive, and more will be added to you.

4:25 For whoever has, more will be given to you, and whoever does not have, what he has will be taken from him."

Jesus tells another set of parables: the lamp and the measure. With the lamp image, Mark brings together what the other Gospels have in distinct contexts (Matt 5:15; 10:26; Luke 8:16 with no parallel to Mark 4:22). The same is true for the image of the measure (Matthew 7:2; 13:12; Luke 6:38; 11:33; 12:2; 19:26).[182] The general call to hear likely looks to a broad audience, as does Mark 4:26 and 33, though some see only disciples in view in light of Mark 4:13–20. Mark's transitions are not always clear.

In the lamp (**v 21**), Jesus shifts to the picture of the word of the kingdom brought by Jesus as a light that shines and exposes (Ps 119:105). So the lamp "comes." Oil lamps are in view in the imagery. The context points to the kingdom's arrival as the topic. The picture ultimately is eschatological. This word will reveal where hearts are. What seems hidden will be revealed (**v 22**). This word is not covered by up to a two-gallon, peck measure basket or placed under a bed, but placed where it can shine and show the way things are. The first question expects a negative reply, whereas the second looks for a positive reply. One does not hide the lamp. Rather the light shows what is there and exposes the initially secret things. Jesus points to the accountability the word's exposure is to bring. Jesus ends the short summary with another call to understand and respond (**v 23**; Mark 4:9).

The parable of the measure adds to the note of accountability (**v 24**). It is yet another call to hear, something the entire chapter has stressed (Mark 4:3, 9, 23–24 [three times]). The measure you use to respond to the word of the kingdom will be used on you (Matt 7:2; Luke 6:38, but in a distinct context of judging others, not how you hear the word as here). The one who has gets more (**v 25**), but the one who does not have loses what he has (Matt 13:12; 25:29; Luke 8:18; 19:26; *Thomas* 41).[183] This sounds odd, but the point is that the one who responds gets more benefit, whereas the one who does not respond ends up absolutely empty. Jesus is giving more reason to respond. Not only is there exposure and accountability, but the one who lacks also ends up with nothing at all, stated rhetorically as emphatically as it could be said. Whatever little understanding one may have had is lost without an open, welcoming heart. In contrast, the one who welcomes light receives more light. The verbs "is given" and "is taken away" say what God will do in the judgment. The warning makes sense only if outsiders are also being addressed. A person is very responsible for how he or she responds to

---

[182] We likely are dealing with variations in a repeated image in the oral tradition versus a singular saying. The imagery is also like *Thomas* 3, 35, and 41.

[183] These themes also show themselves in later Judaism: verse 24 is like *Mekilta on Exod* 13:19ff., *m. Sotah* 1:7; verse 25 is like *Mekilta on Exod* 15:26; Lane, *Mark*, 167.

God and for the consequences that come from that response or the lack of it. So where the earlier parable pictured the various responses to the word, these last two short parables picture how the word enlightens and exposes, which is why it should be heeded.

4:26–29 The Parable of the Growing Seed

> **4:26 And he said, "The kingdom of God is like someone who scatters seed on the earth.**
>
> **4:27 He goes to sleep and rises up, night and day, and the seed sprouts and grows, though he does not know how.**
>
> **4:28 Automatically the soil produces a crop, first the stalk, then the grain, then the full grain in the head.**
>
> **4:29 And when the fruit permits, he immediately sends in the sickle because the time for harvest has come."**

The Parable of the Growing Seed is unique to Mark, though it looks like the kind of parable one might see in Luke, as it is introduced with a certain man who sows seed. The parable is about the mysterious yet inevitable way the kingdom grows. It is compared to how a farmer sows seed and allows time to pass, and then automatically the seed sprouts and grows. The idea of sprouting might evoke a messianic image (Zech 3:8; 6:12; Jer. 23:5–6; 33:14–16; 4QpGena 5),[184] but that is less likely here. We have a simple picture of the growth of the impact of the seed. The parable is not focused on Christology alone.

The farmer has no idea how it works (**vv 26–27**), but he is the beneficiary of the harvest that results (*4 Ezra* 4:1–12). This detail shows that we are not speaking of Jesus alone, but of the entire work of kingdom preaching. Something in the seed brings the growth (**v 28**). The kingdom will grow and do its work over time. There will be a harvest at the end when all things are sorted out (**v 29**). The language of the harvest in sending forth the sickle echoes Joel 3:13 (1QHab 7:13–14 – the time will come; *Thomas* 21 – sickle image). The parable is less about growth over time than a contrast of the start with the finish, along with the mystery of how we get to the end. The goal is to reach the harvest, and the seed brings forth its fruit. A harvest both gathers and separates. This is a confident parable that the seed of the kingdom will do its work and that all will be held accountable for the response. Accountability is suggested by the contextual link back to the

---

[184]   Marcus, *Mark 1–8*, 322.

measure in Mark 4:24–26, but the thrust is positive. There will be a yield in the end.

4:30–32 The Mustard Seed

> 4:30 And he was saying, "To what shall we liken the Kingdom of God or in what parable can we lay it out?
> 4:31 It is like a mustard seed when sown in the ground, even though it is the smallest of seeds for the ground,
> 4:32 when it is sown, it grows up, becomes the greatest of all garden plants, and grows large branches so that the wild birds can nest in its shade."

Jesus' final parable in this chapter is the Parable of the Mustard Seed. Again the contrast is the mystery of the seed's small size at the start with its size at the end. Matthew 13:31–32 and Luke 13:19 have the same image with slightly different wording, suggesting a well-circulated parable in slightly distinct versions.[185] This is the type of thing Jesus could have taught regularly as he traveled.

The mustard seed here is proverbially called the smallest of seed as a very common plant in use (TDNT 7:288–89; *m. Tohar* 8.8; *m. Nid* 5.2; *b. Ber* 31a; *b. Nid* 5a, 13b, 16b, 40a, 66a[186]), so the language should not be horticulturally pressed (**vv 30–31**). It is likely the *Braasica nigra* that is meant, which produced oil and grew to about 9 feet or so. The anticipation had been that the kingdom would be glorious from the start. In contrast, Jesus says the Kingdom starts out as small as the smallest of seed but one day will be large enough to be like a place of shelter for birds (**v 32**).

Such a mustard seed shrub could be 8 to 10 feet in size, making nesting possible. The background is likely Ezek 17:23 (also Ezek 31:6; Ps 104:12; Dan 4:9–21; *Joseph and Aseneth* 15:6).[187] There a stump of Jesse becomes replanted and will become a great place of shelter. The contrast of the start with the finish is the point.[188] The note is again a confident one about where God's program is headed. However insignificant the kingdom looks

---

[185] This could be evidence of some overlap between Q and Mark on content. *Thomas* 20 also has a version of this parable. Witherington, *Mark*, 171, notes that this is the only parable attested across those three sources as he argues for its authenticity.

[186] Stein, *Mark*, 235.

[187] Collins, *Mark*, 255–56, in discussing the background rightly calls Ezekiel a "messianic parable."

[188] Cranfield, *Mark*, 163, "the key feature of the parable."

now, that will not be the end story for the kingdom. So the application is: do not underestimate what is taking place simply because the start appears small. This is the point that underlies the choice of the mustard seed as the point of comparison.

4:33–34 Summary: How Jesus Used Parables

4:33 So that with many parables such as these he was speaking the word to them, even as they were able to hear.

4:35 He did not speak to them without a parable. But privately he explained everything to his own disciples.

Mark summarizes that parables were a key way Jesus taught the word about the kingdom (**v 33**). Mark has given but a sample of those parables. They were of value as long as they were heard. His remark that Jesus did not teach without parables means that they were a key means of teaching. Jesus does use other forms of teaching in Mark. Disciples had an added advantage over the larger crowds, as Jesus explained the parables privately to them (**v 34**). The explanation of parables goes to more than the Twelve, however; it goes to those who have chosen to follow Jesus.

So ends the first of only two discourses in Mark.[189] Jesus has used three seed parables to note that the kingdom produces an array of responses and that it will start by appearing to be of insignificant size, and yet will end up being a place of rest, with all, even those who do not rest in its shade, being accountable to it.

4:35–5:41 Jesus Performs a Series of Miracles

4:35–41 Jesus Calms a Storm

4:35 He said to them on that day when evening came, "Let's go to the other side of the lake."

4:36 So leaving the crowd, they took him just as he was, in the boat, and other boats were with him.

4:37 Now a giant windstorm developed, and the waves were beating over the boat, so that the boat was nearly full.

4:38 And he was in the stern of the boat sleeping, resting his head on a cushion. They woke him up and said to him, "Teacher, do you not care that we are about to perish?"

---

[189] Mark 13 on Jerusalem's destruction and the end of time is the other.

4:39 So he arose and rebuked the wind and said to the sea, "Silence! Calm down." And the wind ceased and there came a great calm.

4:40 And he said to them, "Why are you cowardly? Do you still not have faith?"

4:41 They were full of fear and were saying to each other, "Who is this that the wind and the sea obey him?"

Jesus' calming of the storm is the first of a series of four miracles Mark will tell in Mark 4–5: calming the storm, the demoniac, healing the woman with a flow of blood, and raising Jairus' daughter. It is an A to Z portrayal of Jesus' power: nature, demons, disease, and death. This miracle of calming the storm also appears in Matthew 8:18, 23–27 and Luke 8:22–25. It is a nature miracle and a rescue account. Jesus has authority over creation like God (Ps 107:23–32; Jonah 1:1–16), so it also is an epiphany account. It is very parallel in structure to the exorcism in Mark 1:21–28.[190] Luke has the same miracle sequence as Mark. Matthew breaks up the sequence of miracles. The story has several Semitisms, so it reflects early tradition.[191]

At the end of the day (**vv 35–36**), Jesus heads to the other side of the Sea of Galilee in the boat in which he taught noted in Mark 4:1, as the text says they went "as he was." He is not alone; he travels in a boat along with other boats traveling with him. This is part of Mark's "growing crowds" motif. The journey takes Jesus into more prominent Gentile territory, as the next encounter will involve pigs. Jesus is ministering to more than Israel.

The bowl that is the Sea of Galilee can allow for winds to stir up a storm in a hurry (**v 37**). Hills surround it except for where the Jordan River exits it. The description of a great windstorm recalls the story of Jonah (Jonah 1:4). That is what happened on this trip. But this was not just a minor storm; the winds produced waves that were dangerous, catching the travelers as they were crossing, filling the boat with water from the waves spilling over the boat. It is possible that the first-century fishing boat found in the Sea in 1986 and now displayed at Ginnosar found its fate in this way. At day's end, as darkness is falling, this situation is especially dangerous. Jesus was sleeping and had to be roused by those with him (**v 38**). His head is on a cushion, probably a sandbag used for ballast.[192] Mark simply describes this. It is a detail many have sought to explain, but Mark simply notes it and moves on.

---

190   Kuruvilla, *Mark*, 95.
191   Guelich, *Mark 1:1–8:26*, 262. He notes that there are paratactic sentences, impersonal plurals, and unrelated imperatives in verse 39, an interrogative pronoun in verse 40, and the use of a cognate accusative with the verb they feared in verse 41.
192   Marcus, *Mark 1–8*, 333.

Clearly the narrative has Jesus calm in the midst of the storm.[193] He trusts God.

In verse 38, rhetorically they ask if he cares that they are about to be consumed in the sea and perish, the same verb used in Jonah 1:6, 14 and 3:9. The question (*ou*) expects a positive reply. Surely he does care, but their panic shows a lack of faith, as Jesus' later remarks demonstrates. Their faith in him is at a tipping point. Jesus is addressed as "teacher," the first use of what will be a common title for him. The disciples are quite nervous. This is the first hint in Mark of a failure in the disciples to trust Jesus, the first of several such moments as they grow to appreciate who he is (Mark 6:52; 8:17, 32–33; 9:18–19, 33–37; 10:13–16, 35–45; 14:3–9, 27–31, 32–42, 53–54, 66–72; with rebuke: 7:18; 8:17–18, 21, 32–33; 9:19).

Jesus responds by rebuking the wind and telling it to calm down (**v 39**). The almost personal feel of the term *rebuke* makes Jesus' response to nature one of challenging the presence of evil. As noted earlier, this handling of creation is almost like an exorcism (Mark 1:25; 3:12; 9:25; *T. Sol* 16). It is a point of his authority that he acts directly against nature. There is no call to another to act, no prayer, no ritualistic formula. Creation is told to be muzzled (BDAG, 1060; Deut 24:5 LXX). Creation simply obeys and all is calm (Ps 104:7 – of God's power; 107:29; contrast 2 Macc 9:8 of Antiochus Epiphanes' arrogant self-belief he could calm the waves).[194] As Stein says, "Like Yahweh, Jesus is also Lord over nature."[195]

Jesus rebukes his disciples as well (**v 40**). He calls them cowardly (Deut 20:8; Judg 7:3; 1 Macc 3:56) and implies that they lack faith. This lack of faith is not merely in Jesus as a miracle worker, as Mark is consistently against seeing Jesus in such limited terms. Faith here is about trusting God for his care and program. God will care for Jesus and for the disciples to accomplish his program. For Mark, fear is the opposite of faith (Mark 5:15–17, 36; 6:49–52; 10:32; 11:18; 16:8). This theme sets up the way the Gospel ends. Will one trust in what God has done and is doing? Jesus knows his disciples will

---

[193] Collins, *Mark*, 259, seeing the image of a sleeping deity and an epiphany scene, citing the work of B. Batto, "The Sleeping God: An Ancient Near Eastern Motif of Divine Sovereignty," *Bib* 68 (1987) 153–77. Perhaps this is meant, given that Jesus acts directly. Unlike Jonah, he will not pray to God to solve the dilemma, but will act on his own. The image of the teacher works in another less dramatic direction, but the disciples do not yet get who Jesus is fully.

[194] Marcus, *Mark 1–8*, 334.

[195] Stein, *Mark*, 244; Collins, *Mark*, 260, Jesus is "behaving not like a devout human person but like God."

be in many difficult spots. They will need to look to God. So he redirects them to deepen their trust and have courage.

The miracle closes with reflection over what the disciples have just seen (**v 41**). They "feared a great fear," a Semitic cognate accusative construction retained in Greek that alludes to a deep amazement and awe (Jonah 1:16 LXX). They are asking themselves, "Who is this that the winds and sea obey him?"[196] The question speaks to a control of creation that only God has (Ps 107:29; 89:8–9) or those, like Moses or Elijah, who worked very closely with God. At Qumran, this kind of power where heaven and earth obeyed was tied to the Messiah (4Q521 2 ii 1). It is beginning to dawn on the disciples that Jesus is a most unusual messenger from God. The scene ends here, leaving Mark's reader to contemplate the same question with no answer except to ponder what has just been described. The event represents an epiphany of divine authority. The scene sets up a direct confession coming in Mark 5:7: he is "son of the Most High God." In light of this, will fear lead to trust?[197]

5:1–20 *Jesus Exorcizes a Demon-Possessed Man in Gentile Territory*

5:1 And they came to the other side of the sea into the region of Geresene,

5:2 and as Jesus was coming out of the boat, immediately a man with an unclean spirit came from the tombs and met him.

5:3 He had dwelt among the tombs, and no one could bind him, not even with a chain.

5:4 For his hands and feet had often been bound with chains and shackles, but he had torn the chains apart and broken the shackles into pieces. No one was strong enough to subdue him.

5:5 Each night and every day among the tombs and in the mountains, he was crying out and cutting himself on the stones.

5:6 When he saw Jesus from some distance he ran and bowed before him

5:7 and crying out in a loud voice said, "What is there between me and you, Jesus Son of the Most High? I implore you by God – do not torment me."

5:8 For Jesus had been saying to him, "Come out of that man, you unclean spirit."

5:9 And Jesus asked him, "What is your name?" And he said, "My name is Legion, for we are many."

---

[196]   Witherington, *Mark*, 177, sees the force as "Who is this masked man?"
[197]   So asks, correctly, Edwards, *Mark*, 152.

5:10 And he was begging him a great deal not to send him out of the region.

5:11 There was on the hillside a great herd of pigs feeding.

5:12 And they requested of him, saying, "Send us into the pigs, that we may enter them."

5:13 And he permitted them. So the unclean spirits came out and went into the pigs. And the herd rushed down the steep slope into the sea, and about two thousand were drowned in the sea.

5:14 Now the herdsmen ran off and spread the news in the town and countryside, and the people went out to see what had taken place.

5:15 They came to Jesus and saw the demon-possessed man sitting there, clothed and sane – the one who had the "Legion" – and they were afraid.

5:16 Those who had seen what had taken place to the demon possessed man reported it, and they also told about the pigs.

5:17 Then they began to ask Jesus to leave their region.

5:18 And as he was getting into the boat, the man who had been demon possessed asked if he could go with him.

5:19 But Jesus did not permit him to do so. Instead, he said to him, "Go to your home and to your own and tell them what the Lord has done for you, that he had mercy on you."

5:20 So he went out and began to preach in the Decapolis the things Jesus did for him, and all were amazed.

From a nature miracle pointing to the powerful presence of God, we turn to a very expanded exorcism account, the longest such account in the Gospels. Exorcisms dominate Mark, of which this is the third so far (Mark 1:21–28, 32–34; 3:11–12, 15, 22–30; 6:7; 7:24–30; 9:14–29). Jesus' battle goes beyond human struggle. This miracle is told with far more detail than most, so it is unusual in its portrayal. Some have called it a mission story, but that is hard to see clearly, given that the healed man is to remain where he is.

Jesus crosses the Sea successfully, having calmed the storm (v 1). He ends up in the region of Geresene. There is a complex textual issue here about the location that also shows itself in the parallels in Matthew and Luke. Geresene is the best attested in terms of external evidence (א*, B, D). Luke 8:26 reads like Mark. Gadarene is the best-attested reading for Matthew 8:28. These are overlapping regional references. Geresene is Geresa, which is the major city of the Decapolis, but is about 37 miles from any water.[198]

---

[198] S. T. Parker, "The Decapolis Reviewed," *JBL* 94 (1975): 437–41, reviews the ancient textual discussion of the region.

Gadarene refers to a location closer to water (A, C, 𝔐), some 6 miles removed. Gergesa, yet a third option (א², L) is located on the eastern edge of the Sea. These are references to a region or territory versus a specific location. It may well be the best known general location has been noted. The similarity in the spelling and the proximate locales by those who knew the geography has led to the textual confusion. Mark likely had Geresene as original.[199] The important observation is that this is predominantly Gentile territory, as the prominence of pigs in the scene shows, although it also had much contact with Judaism.

Mark describes someone who is seriously possessed by an evil spirit (**v 2**; Mark 1:23). The scene is paralleled in Matthew 8:28-34 and Luke 8:26-39, but it is clear Mark tells it with much more detail. Actually, the man is multiply possessed, as later verses make clear. He lives in a permanently unclean state among the tombs (Num 19:11-14; Ps 68:6; Isa 65:4; *m. Oholot* 17-18; *b. Sanh* 65b), tied to death. In later Judaism, spending the night on a grave was a sign that one had gone mad (*b. Hagigah* 3b).[200] People would want a cemetery cleansed so they could visit the graves of their loved ones.[201] Cave tombs hewn out of the mountains are probably the setting. The later mention of pigs adds to the unclean imagery (Lev 11:7; Deut 14:8; Isa 66:17; *m. B. Qam* 7:7). In fact, there are three layers of uncleanness: the demons, death, and the pigs. Everything about this scene would make Jewish readers squeamish, and the man is likely a Gentile, not an expectant candidate for one ministering Jewish hope.

Some of the details in verses 2-5 about the severity of the power and destruction of the man are unique to Mark, though Luke 8:29 does note the inability of chains to contain him (**v 3**). He was strong enough to break any

---

[199] Cranfield, *Mark*, 176; Lane, *Mark*, 181, opts for the specific location of Kersa (Koursi) as intended here; Metzger, *Textual Commentary* (1994), 72. Kersa is located on the sea's edge and has a steep slope about one mile to the south. This equals Gergesa. Origen (*Comm. on John* 6:41, chap. 24) and Eusebius (*Onomasticon* 64.1) make this identification. Guelich, *Mark 1:1–8:26*, 275-77, has a full discussion of options, though his option of a later redaction (of bringing in the sea, as the event was connected to the other miracles) is complicated, unlikely, and unnecessary.

[200] Marcus, *Mark 1–8*, 343, who notes that the chains may reflect efforts to bind the man long enough to try and perform magic over him to stop him. Demons were often pictured as fettered; M. J. Geller, "Jesus' Theurgic Powers: Parallels in the Talmud and Incantations Bowls," *JJS* 28 (1977): 141-55.

[201] Gundry, *Mark: A Commentary on His Apology for the Cross* (Grand Rapids: Eerdmans, 2004), 258, who also explains why a full allusion to Isa 65:1-7, 11 LXX and its association of demons with tombs is not present, although the text from the prophet does show that such a demon-tomb connection was sometimes made. The terminology does not match that text, so, correctly, Stein, *Mark*, 251. We have at best an echo here, not a full midrash.

chains placed on him (**v** 4). No one could subdue him. He cut himself among the stone where he lived and was constantly crying out (**v** 5). He was isolated, destructive, and self-destructive. He was in a completely desperate state. He had been left on his own, as there was nothing that seemingly could be done. He is "consigned to the land of the dead."[202] In fact, he is the living dead, left with no life.

Jesus will confront this isolating and terrifying power with a liberating and saving power of his own (Mark 1:7). Mark likes to reflect on the power tied to Jesus, used on behalf of others, as Jesus is the stronger one who overcomes the strong one (Mark 3:27). Jesus has no fear of all the uncleanness and bleak forces present in this scene. Jesus ministers among the untouchables here.

As was the case in the exorcism of Mark 1:24, the demon bows before Jesus and responds by asking why he would come and what they have to do with one another (**v** 6). There he was named Jesus of Nazareth and the Holy One of God, but here he is identified as Jesus Son of the Most High God. In 3:11 he had been called the Son of God. The title "Most High God" is common in the LXX; Gentiles in Scripture used it to refer to God (Gen 14:18–20; Num 24:16; Isa 14:14; Dan 3:26; 4:2 [3:32, LXX]; cf. 1 Esdras 2:3; 6:31; 8:19, 21; 2 Macc 3:31; 3 Macc 7:9; Acts 16:17). The title acknowledges God's residence in heaven and his sovereignty (Deut 32:8; Dan 4:17). It also is a sign of respect in a polytheistic context as a reference to Zeus where many gods are seen as operating (Acts 16:17).[203] The title "Son of God" was discussed in detail in 1:1. 4Q246 uses the title of Messiah in a context like this, but that is less than what is intended here by these beings who know who Jesus is and fear his power as a transcendent presence. Once again, supernatural forces make this confession (1:24).

In verse 6, the bowing is a show of respect, but here it is not likely to mean worship, as demons are directing the action. It is ironic to see this powerful presence bow before Jesus, given what has just been described.[204] The authority Jesus has shown in Mark up to this latest exorcism helps to explain the difference in the naming. The demon pleads for Jesus not to torment him. The demon speaks in a singular voice here even though in verse 9 it will be noted that many demons are present in possession of the

---

202 Edwards, *Mark*, 154.
203 Marcus, *Mark 1–8*, 344, notes the use by Pindar in *Nemean Odes* 1.60, where Most High is the name of one of the gates that give entry to Zeus.
204 Guelich, *Mark 1:1–8:26*, 278.

man (**v 7**). Everything about the remark indicates Jesus has authority and power over these malevolent forces and they know it.

In verse 7, the demons recognize Jesus' authority in the request not to be punished. They use a term for torment that often refers to the punishment of prisoners (BDAG 168). This is ironic because the man is already suffering, as is often the case with demon possession (1:26; 5:2–5; 9:17–18, 20–22, 26). These demons desire not to be judged. The request is confused, as the spirit has just acknowledged Jesus' relationship to the God he is invoking. It also is the reverse of what normally takes place in such scenes, as usually the exorcist requests of the demon not to torture him.[205]

Jesus did exorcize the demon, commanding it to come out of the man (**v 8**).[206] There are no formulas or prayers to invoke another. He just speaks. His authority is direct and singular. Jesus also inquired as to the name of the demon (**v 9**). It is not unusual to seek the name of a demon (*T. Sol* 2.1; 3.6; 4.3–4; 5.1–2; 11.4–6 – also a legion is present; 13.1–4; *PGM* 4.3035–50). "Legion," he replied, noting that they were many. So this was a multiple possession. Such multiple possession is rare in the Gospels (Luke 8:2; alluded to in Matt 12:430–45). Legion refers to thousands as a military term, a combination of almost six thousand infantry and cavalry that could include up to six thousand auxiliaries (BDAG 587).[207] The point is not a specific number, but the presence of a vast opposing force. This is not merely a one-on-one battle; Jesus is confronting a full army of demons. The battle Jesus wages for the kingdom is a spiritual one against transcendent forces.

Recognizing he could not stop Jesus (**v 10**), the demon was begging (note the imperfect verb) not to be cast out of the region and noted the herd of swine that were feeding near them (**vv 11–12**). The presence of unclean animals indicates we are in a Gentle region (*m. B Qam* 7:7). The demon's desire to reside there as an alternative underscores the lack of sensitivity of the demon to the ways of God. It is not clear why the demons wanted to remain in the region, except to continue to have a presence and influence there. They are trying to limit the damage of the judgment that is to come. Did they not want to go immediately to the torment of the abyss (Mark 5:7b)? Did they simply want to remain in an area they knew? This text gives

---

[205] Guelich, *Mark 1:1–8:26*, 279.
[206] It is clear the narration reaches back in time here to why the demons sought not to be tormented. The imperfect here functions as a pluperfect (had been saying).
[207] Marcus, *Mark 1–8*, 345, speaks of three thousand to six thousand troops. The term refers to the largest unit in the Roman army.

us no clue as to the reason, but Luke 8:31 says the abyss is the concern. What is clear is that the demons are speaking through the man, showing the possession and "alien occupation."[208]

The unclean spirits ask to be sent into the unclean pigs. Jesus grants the request, but the result is still disaster and judgment for the demons (**v 13**). About two thousand pigs rush into the sea and drown. The pigs are evidence of the exorcism as well as the demons' destructiveness. The scene also vividly displays that the demons have been judged, left to the abyss. The one has overcome the thousands. The moral questions about the destruction of the pigs that modern Westerners raise would not have been questions to the ancients. To them it would have been better that the pigs be destroyed by the demons than that the man who was exorcized be destroyed.[209] The herd is indicative of a large owner. Most herds ran in the low hundreds.

One of the unusual features of this miracle is the long time spent on its aftermath, namely, a full seven verses (**vv 14–20**). The detail shows that not all responses to miracles were positive, even when people recognized that something good had been done. Those caring for the pigs went into town and told what had taken place (**v 14**). So people from the town went out to see (**v 15**). There they found Jesus and the man, no longer possessed, simply sitting with Jesus. This man was much different from the man who was unable to be restrained in Mark 5:4. In their view, this man is the demon-possessed man (note the present participle), yet he is now a completely different person.[210] Rather than being crazed, he was a restored human. The realization of what had taken place left the city afraid. The value of pigs was more important than the restoration of human well-being. This was not a positive fear but one that caused them to not have anything to do with what God was doing. Often fear in Mark is debilitating (Mark 5:36; 6:50; 9:32; 10:32; 11:18, 32; 12:12; fear is positive in 4:41; 5:33; 6:20). This theme sets up Mark's open ending at Mark 16:8. The presence of God can be an invitation or something to distance oneself from accepting, both in Jesus' life and in his resurrection. One will see both reactions to the same

---

[208] France, *Mark*, 230.
[209] Edwards, *Mark*, 159; Witherington, *Mark*, 183. The pigs' part of the miracle is not secondary, as some argue (so, contra, Guelich, *Mark 1:1–8:26*, 282). Without the act against the pigs, the reaction of the town makes no sense and cannot exist. Their reaction is a core part of the scene. Nor is there any political allegory about Rome present. Jesus' battle in Mark is with Satan. So this is a straightforward exorcism, not a parabolic event.
[210] France, *Mark*, 231.

phenomenon. Given the fear, will one respond with faith or distancing from what God is doing? Note also how this fear looks back to Mark 4:41. There the acts of Jesus caused the disciples to ponder who Jesus is. Mark is driving to the same place. Both events share a calm after a traumatic experience. The winds die, and the soul is calm and restored. Mark asks those who encounter his Gospel to ponder who Jesus is and what one will do with what God is doing through him.[211]

The townspeople who had seen Jesus' act of powerful cleansing spread the word about what had taken place to the man and the pigs (**v 16**). Both points are important.[212] With sanity and loss side by side, how would they weigh the contrast? They asked Jesus to leave the region (**v 17**). Economic concerns over pigs had trumped human need and restoration, a common but sad choice. More importantly, Jesus' power had been misread. They read him as a problematic miracle worker, whether economics was involved in the choice or not. It is an unusual end to a miracle story of any sort, biblical or non-biblical, which normally praises the healer.[213] Something is awry in the assessment of Jesus and what he is doing.

So Jesus departs (**v 18**). The man asks if he might come with him. Jesus gives him a different assignment (**v 19**). No reason is given for the refusal. Still the man is to go to his own home and people and tell them about the Lord's mercy. God's kindness had healed him. "Lord" is a reference to God, as Mark does not use it as a title for Jesus. There is no hesitation to tell what God had done, no secret here (contrast Mark 7:31–37 also in Gentile territory). However, what God had done is wrapped up in Jesus' act. So the man returned to the Decapolis and told what Jesus had done for him (**v 20**).[214] He could not tell the story without mentioning Jesus. The report amazed all who heard it. Gentiles heard about Jesus, just as will be the case in Mark 7:24–28. Jesus has now shown power over creation and the demons. His authority over exterior forces is clear. His ministry now extends beyond the borders of Israel.

---

[211] Edwards, *Mark*, 159.

[212] Contra Stein, *Mark*, 258, who argues that Mark has no note about economic loss. The mention of the pigs in the report alongside the man implies this concern as a part of the reaction.

[213] Marcus, *Mark 1–8*, 346.

[214] Donahue and Harrington, *Mark*, 168, note the ten cities of the Decapolis are: Damascus, Philadelphia, Raphana, Scythopolis, Gadara, Hippos, Dion, Pella, Gerasa, and Canatha.

5:21–41 *Jesus Heals a Woman and Raises a Girl*

5:21 When Jesus had crossed again to the other side, a great crowd gathered around him, and he was by the sea.

5:22 Then one of the synagogue rulers, named Jairus, came up and when he saw Jesus, fell at his feet.

5:23 And he asked him urgently saying, "My little daughter is at the end. Come and lay hands on her so she may be delivered and live."

5:24 Jesus went with him. A large crowd followed him and pressed around him.

5:25 Now there was a woman who had suffered with a flow of blood for twelve years

5:26 and she had suffered much under many doctors and spent all she had. And it did her no good but rather she got worse.

5:27 When she heard about Jesus, she came up behind him in the crowd and touched his garment,

5:28 for she was saying, "If only I touch his garments, I will be delivered."

5:29 And immediately the flow of blood dried up and she knew her body had been healed from her torment.

5:30 And immediately Jesus recognized power had come out of him. Turning to the crowd, he said, "Who touched my garments?"

5:31 His disciples were saying to him, "See the crowd pressing against you and you say 'Who touched me?'"

5:32 But he looked around to see the one who did this.

5:33 Then the woman with fear and trembling, knowing what had happened to her, came and fell before him and told the entire truth.

5:34 He said to her, "Daughter, your faith has delivered you. Go in peace and be healed from your torment."

5:35 While he was speaking, people came from the synagogue ruler's house saying, "Your daughter died. Why still trouble the teacher?"

5:36 But Jesus, overhearing what was said, said to the synagogue ruler, "Do not fear. Only believe."

5:37 He did not permit anyone to follow him but Peter, James, and John, the brother of James.

5:38 And they came to the house of the synagogue ruler and he was seeing commotion, weeping, and great wailing.

5:39 And coming into he said to them, "Why are you distressed and weeping? The child is not dead but is sleeping."

5:40 And they mocked him. But he put them all outside and taking the father and mother of the child and those with him and entered to where the child was.

5:41 And grasping the hand of the child he said to her, *"Talitha Koum,"* which means "Little lamb, I say to you, get up."

5:42 And immediately the girl got up and walked. For she was twelve years old. And they were greatly astonished.

5:43 And he strictly ordered them that no one should know about this, and said to give her something to eat.

This scene involves an intertwined double miracle. It has gender balance, as a man makes one request and two females are healed. It has social balance, as the man would have had high social status, whereas the woman with the flow of blood would be on the cultural fringe. The story is abbreviated by Matthew 9:18–26, who also separates it from the previous two miracles, while Luke 8:40–56 keeps the miracles intact and uses much of the detail.

Jesus leaves the Decapolis and returns to the Jewish side on the western edge of the sea (**v 21**). Jesus ministers among a great gathered crowd. There he meets a key civic leader of the synagogue, Jairus (**v 22**). He would have been a lay leader who directed worship services in terms of designating the readers and preachers of the text, those who prayed, and overseeing the building (*m. Yoma* 7:1; *m. Sota* 7:7–8). Some synagogues had more than one such leader (Acts 13:15). He is one of very few Jewish leaders who responds to Jesus and seeks him out. His position could have been by election or heredity.[215] His bowing at Jesus' feet is a cultural sign of respect. The use of a name for a figure healed is rare (see Bartimaeus in Mark 10:46).[216] Still his stature may have led to his name being recalled, whereas the girl who gets healed remains nameless. It would have been striking to see him bow before Jesus.

Jairus has a very sick little girl near death (**v 23**). Mark 5:42 tells us she is a twelve-year-old. Her condition is described idiomatically as she "is having her last," what we might idiomatically express as being on one's last leg. In Matthew 9:18, she is portrayed as having already died, but this difference probably is a result of Matthew's compressed account and presenting her state by the time Jesus shows up. Jairus has a simple request: come and lay hands on the girl so she can be saved from her condition and live (*Genesis Apocryphon* 20:20–22). The expression "being saved" here actually means being delivered from her condition, as the context and so the translation

---

[215]   Stein, *Mark*, 265; C. J. Setzer, *ABD* 5:841–42. Edwards, *Mark*, 161, notes inscriptions that apply the title to women and children, but argues that these are honorific and tied to the men who ran the service, as was the ancient Jewish practice.

[216]   Text critically the external evidence for omission of the name is not strong; Metzger, *Textual Commentary* (1994), 85–86. Omission is mostly a Western reading.

indicates (Mark 3:4; 5:28, 34; 6:56; 10:52; 13:20; 15:30–31; only 8:35, 10:26, and 13:13 look to being spiritually saved). Laying on of hands would be how the healing was communicated in popular terms. The Hebrew Bible has no such example, but 2 Kings 5:11 LXX does (common with Jesus: Mark 6:5; 7:32; 8:23, 25). The man is confident Jesus can heal the girl. He has faith. Jesus goes with him and a great, pressing crowd follows them (v 24). Luke 8:42 describes the crowd as choking them (Mark 3:9–10). This miracle will not be done in a way that leaves people unaware of what has taken place.

As they go to the synagogue leader's home, a woman approaches. Her condition and response in seeking Jesus are described in great detail using seven participles: having, suffering, spending, profiting, becoming, hearing, and coming. Much history had gone into her decision to seek out Jesus and touch him for healing.

She had a flow of blood for twelve years (v 25). The idiom "flow of blood" speaks of a perpetual bleeding condition much like a continuous period. Collins notes how in the ancient world this was seen as a disease, which of course it could well have been (menorrhagia, DUB, or VWD).[217] She lives on the fringe of society because by Jewish standards she is perpetually unclean (Lev 12:1–8; 15:25–30, esp. 15:25; 11QTemple 45:7–17; 46:16–18; 48:14–17; Josephus, *Ant* 3.261; *War* 5.227; and *m. Nid* 7:4). She also might be seen to be at risk in terms of life, since her condition is so lingering.[218] At the least her condition would have produced anemia. The twelve years indicates the condition is long standing and particularly difficult, just like the multiple possession of the previous scene. These are not the simplest of miracles. She is unclean, as the demon-possessed man was in the previous scene. The woman's social status is the exact opposite of Jairus'. Jesus ministers to all levels of people.

She had been attended to by many doctors (v 26), but it had done her no good. She had suffered in their hands. In Judaism, doctors were viewed on a spectrum between esteem (Sir 38:1–5) and contempt (*m. Qid* 4.14 – the best

---

[217] Collins, *Mark*, 280, cites Aristotle, *Historia Animalum* 3.19 (521a.25–27) and Galen, *On the Affected Places*, 332, 336, among other texts, and Soranus (3.10–11 §40–44), who did distinguish between sudden hemorrhages and other more common discharges. Remedies include magic as well as various washes or attempts to simply relieve the pain.

[218] Marcus, *Mark 1–8*, 357–58, details the social isolation and fear for one's life, given the loss of blood, that this condition would have produced. So her condition might be seen as not being much different from the daughter's in terms of the threat. The condition led to the woman being called a *zab*, a sacrifice.

doctor is worthy of hell!; Tob 2:10 – of failure to heal; 1QapGen 20:20).[219] Not only was her money gone, having spent it all, but she had come into a worse condition. Whatever they had given her to take care of the problem only accentuated her lingering condition. This might include various combinations of wine and powder taken from rubber, alum, or garden crocuses or simply wine and onions.[220] She had profited nothing from her efforts. Her social status had gone from being wealthy enough to seek out many doctors to having nothing.

So upon hearing about Jesus' coming (v 27), she decides to try and come up behind him and secretly touch his garments. This reflects a populist, almost magical kind of faith (Mark 3:10; 6:56; Acts 19:12). Her faith was that all she needed to do was touch him and she would be delivered (v 28). The idea is expressed as a third-class condition with no presumption that the faith is automatic. It reflects a resolve to be healed. She does as she planned. Her willingness to go into public and risk it shows both her faith and desperation. The verb here for her hope is the same as that Jairus uses of his daughter (*sōzō*). Again the expectation is of being healed, delivered from her condition and returned to restored life.[221]

Upon touching Jesus she senses that she is healed and that the bleeding has stopped (v 29). Her uncleanness did not defile Jesus upon her touch, but his cleanness cleanses her. Jesus honors her populist faith because it is directed at him (Mark 5:34). He does what an army of doctors could not do. More than that, the healing had cost her nothing but having faith. The description is vivid. The flow of blood immediately dried up and she sensed her body had been relieved of its torment or suffering (on *mastix*, BDAG 620). The term for suffering pictures a whip and the lashing that disease gives a person. The idea that her flow stopped echoes Lev 12:7 LXX and points to her being made clean. The suffering was over.

Jesus noted the power that had departed from him so he asked who had touched him (v 30), a query that amazes the disciples given the press of the crowd (v 31). Still, Jesus sought out the one who touched him. It is easy to

---

[219] Collins, *Mark*, 281, cites Greco-Roman sources that show doctors had a reputation of taking financial advantage of people (e.g., Martial, *Epigrams* 1.47; 5.9; 8:74; 9.96; Plutarch, *Moralia* 177F [9]). In contrast, she notes the Hippocratic work *Precepts* 4 and 6 calls for doctors not to worry about their fees and to treat the poor fairly.

[220] Lane, *Mark*, 191, n. 46.

[221] Stein's reading, *Mark*, 268, that being cleansed is not a concern here ignores the entire cultural context of the restoration. Mark does not need to mention it explicitly. It comes with the territory of restoration. The remark ignores the significance of the allusion to language from Lev 12:7.

forget about Jairus in the midst of this delay. One can only imagine what Jairus felt as Jesus' arrival to his house was delayed. However, Jesus is going to develop the faith of this woman first.

The feminine participle in Mark 5:32 shows that a woman is being looked for here. Either Jesus or the narrator knew that this was a woman. A narrative comment to that effect seems superfluous as the story makes this clear, so there is a hint here that Jesus was aware of who it was. Jesus sought her out for her sake, not his own. It is also easy to give the disciples a hard time here, as many commentators do and argue that Mark does, but the disciples have no idea that the touch of the woman has led to a healing, so the question from Jesus seems odd to them and is not deserving of their being criticized, given the limits of what they know. The entire exchange shows how aware Jesus is of what is taking place.

The woman, recognizing she has been discovered (v 33), and with fear and trembling for the recognition of power present (Mark 4:41; 5:15), falls before Jesus. Would he expose the fact she had touched him while unclean?[222] Would public shame be on the way? She takes the high road and decides to tell her story, all of it, the whole truth out of respect for what she senses Jesus already knows. Fear has led into trust and faith. Jesus has forced a personal encounter and growth.[223] This is where fear of God's presence and action should take one. Again the theme sets up the climactic events of Mark 16.

Jesus responds in four steps (v 34): a gentle address, a declaration, a blessing, and a promise. Jesus addresses her gently as daughter, a reassuring address unique in the Gospels. He commends her faith in return (Mark 2:5; 4:40; 5:36; 9:23–24; esp. 10:52; 11:22–24; Luke 7:50; 17:19). Her belief in Jesus has delivered her, not her touch.[224] There is a benediction/blessing

---

[222] On the debate as to how important cleanliness is to this story, pro and con, Collins, *Mark*, 283–84. She argues that although it is not explicit, it works in the cultural background of the account. It is not at all clear that the woman's condition required complete social isolation, although in some circles it might have; see Shaye J. D. Cohen, "Menstruants and the Sacred in Judaism and Christianity," in *Women's History and Ancient History*, ed. Sarah B. Pomeroy (Chapel Hill/London: University of North Carolina Press, 1991), 273–99, esp. 278–79, and Amy-Jill Levine on Matthew 9:18–26, "Discharging Responsibility: Matthean Jesus, Biblical Law, and Hemorrhaging Woman," in *Treasures New and Old: Recent Contributions to Matthean Studies*, ed. David R. Bauer and Mark Allan Powell (SBLSymS 1; Atlanta: Scholars Press, 1996), 379–97.

[223] Witherington, *Mark*, 188.

[224] Lane, *Mark*, 193; see Marcus, *Mark 1–8*, 360–61, on faith and miracles and how this account is distinct from Greco-Roman parallels. There miracles lead to faith, but here faith leads to miracles. Speculation exists that these were originally two separate miracles stories now combined, but such arguments are hypothetical and lack solid

and a promise. She can go in peace (Judg 18:6; 1 Sam 1:17; 2 Sam 15:9; 1 Kings 22:17; Luke 7:50; Acts 16:36; James 2:16). This is a common blessing that also shows God is pleased with what has taken place. She also can know that she is permanently healed from her tormenting suffering. Note the repetition of the vivid term for tormented suffering in Mark 5:29. This healing was not magic, but an act of God. Grace with faith has brought not shame but peace.[225]

At this same time, bad news arrives. During the delay, Jairus' daughter has died (**v 35**). There is an interesting juxtaposition with the term *daughter* in verses 34–35. One daughter is saved while the other dies in the meantime. Members from the household bring the announcement. What was gained in one quarter now seems lost in another. The emissaries suggest there is no longer need to bother the teacher. There is no expectation of being able to raise someone from death. The delay appears to have been devastating for Jairus' request. All the miracles in this series are consistently great: nature, multiple demons, a long-term disease, and now death. These are acts beyond what normal humans might hope to experience (Mark 4:37–38; 5:3–5, 25–26).[226]

Jesus overhears what is said (**v 36**). Some translations have "ignored," but Jesus reacts to what is said. In effect, he ignores it, but it is a conscious response to the suggestion that there is nothing that can now be done.[227] He goes a different direction than the messengers suggest. He reassures Jairus, telling him not to fear but only to believe. The present imperative calls for an ongoing trust, a faith like that Jesus just commended the woman for having. It also is a call to maintain the faith Jairus had when he approached Jesus. Collins calls it "a call for courage," and Lane says it is a "radical trust."[228] Once again Mark raises the fear-faith contrast with a call to believe.

Jesus takes only Peter, James, and John, the brother of James (**v 37**). His inner circle will see this ability to challenge death, and will be there later at the Transfiguration, Gethsemane, and at the Mount of Olives with Andrew. Luke 8:51 also notes that the parents went in with Jesus. They

---

demonstration. The very uniqueness of the intertwining speaks for authenticity in the tradition, not a created juxtaposition. It is dissimilar to other miracle accounts.

225 Lane, *Mark*, 194 notes that this story made a deep impression on tradition. The woman received the name Berenice in the Coptic tradition and Veronica in Latin (Acts of Pilate 7; Eusebius, *Eccl His* 7.18.1–4, says she came from Caesarea Philippi).

226 Guelich, *Mark*, 300.

227 Lane, *Mark*, 195, says, "Jesus heard what they said but deliberately ignored its import."

228 Colllins, *Mark*, 285; Lane, *Mark*, 196.

will also serve as multiple witnesses. Upon arriving at the home, full-blown mourning is taking place. These would be friends and/or professional mourners. Poor families would often have at least two flute players to participate in the mourning (Jer 9:17–20; Josephus, *War* 2.1.3. §6; 3.9.5.§437; *m. Ketub* 4.4).[229] Jairus was not poor, so there likely was a crowd. So Jesus arrives to commotion and much weeping and wailing. It is a sad indication that the girl had truly died.

Jesus tells the crowd the girl is not dead but sleeps (**v 39**; Matt 27:52; John 11:11; Acts 7:60; 13:36; 1 Thess 4:13–15; 5:10; *Genesis Rabbah* 17.5). It is not a denial that she has died but rather a consideration of the fact that here death is not permanent and the power of God he accesses can bring her back to life. This is a figurative use of the term *sleep*. Mark is seeing a potential resuscitation back to life out of death as Luke 8:55 did. It is a ludicrous claim, if Jesus does not possess the power he will utilize. So the crowd laughs at him in skepticism and unbelief (**v 40**).

Jesus now moves to heal the child. He sends all those mourning outside and moves into the room where the girl is. With his three companions and the parents, he goes into the girl. The fact that there is more than one room in the house indicates that Jairus is not poor.[230] Jesus touches the child, grabbing her hand. Touch is sometimes included in Jesus' miraculous work (Mark 1:31; 9:27). Just as with the woman with a flow of blood (Mark 5:30–34), the touch does not render Jesus unclean because he is reversing that which communicated uncleanness. In Aramaic, which Mark renders literally and with translation, he tells the girl to get up, picturing her as a little lamb (**v 41**).[231] This is a simple command to awake and arise from the dead. It is not a magical formula. Unlike the resuscitation from Elijah and Elisha (1 Kings 17:17–23; 2 Kings 4:18–37), Jesus does not pray to bring healing. His word is enough.

Immediately she is healed and walking around (**v 42**). Because she has been described as a little girl, Mark notes she is twelve years old, so we appreciate she is not a toddler, but at the cusp of moving into society. As the just healed woman had bled for twelve years, this girl had been alive for

---

[229] Stein, Mark 273; Strack-Billerbeck 1:521–23.

[230] Marcus, *Mark 1–8*, 362–63, makes this perceptive observation, but his claim that this mirrors magical papyri does not follow. Jesus does not use a foreign language or secret words. Mark says clearly what Jesus says, an expression of simple command rendered in Jesus' own tongue; correctly, Guelich, *Mark 1:1–8:26*, 302; Witherington, *Mark*, 190.

[231] France, *Mark*, 240, n. 30; Mark often cites an Aramaic expression (Mark 3:17; 7:11, 34; 11:9–10; 14:36; 15:22, 34). The Aramaic term *talitha* can refer to a lamb or a little child. It is clearly a term of endearment. The previous translation reflects this ambiguity.

the same period of time. Her life has been restored to a usefulness that will soon make her able to pursue life to the full.

Jesus instructs them not to make known what has taken place (**v 43;** Mark 1:41–45; 7:31–36). Now there is no way people will not suspect what took place, as mourners had been to the house and knew about the girl's death. The goal rather is to prevent more attention coming just to Jesus' healing. He does not want it publicized and emphasized. Jesus then tells them to give her something to eat. He cares for her well-being now that she has been restored to life. This act of eating also shows she is truly raised. This was no phantom or visionary experience. The entire experience left those who saw it amazed. This is a rare term appearing only here in Mark 16:8 and in Luke 5:26. So Jesus performs a double miracle, showing his power over disease and death and completing a sequence where nature, demons, disease, and death are subject to his power and authority.

6:1–6 Jesus Speaks in the Synagogue and Encounters Skepticism

6:1 Now Jesus left that place and came to his hometown, and his disciples followed him.

6:2 When the Sabbath came, he began to teach at the synagogue. Many who heard him were astonished, saying, "Where did he get these things? And what is this wisdom that has been given to him? What are these miracles that are done through his hands?

6:3 Is this not the craftsman, the son of Mary and brother of James, Joses, Judas, and Simon? And are not his sisters here with us?" And so they took offense at him.

6:4 Then Jesus was saying to them, "A prophet is not without honor except in his hometown, and among his relatives, and in his own house."

6:5 And he was not able to do any miracle there, except when he laid hands on a few people, he healed them.

6:6 And he was amazed because of their unbelief. Then he went around among the villages teaching.

This scene is a biographical pronouncement account. It shows how people are responding to Jesus. Jesus now returns to Nazareth with his disciples (**v 1;** Luke 4:16). Mark does not name the specific locale, probably because Jesus' origins were well known in the church. Luke 4:16–30 presents what Jesus taught in terms of fulfilling promise in a description of his mission, but Matthew 13:53–58 and Mark lack this detail. In fact, what likely has happened is that Luke has moved forward this event to be representative of Jesus' Galilean ministry. In doing so, Luke has given more detail.

Jesus goes to the synagogue to teach (**v 2**). Many in the audience were astonished, caught off guard by his teaching. This reaction by a crowd is common in Mark and usually is positive (Mark 1:22; 7:37; 10:26; 11:18). Here it is not a term picturing belief, as the end of verse 3 makes clear, but simply a reaction that says we did not expect this. A series of reflective, rhetorical questions emerge (**vv 2–3**). From where did these things emerge for this man? How did he acquire this wisdom? How can one explain the miracles he does? The remark appears to suggest the miraculous activity of Jesus has been recent, whereas some apocryphal gospels portray it as having taken place throughout Jesus' life. It also suggests they sense what he has comes from somewhere other than the natural flow of his life, from beyond in one way or another. There is a kind of disconnect. How did the Jesus we know and grew up with come to this? The response is reflective, neither positive nor negative in itself. It is perplexity, reflecting having pause about the power of what Jesus is doing alongside their past knowledge of him.[232]

On the other hand, is this not the carpenter, the son of Mary?[233] The term for carpenter really refers to a craftsman, someone who builds with wood or stone. The work we see reflected in Sepphoris, a major city a few miles away, points to this kind of combination. It is likely Jesus did this kind of work there. That is what they remember about him before he started to engage in ministry near the age of thirty. He would have engaged in such trade for about two decades before he launched out to preach and teach about the kingdom of God.

The absence of Joseph's name is unusual. It may indicate that he is now dead or that he is the less prominent of the two parents for some reason.[234]

---

[232] Guelich, *Mark 1:1–8:26*, 308; contra Stein, *Mark*, 281, who sees these verses positively, something that can be done only if one does not give the remark about taking offense enough weight.

[233] The reference to carpenter or craftsman here refers to Jesus, not directly to Joseph, who goes unmentioned. The bulk of the manuscript evidence from the uncials, minuscules, and versions makes this clear; Metzger, *Textual Commentary* (1971), 88–89. Even a text like p[45] assimilates the text to Matthew 13:55 or Luke 4:22 and has a reference to Joseph, probably on the basis that describing Jesus as a carpenter undervalues who he is. The point of the various parallels is that Jesus' family is known to them. For the tradition of Jesus' vocation, see Justin Martyr, *Dialogues*, 88.

[234] Among the suggestions are: a veiled reference to the virgin birth, an attack on Jesus' legitimacy (Lane, *Mark*, 203; Marcus, *Mark 1–8*, 375; possibly, Edwards, *Mark*, 272), his mother's prominence (Edwards, *Mark*, 171), the possibility Joseph had other children from an earlier marriage, that he had already died (France, *Mark*, 242), some kind of slur,

The question expects a positive reply. He is just Mary and Joseph's son. Do we not know his brothers, James, Joses, and Simon, as well as his sisters? James became the leader of the church in Jerusalem. Joses is sometimes equated with Jude, the letter writer. Of the other we know nothing else. How can someone like that come from origins like this? So it says they took offense at him, possibly because he was claiming more than they thought he had the right to claim. The reference to offense shows that, in the end, the crowd found Jesus fascinating but not one to embrace. They are asking, how could our Jesus have teaching, wisdom, and miracles? Their answer is that it is a curious situation.

Jesus' response is a pronouncement in a proverb (**v 4**). A prophet has honor everywhere but in his hometown, among relatives, and in his home (Luke 4:24; John 4:44; *Thomas* 31; P. Oxy 1.6; Plutarch, *De Exilo* 604D). Mark's version is the most emphatic, as it mentions relatives, and not just homeland as Matthew and Luke do or home as Mark does with Matthew. It is a variation of our saying that familiarity breeds contempt. Jesus is noting that what is causing the crowd to hesitate in this case is a common thing. They had too much everyday experience with Jesus, especially in the many years he did not engage in ministry.

So Jesus was not able to perform many miracles (**v 5**), except lay hands on a few people. Their lack of faith made for a restriction on his activity. The issue was not so much on Jesus' inability to do works of power (*dunamin*); rather, the intended linkage between faith and works of power meant that Jesus would not randomly perform such works for their own sake. Apparently the rise in opposition led to fewer coming to him.[235] His work was not only about healing, so without some openness to the message, healing made no sense and had no opportunity to take place. As Guelich says, "Jesus did not come as a magician or a miracle worker to display and dazzle his audience."[236] Mark emphasizes the relationship between faith and healing (Mark 2:5; 5:34, 36; 9:23-24; 10:52; 11:22-24).

(Witherington, *Mark*, 193), or simply Mark's lack of interest in Joseph. So little is said that there is no way to know. Edwards, *Mark*, 173, and n. 67, treats the issue of these being half-brothers or cousins, rejecting both options. Marcus, *Mark*, 375, also rejects the earlier marriage view, arguing that then another mother would have been mentioned. Why connect the siblings to one who was not their mother? On the unusual nature of referring to the mother, Collins, *Mark*, 290-91.

[235] Commentators who spend energy explaining Jesus as "not being able to heal" may be overlooking a rather simple explanation. Where faith was absent, people were not coming forward and seeking him out.

[236] Guelich, *Mark 1:1-8:26*, 311.

The unbelief amazed Jesus (**v 6**), so he went to other villages and taught.[237] This is the only passage in Mark where Jesus is described as amazed. Jesus' experience in his hometown was a microcosm of what was coming in ministry. He would teach, act, and heal, but many would not respond. At one level, the rejection of such clear divine activity is amazing and tragic to Mark. Even those acting faithfully meet with rejection, as Jesus' example shows. This is a key theme of Mark. You can be faithful and yet be rejected by many who will not see the good you represent.

6:7–8:26 JESUS IN GALILEE: JESUS' ACTS YIELD A CONFESSION

6:7–13 Jesus Sends the Twelve Out into Mission

6:7 Jesus called the twelve and began to send them out two by two. He gave them authority over unclean spirits.

6:8 He instructed them that they take nothing along the way except a staff alone, no bread, no bag, no money in their belts,

6:9 but to put on sandals, and not to wear two tunics.

6:10 And he was saying to them, "Wherever you come into a house, stay there until you leave the area.

6:11 And whatever place does not receive you or listen to you, going from there, shake the dust from your feet as a testimony against them."

6:12 And going out, they preached that they might repent

6:13 and cast out many demons and anointed with oil many who were sick and healed them.

Mission in the face of rising opposition now becomes a key theme for Mark. This scene is a summary report on mission. Jesus expanded his message by commissioning the Twelve to minister on their own. The commission is noted here in Mark 6:7–13 with the report coming back to Jesus in 6:30. The bookends form yet another Markan sandwich in the Gospel.

He sent them out two by two with authority to cast out demons as he had been doing (**v 7**). Traveling in pairs was not unusual (Luke 7:18; 24:13; John 1:37; Acts 8:14; 9:38; 11:30; 13:1–3; 15:22, 39–40). It might be rooted in the two-witness requirement (Num 35:30; Deut 17:6; 19:15; just the idea of the benefits of pairing: Eccl 4:9–10). Mark presents this authority as something

---

[237] Mark 6:6, especially 6b, is often seen to introduce the next unit. That is possible. It is really a transition verse, explaining what Jesus did after he left his home. The verse pictures Jesus moving "in a circle" (*kuklw*) in the region.

Jesus himself gives to them. It is yet another evidence of his prerogatives. *T. Levi* 18:12 expected this of messiah, as the messianic high priest would "grant authority to his children to trample on wicked spirits."[238] So these commissioned disciples will speak and minster, giving words of grace and performing deeds to support it. These disciples are still learning, but they also are to be witnesses for God. Jesus does not wait until they have full understanding before he sends them out.

They are to travel with the bare necessities, nothing extra (**vv 8-9**). Their ministry will be on the move. They can take a staff, but no bread, traveler's bag, or money in their belts. The reference to bread could be to food in general, as the point is to depend on others to provide for them. A staff helped one walk and could be used for protection against wild animal and bandits.[239] Matt 10:9-10 and Luke 9:3 have similar lists with a few differences, such as taking no staff or sandals. A distinct commission in Luke 10:4 is also similar when the seventy-two are sent out. Exod 12:11 have people going with sandals on and staff in hand.[240] As with the Exodus, they are to travel light and be ready to move on, so the point may be that they can take nothing extra, which can be expressed in a variety of ways. Another possible point of background is that *m Ber* 9:5 forbids a person to enter the temple with staff, sandals, or wallet, so we may have an indication of a sacred task.[241] These points show how these items were seen culturally. It is clear that Jesus is making a point about the humble values attached to mission.

Beggars and itinerant philosophers who sought donations often used a traveler's bag to collect money (*Diogenes Laertius* 6.13, 22). Jesus forbade its use on this trip. They could take sandals, but they were to wear only one tunic. The second tunic often served as a bedroll for the poor. They were to trust that God would care for them through the hospitable reception of others. The Essenes gave such care to other travelers from their own communities (Josephus, *War* 2.124-27). There is nothing ostentatious about the way they would travel.[242] The travel with little provision is like

---

[238]   Edwards, *Mark*, 178.

[239]   Marcus, *Mark 1-8*, 383.

[240]   Stein, *Mark*, 292, objects that the term for staff is not the same as the LXX, but in dealing with a translation from Aramaic, the use of synonyms does not discount an allusion; Lane, *Mark*, 207, n. 31; Marcus, *Mark 1-8*, 389; E. Power, "The Staff of the Apostles, A Problem in Gospel Harmony," *Bib* 4 (1923): 241-66, has an older, full discussion.

[241]   T. W. Manson, *The Sayings of Jesus* (London: SCM, 1957), 181.

[242]   This stands in contrast to the warning about the advantage later missionaries took in *Did* 11:4-6, where two days were said to be sufficient. The difference is that the Twelve were starting communities, whereas *Didache* addressed established communities.

Cynic philosophers, who did use the traveler's bag (BDAG 656) Jesus prohibits, but this light travel was not intended as imitation of them, as they were not prominent in Galilee.[243]

They were to stay in the home they entered in any place where they were, accepting the hospitality offered (**vv 10–11**). If they were not received, then they were to depart, shaking the dust from their feet as a testimony against them.[244] The people were still accountable before God, even with their rejection. Culturally, this act meant that the "unclean" state of the town (for rejecting those whom God had sent) was no longer attached to the feet of the messengers (Matt 10:14; Mark 6:11; Acts 13:51; 18:6; cf. Neh 5:13). The act was a sign that the responsibility was theirs and the Twelve had "washed their hands" of it. A variety of more detailed explanations include treating the area like Gentiles, a separation of future contact, or responsibility for future judgment.[245] Accountability for judgment is the key point (Matt 10:15; Luke 9:5; 10:12).

So they went out and preached that all should repent (**v 12**; Mark 1:15). They cast out demons and healed the sick, anointing them with oil (**v 13**). Mark clearly distinguishes between disease and demon possession here. This is the only mention of anointing with oil in the Gospels (Isa 1:6; James 5:14–15). It was designed to soothe wounds and represents the presence of God. The ministry of word and deed Jesus has started will be continued with the Twelve. They are to mirror his work.

6:14–29 As Herod Contemplates Who Jesus Is, the Execution of John the Baptist Is Told

> **6:14 Now the King Herod heard, for Jesus' name had become known, and they were saying, "John the Baptist is raised from the dead, and because of this miraculous works are worked by him."**

---

[243] For the Cynics' practice, Arrian, *Discourses of Epictetus*, 3.22.50; Diogenes Laertius 6.85 and Pseudo-Diogenes, *Epistles* 30.4. For the non-imitation of Cynics in this instruction, see France, *Mark*, 248, n. 16; Edwards, *Mark*, 179–80; and H. D. Betz, "Jesus and the Cynics: Survey and Analysis of a Hypothesis," *JR* 74 (1994): 453–75. On stoic practice and poverty, Musonius Rufus 19.

[244] A text-critical issue here exists where some later manuscripts add a reference to it being more tolerable for Sodom and Gomorrah in the judgment, an expansion that assimilates this text to Matt 10:15. It is not likely to be original to Mark.

[245] Treat like Gentiles, as rabbis viewed Gentile dirt as unclean, *m. 'Ohol* 2:3; *m. Toh.* 4:5; Edwards, *Mark*, 181; separation, Marcus, *Mark 1–8*, 384; judgment, Cranfield, *Mark*, 201. It is not clear that these are mutually exclusive explanations, as Lane, *Mark*, 209, argues for both judgment and separation of broken communication, while France, *Mark*, 250, argues for the Gentile parallel and judgment. See especially Neh 5:13 and 2 Esdr 15:13.

6:15 Others were saying, "He is Elijah." But others were saying, "He is a prophet, like one of the prophets."

6:16 Upon hearing this, Herod was saying, "John, whom I beheaded, has been raised."

6:17 For Herod himself, having sent men, arrested John and bound him in prison on account of Herodias, his brother Philip's wife, because Herod had married her.

6:18 For John was saying to Herod, "It is not lawful for you to have the wife of your brother."

6:19 So Herodias held a grudge against John and wished him to be killed, but she could not,

6:20 for Herod feared John, seeing him as a righteous and holy man, and so he protected him. And he was greatly perplexed by John and liked to listen to him.

6:21 But a favorable day came, when Herod gave a banquet for his court officials, military tribunes and the prominent of Galilee.

6:22 When Herodias' daughter came in and danced, she pleased Herod and his dinner guests. The king said to the girl, "Ask of me whatever you wish and I will give it to you."

6:23 He swore to her, "Whatever you ask of me I will give to you up to half my kingdom."

6:24 And coming out, she said to her mother, "What should I ask for?" Her mother said, "The head of John the Baptist."

6:25 And coming in immediately she hurried back to the king and asked saying, "I want the head of John the Baptist on a platter immediately."

6:26 And becoming exceedingly sad, the king, because of the oaths and those reclining with him, did not want to deny her.

6:27 So the king immediately sent an executioner to bring John's head. And going out he decapitated him in the prison.

6:28 And he brought his head on a platter and gave it to the girl, and the girl gave it to the mother.

6:29 And upon hearing John's disciples came and took his body and set it in a tomb.

The next scene involves two intertwined reports: popular views of Jesus juxtaposed to the account of John the Baptist's death. The link is the popular association of Jesus with the return of John the Baptist. The cloud of potential opposition noted in the previous mission also leads at a narrative level into the report about Jesus to Herod and his reflection about John and Jesus. The mission of Mark 6:6–13 may have been part of what got Jesus the attention, although he had done much in the region to gain attention otherwise and there is no mention of the disciples in the report. The report on John is the only account in the Gospel not about Jesus. It shows that God's messengers may not always be well received, something the warning about opposition to the disciples in their mission also indicated. John's story will parallel that of Jesus.[246]

The popular reflection in verses 14–16 leads into the retelling of how John died.[247] Opposition to the prophets of God had already led to a martyr. In fact, the telling of the story of John's death might be considered a martyrdom account (Azariah – 2 Chron 24:20–22; Eleazar – 2 Macc 6:18–31; the Maccabean brothers – 2 Macc 7).[248] The speculation, perhaps out of a sense of guilt for Herod, was that Jesus was John raised (v 14). Some in the public raised that possibility and Herod appears to have taken it seriously. The idea of John being raised may simply mean John's spirit worked in Jesus, as resurrection was strictly an idea left to the end of history for Jews. The example is Elijah's spirit resting on Elisha (2 Kings 2:1–15).[249] Others thought Jesus was Elijah (v 15), heralding the end time (Mal 3:1; 4:5–6), or one of the prophets. The association with miracles and John is somewhat odd, since there is no tradition of John working miracles (John 10:41).

Another key point is that messianic speculation is not a part of this popular report, perhaps because Jesus was not as overtly political as the Messiah was anticipated to be. The crowd does not get who Jesus is, but

---

[246] C. Wolff, "Zur Bedeutung Johannes des Taufers im Markusevangeliums," *TLZ* 102 (1977): 857–65. Wolff shows the structural parallels between the sequence of the two stories: arrest, death plot, fear, innocent executed under pressure and burial; also Witherington, *Mark*, 213. Especially noteworthy is that both sense that the person they hold is innocent (Mark 6:20, 26 and 15:14).

[247] Read in verse 14b "they were saying" (*elegon*) here, not "he was saying." The plural is the more difficult reading and has better, older manuscript support (B, W, key old Latin witnesses).

[248] Guelich, *Mark 1:1–8:26*, 326. Josephus also discusses John's death (*Ant* 18.116–19). On page 331, Guelich argues that Josephus and Mark look at events from complementary angles. Josephus mentions the war with Aretas IV, king of Nabatea, that Herod faced for divorcing his first wife to marry Herodias, exacting the earlier wife's father's revenge. This act violated Lev 18:16 as Herodias was Herod Antipas' brother's wife while he was still alive, and Herodias initiated that divorce. Jewish law also forbade a wife to divorce a husband, so there was a double violation; France, *Mark*, 256. Herod Antipas also was Herodias' uncle, as Herodias was a granddaughter of Herod the Great (a marriage prohibited in CD 5:8–11). Josephus says this was seen by some as divine revenge for immorality. For both writers, the ruler's morals were seen as less than stellar. The role of Herodias is at the center of Mark's account starting in Mark 6:17; also Harold Hoehner, *Herod Antipas* (Cambridge: Cambridge University Press, 1972), 136–46. Potential sources for such a story are Joanna, wife of Herod's steward (Luke 8:3) and Manaen (Acts 13:1); Stein, *Mark*, 303.

[249] Stein, *Mark*, 301; France, *Mark*, 203. Mark 1:6 alluded to Elijah's connection to John the Baptist. Matthew 11:14 presents John as Elijah.

leaves him in a popular and high category where people often like to leave him. Such a view blocks the way to real faith.[250] For Mark, Jesus is far more than a prophet (Mark 15:39). Matthew 14:3–12 and Luke 9:7–10 also treat the speculation about Jesus, and Matthew also tells the story of John's death.

Herod was one of the client-kings of Rome, the son of Herod the Great, and of Idumean descent. He was born in 20 BCE. He had authority over the neighboring regions of Galilee and Perea from 4 BCE to CE 39. Officially he was a tetrarch, which was lower than a full client-king. Still the title king was popularly applied to him. The presence of tetrarch in Luke 9:7 and Matt 14:1 versus king in Matt 14:9 shows the usage. He was insensitive to Jewish concerns, as he founded a major city on the site of a cemetery, ignoring concerns for ritual cleanliness (*Ant* 18.36–38). He did so to give land and property to some in his region in an area many Jews would hesitate to inhabit.

John is imprisoned by Herod because of his illegal marriage to Herodias (**v 17**; Lev 18:16; 20:21; Luke 3:19). The arrest was already noted in Mark 1:14. In contrast to Jesus sending out messengers to tell them about God's program (Mark 6:7), Herod sends out men to arrest John. John likely was held at Machaerus, a military headquarters east of the Dead Sea not far from Perea (*Ant* 18.119). It is possible he was moved to Tiberias, as the banquet has Galilean attendees.

John had criticized this breach of Torah when Herod married his brother Philip's wife (**v 18**), and so Herod took him into custody.[251] Herodias wanted John dead, but Herod protected him because he saw John really as a righteous and holy man. In fact, the text says Herod feared John, in contrast to Herodias who held a grudge against John (**vv 19–20**). The idea of a grudge is rare in the NT, appearing only here and in Luke 11:53 of the Pharisees against Jesus. The prophet was confusing to Herod, for the prophet's rebuke was a sharp and embarrassing public critique, but he liked listening to the prophet. Matthew 14:3–5 says Herod wanted him dead.

---

[250] Edwards, *Mark*, 185; Hooker, *Mark*, 159–60.

[251] Some argue that Mark erred here in referring to Philip the tetrarch, but Mark probably referred to another Herod, who also may have been called Philip, adding only the second name Philip to make his identity clear (Guelich, *Mark 1:1–8:26*, 331). The multiple wives Herod the Great had (ten total) makes tracing descent difficult. Herod the Great also had two wives named Mariamne. Josephus called him only Herod according to Lane, *Mark*, 216, referring simply to his family name. There is no source that has both names. Some do see her married to Philip the tetrarch; noted by Collins, *Mark*, 307, n. 101, but she is skeptical about the account seeing assimilation to Jezebel (1 Kings 19:2). Guelich, *Mark 1:1–8:26*, 331, notes that Herodias succeeds where Jezebel fails and so questions this typology as the key detail here.

Mark has more detail here and shows Herod conflicted. The Greek term *aporeō* means to be at a loss about something (BDAG, 119).[252] It describes the disciples' reaction when Jesus initially announced that he would be betrayed by one of them (John 13:22). It was the women's first reaction when they discovered the empty tomb (Luke 24:4). Herod was at an impasse about what to do with John. Should he heed him or kill him?

Things change at a banquet given on his birthday with governmental nobles, and military and social leaders of Galilee present (**v 21**). The mention of Galileans makes the scene appear to be located in Tiberias. His daughter, Herodias, dances for the crowd and pleases them all (**v 22**).[253] She would have been in her mid-teens, of marriageable age. The term *pleased* (*areskō*) can refer frequently to sexual arousal (Gen 19:8; Esth 2:4, 9; Job 31:10; Jdt 12:14). Herod offers her whatever she wishes (**v 23**), seals it with an oath, and says whatever she desires he will give her up to half the kingdom – clearly hyperbole but an indicator of Herod's being quite pleased with her.[254] The promise echoes Esth 5:3. These banquets usually have the feel of symposia, a celebratory meal where drinking and carousing takes place, that was criticized by Jews (*m. 'Abod Zar* 1.3). However, since this is a family member, it is debated how raucous this scene would have been. It may have simply been the display of a child's talent.[255] Either way, Herod makes a rash promise with a public oath that binds him.

The daughter did not know what she wanted to do (**v 24**), so she ran to her mother to ask what she should request. The mother told her to ask for the head of John the Baptist, which she did with enthusiasm when she asked for his head on a platter (**v 25**). Herod was caught. He was very sad because he sensed that the oath (Num 30:2; Judg 11:29–40) and the public nature of making it in front of guests gave him no other option (**v 26**). He had to honor her request.

---

[252] The imperfect of this verb is the likely reading here (with ℵ and B). The variant (*epoiei*) is likely a fix for this rare term.

[253] In Mark 6:24, Herodias is called his daughter by ℵ, B, D and L. Technically she is his stepdaughter. Alternatives smoothing out the text call her the daughter of Herodias. We are dealing with popular expression in the more difficult reading, since she is the daughter of Herod's wife. She is known as Salome (Josephus, *Ant* 18.136). We may also be dealing with an alternate name.

[254] The reading without *polla* in Mark 6:23 is slightly more likely to be original. NA 28 brackets it. ℵ and B lack it with the majority text and some Western witnesses, although p⁴⁵ has it, making it possibly original.

[255] For a raucous dance, Lane, *Mark*, 221; for a child's performance, Donahue and Harrington, *Mark*, 198–99. Noting that Herod was not a paragon of virtue, Marcus, *Mark 1–8*, 396, and Hooker, *Mark*, 161, hold the scene as plausible, even though this is a family member.

So Herod sends an executioner to carry out the promise (**v 27**). The executioner is actually a bodyguard (the Latin loan word is *spekoulatora*) who does what the king requires. John is beheaded in prison and the head is brought to the girl (**v 28**), who in turn gives it to her mother. The plan now carried out, the disciples of John come and collect the remains and place the body in a tomb, giving him an appropriate burial (**v 29**). The notice echoes Mark 15:42–46 about Jesus' burial. *The Midrash on Esther* 1:19–21 has a similar story where the head of Vashti is brought to the king on a platter. John dies unjustly for standing up for righteousness. Sometimes death is the fate of the one who speaks for God. It is a lesson not lost on Jesus (Mark 9:12–13). Herod is portrayed as conflicted: fascinated by John but afraid of the moral challenge he represents. In the end, Herod opts to protect his own interests and behavior. The guilt of the choice shows up in Herod's reflection that Jesus may be John raised from the dead, which probably means his spirit now guides Jesus, as Jesus was John's contemporary.

6:30–44 Jesus' Compassion Is Displayed and the Miracle of the Feeding of the Five Thousand

6:30 **Then the apostles gathered around Jesus and told him everything they had done and all they had taught.**

6:31 **And he said to them, "Come with me privately to an isolated place and rest for a time" (for many were coming and going, and there was no time to eat).**

6:32 **So they went away by boat to an isolated place.**

6:33 **But many saw them and they ran out from all the towns and came to them.**

6:34 **As Jesus arrived, he saw the large crowd and had compassion on them for they were as sheep without a shepherd. So he began to teach them many things.**

6:35 **And when it was already late, his disciples came to him and were saying, "This is an isolated place and the hour is advanced.**

6:36 **Send them away in order that going onto the surrounding country and villages they may buy something for themselves to eat."**

6:37 **But he replied to them, "You give them something to eat." And they said, "Should we go and buy bread for two hundred silver coins and give it to them to eat?"**

6:38 **He said to them, "How many loaves do you have? Go and see." When they found out, they said, "Five and two fish."**

6:39 Then he commanded them all to sit down in groups on the green grass.

6:40 So they reclined in groups of hundreds and fifties.

6:41 And taking the five loaves and two fish and looking up to heaven, he blessed and broke the bread and gave to the disciples that they might set before the people, and he divided the two fish among them all.

6:42 They all ate and were filled,

6:43 and they picked up the broken pieces of bread that were left over, twelve baskets full, and from the fish.

6:44 Now those eating the bread were five thousand men.

This scene comes in two parts: a ministry summary (6:30–34) and the provision-gift miracle of the feeding of the five thousand (6:35–44). The miracle is the only miracle of Jesus in all four Gospels (Matt 14:13–21; Luke 9:10–17; John 6:1–15). It recalls some OT scenes, where God is the provider of food and care (Exod 16; Num 11; Ps 78:18–30; 105:40; 1 Kings 17:8–16; 2 Kings 4:1–7). The miracle of provision of food stands in contrast to the viciousness of the meal just described where John is slain. Jesus' care and provision are the focus. A feeding of four thousand will come later in Mark 8:1–10.

The apostles, Jesus' commissioned representatives, returned from the mission noted in Mark 6:6b–13, completing the sandwich structure (v 30). This is the only time Mark uses the term *apostles*. It is time to rest (v 31). The association of rest in the wilderness is a biblical theme (Deut. 3:20; 12:9 f.; 25:19; Josh. 1:13, 15; 21:44; Ps. 95:7–11; Isa. 63:14; Jer. 31:2; Heb. 3:7–4:13).[256] So Jesus calls them to go with him to a private place to eat and rest (v 32), as they had been so busy with people coming in and out they could not eat (Mark 3:20). The locale was an isolated spot in the wilderness (*erēmos*). As in Mark 1:35 and 1:45, Jesus withdraws for a time to collect himself and those with him (also Mark 6:46; 7:24).

The withdrawal fails to gain the respite (v 33). Upon arriving, a great crowd has come out from all the towns. Luke 9:10 has associated the event with Bethsaida, and John 6:2 ties it to the Sea of Tiberias, naming the water after its most prominent town, and John 6:23 also ties the event to Tiberias. So we may be thinking of an area between these two locales, as Mark 6:45 has Bethsaida on the "other side of the sea" from where they now are.[257] Tradition suggests a site near Tabgha, next to Capernaum, which might fit.

---

[256] Lane, *Mark*, 225.

[257] Guelich, *Mark 1:1–8:26*, 340; France, *Mark*, 264.

Jesus has compassion for them as they are compared to sheep without a shepherd (**v 34**; compassion: Mark 1:41; 6:34; 8:2; 9:22; Matt 9:36; 14:14; 15:32; 20:34; Luke 7:13). People with no shepherd lack true leaders, who are often seen as fighting the battle for them (Num 27:17; 1 Kings 22:17; 2 Chron 18:16; Ps 78:71; Ezek 34:5; Nah 3:18; Zech 10:2; of a Gentile leader as shepherd, Jdt 11:19). The nation is pictured as being adrift at sea. Moses and David had been shepherds, but no one like them was leading the people now. God promised the people a shepherd one day (Jer 23:1–6; Ezek 34:22–23; 37:24). That also was a Jewish expectation in the period (*Ps Sol* 17:40–41). The figure is old and broad, going back as far as Hammurabi (*Code of Hammurabi*, Prologue 1).[258] Lost sheep are those who stray from God's way (Ps. 119:176; feeding as teaching: Torah, 2 Bar 77:13–15). Moses is seen in this light, especially when people longed for leadership (Isa 63:11). So out of compassion for their need, Jesus begins to teach them many things.[259] Jesus is that good shepherd and cares for them through his teaching them the way of God. Jesus appears as a "greater Joshua" (Hebrew Joshua = Jesus in Greek) here (Num 27:18–23; Mark 14:27; John 10:1–18).

As the day grew dim (**vv 35–36**), the disciples come to Jesus and suggest releasing the crowd so they can find food, as they will not find it in the isolated locale where they are meeting. In the area and villages around them, they can go and buy something to eat. Jesus surprises the disciples by saying that they should provide the food (**v 37**). He gives the command with the personal pronoun included, so the response is emphatic. The disciples ask if they should go and spend the two hundred silver pieces it would take to feed the crowd (**v 38**). This was not cheap, but equivalent to more than two-thirds of a year's labor for someone, as John 6:7 says it would cost more than 200 denarii. Even split across the twelve, it would be an expense. The question might echo a similar scene of provision involving Moses (Num 11:13, 22). Here, not only was there the expense, but there also was the sheer logistics of such an operation to consider. The disciples are clueless as to what Jesus really intends. For the disciples, Jesus' idea of providing food is an impractical suggestion. Collins is surely right that they would have been puzzled by Jesus' approach, having no idea what is coming.[260] So Jesus asks for an inventory. They return having determined there are five loaves and two fish, hardly enough to deal with the crowd. A loaf was about 8 inches

---

[258] Marcus, *Mark 1–8*, 406.
[259] One could also read Mark 6:34 as saying he taught them at length, reading *polla* as adverb. The point is the same. Jesus taught them much.
[260] Collins, *Mark*, 324.

long and an inch thick. Each person would get a crumb, if that. Neither the numbers nor the material are symbolic; they simply show the paltry resources available.[261]

Jesus has the people recline on the green grass in groups of fifty and a hundred (**vv 39-40**). They recline (*anaklinai*) as at a banquet (Matt 8:11; Luke 12:37; 13:29). The green grass possibly points to spring time when grass grew on the desert hills of Galilee. These are very vivid details. The scene has a serene, pastoral feel (Ps 23:1–2), even though it was not yet clear where all the food would come from. The mood contrasts with the dilemma. The gathering in fifties and hundreds partially echoes the Mosaic camp of the wilderness (Exod 18:21–1000, 500, 100, 10; also CD 13:1–8).[262] The phrase "in groups" uses the term συμποσια, pointing to a company, but also to a symposium or banquet meal (BDAG, 959). A new exodus is taking place. This is a second Moses.

After a prayerful glance to heaven, Jesus breaks the bread so the[263] disciples can distribute it and then divides up the fish for all to eat (**v 41**). The glance to heaven is rare in a miracle (Mark 7:34; John 11:41). Luke 9:16 has the food blessed by Jesus. A common Jewish blessing over bread or a meal was, "Blessed are you. Lord our God, King of the world, who brings forth bread from the earth" (*m. Ber* 6:1). Jesus is not seeking power for the miracle but is thanking God for the provision, as was commonly done at meals.[264]

The Greek in verse 41 is clear: the two fish are divided among the entire crowd. Some see an echo of the Last Supper here, because much of the terminology overlaps with that of the meal,[265] but it really is an expression of divine provision for all meals, especially since there is no wine and the leftovers point to a focus on provision in general. Still, John 6 does lean in this direction in terms of the significance of the act. The provision of food for people mirrors the provision of manna in the desert (Exod 16; also

---

[261] Marcus, 407, suggests bread for Torah (Deut 8:3; Prov 9:5). Though possible, the fish have no clear symbolic force, weakening the supposed link; correctly, Hooker, *Mark*, 166.

[262] Although this is not exact in number, the other overlaps with Moses point to a new era and a typology appealing to the arrival of a new era.

[263] Some manuscripts, such as p⁴⁵, A, and D read "his" disciples here, but ℵ and B, among others, lack it. The shorter reading with the disciples is slightly more likely; Metzger, *Textual Commentary* (1994), 78.

[264] Guelich, *Mark 1:1–8:26*, 342.

[265] Lane, *Mark*, 230. Those terms are *taking, bread, blessed, broke, gave,* and *to the disciples* (Mark 6:41; 14:22). Except for giving to the disciples, the language would fit any meal.

Elijah and Elisha, 1 Kings 17:7–16; 2 Kings.4:1–7, 42–44). Jesus' creative power is illustrated, as is his ability to give the sustenance of daily bread. God cares for his people through Jesus and the disciples.

The people ate their fill (**vv 42–44**), expressed in a way that echoes Psalm 78:29 and 42, with the picture of manna in the wilderness.[266] Five thousand men in all, plus whoever else had come, partook of the meal. Matthew 14:21 speaks of the count "besides women and children." The count is possible because of the way people were organized to eat the meal. When the leftovers were gathered, twelve baskets full remained. The bread is highlighted over the fish in the Greek word order. These baskets were either as small as a wicker basket or as large as fish baskets, which could have been large enough to hold a person squatting down (Acts 9:25).[267] Jesus had more than satisfied the need. It is hard to know if the capability of meeting Israel's need is meant in the number twelve, but perhaps it is. What is clear with the picture of bringing blessing is that Jesus can provide and minister through those who serve him. The miracle ends here, somewhat surprisingly without a note of reaction. It may be that the people did not realize what had taken place, and that only the Twelve did.[268] The focus is totally on what Jesus has done as a shepherd (John 10:10).

6:45–52 Jesus Walks on Water

6:45 And immediately Jesus urged his disciples get into the boat and go on ahead to the other side, towards Bethsaida, while he dismissed the crowd.

6:46 After saying farewell to them, he went to the mountain to pray.

6:47 When evening came, the boat was in the middle of the lake and he was alone on the land.

6:48 And as he saw them straining at the oars, for the wind was against them, during the fourth watch of the night, he came walking on the sea to them, for he wanted to pass by them.

6:49 Those seeing him walking on the water thought he was a ghost, and they cried out.

---

[266] Collins, *Mark*, 326. See also Isa 25:6–9.

[267] Taylor, *St. Mark*, 325, opts for a large basket. BDAG, 563, speaks of baskets of a variety of sizes with this word (*kophinos*).

[268] Lane, *Mark*, 232. Mark lacks any note about people wanting to make Jesus king such as exists in John 6:15. This means some may have had political hopes for Jesus versus Rome. Jesus did not go there in John. Mark mentions nothing like this at all. The Kingdom Jesus brings is about something more profound than political power.

6:50 For they all saw him and were terrified. But immediately he spoke to them, "Have courage. It is I. Do not fear."

6:51 And he went up with them into the boat, and the wind ceased. They were totally astonished,

6:52 because they did not understand the loaves but were hardened on their hearts.

The next scene is yet another nature miracle and also an epiphany, like the Transfiguration.[269] The scene also is described in Matt 14:23–33 and John 6:15–21, likely making it multiply attested.[270] Matthew's account has the additional detail of Peter's attempt to walk on the water as well. In this Markan scene, the juxtaposition of Jesus showing his authority over creation here versus the provision he just accomplished is the account's key point. That is its sole purpose, as no one gains any benefit from what Jesus does here, unlike many other miracles. Some see a rescue miracle here, but the disciples are not really in danger. They simply have to take their time to cross the lake against the wind.[271]

This is another Markan scene where Jesus has divine prerogatives, as God controls the seas (Job 9:8; Ps 77:19–20; Isa 43:16; 51:10). The background to such a theme is extensive but also complex.[272] It is clear that some entertained the idea for gods and exceptional rulers. Ps 77–78 are important, as they depict the crossing of the sea under Moses. Combined with the picture of food provision of the previous scene, we again look back at the first great corporate saving event God performed for his people (Ps 78:13–25). The key Markan theme of fear also reappears in this passage.

---

[269] Hooker, *Mark*, 169, develops the background of this scene as a whole.

[270] This judgment depends on whether one sees John as knowing and using the Synoptics or as independent. In all likelihood, John is independent, though he certainly knows some of the events the Synoptics depict.

[271] The text is similar to but distinct from Mark 4:35–41; France, *Mark*, 269–70.

[272] In the Greco-Roman world, such control was seen in the figures of Poseidon and Neptune, as Collins, *Mark*, 328–33, details the texts we note. In Jewish materials, God divides the sea (Exod 14:21–29), as do Joshua, Elijah, and Elisha with God's help (Josh 3:7–4:18; 2 Kings 2:8; 2:14). This dividing of the sea is not quite the same thing as walking on it. Striding over the sea was attributed to Euphemus of Taenarum (Apollonius Rhodius, *Argonautica* 1.182–84) and Orion (Apollodorus, *Library* 1.4.3; Pseudo-Hesoid, *Astronomy* 4; other examples include Seneca, *Hercules furens* 319–24). What is hard to know in some cases is whether these are figures of speech for being able to survive as one travels over the sea, but the scene in Seneca is not. Zeus is said to enable Xerxes to do this (Herodotus 7.56). The skill is extolled to Socrates in a later text, but Socrates rejects the idea (Dio Chrysostom 3.30–31). It is hard to determine whether this is literal or figurative in the Menander text on Alexander (frg 924K) and also in 2 Macc 5:21, which describes Antiochus' arrogance.

The disciples are still struggling to figure out who Jesus is and what he is capable of doing. This struggle to truly perceive how Jesus can do such things is the second key theme of the account.

It begins with a boat journey for the disciples as Jesus sends them ahead of him to cross the lake (**v 45**). Unlike John 6:14–15, Mark gives no motive for the action. We simply are moving on. John has the pressure to be made a political king as the reason for getting in the boat and moving on.

He sends them to Bethsaida. They will end up at Gennesaret, between Tiberias and Capernaum southwest of Bethsaida (Mark 6:53) and arrive at Bethsaida later (Mark 8:22). It is located at the northern tip of the Sea of Galilee at the mouth of the Jordan River. In Mark 8:22, it is the setting for the healing of a blind man. In Matt 11:21 (Luke 10:13), it is one of the villages over which Jesus pronounced a woe. Jesus takes some time to withdraw and pray (**v 46**). This is the last prayer by Jesus mentioned until Gethsemane (Mark 1:35; 6:31). That evening the disciples are halfway across the lake (**v 47**), having gotten a late start after the feeding at the end of the day. Jesus is still on the land alone. When Jesus separates from the disciples in Mark, there always is a crisis that follows.

It is the fourth watch of the night (**v 48**), which involves the hours before dawn sometime after 3:00 AM. Four watches means Mark is reckoning by Roman standards, as Jews had three watches (also in Mark 13:35). This timing meant that since they left shore, they had been rowing for hours. Jesus saw the disciples stuck at sea, rowing but going nowhere as they fought against the wind. The Greek says they were "being tormented in their rowing." They were struggling. So Jesus walks out on the sea toward them. In the OT, only God walks on the water (Job 9:8; 38:16; Ps 77:19; Isa 43:16; Sir 24:5–6, *Odes Sol.* 39:10).[273] Jesus is taking on this divine prerogative. Clearly Mark portrays a miracle here, as the seeing a ghost makes it clear something unexpected was taking place.

The text in verse 48 says he wanted to pass them by, an expression with OT significance for God revealing himself (Exod 33:22; 33:19; 34:6; 1 Kings 19:11; Job 9:8, 11). At another level, his presence is a reminder that he knows what is happening to them.[274] His power shows he can care for them. The event is much like the earlier calming of the storm when he was with them sleeping, and they were to have faith. But his presence disturbed them (**v 49**). They thought he was a ghost and cried out with a terrified fear. So he

---

[273]   Edwards, *Mark*, 198.
[274]   Witherington, *Mark*, 221.

told them to have courage (**v 50**). He affirms it is he and they are not to fear. Although some see an allusion to the divine name "I am" here (Exod 3:14; Deut 32:39; Isa 41:4; 43:25; 47:8, 10; 48:12; 51:12), if the name is the point it is very subtly expressed, as his power, presence, and awareness are the point of the scene. This presence should relieve their fear. He is with them as one who walks through creation is more the point (Ps 23; Heb 13:5). This is an epiphany, but not at the level of the divine name as much as at the level of divine activity. The scene is rooted in OT expression and worldview. Jesus' actions reveal who Jesus is. Once again Mark notes that fear should lead not to being disturbed or bothered but to faith.

Jesus enters the boat, and the wind working against them ceases (**v 51**). The disciples are completely astonished. The Greek piles on the language of the reaction ("very, exceedingly astonished"). This is the third and last time Mark notes amazement using *existēmi* (Mark 2:12; 5:42; in 3:21 the term has a different meaning).[275] Each time involves a divine prerogative (forgiveness of sins, raising from the dead, walking on water). Awe is a part of the calming of the storm in Mark 4:41.

A narrative comment notes that their hearts were hardened and they did not understand the loaves (**v 52**). Hardening had been mentioned of opponents in Mark 3:5. Some say Mark portrays the disciples as outsiders, or like outsiders,[276] but this comparison is overdrawn, given texts like Mark 4:10–12. Here it is not hostility, but simply being slow to perceive what is taking place and understand what is meant in terms of being an epiphany. Jesus' capabilities have not registered with them.[277] The previous miracle should have registered with them, but had not. This is part of what these miracles indicate, as they extend beyond the act to the person. It is that their hearts did not totally perceive. Unlike opponents, they were open to Jesus, but like them, they did not yet understand all that Jesus was. Still, their openness will let them, unlike opponents, get there.

Matthew 14:33 shows that they did eventually sense the point as they responded to Jesus as Son of God. Mark describes and points to their failure to understand how the event could be taking place. Matthew deals with the result of the event after it was done. Mark shows the disciples as needing to grow, as well as indicating that Jesus is about more than performing miracles. These miracles are pointers to his person.

---

[275] Mark also uses *thaumazō* to describe amazement (Mark 5:20; 6:6; 15:5, 44).
[276] Collins, *Mark*, 336.
[277] Lane, *Mark*, 237–38.

6:53-56 Another Summary: Jesus Heals Those Brought to Him

6:53 After they had crossed over, they came to land at Gennesaret and anchored there.
6:54 And as they came out of the boat, immediately people recognized Jesus
6:55 and ran through the entire region and began to bring the sick on mats to wherever he was heard to be.
6:56 And wherever he would go – into the villages, towns, or countryside – they would set the sick in the marketplaces, and would ask if they could touch the hem of his garment, and all who touched it were healed.

This is Mark's third summary (Mark 1:35–39; 3:7–12). Matthew 14:34–36 is parallel. The locale of Gennesaret is not known and is only noted here and in Luke 5:1 (**v 53**). It is related to Gennesar (1 Macc 11:67; Josephus, *Ant* 5.7; *War* 3.506–507). It is either on the northwestern shore of the Sea south of Capernaum between it and Tiberias or a town on the plain that runs for 3 miles near that shore. Neither is it clear if they crossed over from Bethsaida (Mark 6:45) or from the middle of the sea (Mark 6:47), but given the situation, the latter is more likely. Still with the wind having died down, they now could reach their goal. So, why they ended up here versus the seeming goal of Bethsaida is discussed. Mark 6:45 likely speaks of travel in the direction of Bethsaida or toward Bethsaida versus to a specific locale, so there is no need for this discussion. If the travel note is broad, then this means appeals to Mark's confusion about geography or a combining of sources is not at work here. We are speaking of ministry in a region.

The people recognized Jesus and sent out word into the entire region that he was there (**v 54**). So the people brought the sick on mats to him wherever he was. They would place them in the marketplace and ask to touch the edge of his clothes. The attitude here is like that of the woman in Mark 5:25–28 (Matt 9:20; Luke 8:44; Acts 5:15; 19:11–12 for healing through touch). It reflects an almost magical view of Jesus' power that the populace had, since it is not Jesus' word alone that is required but actual contact with him. Regardless Jesus still showed his care by extending his healing power. The reference to the garment is probably to the tassels on the fringe of Jewish clothes that signified dedication to God and served as reminders of God's commandments (Num 15:38–40; Deut 22:12; Matt 23:5; *Aristeas* 158). Those that did touch him were healed.

The power and compassion of Jesus continued to minister to people (vv 55–56). In this summary, the stress is completely on Jesus' healing and what he does with the faith of those healed, noted in passing as they seek Jesus' power out. Nothing is said about his teaching. The draw for people was his work of compassion, which Jesus offered freely even though it was not the ultimate point of his work. God cared, and so his messenger ministered comfort to any who came. Jesus cared about more than healing the sick, but he did so nonetheless. Marcus calls the scene unrealistic, because people would just seek to touch Jesus and not ask him to heal, but this reads the text too literally. The language likely expresses the intent of their action and also ignores the fact that the sick on mats were set before Jesus as he went down the line to heal because most of the sick would not have been able to move.[278] The term for healing here is the everyday use of the term for being saved (*esōzonto*), which means being delivered from a particular circumstance. Jesus continues to reach out and meet needs even as people as are trying to figure out exactly who he is.

7:1–23 Jesus Discusses that True Cleanliness Comes from the Heart

7:1 **And some Pharisees and some of the scribes coming from Jerusalem gathered around him.**

7:2 **And they saw that some of the disciples ate their bread with unclean hands, that is unwashed –**

7:3 **For the Pharisees and all the Jews do not eat unless they wash the hands with the fist, holding fast to the tradition of the elders.**

7:4 **And when they had come from the marketplace, they do not eat unless they wash. They hold fast to many other traditions; the washing of cups, pots, bronze vessels, and dining couches.**[279]

7:5 **The Pharisees and scribes asked him, "Why do your disciples not live according to the tradition of the elders, but eat with unwashed hands?"**

7:6 **He said to them, "Isaiah prophesied correctly concerning you hypocrites as it is written, 'This people honors me with the lips, but their heart is far from me.**

7:7 **They worship me in vain, teaching as doctrine the commandments of men.'**

---

[278] Marcus, *Mark 1–8*, 436–37.

[279] A textual issue is tied to this last entry in the list. Should it be included or not? It could reflect harmonization with Lev 15 or it could have been accidentally omitted with all the words ending in –*ōn* in the list. It is hard to be sure. Metzger, *Textual Commentary* (1971), 93–94.

7:8 Abandoning the commandment of God, you hold fast to the tradition of men."

7:9 He also was saying to them, "Well you set aside the commandment of God that you might establish your tradition.

7:10 For Moses said, 'Honor your father and your mother' and 'whoever insults his father or mother must be put to death.'

7:11 But you say if anyone says to the father or mother, 'whatever benefit you would have received from me is *korban*, that is a gift for God,'[280]

7:12 then you no longer permit him to do anything for the father or mother.

7:13 You nullify the word of God by your tradition which you handed down. And you do many things like this."

7:14 And calling the crowd again, he was saying to them, "Listen to me, everyone, and understand.

7:15 There is nothing outside the man coming into him that can defile a person, but it is what comes out of a person that defiles him."[281]

7:17 Now when Jesus had entered the house having left the crowd, his disciples asked him about the parable.

7:18 And he said to them, "So also are you without understanding? Don't you understand that whatever goes into a person from the outside is not able to defile him?

7:19 For it does not enter the heart, but the stomach, and then goes into the latrine." (Cleansing all foods)

7:20 He was saying, "What comes out of a person defiles the person

7:21 For from within out of the heart come evil ideas, sexual immorality, theft, murder,

7:22 adultery, greed, evil, deceit, debauchery, a wicked eye, slander, pride, and folly.

7:23 All these evils come out from within and defile a person."

This scene is a controversy account that contains pronouncements as part of a teaching. It is likely an anthological treatment of a dispute that was ongoing between Jesus and the leaders. It is the longest controversy scene in Mark, making it an important passage that reveals an ethical core to Jesus' teaching. Morality and defilement are about the heart, not superficial activity from outside the person.

Jesus has now received the attention of those in Jerusalem (v 1). They now have a group of Pharisees and scribes coming up from there to see what Jesus is doing. They observe some of Jesus' disciples now washing

---

280   Korban in this context means something dedicated to God.
281   Verse 16 is not present in most early manuscripts.

their hands to render themselves clean before a meal (**v 2**). Jesus is responsible for the activity of his followers. Mark notes that the Pharisees and Jews do this as they follow the tradition of the elders, or the oral law from teachers who ruled about legal disputes (**v 3**), to wash their hands up to the fist before a meal to prevent being unclean. Unclean hands were seen as "common." The fact that Mark has to explain this practice shows that his audience is Gentile. Oral law was seen as a "fence around the Torah" to protect it being faithfully kept (*m. 'Abot* 3.14' *m. Yadim* deals with this custom).

Mark says in verse 3 that all Jews keep this law, an expression that is hyperbolic to refer to most Jews. The fact the Pharisees are singled out as doing so shows the hyperbolic nature of the remark. Mark uses the term *all* (*pas*) this way (Mark 1:5, 32–33; 6:33; 11:11; also *Aristeas* 305). The practice is rooted in priests washing their hands before offering a sacrifice and being clean at the temple (Exod 30:19; 40:13; Lev 22:1–6; Num 18:8–13), a practice extended to the home for all by the Pharisees and Essenes, perhaps with the view that the home was a small version of the temple (*m. Hag* 2.5).[282] Most of the traditions we have noting this view are late, from the fifth or sixth century (*b. Hullin* 105a; *b. Shab* 13b–14b). The reference to the fist means either that a fistful of water was used, that the water was poured onto hands cupped at the fist, or that the hands were washed up to the fist (*m. Yad* 1.1; 2.3).[283] The Mishnah notes that the amount of water is compared to an egg and a half. Contracting uncleanness from the marketplace among other locales is in view (*y. Shev* 6.1, 36c).[284] Other possibilities include from uncleanliness include lepers (Mark 1:40), contact with tax collectors, and women during their periods or dead bodies.[285] The range of washings is covered in Lev 11–15, which is why Mark notes various objects (cups, pots, bronze vessels, and dining couches) covered for cleanliness (**v 4**).[286] Jewish tradition came to expand this practice to discuss the specific objects washed in detail so as to protect a person from uncleanliness. This raised issues of *teharot* (cleannesses) for the Jews. This practice was seen as an important expression of faithfulness to being Jewish in a context where Hellenistic

---

[282] Guelich, *Mark 1:1–8:26*, 363–64.

[283] Hooker, *Mark*, 174–75.

[284] Marcus, *Mark 1–8*, 442.

[285] Edwards, *Mark*, 205.

[286] A reference to couches or beds is uncertain, as several manuscripts lack it (p[45], א, B). It is a harder reading and pulls in Lev 15, so it may well be original (also *m Kelim* 19.1). Edwards, *Mark*, 207–208, notes how important this theme of purity was to Judaism, noting that 25 percent of the *Mishnah* covered such issues.

practices risked overwhelming Jewish distinctiveness. Archaeological evidence shows many Galileans were Torah observant because stone vessels for such ritual water were found.[287]

The Pharisees and scribes ask why Jesus' disciples do not live according the tradition of the elders and instead eat with unwashed hands (v 5). Josephus notes how much of what the Pharisees practiced was not in the Law (*Ant* 13.297). To walk is to live in a certain way. Jesus calls them hypocrites and cites Isaiah 29:13. The prophet says the people honor God with their speech and words (vv 6–7), but their heart is far away from God. This contrast is a common prophetic theme (Isa 1:12–17; Ho 6:6; Amos 5:21–24; Mic 6:6–8). Josephus notes a similar condemnation of Pharisees (*Ant* 17.41) and the Dead Sea community called them the "seekers of smooth things," who suffered from a "stubbornness of heart" (1QH 4:7–15).[288] Mark uses a version close to the LXX, but the Hebrew wording makes the same core point. Their worship is empty because they keep the traditions of men and do not do God's will. This is the only place in Mark where Jesus calls the Jewish leaders hypocrites, in comparison to Matthew who does it thirteen times and Luke who does it thrice. Also different from Matthew 14 is the sequence, as Matthew has not following God's commandment, the *korban* illustration, and then the citation. Mark has the citation, not following God's command, and then the illustration. In citing Isaiah, Jesus compares the current generation to a failure in Israel from long ago. The principle from the prophet applies to them. Jesus charges them with holding fast to tradition and separating from the commandment of God. The singular commandment may be a focus on the call to love in line with God's will, given the illustration that follows (Deut 6:5; Mark 12:29–30).

So they reject God's command and establish their tradition (v 8). This gives the result of their way of spirituality. What was set up to protect the keeping of the Law now ends up nullifying it. Tradition that does not lead to following God's will is worthless. It results in a false piety. Jewish texts also sometimes made this charge (*T. Levi* 14:4; *T. Asher* 7:5).[289] Jesus is ironic here (v 9), saying that they set aside God's command "well" or "beautifully" (BDAG 505). The term for honor (*tima*) links back to the idea of honor from the earlier Isaiah 29:13 citation, forming a *gezerah shewa*. Another link is the contrastive use of the term *kalōs* in Mark 7:6 and 9. The practice Jesus is about to describe is a very effective nullification

---

[287] Collins, *Mark*, 346.
[288] Marcus, *Mark 1–8*, 444.
[289] Focant, *Mark*, 289.

of God's command. The contrast between rejecting God's command and what this tradition does is stated three times in this text, adding intensity as it goes (Mark 7:8, 9, 13).

Jesus uses the example of honoring one's parents, one of the Ten Commandments and a core social value (**v 10**). Parents should be honored and not insulted. The texts are from Exod 20:12; 21:17; Deut 5:16; and Lev 20:9 (also *m. Sanh* 7:8). That such dishonoring could lead to death shows how serious this act of disrespect is in God's eyes. The LXX has a term that means "insult," which renders a Semitic idea of cursing from the Hebrew text, and surely is the opposite of loving and giving honor. Jesus argues the oath of *korban* nullifies this command (**v 11**).[290] The term *korban* means a gift (Josephus, *Ant* 4.72–73; *Ag Apion* 1.167; *m. Nedar* 5.6 – shows how binding this was, 8.7 and 9.1 – shows honoring parents can nullify it in the view of some, but the point was disputed). To declare something *korban* is to say it is dedicated and reserved for God. For whatever is called a gift for God is not available to help the father or mother (**v 12**). It is unclear whether it had already been given or was declared such. Either way, it could not help the parents, as it was reserved for the temple either with the vow or upon death. Such a vow would need to be honored (Num 30:1–2; Deut 23:21–23). The result is that the word of God is nullified by tradition (**v 13**). By the third century, this practice was rescinded, so some may have been aware of the misuse of this act of dedication.[291] Jesus adds to the charge of a lack of love and its implicit rebuke by saying in verse 13b that this is only one example of such inconsiderate behavior. The five uses of what "you" do in Mark 7:12–13 underscore the example. Jesus' initial reply to the query about keeping tradition is that tradition can result in God's command not being followed. So it is not binding.

The second part of Jesus' reply involves remarks to the crowd about what defiles (**v 14**).[292] He issues a call to hear as he makes the declaration

---

[290] Witherington, *Mark*, 226, argues that the illustration gives evidence of being authentic, as a dispute over the practice of *korban* is not likely to have been an early church dispute.

[291] Marcus, *Mark 1–8*, 445–46.

[292] *Thomas* 14 has a variation of this saying in another context. Witherington, *Mark*, 228–30, defends the originality of the Markan form of the saying in Mark 7:15. Hooker, *Mark*, 178–79, may be right to read 7:15 as a Semitic comparison stated as a contrast; so Kuruvilla, *Mark*, 147–48. One thing defiles more than another (Isa 1:11–17; Hos 6:6; Amos 5:21–27; Jer 7:22–23). It is important to note that uncleanness is not always about sin, even in the Old Testament, so there is an inherent gradation even in the Torah. However, Mark 7:19 appears to suggest that the contrast ultimately is intentional and far reaching, extending to how food is seen. The remark by Mark there is reflective of something realized later as implied in what Jesus said. If so, then Jesus makes a

(Mark 4:3, 9, 23–24). It is not about what goes into a person but what comes out of the heart (**v 15**).[293] The complaint that the saying is off-target because it is the condition of the eater as unclean that was the point of the question in Mark 7:5, not the nature of the food, misses the point that the contraction of defilement comes from contact with something unclean and thus extends to the food, not to mention that certain foods were also prohibited by such laws.[294] The saying "attacked the delusion that sinful men can attain to true purity before God through the scrupulous observance of cultic purity which is powerless to cleanse the defilement of the heart."[295] Jesus seeks a true purity and cleanliness, one that comes from the heart. When Jesus returned to the house, the disciples asked him what he meant (**v 17**). Such private teaching is common in Mark (Mark 1:32–34; 2:1–2, 15; 5:37–40; 7:24; 9:28, 33; 10:10; 14:3).

After a short rebuke about lacking understanding (**v 18**; Mark 4:13; 6:52; 8:17), Jesus repeats the principle that what goes into the person cannot defile him (Mark 7:15).[296] The remark is stated as a rhetorical question that expects a positive reply given the interrogative used (*ou*). The explanation is that what goes into the person goes to the stomach and then passes out of the body as waste. What defiles involves what comes out of the person in terms of actions – what comes from the heart. Jesus has shifted attention from hands to what they handle, because it is eating with unwashed hands that is the issue with the food. By arguing that food also does not defile, then the hands cannot impact the food that is consumed.[297]

In the midst of this reply in Mark **7:19b** is a parenthetical remark that Jesus' remark made all foods clean.[298] Mark often makes such asides

---

declaration about what is clean that shows yet another exercise of a divine prerogative in Mark. He can declare what is clean and unclean. France, *Mark*, 289, correctly observes that some issues of uncleanness do not involve what goes into a person (like touching the dead or certain skin conditions), so the remark about defilement here is specific to food. It also seems likely that the most radical reading emerged on reflection, so later disputes about clean and unclean food in the church preceded this more reflective reading of the saying. The reflection might emerge from seeing the range of situations in which Jesus allowed himself to be defiled, only to reverse the effect (a leper, Mark 1:41; a corpse, Mark 5:41; a bleeding woman, Mark 5:27–29).

[293] Mark 7:16 repeats Mark 7:14 and is only attested in later manuscripts. It is omitted in ℵ and B, among other earlier manuscripts. It is not likely to be original to Mark.

[294] H. Hubner, *Das Gesetz in der synoptischen Tradition* (Witten: Luther, 1973), 160–64.

[295] So Lane, *Mark*, 254.

[296] Other Markan texts on "not getting it" are Mark 4:40–41; 8:32–33; 9:5–6, 32; 10:24; 14:40.

[297] Guelich, *Mark 1:1–8:26*, 378.

[298] The parenthetical nature of the remark is clear from the fact that the participle for *clean* is syntactically unattached, having no masculine singular antecedent subject in the sentence; France, *Mark*, 291.

(Mark 3:30; 5:8; 7:3–4; 13:14). The detail is unique to Mark's Gospel and presents a reflection on the implications of what Jesus was saying. What goes into a person cannot defile him, so no food can defile. The vision of Acts 10:9–16 and its exposition in Acts 11:2–18 makes the same point about diet, something also suggested by the discussions in Rom 14 and Gal 2:11–14. Jesus is demonstrating his authority to make judgments about the Law. It is likely, given the Torah's teaching on clean and unclean foods, that Jesus is making a declaration about a new reality coming as a result of the eschatological arrival of the kingdom.[299] This is part of the "new wineskins" that Jesus brings as the promise is realized (Mark 2:22). Defilement is now exclusively moral and not cultic (**v 20**). The following of food laws is not obligatory, but optional (1 Cor 8:8). Jesus' point is that ultimate purity is a matter of the heart (Rom 14:14, 20).[300]

So Jesus lists thirteen vices that come from within (**vv 21–22**): evil ideas, sexual immorality, theft, murder, adultery, greed, evil, deceit, debauchery, a wicked eye, blasphemy, pride, and folly. These are the acts that defile a person (**v 23**). It appears we have a general category of evil ideas followed by a list of six things in the plural for a series of acts and six in the singular for core vices.[301] The echo in the general term, evil ideas, comes from Gen 6:5 on the inclinations of the human heart toward evil (also *4 Ezra* 3:21 of Adam).[302] Washed hands are nothing compared to these acts that we are responsible for doing and that do damage to others. Defilement is not only about what we do but also about how that impacts others. This list of vices resembles the "deeds of the flesh" in Gal 5:19–21 (Wis 14:25–26; 1QS 4:9–11; Rom 1:29–31; 1 Cor 5:10–11; 6:9–10; 2 Cor 12:20–21; Col 3:5–8; 1 Tim 1:9–10; 2 Tim 3:2–5; 1 Pet 4:3, 15). Such lists were common, and some were very long (Philo, *Sacrifices of Cain and Abel* 32 has 150 items; *T. Isa* 7:2–4; *T. Gad* 5:1; *T. Reub* 3:2–7).[303] Mark's order of adultery, stealing, and murder follows the LXX of the Ten Commandments, in contrast to Matthew who follows Hebrew order and has a shorter list of seven vices, with the first being general and then six items (Exod 20:13–15). These destructive behaviors damage relationships. How one handles the sexuality of the body,

---

[299]   Stein, *Mark*, 345. Hooker, *Mark*, 180, points to the authority of Jesus this implication reveals, citing Mark 1:22. He is not merely a scribe who debates; he declares God's commands directly. Witherington, *Mark*, 231, notes that the view takes us back to a place before the Mosaic Law where all food was clean (Gen 9:3).

[300]   Lane, *Mark*, 255.

[301]   France, *Mark*, 292–93, is correct to point out that vices also appear in the plural listings.

[302]   Collins, *Mark*, 357–62 covers the list in detail; also Cranfield, *Mark*, 242–44.

[303]   Marcus, *Mark 1–8*, 459.

possessions, and life completes the list in 7:21–23. The "evil eye" likely refers to jealousy or envy and is not language of giving someone a curse, as is often the case in usage today (Deut 15:9; Prov 28:29 – the man with an evil eye runs after riches; Sir 14:8–10; BDAG, 744). Defilement that dishonors is about damage to reputation and relationships. This point is the key to Jesus' response. Jesus is prioritizing in this dispute over handwashing. More important than following traditions built up around the law is considering the heart and what defiles relationships.

7:24–30 Jesus Honors the Humble Faith of a Syro-Phoenician Woman

7:24 And arising from there, Jesus went out to the region of Tyre. And he went into a house, he did not want anyone to know, but he was not able to escape notice.

7:25 But immediately having heard about him, a woman, who had a daughter with an unclean spirit, came up to him and fell at his feet.

7:26 The woman was a Greek, a Syro-Phoenician in descent. And she asked him to cast out the demon from her daughter.

7:27 He was saying to her, "Let the children be satisfied first, for it is not good to take the children's bread and throw it to the dogs."

7:28 She replied and said to him, "Yes, Lord, but even the dogs under the table eat the children's crumbs."

7:29 Then he said to her, "Because you said this, go. The demon has left your daughter."

7:30 And going to her house, she found the child lying on the bed, and the demon having gone.

This healing scene is the one miracle that involves a Gentile in Mark. It also has features of a pronouncement account. As we shall see, it is the pronouncement exchange that drives the passage. Gundry rightly calls this a "duel of wits," and the resolution in favor of the woman makes an important statement for Mark.[304] Matthew 15:21–28 is parallel.

With this act, Jesus moved across all kinds of boundaries: geographical, ethnic, gender, and theological.[305] However, the scene is exceptional for Mark. There is no account of Jesus having a sustained mission to Gentiles.

---

[304]   Gundry, *Mark*, 374.
[305]   Witherington, *Mark*, 231. He also notes that the passage, with its difficult remark about Gentiles from Jesus, must be authentic (also Hooker, *Mark*, 182). The church would not invent such a scene with such a saying.

The best we have is a trip briefly into the land of the Decapolis. Still, there is no accident that the preceding scene involved a debate over cleanliness and now we are in contact with Gentiles, who often were seen by Jews as unclean. It is interesting that healing from a distance involved Gentiles, with the centurion's son as another example (Matt 8:5–10/Luke7:1–10), which Mark lacks.[306]

Jesus now moves into Tyre to the north and west of Galilee (**v 24**), a locale that had an ethnically mixed population.[307] Relations were strained between Galilee and Tyre because agricultural resources often migrated from Galilee to Tyre, leaving some Jewish folks in Galilee with little to eat (Josephus *Against Apion* 1.70 notes the ill will between the two groups, "our bitterest enemies"; *War* 2.478).[308] The roots of this go way back (Isa 23:1–12; Jer 47:4). So people there were often resented by Galileans. The move was an attempt to withdraw and gain some quiet, but the effort failed. Jesus was noticed and word went out about his presence. A Greek, Syro-Phoenician woman had a daughter who was possessed by an unclean demon (**v 25**).[309] Everything about her background and the situation made her look like an unlikely candidate for help: a Gentile, a woman, a girl with spiritual uncleanness, later described as demonic possession in Mark 7:29–30. She had no commending credentials. The description also makes it clear she is not from Libophoenicia in Africa, but is from the region of Syria, a native not from Coele-Syria, perhaps a Phoenician married to a Syrian.[310] Whatever the detail, she is not a normal candidate for ministry from a Jew.

She came to Jesus, fell at his feet, and asked him to cast out the demon (**vv 25–26**). In Mark, only she and Jairus fall at Jesus' feet as a sign of respect, besides those possessed by demons (demon-possessed: Mark 3:11; 5:6; Jairus: 5:22).

Jesus' response seems harsh (**v 27**). He says food is for children, not dogs. The term *kunariois* is diminutive and can look to a puppy, a domesticated dog, although whether it has this exact force is less than clear given how many diminutives are in the scene (BDAG, 575).[311] The term is describing a

---

[306] Guelich, *Mark 1:1–8:26*, 382–83.
[307] The words "and Sidon" are likely an addition in Mark to assimilate to Matthew 15:21.
[308] Edwards, *Mark*, 217, says the locale of Tyre is "the most extreme expression of paganism . . . a Jew could expect to encounter."
[309] Later tradition named her as Justa and her daughter as Bernice (Pseudo-Clem. *Hom* 2:19; 3:73); Guelich, *Mark 1:1–8:26*, 385.
[310] Marcus, *Mark 1–8*, 462–63.
[311] Guelich, *Mark 1:1–8:26*, 386.

house dog.[312] However, this is not the tender, emotive image it is to modern people. Dogs normally were seen in a negative light (2 Sam 16:9; Ps 22:16; Isa 56:10 – of useless dogs because they are mute and only sleep; Matt 7:6; Luke 16:21; Phil 3:2), although there are a few Jewish texts where the dog is seen as a companion (Tob 6:1; 11:4; Eccl 9:4; *Midr Ps* 4:11).[313] The image is very much within a Jewish mentality, with the point being that Jesus came to minister to his own, at least initially.[314] The term "first" (*prōton*) points to priority, not exclusion (Rom 1:16–17; Acts 13:46), but his attention is aimed at Israel.[315] Jesus had been in the Decapolis when he healed the Gerasene demoniac, but his mission was to his own people. They are the children who are in the line of the promise (Exod 4:22; Hos 11:1; *m. Abot*3.15) and thus are to have the food.[316] Jesus' remark is a challenge to the woman's request, but not a closed door. The woman persists, sensing the opening.

The woman's reply does not challenge the premise and comes with intense respect as she calls him Lord, probably in a simple cultural sense based on his role as a respected teacher (**v 28**).[317] Given the ethnic history between the groups, she may well understand the difference of perspective Jesus has as a Jew. This is how Jews think of us. Still she argues that beyond what the children get are the crumbs that fall down to the dogs.[318] As politically incorrect as this reply sounds today, it indicates that she is not entitled to what she is requesting. She is asking for mercy. In effect, she argues that she does not deserve anything but those meager leftovers. Jesus is clearly impressed (**v 29**). He tells her she can depart because her daughter is healed on account of the word she said. This was a word of faith. The

---

312   Stein, *Mark*, 351–52.
313   Edwards, *Mark*, 219–22, who notes Luther's words, "She took Christ at his own words. He then treated her not as a dog but as a child of Israel." Collins, *Mark*, 366–67, probably speaks too negatively in saying we are dealing with scavenger dogs. Some dogs herd and guard. The term here is not positive as it is for moderns, but it likely is not as negative as it could be for ancients. The idea that first the children are fed suggests that the reference to dogs is not entirely negative.
314   On Gentiles as dogs, *1 En* 89:4, 46–47, 49.
315   Marcus, *Mark 1–8*, 463, notes how Mark uses the term first to indicate such a divinely ordained order: Mark 3:27 – Satan bound first; 9:11–12 – Elijah comes first before Messiah; 13:10 – Gospel proclaimed before the end.
316   The perspective shows this is not an early church perspective and thus points to an authentically rooted event; Hurtado, *Mark*, 115.
317   Some translations have a "yes" here reflective of some manuscripts, but the remark is not likely original, as it looks like assimilation to Matthew 15:27; Metzger, *Textual Commentary*, 95.
318   Israel's history gives precedent for this kind of "outside" activity, as Elijah healed a Gentile woman (1 Kings 17:8–24).

word to go is how Jesus notes healing (Mark 2:11; 5:34; 7:29; 10:52). The woman leaves and finds the child in bed and exorcized of the demon (v 30).

The account is an unusual pronouncement account in that the last word is left to the woman. The exchange is the key to this text more than the miracle. As harsh as the exchange seems, the passage as a whole actually ends up affirming the woman by allowing her final word to dictate events and reveals an intent to minister to anyone who approaches God with humility. This is part of what Mark is intending to show, so one should not isolate the initial reply and sever it from the rest of what happens. The text shows that Jesus came as "glory for Israel and revelation to the Gentiles" (Luke 2:32). It is also interesting that the humility and persistence of the woman are like that of the centurion in Matthew 8 and Luke 7, and there is yet a second similarity in how the event is recounted, along with the healing from a distance. The fact that the next event involves a deaf mute shows how common people are doing well in responding to Jesus. The woman in this scene also stands in profound contrast to the religious leaders of the previous scene. She seeks mercy from Jesus and does not make a critique of him because her heart is right. In the end, despite being initially compared to a dog, she is affirmed and lifted up as an example. Faith and humility have transformed her worth. The woman comes off as one who understands Jesus profoundly, looking as sensitive as the disciples, if not more so, in her appreciation of Jesus.

7:31–37 Jesus Heals a Deaf Mute, but His Effort Not to Publicize the Healing Fails

> 7:31 **And again coming out from the region of Tyre, he came through Sidon to the Sea of Galilee in the region of the Decapolis.**
>
> 7:32 **And they brought to him a deaf man who also was muted, and they asked him that he might lay hands on him.**
>
> 7:33 **And taking him away from the crowd privately, Jesus placed his fingers into the man's ears, and after spitting, touched his tongue**
>
> 7:34 **and looking up to heaven, he sighed and said to him, "*Ephphatha*" (that is, "be opened").**
>
> 7:35 **And immediately the man's ears were opened, the bonds of his tongue loosened, and he spoke plainly.**
>
> 7:36 **And Jesus ordered them that they should say nothing to anyone. But as much as he ordered them, they proclaimed it all the more.**
>
> 7:37 **People were completely astounded and said, "He has done everything well. He even makes the deaf hear and mute speak."**

This scene contains another healing account. Jesus returns to the place of his primary ministry in Galilee (v 31), having passed through Tyre and Sidon. He ends up to the east in the Decapolis area again, a mostly Gentile region to the east of the Jordan River where the Gerasene demoniac also was healed. The route seems odd, as Sidon is 22 miles north of Tyre, whereas the Decapolis is to the south and east. This route is not exactly as the crow flies! Some have argued that it shows Mark's ignorance of geography, but it more likely indicates that Jesus did make a circuit through the neighboring region before returning.[319] There was biblical precedent for such a route (2 Kings 2:2–6, 23–25).[320] What the description of the route does not make entirely clear is whether we are to think of this healing as also involving a Gentile, since the Decapolis could point that way, whereas the Sea of Galilee could suggest a Jewish setting. We have gender balance here at the least with the previous scene. We may have ethnic balance (Gentile and Jew) as well, as opposed to an ethnic emphasis only on Gentiles. Matthew 15:29 seems to read the text as involving a Jewish setting.[321]

Here some people bring Jesus a deaf and a partially or fully mute man and urge Jesus to heal him by laying hands on him (v 32).[322] This "bringing" by people will be mirrored in the description of the healing of a blind man in Mark 8:22. The laying on of hands is almost always for healing (Mark 5:23; 6:5; 8:22, 25; similar "by the hand," 1:31, 41; 5:41; 9:27; one exception – 10:16). The term *mogilalos* used here can mean partially or completely mute. It is important, as it appears only here and in Isa 35:5–6, which is about healing that will take place during the time of salvation (BDAG, 656). The idea that the man is not completely mute is suggested by his being able to speak correctly, that is, more plainly in Mark 7:35 after he is healed (although, for full muteness, could be the term used in Mark 7:37).[323]

Jesus works hard to keep this healing as private as possible (v 33), as he did in Mark 5:40–43 and will do in 8:23. So he takes him away privately.

---

[319]   F. G. Lang, "'Über Sidon mitten ins Gebiet der Dekapolis': Geographie und Theologie in Markus 7,31," *ZDPV* 94 (1978): 145–60.

[320]   Edwards, *Mark*, 223–24.

[321]   Mark 8:11 also suggests a Jewish setting, as the next event has Pharisees present. They are not likely to have been in a Gentile area; Stein, *Mark*, 358, versus Guelich, *Mark 1:1–8:26*, 391, who argues for a Gentile setting.

[322]   The ambiguity of the term *mogilalos* explains our translation "was muted" where the degree is left open. See the following discussion.

[323]   Full muteness would have likely used *alalos*, but the fact that the term appears in Mark 7:37 means the exact condition is not clear. Either way the healing fully restores the man.

Jesus is working hard not to draw attention only to his healing, which is what many are focused on when it comes to his ministry. This is another indication we are on the Jewish side of things, as in the Decapolis before he had no such hesitations for Gentiles would not have had messianic expectations.

Jesus places his fingers in the man's ears and spits, probably on his own fingers, to touch his tongue. Spit was believed to have medicinal or healing power (Galen, *Natural Faculties* 3.7; Pliny the Elder, *Natural History* 28.5.25; 28.7.37 are but two examples from him).[324] So Jesus was using means familiar to the culture. Although some see elements of magic here or see this as pointing to a particularly difficult miracle, the act of spitting may have the simpler explanation that his actions allow the deaf man to sense the healing and the directness of it (Mark 8:23; John 9:6; and the healings alleged of Vespasian, an emperor who came after Jesus – Tacitus *Histories* 4.81; Suetonius *Vespasian* 7.2–3 – at the behest of Serapis; later Jewish text, *b. Baba Bat* 126b).[325] He can both see and feel Jesus act, even though he cannot hear what Jesus says. Jesus "entered into the mental world of the man"[326] and showed his care for him with intimate touch. Interestingly, neither Matthew nor Luke have this miracle, which is unusual, as between the two most of Mark is present in their Gospels. Matthew 15:29–31 has a more general summary about the array of Jesus' healing at this point in his narrative. This healing also echoes Isa 35 among other texts and looks like Jesus' reply to John the Baptist in Luke 7:22 and Matt 11:5.

Jesus looks up to heaven (**v 34**), possibly praying with a compassionate sigh (Mark 9:25; Rom 8:26). The act of sighing also parallels magical healings, but here we are dealing with appeals to God, not a conjuring up of spirits. Jesus says to him in Aramaic that his ears be opened (*ephphatha* – BDAG, 419).[327] His ears opened, the "chains" of his mouth were loosed, and he spoke correctly.[328] It is interesting that Jesus speaks in private a command the man

---

[324] Collins, *Mark*, 370–71.

[325] See discussions in Hurtado, *Mark*, 117, and Taylor, *St. Mark*, 354; for spit and healing, Marcus, *Mark 1–8*, 473–74.

[326] Lane, *Mark*, 266–67.

[327] Citing Aramaic occurs here and there in Mark (5:41; 14:36; 15:22, 34). Whether this is Aramaic or Hebrew is debated, but Mark normally notes Aramaic; see details on parallels with magic, Marcus *Mark*, 474; and on the language of Jesus' response, Guelich, *Mark 1:1–8:26*, 395–96.

[328] Is this a hint that this is an exorcism? Perhaps, even likely, but this conclusion is not entirely clear. Nothing else in the text points to an exorcism. What especially is missing is any exchange pointing to an exorcism or the mention of a spirit. See Lane, *Mark*, 267.

cannot hear. The utterance produces the healing (v 35), a speech act in the full sense of the term. So the tongue is pictured as being freed from prison. Jesus then tells the man and his companions not to say anything, as elsewhere in Mark (1:34, 44–45; 3:12; 8:26). Jesus' goal is simply to keep the focus from being on his healing alone. The effort fails. The reality is that Jesus' work is too amazing to engender silence. He cannot be hidden.

They went out and proclaimed extensively what had taken place (v 36). The verb here is one used for preaching and generally is not seen as negative. The crowd's reaction is acclaim for Jesus that he has done all things well, even to the point of curing the deaf and mute – a hope of the eschaton, as Isa 35:5–6 shows (Wis 10:20–21). They were astounded "above and beyond" (*huperperissōs* – BDAG, 1034). The healings of Jesus are creating an impression about him, although the focus is on something other than the main point of Jesus' work. The kingdom comes with continuing acts of compassion that are noticed but not entirely appreciated for all they are. Jesus is an agent of divine fulfilment, not just a healer.

8:1–9 Jesus Feeds the Crowd a Second Time

> **8:1** In those days there was another large crowd with nothing to eat. So calling his disciples, Jesus said to them,
>
> **8:2** "I have compassion on the crowd, for already they have been here three days with me, and have nothing to eat.
>
> **8:3** If I send them to their home hungry, they will become weary on the way, and some of them came from a great distance."
>
> **8:4** And his disciples replied, "From where can someone get enough bread in this desolate place to satisfy these people?"
>
> **8:5** He asked them, "How many loaves do you have?" They replied, "Seven."
>
> **8:6** Then he directed the crowd to sit down on the ground. After taking the seven loaves and giving thanks, he broke them and began giving them to the disciples to serve. So they set them before the crowds.
>
> **8:7** And they had a few small fish. After giving thanks for these, he told them to set these before them as well.
>
> **8:8** Everyone ate and was satisfied, and they picked up the left over broken pieces, seven baskets full.
>
> **8:9** There were about four thousand who ate. And he dismissed them.

This gift miracle of provision repeats the earlier feeding of Mark 6:35–44. A parallel is found in Matt 15:32–39. Mark has it reinforce what the disciples are to learn about Jesus. Despite the view of some that this is the same event or tradition used twice, it makes little sense of Mark's remarks in 8:19–20.[329] So either one takes Mark's direction seriously or else we are left with a doublet that Mark knew was not. The latter is an unlikely scenario.[330]

The scene starts simply (v 1). We are somewhere on the Sea of Galilee. It is discussed whether we are on the eastern side or the western. The presence of Pharisees in Mark 8:11 without a note of crossing points to the west. It is true the last locale noted is the Decapolis in Mark 7:31, which might point to the east. Yet it is clear Jesus is working his way back to Galilee, so he could be anywhere in between.[331] Still, a Jewish setting is more likely, although a reference to the distance some have come may well suggest Gentiles are included, perhaps having tracked with him in his earlier circuit. The discussion has some significance, as a ministry in the east points to a Gentile audience, one in the west looks to a Jewish setting.

A crowd has gathered with Jesus and has been with him for three days (v 2). Jesus is spending a great deal of time and effort teaching them. This is the first mention of a crowd in Mark since that last feeding. Jesus desires to send the multitude away but knows after three days they would be made weary from a journey and no real provisions. In effect, they have been fasting or eating a minimal amount of food. His compassion tells him that he needs to act on their behalf (Mark 1:41 – of lepers; 6:34 – of the people; 9:22 – demon-possessed). This compassion is distinct from Mark 6:34, where it was for the lack of leadership the people had. Here it is simply about caring for their need. A second distinction is that Mark 6:35–37 has the disciples tell Jesus to dismiss the crowd so they can get food. Here Jesus takes the initiative (v 3). The dilemma leaves the disciples perplexed (v 4). They do not draw on the previous experience, and that is not entirely surprising.[332] Mark wants you to sense how slow they were to respond. So they ask where they can get enough bread for the crowd (v 5). Jesus asks how many loaves are present. Seven is the reply. There is no clear symbolism in the number.[333]

---

[329] Guelich, *Mark 1:1–8:26*, 401–402, speaks of "an independent traditional variant of the Feeding tradition." He sees Mark as having understood it as a second miracle because of the way he found it in the tradition. So Mark is confused. However, this also is an unlikely scenario given Mark 8:19–20. The hardest point for seeing two events is the disciples' lack of reference to the previous event, a response seen by some as unlikely. It is hardly the case that they expected such unusual acts as a matter of course. They defaulted to the normal response to this scenario.

[330] Lane, *Mark*, 272; France, *Mark*, 306–307.

[331] Collins, *Mark*, 369, 378; Hooker, *Mark*, 187–88.

[332] Edwards, *Mark*, 231, notes how Jesus is not a "vendor" of miracles in Mark.

[333] Stein, *Mark*, 369–70, presents the various options and notes that no clear answer emerges from the choices.

The actual miracle is told in a simple, matter-of-fact manner, similar to the telling of the previous feeding (**v 6**). Jesus has the crowd sit. He takes the bread, as well as the few fish they had, and gives thanks for the bread and fish separately (**v 7**). The presence of the fish speaks against a Eucharistic allusion here, especially given that its mention is almost like an afterthought. He hands the food to the disciples to distribute. Everyone ate and was satisfied (**v 8**). Around four thousand were present. Seven baskets full were left over, so there was more than enough.[334] In Mark 8:8, the term for baskets, *spyridas*, differs from the earlier account (*kophinōn* in 6:43). It is not clear what size the baskets were or if there is any real difference in the choice, but this term usually refers to larger kinds of baskets. The term used can describe a basket that can hold an entire person (Acts 9:25). It is the mere superabundance that is the point. There is no comment or crowd reaction. Jesus simply got the crowd fed (**v 9**); needs were met, with Jesus providing as God did in the past. The disciples are to appreciate that Jesus can provide and does so through them.

8:10–13 Jesus Rebukes the Request for a Sign

8:10 And immediately he got into the boat with his disciples, he came to the region of Dalmanutha.

8:11 And the Pharisees came out and began to argue with him, seeking from him a sign for heaven, testing him.

8:12 And sighing in his spirit he said, "Why does this generation seek a sign? Truly I say to you, no sign will be given to this generation."

8:13 Then he left them, and getting back into the boat, he went out to the other side.

This scene is a pronouncement account. It is triggered by the presence of Pharisees and their reaction to Jesus' work in a request for a sign in the midst of a series of miracles. The sense is: what would it take to be convincing? Parallels are Matt 16:1–4, as well as Matt 12:38–39 = Luke 11:29. Jesus refuses the request emphatically.

In a transition verse (**v 10**), Jesus then traveled in the boat to a new region, Dalmanutha (read by all key manuscripts but D).[335] The locale is unknown today, but the parallel in Matt 15:39 reads "Magadan," whereas

---

[334] There is much discussion of possible symbolism in the numbers seven and four thousand, but the fact that no association is clear makes such a meaning unlikely.

[335] Metzger, *Textual Commentary* (1994), 83.

variants for Mark read "Mageda" (D^c) or "Magdala" (Θ). Lane suggests that this is an alternate name for Magdala.[336] Others have placed the event in the Gerasa region. Taylor mentions Eusebius and Jerome for this view, while suggesting that the locale was near Tiberias and that the obscure name shows that the tradition was primitive.[337] So the exact locale is not clear except for being on the western side of the Sea.

The Pharisees ask Jesus for a sign (**v 11**), an indicator by an unusual act that God is at work. This must be some type of specific request, perhaps for a sign from heaven or some type of specific divine confirmation, given that Jesus has been performing all kinds of miracles. So something very specific is likely. John 2:18 has another such challenge about his authority to act. The last week will have a final such challenge (Mark 11:28). The request shows that the person of Jesus is becoming an issue to the leadership. Show us you have the right to do what you are doing is the point of the question. The synoptics never call a miracle a sign, as John's Gospel and the book of Acts do. A miracle is "power" (*dynamis*), but the source of the power and the nature of the miracle points to the same thing. That activity makes this request look hard-hearted, even though it is asked because they think Jesus' work is from the devil (Mark 3:22). In sum, it seems little would have sufficed here. Later, even resurrection will not suffice.

In verse 11, Mark calls this challenge a test, clearly a critique of their motive (Exod 17:1–7; Mark 1:13; 10:2; 12:15).[338] So it appears to be an attempt to have Jesus prove who he is with a specific indicator they are demanding be shown (1 Cor 1:22). Jesus' reaction is strong and somewhat emotional as the response comes with a sigh (**v 12**; the noting of emotions in Mark: 1:41; 3:5; 6:6; 10:14; 14:34).[339] This kind of dispute is common in Mark (Mark 2:6–12, 16–17, 18–22, 23–28; 3:1–5; 7:1–23). There will be no sign given, as here is plenty of indication of Jesus' authority all around. The reference to "this generation" is a rebuke that is common in the OT (Gen 7:1; esp. Ps 95:10; Deut 32:5, 20). The use of the conditional particle *ei* without an apodosis is Hebraistic and reflects an emphatic negation (BDAG 278, 4). Its full sense is to invoke a curse if something done. So, "May I die, if a sign is given."[340] No sign is given in part because no sign is good enough, as Jesus' past activity

---

[336] Lane, *Mark*, 275.
[337] Taylor, *St. Mark*, 361.
[338] Requests for signs are not always negative (Judg 6:36–40; 2 Kings 20:8–11; Isa 7:10–12). Such a request, when wed to unbelief, as it is here, is negative.
[339] Sighing texts in the LXX include Sir 25:18 and 2 Macc 6:30.
[340] Guelich, *Mark 1:1–8:26*, 415. 2 Kings 6:31 has a full example.

has shown. Matt 16:1–4 and Luke 11:29 do mention the sign of Jonah, but that is not the kind of sign requested, as it is either repentance or a resurrection that is meant versus a heavenly sign, so Mark speaks of no sign.

With that said, Jesus departs (v 13). Jesus supplies the evidence for who he is. No one can demand how he should do that. The departure points to a growing distance between Jesus and the Pharisees. Unbelief has created that distance. Jesus' interaction with the Pharisees in Mark is one continual story of conflict (Mark 2:16–18, 24; 3:6; 7:1–5; 10:2; 12:13–15).

8:14–21 Jesus Reviews the Two Feedings, Making a Call to Faith

8:14 And they had forgotten to take bread, except for one loaf they had with them in the boat.

8:15 And Jesus commanded them, "Watch out! Beware of the yeast of the Pharisees and the yeast of Herod."

8:16 So they began to discuss with one another about having no bread.

8:17 And when Jesus knew, he said to them, "Why are you discussing that you have no bread? Do you neither perceive nor understand? Have your hearts been hardened?

8:18 Though you have eyes, do you not see and having ears, do you not hear? And do you not remember?

8:19 When breaking the five loaves for the five thousand, how many baskets full did you pick up?" They replied, "Twelve."

8:20 "When breaking the seven loaves for the four thousand, how many baskets full did you pick up?" They replied, "Seven."

8:21 Then he said to them, "Do you still not understand?"

This scene is another didactic pronouncement. Matthew 16:5–12 is the parallel passage. It contains a warning and a rebuke. The disciples are traveling with only one loaf of bread (v 14). Although some argue for some type of symbolism here for the number one, the issue is simply a lack of provision. The dilemma leads Jesus to warn the disciples about the leaven of the Pharisees and Herod – one religious, the other political (v 15). Herod had shown his rejection by slaying John the Baptist. Leaven here is negative, looking to corruption or that which is destructive, driven by evil impulses in people (1 Cor 5:6–8; Gal 5:9; of hypocrisy, Luke 12:1).[341] They are to be careful not to be like them. Matthew speaks of the Sadducees, not Herod. Luke 12:1 in a distinct context only speaks of Pharisees. The allusion

---

[341] Marcus, *Mark 1–8*, 510–11.

is to their lack of openness to what God is doing, something the last scene showed of the Pharisees.[342] The disciples are more concerned with having bread in the movement of normal life than the spiritual warning Jesus gave them as they go back to discussing the lack of bread (**v 16**). They still show themselves to be slow to understand what Jesus is doing, as has been the case in a sequence of texts in Mark (4:13, 41; 6:37, 52; 7:18; 8:4). The passage treats both their incompetence and Jesus' power. One need not choose between these themes.[343] The disciples should have been perceptive enough to know that Jesus and his presence had the ability to care for them.

When Jesus heard that they were discussing the lack of bread, he moved to remind and teach them (**v 17**). Five questions follow: (1) Why they are discussing this? (2) Do they not see? (3) Do they not understand? (4) Do they have hardened hearts (Mark 4:13, 40; 6:52)? (5) Without eyes that see or ears that hear, do they remember (**v 18**)? The fifth question alludes to a theme expressed in texts like Ps 115:5–6, Isa 6:9, 40:21, Jer 5:21, and Ezek 12:2. In many contexts, the issue is correctly the perception of what God is able to do. This is a rebuke that calls them to see hear, understand, and recall, as other earlier texts in the Old Testament had done (Deut 29:2–4; Ps 63:17; 95:8). The language echoes back to earlier rebukes (Mark 6:52; 7:18). Jesus can sustain them.

So he reviews when they fed the multitudes (**vv 19–20**). First to be recalled, the twelve baskets of leftovers that came from feeding the five thousand. Then they recall the collecting of seven baskets after feeding the four thousand. The second scene is evoked with elision, so that the actions need to be supplied from the previous event. They do recall details of these events.

Jesus simply asks a reflective question (**v 21**). Do they not yet understand? The open-ended conclusion is left for the disciples and readers to ponder. They recall the event but have not yet grasped its significance. Unlike the earlier Pharisees, the disciples are not hostile, seeking specific signs, but they still fall short of being where events should have taken them. They need to appreciate what Jesus' ability to provide means and also what it implies about who he is. Just as God had supplied manna, so he provides. He is the one through whom God is bringing a new opportunity for salvation. With Peter's confession about to take place, the question sets

---

[342] Edwards, *Mark*, 239.
[343] Stein, *Mark*, 382, argues that Jesus' power is the only point.

up that scene and shows that the disciples will begin to get it. They should already be there, but they are not.

8:22–26 Jesus Heals a Blind Man

> **8:22 And they came to Bethsaida. And they brought him a blind man and asked him to touch him.**
> **8:23 And taking the blind man by the hand, he brought him outside the village. Spitting on his eyes and placing his hands on his eyes, he was asking him, "Do you see anything?"**
> **8:24 And regaining sight, he was saying, "I see people, that I see walking like trees."**
> **8:25 Then again he placed his hands on his eyes. And he opened his eyes, was restored and saw everything clearly.**
> **8:26 Jesus sent him to his house, saying, "Do not come into the village."**

The final scene before Peter's confession, the healing of a blind man in Bethsaida, serves as a bridge into the latter part of the Gospel, as Peter's confession is a turning point in this Gospel.[344] One can see this event as closing the first part of Mark or beginning the second half of the Gospel.

This miracle appears only in Mark. It is the first healing of a blind person in Mark. John 9 has a similar kind of healing.[345] The opening of blind eyes to light also serves as symbolic of the process the disciples are going through. Their eyes are being opened as to who Jesus is. It is an "acted parable of faith."[346] The opportunity to really see Jesus' identity is there. Jesus is touching them.

Bethsaida is a town of a few thousand located on the northeastern shore of the Sea of Galilee (**v 22**; only other mention: Matt 11:21; Luke 10:13). It is in the region overseen by Herod Philip, who had fortified it recently and renamed it after Augustus' daughter, Julia (Josephus, *Ant* 18.28).[347] Thus, it could be called a village or a city, depending on whether one thinks of its

---

[344] France, *Mark*, 321–22.
[345] On ancient claims of healing of the blind, see Collins, *Mark*, 391–92. She notes healings tied to Asclepius in Epidaurus (Inscription nos. 4, 9, 11, 18, 20, 22, 32, and maybe 40). She cites 18, as it involves gradual seeing. She also notes a later report of Suetonius in *Twelve Caesars*, *Vesp* 7.2–3, where spitting at the behest of Serapis leads to a healing of a partially blind person. The much later report of Philostratus about Indian sages is also noted (*Life of Apollonius* 3.39). Of these claims, only those tied to the god Asclepius predate Jesus.
[346] Hooker, *Mark*, 197–98.
[347] Marcus, *Mark 8–16: A New Translation with Introduction and Commentary*. Yale Anchor Bible 27 (New Haven: Yale University Press, 2009), 593.

size or its more recent, more official status.[348] The miracle is told very simply, very much like the healing of the deaf mute in Mark 7:32-37 and the healing of Bartimaeus to come in Mark 10:46-52. Isa 29:18 and 35:5 are evoked.

In the Bethsaida scene, some simply bring the blind man to Jesus and ask for his healing touch (on touch: Mark 3:10; 6:56). The advancing stages of the healing are out of character for Jesus' miracles and point to a symbolism beyond the mere healing. It shows the gradual nature of things coming into view for the disciples.

The healing comes in two stages as Jesus takes the man by the hand outside the city (**v 23**), just like Mark 7:33 where Jesus acted in private with the deaf mute. This is yet another act in Mark to make sure excessive attention to the healing is not the focus of attention, something Jesus does now and again (Mark 5:35-43; 7:33; on such concerns: 1:35-39, 45; 3:7-9; 6:45).[349] First, Jesus spits on his eyes and places his hands over them, again just as he did in Mark 7:33 (also John 9:6-7).[350] When Jesus asks what the man sees, the man says he sees people moving like trees (**v 24**). So the sight is back, but not clear. The fact that the man could sense what trees looked like may mean he had not been blind from birth. This is the only miracle account where Jesus asks about the state of the one being healed after acting. It also is the only miracle that takes place gradually.

So Jesus places his hands on the man's eyes again (**v 25**). With this second step, the man's sight is restored as he reopens his eyes, and now he can see everything clearly. The healing is underscored by using three verbs to describe the recovery: opened his eyes seeing clearly, he is restored, and saw everything distinctly.

Jesus sent the man home, telling him to not return to the village (**v 26**). Mark 5:19 is distinct in that the demoniac there is not to travel with Jesus but is to tell those among his people what the Lord had done. Mark 7:36 has Jesus command those who know about the healing to say nothing, but they do not keep silent. Once again here Jesus tries to keep miracles from being a focus of his work. It is a hard thing to accomplish.

With Mark's placement, the entire exercise is symbolic of how the disciples' eyes were being gradually opened, although the miracle itself

---

[348] Efforts to express that Mark speaks inaccurately by calling it a village versus a city fail to recognize how recently the status of the location had been lifted up; Lane, *Mark*, 283, n. 42.

[349] Lane, *Mark*, 285.

[350] 2 Kings 5:11 is the only example of healing coming from touch in the OT. In Mark 1:41; 7:33; and here we have touch.

had been passed on as a healing in stages.[351] When Peter calls Jesus the Christ in the next scene, they are beginning to see more clearly; total sight is on the way. The point of the symbolism is not to read it strictly as two stages and identify which events are in view, but to simply see it as pointing to a gradual dawning of understanding the disciples have in coming to appreciate who Jesus is.[352]

8:27–10:52 AFTER A KEY CONFESSION, JESUS HEADS TO JERUSALEM AND PREPARES HIS DISCIPLES FOR THE SUFFERING THAT IS TO COME

8:27–30 Peter Confesses Jesus as the Christ

> **8:27 The Jesus and his disciples came out to the villages of Caesarea Philippi. And on the way he asked his disciples, saying to them, "Who do people say I am?"**
> **8:28 They said, "John the Baptist, others say Elijah, and still others one of the prophets."**
> **8:29 He asked them, "Who do you say I am?" Peter said to him, "You are the Christ."**
> **8:30 And he warned them not to tell anyone about him.**

This scene is the pivot in Mark's Gospel. It is a dialogue and confession scene, in which the disciples compare their view of Jesus with that of the public.[353] The parallels are Matt 16:13–20 and Luke 9:18–21. Matthew's version has far more detail, especially with a full commendation of Peter and his reply, than Mark or Luke.

Whereas the public sees Jesus as some kind of a prophet (**vv 27–28**) – John, Elijah, or someone else – that is, Jesus as one of the prophets (Deut 18:15, 18; Mark 6:14–16), Peter confesses Jesus to be the Christ, the one at the

---

[351] So, correctly, Guelich, *Mark 1:1–8:26*, 433.

[352] Stein, *Mark*, 392–93, questions the symbolic view, arguing that the clear seeing does not take place until Easter. This critique interprets the imagery in too precise a way. The point is not two events, but an unfolding of understanding. Clearly Peter's confession is a first step that puts the disciples ahead of both the Pharisees and the crowds. The existence of continued dullness until the resurrection simply shows that seeing clearly is going to take them time, and the confession is only the start, not the finish; see Collins, *Mark*, 394–95.

[353] Bultmann called the scene a "legend," *History of the Synoptic Problem*, 257–58, but the case for it being an authentic event in Jesus' life is strong; see the full discussion by Wilkins, "Jesus' Declaration concerning Jesus' Identity in Caesarea Philippi," in Bock and Webb, *Key Events*, 293–381.

center of God's program and promise. The difference may seem slight, but it is huge. Prophets come regularly to Israel in her history, but there is only one Messiah for most in Israel. John the Baptist and Elijah were associated with the eschaton (Isa 40: 3 cited in Mark 1:2–3; Mal 3:1: 4:5–6), but only point to it. The expectation for Elijah had been of a return from the dead. Something similar is in view with John, perhaps directed by his spirit (Luke 1:16–17; 2 Esd 2:18 looks to a return from the dead for Jeremiah and Isaiah).[354] Jesus is unique. What lies ahead is "the way," a theme Mark consistently invokes in Mark 8–10 (8:3, 27; 9:30, 33–34; 10:1, 17, 32, 46, 52). Jesus' calling and destiny lie before him. The disciples must learn about what is in store for Jesus and for them.

The confession takes place among the villages of Caesarea Philippi. This also is significant, for the site was full of sacred Hellenistic sites, including temples to the emperor Augustus built in 20 BCE and to the god Pan, guardian of the flocks.[355] The dedication of the temple to Pan explains why the site was also known as Panion or Paneas (Banias today; Josephus, *War* 1.404–406; 2.168; *Ant* 15.363–64; 18.28). The major village is located north of the Sea of Galilee at the source of the Jordan River, southwest of Mount Hermon. It was a predominantly non-Jewish area ruled by Herod Philip. Philip named it after Caesar and himself in 3 BCE, no doubt to underscore his connections to Rome. It was known for its beauty. This is the only reference to the locale, and the reputation of the locale is out of character with much of Jesus' ministry to Israel, so the detail points to authenticity. Jesus as the Christ has come to take on the spirituality of the world.

Jesus then asks the disciples for their understanding of who he is (**v 29**). Jesus asks, "But who do you say I am?" The "you all" in this question is plural and emphatic in Greek. Peter replies for the group that Jesus is the Christ. Peter often has this role in Mark (Mark 9:5; 10:28; 11:21). The Messiah is the Christ, or anointed one. It is the first time this title has appeared in Mark since the opening verse.

The point of Peter's answer stands in the contrast between Jesus as merely a prophet versus the promised, chosen One of God. If Jesus was the Messiah, then he stood at the center of God's plan and there was no other like him. The disciples understood this much, but they had much more to learn about the Messiah. Many saw this role in Judaism as involving a key figure of deliverance for the nation, a Davidic-like king,

---

[354] Witherington, *Mark*, 239–40.
[355] Collins, *Mark*, 399–401.

the one who brought God's promise of salvation. It is likely the disciples shared this expectation, which was only partially correct. Their view of who the Messiah is will need reshaping.

Jesus accepts the remark but warns them not to tell anyone (v 30).[356] This hesitation to disclose has been called the messianic secret. To some it means that Jesus really did not claim to be a Messiah, and so Mark overlaid the story with this secrecy theme to cover up that fact.[357] But it is highly unlikely the church would take up such a risky messianic claim about Jesus if he denied or completely discouraged it. A better explanation is an appreciation of the delicacy of the claim in its historical context.

Such a public disclosure would be dangerous. Most messianic expectation involved a political ruler, and Rome was careful to protect Caesar's interests. Whether one thinks of *Psalms of Solomon* 17–18 or *1 Enoch* 37–71, Jewish expectation involved either a human figure or some kind of transcendent figure who would defend and vindicate God's people against the nations.[358] It was rooted in texts from the OT (2 Sam 7:14–16; Pss 2; 110:1–4; Isa 55:3–5; Jer 23:5).[359] So the title bore significant political expectation. Such hope carried revolutionary overtones for many. So the disciples were to keep this to themselves for now because of potential misunderstanding of what Jesus meant by it.[360] There would be a time to reveal it, but not yet.

---

[356] Stein, *Mark*, 399–400, has a long discussion showing that Jesus accepted this title and challenging the view that he rejected it here. Among the key points are Mark 1:1, Jesus' acceptance of the title in Mark 14:61–62, and Jesus' crucifixion for being King of the Jews in Mark 15:2, 12, 18, and 26. Weeden, *Mark – Traditions in Conflict* (Philadelphia: Fortress, 1971), 64–69, is among those who argue that Jesus rejected the title.

[357] This view is tied to W. Wrede, *The Messianic Secret*. Trans. J. C. G. Grieg (Greenwood, NC: Attic, 1971).

[358] Qumran apparently held to two Messiahs, one political and conquering Davidic leader and one Aaronic, who served side by side (CD 12:23–13:1; 14:17–19; 19:10–11, 20:1; 1QS 9:11; 1QSᵃ 2:11–22). *Ps Sol* 17:23–30 says things like "gird him with strength that he might shatter unrighteous rulers" and "he shall gather together a holy people, whom he shall lead in righteousness, and he shall judge the tribes of the people that have been sanctified by the Lord." *1 Enoch* has a more transcendent figure who sits with God in heaven, is called Son of Man, and is pre-existent. On these texts, see Darrell L. Bock and James Charlesworth, eds., *Parables of Enoch: A Paradigm Shift* (London: Bloomsbury, 2013). Craig Evans, *Mark 8:27–16:20* (Dallas: Word, 2001), 15, notes that the key messianic text at Qumran 4Q521 (=4QMess Apoc) 2 and 4 ii 1 speaks of the gospel of the poor and of healing, as well as the Messiah raising the dead (lines 8–12).

[359] For a detailed look at such expectation, Herbert Bateman IV et al., *Jesus the Messiah: Tracing the Promises, Expectations, and Coming of Israel's King* (Grand Rapids: Kregel, 2012). For a focus on Second Temple expectation, J. Neusner et al., *Judaisms and Their Messiahs at the Turn of the Christian Era* (Cambridge: Cambridge University Press, 1987).

[360] Taylor, *St. Mark*, 377.

Instead, the disciples needed to appreciate what kind of Messiah Jesus would be. Next Jesus turns to describing those features of his calling.

8:31–33 Jesus Predicts His Coming Suffering as the Son of Man

8:31 And he began to teach them that it is necessary the Son of Man suffer many things and be rejected by the elders, chief priests, and scribes, and be killed, and after three days rise again.

8:32 He was speaking openly about this matter. So taking him aside, Peter began to rebuke him.

3:33 But turning and looking at his disciples, he rebuked Peter and said, "Get behind me, Satan. You are not thinking about God's interests, but man's."

This scene continues the dialogue emerging from the confession of Jesus as the Christ. It has parallels in Matt 16:21–23 and Luke 9:22. It is a proclamation and prediction by Jesus of his coming suffering using Jesus' favorite self-designation, the Son of Man (Mark 8:38; 9:9 12, 31; 10:33, 45; 13:26; 14:21, 41, 62). Certain things must be (*dei*) for him as a part of his divine calling (Mark 9:11; 13:7, 10, 14; 14:31). This is the first of three such predictions in Mark (Mark 9:31; 10:33–34).[361] It is the rejection of Messiah and his suffering that is an unanticipated feature of Jesus' messianic calling. The disciples need to understand the kind of Messiah Jesus will be before they proclaim him as such.

That this theme is missing for the promised one is somewhat surprising given texts on the suffering of the righteous (Pss 22, 69, 118), a smitten messianic figure in Zech 9–14, and the picture of Isaiah 52:13–53:12.[362] Nonetheless, this dimension to God's sent one was lacking in eschatological expectation.

So Jesus will be rejected by the leadership (**v 31**): elders, chief priests, and scribes. Some of the language ties to Ps 118:22. He will be put to death and after three days rise. The disciples will have a hard time processing that the Messiah can suffer like this. It does not make sense to them how such a glorious figure can suffer such a fate. The three days to the resurrection are

---

[361] For a full study and defense of the historicity of these predictions, see Hans Beyer, *Jesus' Predictions of Vindication and Resurrection* (Tübingen: Mohr/Siebeck, 1986). That Jesus could have foreseen his suffering and death is rooted in as simple an observation as his being able to sense the level of opposition he was facing and the example of John the Baptist. Knowing his kingdom claims, a response by Rome was not difficult to anticipate. The hopes of vindication are rooted in trusting God in this calling.

[362] France, *Mark*, 334–35.

counted inclusively. The disciples do not get that far in the prediction. The idea that the Messiah will be killed by the nation's leaders just does not seem right, as the following conversation with Peter reveals.

Jesus was speaking of his coming suffering openly (**v 32**). It was shocking to the disciples. So Peter took him aside and began to rebuke him. In his view, this was not what would happen to the Messiah. Matt 16:22 says "God forbid, Lord. This shall never happen to you." Jesus' response was pointed and directed at all the disciples, not just Peter (**v 33**). This may suggest that Peter was speaking for more than himself. Addressing a rebuke to Satan, Jesus declared that Peter was not thinking the thoughts of God, but of men. The directness of the address is another indication of authenticity, as it is hard to imagine the church making up and circulating such a rebuke of what was then one of her major leaders. Peter's view is a hindrance to Jesus that needs to be altered. Peter needs to return to being the disciple.[363] Peter is addressed as Satan not because he is possessed but because he is thinking in ways opposed to God. What was an expectation of deliverance by power would be accomplished in another way, by suffering and sacrifice. Of this the disciples should be assured. The following teaching on the cost of discipleship and suffering only underscores the point. Instruction is needed because of the lack of real understanding Peter has of his earlier confession.

8:34–9:1 Jesus Calls for Total Commitment from Disciples

8:34 Then Jesus called the crowd together with the disciples and said to them, "If anyone wants to follow after me, he must deny himself and take up his cross and follow me.

8:35 For whoever wishes to save his soul will lose it, but whoever loses his soul for my sake and for the gospel will save it.

8:36 For what benefit is it for someone to gain the whole world and lose his soul?

8:37 For what can a person give in exchange for his soul?

8:38 For if anyone is ashamed of me and my words in this adulterous and sinful generation, the Son of Man also will be ashamed of him when he comes in the glory of his Father with the holy angels."

9:1 And he was saying to them, "Truly I say to you, there are some standing here who will not taste death before they see the kingdom of God has come with power."

---

[363]   Marcus, *Mark 8–16*, 607, nicely covers what "get behind me" means as a call to return to discipleship. It is not a dismissal of Peter, as Peter is very much still around after this.

Jesus presents a short discourse on discipleship. It is an individual address to anyone, male or female (**v 34**). The parallels are Matt 16:24–28 and Luke 9:23–27. It is about the cost and total commitment it will require to walk the same path as Jesus is taking. Discipleship involves self-denial, rejection with suffering and preparation for martyrdom as pictured by a crucifixion, and following the path and example Jesus is setting.[364] The idea of crucifixion was widespread enough and so well known we need not think of a post-Easter perspective.[365] This focus on suffering and rejection is a lesson that reverses all the expectations the disciples had of how Jesus would bring promise. Jesus says this to the entire crowd. He wants them to know what he is calling for from them to walk in God's kingdom ways. It will take initial commitment (deny, take up the cross) and perseverance (follow). The first two verbs are aorist imperatives, whereas the last one is a present imperative pointing to this difference.

Jesus explains himself that to preserve a soul only to really lose it is no gain (**v 35**). He gives what looks like four reasons, using *gar* three times, in verses 35–37, but there really is one point: nothing is worth giving up real life. To lose the soul in self-denial and identification with God is to gain it. The reference to losing one's life for Jesus' sake and for the Gospel points to life's connection to God and promise. Note how the two are linked. Jesus and the fate of people are linked in several texts (Matt 7:21–23=Luke 13:25–27; Matt 10:32–33=Luke 12:8–9; Matt 10:35–36=Luke 12:51–53; Matt 10:37–39=Luke 14:26–27; Matt 11:6=Luke 7:23).[366] The Gospel is tied to the Jesus who brings it. In this passage the soul is seen as the inner life, that which represents real life, the self in the full sense of that term.[367] To gain the world and have the things of it but lose the connection to the Creator which is life is of no benefit (**v 36**). To preserve one's life and lose the spiritual life that one really has and that really matters is a tragedy. Nothing is more precious than that spiritual life connection.

The language of gain and exchange is the language of commerce (**v 37**). This is a loser's deal, as nothing can replace the life that has been lost. The

---

[364] Lane, *Mark*, 307, discusses Jesus as describing a "death march" with this image of the cross.

[365] Donahue and Harrington, *Mark*, 263, make this correct observation, as does Taylor, *St. Mark*, 381. Josephus notes many such examples in passing (*War* 2.241, 306; 5.449–51; *Ant* 17.295); see Marcus, *Mark 8–16*, 617. Also Plutarch, *De sera numinis vindicta* §554b, where he describes the fact that the crucified normally carries his own cross, something Jesus did not do because of weakness later; Stein, *Mark*, 407, notes that this difference is another point for authenticity here. *Thomas* 55 is a parallel.

[366] Stein, *Mark*, 408.

[367] Donahue and Harrington, *Mark*, 263; France, *Mark*, 340–41; BDAG 1098–99.

ideas expressed reflect themes from the OT and Judaism (Ps 47:7–9 – of choosing riches; 2 *Bar* 51:15 – did not choose glory to come). The term *antallagma* looks to an exchange rate and here points to no amount being worth real life (BDAG, 86). There is irony throughout the imagery, as to gain one must lose, whereas seeking to gain in one's own way results in loss. To be without God's promise is to be in the red and quite dead, having nothing.

Jesus warns of his coming authority in the face of the rejection disciples will face. This is a reminder of accountability before God. Anyone ashamed of the Son of Man in response to this adulterous and sinful generation will experience shame from the Son of Man when he comes with the angels on behalf of the Father at judgment time (v 38). It is a reminder that connection to the kingdom and faithfulness to it is the primary relationship one should prioritize, especially in the face of pressures that pull people away from God. So rejection of Jesus and persecution of those allied to him are in view as the dangers of this generation. Shame here would refer to denying Jesus or failing to confess him.

Only Mark has the warning about being ashamed of the Son of Man. The positive side of acknowledging the Son is in the parallels (Matt 10:32–33; Luke 12:8–9). Of course, Jesus is the Son of Man, as this is his favorite way to refer to himself. Matt 10:33 simply speaks of "I" instead of using the title. The authority background tied to judgment comes from Daniel 7. The reference to "his Father" means that the images of the Son of Man and Son of God are juxtaposed here as well. Everything tied to promise, salvation, and judgment converges around Jesus.

So Jesus raises a core question at this point of his teaching the crowds. Will one identify with Jesus, the Son of Man to whom one's soul is ultimately accountable? To shun the Son is to face the prospect of being shunned by him when he returns with the angels to exercise judgment in the power and glory of the Father (14:62). The risk is that one will lose one's soul. This is the first clear reference to a return in Mark, though 4:21–22 and 30–32 have suggested it. Of course, it is merely presented as a time when judgment will take place, so the return element is not clear to those hearing Jesus. The idea of a return becomes clearer later (Mark 13; 2 Thess 1:7). This is the only public reference to the Son of Man before Jesus replies to the High Priest in Mark 14:62. Lane says it this way: Mark "8:38 served to warn those who choose to stand with the world in its contempt for Jesus that his apparent weakness and openness to humiliation will be reversed in an awesome manifestation of his glory as the eschatological

Judge."[368] No matter how things look now, there will be glory and vindication to come. This makes the choice to side with Jesus worth it.

Jesus also promises that some present with him will see the kingdom in power before they taste death (9:1). "Tasting death" is a metaphor for experiencing death (Matt 16:28; Luke 9:27; John 8:52; Heb 2:9). This is a controversial text.[369] What event does Jesus have in mind? Is it the judgment he just described? That would seem natural enough. However, given the timing of when Mark is written and the fact Jesus suffered without bringing consummation, this judgment is unlikely to be the meaning.[370] Is it some other event that points to the presence and power of the kingdom? Could it be the resurrection?[371] This seems possible, since salvation and its provision from Jesus are tied to resurrection. Might it be the Pentecost and the evidence of Jesus' saving power at work? That could fit Luke-Acts, but Mark has no sequel to point to this event specifically. Could it be the Fall of Jerusalem? This is unlikely, since the scene assumes acceptance and shame, not mere power. Is it the simply already presence of the kingdom? However, this is already present with Jesus, so what then is the point of saying it is in the future? Better to point to the resurrection itself and the exaltation and benefits of the life in the Spirit tied to it, if this is the point. The juxtaposition of this saying to the Transfiguration that follows immediately suggests at the least that that event is a preview of what he is describing here. As such, the Transfiguration serves at least as an indicator for the authority still to come. It seems likely this is what is referred to and the connection to consummation is in the preview that the Transfiguration represents. Not far away is the experience of resurrection-exaltation that discloses more fully who Jesus is and what he is ultimately to bring. Jesus may suffer and experience rejection. So will his disciples. However, that is

---

[368] Lane, *Mark*, 313.

[369] Cranfield, *Mark*, 286–89, notes seven views about what is being referred to here.

[370] Nonetheless, Hooker, *Mark*, 211–12, argues that Jesus was wrong in some sense to anticipate the kingdom as soon as he suggests here, although he was right in that the vindication pointing to this did take place. One could argue that Mark holds out hope the consummation may still come in the lifetime of those who are left, but his placement of the Transfiguration as a full epiphany after this remark suggests he had something else in mind. See Witherington, *Mark*, 261. Idiosyncratic is the view of France, *Mark*, 343–45, who sees the fulfilment as not involving a coming to earth in judgment at all, but as tied to Jesus' vindication only. Marcus, *Mark 8–16*, 620–21, has a good overview of the debate about authenticity and opts for the saying being authentic, seeing it as unlikely the church would create such a statement that raised so many questions about "Jesus' predictive powers."

[371] Edwards, *Mark*, 260, and Marcus, *Mark 8–16*, 622.

not the last act in this drama surrounding the kingdom and Jesus' authority.

9:2–8 A Voice from Heaven Commends Jesus as the Beloved Son as He Is Transfigured before a Few Disciples

> **9:2 Six days later Jesus took Peter, James, and John and led them alone up a high mountain in private. And he was transfigured before them,**
> **9:3 and his clothes became radiantly white, more than a launderer in the world could bleach them.**
> **9:4 Then Elijah appeared before them along with Moses, and they were speaking together with Jesus.**
> **9:5 So Peter said, to Jesus, "Rabbi, it is good for us to be here. Let us make three shelters – one for you, one for Moses and one for Elijah."**
> **9:6 For they did not know what to say, for they were very afraid.**
> **9:7 And a cloud overshadowed them, and a voice came from the cloud, "This is my beloved Son. Listen to him."**
> **9:8 Suddenly, looking around, they no longer saw anyone but Jesus alone with them.**

This scene is an epiphany and a theophany wrapped together. Its parallels are Matt 17:1–8 and Luke 9:28–36. It parallels the voice from heaven at the baptism and serves as a confirmation of all that has been said since Peter's confession. Jesus says nothing in this scene. It is a disclosure about him. He is more than a teacher; he is a Messiah – Son of God of cosmic proportions.[372]

Six days after the remarks on discipleship (**v 2**), Jesus takes three disciples in his inner circle to a high mountain for a private experience.[373] Outside the Passion Week in Mark 14:1, this is the most precise note of timing we have in Mark. It points to the importance of this event. 2 Peter 1:16–18 alludes to this event. Six days was the time tied to the revelation at Sinai (Exod 24:16–17). The later mention of Moses also points to a key event like the disclosure at Sinai in Exod 24. The mountain is simply described as being high and is not named. Three sites are proposed: Mount Tabor, Mount Hermon, or Mount Meron.[374] Mount Tabor is the traditional site, but it is not such a high peak as Mount Hermon. There is no clear way to decide.

---

[372] France, *Mark*, 347–48.
[373] On an inner circle among the Twelve, Mark 5:37 and 14:33 have these same three with Jesus, while 13:3 adds Andrew.
[374] France, *Mark*, 350. Collins, *Mark*, 421, opts for Mt. Hermon as a more sacred site, as does Edwards, *Mark*, 262–63.

It begins with Jesus being transformed before them into a dazzlingly, bright appearance (Dan 12:3; 2 *Baruch* 51:3, 5, 10, 12; 1 *Enoch* 38:4; 104:2; another conceptual parallel could be the Transfiguration of Moses' face at Sinai).[375] His clothes shone brighter than anyone could wash them. This was a glimpse of his glorified state, Jesus as a figure come from the side of heaven, a cosmic character (Dan 7:9; Matt 28:3; Mark 16:5; John 20:12; 1 Cor 15:43, 49, 51–53; Rev 1:9–18; 1 *Enoch* 14:10; 2 *Enoch* 22:8–9).[376] The comparison is made that Jesus' appearance is brighter than what a launderer (**v 3**; *gnapheus*) could do with a piece of wool or cloth (BDAG, 202). This person does all kinds of things with clothes, including washing them with lye. Usually such cleansing is tied to a spiritual washing in the OT (Ps 51:7; Jer 2:22; Mal 3:2–3).[377]

Next Elijah appeared with Moses, conversing with Jesus (**v 4**). The presence of these two indicates restoration in the eschaton. Moses appears as the father of deliverance, while Elijah points to the promise and hope of a new era as the promised herald of that period (Mal 4:5–6). They also are associated with revelation at Sinai (Exod 19–24; 1 Kings 19). It is a little unusual that Elijah would be named first, and both Matt 17:3 and Luke 9:30 reverse the order. It may be the stress on restoration is the point in the unusual word order, as well as the fact Elijah is discussed again in the next scene. The common idea that they point to the Law and the Prophets is probably too vague to work, and Mark's order of presentation is against that suggestion.[378] Moses certainly is associated with the idea of restoration in the image of the prophet like Moses (Deut 18:15–19). The age of salvation and messianic presence is the point. Might we understand that we have two great witnesses to the new era here? Mark notes no detail about the conversation. Luke 9:31 says they spoke of Jesus' coming exodus from Jerusalem.

The disciples are overwhelmed with fear according to verse 6b. This is a common reaction to the presence of heavenly power and shows respect for

---

[375] Hellenistic parallels starting with the *Illiad* 20.81–82, 131, and *Odyssey* 7.20, 13.222–23, 13:288–89, 17.485–87, are noted by Collins, *Mark*, 418–19. Most of these are more general in the idea of a god taking on human form. The closest parallel in terms of brightness is the *Homeric Hymn to Demeter*, 275–80. Jewish analogies from angels are closer parallels.

[376] Lane, *Mark*, 313–14.

[377] Marcus, *Mark 8–16*, 632.

[378] Collins, *Mark*, 422, suggests the fact that both are tied to traditions of being taken up to heaven is also in play (Elijah in 2 Kings 2:11). That might be the case, although Moses is portrayed as having experienced a normal death in Deut 34:5, despite that tradition Josephus, *Ant* 4.325–26, notes (also *Assump Moses*).

the transcendent. The uncertainty their emotional state produced explains how they reacted. Peter had spoken up, suggesting building booths for the three of them—one for Jesus, one for Moses, and one for Elijah (v 5). The background is the feast of Tabernacles (Lev 23:39–43), and Peter is suggesting prolonging the experience along similar lines of reflection. The request is not so foolish at this level, as Mark's narrative comment might suggest in that there was the hope that in the new day God would tabernacle with his people again (Tob 13:11).[379] That feast celebrated the Exodus, the original event of deliverance, and God's provision and care during that time. The problem with the request lies elsewhere. The equality of the three of them is also implied in his remarks (v 6). It is this presumption that the voice from heaven addresses, showing yet another need for the disciples to learn. Peter has missed the import of his earlier confession and that only Jesus appears glorified.[380]

The correction comes in a voice from heaven announcing Jesus to be the beloved Son and a command to listen to him. The voice comes out of a cloud that overshadows them (v 7). This seems to suggest they have been brought into the cloud and God's presence with access to revelation; but discussion does exist about whether Jesus, Moses, and Elijah only are in the cloud or the disciples as well, since one can argue that the voice came out of the cloud, making it a distinct locale from those who were intended to hear the voice. The text is not entirely clear on the point. The symbolism does point to the revelation and presence of God, the Shekinah, just as at Sinai (Exod 19:9, 16; 24:15–16; 33:9; 40:35; 1 Kings 8:10–11; Isa 4:5).[381] This is a theophany (Matt 17:5 and Luke 9:34–35 are the parallels). What is interesting is how in the NT clouds are often tied to Jesus or the revelation of his return (Son of Man on the clouds: Matt 24:30=Mark 13:26=Luke 21:27; Matt 26:64=Mark 14:62; Rev 14:14–16; cloud tied to ascension, Acts 1:9; Shekinah presence in the wilderness, 1 Cor 10:1–2; future meeting with a returning Jesus, 1 Thess 4:17; return of Jesus, Rev 1:7; angels and clouds, Rev 10:1; two witnesses taken up, Rev 11:12). The disciples are clearly intended as the recipients of the voice's testimony. 2 Macc 2:8 shows that some Jews expected a return of the cloud to reveal the things of the end.[382]

---

379 Edwards, *Mark*, 266.
380 Stein, *Mark*, 418.
381 Lane, *Mark*, 320, notes that the voice and cloud combination appears only at Sinai in the OT.
382 Marcus, *Mark 8–16*, 634.

What is said here about being the beloved Son was said earlier at Jesus' baptism to him (Mark 1:10–11). This statement alludes to Ps 2:7 and Isa 42:1. Jesus is the royal son who serves the program of God (Mark 12:6; Heb 1:1–2). Peter's confession in Mark 8:29 is affirmed. Unlike the earlier declaration, there is no declaration that the speaker is pleased with the Son, and the address is now to the disciples ("this") versus the earlier direct address to Jesus ("you"). Added to the earlier declaration is the call to hear what he says, an allusion to Deut 18:15, and the prophet like Moses, a leader-deliverer-prophet. The disciples have shown they have much to learn. So they need the instruction he will give.

They also need to appreciate who Jesus is. That this word comes in the midst of teaching on the impending suffering points to one key thing that still needs to be learned – Jesus will suffer despite who he is. Jesus' power is unique and yet will show itself in unique ways.[383] It is important that this divine attestation and vindication has followed right after Peter's confession and Jesus' announcement of coming suffering.

After the voice, Jesus is left alone (**v 8**). The need for witnesses has passed. Jesus has been shown not to be equal to Moses and Elijah, as Peter's remark had implied, but unique in God's program. The unusual moment of disclosure and preview is done. Jesus teaches on suffering, but he does so as Son who is to be heard. Suffering is not a disqualifier for bringing the new era or for Jesus' status. It is a part of his calling as Son.

9:9–13 Jesus Commands Silence until the Resurrection about the Transfiguration and Discusses Elijah as Having Come

9:9 As they were coming down from the mountain, he gave them orders not to tell anyone what they had seen until the Son of Man had risen from the dead.

9:10 They held this matter to themselves, discussing what rising from the dead meant.

9:11 Then they were asking him, "Why do the scribes say that Elijah must come first?"

---

[383] There is no need to choose between these two themes of Christology and suffering tied to discipleship, as Stein, *Mark*, 419, and Edwards, *Mark*, 268, opt for the Christological point and Marcus, *Mark 8–16*, 81, points to the need for more instruction tied to discipleship. The two themes are related and go together. Part of Jesus' unique role as Son is that his sonship will also emerge from his suffering. Power comes out of weakness.

9:12 He said to them, "Elijah does indeed come first and restores all things. And why is it written that the Son of Man must suffer many things and be despised?
9:13 But I say to you that Elijah has come, and they did to him what they wanted, even as it written about him."

This scene contains short didactic dialogue about what has just taken place. Matthew 17:9–13 is a parallel. The program of God is affirmed as announced and arriving with Elijah having come and suffered. The character of the new era as including suffering is highlighted once again. The idea is so surprising that it needs repeated affirmation. It also took some time to sink in and be understood.

As they were coming down from the mountain (v 9), he commanded them not to discuss with anyone what they had seen until the Son of Man is raised from the dead.[384] Full disclosure awaits a fuller understanding of what is taking place and requires other events before that, such as his death (Mark 10:45). That more complete understanding takes place with the raising of the Son of Man from the dead. This remark echoes Mark 8:31. The call to be silent reaches back to Mark 1:25, as do similar commands elsewhere (Mark 5:43; 7:36; 8:30).

These three disciples did keep silent (v 10). They guarded (*krateō*) this matter and kept it to themselves (BDAG, 564). The one thing they did discuss was the meaning of the resurrection from the dead. This was anticipated to be at the end of history before the judgment, so how could this work? Was Jesus discussing a singular resurrection by itself? The disciples had no idea.

The disciples then raise the topic of Elijah (v 11), asking why those who study Scripture say Elijah must come first before a Messiah (Justin Martyr, *Dialogue* 49:1). Jesus affirms with the OT hope (Mal 3:1; 4:5–6; Sir 48:10) that Elijah does come and will restore all things. Although this hope only had

---

384 This is a key text in the messianic secret view tied to William Wrede in 1901 that Mark overlaid a messianic understanding projected back to Jesus that did not originally exist with the command to silence being the way he made the move. Wrede actually stepped back from this view, but it continued to influence many scholars in NT studies; see Wilkins, in *Key Events*, 333, n. 143, and Martin Hengel and Anna Maria Schwemer, *Der messianische Anspruch Jesu und die Anfänge der Christologie: Vier Studien* (Tübingen: Mohr/Siebeck, 2001), ix. The major problem is why the disciples would turn to a category that would only bring trouble for them if Jesus had not taken them there earlier. In addition, the tradition with these messianic themes is too widely attested to be only a later construct. Even Jesus' death for sedition assumes some type of regal claim, and the *titulus* over the cross claimed Jesus as a regal figure, a messianic category in this context.

Elijah coming at the end, it is not a far step to think this is before the Messiah as well, since the Messiah is a key figure of the end.[385] A question is raised whether Jesus makes a statement or raises a question about Elijah's coming.[386] Even if this is a question, which is not at all certain, a query using the Greek *men* looks to expect a positive reply. More commonly, it reflects the first part of a two-part statement, making a statement more likely here. The parallel in Matthew 17:11 also reads it as a statement. The claim that Jesus' later remark about the Son of Man contradicts this claim about Elijah ignores another possibility being raised by Jesus. Elijah has come and apparently will come as well. As Jesus is about to show, Elijah has come now in the figure of John the Baptist. This sets up restoration with the coming of Messiah. The Messiah's work will complete it when it looks as though Elijah or a figure like him also will reappear.

Jesus has a question of his own (v 12). Why must the Son of Man suffer and be despised? This idea recalls Isa 53:3 where the Servant is despised, and the language reflects a related verb of being despised in Ps 22:6 (= 21:7 LXX) or the verb used in the Acts 4:11 citation of Ps 118:22.

There also is the righteous sufferer of the Psalter (Ps 22, 41, 69). Jesus is again returning to the theme of suffering tied to his work, whereas the disciples are focused on victory. Jesus goes on to say that Elijah has come already (v 13). This is almost certainly an allusion to John the Baptist. He continues by saying that they did to him whatever they wanted. This points to his suffering, death, and martyrdom (Mark 6:14–29). It is the template for what Jesus is saying about discipleship. If John did not survive rejection, neither will he. If he does not survive rejection, neither will the disciples. This fits with what was said about him. Here it is harder to know what is being alluded to beyond the picture of the righteous sufferer and the general precedent that prophets in general, including Elijah, did not fare well in Israel's history. So we should expect that pattern to continue. Elijah's conflict with Jezebel comes to mind as the basis for the evocation of a pattern of suffering (1 Kings 19:1–3, 10, 14).[387] Yet the differences are important. Elijah does not die at the hands of a ruler who opposed him, as John the Baptist did, and yet the text is rooted in the pattern the historical Elijah established, not the eschatological figure. Still, Jesus' point is that suffering attends the work of this key prophet, something the precedent of

---

[385] Marcus, *Mark 8–16*, 644.
[386] Marcus, *Mark 8–16*, 645.
[387] Taylor, *St. Mark*, 395; Witherington, *Mark*, 265.

Scripture points to as possible. The innovation in thinking has roots in the example of Elijah. So when heaven speaks, earth often resists.

Interestingly, this is a role John denied having (John 1:21), when he said he was not Elijah. Luke 1:16–17 says John came in the spirit of Elijah. The denial may be seen as an attempt to preserve a role for Elijah coming at the end or a denial that John will restore all things versus setting up its restoration through the call to repent. The parallel in Matt 17:13 makes a connection to John explicit. Elijah may well be functioning as a type or pattern category here. John is a type of Elijah.[388] The evocation of Elijah tied to John says that the new era has come and that restoration will follow.

9:14–29 Jesus Heals a Demon-Possessed Boy Who Is Epileptic after the Disciples Fail to Heal Him

> **9:14 And when they came up to the disciples, they saw a large crowd around them and the scribes disputing with them.**
>
> **9:15 And immediately when the entire crowd saw him, they were amazed and greeted him.**
>
> **9:16 And he asked them, "What are you arguing about with them?"**
>
> **9:17 One of the crowd replied to him, "Teacher. I brought you my son, having a spirit that makes him mute.**
>
> **9:18 Whenever it seizes him, it throws him down, causes him to foam at the mouth, grind his teeth, and he becomes rigid. I requested your disciples cast it out, but they were not able to do it."**
>
> **9:19 He answered them, "O unbelieving generation! How much longer shall I be with you? How much longer will I have to endure you? Bring him to me."**
>
> **9:20 So they brought the boy to him. And when the spirit saw him, it immediately convulsed the boy. And falling to the ground, he was rolling around, foaming at the mouth.**
>
> **9:21 Jesus asked his father, "How long has this been taking place with him?" And he said, "From childhood.**
>
> **9:22 And many times also into fire he has cast him and into water that he might destroy him. But if you are able, help us. Be merciful to us."**
>
> **9:23 Then Jesus said to him, "If you are able – all things are possible for the one who believes."**
>
> **9:24 Immediately the father of the child cried out, saying, "I believe; help my unbelief!"**

---

[388] Lane, *Mark*, 326.

> 9:25 Now when Jesus saw that a crowd was quickly running together, he rebuked the unclean spirit, saying to it, "Mute and deaf spirit, I command you, come out of him and never come into him again."
>
> 9:26 And crying out and with many convulsions, he came out. And the boy became like a corpse, so many said, "He is dead."
>
> 9:27 But Jesus, taking his hand, raised him up and he stood up.
>
> 9:28 Then after coming into his house, the disciples asked him privately, "Why could we not cast it out?"
>
> 9:29 And he said them, "This kind can only come out by prayer."[389]

This long miracle account shows that despite all the revelation that had been taking place, the disciples are still learning. It is the last of four exorcisms in Mark (Mark 1:21–28 – a Jew; 5:1–20 – a Gentile; 7:24–30 – a Gentile daughter; now – a Jewish son). The parallels are Matt 17:14–21 and Luke 9:37–43, but Mark's account is far more detailed, being more than twice as long as the parallels. While Jesus had been up on the mountain with the three, the rest of the disciples had been struggling to perform a healing of a demon-possessed boy who had seizures and was mute.[390] This is the only scene in which the disciples fail at such an effort.

The four returned to find the disciples in dispute with some scribes about what was taking place (**v 14**). When the crowd that had gathered around the discussion saw Jesus, they came and greeted him, being amazed (**v 15**). They seem to be surprised that he had shown up. Normally such notes of amazement follow a miracle, but here the mere appearance of Jesus is enough. The use of *exthambēthēsan* here is the first of four uses of this verb in Mark (14:33; 16:5–6), the only NT writer to use the word. It refers to great surprise or perplexity (BDAG 303).

Jesus asks the crowd or the scribes within the crowd what is taking place and what the fuss is about (**v 16**). Scribes are more likely here, as the crowd has no disagreement with the disciples. They are simply witnessing what is going on.

However, the one in the crowd who brought the boy to the disciples explains why there is an argument (**v 17**). As he comes forward to explain, he respectfully calls Jesus teacher. Usually Mark uses this term when an issue needs resolution (Mark 4:38; 5:35; 9:17, 38; 10:17, 20, 35; 12:14, 19, 32;

---

[389] There is a textual problem here, as many manuscripts add a reference to fasting. It could well be original, given some early support in p[45], but it seems more likely to have been added by a scribe versus being deleted. Metzger, *Textual Commentary* (1994), 101.

[390] On the ancient background of how epilepsy was seen by the ancients as a "sacred disease," an affliction from the gods, Collins, *Mark*, 435–36; Pseudo-Hippocrates, *The Sacred Disease*; Lucian, *Philopseudes, Lover of Lies*, 16; Apuleius *Apology*, 42–51.

other uses are simply as a title, Mark 13:1; 14:14). The father notes that his son has a spirit that makes him mute. It also seizes him and throws him down to the ground, making him foam at the mouth, grind his teeth, and become rigid (**v 18**). When the attack is done, the child lies paralyzed. The condition appears to reflect epilepsy. Matt 17:15 says as much, calling him "moonstruck," an ancient description of that condition. Later, in Mark 9:25, we are told that he is deaf. This is a disturbing condition for a parent to watch a child go through. In fact, the condition is described four times in the scene, showing how violent and painful it is (Mark 9:18, 20, 22, 26). He came and asked the disciples to cast out the demon, but they had met with no success. The verb used to describe the failure is vivid (*ischuō*), as it means to have the power or strength to do something (BDAG, 481). They did not have the power or strength to overcome the demon that possessed the son. The failure had likely precipitated the disagreement.

Jesus responds with a rebuke for a generation lacking faith (**v 19**). He asks how long must he be with them and endure them. The absence of belief is painful. Who is in view? Is it the crowd apart from the disciples,[391] the disciples alone,[392] or the whole group?[393] The rebuke is more like Num 14:11 than Deut 32:20, since in Numbers a rationale for the rebuke appears. However, it is a theme that is at work here as Matthew 17:17 and Luke 9:41 echo Deut 32:5, speaking of a perverse generation. In those OT texts, it is God who is reacting; here it is Jesus in line with the Christological elevation Mark consistently gives to Jesus.[394] It is hard to be sure why this particular failure provoked such a thorough rebuke, but the persistent failure of the disciples is something Mark has been noting, so it may not be just this one situation that brings the rebuke but a cumulative set of responses. After all, they failed twice to get the provision of food, failed to accept the idea of coming suffering, mistook the presence of Moses and Elijah as pointing to people equal to Jesus, and now this. So Jesus' labor to encourage faith has met with many exasperating hurdles, even from those closest to him. Of course, the crowd and others have been slow to embrace Jesus as well. The term "generation" (*genea*) normally refers to a broad group in Mark (8:12 [twice], 38; 9:19; 13:30), so the crowd is probably included in the rebuke, and the lack of faith in the father confirms this. The point is to issue a call for a renewed faith.

[391] Edwards, *Mark*, 278.
[392] Cranfield, *Mark*, 301.
[393] Hooker, *Mark*, 223; Witherington, *Mark*, 267; Stein, *Mark*, 433.
[394] Marcus, *Mark 8–16*, 653.

Nevertheless, Jesus asks that the boy be brought to him (**v 20**). This leads to an episode as the spirit takes the boy and throws him to the ground and into convulsions. On the ground, the boy rolls around and foams at the mouth. Jesus now sees the desperate and dangerous condition that has been described. The spirit has responded to Jesus' presence, and a power encounter is set up by the language about Jesus' ability to heal.

In an exchange unique to Mark (**v 21**), Jesus asks how long this condition has existed. The father has to speak, since the boy is mute, and replies from childhood. It may be that the duration of the condition points to a chronic condition and a sense that it will never change.[395] He also adds that many times the spirit throws the child into fire or water to destroy him, either by burning or drowning (**v 22**). The demon is portrayed as destructive, looking to damage the one occupied. So he asks again for Jesus' help, compassion, and mercy. This is the final note about compassion from Jesus in Mark, but it is the first time it is requested (1:41; 6:34; 8:2). Help will be requested again in the scene in 9:24 for a lack of faith. This unique exchange means that the development of faith is being highlighted beyond the fact of the miracle.

The father predicates the request on Jesus' ability to do something, "if you are able." The failure of the disciples has led to uncertainty. The father is proceeding, but is not confident something will happen. Jesus responds by asking, with some mild rebuke (**v 23**), "If you are able?"[396] He breaks up the thought, as if it is not appropriate to finish, and instead turns to a call for faith. All things are possible for the one with faith, another consistent Markan theme (Mark 5:36; 10:27). The remark is purposely open in terms of audience, but is aimed at the father. The father confesses he is torn (**v 24**). He believes, but needs help for his unbelief. He has brought his son for healing, but is Jesus really able to help? That is enough for Jesus to act and show that faith is honored. Doubt is met with affirming action. Imperfect faith can be perfected (Mark 5:34, 36). He can believe in Jesus and that he is able.

A crowd comes running toward the scene (**v 25**), adding to those already present in Mark's account (Mark 9:14–15, 19). Jesus performs the miracle with a command to the demon to come out and never come back again.

---

[395] This sense is raised by Collins, *Mark*, 438, who notes that once a child reaches puberty, the sense settled in that one would not outgrow a condition like this. The reference to childhood may indicate that the boy had reached such an age, and was not a child.

[396] France, *Mark*, 367. He says the force is "If you can indeed!" For the Greek on an article before a set of quoted words, see BDF §267, 1.

The idea of a demon returning is present in other Synoptic accounts of another saying (Matt 12:43–45; Luke 11:24–26), but this is not like other exorcisms in Mark (Mark 1:25; 5:8).[397] His word is able and strong enough to overcome the demon. Mark had used various terms for a command or rebuke for previous miracles (*epitiman; epitassein*; Mark 1:25, 27; 4:39). The demon is said to have made the boy both deaf and mute here. Jesus is about to shatter the world of the boy's silence. Shaking the boy into convulsions as he left (**v 26**), the boy was dropped to the floor one final time. Those watching thought he was dead, since he was as still as a corpse. They thought Jesus had failed and the result was disaster for the boy. But Jesus took his hand and raised him up alive and well (**v 27**), a description that mimics resurrection, given what was said about being dead, and echoes Mark 5:41–42 and the raising of Jairus' daughter. Unlike many miracles, no reaction is narrated for the healing. The miracle and power over the demon are the story.[398]

Alone at home (**v 28**), later the disciples asked him why they could not exorcize this demon. Jesus' private teaching is another common Markan theme (after public teaching: Mark 4:10; 7:17; 9:14; 10:10). Jesus responded that this kind could be removed only with prayer (**v 29**).[399] Only here and in Mark 11:17 does Mark use this term for prayer that points to petition (*proseuchē*), although other texts use other terms (Mark 1:35; 6:46; 11:24–25; 12:40; 13:33; 14:32–39).[400] Their healing gift was not automatic. Dependence was the lesson of faith for the disciples. Inadequacy outside of God must cause them to turn to him. They must rely on God as they minister with the enablement God has given them.

9:30 32 Jesus Predicts His Suffering One More Time

9:30 And going out from there, they passed through Galilee, and he did not wish anyone to know,

---

[397] Foucant, *Mark*, 374, adds the note from Josephus that exorcism often came with a casting out that did not allow a return; *Ant* 8:45–47.

[398] Lane, *Mark*, 336, comments, "When faith confronts the demonic, God's omnipotence is its sole assurance, and God's sovereignty is its only restriction."

[399] This association of prayer and healing left its mark on the early church; James 5:15; Acts 9:40, as did invoking Jesus, Mark 9:38–39; Matt 7:22; Luke 10:17; Acts 3:6; Collins, *Mark*, 439, though she makes too much of the fact that Jesus himself does not pray for this healing. This is because his power is seen by Mark as unique. His word is enough.

[400] Some manuscripts add a reference to fasting here, but a key array of witnesses lack the term, pointing to its not being original; Metzger, *Textual Commentary*, 85. God alone acts to make this possible, so what is required is faith, another indication of the close connection between Jesus and God (Mark 9:23).

9:31 **for he was teaching his disciples and saying to them, "The Son of Man is being given over into the hands of men, and they will kill him, and being killed after three days he will rise."**
9:32 **But they did not understand this statement and were afraid to ask him.**

This scene involves another pronouncement and passion prediction. The first was in Mark 8:31. Matt 17:22–23 and Luke 9:43–45 are the parallels. Jesus continues to travel through Galilee, teaching his disciples and seeking not to be detected. His attention is turning to preparing his disciples for what is ahead. This is the last time Galilee is noted until we are well into the Passion Week (**v 30**; Mark 14:28; 16:7).[401]

The text predicts in a general way what Jesus was teaching them about his coming suffering (**v 31**). This uses an imperfect tense, underscoring these repetitions as a theme. He offers a second prediction of what is coming: handing over, death, and then resurrection after three days. It is the least detailed of the three predictions. The handing over to men is the new feature in this prediction. The passive is a divine passive. God's program is at work. It is portrayed in a vivid present tense as in process (is being handed over).[402] The following verbs are future: he will be killed and raised. As in Mark 9:10, the disciples still do not get it and are afraid to ask him (**v 32**; Luke 9:45). The remark had to have struck fear in them and produced some uncertainty.[403] The expectation of a deliverer who suffers death is hard for them to comprehend. The Son of Man is a figure from Daniel 7 who vindicates the persecution of the righteous who are delivered into the hands of men (Dan 7:25). What had not been anticipated is that he himself would suffer, leading God's people in and out of rejection. The image of the leader-sufferer is a theme of the righteous sufferer of the Psalter and of the Servant figure of Isaiah. Marcus sees an allusion to Isa 53:6 and 12, as well as to language in Dan 7:25–27.[404] A general resurrection is affirmed in Dan 12:2. So a specific individual resurrection is a distinctive teaching.

---

[401] Edwards, *Mark*, 283.
[402] The alternative is a futuristic present tense, pointing to the certainty of what is coming. Though true, it is perhaps better to see the wheels already turning for Jesus' fate in the reaction he has been facing and where God is taking him on this journey to Jerusalem. The verb given over (*paradidonai*) dominates from here (Mark 10:33; 13:9, 11–12; 14:10, 11, 18, 21, 41, 42, 44; 15:1, 10, 15).
[403] France, *Mark*, 372, citing Best, *Following Jesus: Discipleship in the Gospel of Mark* (Sheffield: JSOT Press, 1981), 73, explains, "They understand enough to be afraid to ask to understand more." Lane, *Mark*, 337, says, "They suspect that to know would be more painful."
[404] Marcus, *Mark 8–16*, 667. Focant, *Mark*, 377, argues that the language is closer to Dan 7:25, but, even so, a theme is in play.

There are three such prediction scenes in Mark. One was in the north near Caesarea Philippi, the second in Galilee, and the third as they head to Jerusalem. Jesus is on his journey with divine destiny. He wants the disciples to be ready. Mark 10:33–34 is yet to come. Each prediction is followed by a failure by the disciples: Peter's refusal to see suffering, the debate about who is the greatest here, and the request to sit on thrones with Jesus in the last.[405] Power drives the disciples' hope. Jesus is taking them to another place: suffering and service. They sense danger and fear asking. Fear, usually out of a sense of self-preservation, is another key Markan theme (Mark 4:41; 5:15; 10:32; 11:18, 32; 12:12), which is likely to be what is at work here, in contrast to a "holy fear" that the lack of understanding would not generate.[406]

9:33–50 Jesus Teaches on Humility, Service, and Sin

9:33 Then they came to Capernaum. And after Jesus was in the house, he asked them, "What were you discussing on the way?"

9:34 But they were silent, for they had argued with one another about who was the greatest.

9:35 After sitting down, he called the twelve and said to them, "If anyone wishes to be first, he must be last of all and a servant of all."

9:36 He took a little child and had him stand in their midst. Taking him into his arms he said to them,

9:37 "Whoever welcomes one of these little children in my name welcomes me, and whoever welcomes me does not welcome me but the one who sent me."

9:38 John said to him, "Teacher, we saw someone in your name casting out demons and we tried to stop him, because he was not following us."

9:39 But Jesus said to him, "Do not hinder him. For no one who performs a miracle in my name will be able soon afterward to say anything bad about me.

9:40 For whoever is not against us is for us.

9:41 Truly I say to you, whoever gives you a cup of water because you bear Christ's name will never lose his reward.

9:42 If anyone causes one of these little ones who believes in me to sin, it would have been better for him to have a huge millstone hung around his neck and be thrown into the sea.

---

405 Witherington, *Mark*, 269.
406 Contra Stein, *Mark*, 440.

9:43 If your hand causes you to sin, cut it off. It is better for you to enter life crippled than to have two hands and depart into Gehenna, into unquenchable fire.[407]

9:45 If your foot causes you to sin, cut it off. It is better to enter life lame than to have two feet and be tossed into Gehenna.[408]

9:47 If your eye causes you to sin, tear it out. It is better to enter into the kingdom of God with one eye than to have two eyes and be tossed into Gehenna,

9:48 where their worm never dies and the fire is never quenched.

9:49 Everyone will be salted with fire.

9:50 Salt is good, but if it loses its saltiness, how can you make it salty again? Have salt in yourselves, and be at peace with each other."

This section contains a short discourse of related teaching on discipleship. It is linked by a series of catchwords that tie the parts together (e.g, "servant," 9:35–36, assuming an Aramaic background from the word for servant, *talya*; "in my name," 9:37–38, 39, 41). The parallels for Mark 9:33–37 are Matt 18:1–5 and Luke 9:46–48. Parallel to Mark 9:38–40 is Luke 9:49–50. The parallels to Mark 9:41–50 are Matt 5:13; 18:6–9; and Luke 17:1–2 and 14:34. The nature of the parallels suggests we may be dealing with either themes Mark has pulled together into one place or teaching Jesus repeated. Once again the disciples need instruction and correction, a theme of the last few chapters.

Jesus returns to Capernaum and asks the disciples what they had been discussing (v 33). This is the final mention of Capernaum, as Jesus is moving on to Jerusalem. The verb here (*dialogizesthai*) is often used of arguing in Mark (2:6, 8; 8:16–17; 11:31). The discussion of status had resulted in disagreement and debate. They were reluctant to let Jesus know this (v 34), so they initially were silent, because they had argued over their relative greatness. The comparative (*meizōn*) is used for the superlative here. It may be that Jesus' earlier separating out of three for the Transfiguration led to the discussion (Mark 9:2). Qumran had such a ranking, and seated people accordingly (1QS 2:19–23).[409]

So he sat them down to teach them a lesson (v 35). The seated posture points to formal teaching. The position of being first is for those who are

---

[407] Matt 9:44 is missing in key early witnesses and looks to be added to create a parallel to verse 48.

[408] As with Mark 9:44, the earlier manuscripts lack this verse, as the phrasing matches verses 44 and 48.

[409] Edwards, *Mark*, 286, who calls the discussion a debate on the "whine of rank."

last and serve all. The term "first" normally would refer to those at the top of the social ladder (Mark 6:21; Luke 19:47; Acts 25:2; 28:17; Josephus, *Ant* 11.140–41; 18.121).[410] Jesus says this more than once in this Gospel, showing its importance (Mark 10:43–44; Luke 10:16; also Matt 20:26–27; 23:11; Luke 22:26). The term servant (*diakonos*) points to one who aids another like Elisha for Elijah (Josephus, *Ant* 8.354), government servants (Rom 13:4), or messengers on behalf of another (Col 4:7). Service is like household service and points to a form of self-denial (Mark 8:34). Plato (*Gorgias* 491e) asks, "How can a man be happy when he has to serve someone?" Here is the contrasting attitude of the larger culture. Luke 22:27 shows Jesus as the example of such service.

To drive home the point (v 36), he took a child and put him in front of them. In the ancient world, a child had virtually no status until he or she was useful. A later text in *Pirqe 'Abot* 3:10 reads, "Sleep in the morning, wine at noon, babbling with children, staying at the synagogue with 'people of the land' accelerates the loss of humanity."[411] In fact, young children, who were unwanted, were abandoned and left to die in some Greco-Roman contexts.[412] These examples show the Greco-Roman attitude about children is different from that in modern times. The OT saw children as a blessing, but this was often because of the role they performed in helping around the home and perpetuating the family name (Ps 128). Jesus takes a different route. Jesus told them that the one who welcomes a child in his name welcomes him (v 37). They are to follow his example in welcoming and lifting up the child.

Jesus' action and remark in verse 37 raised the status of the child and presented the child as important. Then he also noted the one welcoming him also welcomed the one who sent him. So to welcome a child was to welcome God and be responsive to him. Matt 25:31–46 is a conceptual parallel. The point not only affirms the importance of all people; it also, in the context of this dispute, is a call to humility. One is to love one's neighbor, even ones the culture sees as irrelevant. In fact, rather than thinking that such "lesser" people should serve us, disciples should serve

---

[410] Focant, *Mark*, 381.

[411] P. Achtemeier, "An Exposition of Mark 9.33–37," *Int* 39 (1976), 182; Donahue and Harrington, *Mark*, 285, call children "a 'non-person' who is totally dependent"; Witherington, *Women in the Ministry of Jesus* (Cambridge: Cambridge University Press, 1984), 13–15.

[412] Collins, *Mark*, 445–46. She sees a direct contrast to such exposure in the picture of acceptance of the child, but this applies too narrow a meaning to the text. It is the social status of the child in general that is in view in the choice of a child as an example. Collins's example is but a vivid illustration of the point.

them. The remarks turn the tables on how one sees issues of rank and power; a hierarchy has become a lowerarchy. In making the low important, all are made important.

Such humility also means that others may serve in Jesus' name. John raises the issue, noting that someone was casting out demons in Jesus' name (v 38). The disciples tried to stop him because he was not among the followers. Jesus responded not to try and stop him (v 39), because the one who does a miracle in Jesus' name will not speak badly about him. This appears to foresee the experience of invoking Jesus as solidifying a sense of connection to him. Is the one invoking Jesus a believer outside the circle or anyone just trying to use the power of his name? The text is not clear and may be purposely open in terms of its scope. Still, the text seems to assume that the one who is effective in the use of the name has a relationship to the kingdom, or at least, an openness to it (1 Cor 12:3; counterexample, Acts 19:13–16).[413] Simply put, the one who is not against us is for us (v 40). So, support for the ministry or openness to it is to be encouraged. Jesus is not offering a closed club, but one with an open invitation to enter into ministry on Jesus' terms. Disciples are to be generous to the array of support Jesus garners from wherever it comes.

In fact, service in Christ's name should be honored as God honors it (v 41). So Jesus uses the example of someone giving disciples a cup of water in the Christ's name. This is the only text in Mark where Jesus makes a self-reference to the Christ or explicitly refers to reward, though Mark 10:28–30 is close.[414] The scorching sun made the offer of water a gift in this region. That person will receive his reward (Wis 5:15–23; 4 Ezra 7:83; 13:56; *m. Abot* 2:1–2, 14–16; 5:1). The implication is that God will supply the commendation.

On the other hand, to drive a follower into sin is to commit a crime before God (v 42). The picture is leading a person into serious sin, to cause them to stumble over the kingdom. France speaks of "spiritual shipwreck."[415] The verb *skandalizō* refers to stumbling over an obstacle and is a link word tying the passage together.[416] It would be better for that person to drown in the sea, having been tossed in with a millstone around his or her neck, than to face the judgment that is the outcome for causing followers to stumble. A millstone was a heavy stone driven by a donkey to grind grain (BDAG, 661). Capital punishment in Rome sometimes

---

[413] Lane, *Mark*, 343.
[414] France, *Mark*, 378.
[415] France, *Mark*, 380.
[416] Cranfield, *Mark*, 313; BDAG, 926, speaks of leading to a downfall.

involved drowning.[417] One is warned not to be a cause of spiritual defection. It will have severe consequences.

Three examples to avoid personal sin follow in verses 43–47 involving hands, feet, and eyes – the parts of the body that carry out action (Job 31:1, 5, 7). Note how the attention has moved. It has gone from the previous example of causing another to sin to the issue of personal responsibility for sin, personal stumbling.[418] If your hand causes sin (v 43), then cut it off. For it is better to continue life crippled than to allow sin to lead you into judgment (v 45), to be sent into Gehenna with its unending flames of torment. The picture is figurative, for otherwise only two violations would be permitted, and Deut 14:1 prohibited self-mutilation, so this is a shocking image out of line with aspects of the Law to show the seriousness of the exhortation.[419] Nonetheless, the cutting off of body parts was a punishment rendered in some situations (Deut 25:11–12; Exod 21:23–25 – "eye for eye"; Josephus, *Life* 34–35; *War* 2.642–46; *m Niddah* 2:1). Life (Mark 9:43, 45) and the kingdom of God (Mark 9:47) are in parallelism across the three examples showing they are connected. One's fate in life is related to the presence of the kingdom. Jesus is urging separation from sin as part of the kingdom's call.

This is not a literal cutting off of the hand, but a separating from that which causes one to sin. It is better to do without such destructive freedom that leads into spiritual accountability and death. The challenge points to the seriousness of sin and the reality of accountability to God for it. The picture of unquenchable fire also is figurative of a torment and judgment that has no end. That is the result of being permanently separated from a God you knows exists and with whom fellowship had been possible. The Greek term for hell is *Gehenna*, named after a place, the valley of Hinnom in south Jerusalem, where infants were sacrificed to Molech and in later times where refuse was burned (BDAG, 191; 2 Kings 23:10). The picture of endless torment reflects imagery like we see in Jdt 16:17, where the condemned weep forever, and Sir 7:17, where fire and worms await the dead (also *1 Enoch* 27:2; 90.26–27; *4 Ezra* 7:36). Annihilation does not look to be present, but unending torment.

As with the hands, so it is to be with the feet and eyes.[420] With the final example of the eyes, the picture of the permanence of judgment is

---

[417] Hooker, *Mark*, 231–32.
[418] Stein, *Mark*, 447.
[419] France, *Mark*, 382; Edwards, *Mark*, 293–94.
[420] Mark 9:44 and 46 (with their "where their worm never dies and the fire is never quenched") is not as well attested as original as the appearance of the same phrase in 9:48. Although the majority text and D have it, most early manuscripts, including ℵ and B, lack it. So it is likely a scribal addition to bring more balance to the text with verse 48.

reinforced (**v 47**). The image of a non-perishing worm and an eternal flame is invoked (Isa 66:24). The suffering depicted from judgment is unending. If your actions cause you to sin, separate from what causes the sin, for entry into heaven with a loss of freedom is better than to exercise those destructive acts and face a judgment that has no end. The picture is rhetorical, not literal. The call of the disciple is to take responsibility to separate oneself from the causes for sin.

Jesus closes the short discourse with an enigmatic (**v 48**), quickly shifting phrase about salt that makes three distinct points. First, everyone will be salted, that is, tested with fire, as Jesus puts it (**vv 49-50**). All are accountable and tested (Ezek 16:4; 43:24; 1 Cor 3:15). The imagery appears rooted in the OT where sacrificial flames were purified with salt that symbolized a special connection to God. Lev 2:13 reads, "Do not let the salt of the covenant be lacking from your cereal offering."[421] Fire purges and shows what remains of worth. Salt pictures that which is special in a connection with God. It is to be utilized.

Second, Jesus shifts the image. Salt is good, but once the saltiness is lost, it cannot be regained. It becomes useless. Salt mixed with gypsum at the Dead Sea could show such characteristics.[422] The point here is not to lose the salt and become useless.

Third, and as a summation, Jesus urges them to have salt in themselves, to put to use the covenant relationship that they have been given and exercise capabilities they have received that are distinctive. If they do that by working together, they will be at peace with themselves. The rivalry of trying to determine rank will be gone. So Jesus ends by coming full circle to where he started. Humility will lead to peace.

10:1–12 Jesus Discusses Divorce and Emphasizes the Design of Marriage as Male and Female Made One for Life

10:1 Then Jesus having gotten up from there came into the region of Judea beyond the Jordan River. And again crowds gathered to him, and again as was his custom, he taught them.

It is harder to explain how the verses dropped out later, if original, than to explain their addition.

[421] Some manuscripts (D, *it*) of the verse actually allude directly to this Leviticus text with additional wording, but that is unlikely to be original.

[422] Witherington, *Mark*, 273, who also notes Num 18:19 for covenant imagery; also Exod 30:35 for purity and holiness.

10:2 And coming, some Pharisees asked him, testing him, "Is it was lawful for a man to divorce his wife?"

10:3 He replied to them, "What did Moses command you?"

10:4 They said, "Moses permitted a man *to write a certificate of dismissal and to divorce* her."

10:5 But Jesus said to them, "Because of your hardness of heart he wrote this commandment for you.

10:6 But from the beginning of creation *he made them male and female.*

10:7 *For this reason a man will leave his father and mother, and the two will become one flesh.*

10:8 *So they are no longer two, but one flesh.*

10:9 Therefore what God has joined together, let no one separate."

10:10 In the house again, the disciples asked him about this.

10:11 So he told them, "Whoever divorces his wife and marries another commits adultery with her.

10:12 And if she, having divorced her husband, marries another, she commits adultery."

This scene is a controversy account that ends in a pronouncement. Matt 19:1–12 is the parallel and appears to be a more detailed account. Luke 16:18a is like Mark 10:11.

Jesus' journey moves on (v 1). He now enters Judea. Galilee is left behind. He comes south probably by way of the eastern side of the Jordan River or Perea, so he comes from the other side of the Jordan. On this trip he apparently avoids Samaria, as was common (contrast John 4). There is a textual issue here, but the more difficult reading refers only to the other side of the Jordan. The variants appear to clean up what is otherwise a somewhat unclear description, given that Judea was not on the other side of the Jordan. The expression is probably a highly condensed reference to the route.[423]

Crowds are drawn to him, and he teaches them as is his custom (v 2). In a test, the Pharisees ask him a question about divorce. Is it lawful for a man to divorce his wife? Matt 19:3 presents the question in a more detailed way as being about divorce for any reason, which would be the point of such a question. Collins reads the question as artificial by reading it too narrowly and literally about allowing divorce at all.[424] The OT allowed this for something unseemly (Deut 24:1), but the interpretation of this was disputed. In addition, Mal 2:13–16 expressed the view that God disliked

---

423 Metzger, *Textual Commentary* (1994), 88. The addition speaks of "into the coast of Judea by the far side of the Jordan" (A, K, X, Π).

424 Collins, *Mark*, 465.

divorce, so it may have been permitted but was not advised. When permitted, was it for immorality alone (School of Shammai) or could it submitted for something as simple as a poorly cooked meal, finding another more beautiful, or general insubordination (Sirach 25:26; Josephus, *Life* 426; *Ant* 4.253; *m. Gittin* 9.10; School of Hillel)?[425] At Qumran, CD 4 may preclude divorce as an option.[426] This was the range of views in Judaism. The question assumes a patriarchal right to divorce, but generally in Judaism women do not divorce men, though there are exceptions as the example of Herodias showed.[427] Greco-Roman divorce was more open for an array of causes and involved both genders.[428]

Another element of the test is more likely to have been to draw him into the dispute over Herod's marriage to Herodias.[429] This challenge had led to John the Baptist's death according to Mark 6:14–29. Jesus has passed through Perea where Herod rules. The account looks to be authentic, since Paul is aware of it in 1 Cor 7, where the apostle expands on what Jesus is known to have taught.

Jesus asks what Moses commanded, pointing to Scripture for guidance (v 3). They note that Moses permitted a man a certificate of divorce (v 4), citing Deut 24:1, but not presenting the reasons. Technically this does not permit divorce but regulates it.[430] Jesus' response is that it was hardness of heart that caused Moses to say this (v 5). Stubbornness and sin meant divorce was acknowledged in certain situations. So this was how to do it, giving protection to the woman with a certificate of release. In Greek the reference to "hardness of heart" is thrown forward for emphasis. The

---

[425] The *Gittin* text reads, "The School of Shammai say: A man may not divorce his wife unless he has found unchastity in her, for it is written, 'Because he hath found in her indecency in anything.' And the School of Hillel says: [He may divorce her] even if she spoiled a dish for him, for it is written, 'Because he hath found in her indecency in anything.' R. Akiba says: Even if he found another fairer than she, for it is written, 'And it shall be if she finds no favour in his eyes.' " In 9:1, the Mishnah presents a divorce decree that provided for remarriage if it was granted. A woman got to keep her dowry unless she had been unfaithful.

[426] There is dispute about whether this is about divorce or simply prohibiting polygamy.

[427] See Ernst Bammel, "Markus 10,11f und das jüdische Eherecht," *ZNW* 61 (1970), 95–101. The Jewish Elephantine community allowed this. There also is the example of Salome with Costobarus, but Josephus noted that it was exceptional (*Ant* 15.259). On Jewish Second Temple practice, John D. Rayner, "Unilateralism to Reciprocity: A Short History of Jewish Divorce," *Journal of Progressive Judaism* 11 (1998):48–49.

[428] Collins, *Mark*, 465, who notes that immorality, infertility, or mutual agreement of the families could lead to divorce.

[429] Hurtado, *Mark*, 160; Evans, *Mark 8:27–16:20*, 85–86.

[430] France, *Mark*, 390–91.

answer slips the trap, for he is not affirming divorce nor pointing to it being the right thing to do.

Jesus is focusing on the fact that marriage was not designed to be entered into with the hopes of getting out of it. So he turns to the beginning of creation (vv 6–8). He starts with Adam and Eve, looking to the start of marriage. He notes that God made humans as male and female, citing Gen 1:27. He then cites Gen 2:24 where a man leaves his father and mother and the two become one flesh. So the marriage of a man and a woman makes the couple a one-flesh unit, their own family. What God brings together is not to be put apart. Jesus defines marriage by this remark (v 9). As Edwards says, "By expressly mentioning the two sexes, Jesus declares that maleness and femaleness are rooted in the creative will of God and are foundational for marriage."[431] The verb for "put together" is *suzeugnumi,* referring to yoking together, fusing into a unit something that was in two parts (BDAG, 954). That was the intent in the design of marriage. It was a relationship, not merely a contract. This is what Jesus chooses to emphasize. Marriage was intended to be for life. It is God's will, not what the Torah permits, that is the point.[432] So to separate or divorce what God has brought together is not desired. The verb is the term also used for divorce (*chōrizō* – BDAG, 1095; 1 Cor 7:10–11). Jesus is asking not what is the least one can do, but what one should seek in pursuing marriage. These are the high standards Jesus says God has set for marriage, and those in his community should seek to follow it.

In a private discussion after the exchange with the Pharisees (v 10), Jesus reaffirms the oneness of the marriage bond. Interestingly, Matthew omits reference to a private teaching at this point, as he lacks anything like Mark 10:10. Teaching in private is common in Mark (4:1–12, 33–34; 7:17–23; 9:28–29; 13:1–4). Hooker speaks of a contradiction between Mark 10:9 and Mark 10:10–12, since in verse 9 divorce is prohibited, but in verses 10–12 it is remarriage that is in view after a divorce.[433] However, we are dealing with real life here. People did get divorced and did so to get remarried, so both circumstances are relevant.[434] Both took place, so how should those realities be seen?

Jesus notes that remarriage after a divorce leads to adultery because the bond of marriage is an issue tied to God bringing the couple together and

---

[431]   Edwards, *Mark,* 303.
[432]   Hooker, *Mark,* 235.
[433]   Hooker, *Mark,* 236.
[434]   France, *Mark,* 393.

making them one (**vv 11–12**). The seventh commandment is violated (Exod 20:14). This is the result regardless of whether the man or the woman seeks the divorce.[435] An effect of Jesus' remarks was that women, who were often regarded as property in marriage, should be seen as equal partners, since marriage is a male-female unit with no special preference given to men[436] The fact that the same rules apply to the man and woman is important, since normally an adultery was seen as an offense against another husband and not against the wife.[437] Mark's mention of the woman's divorcing is a detail not in the parallels. Some suggest Mark has added it to take account of Greco-Roman practice,[438] but the example of Herodias shows the possibility in the mixed context of first-century life, so a later Markan addition is not a given at all.[439]

One impact of Jesus' remarks about divorce is to protect women, who in a patriarchal society were vulnerable to arbitrary divorce.[440] The act is "against her." Matthew 5:32 makes the same point. Jesus' teaching protected the mother and children from capricious neglect. To value marriage is to value the family formed by it. Adultery is not an independent act of an adult exercising privileges of freedom of choice. It has implications for the social relationships one has made commitments to honor. It is a violation of ties made with another before God.

Mark's version notes no exceptions. This differs from Matthew where *porneia* is noted in both Matt 5:32 and 19:9. Although it is common to argue that Matthew is responsible for this addition, it may simply be that Mark has focused on the emphasis that marriage is designed to be permanent. For this idea, Paul in 1 Cor 7 knows what Jesus taught and is comfortable

---

[435] Textual variants in a few Western and Caesarean manuscripts raise the issue of a woman's desertion and remarriage and speak of the woman leaving the husband versus divorcing, but that reading is less well supported and is not original.

[436] Hurtado, *Mark*, 160–61.

[437] Cranfield, *Mark*, 321; Hooker, *Mark*, 236.

[438] Hooker, *Mark*, 236–37. Marcus, *Mark 8–16*, 706–707, notes the right of women to seek divorce, as noted in Cicero, *Letters to His Friends* 8.7.2; Gaius, *Institutes* 7.137a, but says too much in saying that this cannot fit Jesus' context; again, see Ernst Bammel, "Markus 10,11f und das jüdische Eherecht," *ZNW* 61 (1970), 95–101. Marcus's later discussion shows how complex this debate is, as there is some indication that even though divorce rights were primarily patriarchal, exceptions did exist; however, they were viewed as less than ideal. Edwards, *Mark*, 304–305.

[439] Yet another example is Salome, Herod the Great's sister, whose divorce Josephus described as exceptional (*Ant* 15.259–60). To claim only a Hellenistic context for this is to claim too much, given how prominent these Herodian examples were.

[440] Placed with the example of the Syro-Phoenician woman with great faith, one can argue Mark is positive toward women in the book.

adding his own exception, unbeliever desertion. If Jesus had taught an absolute view with no exceptions, then it would seem that Paul would have been less comfortable with making his own move. Luke 16:18 also has no exceptions, but Luke is using Jesus' general teaching on divorce as an example of kingdom ethics. He is not making an effort to be exhaustive about what Jesus taught, but is focused on the thrust of his teaching. What Jesus underscores is a person's commitment before God in marriage. Divorce often reflects a selfishness that is not sensitive to how it is an act against the partner as well as a violation of an act that reflects what God has joined together.

10:13–16 Jesus Rebukes the Disciples as He Permits the Children to Come to Him and Urges Them to Have Faith as a Child

> **10:13 Now people were bringing children to him so he might touch them, but the disciples rebuked them.**
> **10:14 But when Jesus saw this, he was indignant and said to them, "Permit the children to come to me, do not hinder them, for the kingdom of God is made up of such as these.**
> **10:15 Truly I say to you, whoever does not receive the kingdom of God like a child will never enter it."**
> **10:16 And taking the children in his arms, he blessed them, having set his hands on them.**

In another short pronouncement scene (v 13), Jesus instructs the disciples yet again. The parallels are Matt 19:13–15 and Luke 18:15–17. The issue here is Jesus' access to children and his availability to bless them. People were seeking to bring children to Jesus. As gatekeepers for Jesus' time and work, the disciples not only were trying to prevent this but also were rebuking people for making the effort. Jesus stopped the disciples indignantly and took the opportunity to teach the disciples of the importance of all people (v 14), using children as an example of faith (vv 15–16). Only Mark has the note about Jesus being indignant, fitting his greater willingness to be critical of disciples and Mark's tendency to show Jesus' emotions. Jesus was not pleased with this action by his disciples and contended that the kingdom of God is made up of such people. He is emphatic. He uses a series of imperatives to say with an aorist "permit", followed by a present imperative not to hinder making the point. The present imperative has the force of "stop hindering."

It is common to turn this text into a discussion about infant baptism, but that issue is not in view here at all. This is not a discussion of membership in the community but simply people from the crowds seeking to gain Jesus' attention and blessing for their children. Baptism as a rite tied to personal faith operates in a distinct context. Jesus makes a comparison using children as an example of a type of faith. His acceptance of children means they are to be appreciated and taken seriously, even welcomed into community, but there is no direct instruction here on whether infants should be baptized. What we see in this passage and in the previous one is teaching Jesus gave to protect women and children.[441]

It is important to note that in this culture children were not appreciated as "cute," as they generally are today. They had no social status until they could be useful to family and others. In fact, we have texts that instruct mothers to leave a child, especially if she is a girl, to be exposed to death (*Oxy* 4.744, lines 9–10).[442] So Jesus is elevating their status and making it clear that even the seemingly unimportant are of value. Those who enter the kingdom, he says, have to do it like a child. This is likely a reference to the dependence that stands at the core of faith. Children know of their need for parents. Without their parents, they are exposed. What they receive, they receive as gifts.[443] One comes to the heavenly Father with respect and a sense of deep need of grace. So Jesus accepted the presence of the children and, taking them in his arms, blessed them. The fact he could hold them indicates these were young children (so Luke 18:15; *Thomas* 22). Jesus is repeating a theme Mark 9:37 had already raised. Some cultural instincts die hard.

10:17–31 Jesus Instructs about the Danger of Devotion to Riches and Urges Disciples to Leave All

> **10:17 And Jesus was proceeding on his way, someone ran up and having fallen to his knees asked him, "Good Teacher, what must I do to inherit eternal life?"**
>
> **10:18 But Jesus said to him, "Why do you call me good? No one is good except God alone.**
>
> **10:19 You know the commandments: '*do not murder, do not commit adultery, do not steal, do not give false witness, do not defraud, honor your father and mother.*' "**

---

[441] Witherington, *Mark*, 281; Marcus, *Mark 8–16*, 714–15.

[442] The issue of how children were seen culturally is treated in the discussion on Mark 9:36–37. Justin, *Apology* 1. 27–29, condemned such exposure of children or the selling of them into prostitution.

[443] Donahue and Harrington, *Mark*, 300.

10:20 The man said to him, "Teacher, these all I have guarded from my youth."

10:21 Looking at him, Jesus loved him and said to him, "One thing you lack. Go, sell whatever you have, give to the poor, and you will have treasure in heaven. And come follow me."

10:22 But at this word, becoming sad, the man went out sorrowful, for he had many possessions.

10:23 And Jesus, looking around, said to his disciples, "How hard it is for those having wealth to come into the kingdom of God."

10:24 The disciples were amazed at these words. Jesus again replying said to them, "Children, how hard it is to enter the kingdom of God.

10:25 It is easier for a camel to go through the eye of a needle than for a rich person to enter the kingdom of God."

10:26 They were even more astounded and said to themselves, "Then who can be saved?"

10:27 Jesus, looking at them, said, "With men this is impossible, but not for God, for all things are possible with God."

10:28 Peter began to speak to him, "Look, we have left everything to follow you."

10:29 Jesus said, "Truly I say to you, no one who has left home or brothers or sisters or mother or father or children or fields for my sake and for the sake of the gospel

10:30 who will not receive in this age a hundredfold as much – homes, brothers, sisters, mothers, children, fields, all with persecutions – and in the age to come, eternal life.

10:31 But many who are first will be last, and the last first."

This scene is another dialogue pronouncement account. It involves Jesus and a rich man. It ends in a pronouncement that produces not only a reaction from the rich man, but also a subsequent dialogue with the disciples. So Jesus uses the exchange to teach his disciples about faith and wealth. The parallels are Matt 19:16–30 and Luke 18:18–30.

Jesus continues his journey on the way to Jerusalem (v 17). Another reference to being on the way (*odos*) makes the journey to Jerusalem reference likely. A man comes and falls to his knees before him and inquires what he must do to inherit eternal life. Matthew tells us he is young, whereas Luke calls him a ruler, so Mark's description is the most general. Mark does not let us know he is rich until later. The question about eternal life is a request to know what it takes to be saved, about entering the kingdom, as Mark 10:23 shows (*1 Enoch* 40:9; *Pss Sol* 14:9–10; *Sib Oracles*

3.46–49; *m. 'Abot* 5:19).[444] He calls Jesus "good teacher" in asking the question and assumes entry into life is something he must do something to get. Jesus will welcome the premise and yet redirect it.

Jesus responds with hesitation about being called good, noting only God is good (**v 18**). Jesus is alluding to Deut 6:4. God is unique. The harsh response is a bit surprising and has caused no lack of comment.[445] The word sequence is "why *me* do you call good." This shows how in Greek the reference to Jesus is moved forward for emphasis. Was Jesus distancing himself from God or was he observing that such a greeting brings him in connection with God? Neither of these explanations is likely, for Mark is unlikely to present a story that has the former idea, and the latter idea is too subtle to be likely.[446] Jesus is probably challenging the flattery that is present and simply redirects the emphasis toward what God desires and God's honor.[447] The man should not think any person or act is ultimately good when it is rendered apart from God.[448] The answer will connect Jesus and God in that to do God's will, he will need to become a follower of Jesus. Mark 10:15 has already noted the one who enters the kingdom must receive it as a child, in dependence, not as entitlement, so a redirection is needed.[449]

Jesus then continues with a list of the commandments (**v 19**). The reply is conceptually like Lev 18:5: the one who keeps God's statutes lives (also Deut 30:15–16; Ezek 33:15). Interestingly, he cites the part of the Ten Commandments that deals with relations with others, numbers 5–10: do not kill, commit adultery, steal, give false witness, or defraud, and honor your father and mother (Exod 20:12–16; Deut 5:16–20). To the list of commandments is added one about defrauding in place of coveting,[450] and the fifth commandment is placed last, whereas the rest are in order. This may be relevant given the man is described later as wealthy. There is an implied warning not to exploit in order to gain wealth (Mal 3:5 LXX).[451]

---

[444] Collins, *Mark*, 476.

[445] The saying is enigmatic enough that most commentators see it as authentic. It is seen as unlikely that the church would have created such a remark; Witherington, *Mark*, 281; Hooker, *Mark*, 241.

[446] France, *Mark*, 402.

[447] Evans, *Mark 8:27–16:20*, 96.

[448] Hurtado, *Mark*, 151.

[449] Lane, *Mark*, 365.

[450] Some manuscripts, including B*, lack this command, but it is likely original, as it is more likely to have been omitted by a copyist than to have been added. Manuscripts including it are ℵ, A, B², C, D, X, and Θ.

[451] Marcus, *Mark 8–16*, 723.

More importantly, Jesus is highlighting that loving God means loving others. God seeks that from people. To live that way is truly to live and have life.

The man claims to have guarded these all from his youth (**v 20**). This is a claim to have kept them faithfully. The response that these things have been kept causes Jesus to extend his answer to the question and to probe more deeply.

Jesus responds out of his own love for the man with one more requirement that tests the man's love for others and shows whether he has kept all these commands (**v 21**). The mention of Jesus' love here shows that challenge and love can go together. This is Mark's only reference to love outside of the great commandments (Mark 12:30–33). To love someone is not always only to affirm them. Sometimes challenge is required.

So what else might be required? Jesus says the man lacks one thing to do. Jesus' response calls for everything.[452] Jesus is testing both obedience to God's commands and whether the man truly loves others, as the Ten Commandments call for doing. The man is to sell what he has, give it to the poor, thereby acquiring treasure in heaven – good deeds to produce recognition and reward from God – and then he is to come and follow Jesus. The focus is on gaining that which pleases heaven. The call to go and sell is expressed with an aorist imperative. It is a call for a single act that leads into the ultimate test. The end of Jesus' answer to the question about life focuses on following him, having left all, an idea Jesus has consistently taught (Mark 8:34–37). He is "challenged to exchange the blessings of this life for those of the life to come" (Matt 6:19–21 *Ps Sol.* 9:5; *2 Bar* 24:1; Sir 29:10–12).[453]

This is a unique challenge. In Luke 19:1–10, Zacchaeus sells half and is declared to be a child of Abraham. This is because Zacchaeus' orientation toward others and God is right. In contrast, in this specific case with this rich man, Jesus presses the matter to expose where the man's heart is. If a choice is forced between possessions and God, as shown in loving others and joining Jesus' program, what is it the man clings to for life? Seen in this light, the Law points to promise and to loving God in such a way that Jesus is followed and people are loved. Lane says, "Keeping the individual

---

452   Hooker, *Mark*, 242. Witherington, *Mark*, 282, n. 98, notes the command is not specifically to sell all, but that might be implied here. On 283, Witherington says, "The ultimate test of obedience, then, is seen as the willingness to take up the yoke of discipleship to Jesus."

453   Evans, *Mark 8:27–16:20*, 99.

commandments is no substitute for the readiness for self-surrender to the absolute claim of God imposed through the call of the Gospel. Jesus' summons in this context means that true obedience to the Law is rendered ultimately in discipleship. This man will achieve the perfect observance of the Law when he surrenders himself and follows Jesus."[454] Is the man willing to go there?

The man reacts with sorrow and departs sad (v 22). The reaction is vivid, since the verb *stugnazō* refers to a face that is crestfallen (BDAG, 949). It contains a mixture of sadness and resentment. He is not affirmed in the direction of his life and he will not join Jesus, unlike the earlier response of Peter, Andrew, John, and James (Mark 1:16–20) – a point Peter will raise in Mark 10:28.[455] He has fallen into a trap Jesus had warned about earlier in Mark (Mark 4:19; 8:36). Wealth had become a barrier to God and loving others.[456] The exchange ends here, but the teaching has just begun.

Jesus notes how hard it is for those with possessions to enter the kingdom (vv 23–24).[457] He addresses his disciples with tenderness, calling them children, even as he issues his hard observation. He says it twice for emphasis, but the second time he notes it is simply difficult to enter the kingdom of God. The remarks surprised the disciples. The text says they were amazed the first time (*ethambounto* – BDAG, 442) and astounded or overwhelmed (*exeplēssonto* – BDAG, 308) the second. For them, it was likely they thought the rich were blessed (Job 1:10; 42:10; Ps 128:1–2; Isa 3:10), possibly even reflecting obedience (Deut 28:1–14).[458]

If the rich could not enter the kingdom, who could? Jesus drives the point home with one further hyperbolic remark. It is easier for a camel to go through the eye of a needle than for a rich man to enter the kingdom (v 25). Later rabbis spoke of an elephant going through the eye of a needle to make a point about the impossibility of something (*b. Ber* 55b; *b. B. Mesia* 38b).[459] Although efforts have been made to equate the eye of a

---

[454] Lane, *Mark*, 367.
[455] Collins, *Mark*, 480.
[456] France, *Mark*, 400–401.
[457] Some manuscripts (A, C, D) add "those who trust in riches" in verse 24. It supplies what is lacking but implied from the previous example. The omission is a harder reading and likely original, especially as it takes a little of the edge off the saying about it being difficult to enter the kingdom without any qualification. With the inclusion of trusting riches, what Jesus says is less shocking, leaving one to wonder why the remark got the reaction of surprise it did. D also repeats the camel reference here.
[458] Lane, *Mark*, 369.
[459] Stein, *Mark*, 472. In *b. B. Mesia* 38b, a date palm made of gold is also noted to make the same point.

needle with a gate and to suggest the illustration is merely of something difficult, the subsequent discussion shows that something impossible is meant.[460] For the disciples ask who then can be saved (v 26), implying that if the salvation of the rich is not possible, they wonder who is left. Inheriting eternal life (Mark 10:17, 21, 23) is now a discussion about being saved, showing the connection of the two ideas. Three terms pointing to wealth have been used in the passage: *katēmata* in verse 22 (BDAG, 572); *chrēmata* in verse 23 (BDAG, 1089); and *plousios* in verse 25 (BDAG, 831). People with possessions and resources are in view and the descriptions cover all the angles. If the Gospels and prophets are to guide us, what wealth can do is to numb people of need for God, creating a sense of self-dependence and a view that others are here to serve them or to be exploited (Luke 12:13–21; 16:19–31). In the OT, it was the rich oppressing the poor that was condemned as a potential misuse of wealth (Amos 2:6; 5:11–12; Isa 1:15–17).

Jesus responds with what is impossible for man is possible with God, for all things are possible with God (v 27; Gen 18:14; Job 10:13, LXX; 42:2; Zech 8:6, LXX). If God reaches the heart, then a rich person can respond properly and enter the kingdom. In the context, it is debated if one is to repent[461] or to be generous.[462] However, one does not get to the second without the first, so it is the starting point that God enables so that the rest is possible. Entry into the kingdom and salvation are the topics focused on here.

Interestingly, in Mark what God makes possible touches on three areas: dealing with demons (Mark 9:23), with possessions (Mark 10:27), and with denying God's will (Mark 14:36). These in turn parallel the three threats in the parable of the soils (Mark 4:14–19).[463]

The exchange leads Peter to seek assurance (v 28). Is he smug or simply querying? Opinions differ, but there is no rebuke in Jesus' response, so a smug reply is unlikely. Peter observes that the disciples have left everything to follow Jesus. Have they not done what the rich man just failed to do? The verb for leaving is aorist, looking at an act of renunciation, whereas the verb for following is in the perfect tense, looking to the ongoing effects of the choice of following. As Mark has made clear, they still have a home (Mark 1:29) and a boat (Mark 3:9), but Peter is contending they have a full

---

[460] Cranfield, *Mark*, 332; France, *Mark*, 405, notes that there is no evidence of a small gate within a double city gate in Jerusalem bearing this name; Marcus, *Mark 8–16*, 731.

[461] Hooker, *Mark*, 243.

[462] Edwards, *Mark*, 315.

[463] Marcus, *Mark 8–16*, 732.

commitment to Jesus and have followed him (Mark 1:17–18).[464] So, have they done that which God makes possible?

Jesus replies positively (**v 29**). He promised a new family and home awaited those who followed him for the sake of Jesus and the Gospel. Peter and Andrew had left all (Mark 1:17–18). Jesus had struggled to gain recognition from within his own family (Mark 3:31–35). What had been lost would be replaced. In fact, they are multiplied a hundredfold. What is lost is more than replaced by what is gained (**v 30**). The order is chiastic: home goes with fields, brothers, sisters, mother, father goes male, female, female, male. Children are added to complete the reference to family. The social isolation and self-sacrifice of leaving all means fields are lost as well. Riches are still in view.

Everything and more that may have been lost, because family might forsake those who come to him, would be regained in the new community. The point here is not declaring a right to neglect family; it is that if making a choice to follow Jesus costs you family because they will not accept your choice, then you will gain new family. This new family will all come with persecutions (1 Pet 4:14–16). Mark is always quick to remind his readers of the suffering of rejection that comes with walking with Jesus. The term for persecution (*diōgmos*) always refers to religious persecution in the NT (Acts 8:1; 13:50; 2 Cor 12:10; 2 Thess 1:4; BDAG 253).

Eternal life also would be gained. This returns us to the original question in Mark 10:17 and forms an *inclusion* for the passage. To follow Jesus is to enter into eternal life. The reference to this age and the age to come reflects the two-stage eschatological perspective of Jewish hope (*1 Enoch* 48:7 with 71:15; *4 Ezra* 7:50), which the NT also alludes to on occasion (Rom 3:26; 8:18; 12:2; 1 Cor 2:6, 8; Gal 1:4).[465]

Jesus closes with a remark about eschatological reversal (**v 31**; Matt 20:16; Luke 13:30; Mark 9:35). Many who are first in the world today will be last, whereas the last will become first. Those who are rich may appear to have life by the tail, but the reality is they are missing the relationship that matters most.

10:32–34 Jesus Predicts His Death and Resurrection for a Third Time

10:32 They were on their way going up to Jerusalem. Jesus was going ahead of them, and they were amazed, but those who followed were

---

[464] Stein, *Mark*, 473.
[465] Marcus, *Mark 8–16*, 733.

afraid. And taking the twelve aside again he began to tell them what was going to happen to him.

10:33 "Look, we are going up to Jerusalem, and the Son of Man will be given over to the chief priests and scribes. They will condemn him to death and give him over to the Gentiles.

10:34 They will mock him and spit on him and flog him, and kill him. And after three days, he will rise again."

As Jesus continues to head to Jerusalem, he issues one more prediction of what will take place there to those who follow him. It is unclear whether this traveling group is the Twelve only or a larger group of followers. It is likely that a larger group of those following Jesus would be afraid, whereas the Twelve would be the ones amazed as the journey of fate draws to completion.[466] Jesus takes the Twelve aside to make his prediction. That note suggests an originally larger group. This is the third such predication.[467] Mark 8:31; 9:31 introduce the other predictions. The parallels are Matt 20:17–19 and Luke 18:31–34.

On the journey there is a note of fear (**v 32**). There is a sense of what Jesus has said about what will take place, plus the mention of persecutions for following him. This will not be a normal trip to Jerusalem. Jesus' restatement reinforces the ominous nature of what is ahead. This will not be the typical pilgrim trip to Jerusalem to celebrate a feast.

There is more detail than what is said here. It prepares one for the description of the Passion Week in Mark 14–16. For the first time (**v 33**), Jerusalem is named explicitly in a prediction. The full exchange first to the high priests and scribes and then to Gentiles is predicted. Jesus will be handed over twice. There also will be mocking, spitting, and flogging (**v 34**; Isa 50:4–6; Ps 22:6–8). The leadership will condemn him to death, but Rome will do the deed, including the acts of insult just described. The resurrection three days in is also noted. An irony is that this will take place for the Son of Man. The one who is exalted by God is rejected by men. Jesus is continuing to prepare his disciples for the suffering ahead. They do not understand this fully yet, but it is a part not only of Jesus' calling but of theirs as well.

---

[466] Stein, *Mark*, 479.
[467] Edwards, *Mark*, 320, defends the authenticity of these predictions, noting their differences from one another and the sequencing versus what comes later.

10:35–45 A Dispute about Greatness Leads Jesus to Teach about Servanthood

10:35 And James and John, the sons of Zebedee, came to him and said, "Teacher we want you to do for us whatever we ask."

10:36 He said to them, "What do you want me to do for you?"

10:37 They said to him, "Give us that one may sit on your right and one on your left in your glory."

10:38 But Jesus said to them, "You do not know what you are asking. Are you able to drink the cup I drink or be baptized with the baptism I am to be baptized with?"

10:39 They said to him, "We are able." Then Jesus said to them, "You will drink the cup I drink, and you will be baptized with the baptism I will be baptized with,

10:40 but to sit at my right or my left is not mine to give. It is for those for whom it has been prepared."

10:41 And when the ten heard this, they were angry with James and John.

10:42 And calling them, Jesus said to them, "You know that those recognized as rulers over the Gentiles lord it over them, and those in high positions use their authority over them.

10:43 But it is not so with you. But whoever wishes to be great among you is your servant

10:44 and whoever wants to be first is a slave of all.

10:45 For also the Son of Man did not come to be served but to serve and give his soul as a ransom for many."

This scene is in two parts: a dialogue with James and John in Mark 10:35–40 that leads to a series of pronouncements and a subsequent teaching that Jesus follows up with in Mark 10:41–45, once again to make a point of emphasis to the disciples on something they need to learn. The parallel is Matt 20:20–28. A partial, conceptual parallel on the latter part of the passage appears in Luke 22:24–27. Another structural point is important. For a second time, the prediction of Jesus' suffering has been followed by a corrective instruction to disciples whose minds are elsewhere (Mark 9:30–35).

Despite all the talk of rejection, persecution, and suffering, some of the disciples are still fixed on power (**vv 35–36**). So James and John make a request to share in powerful roles in the kingdom to come by asking to sit at his right and left when Jesus comes into glory. Jesus has described this glory in terms of the Son of Man (Mark 8:38; 13:26). James and John have been key characters in Mark (Mark 1:19, 29; 3:17, 5:37; 9:2; later, 13:3; 14:33). This is the only time they are mentioned alone.[468] Their special inside group role may have led them to think their request was possible and reasonable. Whether these are seats of honor at a messianic banquet or requests to have a major role in ruling (v 37), the request seeks to trump the other disciples and gain rank over them. It defines Jesus in terms of what he might give as a political figure, but this is to misappropriate the role Jesus has given them. It ignores what Jesus has already taught in Mark 9:34. The likelihood, given the context of kingdom, is that rule is in view, not merely seats at a celebration. Seating versus reclining in the request suggests the same conclusion.[469] The point is that being a part of Jesus' inner group is not primarily about exercising power and privilege, but about serving those they are to shepherd.

In Matt 19:28, before he relates this event in Matt 20, Jesus has given them the promise of sitting on twelve thrones and judging the twelve tribes of Israel. In Matthew's version of this scene, the request for the primary seats of the kingdom comes from their mother. The difference seemingly deflects some blame from the disciples, but it is unlikely that she acted alone, given Jesus' response to teach the disciples as a result. Mark holds the two sons responsible.[470] They form the request almost as a demand – give us whatever we ask. There is irony in this request, as the only other place such a *carte blanche* is made is by Herod to Herodias' daughter, a request the narrative portrayed as foolish and reckless.[471] They may be seeking a reward for having left everything to follow Jesus.

Jesus turns attention to what is ahead in Jerusalem (v 38). Can the disciples drink the cup that Jesus faces (Mark 14:36) and experience the baptism that lies ahead (Luke 12:50)? The reference returns to the suffering and service Jesus will perform when he is left to face death for being faithful. In one sense, they cannot do what Jesus is about to do, but in another sense they can. The cup often refers to experiencing judgment (Ps 23:5; 75:8; 116:13; Isa 51:17–22; Jer 25:15–28; 49:12 – where those innocent drink the cup; 51:7; Lam 4:21 – where God's people also suffer; Ezek 23:31–34).[472] The waters alluded to in the image

---

[468] Edwards, *Mark*, 321, who sees Peter as the source and notes the error, is even more elitist than the remark of John in Mark 9:38.

[469] France, *Mark*, 415.

[470] Stein, *Mark*, 484, speaks of the mother as a possible intermediary in Matthew.

[471] Collins, *Mark*, 495; France, *Mark*, 415.

[472] Taylor, *St. Mark*, 440–41. Marcus, *Mark 8–16*, 747, notes a series of texts that use the expression for martyrdom in later Judaism (*T. Ab.* 1:3; *Tg. Neof.* Gen 40:23 and Deut 32:1; *Martyrdom of Polycarp* 14:2; *Martyrdom of Isaiah* 5:13).

of baptism can refer to being overwhelmed with troubles (Ps 42:7; Isa 43:2). To say that the cup is only about martyrdom is too specific. Losing one's life (Mark 8:35) in the sense of discipleship is in view.[473] Martyrdom may be included, but the suffering pointed to in the imagery is broad. Leadership is not primarily about power for Jesus, but rather service in the context of pressure and calamity. By exercising this type of leadership, they walk the same path as Jesus and witness to his unique ransom in suffering for others (Mark 10:45) and its restorative goals (Col 1:24).[474]

The disciples reply that they are able to do this (v 39), possibly not entirely understanding all that Jesus is asking or saying. Yet Jesus says they will drink that cup and experience that baptism. James was martyred by Herod (Acts 12:2), and John was imprisoned at Patmos for his faith. However, he cannot grant them their request of being seated on the right and left, for that is not his to give (v 40). Certain things in the program are in the Father's hands alone. That belongs to those for whom God has prepared it, using a divine passive to make the point. The saying points to authenticity because it puts certain things in the hands of the Father alone.[475] The seeming limitation on Jesus is not likely to have been made up by the early church after they preached a glorified Jesus. Here, Jesus does not deny that there is a rule to come, but the roles in it are the business of the Father, not of the Son of Man.

Needless to say, when word got out about this exchange, the ten were angry with James and John (v 41). Mark 10:14; 14:4 are the other texts in which Mark uses this term for anger (*ananakteō* – BDAG, 5). The reaction points to one of the effects of an attempt to competitively best another in the community.

So, in classic Markan style, Jesus now teaches them privately to make the correction (v 42). He contrasts the power and authority of rulers in the world at large, often applied in the patron-client context, with the way this newly formed community is to work. Those recognized as rulers react this way as a cultural given.[476] Rank counts in the world of the patron. Honor

---

[473] Stein, *Mark*, 485.

[474] Collins, *Mark*, 497.

[475] On a defense of the core authenticity of the scene, Peter Stuhlmacher, *Versöhnung, Gesetz und Gerechtigkeit: Aufsätze zur biblischen Theologie* (Göttingen: Vandenhoeck & Ruprecht, 1981), 27–42; Peter Stuhlmacher, *Reconciliation, Law and Righteousness* (Philadelphia: Fortress, 1986), 16–29; Stein, *Mark*, 486. Other texts that limit Jesus are Mark 13:32 and Acts 1:7.

[476] The reference to being recognized as rulers is sometimes seen as negative, but it is not negative, as the expression was common. These leaders were seen and experienced as rulers; Edwards, *Mark*, 325.

goes to him. The ruler is served and demands it. They exercise their authority. They "lord it over" others. This term in the LXX can be neutral (Gen 1:28; Ps 72:8 [=71:8 LXX]), reflecting violent acts (Num 21:24; 32:22) or acts that take advantage (Ps 19:13 [=18:14 LXX]; similar with a slightly different term is James 2:6).[477] Rank rests in hierarchy and seeks to take advantage of it. Luke 22:25 in a distinct context has a less radical image by pointing to benefactors and lacking a reference to lording over others.

Jesus teaches something different than the society around him. In the new community first place goes to the servant and slave of all (**vv 43–44**). It is service that counts for rank. The term *diakonos* is an everyday term for a servant, usually describing attendants of one sort or another like those who serve a king or the master of a house (BDAG, 230: Matt 22:13; John 2:5). This one serves a social superior. This could be a freedman or a slave. The term for a slave (*doulos*) adds to the image, reflecting a position most in the ancient world would have sought to avoid, as it was the lowest social status possible. In fact to call a king a slave was to insult his pandering to the people (Plato, *Republic* 569b; Cicero, *On the Paradoxes of the Stoics* 41; Philo, *On Joseph* 35).[478] Although there are Greco-Roman texts that point to the king as a servant, they do not stoop down to slave level.[479] It refers to one who serves out of social obligation (BDAG, 260). Jesus has turned everything upside down. He is reinforcing earlier teaching (Mark 8:35; 9:35; 10:31). One who is great serves the community he is called to lead.

The example for such total sacrificial service is Jesus himself. Jesus again uses the term Son of Man to refer to himself in a pronouncement (**v 45**). He came not to be served but to serve and to give his life as a ransom for many.[480] The background to the image appears to be Isa 53:10, 12 with its

---

477 Marcus, *Mark 8–16*, 748.
478 Marcus, *Mark 8–16*, 748–49. As he says, "Servitude and sovereignty, then, are logical opposites, whereas our passage claims that the former is the pathway to the latter."
479 Collins, *Mark*, 499, cites the example of Antigonus Gonatus who taught his son that a kingdom is "held to be a noble servitude," citing Moshe Weinfeld, "The King as the Servant of the People: The Source of the Idea," *JJS* 33 (1982): 189.
480 Evans, *Mark 8:27–16:20*, 119–25, has a full discussion of issues tied to the unity of this verse with the unit as a whole, the positive role of Isa 53, and authenticity. He argues for the authenticity of the verse. Hooker, *Mark*, 248–49, questions if Isa 53 is in view, contending that ransom links to an offering that brings deliverance (Exod 13:13–16),

picture of the suffering of the servant for many. The image of ransom for many looks to some form of payment substitution (Exod 21:30 LXX; Sir 29:15; 1 Macc 2:50; Isa 43:3–4; 1 Tim 2:6; in Judaism, 2 Macc 7:37–38; 4 Macc 1:11; 6:28–29; 17:21–22; 11QtgJob 38:2–3; *Life of Adam and Eve* 3:1).[481] It could refer to purchasing a slave or war prisoner or some other object (normally plural, Exod 21:30; 30:10–12; Num 35:31; Lev 25:47–55; Isa 45:13, but Mark has a singular). Mark 14:24 speaks of the blood of the covenant poured out for "many" making a similar point. Jesus' service will be his death that opens up the way of God to many. It also is an example to those who seek to reflect him in their own spiritual walk.

10:46–52 Jesus Heals the Blind Bartimaeus

10:46 **And they came to Jericho. As Jesus and his disciples and a large crowd were leaving Jericho, Bartimaeus, the son of Timaeus, a blind beggar, was sitting by the road.**

10:47 **And when he heard that it was Jesus of Nazareth, he began to shout and say, "Son of David, Jesus, have mercy on me."**

10:48 **Many scolded him that he should be silent, but he was shouting even more, "Son of David, have mercy on me."**

10:49 **Jesus stopped and said, "Call him." So they called the blind man and said to him, "Have courage. Get up. He is calling you."**

10:50 **He threw off his cloak, jumped up and came to Jesus.**

10:51 **Then Jesus said to him, "What do you want me to do for you?" The blind man said to him, "My teacher, let me see again."**

10:52 **And Jesus said to him, "Go, your faith has delivered you." Immediately he regained his sight and was following him on the road.**

A messianic miracle account is the final event before Jesus reaches Jerusalem. It is the final healing miracle in Mark. The parallels are Matt 20:29–34 and Luke 18:35–43. The event frames everything about to take place in Jerusalem as set in messianic hope (Isa 35:5 – the blind will be

---

not a sin offering as in Isa 53:11. The problem is that Jesus pictures his death as both. At the Last Supper, Mark 14:24 looks to the inauguration of a new covenant, which assumes an offering to restore from sin. Evans notes the ransom is for "many" (Isa 53:12), which also speaks of making intercession for sinners. She sees a martyr's death for many and appeals to Dan 7 and 4 Macc 6:29 and 17:21, but Dan 7 is not about the Son of Man's death. For a defense of Isa 53 being in the background, France, *Mark*, 420–21.

[481] Evans, *Mark 8:27–16:20*, 122.

healed in this time). Fulfilment is present. It also contrasts with the previous failure of the disciples. Here is someone who simply seeks Jesus' mercy.

Jesus draws near to Jerusalem as he arrives at Jericho, only about 18 miles northeast of Jerusalem (**v 46**). Mark says that as Jesus left the town, a blind man, Bartimaeus, son of Timaeus, was seated by the road. Luke 18:35 puts the healing upon entering Jericho, but he has the unique story of Zacchaeus following, so it may be that he has rearranged the order to place Zacchaeus as a climactic Jericho event.[482] The name of the blind man and his relationship to Timaeus are details unique to Mark and rare for him. It may be a mixed Greek and Aramaic name. Mark spells out the relationship that the name in Aramaic already communicates for those who do not know the language by calling him the son of Timaeus. It is mentioned in a way that looks to point to a known figure to Mark's audience, a vivid detail.

Upon hearing that Jesus of Nazareth was present and with amazing insight as to who Jesus is (**v 47**), the blind man cries out for Jesus as Son of David to be merciful to him. Until this point, only Peter had made such a messianic confession of Jesus in Mark (Mark 8:27–30). That Messiah might perform miracles appears in *4 Ezra* 7:26–29 and 13:50. Son of David as a messianic title appears in *Ps Sol* 17:21. The crowd scolded him (**v 48**), trying to silence him. They thought him unworthy of Jesus' attention and time. Their approach is like the restrictive approach of the disciples earlier (Mark 10:13) in considering some unworthy of attention. Jesus is not so restrictive with people in both cases.

The blind man did not back off but was raising his voice even more and cried out a second time to the Son of David for mercy (**v 48**). The imperfect emphasizes the repetition involved in the call for help. The man cries out to Jesus to help restore him. As he nears Jerusalem, Jesus now begins to ignore the public messianic hesitation he had previously encouraged.

Jesus calls for the blind man (**v 49**). The crowd now encourages him and tells him to get up as Jesus is calling. They tell him to take heart (Matt 9:2; John 16:33; 1 Kings 17:13). Clearly excited (**v 50**), the man throws off his cloak, jumps up, and comes to Jesus. The cloak may have been on the

---

[482]   Stein, *Mark*, 493.

ground to take offerings of alms from other compassionate people.[483] In that case, only an undergarment would have remained on him. The cloak now gets tossed aside. He may not need it anymore. He has left what he has.

Jesus asks what he wants in exactly the terms he had asked James and John in Mark 10:36, but one request was worthy, and the other was not (v 51). The contrast is intentional. The man replies, addressing him respectfully as "my teacher" (John 20:16), that he wishes Jesus to permit him to see again. Jesus tells the man to go – that his faith has healed him (v 52). The address may have the force of "my master" in this personalized form, since there is no request for teaching present and this is the original force of the word (BDAG, 902).[484] The man's faith had been present, respectful yet persistent in the face of the crowd's attempt to prevent him from addressing Jesus. He believed Jesus was able to change his future. He had gone from begging with no status to following Jesus in a new life.

His sight returned by merely a word of report that the man's faith had delivered him (Mark 5:34; Luke 7:50; 17:19). Mark 7:24–30 also has a healing by word alone. Jesus tells the man to go as his faith has saved him. The dismissal with the command to go is typical of dismissal in Mark (Mark 1:44; 2:11; 5:19; 7:29). So the man follows Jesus on the road. The terms "follow" and "on the way" repeat Markan themes for discipleship (Mark 1:18; 2:14–15; 6:1; 8:27, 34; 9:33–34, 38; 10: 21, 28, 32). It evokes that direction as the man's response.

No other reaction by the crowd is given. The focus is solely on the act. Jesus has healed a blind man as Son of David as he travels to enter Jerusalem. The blind man, able to "see" so much better than many, now is also able to see. He sees truly and clearly enough to follow Jesus on the way. A sign of the arrival of the eschaton is present as the curtain goes up on his entry into the city (Isa 35:4–5; 61:1–4; Matt 11:5; Luke 7:22). As Jesus faces death, his ministry continues to serve and draw people.

---

[483] Hooker, *Mark*, 253; Taylor, *St. Mark*, 449. The choice between a descriptive or symbolic act is a false one in one sense. The real act can also be symbolic. The literary echoes in this passage to other parts of Mark point to an intentional symbol here. Even the blind man has left something behind in response to Jesus.

[484] S. J. D. Cohen, "Epigraphical Rabbis," *JQR* 72 (1981–82):1–17.

11:1–16:8 IN JERUSALEM, JESUS MEETS CONTROVERSY AND
REJECTION, LEADING TO HIS DEATH AND RESURRECTION, AS HE
ALSO TEACHES OF SUFFERING, JUDGMENT, AND VINDICATION

11:1–12:24 Jesus' Coming to Jerusalem as a Messianic Claimant Leads
to Controversy

*11:1–11 Jesus Enters Jerusalem to Jubilation as the One Who Comes in the
Lord's Name and Is Tied to the Kingdom*

11:1 And when they drew near to Jerusalem, near Bethphage and Bethany,
at the Mount of Olives, Jesus sent two of his disciples.

11:2 And said to them, "Go to the village ahead of you. And immediately
upon entering it, you will find a colt tied there that has never been
ridden. Untie it and bring it here.

11:3 If someone says to you, 'Why are you doing this?' say, 'The Lord
needs it and immediately he will send it back here.'"

11:4 So they went out and found a colt tied at a door, outside in the street
and untied it.

11:5 Some people standing there were saying to them "What are you
doing, untying the colt?"

11:6 The disciples replied to them even as Jesus said, and they let them go.

11:7 And they brought the colt to Jesus, threw their cloaks on it, and he sat
on it.

11:8 And many spread their cloaks on the road and others spread
branches they had cut from the fields.

11:9 Both those who went ahead and those who followed were shouting,
"Hosanna! Blessed is the one who comes in the name of the Lord!

11:10 Blessed is the coming kingdom of our father David! Hosanna in the
Highest!"

11:11 Then Jesus entered Jerusalem and into the temple. After looking
around at everything, he went out to Bethany with the twelve, as the
hour was already late.

We now enter the last act of the Gospel, the Passion Week. The week is
in three parts in Mark 11–16: Actions and Teaching before the Passion
(Mark 11–13), The Events Leading to Passion (Mark 14–15), and The
Discovery of the Empty Tomb and Resurrection (Mark 16). In Mark, this
is Jesus' only trip to Jerusalem. Mark presents the events that lead into
Jesus' death and resurrection. Most of Mark 11–12 contains controversy
accounts until Jesus is seized. Jesus consciously turned up the heat of his
claims. These actions led to his rejection by those in authority. The hope of

return and vindication comes with teaching in Mark 13 about keeping watch and staying faithful.

The first scene is a simple entrance narrative.[485] The parallels are Matt 21:1–11, Luke 19:28–40, and John 12:12–16. Mark's account is positive, lacking notes of questioning or objection in the parallels. Jesus' entry is purposely provocative. It is loaded with messianic imagery. This and the following temple cleansing give an opportunity and challenge to the religious leadership to recognize what God is doing. However, the entry is "atriumphal" in that Jesus does not receive the kind of citywide welcome a dignitary like Pilate would have received. In that sense, it is an "antientry." Jesus comes with no entourage like an army to show his power. He comes with no welcoming committee from the city he enters. Disciples speak up for him, not the city.[486] Some who join in may well reflect celebration tied to participating in a feast. Unlike Matthew and Luke, Mark does not note any rejection of the entry. Subsequent events will show that dimension of reaction to Jesus' arrival. Still, the act is messianic, juxtaposed to the cry of Bartimaeus in the previous event, as well as associated with the Mount of Olives, the riding of an unused animal, and the cry of the crowd in Mark 11:10.

Jesus now approaches Jerusalem as he enters Bethphage and Bethany at the Mount of Olives (v 1), given that Jerusalem is on the other side of the Mount, which rose more than 2,600 feet above sea level and a few hundred feet over Jerusalem, overlooking the eastern side of the Temple. The order goes from Jerusalem as the goal back out to where they stayed. Bethany is simply on the other side of the Mount of Olives from Jerusalem, only 2 miles away, whereas Bethphage is a half-mile away, with its outer wall touching the edge of Jerusalem according to later sources (*b. Men.* 78b). The Mount had messianic associations tied to it in Zech 14:1–9.

---

[485] Ancient entries to honor a dignitary are common. We have evidence of twelve such scenes in ancient literature; Evans, *Mark 8:27–16:20*, 139 (Alexander–Josephus, *Ant.* 11.8.325–39; Apollonius – 2 Macc 4:21–22; Judas Maccabees – 1 Macc 4:19–25; Josephus, *Ant.* 12.312; 1 Macc 5:45–54; Josephus, *Ant.* 12.348–49; Jonathan Maccabees – 1 Macc 10:86; Simon Maccabees – 1 Macc 13:43–48; 1 Macc 13:49–51; Antogonus – Josephus, *War* 1.73–74; *Ant* 13.304–6; Marcus Agrippa – 16.12–15; Archelaus – 17.194–239). A full discussion of the scene, including issues tied to authenticity, comes from Brent Kinman, "Jesus' Royal Entry into Jerusalem," in Bock and Webb, *Key Events*, 383–427. On entries, D. R. Catchpole, "The 'Triumphal' Entry," in *Jesus and the Politics of His Day*, ed. E. Bammel and C. F. D. Moule (Cambridge: Cambridge University Press, 1984), 319–35; also Kinman, "Parousia, Jesus' 'A-Triumphal' Entry, and the Fate of Jerusalem (Luke 19:28–44)," *JBL* 118 (1999): 279–94.

[486] France, *Mark*, 429–30.

Jesus sends two of his disciples to a neighboring village to get a colt to ride (**v 2**). The instructions are very specific. The account is told without any sense of whether there had been an arrangement or understanding ahead of time. There simply is the sense that Jesus is completely aware and in control of what is taking place. He tells them they will find a previously unridden colt of a donkey tied up as they enter the city (*m.* Sanh 2:5 – a horse for a king is not for anyone else to ride; BDAG, 900, *pōlos* – of any colt, but here of a donkey as is common in the region; Gen 32:15; 49:11; Judg 10:4; 12:14; 1 Kings 1:33, 38; Zech 9:9). They are to untie it and bring it back. If anyone asks what the two disciples are doing, they are to simply explain that the Lord has need and will return it (**v 3**). The promise to return it makes a reference to the owner as the one addressed here unlikely.[487] Jesus is the one calling for the animal's use.

Things happened exactly as Jesus described (**v 4**). The colt is there as they enter the city. When asked, they respond as Jesus communicated. Those who ask let them take the colt, probably on the principle of *angaria*, "pressed transportation," where a dignitary is loaned the use of something (**vv 5–6**).[488] Jesus had enough status for this to be done. Thus he is called "the Lord" here, a sign of social respect. The reference to Lord is neither to the owner of the colt or to God. It is simply a note that the need of someone with social rank exists for a time and he will return the colt when done (possible similar uses of *kurios*: Mark 7:28; 12:9; 13:35).

When the disciples return with the animal, they prepare it for Jesus and his entrance into Jerusalem, placing their cloaks over it (**v 7**). These cloaks are like the outer garment Bartimaeus had left behind in the last scene. Jesus sits on the donkey and enters the city, with many spreading their cloaks before him and others spreading branches (**v 8**), much as people did at the Feast of Tabernacles (2 Macc 10:7; *m Sukkah* 3–4).[489] Jesus is entering the city as a king, something Zech 9:9 had anticipated (rule and a colt are also linked in Gen 49:10–11). This is a text Mark does not cite, unlike the parallels in Matt 21:5 and John 12:15.

Disciples were paving a way of honor for Jesus, like the "red carpet" greeting of a king (1 Kings 1:38–40 – Solomon at his coronation; 2 Kings

---

[487] Stein, *Mark*, 504, notes that the possibility the owner was originally in view here is unlikely.

[488] J. D. M. Derrett, "Law in the New Testament: The Palm Sunday Colt," *NovT* 13 (1971): 241–58.

[489] France, *Mark*, 433. An objection to the event's historicity that the feast time does not match is not persuasive. The actions here are spontaneous responses with cultural conventions at work.

9:13 – when Jehu was anointed king; 1 Macc 13:51 – of Simon Maccabees).[490] That honor was bestowed by acknowledging him publicly with cries of "Hosanna!" They confessed him as coming in the name of the Lord in line with Ps 122:26, a psalm portraying an affirmation of welcome to the temple (**v 9**). It is part of the "liturgy of entry and the gate."[491] They also acknowledged praise for the coming kingdom of our father David (**v 10**; 2 Sam 7:6–16; Ps 132).[492] So here we see kingdom and the person from David placed together in a messianic proclamation (Mark 10:47–48).[493] God has sent the one who brings the promised kingdom, so the highest praise is to be offered. Hosanna also adds the note of expected deliverance (Ps 118:25), for it reflects a request to "save now" (Ps 117:26 LXX) or "help, I pray" (BDAG, 1106). It was used as a call to praise, as one calls on God to be responsive. Jesus is associated with God activity to save.

The act would have blended in with the general celebratory atmosphere of a feast, so there was no need for Roman soldiers to have reacted. Jesus' act was modest and symbolic. It also would have been just a part of the entering the tumult that pilgrims would have been generating, with its significance easily missed.[494]

Mark ends the entry here (**v 11**). Unlike Matt 21:15–16, Luke 19:39–40, and John 12:19, there is no discussion or hint of the reaction and criticism of these notes of praise. Mark's presentation is strictly focused on Jesus, sharing only the positive. The messiah Jesus enters the city, surrounded

---

[490] Such acts took place on occasion (Plutarch, *Cato Minor* 7); Evans, *Mark 8:27–16:20*, 143–44.

[491] Collins, *Mark*, 520, citing Kraus on the Psalm.

[492] On messianic hope, Bateman, Bock, and Johnston, *Jesus the Messiah*.

[493] Contra Lane, *Mark*, 396–97, who sees no explicit messianic emphasis because there is no affirmation of Jesus' majesty, and Hooker, *Mark*, 260. We should distinguish between Jesus' intent in permitting the praise and having set up the act and what people may have been aware of in joining in the praise. John 12:16 recognizes the disciples did not understand completely the significance of the event and its tie to Scripture at the time. Curious also is the remark of Edwards, *Mark*, 337, that the reference to the kingdom of our father David does not evoke overt messianism, but is eschatological. He is correct to see the portrayal as subdued, but it is quite present in the combination of symbols applied, so, correctly, Collins, *Mark*, 520. To evoke David in an eschatological context is to point to messianic and salvation hope. As is often the case in the Gospels, what Jesus does points to who he is. Especially misdirected is to distinguish the kingdom of God from the coming kingdom of David. The two are part of the same promised and hoped for rule package.

[494] Stein, *Mark*, 507; Hooker, *Mark*, 261; Evans, *Mark*, 140; Edwards, *Mark*, 338, who says what does not happen with this act is just as significant, given that Jesus is not welcomed by the religious leaders who see what is taking place.

by the praise of those who enter with him. For Mark, Jerusalem has her chance to accept her king and her promise.

In this way, Jesus enters the city and comes to the temple. Nothing happens.[495] He looks around and receives no welcome. Given what happens in the next event, Jesus clearly saw something he did not like. So this inspection comes out of the regal context just invoked by his entry.

He returned for the night to Bethany as it was late. Jerusalem swelled to up to triple its size for feasts, so pilgrims often stayed just outside of town. So, the opportunity for Jerusalem to accept the offer of her king had come and gone. Instead, Jesus was headed in another direction, as he is going more public with his claims, leading to the reaction those acts will generate.

11:12–25 Jesus Juxtaposes the Cursing of the Fig Tree with the Cleansing of the Temple as He Makes Israel Accountable

> 11:12 **And the next day, as they were coming out of Bethany, he was hungry.**
>
> 11:13 **And seeing a fig tree from afar with leaves, he came to see if he might find anything on it, and coming to it, he found nothing except leaves, for it was not the season for figs.**
>
> 11:14 **And responding, he said to it, "May no one ever eat fruit from you again." And his disciples heard it.**
>
> 11:15 **Then they came to Jerusalem. Jesus entered the temple area and began to drive out the moneychangers and those who were buying in the temple. He turned over the tables of the moneychangers and the chairs of those selling doves.**
>
> 11:16 **And he would not permit anyone to carry anything through the temple courts.**
>
> 11:17 **Then he was teaching and saying to them, "Is it not written, *'My house will be called a house of prayer for all the nations'*? But you have turned it into a *hideout for bandits*."**
>
> 11:18 **The chief priests and scribes heard it and were considering how they might destroy him, for they feared him, because the entire crowd was amazed by his teaching.**
>
> 11:19 **When evening came, Jesus and his disciples went outside the city.**
>
> 11:20 **In the morning as they passed by, they saw the fig tree withered from the roots.**
>
> 11:21 **And Peter, remembering, said to him, "Rabbi, look the fig tree you cursed has withered."**

---

495 Evans, *Mark 8:27–16:20*, 147, says simply that "Jesus was ignored."

¹¹:²² Jesus, responding, said to them, "Have faith in God.

¹¹:²³ Truly I say to you, if someone says to this mountain, 'Be lifted up and thrown into the sea,' and does not doubt in his heart but believes that what he says will take place, it will be done for him.

¹¹:²⁴ Because of this, I say to you, whatever you pray and ask for, believe that you have received it, and it will be yours.

¹¹:²⁵ And whenever you stand praying, if you have anything against anyone, forgive him, so that your Father in heaven will forgive you your sins."

This scene has to qualify as one of the most unusual in all of the Jesus tradition. It is a nature miracle account that is one of the few places in the NT where the miracle performed has a negative effect.[496] It is a symbolic judgment miracle, as a fig tree is cursed. The symbolism has OT roots. Often associated with the vine and having a rich and varied symbolic role there, this tree and its fruit frequently represent the people of God (Isa 28:4; Jer 8:13; 24:1–10; 29:17; Hos 9:10, 16–17; Mic 7:1).[497] It is included in a sandwich construction that also is common in Mark. So we get the curse, then the cleansing of the temple, and only after that event do we see the effects of the curse. The unit is very intentionally constructed. The fig tree and temple scene are of one cloth. The temple scene is an act of judgment that results in a pronouncement. The parallels are Matthew 21:12–22, Luke 19:45–48, and John 2:13–17 (also *Thomas* 106).[498] The following unit on faith is more closely tied to the curse in Matthew 21:20 as the disciples ask how the fig tree was able to wither at once. The pall of judgment for Israel and her need to return to God is a shadow cast on the events leading to Jesus' death. Some expected such cleansing acts of Messiah, but it was of a purge of the unrighteous and of Gentiles (*Ps Sol* 17:22–30). Jesus' cleansing is setting up spiritual renewal that extends beyond Israel.

---

[496] Similar kinds of events are the temporary judgment on Zechariah in Luke 1, Paul's temporary blindness in Acts 9, and Paul's judgment on Bar Jesus in Acts 13:8–12. For Jesus' acts, it is unique in its negative impact. Evans, *Mark 8:27–16:20*, 151, notes that Luke 9:51–56 is a contrastive text where a judgment is prevented. Of course, that text was having the disciples contend for judging people, not a symbolic act.

[497] France, *Mark*, 439–40.

[498] John's placement of the incident early in his Gospel has led to discussion of whether two such events existed, who moved it, or both. It is unlikely that Jesus could have gotten away with this kind of disruptive act twice. It also seems likely that the Synoptic placement is correct and that John moved the event forward because it typifies what Jesus knew was in man, as an introduction to the rejection his Gospel also will describe. Hooker, *Mark*, 262–63, argues the tradition knew of the event but not its chronological locale, so each chose its placement.

It is the day after Jesus' entry into Jerusalem (**v 12**). The specificity of the timing is also unlike the way Mark normally introduces events. Jesus was hungry, and seeing a fig tree from a distance, he went over to it to look for fruit. But there was nothing. Mark notes it was not yet the season for figs (**v 13**).[499] It was early to mid-April, and during this time of year figs became ripe in May or June. The timing between God's program and God's people was off. This led Jesus to curse the tree and say that no one would ever eat fruit from it again (**v 14**). Mark notes that the disciples heard him make the remark. As the next event shows, there is symbolism here. Israel is not bearing fruit at the time God's program calls for. It looks to be coming later. The idea is expressed distinctly in Luke 13:6–9 with its parable of the fruitless vine.

The scene abruptly shifts to the temple, and Jesus acts immediately upon his arrival there (**v 15**). He drove out those who were buying and selling in the temple courts. He turned over the tables of the moneychangers and those selling doves for sacrifices. No one was allowed to carry materials through the area of the temple courts, likely located at the southern portico. The act is contained in a relatively small space where a bottleneck could form for worshippers and was itself symbolic of larger concerns about the activity of the temple, as we shall see.[500] It is quite possible Caiaphas had just moved this activity into the temple courts from a slightly further locale at the Mount of Olives.[501] These services allowed for the use of the Tyrian shekel as the sanctioned coin for the half-shekel temple tax (Exod 30:11–16) and for unblemished doves for sacrifices (Lev 12:6; 15:14, 29; *m. Sheqalim* 1:1, 1:3).[502]

Jesus' objection to the activity is summed up in a scriptural rebuke he gives (**vv 16–17**), using two texts, Isa 56:7 and Jer 7:11. The first OT text says

---

[499] Evans, *Mark 8:27–16:20*, 155, asks whether Jesus was looking for lingering winter figs or early buds (so also Edwards, *Mark*, 339–40), but prefers to see the timing explanation as simply saying it would be a difficult time to find figs so Jesus went to check. However, because we are in a scene that becomes a carried-out prophetic and symbolic act, the ultimate point seems to be more about a lack of congruence between what God's messenger sought and what was found, as Evans also notes. Lane, *Mark*, 401, sees Mic 7:1 in the background, with the idea stated negatively in Jer 8:13. Jesus was looking for the first figs and there were none. They had squandered the gifts God had given, and there was not even hope of fruit. It may be the odd note about timing from Mark that explains why the disciples were impacted by Jesus' act of cursing the tree that leads Peter to make an observation about it later in verses 20–21.

[500] Stein, *Mark*, 516–17; Edwards, *Mark*, 342.

[501] France, *Mark*, 444; V. Eppstein, "The Historicity of the Gospel Account of the Cleansing of the Temple," *ZNW* 55 (1964): 42–58.

[502] Lane, *Mark*, 405.

what the temple should be, whereas the second argues what it has fallen into becoming. The first measures what should be going on, whereas the second cries out against what is taking place.

Citing Isa 56:7, Jesus notes in verse 17 that God's temple was designed to be "a house of prayer for all nations." That stands written and that is what the temple should be. The southern portico led into the Court of Gentiles, the closest Gentiles could get to the temple proper. So the crowding of this area with merchants prevented the opportunity for Gentiles who came to the temple to pray undistracted. The action was symbolic of the wrong spiritual priorities.

It gets even worse, because those who are doing commerce in the courts and the leadership sanctioning it have turned that sacred space into a habitat for bandits. This language is from Jer 7:11.[503] The compliant is of taking advantage of others, leading to a demeaning of the temple from what it should be. It also appears to speak to the sin of the people who participate in such a system (Mal 3:3–10). The Jeremiah 7 passage as a whole makes the point that sin can be judged, and the temple is not an elixir to judgment when sin exists. What was a sacred place of prayer is now a place where petty thieves reside.

The entire prophetic act is a current rebuke of the leadership's operation of the temple and the people who submit to it, an act they could hardly ignore.[504] It is a prophetic indictment that explains why Jesus must face death for others. It also explains why the leaders get more active to deal with Jesus (**v 18**). His indictment in public at the most sacred spot on earth for a Jew leaves them no choice. Jesus has tuned up the heat, claiming the temple back for what he represents and for God.

Yet there is more. Just as the temple was cleansed in the past by Josiah (2 Kings 23) and after its pollution by Antiochus Epiphanes, and Judas Maccabees cleansed it (1 Macc 4:39–59), so now Jesus offers to cleanse the temple and, more importantly, to renew the people.[505] This is why he comes to Jerusalem, though ultimately and ironically that cleansing will lead to and require his death, and also will mean judgment for some.

There is a significant debate about whether the temple act is a cleansing or a prediction of destruction, given the fig tree image. It is a complex

---

[503] For details on how Isa 56 and Jer 7 fit into the understanding of this event, Evans, *Mark 8:27–16:20*, 175–78.
[504] Lane, *Mark*, 407, is correct to stress that Jesus' act has immediate relevance and is not just about the future.
[505] Hooker, *Mark*, 264–65.

debate, and a good case can be made on both sides. We have already noted that the critique has relevance for Jesus' time that should not be underestimated. However, the eschatological nature of Jesus' actions also looks to the future.

For a cleansing: Jesus says what the temple is to be, not that the temple is going away. The problem is not the temple, but the people who occupy and direct it. For the act pointing to destruction: the reality of the judgment that followed in CE 70. Other images in the context also can point in this direction, including Jesus' predictions of the temple's destruction (Mark 13:1–2), and the image of the cursed fig tree in the previous scene.

It may be that the debate exists in part because CE 70 is connected in the Gospels with a judgment of Israel for her unfaithfulness, something other Gospels texts also teach (Luke 13:33–34; 19:41–44). The more difficult question is whether such a judgment on Israel, which did come in CE 70, was anticipated to be permanent. Here texts like Acts 3:18–22 or Romans 11 speak to a hope for a restoration of the very people now subject to judgment. So it may be best to see a judgment of an unfaithful people, a cleansing of a temple where they are to gather, and a picture of Jesus as the bearer of a new kind of sacredness that brings it all with him in his call for spiritual renewal and accountability.[506]

Jesus' direct prophetic challenge to the leadership in verse 18 does not gain a receptive response. Jesus' act required some response: either change the way things were being done at the temple, or reject what Jesus is doing. The latter course is chosen by the chief priests and scribes. It is the ruling priests in Jerusalem who are responding, along with those who helped

---

[506] For a more complete look at this debate, see Klyne Snodgrass, "The Temple Incident," in Bock and Webb, *Key Events*, 430–80. He opts for a "prophetic protest that pointed to future eschatological hope" (471). He sees both judgment and cleansing, looking to a day of a future pure temple as fits broader Jewish expectation in this period. He cites an array of texts supporting this expectation (4Q174, 11Q Temple 29:8–10; *1 Enoch* 90:28–29; Tobit 13:16–17; *Jubilees* 1:15–17; *Syb Oracles* 3:286–294; *2 Baruch* 68:5–6; Benediction 14 of the *Shemoneh Esreh*). The point is that calls for eschatological restoration, such as we see in Acts 3, assume something like this (Isa 2:1–4=Mic 4:1–4), looking to a day when the temple is restored (Ezek 37:21–28; chaps. 40–48; Isa 56:1–8; Zeph 3:8–20; Zech 6:9–15; 14:4–21, and Mal 3:1–4). Whatever and for all Jesus brings as "new temple" in the NT, it need not entail the exclusion of this element of the eschatological hope which is so affirmed across the OT and so became embedded in eschatological expectation. Marcus, *Mark 8–16*, 782–83, also contends for a both/and reading. He argues that trading on the temple precinct was rebuked as sacrilegious (Zech 14:21 – looking to a day without such) and needing reform, while predicting destruction. Contrast Edwards, *Mark*, 345–46, who sees only a prediction of destruction and no cleansing. The harder question is whether there is foreseen a future for the destroyed temple with all nations present.

them in their work with the Law. The rising attention Jesus is gaining in Jerusalem required that they stop Jesus, if they were not going to join him. So they discuss how they might destroy him. It is an indirect way to say how they might kill him. His teaching was amazing to the whole crowd. He was making an impression on them that could challenge their authority.[507] The unrest could arouse Rome to respond. They sensed a need to act. Something had to be done. In many ways, Jesus' action at the temple was the last controversy that locked in the course the leaders would take with Jesus. Meanwhile, Jesus had left the city for Bethany.

The plan is the working out of events Jesus had predicted in Mark 8:31 and 10:33. It solidified a direction already set after the first round of controversies Mark narrated in Mark 2:1–3:5, culminating in the commitment to destroy Jesus in 3:6. The week is taking on the character it will have until Jesus is crucified. Chief priests, scribes, and/or elders will be key in this movement at several points from here on (Mark 11:27; 12:12; 14:1, 43, 53). It was this Judean leadership that drove the initial response that led to the cross.

In the morning (vv 19–20), Jesus and the disciples passed by the fig tree Jesus had visited earlier. It was now withered from the roots. Matthew 21:19 simply said the tree withered at once, using a typical Matthean literary summary, as he often condenses events. It is not just the leaves that are dead, but the entire tree from head to toe. Peter noticed this (v 21), recalled what Jesus had said (Mark 11:14), and pointed out to Jesus that the tree he had cursed now had withered. The idea of withering from the roots has OT precedent as an expression or picture of the loss of power (Job 18:16; Ezek 17:9).[508] If the fig tree pictures Israel through her leadership, the connection may apply.

What is interesting here is that it is Jesus' word of judgment that has been executed. There was no invoking of God to act. The authority is seen as his directly, although Jesus' response will indicate a connection to God.

Jesus responds by calling them to faith in God (v 22), teaching them that faith can lead to unusual outcomes.[509] Faith in God can allow the disciples

[507] Marcus, *Mark 8–16*, 784.

[508] Collins, *Mark*, 533.

[509] There is much discussion on whether Mark 11:22–25 originally was an independent saying of Jesus, given its topic of faith, prayer, and forgiving and the fact that the saying appears in other contexts in other Gospels (Matt 17:20; Luke 17:6); Hooker, *Mark*, 269. Mark clearly has it connected to the act against the fig tree, so it may have been a proverbial kind of expression Jesus used for an array of situations; so Lane, *Mark*, 409. If Jesus used it as a proverb, it is hard to determine which context is secondary, and all talk

to accomplish much and do amazing things, just as Jesus has done. The remark is vivid and rhetorical. It also is rare, as the exact expression, "have faith in God," appears only here in the Gospels and nowhere else in the NT where the reference to God is an objective genitive.[510] The more common expression is to believe in God. Trust and God's work are present in the healing of Jairus' daughter and in the response to the possibility of the rich being saved by God.[511]

So Jesus speaks about uprooting mountains from the ground to the sea (Matt 17:20; Luke 17:6 *Thomas* 48, 106 – both *Thomas* texts have moving mountains but do not note faith). He uses the vivid image to call people to have faith in what God can do in terms of the request (**v 23**). With faith, it can happen (**v 24**). With belief it can be received – it will be yours. It is significant that he is speaking to the group, so corporate prayer may be in view here.[512] It also is important to recognize that we are in a highly rhetorical and hyperbolic conversation. The point is to believe and trust God that he can work as the opening exhortation indicates (John 12:12–14).[513] It may be that the call is to trust that God will carry out the justice and accountability for the nation that Jesus has been dealing with in his most recent actions.

It may even be that the remark is quite narrow, in that the mountain contextually may allude to the Temple Mount or to the Mount of Olives where the fig tree might have been. If so, then the remark may be about judgment and vindication from God, looking to the completion of what Jesus has just depicted, pointing to the accountability the leaders have for rejecting Jesus. Assumed with this is the deliverance of the faithful, for the return was associated with the Mount of Olives (Zech 9–14).[514] One need not make a choice between the Temple Mount and Olives, since it is the Temple Mount that is the real subject of Jesus' recent actions, and Olives is also tied to ideas of restoration and national responsibility.

---

of a secondary context may even be misguided. Here Mark may be calling for an act of faith that trusts God will render justice one day even though circumstances do not appear to see that as likely.

510 The variant reading, "if you have faith ...," is likely owing to assimilation to Luke 17:6. The expression "truly I say to you" is never part of an "if ... then" construction, which the variant requires; Metzger, *Textual Commentary* (1994), 92.

511 Collins, *Mark*, 534.

512 France, *Mark*, 448.

513 Collins, *Mark*, 536.

514 Evans, *Mark 8:27–16:20*, 188–89; Hooker, *Mark*, 270; Marcus, *Mark 8–16*, 785.

There is reason to question this more narrow reading. Mark refers to an "all things whatsoever" (*panta hosa*) prayer in Mark 11:24. So, even if Mark 11:23 refers to the specific context, which is possible, this verse still broadens the scope.[515] If the remark is more proverbial, a reference that includes the temple and hope of vindication may still be included, explaining why the remark is here at all. James 1:6 is similar in thrust, but focuses on not doubting or being double-minded. Prayer or, more often examples of it, are frequent in Mark (Mark 9:20–27 – prayer and exorcism; examples: 1:35; 6:46; 14:32, 35, 39).

There is a caveat (**v 25**). One is to pray having a forgiving heart, if one has something against another. Our forgiving leads to God forgiving us. So Jesus concludes the explanation by urging a prayer of faith, but in the context of being a forgiving person, even as one seeks justice. Similar but more developed in detail is a parable on forgiveness in Matt 18:21–35. It shows that our move to forgive is motivated by God having forgiven us. This is assumed here. The one experiencing grace exercises it toward others, even if one is also seeking justice. The theme is multiply attested, as it also appears in the Lord's Prayer in the request to forgive sin as we forgive those who sin against us (Matt 6:12 – using debts for sin; Luke 11:4; also Sir 28:1–5). 1 Pet 3:7 applies the point to prayer and marriage. So Jesus has cleansed the temple, warning the nation of her spiritual need and of her fate should she remain stubborn. He also has called on the disciples to have faith in God's justice, but to do so with an eye to being forgiving. Given that Mark is written to a people under pressure, it is an interesting juxtaposition of themes. Disciples are to seek justice, but graciously.

11:27–33 When Challenged about the Source of His Authority, Jesus Responds Raising the Example of John the Baptist, Silencing Those Who Ask Him[516]

> **11:27 And they came again to Jerusalem. While Jesus was walking in the temple, the chief priests, scribes and elders came up to him**
> **11:28 and were saying, "By what authority are you doing these things? Or who gave you this authority to do these things?"**

---

[515] Lane, *Mark*, 410, takes the broadening approach to the verse.

[516] Mark 11:26 is a verse that is unlikely to be original to Mark. It looks to be formed in imitation of Matt 6:15 and is lacking in early manuscripts from various families (א, B, L, W, Δ, Ψ); Metzger, *Textual Commentary* (1994), 93. It reads, "But if you do not forgive, neither will your Father in heaven forgive your sins."

11:29 Jesus said to them, "I will ask you one question. Answer me and I will tell you by what authority I do these things:

11:30 John's baptism – was it from heaven or from men? Answer me."

11:31 And they were discussing with one another, "If we say, 'from heaven,' he will say, 'Then why did you not believe him?'

11:32 But if we say, 'From people –' " (they feared the crowd, for all held John to be truly a prophet).

11:33 So they answered Jesus, "we do not know." Then Jesus said to them, "Nor will I say to you by what authority I do these things."

Most of the sequences that follow from here until the Olivet discourse in Mark 13 are controversy accounts. The disputes cover a range of topics, but the goal of them all together is to show Jesus' competence in comparison to the leadership and to present a range of themes that touch on God's program.

This first controversy hits at a core issue: the source of Jesus' authority.[517] Its parallels are Matt 21:23–27 and Luke 20:1–8. Appropriately enough Jesus is back in the temple (v 27), as was his custom and will be in this final week (Mark 11:11; 15–18, 27; 12:35, 41; 13:1–2; 14:49). The chief priests, scribes, and elders ask where Jesus got the authority to do the kinds of things he is doing (v 28). These are the religious leaders, their support team who knew the Law, and lay leaders. The Sanhedrin was made up of these groups. Jesus' temple action in the preceding passage served as the catalyst for this question. In part the question suppresses an assumption, which is that the authorities have not given him this right, so how can he justify it? The act in the temple was not directed by them, but was a critique of their leadership. Who gave him that right? The question is about doing these things, so more than one action is in view.[518] The leadership is suggesting Jesus is usurping an authority that belongs elsewhere. It also is a trap of sorts. Either Jesus' conduct is unauthorized or he was claiming to supersede the priests, the recognized local authority. The die was being cast for making a political charge by moving Jesus to incriminate himself.[519]

---

[517] Evans, *Mark 8:27–16:20*, 198, defends the authenticity of the scene on the premise that to make a comparison to John without affirming Jesus' superiority is not a move a created scene by the church would make.

[518] Collins, *Mark*, 539, suggests Jesus' entrance into the city is also in view. In light of earlier controversies in Mark, the evangelist probably intends more than recent events the Judean leaders had seen, some of which they were likely to have known. Edwards, *Mark*, 351, lists forgiving sins (Mark 2:5), calling tax collectors and sinners (2:15), redefining the Sabbath (2:28), and raising questions about oral tradition (7:1–13).

[519] Evans, *Mark 8:27–16:20*, 200.

Jesus responds with a question of his own, a move common in rabbinic disputes (**vv 29–30**). He says if they answer him, he will answer them. Who gave John the Baptist his authority, God or man? John's work is made analogous to that of Jesus. For Mark, John pointed to Jesus, so their ministries are linked (Mark 1:2–3, 7–8). As Edwards says, "A decision about John is a decision about Jesus."[520] John also worked without an official appointment of the Judean leadership. So what does one do with him? Jesus almost demands an answer.

The leaders sense their dilemma in answering the question (**vv 31–32**). If they say from God, referred to by the euphemism of saying from heaven, then why did they not go out to him and respond? If they had, they also would sense their need to respond positively to Jesus. If they say from man, then the populace will react because John was highly regarded as a prophet (Mark 2:18). The contrast in how the options are formed is interesting. The heaven option is stated as a third-class condition, a pure hypothetical. The man option is stated without a conditional particle and is cut off before being finished, making it appear the more likely choice, but this option is too hard to confess publically.

So they opt out for appearance' sake (**v 33**), saying they do not know, leading Jesus not to respond to their question. They are shown to be, at best, religiously incompetent,[521] for not having a response, or, at worst, conniving, for not being honest.[522] This is the first indication in Mark that the leadership did not respond to John, unlike Matt 3:7–10; 11:16–19, and 21:32 or Luke 7:29–30.[523] Jesus asks a question they are unwilling to answer publicly about whether or not it is possible that John was sent from God. The deliberation puts them in the second category, deliberations that were reflected in the public handling of John and discussion about him that was likely well known.[524] Jesus' "silence" in refusing as a result to respond also is ironic, for his counter question gives a clear signal to the answer. Jesus' authority comes from God, just as John's did.

---

[520] Edwards, *Mark*, 352.

[521] Evans, *Mark 8:27–16:20*, 207, says it is "an embarrassing surrender of the field."

[522] Evans, *Mark 8:27–16:20*, 207, says this is "an embarrassing public display of cowardice." The common notion of fearing the people as a basis of responding gets at this theology rooted in shallow appearances (Mark 11:18, 32; 12:12)

[523] France, *Mark*, 454–55.

[524] Evans, *Mark 8:27–16:20*, 205, suggests the internal deliberations reflected by an omniscient narrator would have been known on this basis. Another option is that someone who later came to faith knew what had been discussed, perhaps someone like Joseph of Arimethea.

12:1–12 Jesus' Parable of the Wicked Tenants Predicts Both His Death and Vindication, as Well as Judgment for the Leadership

12:1 Then he began to speak to them in parables: "A man planted a vineyard and placed a fence around it, dug a pit for its winepress, and built a watchtower. Then he leased it to tenants and went on a journey.

12:2 And at harvest time he sent a slave to the tenants to receive from the fruit of the vine,

12:3 and seizing him, they beat him and sent him away empty.

12:4 And again he sent to them another slave. This one they struck on the head and dishonored him.

12:5 And he sent another and they killed that one, and many others, some of whom were beaten and others of whom were killed.

12:6 Still he had one, a beloved son. He sent him last to them, saying, 'They will respect my son.'

12:7 But those tenants said to one another, 'This is the heir. Come, let us kill him, and the inheritance will be ours.'

12:8 And seizing him, they killed him and cast him outside the vineyard.

12:9 Then what will the owner of the vineyard do? He will come and destroy those tenants and give the vineyard to others.

12:10 Have you not read this scripture: 'The stone the builders rejected has become the cornerstone.

12:11 This is from the Lord, and it is remarkable in our eyes?' "

12:12 Now they were seeking to arrest him, and they feared the crowd, because they knew that he spoke this parable against them. So they left him and went away.

The second controversy account in this final public Markan sequence involves an allegorical parable that reviews the history of Israel's unfaithfulness, The Parable of the Wicked Tenants. The controversy is found in Jesus' direct challenge of the leadership. Despite the question about his implied lack of authority, Jesus is not backing off. The parable's climax is the death of the son and the promise of judgment for those responsible.[525]

---

[525] Hooker, *Mark*, 274, observes that the lack of mention of resurrection points to the parable's origin with Jesus. An early church creation would be unlikely to omit this. She sees the addition of a scriptural proof text from Ps 118:22–23 as a later addition, but it is unclear why Jesus could not have connected such a text to his story in anticipation of some form of divine vindication, especially if his passion predictions go back to him and he believed he had come in the name of the Lord (Ps 118:26). On the authenticity debate, see Evans, *Mark 8:27–16:20*, 215–31, who notes that *Thomas* often compresses parables and contends that Mark's form of the parable is the oldest. Collins, *Mark*, 541–44, surveys the various views on the origin and point of the parable in recent discussion.

The parable foresees care of the vineyard, the promise and people of God, going to others who will be faithful, an allusion to the Twelve among others. It is easily the most allegorical of Jesus' parables. It builds on the example in first-century real life of absentee landlords, who gain profit from the produce of their rented-out lands.[526] In fact, produce was often how rent was paid. The agreement was housing and food for working the land and protecting it with a part of the produce to the owner.[527] The parallels are Matt 21:33–46, Luke 20:9–19, and *Thomas* 65–66. Hostility and tension dominates the parable and the controversies surrounding it. Rejection of Jesus is setting in. So is Jesus' continuing public challenge of the leadership (Mark 12:12). A confrontation emerges that has to be resolved.

Jesus begins to teach the public in parables again, much as he had done in Mark 4 (**v 1**). The practice was common among the rabbis as well.[528] The key image involves the keeping and harvesting of a vineyard, a symbol for Israel (Isa 5:1–7; also Ps 80:8–13; Jer 2:21). Where Isa 5 is about Israel as a whole, here the focus is on those who tend the vineyard, the leaders who are to care for it, as Jesus adds the leasing of the land to tenants to the standard imagery (**v 2**). That vineyard is built with a watchtower wall and winepress. It is rented out to tenant farmers. They are to care for and nurture it. The owner departs. After some time to allow the vineyard's development (usually three to five years in real practice), three times the owner sends servants to collect the fruit of the harvest (**vv 3–5**). Each time they are not only rejected but also sent away, beaten, struck on the head, and killed in turn. Still others are sent, but all are beaten or killed. These scenes picture the internal persecution and rejection of the prophets, as was common in the OT (prophets as servants: Jer 7:25; 25:4; Amos 3:7; Zech 1:6; rejection texts: 2 Sam 10:2–5; 2 Kings 17:7–20; 2 Chron 24:20–22; 36:15–16; Isa 3:14; Jer 12:10; 25:3–7; 26:20–23).[529] John the Baptist was the last in the line. The more

---

[526] Hurtado, *Mark*, 197; France, *Mark*, 459, suggests that some of the leaders may have even been such land owners; especially J. D. M. Derrett, "Fresh Light on the Wicked Vinedressers," in *Law in the New Testament* (London: Darton, Longman & Todd, 1970), 286–312. The Zenon papyri detail such practices; M. Hengel, "Das Gleichnis von den Weingärtnern Mc 12,1–12 im Lichte der Zenonpapyri und der rabbinischen Gleichnisse," *ZNW* 59 (1968): 1–39.

[527] Lane, *Mark*, 417.

[528] For the use of parables in the Old Testament, the Second Temple period, in the Greco-Roman context, and among the rabbis, Klyne Snodgrass, *Stories with Intent: A Comprehensive Guide to the Parables of Jesus* (Grand Rapids: Eerdmans, 2008), 37–59.

[529] France, *Mark*, 460.

messengers God sent, the harder the resistance. The versions in Luke and
Thomas are shorter.[530] The point of the parable is to challenge the leaders'
lack of stewardship and care, a consistent problem throughout Israel's
history. The critique is Deuteronomistic in thrust, mirroring earlier cri-
tiques of Israel's history running through the Old Testament (like Matt
23:29–35).[531]

Finally the owner sent his beloved son (**v 6**; Gen 22:2; Mark 1:11; 9:7),
thinking surely they will respect him. This pictures Jesus and his unique
status in relationship to God. He is more than a mere commissioned
messenger for God, as pictured by the slaves symbolizing the prophets.
The tenants decide that killing the son is best (**vv 7–8**).[532] It is sometimes
suggested that the owner would never have risked a son like this, so the
parable was created by the early church for theological reasons and is not
credible as having come from Jesus. However, the respect for the son might
reflect the view that someone sent with the right social and legal status
would prove his right to the land and get the response of the tenants. After
all, they would want to continue to have a livelihood. On the other hand,
when the son shows up, the tenants might have thought the owner was
dead, so removing the son would allow the land to fall to them, as was
common practice (assuming no one knew how the son had died).[533] The
unnaturalness of all this is actually part of the point. There is something
foolish and irrational about what is taking place with God's messenger. The
sin of rejecting the one the owner sent means acting foolishly and blindly.
So they seized the son, killed him, and tossed his carcass out of the
vineyard. Matt 21:39 and Luke 20:15 change the order, having the murder
come after the casting out from the vineyard, a detail that fits the sequence
of Jesus' death and a crucifixion outside the city (John 19:20; Heb 13:12). The

---

[530] Witherington, *Mark*, 321, suggests a de-Judaizing simplification for Gentile audiences by
Luke and *Thomas*.

[531] Stein, *Mark*, 536, cites a series of OT and NT texts showing prophets "persecuted (1 Kings
19:10–14; 2 Chron. 36:15–16; Matt. 5:12) and killed (1 Kings 18:13; 2 Chron. 24:20–27; 36:15–
16; Neh. 9:26; Jer. 26:20–23; Matt. 23:29–36/Luke 11:47–51; Matt. 23:37/Luke 13:33–34; 1
Thess. 2:15)."

[532] Is there OT background here? Marcus, *Mark 8–16*, 803, sees an allusion to the initial
decision by Joseph's brothers to kill him (Gen 37:20), who does get thrown in a pit.
Though possible, given Joseph is a beloved son, the fit is not quite exact. Evans, *Mark
8:27–16:20*, 237, also notes 1 Kings 21 as possible, where Ahab murders Naboth to obtain
his vineyard and suffers divine judgment.

[533] Lane, *Mark*, 418–19, shows that often those who worked the land would get it if no heir
was left; J. D. M. Derrett, "Fresh Light on the Wicked Vinedressers," in *Law in the New
Testament* (London: Darton, Longman & Todd, 1970), 286–312.

son was left dishonored, given no burial, his body left to rot.[534] The rejection of the son represented a total rejection of the owner. The tenants have acted to claim total ownership of a program that is not theirs.[535]

So what will the owner do (**v 9**)?[536] The owner is now called the Lord (*kurios*) of the vineyard. It is his. He will destroy those tenants and give the vineyard to others. Such an expectation for unfaithful leaders was seen at Qumran, who pictured a judgment that left the vineyard unwalled so it would become a pasture, flattened by those who trample it (4Q162 [4QpIsa]).[537] He will find stewards who carry out their responsibilities. This is a reference to the Twelve (Matt 19:28; Luke 22:30) and others who affirm their loyalty to God by embracing the one he has sent (Matt 21:43, looking to include Gentiles).[538]

Scripture makes the point, as elsewhere in this Gospel (**vv 10–11;** Mark 2:25; 12:26). Jesus cites Ps 118:22–23. The wording matches the LXX. Originally the psalm pictured a king under pressure of rejection by the nations being welcomed to the temple. Some appreciate who the rejected one is and acknowledge the central place he has before God. This part of the psalm is one of the most cited texts for Jesus' vindication by God (Luke 20:17; Acts 4:11; 1 Pet 2:4, 7; Rom 9:32–33). Another part of the Psalm (vv 25–26) is cited in other texts (Luke 13:34–35; 19:38; Matt 21:9; Mark 11:9). The stone rejected by the builders is the keystone, the cornerstone that supports everything. The son will be vindicated in his rejection. God will use him to carry out the task assigned to him. What God has done is remarkable (*thaumastos* – BDAG, 445). Matt 21:42 also has this additional verse, whereas Luke omits it. Hooker claims the text is out of place and was added later but relatively early on, since the emphasis is on the punishment of the tenants. However, the point is that despite the current rejection, God's plan will be carried out, a point that completes the story.[539] With confidence of vindication, it is a point Jesus could well make. There is no need or compelling reason to see the text as out of place or the insertion as

---

[534] Taylor, *St Mark*, 475.

[535] Witherington, *Mark*, 322.

[536] Stein, *Mark*, 536–37, shows that Jesus' use of rhetorical questions is common in Mark (3:23, 33; 4:13, 21, 30, 40; 7:18; 8:12, 17–18, 21, 36–37; 9:19, 50; 11:17; 12:24; 13:2; 14:6, 37, 41, 48).

[537] Edwards, *Mark*, 359.

[538] It is wrong to choose between these groups in the verse that is open and looks to the future.

[539] Hooker, *Mark*, 276–77. Collins, *Mark*, 547–48, notes the idea the citation is integral to the completion of the parable on rabbinic models and has a word play between son and stone (*bēn/'eben*).

late. In the face of rejection, Jesus surely contemplated what God was doing and how vindication for his ministry might take place.

There is debate about whether a cornerstone or a capstone is intended (v 10). Those who argue for a cornerstone point to the application of the image in Eph 2:20–22 and 1 Pet 2:6–7, and the fact that it is linked with Isa 28:16 and the idea that one can stumble over the stone, as Luke 20:18 suggests. Those who point to a capstone cite the image pointing to resurrection as a picture of exaltation, the use of the term head (*kephalē*) pointing to a prominent stone, and the example of *Test Sol* 22:7–9.[540] The choice is not clear, but a cornerstone seems more likely, given that the early church read the image consistently this way.[541]

The leaders' reaction shows their commitment to a path they had already set (Mark 3:6; 11:18). They wanted to arrest him (v.13), but their fear of the crowd prevented them from acting. The effort is expressed as an imperfect, so the desire is expressed as ongoing. They would have to find another time. They knew the parable had been told against them. So they left and went away. Their time would come under better circumstances. Again, given the choice to accept or reject God's sent one, they have opted to reject. What Jesus pictures, they commit themselves to do. Despite that rejection, Jesus says God's program and providence will prevail because vindication comes as a part of it.

12:13–17 Jesus Avoids a Trap on Whether to Pay Taxes to Caesar by Saying One Should Render Caesar's Things to Caesar and God's Things to God

> **12:13 And they sent to him some of the Pharisees and Herodians that they might trap him in a word.**
>
> **12:14 And coming, they said to him, "Teacher, we know that you are truthful and do not curry favor from anyone, because you show no favoritism, but truly teach the way of God. Is it right to pay taxes to Caesar or not? Should we pay or not pay?"**
>
> **12: 15 But knowing the hypocrisy, he said to them, "Why are you testing me? Bring me a denarius and let me see it."**
>
> **12:16 And they brought one, and he said to them, "Whose image and whose inscription is it?" They replied, "Caesar's."**

---

[540] Evans, *Mark 8:27–16:20*, 238, and Marcus, *Mark 8–16*, 808–809, who argue this is a capstone.

[541] Collins, *Mark*, 548.

12:17 Then Jesus said to them, "Give to Caesar the things that are Caesar's, and to God the things that are God's." And they were amazed at him.

This is another controversy pronouncement account or *chreia*, preserving a key saying of Jesus.[542] Its parallels are Matthew 22:15–22, Luke 20:20–26, and *Thomas* 100.[543] It is the first of four consecutive pronouncement accounts. A controversy scene and a parable that also engenders controversy precede these four scenes. Only in the interaction with the scribe in Mark 12:28–34 is there a lack of controversy in the foru units that follow. In these scenes we meet Herodians, Pharisees, Sadducees, and a scribe. The scope of the leadership is covered. So five of six scenes in succession in Mark show the distance between Jesus and the leadership.

Another attempt to catch Jesus involves questions from some Pharisees and Herodians about how Jesus deals with Rome and her taxes (v 13–14). This is the second time they have been paired together in responding to Jesus (Mark 3:6). They likely supported the tax they ask about, but in different ways. Herod ruled at Rome's behest, which Herodians surely supported. Meanwhile, the Pharisees participated in the oversight of the people, and may have supported the tax somewhat grudgingly, as they might have seen the payment as acknowledging too much to Caesar because of the idea the emperor was related to divine figures (see the following discussion about the coinage). In fact, when the tax was introduced, a Pharisee, Sadduc, had helped Judas the Galilean lead a revolt against paying it (Josephus, *Ant* 18.3–8).[544] The fact that Herodians and Pharisees, despite their differences, have gathered together against Jesus shows how much they see him as a threat.

They try to trap Jesus in a public statement they can take to Rome. The Greek term for trap (*agreuō*) means to snare something, like catching an animal or a hunt or surprising an unsuspecting person (Job 10:16 LXX; Prov 5:22; 6:25; BDAG, 15). This trap involves asking whether one should pay taxes to Rome or not. This poll tax (*kēnsos*) was unpopular because it came on top of the required temple tax and showed Israel to be subservient to Rome, being instituted in CE 6 when the prefect was sent to rule in Judea (a Latin loanword, BDAG, 42). The anticipated reply involves either

---

[542] Witherington, *Mark*, 323–24.
[543] Egerton Papyrus 2 frag 2 also has a version of this scene; Evans, *Mark 8:27–16:20*, 243.
[544] Lane, *Mark*, 423. Those who totally opposed the tax hoped for a day to revolt against Rome, an attitude that came to form the Zealots later in views like that of Judas the Galilean.

supporting taxes and thus incurring the displeasure of those who do not like Rome and want her out, dampening the messianic hope Jesus evoked, or denying the payment of taxes, which would be a seditious offense and make Jesus subject to Roman law. The flattery that Jesus teaches the truth and shows no favoritism is clearly ironic in light of the whole of the narrative in which these groups have not been responsive at all to Jesus.

Jesus' response signals his awareness that they ask not out of a sincere desire to learn, but rather to test him (v 15). He still goes on the answer the question. He asks for a denarius, the coin used to pay the tax, to be produced. The very fact that they have such a coin shows they participate in Roman society with its currency (v 16). He asks whose image and inscription is on it. They note that it is Caesar's. The inscription on some Roman coins described Tiberius as "Son of the Divine Augustus," which pious Jews regarded as blasphemous. On the back side was the declaration that Caesar was *pontifex maximus,* or high priest for the people. Others still would have had the image of Augustus. The leaders did not object so much to the existence of an economy that they refused to use the coins to meet their daily expenses.

Jesus then concludes, render to Caesar the things that belong to him and render to God the things that belong to him (v 17).[545] Jesus' reply recognized that Caesar had a sphere of responsibility and that God had one as well. Those coins belonged to Caesar and ran the economy he oversaw, so they should give him his due. However, they should also be sure that God was given what was owed to him. Implied is that Caesar is not God and is not to be followed blindly. Caesar and God each has their role to play in life and should be honored accordingly. The previous parable (12:1–12) had already warned that the leaders failed to do exactly that with God.

What the Jewish leaders had set up as a choice between rival options, Jesus turned into a set of relationships where no absolute choice is required, merely discerning what belongs to whom. Jesus is no revolutionary, nor is he a servant of Rome. He urges that government be honored and God obeyed. So Jesus avoids the trap, leaving his listeners amazed. The text is not so much speaking of two realms, so that one should separate church and state, as it is affirming that government and God are each a part of the creation with their own set of relationships, with God having priority

---

[545] *Thomas* 100 adds "and what is mine give me." This is clearly a secondary addition; Marcus, *Mark 8–16,* 818.

(Rom 13:7; 1 Tim 2:1–6; Titus 3:1–2; 1 Pet 2:13–14).[546] So their roles are distinct, but not entirely separate, as governments ultimately also are accountable to the Creator God.

12:18–27 Jesus Defends the Resurrection to Sadducees

12:18 And Sadducees came to him who said there is no resurrection and asked him saying,

12:19 "Teacher, Moses wrote for us: '*If a man's brother dies* and leaves a wife *but no children, that man must take the widow as a wife and raise up offspring for his brother.*'

12:20 There were seven brothers. The first one married, and when he died, he had no children.

12:21 The second married her and died, not having any children, and likewise the third.

12:22 None of the seven had children. Finally, the woman died too.

12:23 In the resurrection, when they rise again, whose wife will she be? For all seven had married her."

12:24 Jesus said to them, "Are you not mistaken for this reason, because you do not know the scriptures or the power of God?

12:25 For when they rise from the dead, they neither marry nor are given in marriage, but are like angels in heaven.

12:26 Concerning the dead being raised, have you not read in the book of Moses, in the passage about the bush, how God said to him, '*I am the God of Abraham, the God of Isaac, and the God of Jacob*'?

12:27 He is not the God of the dead but the living. You err greatly."

In another controversy pronouncement account, Jesus affirms the resurrection in the face of Saducean denial. The parallels are Matt 22:23–33 and Luke 20:27–40.

The Sadducees (**v 18**) were a powerful priestly party of Jews who came from the upper classes, first mentioned during the reign of John Hyrcanus (135–104 BCE; Josephus, *Ant* 13.293–97), yet they are mentioned in a way that makes their existence appear to be far older (Josephus, *Ant* 18.11). Their name either comes from the Hebrew word for "righteous" (*ṣaddîq*) or more likely after Zadok, high priest under David and Solomon (2 Sam 8:17; 1 Kings 1:34), who fathered the genuine priestly line (Ezek 40:46). Sadducees did not hold to resurrection and created a story they thought

---

[546] The Book of Revelation and the prophets of the Old Testament show that government does not get a blank check to do what it wants and is accountable to God.

showed the ridiculous nature of the idea (Josephus, *Ant* 18.16; Acts 4:2; 23:6–8). They also preferred the Torah over other parts of the Hebrew Scripture and especially oral tradition (Josephus, *Ant* 13.297). They were the most politically powerful group during Jesus' time, but were a minority on this point of doctrine. They had compromised to share power with Rome (Josephus *Ant* 18.16–17; *War* 2.164–166).[547] This is Mark's only mention of them.

They asked Jesus as a religious teacher about their critique of resurrection (v 18). The address as "teacher" replicates the earlier query in Mark 12:14. It might seem such a question is out of place,[548] but Jesus raising the idea of divine vindication earlier in his telling of the parable of the wicked tenants implies his belief in this kind of an idea, as do other elements of Jesus' public teaching.[549] The goal is to undercut this possibility and thus seek to discredit a key part of his claim that the kingdom he brings has a future. Resurrection is seen in three OT texts (Isa 26:19; Ezek 37 – as a metaphor; Dan 12:2), as well as at Qumran (4Q521 2 ii 12).

The Sadducees raise what they think is a dilemma for resurrection using a scenario that is exaggerated but raises a seeming problem (v 19). Tobit 3–7 had a story of a woman with seven husbands but did not raise this problem. The Sadducees press the example. It involves a family with seven brothers and the command of levirate marriage (Deut 25:5 is cited in a conceptual summary from the Law in 25:5–10; examples: Gen 38:8; Ruth 4:1–12; Tobit 6:9; 7:11; *m. Yevamot*; Josephus, *Ant* 4.254–56, who is clear a marriage is involved). Lev 18:16 and 20:21 prohibited a brother-in-law and a sister-in-law from marrying, but this was read as outside of a levirate situation. Deuteronomy 25:5 refers only to a son, whereas the LXX, Josephus (*Ant* 4.254), and rabbis limited it to no children of either gender. The Sadducean example follows the broader reading. Also unclear is whether this law was actually practiced in Jesus' time, but the existence of Mishnah on the topic means it was at least discussed.[550] With only two examples from the OT

---

547   Marcus, *Mark 8–16*, 1121–23, has an appendix on the Sadducees with many of these points.
548   Evans, *Mark 8:27–16:20*, 251–52, who sees Mark giving the genuine dispute a new setting.
549   The issue here is affirmation, not of the timing of the resurrection as being near for Jesus, but simply of its eventual coming on his behalf. Jesus taught resurrection (privately: Mark 8:31; 9:42–50; publically: Matt 12:41–42=Luke 11:31–32; Luke 14:14; 16:19–31). Jesus' public remarks about accountability in a judgment to come assumes resurrection; Marcus, *Mark 8–16*, 827.
550   Collins, *Mark*, 560. She also notes on page 561 how the expectation of Jews about whether there would be marriage after resurrection expresses uncertainty, as no text says so explicitly, and passages looking to an earthly kingdom precede a resurrection to the

and Josephus' remarks, it looks as if it was practiced, at most, rarely. So we are dealing with a fairly uncommon, mostly hypothetical situation (seven brothers) at best. Still, such theoretical cases were used to make a theological point. When a brother dies without progeny (*sperma*), then a surviving brother must take the widow as a wife and produce seed for his brother's legacy. The expression "take the widow" (*lambanō + gynē*) refers to marriage (BDAG, 583, 3).[551] Such a marriage also provided protection for the widow.

In the example, each of the seven brothers has an opportunity to leave a child but dies without success (**vv 20–22**). Finally, the woman dies. The question is, in the resurrection, whose wife will the woman be (**v 23**)?[552] She had had seven husbands! All seven had married her. The picture is of a woman who has too many to care for, too many places to go. There is supposed to be some humor in the example. It is designed to make resurrection look silly. One assumption in the example may be that if descendants are needed through the brother, then there is no resurrection, no later remedy.[553] Another assumption is that monogamy is the ideal for marriage, and that the lack of a child meant no one could claim her as his wife. There was no way to adjudicate to whom she was wed.[554]

Jesus responds by saying they have erred (**v 24**). That erring is the point in the verb *planaō* is seen in the reuse of the verb in Mark 12:27, where the point is they have erred badly.[555] Jesus is pointing out where their mistake is. The rhetorical question expects a positive answer using the particle *ou*. They do not understand either the Scripture or God's power, so they misread what resurrection means. They underestimate God's power to produce a resurrection and do not understand the teaching on the afterlife that results from his work. This is a direct challenge, as Scripture is what

---

eternal kingdom. Life in that earthly kingdom is described in normal terms, but marriage in the afterlife is not explicitly addressed.

[551] As is common in the OT, the term *sperma* or seed means descendants (Gen 12:7 LXX; 13:15 LXX; 17:7 LXX; 24:7 LXX; also Rom 4:16, 18; Gal 3:16).

[552] There is a textual issue here. Does Mark make a double reference to resurrection here with an additional reference to "when they rise," using Mark's common pleonasm? Many good manuscripts omit the phrase (א, B, C, L, Δ), but it also is hard to see a copyist adding it. So Nestle-Aland has the phrase in brackets to express uncertainty about its inclusion, though its presence in this case is more likely than not; Metzger, *Textual Commentary* (1994), 93.

[553] Hooker, *Mark*, 283.

[554] Stein, *Mark*, 553, who notes that if the other brothers also had been married, as might be expected, the tension in the example was even multiplied.

[555] This verb can refer to deception, which is the result of their error. The reference to a lack of understanding in the context is a reference to error.

they are supposed to know best, and to underestimate God is a major failing for a theologian and priest.

Jesus makes two affirmations in responding. First, Jesus points to a lack of continuity in the afterlife with this life (v 25). People neither marry nor are given in marriage (*1 En* 15:7). Later, in the Babylonian Talmud, a statement appears in a context explaining that the world to come is not like this world. It says that "in the world to come there is neither eating, nor drinking nor procreating" (*b.* Ber 17a). In a world with no death, there is no need to replenish the earth. So people are more like angels, another detail noted in a Second Temple text (2 Bar 51:5–12; *1 En* 51:4; 104:4, 6). Paul has a more detailed discussion of resurrection in 1 Cor 15, including an emphasis on it involving a spiritual body that is able to inherit the kingdom (esp. vv 40–58). Jesus' mention of angels is provocative, because it is possible some Sadducees also did not believe in angels (Acts 23:8), even though they are mentioned in the Torah.

Second, he cites the Torah, in Exodus 3:6, where God identifies himself as the God of Abraham, Isaac, and Jacob (v 26). He is the God of the living, not the dead (v 27). So if God says this to Moses, long after the patriarchs have died, these luminaries must be alive and raised or they will be such, a view that is in concert with other Second Temple texts (4 Macc 7:19; 16:25).[556] He is not the "God of dead heroes."[557] The remark may well also assume that God keeps his commitments to them, pointing to a connection between resurrection and faithfulness.[558] The argument is made from the Torah because that is the portion of the Hebrew Scripture the Sadducees most respect. The failure to recognize these two things means his questioners err greatly. Mark ends here, while Matt 22:33 and Luke 20:39–40 note the reaction of those who listened. The influence of Jesus' answer can be seen in Rom 13:10; Gal 5:14, and James 2:8.[559]

---

[556] Evans, *Mark 8:27–16:20*, 256, opts for a future resurrection, while Marcus, *Mark 8–16*, 828–29, sees the patriarchs as currently alive and therefore raised (4 Macc 16:25; 17:18–19). Either option is possible, but the point seems to fit better if the patriarchs are seen as currently alive. The picture Jesus paints in the rich man and Lazarus (Luke 16:19–31) pictures a functioning Abraham to greet those who have died and gone to Abraham's bosom. It does not assume a future resurrection for Abraham. This also favors a current view of resurrection. Collins, *Mark*, 564, makes no choice between the options.

[557] Hooker, *Mark*, 285, who notes that the Jewish view of the afterlife was a resurrection, so this would not be a reference to immortality of the soul. One can add that this is correct, especially since Jesus is defending resurrection by the remark.

[558] Lane, *Mark*, 430.

[559] France, *Mark*, 478.

12:28–34 Jesus Affirms the Need to Love God and One's Neighbor as the Greatest Commandment

12:28 And coming up one of the scribes heard them debating. Seeing that Jesus answered them well, he asked him, "Which commandment is first of all?"

12:29 Jesus answered, "First is '*Hear, O Israel, the Lord your God is one.*

12:30 Love the Lord your God with all your heart, with all your soul, with all your mind, and with all your strength.'

12:31 Second is '*Love your neighbor as yourself.*' There is no other commandment greater than these."

12:32 The scribe said to him, "Good, Teacher, you speak truly that *he is one, and there is no one else besides him.*

12:33 And *to love him with all your heart, with all your mind, and with all your strength* and *to love your neighbor as yourself* is more important than all burnt offerings and sacrifices."

12:34 And Jesus seeing that he answered thoughtfully said to him, "You are not far from the kingdom of God." And no one no longer dared to ask him anything.

Another pronouncement account is less controversial than it is revealing. A parallel is Matt 22:34–40, along with a conceptual parallel in Luke 10:25–28 in a completely distinct scene and context. As we shall see, the discussion is so thoroughly Jewish that it has a good claim to authenticity, lacking elements one might expect a later Christian creation to possess.[560]

A scribe and Jesus exchange views on the greatest commandment. The scribe is portrayed more favorably than other Jewish leaders in the chapter, as it is said he saw that Jesus had answered the resurrection dispute well (**v 28**). The scribe, then, may well have been a Pharisee, since they were believers in resurrection. He asks Jesus what is the first or primary commandment. The question may have been motivated by a discussion of which commandments were light or heavy among the 613 commanded (*m. 'Abot* 2:1; 4 Macc 5:20; *b. Mak* 23b numbers the commandments and notes that 248 are positive and 365 are negative).[561] The point is not to disqualify any of the commands but simply to ask which is the most important.

Jesus cites the *Shema* (Deut 6:4) with the call to love God completely (Deut 6:5) and the commandment to love one's neighbor (Lev 19:18) (**v 29**).

---

560   Evans, *Mark 8:27–16:20*, 261–62; Stein, *Mark*, 558–59.
561   Stein, *Mark*, 560.

The *Shema* was probably the most well-known Jewish text of confession (also in Deut 11:13-31; Num 15:37-41). The Mishnah notes at its later time of composition that Jews recited it twice a day (*m Ber* 1.1-2). This is likely to be an older practice (Josephus, *Ant* 4:13). This is a call to only recognize the one God and to live well with others in his creation. The mention of heart, soul, mind, and strength is a way to say that one should love God fully at every level (**v 30**). Deut 6:5 does not mention strength. Matthew and Luke lack a reference to Deut 6:4, keeping only the ethical call to love God fully. Matthew makes no mention of strength, but the point is the same.

The love for one's neighbor (**v 31**) is also a significant Jewish text (Akiba in *Sifra* 89a [§ 200 on Lev 19:15-20]; Hillel in *b. Shabbat* 31a says that "What is hateful to you, do not do to your neighbor" is the whole of the Law; Philo *Decalogue* 109-110 and *Spec Laws* 2.63, although Philo elsewhere sees the Ten Commandments as having this position; *Decalogue* 19-20; *Aristeas* 168).[562] Love for God and neighbor is also the summary of the Law in *T. Iss* 5:2 and *T. Dan* 5:3, but there is some question of whether Christian influence had impacted these texts. Other Jewish writers had other emphases. So Simeon the Just (c. 200 BCE) taught, "The world rests on three things: the Law, the sacrificial worship, and expressions of love" (*m. Avot* 1.2).[563] One can see the inner Jewish points of view in the contrast.

The scribe affirms the reply with a "good!" and recognizes several things while agreeing in his response (**v 32a**). He affirms that God is one (Deut 6:4b, 35; Isa 45:21 LXX). He repeats the commands to love God and neighbor (**vv 32b-33**). And he adds that these are more important than burnt offerings and sacrifices, leading to Jesus' commendation. Other Old Testament texts say that God desires mercy, not sacrifice (1 Sam 15:22; Isa 1:11; Hos 6:6; Jer 6:20; 7:22-23; Mic 6:6-8).[564] Texts at Qumran, interestingly enough, also say this (1QS 9:4; 4Q266 [= 4QD^a] 10 i 13). Jesus says that this understanding leaves him not far from the kingdom (**v 34a**). He is close to being in a place of blessing. All that is left is responding to the one God has sent, as the next passage suggests.

For Jesus, God's existence as Creator and Lord God carries a corollary: our love for him must involve the entire person (Rom 13:8-9; Gal 5:14;

Hooker, *Mark*, 288. Of course, the Ten Commandments, in their two tables, cover the response to God and to one's neighbor. *Jub* 36:7-8 juxtaposes love for God and for one's brother, by which is meant one's fellow Jew.

563 Lane, *Mark*, 434.

564 Evans, *Mark 8:27–16:20*, 265–66.

James 2:8; for the opposite, 1 John 4:11, 19–20). Everything we do radiates from this theological core. Faith, life, and theology begin at the same place, from a love relationship with the living God to whom one submits as to the one and only Lord. That also impacts our relationships as we interact with others also made in God's image. Jesus sees the two commands as a package that together make up the one great commandment. The scene closes with a note that no one dared ask him any more questions (**v 34b**). Mark 12 has demonstrated the authority of Jesus and his qualification to represent God.

12:35–37 Jesus' Query about the Christ as David's Son and Lord

12:35 And Jesus replying said, as he was teaching in the temple courts, "How is it the scribes say that the Christ is David's Son?
12:36 David himself said, by the Holy Spirit, '*The Lord said to my lord, "sit at my right hand until I place your enemies under your feet."* '
12:37 If David himself calls him 'Lord,' how can he be his son?" And the large crowd listened gladly.

This scene is a pronouncement account that simply raises a dilemma about the claims tied to the Messiah. Once again we are in the temple area as Jesus teaches (Mark 11:15–16, 27, 13:1; 14:49). The parallels are Matt 22:41–46 and Luke 20:41–44. The theme that emerges is that Messiah is an authority, since David calls him Lord (**vv 35–36**). The dilemma is twofold: (1) why do people call the Messiah David's son, when David calls him Lord, and (2) why would an ancestor call a descendant Lord? Jesus' remarks assume the Psalm is Davidic and ultimately about Messiah.

At the base of the question is Ps 110:1, which becomes a major Christological text in the rest of the New Testament (Mark 14:62; Acts 2:34–36; Rom 8:34; 1 Cor 15:25; Eph 1:20–23; Col 3:1; Heb 1:13; 10:12; 1 Pet 3:21–22), and Jewish expectation of the time, which in many quarters was tied to the Davidic dynasty (2 Sam 7:12–16; Isa 9:2–7; 11:1–9; Jer 23:5–6, 33:15; Zech 3:8; 6:12; Amos 9:11; *Ps Sol* 17–18; 4QFlor 1:11–13; CD 7:16). By noting David calls him Lord, so how is he son, Jesus simply raises the question to ponder and leaves it hanging (**v 37**). He does not indicate where the right hand is, even as he points to the total power Messiah will have. This simply evokes the presence of God and his proximity to the one David describes. The stress is on the priority given to the name Lord. What is clear is that God and the Messiah share rule, a point that begins to suggest why David may have addressed the figure with such respect. The question is about messianic status next to God.[565] The crowd is delighted with the dilemma Jesus poses. With no response, the scene closes simply with the question posed for reflection.

The rest of Mark's narrative will supply part of the answer when Jesus returns to the text at his Jewish examination at the end of Mark 14. The point appears to be that thinking of Messiah as David's son is not enough.[566] He is far more than David's Son, one whom the founder of the line sees as Lord. The way the ancestor treats the descendant by addressing him with such respect shows this. What more this text means beyond this is not made clear here.[567] The very indirectness of the point speaks for authenticity.[568] Still the implication of raising the point shows Jesus making his messianic mission public again as he winds up his public teaching in Mark. He also is pushing people to see how close the sent one is to God. In terms of public acts, the entry and this teaching bookend his self-presentation in Jerusalem for Mark. The New Testament also makes much of these links to David (Rom 1:2–4; 2 Tim 2:8; Matt 1:20; Luke 1:27, 32, 69; 2:4, 11; Rev 5:5; 22:16).

12:38–40 Jesus Warns about the Scribes

12:38 And in his teaching, he was saying, "Beware of the scribes, those who like walking around in long robes and receiving greeting in the marketplaces,

12:39 and the best seats in the synagogue and the places of honor at the banquets.

12:40 They devour widows' property, and as a show make long prayers. These men will receive a more severe judgment."

---

[565] Edwards, *Mark*, 377.

[566] O. Betz, "Die Frage nach dem messianischen Bewusstsein Jesu," *NovT* 6 (1963): 20–48.

[567] Mark argues juxtaposing themes throughout his Gospel tied to the titles Lord, Son of God, and Son of Man. He sees one who is directly in God's presence, as Mark 14:61–62 especially affirms. Mark 1:1 raised the note about sonship from the start.

[568] Taylor, *St Mark*, 493. The idea the saying denies Davidic sonship is problematic in two ways: (1) Mark has already signaled that this is an acceptable category (Mark 10:47; 11:9–10), and (2) the entire NT thrust about Jesus' Davidic connection is unlikely if he denied such a point; also Cranfield, *Mark*, 381. Jesus makes the points far too indirectly for this to be a church creation. Neither does the scene require the LXX for this argument. An oral Semitic rendering of the text with respect for the name of God would have the same result, and the title Lord coming from David for Messiah is not impacted by the difference. That title is the key point; Evans, *Mark 8:27–16:20*, 273.

Jesus closes his public discourse with a warning and a contrast in another brief pronouncement. The parallel is Luke 20:45–47, whereas a far more extensive conceptual parallel is Matt 23:1–36, a long rebuke to Pharisees and scribes. It recalls another warning to beware of Pharisees and Herodians in Mark 8:15.

Jesus warns the crowd away from the way of certain scribes (v 38).[569] He tells people to "beware of them," using a present tense that calls for a constant watch (Mark 8:15). They do not love their neighbor by their actions. They like long ceremonial robes (BDAG, 946), greetings in the market (Mark 23:7), best seats in the synagogue, and places of honor at banquets (v 39; Luke 14:7–11; seating by rank: 1QS 6:8–9). They want attention and honor. They like the attention. The robes may have been long prayer shawls of wool or linen with tassels on four corners, with a white mantle-like look; they were known as *tallits*. This dress was unique to religious offices. Other robes may simply have been expensive garments pointing to status. These robes had a reputation tied to them of enhancing a person's stature, communicating they were somebody (Josephus, *Ant* 3.155; Sir 50:11). In addition, these scribes take advantage of widows (v 40a),[570] taking their property (Isa 10:2; Mal 3:5; *T. Moses* 7:6–10), and pray for show. It is not entirely clear what is meant here in their exploitation. Was it excessive appropriation of a widow's inheritance by over-charging for services that were to be offered without charge (*m. 'Abot* 1.13), by seizing assets for payment of nonpayment of tithes (Josephus, *Ant* 20.206), urging temple gifts and taking the proceeds (Josephus, *Ant* 18.81–84), or some unspecified means of taking money that was not theirs to take?[571] Regardless of the unspecified detail, the point is exploitation of the vulnerable, something the Hebrew Scripture addressed with regard to widows (Deut 14:29; Ps 68:5; 146:9; Isa 1:17; Jer 7:6; 49:11).[572]

---

[569] On the restrictive and limited scope of the scribes described here, Marcus, *Mark 8–16*, 852. Jesus is not speaking of all scribes here, but those of this type. He notes the previous scene has a scribe who is not seen so negatively.

[570] Some manuscripts (D, W, and other mostly Western witnesses) add a reference to orphans here, but it is unlikely they have property to exploit. The addition is likely scribal to mirror OT expressions (Exod 22:22; Deut 14:29).

[571] J. Fitzmyer, *The Gospel According to Luke (X–XXIV)* (New York: Doubleday, 1985), 2:1318, notes six options and also observes that the text does not make clear the exact act in view. It may well be a variety of abuses are in view; see also J. D. M. Derrett, "'Eating Up the Houses of Widows': Jesus's Comment on Lawyers?" *NovT* 14 (1972): 1–9, and H. T. Fleddermann, "A Warning about the Scribes (Mark 12.37b–40)," *CBQ* 44 (1982): 52–67.

[572] Stein, *Mark*, 575.

Criticisms like this of the Sadducees are noted by Josephus (Ant 20.180–81, 205–207).[573] So Jesus is not alone in raising such issues. The term *prophasis* tied to prayer points to an act done out of a pretext (BDAG, 889, 2).

What lies ahead is a more severe judgment (**v 40b**). Is this eschatological or is it indicative of the vineyard being given to others, as the displacement of many Jewish leaders in 70 CE accomplished, or both? Beyond the dire result, Jesus does not say. What is clear is that there is accountability to God who sees and will act. God will judge those who sought first place in attention, pretense, and self-exaltation, while taking advantage of others (Matt 23:12; Luke 14:11). What they have done is the exact opposite of the greatest commandment Jesus has just affirmed and commended. The OT also expresses such concerns and outcomes (Isa 10:1–4), as did Qumran (CD 6:16–17).[574] God will honor those who love him and do not take advantage of others while seeking self-interest.

12:41–44 Jesus Commends the Sacrifice of the Poor Widow

> **12: 41 Then he sat down opposite the offering box, and was observing all the crowd putting coins into it. Many rich people were throwing in large amounts.**
> **12: 42 And a poor widow came and put in two small copper coins, worth less than a quadrans.**
> **12:43 He called his disciples and said to them, "Truly I say to you, this poor widow has put more in the offering box than all giving to the treasury.**
> **12:44 For they all gave out of their wealth. But she, out of her poverty, all that she had put in her whole life."**

A final pronouncement gives the contrast. The parallel is Luke 21:1–4. We are again at the temple, near the offering boxes (**v 41**), located either as one of thirteen receptacles shaped like trumpets in the Court of Women (*m. Sheqal* 6:5) or at the treasury that stored such contributions in the inner court (Josephus, *War* 5.200), which is the normal meaning of the term used (*gazophylakion* – BDAG, 186, 2). However, the treasury was not in a locale where a woman could give an offer, so the fact that a widow is involved favors one of the receptacles as the more likely location. Jesus was

---

573   Witherington, *Mark*, 334.
574   Evans, *Mark 8:27–16:20*, 284.

observing people giving offerings, including the rich throwing in a lot of money, but it was a poor widow who caught his eye (**v 42**). The way she was dressed may have pointed to her status (Luke 7:11–19). She put in only two small copper coins, what were called lepta or quadrans, the lowest currency possible (BDAG, 592). *Quadrans* is a Latin term to explain the lepta (BDAG, 550).[575] There even was saying about paying the last quadrans (Plutarch, *Cicero* 29.5; Matt 5:26), as we speak of the last penny.[576] This equaled about fifteen minutes of average labor. It was next to nothing, but here it was genuine piety.

So she gave more than all (**vv 43–44**). Jesus' remarks here are privately made to the disciples. It is a teaching moment for them, dealing with issues of character. In contrast to others who gave out of excess and wealth, she offered out of her poverty what she needed for life. Something about her appearance led to the understanding her sacrifice was great.[577] The picture of self-sacrifice and genuine appreciation for God is where Jesus ends these public remarks. Even the poor can be rich toward God, and he will notice.

There is discussion about whether Jesus is commending the woman (most scholars agree) or complaining about what she has done under social pressure.[578] In this latter view, human need has been forced to succumb to religious practice. However, Jesus' remark has no real hint of lament in it. There is no "beware" here, but rather the observation that her sacrifice is genuine. Jesus may sense that the dilemma the woman was put in was not right, but what he comments on is the sacrifice of her act. A woman of no social status serves as a rebuke to the behavior of others who regard social

---

[575] On the debate about whether explaining the lepta by appeal to the Latin quadrans is evidence for the origin of Mark's Gospel in Rome or southern Syria, see G. Theissen, *The Gospels in Context: Social and Political History in the Synoptic Tradition* (Minneapolis: Fortress, 1991), 247–49. He opts for southern Syria, even though this is a coin that did not circulate in the East. Its name was known there, as Matt 5:26 shows. Theissen argues that it simply meant the "smallest" coin. What this shows is that the naming need not require a Roman context, but neither does it preclude it, given the coin circulated there and not in the East. On the other hand, Hengel, *Studies in the Gospel of Mark* (Philadelphia: Fortress, 1985), 28–30, argues for a Roman origin, placing this example as reflecting a need to explain to Romans what a lepta was using quadrans, alongside another example in Mark 15:16, with its Latin explanation of the praetorium, which argues against a Syrian origin in that case, as they would be less likely to need to be told where the palace was. His larger argument is that the larger number of Latinisms points to this setting over Syria. Hengel has the more substantial case.

[576] Marcus, *Mark 8–16*, 858.

[577] Were her clothes tattered? Was she wearing black for mourning? Was she gaunt? No detail is given as to how we know she was a widow.

[578] Evans, *Mark 8:27–16:20*, 282–83, discusses the options and opts for a lament here.

status as important and seek to exploit those of the woman's status, as the previous scene has indicated. That is where the contrast lies: her sacrifice versus the way the rebuked scribes have acted. So, despite much that can be said for the lament view, and though it might be in the background, the point is that the woman acted out of a sense of sacrifice, and sacrifice is what Jesus has spent much time teaching disciples about as they traveled to Jerusalem.[579]

13:1–37 Jesus Describes Events Surrounding the Destruction of the Temple and the Return of the Son of Man That Mean Redemption and Vindication for His Disciples

> 13:1 And going out of the temple courts, one of his disciples said to him, "Teacher, look at these glorious stones and buildings."
>
> 13:2 And Jesus said to him, "Do you see these great buildings? Not one stone will be left on another, which will not be torn down."
>
> 13:3 And while he was seated on the Mount of Olives opposite the temple, Peter, James, John and Andrew asked him privately,
>
> 13:4 "Tell us, when will these things be? And what will be the sign when these things are about to be completed?"
>
> 13:5 Jesus began to say to them, "Watch out that no one misleads you.
>
> 13:6 Many will come in my name saying, 'I am he,' and they will mislead many.
>
> 13:7 When you hear of wars and rumors of wars, do not be disturbed. It is necessary for these things to come to pass, but the end is not yet.
>
> 13:8 For nation will rise up against nation, and kingdom against kingdom. There will be earthquakes in various places, and there will be famines. These things are the beginning of birth pangs.
>
> 13: 9 Watch out for yourselves. You will be handed over to councils and beaten in the synagogues. You will stand before governors and kings on account of me as a testimony to them.
>
> 13:10 First, the gospel must be preached to all nations.
>
> 13: 11 And when they arrest you and hand you over to trial, do not worry about what to say. But whatever is given to you in that hour, speak this. For it is not you speaking but the Holy Spirit.
>
> 13:12 And brother will hand over brother to death, and a father his child. Children will rise up against parents and have them put to death.
>
> 13:13 You will be hated by all because of my name. But the one who endures to the end will be saved.

---

579 Collins, *Mark*, 590.

13:14 But when you see *the abomination of desolation* standing where he should not be (let the reader understand), then those in Judea must flee to the mountains.

13:15 The one on the roof must not come down nor go inside to take anything from his house.

13:16 The one in the field must not turn back to take his cloak.

13:17 Woe to those who are pregnant or nursing their babies in those days.

13:18 Pray that it may not come in winter.

13:19 For those are days there will be tribulation unlike anything from the beginning of creation that God created until now, or will ever happen again.

13:20 And if the Lord had not cut short those days, no one would be saved. But because of the elect, whom he chose, he has cut them short.

13:21 And then if anyone says to you, 'Look, here is the Christ,' or 'Look, there he is,' do not believe him.

13:22 For false messiahs and false prophets will appear and perform signs and wonders to deceive, if possible, even the elect.

13:23 Watch, for I have told you everything.

13:24 But in those days, after that tribulation, *the sun will be darkened and the moon will not give its light;*

13:25 *the stars will be falling from heaven, and the powers in heaven will be shaken.*

13:26 And then they will see *the Son of Man arriving among the clouds with great power and glory.*

13:27 Then he will send angels and they will gather his elect from the four winds, from the ends of the earth to the ends of heaven.

13:28 Learn from the parable of the fig tree: Whenever its branch becomes tender and puts out leaves, you know summer is near.

13:29 So also you, when you see these things taking place, know that the end is near, right at the door.

13:30 Truly I say to you, this generation will not pass away until all these thing take place.

13:31 Heaven and earth will pass away, but my words will never pass away.

13:32 But as for that day or hour no one knows it – neither the angels in heaven, nor the Son – except the Father.

13:33 Keep watch. Stay alert. For you do not know when the time will come.

13:34 It is like a man going on a journey. He left his house and gave his slaves authority, giving to each his own work and commanded the doorkeeper to stay alert.

13:35 Therefore, stay alert, because you do not know when the owner of the house will return – whether during evening, at midnight, when the rooster crows, or at dawn –

13:36 so that he might not find you asleep when he returns suddenly. 13:37 What I say to you, I say to all, stay alert."

The Olivet discourse is one of only two major discourses in Mark. The other was Mark 4:3–32 on the parables. The parallels to this scene are the more extended version in Matt 24–25 and a similar treatment to Mark in Luke 21:5–38. It is an apocalyptic-like, eschatological prophetic discourse, as it looks at judgment on the nation with its prediction of the destruction of the temple and culminates in the coming of the Son of Man in vindication of the saints.[580] Apocalyptic discourse is an unveiling or disclosure of realities about the divine program that pulls the veil away to reveal the resolution of the cosmic conflict God is resolving, often written to assure God's people he will vindicate them despite the tough times. However, the discourse lacks a few key features of normal apocalyptic discourse, such as visions and otherworldly tours, as well as any feel of this age and the age to come, though that is implied in the Son of Man's coming and the vindication he brings.[581] So the discourse is better regarded as eschatological and prophetic with apocalyptic features.[582] The discourse is introduced in Mark 13:1–2 with a short pronouncement about the temple's destruction that triggers a question in verses 3–4 and the discourse in verses 5–37.

The discourse is complex in that it juxtaposes the temple's destruction and the end tied to Day of the Lord imagery and treats the signs indicating that each is going to take place. The relationship between those two events is not entirely clear, although some separation appears likely.[583] There is a tension between specific signs being given and not knowing exactly when the culmination comes. God has a plan, but it also is part of a mystery not completely disclosed. One can rest assured these things will happen, but do

---

580   For other examples of apocalyptic discourse in the Second Temple period or in Jewish sources, Dan 7–12, *1 Enoch* 37–71, and *4 Ezra* 13; Hooker, *Mark*, 297. It is not a farewell discourse. That description is better tied to the Last Supper.

581   Witherington, *Mark*, 336, claims it lacks other such features, such as an otherworldly mediator, but that surely is the Son of Man, coming on the clouds. He adds a lack of apocalyptic verbiage and date setting. However, the language surrounding the Son of Man's return has such cosmic descriptions, and although no dates are set, the time is declared as known by God, with signs pointing to a divine calendar. All of this means that we are in a type of apocalyptic discourse.

582   Edwards, *Mark*, 384–85.

583   Stein, *Mark*, 584–85, charts four primary options for how the discourse is broken down in terms of events for commentators. They range from a mix of the lead-up to the destruction and, distinctly, the parousia, all the way to being just about the destruction. Particularly debated is whether verses 14–23, 24–27, and 32–37 include the parousia or not, either exclusively or as a parallel experience to the time of the destruction. The point of agreement is that verses 5–13 are the lead-up to the temple's destruction.

not try to put a calendar on them. One can see progress toward that vindication, but the exact time is God's business alone. In the meantime, keep to the task, despite the difficulty of current times. Jesus' point is to call for watchfulness and faithfulness until that deliverance comes. It is part of Mark's point about discipleship requiring perseverance, suffering, and watchfulness. The discourse also shows Israel accountable for her rejection of the one God has sent. An exilic-like experience of judgment, even greater than the one already present with Rome, awaits the nation.

What triggered the discourse was a disciple's remark made in the temple courts about how glorious the temple buildings were (**v 1**). The mount itself was under major renovation at the time, as Herod was expanding the location. The work on the temple took eighteen months and the outer buildings eight more years, but work was still going on at the time of Jesus (Josephus, *Ant* 15.5–6). In fact, it continued until at least 62 CE, having started in 20 BCE. Josephus compared the temple's appearance to a snow-capped mountain rising in the midst of Jerusalem (*War* 5.184–226, esp. 222–23; also *Ant* 15.380–425). Large stones of 15 meters by 2.5 meters and weighing 420 to 600 tons provided the structure.[584] It was a massive structure. Jews felt secure in its presence.

Jesus' response was surprising (**v 2**), although such warnings had OT precedent (Jer 7:14; 26:6; Mic 3:12). He noted that from these great buildings not one stone would be left on another. The destruction predicted here took place in 70 CE. Josephus describes it in detail (*War* 6.271–373; 7.1–20). What seems not to have taken place is the return of the Son of Man, leading to all kinds of interpretive discussion. That Jesus could foresee this is not surprising. The nation was in covenantal unfaithfulness in his view, having rejected him as the one God had sent. The punishment for such, according to Deut 28–32, was the danger of exile or being overrun by the nations. If Rome did this, it would be in typical Roman ruthless style. Even Josephus notes senses of foreboding in the years before Rome finally crushed the city (Josephus *War* 4.128, 388). Destruction would come in its wake.[585] The fact the temple was going to be destroyed also did not bode well for Jerusalem or the nation.

The prediction of the destruction of such a sacred site piqued the curiosity some of the disciples as they moved past the temple to the

---

[584] Evans, *Mark 8:27–16:20*, 299.
[585] Hooker, *Mark*, 304, regards such a prediction as authentic. Evans, *Mark 8:27–16:20*, 295–98, notes that the lack of mention of the devastating fire of the destruction and other lack of detail suggest this is not a prophecy after the fact, but point to authenticity.

Mount of Olives. They sensed that Jesus was speaking about very important events, since the temple was such a sacred site. Peter, James, John, and
Andrew were with him at the Mount of Olives and asked him two questions (vv 3-4): (1) when will these things be, and (2) what will be the sign
they are about to be completed? Stein summarizes these two questions as
asking about the time and the sign.[586] The location of the Mount of Olives
was often associated with judgment (Ezek 11:23; 43:2; Zech 14:3-4). The
wording even echoes Zech 14:4 (Mark: Mount of Olives, opposite the
temple; Zechariah: Mount of Olives, to the east of Jerusalem). The mount
lay to the east of the temple mount, providing a stunning look down on the
spectacle. As is common in Mark, it is an inner circle that hears the
teaching, though here Andrew is added to the more common threesome
of Peter, James, and John. They sensed that something this catastrophic
had to have significance, so they wanted to know what would augur its
arrival. In asking about "these things," there is a hint that there must be
something more to this than the destruction. Jesus' response confirms that
suspicion. In asking for "the" sign, they request an indicator that will tell
them, "This is it." Jesus will give many indicators that the time is approaching, but the key indicators are found in a shameful act in the temple and the
catastrophic cosmic signs that come with the Son of Man's return. All else
is preparatory.

Jesus begins a series of indicators, which point to the event but are not
"the sign." The list leads up to the remark about abomination in Mark 13:14.
The first indicator is that many will come in the name of Jesus claiming to
be the one (vv 5-6). They are not to be misled by these messianic pre-
tenders, though many will be. So they are to beware not to be misled by
such claims. The idea of taking heed or paying attention runs throughout
the discourse (Mark 13:9, 23, 33, 35, 37). They are not to fall into the trap of
thinking another brings the program of God. The fact that Jesus is facing
death and will be absent leads into this possibility.

The claim "I am he" is a claim to be Messiah or to bring deliverance in
God's program, perhaps at Jesus' instruction. However, the one fulfilling
that role has already been announced along with the kingdom program
that comes with it. Jesus and no one else brings this deliverance, even with

---

[586] Stein, *Mark*, 590. He also notes that Mark spends much time on the destruction, while
Matthew looks more to the end. Luke follows Mark in this emphasis. What is being set
up is a kind of pattern prophecy, or typology, where the time of the destruction and the
time of the end mirror each other in many ways.

his upcoming departure. So they are not to be led astray by such claims.[587] They are to ignore them. In an ironic way, Jesus is using apocalyptic rhetoric to dampen some apocalyptic fervor that events might drum up. Warnings about such potential deception are common to end-time teaching in Judaism as well as among those who responded to Jesus (CD 5:20; 1QH 4[12]:7, 16, 20; *T. Moses* 7:4; Acts 20:29–30; 2 Thess 2:9–12; 1 John 2:18, 22; 4:1–4; 2 Pet 2:1; 2 John 7; Rev 13:14; 19:20; *Did.* 16:4; *2 Apoc. Bar.* 70:2).[588]

The second set of indicators Jesus notes are about national conflicts, wars and rumors of wars, political chaos (**vv 7–8a**). Jesus says not to be alarmed. 2 Thess 2:2 shows the tone of this verb in this kind of a chaotic context. Such things must happen. Such conflict should not throw them off or disturb them. Rome was full of conflict, both locally and with some of their neighbors, like the Parthians with whom they fought in 36–37 CE and the civil war after Nero died in 68 CE. The term used here for "must be" is *dei*, often used of something in God's plan (also in v 10; Mark 8:31; 9:1; see Dan 2:28–29 LXX for this use of the verb; especially prevalent in Luke-Acts). Prophetic Jewish texts on the end times are full of such descriptions of end-time events (*1 En* 99:4; *2 Bar* 27:5; *4 Ezra* 13:31; 15:15; note also Isa 8:21; 13:13; 14:30; 19:2; Jer 23:19; 51:46; Ezek 5:12; Hag 2:6; Zech 14:4).[589] These things are not the end, but chaos will precede the temple's destruction and acts against it. That is still to come. So this is another indicator that moves us toward the end but is not its sign. Nation will rise against nation and kingdoms against each other. When things got difficult with Rome, these served as words of encouragement that God was still in control and had a plan.

Everything about what Jesus is saying argues that the disciples are already in the *eschaton*, the last days, and moving toward its completion. The destruction of the temple and the movement toward it is included in this preparatory period.

A third indicator involves earthquakes and famines (**v 8b**). Such events were common in the first century: Jerusalem in 67 CE (Josephus, *War* 4.286–87), Philippi had one (Acts 16:26), Pompeii (a minor one in 62 CE

---

[587]   Evans, *Mark 8:27–16:20*, 306, notes several such deliverance or revolutionary figures in the run-up to the temple's destruction in 70 CE (Judas the Galilean, Simon of Perea, Athronges, Menahem, Simon bar-Giora; see Josephus, *Ant* 17.273–84; *War* 2.56–65, 2.433–48; 4.503–44). It is figures like these that Jesus may have in mind. They are messianic-like.

[588]   Marcus, *Mark 8–16*, 874–75.

[589]   Taylor, *St. Mark*, 505.

that partially destroyed the city before the more famous, permanently destructive one in 79 CE), Herculaneum in 62 CE, and Laodicia in 61 CE. There was a famine in the forties under Claudias (Acts 11:28; Josephus, *Ant* 3.320; 20.101).[590] Jesus has given three indicators so far, but none are the sign; none stop God's program. Jesus simply says these are the beginning of birth pangs. The picture is of a process of birth that is just at its start, another prophetic theme (Isa 13:8; 26:17; Jer 4:31; 6:24; 13:21; 22:23; 49:22; 50:43; Hos 13:13; Mic 4:9–10).

A fourth event is persecution. Now Jesus gets more personal and points attention to events that will impact the disciples directly (**v 9**). Disciples will have to watch out for themselves. The present imperative *blepete* looks to a constant watchfulness. They will be given over to councils, beaten in the synagogues, and stand before governors and kings. Matt 10:17–22 discusses this persecution and family betrayal in a pre-Jerusalem missionary call context, whereas Luke 12:11–12 leaves it to itself in yet a third context. Jesus discussed such suffering regularly. They need to be prepared for it. The councils are civil boards that could be Jew or Gentile (Acts 4–5; 17:6–9; 19:35–41).[591] Synagogues look to Jewish persecution, whereas governors and kings look to persecution tied to the Romans. The Book of Acts portrays several such events, especially involving Peter, John, and Paul (Acts chap. 4, 12:1–3; chaps. 22–28). The expectation is this will not be avoidable. They will be witnesses to them on account of Jesus. They will represent him even as they face public rejection and questioning. The expression "to them" could mean "against them," but the stress on the call of what the disciples face means that their faithfulness is in view, not vindication. That means the expression is likely positive. The hope was to draw people to Jesus as the Gospel must go out into the whole world.

So a fifth element is that the Gospel must go out into all of the world, and be preached to all nations (**v 10**). Gentile mission was foreseen in the OT (Isa 42:6; 49:6, 12; 52:10; 60:6; Ps 96) and Judaism (*Ps Sol* 8:17, 43; 11:1).[592] This also will precede the destruction and return. The expression here looks to a breaking out of the Gospel into the world, much like Paul affirms has taken place in Col. 1:6 and 23 (Rom 1:8; 10:18; 15:19; 16:26).

---

590 France, *Mark*, 512.
591 Evans, *Mark 8:27–16:20*, 309.
592 Lane, *Mark*, 461–62, notes this in contending for the authenticity of the remark, as some see this remark as a diversion from the theme of verses 9 and 11. Jesus knew the word of the kingdom was for the world and that word would get out despite the pressure.

This dissemination of the Gospel will come with pressure, so when those sharing the message are arrested or handed over to trial, one might be worried (**v 11**); but that is not necessary (1 Pet 4:14). Instead the Spirit will give one what to say (Acts 4:13). That is what should be shared. The Spirit's presence means there is no need to be anxious about what to say. John 14–16 makes a similar point about the provision of the Paraclete. Brothers will betray brothers to death (**v 12**).[593] Children will act against parents, leading to their death. Divided families were also discussed by Matt 10:35–36 and Luke 12:52–53 in an earlier missions context.[594] Here the allusion is to Mic 7:6, and another common Jewish theme (*1 En* 100:1–2; *Jub* 23:19; *4 Ezra* 6:24; *3 Bar* 4:17). Opposition will result in martyrdom. Some will see faith as betrayal and act against believers.

In a hyperbole, Jesus says all will hate disciples because of Jesus' name (**v 13**). It may refer to all levels of society, but clearly it is not every single human, as some do believe. Tacitus in his *Annals* 15.44 notes how Christians in Rome are "a class hated for their abominations" during the persecutions of Nero. Calling people to be accountable to God, even where grace is being highlighted, is not popular. The one who endures to the end, the faithful one, the one who kept watch while being aware of what is coming: that one will be saved. The end here is not the eschatological end but the end of one's journey, whether it involves suffering or death. The pressure and rejection the church faces for the Gospel is no surprise and should not be surprising to anyone who comes to faith. The calling is to be prepared for it and trust God in his program. There is no "exemption from adversity."[595] Be faithful.

The sign of the temple's destruction, and even the end, is the abomination of desolation standing where he ought not be (**v 14**). A masculine participle (*estēkota*) for standing, even though it modifies a neuter noun (*to bdelygma*), points to a person as a part of the indicator. This is why the translation reads, "standing where he ought not be." This act is a key indicator that things have really changed. So Jesus is now giving a sign that tells those present to act versus not being concerned. They also "see" (**v 14**) versus merely "hear" (**v 7**).[596] Now is the time to respond.

---

[593] The giving up of one's life in Mark 8:35–36 fits here, as one must be willing to give up one's life and face rejection if one accepts the Gospel. That may include isolation from family. Other such warnings include Mark 6:11; 8:15, 17; and 10:30.

[594] That text has a parallel in *Thomas* 16.

[595] Edwards, *Mark*, 395.

[596] Stein, *Mark*, 602.

The desolation is an allusion to Dan 9:27 and 12:11 LXX, so that the reader of the Gospel is called to understand the allusion, see the connection, and act. This is likely a parenthetical narrative remark from Mark or his source, not an utterance of Jesus, who is speaking and has no readers.[597] The picture of this pattern is from Antiochus Epiphanes in the holy place setting up an altar to Zeus in 168 BCE, desecrating the temple (1 Macc 1:54, 59; 2 Macc 6:2; also Dan 8:13; 11:31). Abomination deals with issues that reflect the presence of idolatry (Deut 29:17; 1 Kings 11:5; 7; 2 Kings 23:13, 24; Isa 66:3; Jer 4:1; 7:30; Ezek 5:11).[598] The desecrator stands where he should not be. In 70 CE, this kind of act was seen in Titus' visit to the temple (Josephus, *War* 6.260) or the Zealots falsely appointing Phanni High Priest (*War* 4.163, 182–83, 377–79, 413), but nothing really fits exactly.[599] When Titus came, people fled into the city for protection, not to the hills. Moreover, when he entered the temple it was already destroyed. The satirical act of choosing a clown, Phanni, as high priest is hardly likely. We may have a patterned activity here, so the final desecration is yet to come with the antichrist described in Daniel as part of a final rebellion that itself is like many Temple-desecrating events that have come before it (2 Thess 2:3–4).[600]

It will be a terrible and dangerous time. No one should stay in Jerusalem. Those in Judea are to flee to the mountains. It is important to note that a siege like we had in 70 CE does not fit because that would be fleeing the city into the hands of the enemy, and there was plenty of time to flee given the gradual approach of the Romans.[601] Hills were seen as a place of refuge in the OT (Gen 14:10; Jer 16:16; Ezek 7:14–23; 1 Macc 2:28). The one on the roof is not to come down and get anything out of the house (v 15). The one in the field will not have time to get his cloak (v 16). There is no time to gather

---

[597]   Edwards, *Mark*, 396.

[598]   Evans, *Mark 8:27–16:20*, 318.

[599]   Evans, *Mark 8:27–16:20*, 319. The suggestion of this being about Caligula's order to put up a statue of him as a deified figure is not likely, as it was never carried out and so the abomination never took place; Josephus, *War* 2.184–203. For a defense that events tied to 70 CE are in view, in contrast to what I am arguing, France, *Mark*, 522–28. Stein, *Mark*, 603, notes eight suggestions for what this is, and opts for Phanni. We have highlighted the more common suggestions, and opt for an ultimate eschatological event also mirrored in an act like that of Titus and Antiochus, because no event in 70 CE exhausts the picture.

[600]   So Edwards, *Mark*, 398–99.

[601]   Hengel, *Studies in the Gospel of Mark*, 16–18, who uses the observation to argue that Mark is not writing after 70 CE.

anything to escape; it will be like running to high ground in the face of a tsunami.

It will be hard for those pregnant or those nursing children (**v 17**). How judgment endangers children is an OT theme (Deut 32:25; 2 Kings 8:12; 15:16; Jer 44:7 Lam 2:11; 4:4 Hos 13:16; Amos 1:13; Ps 137:9). The remark has a conceptual parallel (Luke 23:28–29). What is normally a blessing is now a curse. One is to pray it will not be in winter (**v 18**), probably because escaping will be harder in harsher weather and with swollen wadis blocking the way.

The tribulation (*thlipsis*) will be unprecedented, unlike anything that has happened or will happen (**v 19**). The allusion to Dan 12:1 points to the end of the age with the general resurrection following in 12:2–3. These allusions to the unprecedented degree of suffering and to Dan 12 are part of what suggests that the destruction of the temple is also a pattern event for something still to come at the end. The risk to all flesh is about more than people in Jerusalem. The end is being described.[602]

Only God cutting those days of suffering short will result in people being spared (**v 20**). The verbs in this part of the discourse are aorists, expressing as certain what is still future, like a Semitic prophetic perfect.[603] This picture of great suffering is yet another theme of Jewish apocalyptic literature (*T. Moses* 8:1; 1QM 1:11–12; 1 *En* 80:2, 4; *4 Ezra* 4:25–26; 7:27; *3 Bar* 9; 4Q385 3:3–5 [=*Pseu Ezek*]).[604] God cuts the days short for the sake of the elect. He is not literally cutting the days short, but his plan mercifully does not allow the violence to fully play out. He acts to stop it. Vindication comes.

During this time, some will claim to have spotted the Christ (**v 21**), as earlier in verses 5–7. The detail points to the mirroring of the end with earlier events.[605] Such claims are not to be believed. False messiahs and prophets are coming (Luke 17:23; Matt 24:26–27; 2 Thess 2:2; *Thomas* 113). They will even perform signs and wonders that will deceive, even the elect if that is possible – an expression that is rhetorical and points to its power to deceive. (**v 22**). Warnings about false prophets have OT roots (Deut 13:1–5; 18:18–22). This is why one must watch and stay alert (**v 23**). Jesus notes that he has told them what they need to know ahead of time

---

[602] In contrast, France, *Mark*, 527–29, contends that these descriptions are stock phrases for terrible suffering and should not be pressed as pointing to the end.
[603] Marcus, *Mark 8–16*, 893–94.
[604] Evans, *Mark 8:27–16:20*, 323, also sees the influence of Isa 60:21–22 in this theme.
[605] Collins, *Mark*, 613.

(Mark 13:21–27). Jesus clearly is discussing the end beyond the destruction in a new phase of eschatological activity.[606]

Then comes the return, after that time of tribulation (**vv 24–25**). It will be accompanied with catastrophic cosmic signs: a darkened sun, a dimmed moon, stars falling, and powers in heaven shaken. The return is a creation shattering, creation altering, event, a cosmic entry into the affairs of humanity. The lights are going out on the current cosmic order. "God's appearance does not destroy the cosmos; it frightens it."[607] The language is typical of such judgment scenes, but it should not be reduced to only metaphor. Hooker notes that famines and earthquakes were already described in verses 6–8, so something more is in view here.[608] The return brings significant change to the creation's structure and the way God runs it.

No one will need to look for the return of the Son of Man, because when it comes it will be obvious. Such language about the sun and moon is also common in the OT (Isa 13:10; see also Ezek 32:7; Joel 2:10; 2:31; 3:15; Amos 8:9).[609] Language from Isa 34:4 also speaks of stars falling (also Judg 5:5; Ps 18:7; 114:7; Amos 9:5; Mic 1:4; Nah 1:5; Hab 3:6; *T. Moses* 10:1–5; *1 En* 57:2; Rev 6:12–13; 8:10).[610] Yet again standard OT language is present to describe the events leading to the end.

What they will see is the Son of Man arriving among the clouds with great power and glory (**v 26**). Jesus used Daniel 7:13 to describe the coming of the Son of Man. In that passage, one "like a son of man" receives the authority to judge from the Ancient One and rides the clouds, a figure reserved for God or the gods in the Old Testament (Exod 14:20; 34:5; Num 10:34; Ps 104:3; Isa 19:1). Daniel 7 pictures the Son of Man receiving authority from God to execute judgment; in this passage, he is coming to earth to exercise that power. This is not merely a reference to the church's authority nor to the destruction in 70 CE.[611] It is about setting up the

---

[606] What is harder to be sure of is whether verses 14–20 are only of the destruction or of the end, or whether they involve a mirroring of both periods pointing to destruction and the end simultaneously. We suspect a mirroring looking ultimately to the end because some of the features do not match 70 CE.

[607] So Evans, *Mark 8:27–16:20*, 329.

[608] Hooker, *Mark*, 318–19, calls it "more than metaphorical, less than literal." Cosmic disruption seems to be the point.

[609] Lane, *Mark*, 475.

[610] Evans, *Mark 8:27–16:20*, 328.

[611] Contra France, *Mark*, 530–31, 535–36. Everything about the destruction of the temple in these verses as expounded by France is simply imported by not paying sufficient attention to the shifts in the passage and lack of contacts to 70 CE that have been

kingdom's consummation. Who is the "they" who see? This is not clear. It is at the least those who are judged, as often in Judaism it is they who see, when they encounter judgment and justice (*1 En* 62:2–11; *Sib Or* 3.556–57, 693; Wis 5:2; *4 Ezra* 7:78–86; *Apoc Elijah* 35:17; Rev 11:12).[612] These events picture "the doom of the dark side."[613] It may also be general. Those who are present when it happens will see the Son of Man. It will not be able to be missed (note the contrast to vv 21–22 – there will be no need to point out his presence). The center of God's presence will reside in the Son of Man.[614] In other words, when justice finally comes with the Son of Man, no one will miss it and all will experience it, either for good or ill, depending on how they have perceived the one God has sent.

With him are the angels who gather the elect from every direction under heaven and earth (**v 27**; see Deut 30:3–4; Ps 50:3–5; Isa 11:11; 43:6; 66:8; Jer 32:37; Zech 2:6, 10; Tob 14:10; *1 En* 62:13–14; *Ps Sol* 8:28; 11:1–4; 17:28). God's deliverance has come.

Jesus now summarizes with a parable, that is, an extended simile. When a fig tree starts to show its leaves, one can know that summer is near (**v 28**). The fig trees would have been at this point of budding, as it was Passover season. March and April will move into the full bloom of May and June. A second parable on faithfulness and accountability appears in verse 34. The fig tree picture points to the vindicating harvest of believers to come. So when one sees the start to these things, one can know God's plan is unfolding and approaching.[615]

So when one sees these things happening, one can know he is near, at the door (**v. 29**). Standing at the door is a figure for coming to judge and redeem (Luke 12:35–38; Rev 3:20), so he is near.[616] Jesus then declares that

---

noted. The destruction came earlier in the discourse; see Evans, *Mark 8:27–16:20*, 328–29, and especially Stein, *Mark*, 613–15, who argues that how the rest of the NT uses this language dictates this imagery is about the end.

[612] Marcus, *Mark 8–16*, 904. This also fits Jesus' reply in Mark 14:62, where the Jewish leaders see the Son of Man. Marcus also suggests that spiritual evil power is in view. This may help to explain the cosmic imagery.

[613] Edwards, *Mark*, 403.

[614] The corollary often tied to this affirmation that the temple is replaced is another idea read into the passage. The temple is destroyed earlier. The question of whether it is seen as coming back is open and is not decided in this text. If, in other NT texts, the antichrist desecrates the temple at the end, it is implicit that it exists at the end.

[615] Evans, *Mark 8:27–16:20*, 334, connects it to the beginning of birth pangs, in verse 8.

[616] Stein, *Mark*, 618, argues for "it" is near, referring to the destruction of Jerusalem, which is possible given "these things" as a near antecedent. The issue is whether to see the image or the sentence as pointing to the exact sense.

this generation will not pass away until all these things take place (**v 30**). It is less than clear whether "these things" refer to the beginning of the discourse and the false claimants (the things that are budding) or to the things that complete it, such as the abomination and especially the cosmic signs. Probably the latter events are included ultimately, but a stress exists on the earlier events because the appearing of the Son of Man at the end is portrayed as obvious, as signaled by cosmic indicators.[617] In addition, the emphasis is on the signs that let one know that the end is near, not on the timing of the end. So the nearness is related especially to those events coming before the end. This points to events leading to the temple's destruction in verses 5–13.

The expression "this generation" is much discussed and has produced a host of views. The term itself can refer to (1) a specific generation, which might extend forty years or so; (2) a given age, speaking of a broader period; or (3) a given group of people (ethnic or, more commonly, ethical), such as a nation or a righteous or wicked generation (BDAG 191–192, where the "wicked" generation is discussed in point 2). If one reads the term as temporal, then all these events did not occur for that generation, as there was no return (unless one equates the return with the temple's destruction).[618] Other views exist that do not see an erroneous prediction here: (1) The generation referred to is the one that sees the final abomination. Once that climactic event takes place, everything follows quickly. The generation is that of the final great tribulation. (2) Taking the term ethically, it refers to the "righteous" generation and points to vindication. The problem with this is that this ethical sense is rare (Ps 23:6; 111:2 LXX). (3) The term could refer to the more common ethical sense of "wicked" generation, so that the point is that wickedness will remain until judgment comes. It seemingly states the obvious, but that may be to reassure.[619]

---

[617] As Hooker, *Mark*, 320, notes, verse 29 cannot refer to verses 26–27 because they are the "climax to the period of waiting." Also Edwards, *Mark*, 404, makes this point, seeing the allusion to verses 5–13. In contrast again is France, *Mark*, 538, who sees verses 14–22 in view. Marcus, *Mark 8–16*, 911, contends that "these things" in verse 29 are the events leading to temple destruction, while "all of these things" in verse 30 are to everything. So when one sees the early indicators, one can know the end is near, but when the heavens shake, one can know it has come. It is hard to be sure that there is such a distinction.

[618] France, *Mark*, 501–502, argues for the destruction, while Hooker, *Mark*, 321, sees verses 5–27 in view and takes the prediction as wrong on this point.

[619] Evans, *Mark 8:27–16:20*, 335, says "perhaps" for this view. Mark 8:38, Matt 12:39–41 and 45 have this force but are clear in using the qualifying adjective *evil* or *adulterous* with *generation*. The suggestion is that this idea is alluded to by the term *generation* alone. The expression "crooked generation" is similar in force (Matt 17:17; Luke 9:41).

(4) An ethnic use tied to Israel, like one sees in Luke 16:8, is sometimes put forward, so the point is that Israel will be preserved. But this is a very rare use of the term as well. Luke 16:8 may have such a use with the clear qualifier "their own" to make this sense clear, but it also may be only a temporal reference to the generation of a given time period, and not of a particular race. So, even the existence of the category is unclear. (5) The phrase "all these things" actually describes the indicators pointing to the end, and not the end itself. So the current temporal generation will see those signs (the events tied to 70 CE).[620] They guarantee the rest of the events are in view because the end events are in the process of unfolding, and the end is the goal of all the signs.

Of these views, the first, third, and fifth are all possible. Either the first or the fifth is more likely. Either the signs of the end, once abomination takes place, happen within a generation of time, or the signs pointing to the end leading to the temple's destruction in 70 CE (and guaranteeing the end) take place within a generation. Because we are dealing with mirrored events (the temple destruction in 70 CE and the end), it is hard to know which side of the pattern Jesus is highlighting and whether or not they parallel each other.[621] Of the two options, the one looking to the temple destruction that came in 70 CE is slightly more likely, provided one recalls that this near event is a mirror for the end and a prophetic indicator of what is to come at the end. For a more temporal reference is that Mark's use of "this generation" elsewhere is a reference to contemporaries (Mark 8:12 [twice]; 8:38; 9:19).[622]

He assures them with the remark that heaven and earth will pass away, but what he has said will not (v 31, see Isa 40:7–8). Jesus is certain the temple will be destroyed and the Son of Man will return to gather the elect in what will be very difficult times. This is said emphatically with *ou mē*.

In saying the events are close, he goes on to say that no one knows the day or hour, not the angels, not even the Son, but the Father alone (v 32). Jesus' remark on claiming ignorance on this important point was so unusual that it caused a measure of controversy in the early church. There is evidence that it was so controversial that a few later copyists of

---

[620] Witherington, *Mark*, 348; Evans, *Mark 8:27–16:20*, 337.
[621] Interestingly, in the overall telling of the discourse, Matthew 24 highlights events of the end in his rendering, while Luke 21 gives more attention to the near term *fulfilment*. This can be seen even in the way the opening questions by the disciples in the versions read as Matthew refers directly to the end, while Mark and Luke do not.
[622] Lane, *Mark*, 480.

the parallel in Matthew 24:36 omitted it.[623] Acts 1:7 makes a similar point about the Father knowing. In limiting Jesus' knowledge, it points to authenticity, as the early church is unlikely to have created this saying.[624] Lane speaks of God not delegating this knowledge to the Son as he lives in incarnation in dependence on the Father.[625]

So they must watch out and stay alert (**v 33**). Just as Jesus began his reply with a call to be on watch in verses 5 and 9, so he ends it with a double call. The call to be alert and watch out has run through the entire discourse (also in vv. 23, 33, 35, 37). One is to be aware of what God's program is and stay faithful, keeping an eye on what is taking place, for one does not know when the time will come.[626] One is not to try to figure out when the end is, as Jesus just said that cannot be known but is the business of the Father; one is simply to watch and be ready, knowing that chaos will come, but so will judgment and God's program with the return of the Son of Man. Other parts of the NT reflect this expectation (Titus 2:13; 1 Cor 16:22; Matt 6:10; 1 Thess 4:18; 2 Tim 4:8; the book of Revelation, esp. chaps. 19–22).[627]

Jesus closes with a final call to stay alert, having made the exhortation three more times in these final verses (vv 34, 35, 37). He compares it to servants in a household who are given responsibility and a doorkeeper who is to be alert for when the master of the house returns (**v 34**). The door-keeper's responsibility was to protect the home and allow those who came at night to enter.[628] This is a short version of an image we see also in Luke 12:35–40 and Matt 24:45–51. Just the core image of being ready is used. Because none of them knows whether the return will be at evening, at midnight, at the rooster crow (dawn), or at daybreak, all are to stay alert so

---

[623] Only X and some vulgate manuscripts in Mark lack it. In Matthew, ℵ¹, L, W, f¹, vg, and syr lack it. Luke lacks the remark entirely.

[624] The claim that Jesus did not speak openly of himself as the Son, as noted by Hooker, *Mark*, 323, ignores that he did speak of God as Father, an unusual emphasis, and fails to note that Jesus is more overt in his public acts and declarations in this final stage of his ministry (entry and Mark 12:6 – Beloved Son; 14:61–62 – positive reply to being called "Son of the Blessed"; also in Matt 11:27=Luke 10:22).

[625] Lane, *Mark*, 482; France, *Mark*, 544; while Marcus, *Mark 8–16*, 914, opts for taking on the limits of human existence.

[626] Hooker, *Mark*, 323, argues that this end section on keeping watch does not fit with the discourse because it implies that no signs come with the end. There is a difference between being told to keep watch because an event is approaching and being told one need not be concerned because there is no way to know exactly when it will take place. The exhortation prevents indifference by noting that one cannot know exactly when the end will occur.

[627] Stein, *Mark*, 625.

[628] Collins, *Mark*, 618.

that[629] the master does not find disciples asleep when he comes back (vv 35–36).[630] Jesus uses the second-person plural here (v 37). He is speaking to all of them as a group. The call is to keep looking and yet do what God has called you to do in the meantime. There is to be no "dereliction of duty."[631]

14:1–72 Jesus Prepares His Disciples for His Death as Judas Betrays Him and the Jewish Leadership Examines Him, Finding His Claim of Divine Support and Rule Blasphemous

14:1–2 *The Leadership Seeks to Arrest Jesus Secretly but Fear the People*

14:1 It was two days before the Passover and the Feast of Unleavened Bread, the chief priests and scribes were trying to find a way to arrest Jesus secretly so they might kill him.

14:2 For they said, "Not during the feast, lest there be a riot among the people."

This opening unit is actually three scenes that reflect Mark's sandwich style. We have a summary scene on the leaders' desire to arrest and kill Jesus in Mark 14:1–2, the anointing of Jesus for his death in Mark 14:3–9, and the betrayal of Judas, returning to the theme of the movement to Jesus' death in Mark 14:10–11. The parallels to Mark 14:1–2 are Matt 26:1–5, Luke 22:1–2, and John 11:47–53. The parallels to the anointing are Matt 26:6–13 and John 12:1–8. The parallels for Judas' betrayal are Matt 26:14–16 and Luke 22:3–6. The juxtaposition contrasts the act of the woman with that of the leaders and Judas.

The leaders are reacting to Jesus' presence and want to stop him (Mark 3:6; 11:18; 12:12). It is two days before the combined feast of Passover (Exod 12:6–14) and Unleavened Bread (Exod 12:15–20), a feast known by either name, since the opening Day of Passover was followed by a week of celebration of Unleavened Bread (v 1; see 2 Chron 35:17; Jospehus *Ant* 17.203 notes how either term can be used for the whole).[632] It is likely a

---

[629] The use of *mē* in verse 36 is unusual. It introduces a purpose clause that is also negated (BDAG, 646, 2.b–so that . . . not).

[630] Evans, *Mark 8:27–16:20*, 341, notes how the disciples will fail at being alert at Gethsemane (Mark 14:32–42). These are the four Roman night watch points. Three of the watches are alluded to in Mark 14:17, 72 and 15:1.

[631] Evans, *Mark 8:27–16:20*, 341.

[632] Other texts on the Passover include Exod 12:21–51; Lev 23:4–5; Num 9:1–14; 28:16; Deut 16:1–7; on Unleavened Bread, Exod 13:6–10; 34:18; Lev 23:6–8; Num 28:16–25; Deut 16:3–4, 8.

Wednesday, given that Mark portrays the meal as a Passover meal that is on Thursday night, which for Jews counted as part of Friday, with the day starting at sunset when counted inclusively.[633]

The leadership has decided that Jesus must be removed. Jesus had predicted their opposition (Mark 8:31; 10:33). The only question they had was how to arrest him without causing a public riot (**v 2**). The prospect of riots meant that the Romans and other rulers took careful watch during this period (Josephus, *Ant* 17.213–15 notes the example of Archelaus in 4 BCE; also Acts 21:34 shows how easily a crowd could be stirred up about those following Jesus). The arrest has to be in secret or by cunning (so *en dolō*; BDAG, 256). Ironically, it is a stirred-up crowd that eventually convinces Pilate to give over Jesus later in Mark 15:11–13, but the leadership was not confident of such support at this earlier point. So the leadership thought an arrest would not be possible during the feast, when Jerusalem swelled to triple or more of its population, hosting pilgrims for the feast.[634] They may have feared the influx of outsiders from Galilee who would have been present.

14:3–9 Jesus Praises a Woman for Anointing Him for His Death

14: 3 **Now while Jesus was in Bethany at the house of Simon the leper, reclining at table, a woman came with an alabaster jar of costly pure nard perfume. After breaking open the jar, she poured it on his head.**

14:4 **But some who were present, becoming indignant, said to themselves, "Why this waste of expensive perfume?**

14:5 **For this perfume is able to be sold for more than three hundred silver coins and given to the poor." And they were rebuking her.**

14:6 **But Jesus said, "Leave her alone. Why are you bothering her? She has worked a good work for me.**

14:7 **For you will always have the poor with you and when you wish you are able to do good for them. But you will not always have me.**

---

[633] Technically, we may be somewhere between Tuesday sunset and Wednesday sunset if we are counting inclusively, as was done with the three days after Jesus' death to get to resurrection.

[634] Estimates vary as to how large Jerusalem got in these feast periods. A reasonable figure is somewhere in the 75,000–180,000 range, though 50,000–200,000 is sometimes noted; France, *Mark*, 548, notes Jeremias' estimate of 180,000; Jeremias, *Jerusalem in the Time of Jesus* (Philadelphia: Fortress, 1969), 77–84.

14:8 She did what she could. She anointed my body beforehand for burial. 14:9 Truly I say to you, wherever the gospel is proclaimed in the whole world, also what she has done will be told in memory of her."

This scene becomes another proclamation account. It also shows Jesus affirming a leper and a woman. The parallels are Matt 26:6–13 and John 12:1–8. Luke 7:36–50 is a distinct scene in a pre-Jerusalem setting involving a sinner, not Mary. Pharisees are present at that meal, but would be unlikely to be at a home associated with leprosy. John 12 places the event six days before Passover, so Mark may well have moved the event here for the contrast of what is taking place during this last week, enabling him to juxtapose this act with Judas' betrayal. John has it before the entry, which is likely to be correct.[635] With some events, the fact that they happened and their relationship to other events trumps giving a precise timeline.

Jesus is taking a meal at Bethany at the home of Simon the leper (v 3; Mark 11:11. 20 – Bethany was Jesus' home in Jerusalem). Given that we are at a meal, the leper is likely cured now and is better seen as a former leper. The detail is consistent with Jesus interacting with people on the edge of society. A woman takes a very expensive jar of nard perfume and anoints Jesus on the head (v. 4). John 12:1–3 names her as Lazarus' sister, Mary. Nard came from India.[636] Expensive perfume was held in expensive alabaster jars that lacked handles (Pliny the Elder, *Nat.* 13.3.19).[637] Such an anointing was left to kings and other prominent figures (2 Kings 9:6 – of Jehu; Exod 29:7; 1 Sam 10:1; Ps 133:2). As a sign of respect, it may have been a response to the opposition Jesus had been facing. "I acknowledge who you are," she is saying in her act. The use of nard over more normal oil for an anointing may be an indication of respect for the unique role Jesus has.[638] It is an anointing plus. The breaking of the jar is intentional and points to a full anointing. She offered it all, not just a few drops.[639] The perfume is dedicated to Jesus.

Those present are shocked, even angry about what they regard as a waste of money (v 4). Mark says it was some of the people, whereas Matthew 26:8

---

[635] Witherington, *Mark*, 366.

[636] Hurtado, *Mark*, 216.

[637] Lane, *Mark*, 492. It was probably a family heirloom.

[638] It is often objected against a messianic anointing that that requires oil, not nard, based on the OT examples; so Edwards objects, *Mark*, 416. The choice of a verb for pouring out (*katacheein*) versus anoint (*chriein*) also looks to this abundance.

[639] Edwards, *Mark*, 415, observes how contrastive this act is to the widow who gave just two lepta in Mark 12:44. Both are honored by Jesus, because the heart in both acts is the same, and that is the point.

says it was the disciples and John 12:4 singles out Judas. They would have preferred to sell the perfume and use the three hundred silver coins gained to care for the poor (v 5). This would have been around a year's wage, as we are discussing denarii (*denariōn*). The poor were often remembered at feasts like Passover (John 13:27–29; *m. Pesaḥ*9:11; 10:1).[640] On the surface, this is a fair critique; but the circumstances are not normal and change everything. This is a unique moment in which to honor someone sent by God; there will be time to care for the poor in the future.

So Jesus responds that they should stop bothering the woman (v 6). She has done a good work. The "good work" (*kalon ergon*) is a technical expression for an act of charity or kindness.[641] She is described like the virtuous woman of Prov 31:20 and 31.[642]

Jesus goes on to say that there will be other times to serve the poor (v 7), but that he will not be with them much longer. Jesus' remark about the poor comes from Deut 15:11. It goes on to say because the poor in Israel are present, one should have an open hand for their brothers.[643] Here, Jesus is not dismissive of the poor at all; he merely says the current situation is a unique circumstance.

Jesus' key observation is that she has anointed him for his death ahead of time (v 8). It probably was an act done in celebration of the feast and recognition that Jesus is the anointed one, but Jesus' messianism will drive him to die, and to die for others. So, in this office, she anoints him and Jesus ties it to his calling. The verb *murizō* is used only here in the NT and speaks of anointing a corpse (*m. Shab* 23:5 – anointing a body for burial as they wash it; BDAG, 661).[644] It is associated with the word *myrrh* and points to the perfume by referring to the gummy substance – not what we call myrrh – that gave off the smell, as the noun was used in verse 3 to describe the perfume.[645] She has honored him. What she has done will be remembered wherever the Gospel is preached (v 9).[646] This clearly implies that Jesus sees a life for himself after his death. The scene keeps the approaching

---

640   J. Jeremias, "Die Salbungsgeschichte Mc 14,3–9," *ZNW* 35 (1936): 77–82.
641   D. Daube, "The Anointing at Bethany and Jesus' Burial," *ATR* 32 (1950): 186–99.
642   Marcus, *Mark 8–16*, 936.
643   Hurtado, *Mark*, 232.
644   Marcus, *Mark 8–16*, 936, objects to a messianic anointing because this verb is used instead of *chrisai*, but *murizō* is used because of the connection to burial Jesus makes. It is the honoring that is the point. She is accepting him in the way he has come to Jerusalem.
645   Marcus, *Mark 8–16*, 934.
646   France, *Mark*, 555.

cloud of Jesus' coming suffering and death in front of us, but also of its being overcome. It pictures a woman sensitive to what is taking place in contrast to the others around Jesus. The approach of Jesus' death sets a tone for these events. Jesus' remark and reaction to the anointing underscores that point. The disciples should be appreciating what is taking place, but it is passing them by, as is often the case in Mark.

14:10–11 Judas Agrees to Betray Jesus

14:10 And Judas Iscariot, one of the Twelve, went to the chief priests that he might betray him.
14:11 When they heard this, they rejoiced and promised to give him money. And he sought an appropriate time to hand him over.

This scene is a simple summary report on Judas' decision to betray Jesus. It links back to Mark 14:1–2 and completes the sandwich. It also contrasts to the woman's response to Jesus. The parallels are Matt 26:14–16 and Luke 22:3–6.[647]

The leadership had decided there was nothing that could be done about Jesus during the feast. That was before Judas, one of the Twelve, came to them (**v 10**). He went to the chief priests to express his willingness to betray Jesus. An agreement was made with a promise of payment for the act (**v 11**). Matt 26:15 notes that the payment was thirty pieces of silver. So Judas looked for a time when Jesus could be handed over. The verb for "hand over" or "betray" (*paradidōmi*) runs through the chapter (Mark 14:11, 18, 21, 41–42, 44) and was in the earlier predictions (Mark 9:31; 10:33). Judas' act of betrayal is simply to find a good time to hand Jesus over. There is no indication of whether he shared what Jesus had taught with the leaders. Jesus had done enough public teaching to have raised concerns at that level for the leaders who had had opportunity to hear him. Still, it seems likely that the leaders would have asked Judas why he was doing this and that a discussion about Jesus' teaching would have followed.[648]

---

[647] Hooker, *Mark*, 331, calls the historicity of Judas' betrayal as "unquestioned." It would be too embarrassing to have invented this detail.

[648] Evans, *Mark 8:27–16:20*, 365, contends that Judas did share teaching, namely, the temple remark and Jesus' messianism, but both of those were public events (temple declaration of John 2 and/or synoptic parallels; triumphal entry of Mark 11), so they do not indicate inside information. Still, some discussion is likely, as the leaders probably had to determine if Judas' offer was genuine.

Jesus' death, then, is triggered by one of his own. Why Judas did it is not noted,[649] but the leaders could claim that one of his own turned him in. Jesus is a "righteous sufferer," and events are part of God's plan (Ps 41:9 – "my close friend has turned against me").[650] What happens to Jesus is the focus, not why his betrayer did it. With Mark now noting the betrayer in a narrative summary and death drawing even nearer, Jesus continues to prepare the disciples for what lies ahead.

14:12–31 Jesus Predicts His Death at a Meal, Announces the Betrayal, Commemorates His Coming Death for Many, and Predicts Peter's Denials

14:12 And on the first day of Unleavened Bread, when the Passover lamb is sacrificed, Jesus' disciples said to him, "Where do you want us to prepare so we can eat the Passover?"

14:13 He sent two of his disciples and told them, "Go into the city, and a man carrying a jar of water will meet you. Follow him.

14:14 Wherever he enters, tell the owner of the house, 'The Teacher says, "Where is my guest room where I may eat the Passover with my disciples?" '

14:15 He will show you a large upstairs room, furnished and ready. Make preparations for us there."

14:16 And the disciples went out and went into the city and found it just as he said to them, and they prepared the Passover.

14:17 And when it was evening, he came to the house with the Twelve

14:18 and reclining with them and eating, Jesus said, "Truly I say to you, one of you eating with me will betray me."

14:19 They began to be grieved, and one by one said, "Surely not I?"

14:20 He said to them, "One of the twelve, one who dips his hand with me into the bowl.

14:21 For the Son of Man will go as it is written about him, but woe to that man by whom the Son of Man is betrayed. It would have been better if he had never been born."

14:22 And while they were eating, he took bread, and after giving thanks he broke it, gave it to them, and said, "Take it. This is my body."

---

649 Disillusionment (Evans, *Mark 8:27–16:20*, 366) or greed (Matt 26:15; John 12:4–6) is often suggested; Stein, *Mark*, 636, notes options and says no clear indication exists. Both suggestions make sense and are possible. Neither is preferred. Luke 22:3 simply blames Satan entering Judas (also John 13:2, 27), again pointing to larger cosmic concerns behind these events.

650 Lane, *Mark*, 495.

14:23 And taking the cup and giving thanks, he gave it to them and they all drank from it.

14:24 And he said to them, "This is my blood, the blood of the covenant, that is poured out for many.

14:25 Truly I say to you, I will no longer drink the fruit of the vine until that day when I drink it new in the kingdom of God."

14:26 After singing a hymn, they went out to the Mount of Olives.

14:27 Then Jesus said to them, "You will all fall away, for it is written, *'I will strike the shepherd, and the sheep will be scattered.'*

14:28 But after I am raised, I will go ahead of you in Galilee."

14:29 Peter said, "Even if they all fall away, I will not."

14:30 Jesus said to him, "Truly I say to you, today – this very night – before the rooster crows twice, you will deny me three times."

14:31 But Peter even more said, "Even if I must die, I will never deny you." And all of them said the same thing.

This scene is the presentation of Jesus' last meal with his disciples, what is called the Last Supper. It involves the arrangement of the meal (vv 12–16), the announcement of Jesus' awareness that he is being betrayed (vv 17–21), the commemoration of his coming death for others (vv 22–26), and the prediction of Peter's denials (vv 27–31). It represents a series of pronouncements. The parallels are Matt 26:17–35 and Luke 22:7–23, 31–34, 39. It is clear that Luke has unique detail by looking at the verse list for parallels, just as John's Upper Room discourse has much independent material in an event that spanned the evening.

Mark notes that this conversation took place on the first day of the Festival of Unleavened Bread (v 12), reflecting the fact that Passover and Unleavened Bread were treated as one holiday season (Josephus, *War* 5.99). So, for Mark, the day is Passover night-day, when the Passover lamb was sacrificed.[651] By this time, the sheer thousands of lambs needing to be

---

[651] There is major discussion about whether in fact this was a Passover meal, as John 18:28 and 19:14, 31, 42 appear to have Jesus crucified as the Passover lambs are being slain (i.e., a day later). Either Mark has moved up the day and connected it to the season or John has tied the celebration of the eight-day feast to the sacrifice and celebration that opens it; so Lane, *Mark*, 498. The latter is more likely, thinking of events much like the way the Christmas season works for us. Hooker, *Mark*, 332–34, has an overview of the views and opts for John's timing. Her main reason is all the activity on a feast day, if Mark is followed. However, this underestimates the special circumstances Jesus' arrest created as well as getting access to Pilate for a quick action. France, *Mark*, 560, Evans, *Mark* 8:27–16:20, 370–72, and Witherington, *Mark*, 371, opt for Jesus moving up the meal a day intentionally. Though a moved-up Passover meal is quite possible, Lane's view is to be preferred. The shadow of the holiday season and meaning lingers across the week and

slaughtered meant the activity started on Passover eve (Philo, *Special Laws* 2.149; *m. Pes* 5:1; *Jub.* 49:10; Josephus, *War* 6.423; Philo, *Questions and Answers on Exodus* 1:11). For the details of a Passover meal, see *m. Pes* 10:1–7; other elements of procuring the sacrifice are in *m. Pes* 1:1–3. The fact that the meal is purposefully observed in Jerusalem points to a Passover meal, which had to be celebrated there (Deut 16:5–8).

The need to celebrate the meal causes the disciples to ask where they should prepare for the Passover meal. Jesus tells them to look for a man carrying a jar of water once they enter the city, who is going to meet them (v 13). He will seek them out. Since women normally did this, a man, though not completely exceptional, could stand out.[652] They are to follow him when he finds them. When they get to the house, they are to ask the owner for him, as "the Teacher," where his guest room is where he can have a Passover meal with his disciples (v 14). Elements of how this is done are like what we saw in Mark 11:1–6.[653] They will be shown a large room, furnished and ready, which is where they are to prepare for the meal (v 15). It is interesting that Jesus calls it "my" room. So, they went into the city and everything took place as he told them (v 16). They prepared the Passover, picking up the sacrifice at the temple, and then heading to the room. The holiday or sacrifice is mentioned four times in these verses on preparing the meal.

Jesus is completely aware of events. It is not said whether this was all predetermined or whether Jesus' word is all that was needed to secure the locale. To Mark, that is irrelevant. The key is that Jesus is aware and very much in control of the events that surround his disclosure about what is ahead. Nevertheless, it is likely there was some arrangement, given the detail on how to get to the house by a man known to be carrying a jar and Jesus' claim that the room was his.[654]

The meal comes next as, at evening on the 15th Nisan, they gather at the home for this feast meal, reclining as was common in this time for a meal (vv 17–18). Passover meals took place in Jerusalem at night (Exod 12:8; *m Pes* 10:1), whereas normal meals were earlier. Normally it was a family meal,

---

allows for the move either way. All of these issues are considered in detail by I. Howard Marshall, "The Last Supper," in Bock and Webb, *Key Events*, 541–60.

[652] Edwards, *Mark*, 421; See John 4. Marcus, *Mark 8–16*, 945, questions whether this is so unusual, noting that men did do this on occasion (Deut 29:10–11; Josh 9:21–27).

[653] Taylor, *Mark*, 536. The story should not be seen as a doublet. It is simply a stylized summary of two meeting arrangements; Evans, *Mark 8:27–16:20*, 370.

[654] Lane, *Mark*, 499; Witherington, *Mark*, 370–71, speaks of the possibility of a clandestine arrangement out of concerns for safety, also Hurtado, *Mark*, 220–21.

with parents sharing the story of redemption with children. It opened with a child asking, "Why is this night different from other nights (*m Pes* 10:4)?" Then the story is retold. It is likely such a meal had four courses and lasted until near midnight (*m Pes* 10:1–6, 9).[655] The four cups occur (1) with the preliminary course to bless the Passover day; (2) after an explanation of Passover and the singing of some of the Hallel psalms (Pss 113–118); (3) following the meal of lamb, unleavened bread, and bitter herbs; and (4) following the concluding portion of the Hallel. It is not clear where in the meal this exchange is, although bread is a part of the third course.

Jesus uses the occasion to discuss his death. First, he announces the betrayal (**v 18**). It will come from one of those at the table with him. The disciples react with grief and emotional distress (**v 19**). Each one says, "Surely not I." The interrogative (*mēti*) expects a negative reply. It shows disciples more concerned with where they fit and confident they would never betray Jesus than with what is taking place with him.[656] Matt 26:25 has Judas ask as well, with Jesus saying, "You have said so." In John 13:25–26, Jesus hands the morsel to Judas.

Jesus responds that it is one of the Twelve and one who dips his hand in the bowl with him (**v 20**). Mark leaves the culprit vague in this scene, but he has already made clear to his readers that it is Judas, so one should not make too much of this. Food was dipped twice at the Passover meal (*m Pesaḥ*10:4). The picture of one eating with me recalls the righteous sufferer of Ps 41:9 (John 13:18; a popular text, 1QH 5:23–24 [=13:23–25]).[657] Being handed over (*paradidōmi*) appears not only in this Psalm but also in Isa 53:6 and 12. The table shared one bowl of bitter herbs with this meal.[658] There is a disruption in what should be a moment of solemn fellowship. What happens to the Son of Man also is written about him (**v 21**; Mark 8:31; 9:12). Mark noted the betrayal when he introduced Judas (Mark 3:19; also 14:10–11). There is a divine program, but Jesus offers a woe against the one who commits this act of betrayal against the Son of Man (**v 22**). For that person, it would have been better if he had not been born. One can only wonder what Judas thought. Divine design and human accountability are side by side in Jesus' remarks.

Second, Jesus takes the bread as they are eating, gives thanks, and gives it to them (**v 23**). The thanks may well have blessed "the Lord our God,

---

[655] Lane, *Mark*, 501–502.
[656] Witherington, *Mark*, 373.
[657] Marcus, *Mark 8–16*, 950.
[658] Cranfield, *Mark*, 424.

Sovereign of the world, who has caused bread to come forth from the earth (*m Ber* 6:1)." He tells them to take the bread, as it is his body. Jesus is turning the meal into a fresh symbol for his just announced death by betrayal. Bread pictured redemption at the meal (*m Pes* 10:5) and affliction (Deut 16:3), but now it points to a new redemption in death. His sacrifice is food for life. Mark's version, like Matthew's, is short. Luke 22:19 adds "given for you," whereas Paul has "which is for you" (1 Cor 11:24). Aramaic would not have had the verb "is," but we are dealing with a summary of what was said and represented by the elements. On analogy with the Passover is the picture of death and the offer of the body the broken bread reflects.

The blessing over the cup would have been (**v 23**), "Blessed are You, O Lord, our God, King of the Universe, who creates the fruit of the vine (*m Ber* 6:1)." At the Passover, the third cup praised God for salvation brought to his people.[659] It was a communal cup, picturing shared participation. This may be where we are in the meal. For Jesus, the cup pictures the blood, namely, the blood of the covenant, poured out for many (**v 24**). These are shocking words for a Jew, as to drink blood was a forbidden act (prohibitions on drinking blood – Lev 3:17; 7:26–27; 17:14; John 6:52; *1 En* 98:11), but this is what, in part, points to symbolism here (1 Cor 10:16).[660] The allusion here is to Isa 53:11–12 (Mark 10:45). Luke 22:20 and Paul in 1 Cor 11:25 add that it is the new covenant (Jer 31:31) that is alluded to here, which is the point of a sacrifice pointing to the eschaton. Matt 26:28 speaks of "many for the forgiveness of sins." The language also recalls Exod 24:8, where the old covenant was established with the sprinkling of blood. One redemption compares to another. Representational sacrifice is in view (Lev 17:11). Such thinking is rich in Second Temple Judaism (4 Macc 1:11b; 6:28–29; 17:21b–22; 18:3–4; 2 Macc 7:33, 37–38; *T. Moses* 9:6b–10:1).[661] The claim the exact expression "blood of the covenant" is not possible in Aramaic overplays the text, in that we may well have a summary of a much more involved expression now liturgically simplified; some, however, do argue that even the exact expression is possible.[662]

---

[659] Lane, *Mark*, 506.
[660] Witherington, *Mark*, 375; Stein, *Mark*, 651.
[661] Evans, *Mark 8:27–16:20*, 390–91.
[662] France, *Mark*, 570; M. Casey, *Aramaic Sources of Mark's Gospel* (Cambridge: Cambridge University Press, 1998), 241, and "The Original Aramaic Form of Jesus' Interpretation of the Cup," *JTS* 41 (1990): 1–12.

Edwards details a few reasons why transubstantiation is not in view here.[663]

There is nerve and authority in what Jesus is doing here. Who has the right to completely change the imagery of a prescribed sacred rite by adding to it? To equate what he is doing with the core salvation act of Israel's history also says a great deal about the unique work of Jesus, as well as his right to speak forth a new core event.

Jesus' remarks end with the note that Jesus will not drink of the fruit of the vine until the day he drinks it new in the kingdom (v 25). He is refusing the fourth and last cup of the meal at this point. The work is not yet done. There will be more to come and then full celebration will be appropriate. This drinking to come is not an allusion to anything in the era of the church, but at the return and the consummation of the kingdom. Jesus foresees a full vindication (Heb 12:2). This may allude to the messianic banquet (Isa 25:6; 2 Bar 29:5–8; 4 Ezra 6:52; Matt 8:11; Luke 14:15; Rev 19:9; also at Qumran, 1QSa 2; 1QS 6). The group then closed with the Hallel Psalms (Ps 113–18, which in part 2 had pilgrims sing either from Ps 114 or 115 to the end; *m Pes* 5:7; 10:6–7 – notes a difference between Shammai [start with 114] and Hillel [start with 115] here) and headed for the Mount of Olives (v 26).

The final part of the meal scene has Jesus predict that the disciples will fail him and scatter (v 27). He cites Zech 13:7 and a picture of the shepherd being stuck and the sheep scattering to make the point. Jesus would go to the cross alone. That Zechariah passage depicts Israel's apostasy and pictures a strong condemnation, but also looks to the forming of a new people out of the reaction.[664] It foresees a period of testing out of which something better emerges.[665] The imperative of Zechariah is now put in the first-person singular (I will strike), as God is portrayed as acting against the shepherd.[666] God's plan includes this suffering. It is a part of Jesus' call. So

---

[663] Edwards, *Mark*, 426. The words "this is" come after the wine was taken and the demonstrative "this" (*touto*) is neuter, while if it referred to bread or wine it would have been masculine. The blood is what is said to be poured out. Hooker, *Mark*, 342, adds that the lack of protest from the disciples shows that they did not sense they were drinking Jesus' blood in violation of the Law.

[664] Hurtado, *Mark*, 232; see Zech 13:7–9. Marcus, *Mark 8–16*, 969, wonders if Isa 53:4, 6, and 10 are also in view (1 Pet 2:25) as he surveys the influence of Zech 9–14 on the early church, especially Matt 27. One recalls that Jesus' entry evokes Zech 9:9.

[665] Collins, *Mark*, 669–70.

[666] Hooker, *Mark*, 344. Evans, *Mark 8:27–16:20*, 400, defends its use by Jesus, noting that the church is unlikely to have created a remark where God acts directly against Jesus with the picture of a sword without him going there first. He also notes a parallel use at

the remark is a prediction observing that God is at work and a rebuke to the disciples' response. The disciples stumbled by taking offense over him. The verb is *skandalizō* (BDAG, 926). It was used of those who took offense or fell away (Mark 4:17; 6:3; 9:42, 43, 45, 47; 14:29).

But this abandonment is not permanent, as he says they will meet him in Galilee after he is raised (**v 28**). Interestingly, Mark does not narrate the realization of this other than to repeat the idea in Mark 16:7, but Matthew 28 does. Mark, however, has affirmed the reality of resurrection in the predictions. He lets the event speak for itself when it comes. One needs only to decide how one will respond to it. This verse is missing in the Fayyum papyrus Gospel fragment of Egypt, a third-century CE text, but surely is original.[667] Like Israel's exile, the scattering is temporary (Num 27:17; 1 Kings 22:17; 2 Chr 18:16; Ezek 34:8, 12, 15; Zech 10:2; Bar 4:26; *Pss. Sol.* 17:4, 21, 26–28). Regathering will follow.

Peter then denies that he will fall away (**v 29**). Jesus predicts that this very day, before the cock crows twice in the early morning, Peter will deny him three times (**v 30**).[668] In other words, the denial is coming by the time morning comes. Peter was insistent. He would not succumb to a denial, an anti-confession (**v 31**). The verb here (*aparneomai*) means to disown or refuse to acknowledge someone (BDAG, 97). He would die first before denying Jesus. For a third time in the Gospel, Peter misspeaks (Mark 8:31–33; 9:5–7). All the disciples echoed Peter's remarks. Jesus knows the disciples better than they know themselves. Jesus will go to his death on his own. Mark again shows Jesus to be very aware of the events and the storm gathering around him. In Mark, Jesus faces what is ahead with a clear sense of what is being done, why it is happening, and what is at stake.

14:32–42 As the Disciples Fail to Keep Watch, Jesus Submits to God's Will after Asking If the Cup Might Pass

14:32 And they came to a place called Gethsemane and he said to his disciples, "Sit here while I pray."

Qumran (CD 19:7–13). Edwards, *Mark*, 428, sees Peter as a key source for these Petrine exchanges.

[667] It is quite possible that the verse was omitted because of the tension a Galilean appearance placed on the call in Luke 24:49 to remain in Jerusalem and the picture of Acts that the church moved out in mission from the capital city.

[668] France, *Mark*, 579, contends on Petrine memory that Mark is the most detailed account here by noting a double cock crow. He sees the other Gospels as simplifying that detail.

14:33 He took Peter, James, and John with him, and became very troubled and distressed.

14:34 He said to them, "My soul is grieved, even to the point of death. Remain here and keep watch."

14:35 Going a little further, he fell to the earth and was praying that if possible the hour would pass from him.

14:36 He said, "Abba, Father, all things are possible for you. Take this cup away from me. Yet not what I will, but what you will."

14:37 Then he came and found them sleeping, and said to Peter, "Simon are you sleeping? Could you not stay awake for one hour?

14:38 Keep watch and pray that you may not fall into temptation. The spirit is willing but the flesh is weak."

14:39 He went away again and prayed the same thing.

14:40 And again coming, he found them sleeping, for their eyes were weighed down. And they did not know what to tell him.

14:41 He came a third time and said to them, "Are you still sleeping and resting? Enough. The hour has come. Look, the Son of Man is betrayed into the hands of sinners.

14:42 Get up, let us go. Look. The one who is betraying me is near."

This is another summary scene, where Jesus faces up one more time to what is ahead as he submits to God through prayer. The parallels are Matt 26:36–46, Luke 22:40–46, and John 18:1. Jesus goes to an area on the Mount of Olives known as Gethsemane (v 32), an orchard area in the Kidron Valley just to the east of Jerusalem's eastern wall. The name means "oil press" and points to an olive garden, as John 18:1 calls it. He goes there to pray and asks the disciples to sit and wait while he does so. The picture of Jesus struggling with what lies ahead is unlikely to be a created event, given how the church regarded Jesus and the fact that it is multiply attested (Heb 5:7).[669] At a place tied to victory (Zech 14:4), Jesus faces up to the difficult road of what is ahead.

Jesus takes Peter, James, and John with him (v 33). The inner circle is with him again for a key event (Mark 5:37; 9:2; 13:3). All three had made pledges of loyalty about his suffering (Mark 10:35–40; 14:29–31). Mark says candidly that Jesus is troubled and distressed, a hendiadys. The dual reference to distress makes it emphatic (*ekthambeō* – intense perplexity, BDAG, 303; *adēmoneō* – distress, BDAG, 19). Only Mark uses the first term

---

669 Hooker, *Mark*, 346, speaks to its core authenticity and notes that it is in tension with Mark's normal presentation that these events are a part of God's plan. In less likely views, the scene is a creation of Mark or the church, Collins, *Mark*, 673–75.

(Mark 9:15; 16:5–6), and the second term is rare in the NT (Matt 26:37; Phil 2:26). He confesses to them that his soul is deeply grieved, even to the point of death (v 34; Sir 37:2 – sadness unto death; 1QH 8:32; Heb 5:7).[670] This is yet a third term for distress (perilypos – BDAG, 802; Matt 26:38; Mark 6:26; Luke 18:23). The responses are very human, so he turns to God (Ps 42:5–6, 9; 55:4–5). He asks them to remain here and keep watch as he goes to pray. It is the third major prayer scene in Mark (Mark 1:35; 6:46).[671]

Going a little farther, he threw himself down to the ground and asked with an indirect summary that if it were possible, the hour would pass from him (v 35).[672] Still, the core request Mark cites directly (v 36). He opens with a double address as Father, first in Aramaic (abba) and then in Greek (ho patēr).[673] This is the only place Jesus notes this very personal reference to God. He notes that all things are possible with God and asks if the cup of this hour can be taken from him. The cup is one of judgment and wrath (Mark 10:38–39; Isa 51:17, 22; Ezek 23:32–34; Lam 4:21; Ps 11:6 [10:6 LXX]). The pain of experiencing God's judgment is terrifying, especially as a righteous sufferer. In these psalms, the petitioner is seeking vindication and expresses trust.[674] God's sovereignty and power are where Jesus starts. The pain later will lead him to cry out about why God has forsaken him (Ps 22:1 in Mark 15:34). The program he knows is ahead is what he brings up for discussion. But more importantly, he desires the Father's will be done, not what he himself desires. In saying this, Jesus submits to God's plan.[675]

When he returns, he finds the disciples with him asleep (v 37). It is late at night after a long, emotional day. Jesus asks Peter why he is sleeping. Could

---

[670] Stein, Mark, 660.

[671] Witherington, Mark, 378.

[672] To fall on the ground also points to intensity (Gen. 17:1–3; Lev. 9:24; Num. 14:5; 16:4, 22, 45; 20:6; Matt. 17:6; Luke 5:12; 17:16; 24:5; 1 Cor. 14:25); Stein, Mark, 661.

[673] The Aramaic also appears in Rom 8:15 and Gal 4:6. It is a term of relational closeness, but does not always mean "Daddy" as is sometimes said; J. Barr, "Abba Isn't Daddy," JTS n.s. 39 (1988): 28–47. It also is not correct that Jews never used this term for God (4Q460 5:5 [9 1:6]; 4Q372 1:16); Marcus, Mark 8–16, 978. Three elements echo the disciples' prayer of the Sermon on the Mount: Father, God's will be done, and not falling into temptation; Witherington, Mark, 379–80.

[674] France, Mark, 582–83.

[675] Marcus, Mark 8–16, 975–76, raises the question of how they heard the prayer if they were asleep, but nothing is said about at what point they slept, and the response of Jesus speaks of an hour having passed. The distance of a stone's throw in Luke 22:41 is several yards, but still could have been close enough to have been heard. A prayer in agony is unlikely to have been a whisper.

he not stay awake for an hour? They are not up to the moment yet again. Then he urges them to stay alert and pray not to fall into temptation (**v 38**). They need the strength that turning to God can provide, as he observes that the spirit is willing but the flesh is weak. It will take doing more than relying on their own strength to get through what is ahead well. Crisis demands vigilance.[676] Drawing near to God takes conscious effort. Jesus is still standing up to what he faces alone and is alone in approaching God faithfully.

A cycle ensues that is repeated twice more. Jesus goes to pray and he returns to find the disciples sleeping (**vv 39-40**). The stress is not on the content of the praying, as the second time it is simply noted that he prayed the same thing, and the third time he comes back with no mention of the prayer (**v 41**). It is the disciples' failure that is the point. They fail three times, an act anticipating Peter's three failures to come. The warning is that it is easy to neglect being dependent on God and not be prepared. The failure takes place because their eyes were "weighed down" (*katabarynō*), emphasizing that the flesh is weak (BDAG, 514). They could not answer why they were sleeping. It was embarrassing. They had not turned to God, as they had been urged to do.

Finally, Jesus ends the sequence with another question about sleep and resting, along with a simple declaration, either "enough," "finished," or "distant." The word used in the declaration (*apechō*) normally refers to the closing of an account or to be far from something. It is probably idiomatic here, meaning that time has run out or that the matter is now settled (BDAG, 103).[677] He notes that the hour has come (**v 42**). The Son of Man is betrayed into the hands of sinners, just as he had predicted in Mark 8:31, 9:31, and especially 10:33, where being handed over (*paradidōmi*) is specifically noted. He tells them to get up as his betrayer approaches. After time with God, Jesus is ready to face what is ahead, but the disciples are still catching up to what is taking place.

---

[676] Lane, *Mark*, 516.

[677] The word's meaning is difficult. Marcus, *Mark 8-16*, 981, and Evans, *Mark 8:27–16:20*, 416–18, prefer an allusion to distance, as the word in its common meaning can refer to being distant. Is it far away? And the implied answer is, "No, it is here." This is contextually harder and requires a touch of irony. The options the lexicon prefers (enough or finished), and we adopt, are contextually simpler, as they make sense in extending the word's meaning, but this use is much less attested. Stein, *Mark*, 664–65, opts for an allusion to Judas having been paid, but this is an abrupt shift in ideas, as the betrayer is seemingly introduced in a few sentences and not here.

14:43–52 Jesus Is Arrested as He Is Betrayed by Judas

**14:43 And immediately, while Jesus was speaking, Judas, one of the
Twelve arrived and with him a crowd armed with swords and clubs
from the high priests and scribes and elders.**

**14:44 The betrayer had given them a signal, saying, "Whomever I kiss is
he. Arrest him and lead him away securely."**

**14:45 When Judas arrived, he went up immediately to him and said
"Rabbi" and kissed him.**

14:46 They laid hands on him and seized him.

**14:47 One of those standing by drew his sword and struck the high priest's
slave, cutting off his ear.**

**14:48 And Jesus, replying, said to them, "Have you come with swords and
clubs to arrest me like you would an outlaw?**

**14:49 Each day I was with you, teaching in the temple courts, yet you did
not seize me. But this is so that the scriptures would be fulfilled."**

14:50 Then all the disciples left him and fled.

**14:51 A young man was following him, wearing only a linen cloth. They
tried to arrest him,**

14:52 but he ran off naked, leaving his linen cloth behind.

The arrest scene is told in a simple and direct manner. The parallels are
Matt 26:47–56, Luke 22:47–53, and John 18:2–11. As Jesus was speaking,
Judas, again identified as one of the Twelve, arrived (**v 43**). The connection
between Judas and Jesus is stressed because the betrayal is both shocking
and painful. With Judas was a crowd of people ready for a fight. They came
with swords and clubs, having been sent by the chief priests, scribes, and
elders. Mark 8:31 had predicted the leaders' involvement. Luke 22:47, 52 has
some accompany the group. John 18:3, 12 speaks of a cohort, which was
normally about 600 men. The threefold description of the leadership
reflects the makeup of the Sanhedrin, the ruling council. The crowd was
made up of temple guards, likely Levites and others in their employ.[678] It is
unlikely that the Romans were involved yet in an extensive way, although
John 18:12 notes a tribune's presence, perhaps to make clear that this was
not a revolt, but an internal Jewish matter. The posse was not sure what to
expect and was prepared. They are described more like a mob than an
official arrest party (also v 48).

---

[678] Lane, *Mark*, 524; Evans, *Mark 8:27–16:8*, 423; Josephus, *Ant* 20.181, 206–207 describes
their use in another setting. Josephus' description also gives the impression of hired
thugs.

Judas came and gave them a signal so all could focus on the right person (**v 44**). It is sometimes suggested that this means that Jesus was not well known, but the issues were that he may not have been well known to the guards, it was dark, and the way into the arrest needed to look like nothing unusual was taking place, as they did not know what the reaction would be. Judas's signal was that he would kiss Jesus, and call him "Rabbi," a normal greeting of respect (**v 45**). The appearance was to be that perhaps the group had simply run into Jesus. They would do nothing early on to cause initial alarm or reaction. The one Judas kissed was the one to arrest and take away under secure guard. The group was not interested in anyone else.

So Judas kissed Jesus, and those with the betrayer seized Jesus (**v 46**), just as Jesus had just predicted (Mark 14:41). Witherington calls it "the kiss of death."[679] Prov 27:6 says, "Excessive are the kisses of an enemy." 2 Sam 20:9–10 also describes a kiss of betrayal as Joab kisses and then stabs Amasa. This is the only time a kiss is exchanged between a disciple and Jesus.

One of the disciples tries to fight and strikes the high priest's slave on the ear, cutting it off (**v 47**). John 18:10 says that this is Peter and the victim's name is Malchus, whose name is Nabatean and who could be Arab or Syrian.[680] The remark is likely to be authentic, for it is unlikely that, if someone else did this or nothing happened, the church would invent such an act by a disciple, much less Peter.[681] Luke 22:51 says Jesus healed the man. The fact that no arrest of this attacker took place, even as he fled, may mean the situation was rectified.

Jesus simply replies versus fighting (**v 48**). This reply alone stands in contrast to the other Gospels where Jesus rebukes the one who fights (Matt 26:52–53; Luke 22:51). In Mark, the response itself stops the fighting. Jesus observes that the leaders had many opportunities to seize him in the temple when he taught there daily (**v 49**), but they have shown up to arrest him with swords and clubs as though he is a dangerous revolutionary (*lēstēs* – BDAG, 594).[682] The remark about being in the temple day after day may assume that Jesus had been to Jerusalem more than the one time Mark narrates, since at this point Jesus has been present for only a few days on

---

[679] Witherington, *Mark*, 381.
[680] Lane, *Mark*, 526.
[681] Evans, *Mark 8:27–16:20*, 424.
[682] Stein, *Mark*, 672–73, makes the case for revolutionary as the meaning here with Jesus being convicted as "king of the Jews" as a basis for the rendering (Mark 15:1–5).

this trip.[683] The remark also suggests that Jesus is no revolutionary; he has simply taught faithfully in the temple.

There is irony here in light of Mark 11:17. The robbers in the temple arrested the deliverer as though he were a robber.[684] They have accomplished their arrest by stealth (Mark 14:1–2). The theme of Jesus as a righteous sufferer, unjustly evaluated, is the point of this remark. Scripture is being fulfilled in all of this. No specific text is noted, just the themes it raised about rejection of the one sent such as we see in Isa 53:12, Zech 13:7, and Ps 118:22.

The pressure becomes too much for the disciples, who flee (**v 50**). This is just as Jesus had predicted. The sheep are scattered (Mark 14:27). They are not prepared to face the rejection. Jesus is alone. Even a young boy, who had been following them, flees naked when they try to seize him (**vv 51–52**). The identity of this figure has been repeatedly discussed, especially given the vividness of the detail and its seeming unrelatedness to the main line of the story. Was this one showing courage in trying not to flee initially or was he coming to warn Jesus? Is he an ironic picture of "leaving everything" to be spared sharing Jesus' fate, a kind of failure of discipleship?[685] This last option is possible, given what Mark 14:27 says about all the sheep being scattered with the shepherd being struck, and the point that fleeing meant abandoning Jesus in Mark 14:50. Tradition has suggested that this might be Mark, a witness to the events described, but the young man is not identified. Taylor speaks only of an eyewitness known to Mark.[686] It is clear, nonetheless, that the event made an impression on Mark, as it is hard to explain its presence otherwise.[687] So the detail closes the scene on an additional note that things are not right. Jesus is alone as he is taken into custody. As Jesus goes to die to provide for others; no one is there to help or support him.

---

[683] Cranfield, *Mark*, 437.

[684] Hooker, *Mark*, 352.

[685] So Kuruvilla, *Mark*, 317–18; also his "The Naked Runaway and the Embedded Reporter of Mark 14 and 16. What Is the Author *Doing* with What He Is *Saying*? *JETS* 54 (2011): 527–45.

[686] Taylor, *St. Mark*, 652.

[687] Though an allusion to Amos 2:16 is sometimes noted, that text does not really parallel this scene, for there it is the fleeing of the day of judgment. For the myriad of suggestions about why this detail is here, see Collins, *Mark*, 688–93, who does see the unexplained detail as historical.

14:53–72 Jesus Is Found Guilty of Blasphemy by the Leaders as He Proclaims God's Coming Vindication of Him and His Sharing in God's Rule

14:53 And they led Jesus to the high priest, and all the chief priests and elders and scribes came together.

14:54 And Peter followed him from a distance, up to the high priest's courtyard. He was sitting with the guards and warming himself by the fire.

14:55 The chief priests and whole council were looking for evidence against Jesus so they could put him to death but they did not find anything.

14:56 Many gave false testimony against him, but their testimony did not agree.

14:57 Some stood up and gave this false testimony against him:

14:58 "We heard him say, 'I will destroy this temple with hands and in three days build another not made with hands.' "

14:59 And still their testimony was not consistent.

14:60 And standing up in the midst, the high priest asked Jesus, saying, "Have you nothing to answer? What is this they are testifying against you?"

14:61 But he was silent and did not answer. Again the high priest asked and said to him, "Are you the Christ, the Son of the Blessed One?"

14:62 Jesus said, "I am, and you will see the Son of Man sitting on the right hand of the Power and coming with the clouds of heaven."

14:63 Then the high priest, ripping his cloths, said, "Why do we need witnesses?

14:64 You have heard his blasphemy. What is your verdict?" They all condemned him as worthy of death.

14:65 Then some began to spit on him and blindfold him and to strike him with their fists, saying, "Prophesy." The guards also took him and beat him.

14:66 And Peter was below in the courtyard, one of the priest's slave girls came by.

14:67 And seeing Peter warming himself, she looked directly at him and said, "You also were with that Nazarene, Jesus."

14:68 But he denied it saying, "I do not even understand what you are saying." Then he went out to the gateway, and a cock crowed.

14:69 When the slave girl saw him, she began again to say to the bystanders, "This man is one of them."

14:70 But he denied it again. A short time later, the bystanders again said to Peter, "You must be one of them, because you are Galilean."

14:71 Then he began to curse and utter an oath, "I do not know this man you are talking about."

14:72 And immediately a rooster crowed a second time. And Peter remembered what Jesus had said to him, "Before a rooster crows twice, you will deny me three times." And he broke down and wept.

The trial scene is presented in summary form and is juxtaposed to Peter's denial in common Markan sandwich style.[688] A contrast between faithfulness and unfaithfulness emerges that is unlikely to be a church invention. We are told the examination took much of the evening, but it is reduced to a few verses here. The parallels are Matt 26:57–68, Luke 22:54–55, 63–71, and John 18:12–16, 18–23.

Jesus is taken to the high priest at his home (v 53; Luke 22:54).[689] Caiaphas is not named by Mark, but John 18:24 identifies him. He was son-in-law to the powerful Annas I and high priest from 18–36 CE (Josephus, *Ant* 18.35; 18.95). The traditional site of the home is where St. Peter in Gallicantu sits today.

The leaders gather in the three groups Mark has regularly named: chief priests, elders, and scribes. It is discussed whether this is the Sanhedrin with its seventy-one members, since the evidence for its existence is from later sources. At the least it was the major council that existed at the time. A quorum for such a meeting would be twenty-three. Apparently most of the full council was present, given that all of them are said to be there, a remark that could be hyperbolic but still would point to a majority attendance. The dominant sect at the time was the Sadducees. They gathered at night because they wanted to move Jesus on to Roman authority as quickly as possible, and with Pilate in Jerusalem for the feast, this was feasible. They needed a reason for getting Pilate to hear the case. They were acting with urgency under time pressure, while Pilate would still be present.[690]

Peter had not totally abandoned Jesus yet (v 54). He was trying carefully to keep his vow.[691] He followed from a distance up to the chief priest's

---

[688]   Edwards, *Mark*, 441.

[689]   For details about this scene, its background in terms of Jewish practice, and the nature of the decision made as a result, D. L. Bock, *Blasphemy and Exaltation in Judaism and the Jewish Examination of Jesus: A Philological-Historical Study of the Key Jewish Themes Impacting Mark 14:61–64* (Tübingen: Mohr/Siebeck, 1998).

[690]   Much of the study by August Stroebel, *Die Stunde der Wahrheit* (Tübingen: Mohr/Siebeck, 1980), makes the case for this being the setting. Tosepfta, Sanh 11:7 allows for executions tied to feast days for serious crimes such as those discussed in Deut 17:13; Lane, *Mark*, 529–30.

[691]   One should prefer a positive view of this effort versus any negative one. The negatives do not appear until we get the denials; with Stein, *Mark*, 680, against Edwards, *Mark*, 442.

courtyard and ended up warming himself by a fire, seated with the guards. John 18:15–16 has the beloved disciple helping him get access as one who knew people there. Peter's presence in the courtyard may have given him the opportunity to hear some of what was taking place.

They were having trouble finding any cause worthy of death (**v 55**). They had to get this right, because a failure to convince Rome of Jesus' guilt would be a very bad outcome from the leadership's perspective.

Inside, the council was seeking evidence against Jesus to put him to death. They did not have this power (John 18:31); only Rome did.[692] So they were engaged in a judicial examination more than a formal trial. This would have been similar to our grand jury stage, examining whether a charge would be made and, if so, what the charge would be. For this reason, all the Mishnaic rules (*m Sanh* 4:1), often applied to this event and said to be violated in the process on the assumption that this is a formal trial, do not apply.[693] If the configuration had been similar to a trial, the leaders would have been in a semi-circle, with minutes taken by two clerks on each end. The accused and any witnesses would have stood in the midst of the circle (*m Sanh* 4:3–4).[694] They were having trouble putting together a case that

---

[692] Hooker, *Mark*, 354, notes later Jewish testimony to this fact (j. Sanh 1.18a, 34; 7.24b, 41). The appeal to Stephen's death in Acts 6–7 does not contradict this, as this was the response of a popular mob, not a formal judicial act. The execution of James the Just is similar to Josephus, *Ant* 20.200–203, the exception that proves the rule, for Annas II lost his position for executing him and usurping Roman authority.

[693] Bock, *Blasphemy*, 189–95, covers this and the debate over whether Jews had the right to put someone to death.

[694] Lane, *Mark*, 532. Hooker, *Mark*, 354–57, raises a host of issues about the historicity of the scene, claiming that differences between Mark and Luke and John are an issue, as well as where witnesses came from as a source and the portrait of Pilate as vacillating. Collins, *Mark*, 699–700, simply says the examination scene is "not based on any historically reliable tradition," but accepts Peter's denials as tied to a tradition. The source question I have treated in more detail elsewhere, Bock, *Blasphemy*, 195–97; also Stein, *Mark*, 678–79. Several potential sources exist. The Jewish position about Jesus would have been a matter of public debate in Jerusalem. People like Joseph of Arimathea (Mark 15:43) and Nicodemus would have known what took place. Paul, as a chief prosecutor of the new movement, also could have been familiar with the official position. The fact that the family of Annas and that of Jesus contended for Jews in Jerusalem over a thirty-year period also makes it likely the positions and roles were known. The differences raised are matters of editorial selection by different writers about a long event. They are not so great as to undercut the thrust of what the accounts share as the core issue, Jesus' claim to sit at God's right hand as he proclaims he will be vindicated. As for Pilate, he was under pressure for his previous treatment of Jews and possibly recognized how potentially volatile this particular controversy was. So he was moving carefully. In the end, he acted after having consulted with the Jewish leaders and Herod, and having checked all the cultural boxes. The claim that the Romans are treated with some exoneration is exaggerated. They are pictured as executing a man they regarded as innocent, hardly a

reached the capital punishment level. They could not go to Pilate with a mere religious dispute; something involving risk to the state or seriously disturbing the peace was required. Mark says that false testimony was being collected, but it was testimony that did not agree (v 56).

Mark supplies one example involving the temple that is not noted in the other parallels (v 57). The claim is that Jesus said he would destroy the physical temple and that this temple was inadequate, as the expression "not made with hands" is derogatory (v 58). That expression alludes to activity that made idols or false gods (Lev 26:1, 30; Isa 2:18; 10:11; 19:1; 21:9; 31:7; Dan 2:45 of earthly kingdoms; esp. Jdt 8:18; 4QFlor 1 1:2–3; *4 Ezra* 10:54) or to an earthly temple in contrast to a greater temple to come.[695] The idea of a new temple in the era to come was not foreign to Second Temple Judaism (Zech 6:12; 4QFlor 1:6–7; 11QTemple 29:7–10; *2 Bar* 4:3).[696] Other NT texts speak of God not living in a place made by human hands or speak of other rites with the phrase "not made with hands" (Acts 7:48; Heb 9:11, 24; other than a temple context: 2 Cor 5:1; Eph 2:11; Co 2:11).[697] The use of *naos* probably refers to the holy place, adding an emotive element to the claim. The act would have been considered blasphemous and seditious because of the level of public chaos it would have engendered.

This temple saying sounds close to what we see in John 2:19 ("Destroy this temple and in three days I will raise it up again"), especially in the note about three days. Yet there are important differences. First, Jesus does not say he will destroy the temple. Second, he is referring to his body, and not the physical temple. Even Jesus' private teaching about the destruction of the temple in Mark 13:2 does not have him destroy it. Mark notes that their testimony did not agree on this example (v 59). Two witnesses would have been required for this by Jewish law (Num 35:30; Deut 17:6). It appears, then, that this route for making the case was abandoned.

So the high priest takes over the examination (v 60). He is curious why Jesus offers no response to the charges. Does he not have anything to say in reply, in his own defense? Jesus is silent. The allusion is to Isa 53:7.

Caiaphas queries Jesus if he is the Christ, the Son of the Blessed One (v 61). The question is a logical one, since in some views Messiah would

---

flattering picture of Roman justice. Cranfield, *Mark*, 439, says the scene is not as "doctrinally coloured" as one might expect of a church creation.

[695] Marcus, *Mark 8–16*, 1003.
[696] Evans, *Mark 8:27–16:20*, 445–46.
[697] Hurtado, *Mark*, 253.

bring a renewed temple.[698] A messianic confession also would be significant, since that would mean Jesus is a regal figure whom Rome did not
appoint, leading to a potential charge of sedition. Respect for God is shown
in the circumlocution the "Blessed One" (*m Ber* 7.3; *1 Enoch* 77:2).[699]
Caiaphas is asking about the office of Messiah. As a Jew, he is not thinking
of God having a son in any other sense, and the term can have this force
(4Q174 1.11; 4Q246 2.1; 1Qsa 2.11–12).[700] In Matt 26:63c, an oath comes with
the question to show that a reply was required (Prov 29:24; *m Shev* 4.13).[701]

Jesus' reply yields one of the most significant statements about Jesus in
Mark (**v 62**). Jesus replies affirmatively to the question. He says simply, "I
am." This differs slightly from the qualified responses in Matt 26:64 ("You
have said it yourself") and Luke 22:70 ("You say that I am"). Those answers
reflect a qualified yes. The force of those replies is ironically "I am (at least
in part) as you say." This explains the start to the charge that Jesus was
"king of the Jews." After this, Jesus gives them more than they ask for by
elaborating on the reply.

The core of the response is in what follows. First, Jesus speaks of them
seeing the Son of Man sitting at the right hand of the Power. Jesus responds
with his own circumlocution (the Power), an expression tied to God's
saving activity in the midrashim, to show his respect for God.[702] Jesus
will share in God's rule and activity. The allusion is to Ps 110:1. Jesus is
predicting what happens after his death – his resurrection followed by
exaltation into God's very presence. The language must look at a session
next to God, especially given what follows.

Second, he will come on the clouds of heaven. This is an allusion to Dan
7:13–14 and the judging authority that figure receives from the Ancient of
Days. It looks to his return to judge (Mark 13:26).[703] Though the Son of

---

[698] For a defense of the coherence of the summary in Mark here against its historical
backdrop, O. Betz, "Probleme des Prozesses Jesu," in *ANRW* II.25.1 (Berlin: Walter de
Gruyter, 1982), 613–44. For a response to objections by W. Reinbold, *Der älteste Bericht
über den Tod Jesu: Literarische Analyse und historische Kritik der Passionsdarstellungen
der Evangelisten* (Berlin: Walter de Gruyter, 1994), esp. 256; see Bock, *Blasphemy*, 210–13.

[699] Bock, *Blasphemy*, 215–17. Hooker's claim, *Mark*, 360, that these questions look like
Christian formulation, although they might reflect something like what was said, ignores
the unlikely use of circumlocutions by the early church, both in the question and Jesus'
reply. She does not comment on Power at all.

[700] Evans, *Mark 8:27–16:20*, 448–49.

[701] Stein, *Mark*, 684.

[702] Bock, *Blasphemy*, 217–20; *1 En* 62:7; esp. *Sifre Numbers* §12 [on 15:31]; *b Eru* 54b; *b Yev* 105b.

[703] The denial by France, *Mark*, 611–12, that this is not about a return to judge is not
persuasive. It ignores not only the likely context of Mark 13 but also the early hope of the

Man is a human figure, his riding the clouds points to a transcendent act, as only such figures ride the clouds in the OT (Exod 14:20; 34:5; Num 10:34; Ps 104:3; Isa 19:1). Jesus is predicting a vindication from God. They may judge him now, but God will bring him to a place where he shares rule and judgment. One day they will be on trial before him. The claim to share authority with God is what causes the high priest to react. Who sits with God in heaven? Although some texts contemplate this for certain exalted figures (*Exag of Ezek* 68–89; *1 En* 45:3; 46:1–3; 51:3; 61:8; 62:2–8; 70:2; 71:1–17), Sadducees would never have been comfortable with such claims, especially from a teacher from Galilee.[704] It would have been seen as a violation of Deut 6:4. Here is Jesus' answer to his earlier query about how David could call his descendent Messiah his Lord (Mark 12:41–44). It is because God will exalt this figure to share in God's rule.[705]

The juxtaposition of these two OT texts is not an early Christian pesher as Perrin claims.[706] It is stated too indirectly; it uses expression, such as "Power" and "Son of Man," uniquely attested to Jesus; and it uses expressions of those in the council seeing events that would no longer be correct of a later formed saying in terms of the return.[707]

The high priest tears his cloths, a sign that blasphemy has taken place, and asks why do they need any more witnesses (**v 63**). Tearing cloths is what took place when someone heard news they wish they had not heard (Gen 37:34; Jos 7:6; 2 Sam 1:11; 2 Kings 18:37; 19:1). He announces that what Jesus has said is blasphemy (**v 64**). This is not blasphemy in the formal sense of the Mishnah (*m Sanh* 6:4; 7:5), where one needs to say the divine name in an inappropriate way. This is seen as an affront to God's unique

---

church that grew out of Jesus' teaching. France's appeal to the vindication starting with resurrection is correct. That is the point of Ps 110:1.

[704] Rejection of such views is seen in 11Q17 7:4; *3 En* 16:2–3, *b Sanh* 38b, and *b Hag* 15a; Marcus, *Mark 8–16*, 1008–1009.

[705] Collins, *Mark*, 705. She goes on to note on page 706 that the blasphemy was "a human being claiming a greater degree of authority and power than he has a right to do and directly or indirectly, claiming divine status for himself." As a theologian, the high priest sees the issue clearly. Either Jesus is who he claims to be or this is blasphemy. For Mark, the resurrection is the answer vindicating what Jesus claims here. See A. Y. Collins, "The Charge of Blasphemy in Mark 14.64," *JSNT* 26 (2004): 379–401. This article interacts with and updates my own work.

[706] N. Perrin, "Mark xiv.62: The End Product of a Christian Pesher Tradition?" *NTS* 12 (1965–66): 150–55. Pesher was a form of Jewish interpretation of pulling passages together to argue for some type of eschatological fulfilment.

[707] Bock, *Blasphemy*, 220–30; Evans, *Mark 8:27–16:20*, 450–51.

honor by claiming to share directly in his rule and authority, as well as insulting God's rulers (Exod 22:27; 11QTemple 64:7–9).[708]

When he asks for a verdict, they all condemn him as worthy of death. They will take the charge to Pilate so Rome can render a judgment. They will ask for death. In effect, Jesus provides the testimony that sends him to the cross.

Some present communicate their displeasure by spitting on Jesus and mocking him (**v 65**). Blindfolded, Jesus is struck and told to prophesy. The guards who take him also beat him. These acts may allude to Isa 50:6. The point is simply to shame Jesus (Job 30:10; Num 12:14; Deut 25:9).

Mark returns to Peter's denials (**v 66**). The parallels to this scene are Matt 26:69–75, Luke 22:56–62, and John 18:17, 25–27. The Gospel writers made different choices in terms of when to tell this story. Luke tells it before the examination, whereas Mark and Matthew relate it after the questioning. Luke 22:66 has the final exchange as morning is dawning as he presents what looks to be a summary of the entire examination. Peter's denials likely came in the midst of all of this, so each author makes his choices.[709] Peter stands in contrast to Jesus when the pressure comes.

Peter is in the courtyard below where Jesus is being examined. Jesus apparently met the council on a second floor. The area of the traditional site is hilly, so that may also be a factor in this description, if the courtyard is outside the home. Most large homes in this period had an open courtyard in the central area of the house.

A high priest's slave girl sees Peter at the fire and recognizes him as a follower of Jesus (**v 67**). John 18:16 says she was the doorkeeper. She declares that Peter was with the Nazarene, Jesus. Other Markan passages refer to Jesus as a Nazarene (Mark 1:24; 10:47; 16:6). It may be a derogatory reference to someone from the north (John 1:46; 7:41, 52).[710] Peter simply says he does not know or understand the topic she is raising (**v 68**). It is a common way to deny something (*m Sheb* 8:3, 6; *T. Joseph* 13:1–2).[711] He does not even want to broach the question. He hopes that she will move on and leave the matter alone. Peter moves to the vestibule (*proaulion*) leading

---

[708] The main point of Bock, *Blasphemy* is to show this by a full study of blasphemy in Jewish sources. The summary is on pages 234–35.

[709] Stein, *Mark*, 690.

[710] Donahue and Harrington, *Mark*, 425.

[711] Lane, *Mark*, 542.

into the courtyard, which would be called the *aulē*, the word used in Mark
14:66. A rooster crows for the first time.[712]

The slave girl reappears, insisting that Peter was with Jesus and declaring
that this man is one of them (v 69). Peter makes a second denial (v 70). The
imperfect verb here presents it with a feel of duration. Now he directly is
declaring no connection to Jesus or the disciples. Matt 26:72 has Peter deny
this with an oath, saying he does not know the man. Luke 22:58 has him
questioned by a man and replying, "Man, I am not." Peter was likely
responding to many people who now were joining in and considering
connecting him to Jesus.

After a little time, others draw their own conclusion that the girl is right,
for they recognize that Peter is Galilean, and so he must be one of them
(v 71). Why else would he be present in the courtyard area? The event draws
in several participants, something John 18:25 also indicates. Perhaps his
accent (Matt 26:73) or the way he spoke gave him away (Acts 2:7).[713] John
18:26 has someone recognize him as having been in the garden at the arrest.
Peter becomes livid. He curses and swears an oath that he does not know
the man they are describing. It probably had a "May God do to me" flavor
about it.[714] When the verb for cursing lacks an object, it usually means
someone or something has been cursed versus cursing oneself. Mark leaves
this blank, but it may have included a renunciation of Jesus. It is as
emphatic a denial as one can make. Each time Peter's denying has become
more intense.

The rooster crows a second time (v 72), causing Peter to recall the Lord's
words (Mark 14:30), since with this final remark he most emphatically

---

[712] There is a textual issue here regarding whether the mention of the rooster crowing is
original. A copyist's insertion could be present to bring the text into conformity with
Jesus' prediction in Mark 14:30. On the other hand, its omission by a copyist also is
explicable as bringing Mark into conformity with the other Gospels that mention only a
single crowing (Matt 26:74; Luke 22:60; John 18:27). The external evidence is also split,
with key Alexandrian witnesses, among others, omitting the text (א, B, L, W) and the rest
of the families favoring inclusion. Interestingly, B includes a reference to a second
crowing in verse 72, perhaps suggesting a split in the Alexandrian witnesses and favoring
original inclusion. The pressure to make the texts like the other Gospels is likely to be
greater, especially since Matthew and John are the more popular texts. So inclusion is
slightly favored; Metzger, *Textual Commentary* (1994), 97. A parallel issue comes up in
the mention of a second crowing in verse 72. Omissions there are slightly more widespread, but this one also looks like an attempt to harmonize with the other Gospels.

[713] Later Jewish sources make a point about the Galilean dialect (*b 'Erub* 53b; *b Meg* 24b);
Lane, *Mark*, 542. The pronunciation of gutturals was an issue for them; Evans, *Mrk 8:27–
16:20*, 466.

[714] France, *Mark*, 622.

denied Jesus. The cock crow was known as the third watch, covering from midnight to 3:00 AM, because they often did crow at this time of night. However, roosters crowed at all hours, so we are simply before dawn here. The fact that Jesus said he would deny him three times before the rooster crowed twice leads Peter to weep.[715] He has failed to be faithful, by suffering from a loss of nerve. His heart is broken. He had fallen into temptation (Mark 14:38) and sought to save his own life (Mark 8:35). The rest of Peter's life would be very different, as he would speak boldly of Jesus. Those who knew the full story would know that as low as Peter felt here, he learned from the experience, even though persecution can be hard to overcome. That failure can be reversed is probably the point of sharing this event, an experience unlikely to have been a church creation given its initial poor reflection on Peter.[716]

15:1–47 Jesus Is Sent to the Cross by Pilate for Sedition and Dies amid a Series of Cosmic Signs

15:1–15 Amid Some Pressure, Jesus Meets with Pilate and Is Sentenced to Be Crucified

15:1 As soon as it was early in the morning, after forming a plan, the chief priests with the elders and scribes and the whole council tied Jesus up and gave him over to Pilate.

15:2 SoPilate asked him, "Are you the king of the Jews?" He replied, "You say so."

15:3 And the chief priests began to accuse him many times.

15:4 So Pilate asked him again, "Do you reply with nothing? See how many things they charge you."

15:5 But Jesus made no further reply, so that Pilate was amazed.

15:6 During the feast it was customary to release one prisoner to the people, whomever they requested.

15:7 A man named Barabbas was imprisoned with rebels who had committed murder during an insurrection.

---

[715] Knowing how to render *epibalōn* is a matter for discussion, as it can mean to begin or to throw down or out (BDAG, 367, 2b). So either Peter took his cloths to hide his face, cast himself from the location, cast himself to the ground, or began to weep. Taking the cloths to hide his face is the least likely of these options, as a reference to cloths likely would have supplied an object. Any of the last three options is possible here, and there is no way to decide among them; however, the action, whatever it is, is quite dramatic, reflecting the intensity of the moment.

[716] So, correctly, Evans, *Mark 8:27–16:20*, 465.

15:8 And rising up the crowd began to ask Pilate to release a prisoner for them, even as he was doing for them.

15:9 So Pilate asked them, "Do you want me to release the king of the Jews for you?"

15:10 (for he knew that the chief priests had handed him over because of envy.)

15:11 But the chief priests stirred up the crowd to have him release Barabbas to them instead.

15:12 So Pilate again replied, saying to them, "Then what do you want me to do with the one you call king of the Jews?"

15:13 They shouted back, "Crucify him."

15:14 Pilate said to them, "Why? What has he done wrong?" But they shouted even more, "Crucify him."

15:15 Because he wanted to grant the crowd a favor, he released Barabbas to them and gave over Jesus, having had him flogged, that he might be crucified.

This scene is not so much a trial as an examination out of the ordinary (*cognition extra ordinem*),[717] which was a prefect's right as a Roman representative. The parallels are in Matt 27:1–2, 11, 26; Luke 23:1–5, 18–25; and John 18:28–40; 19:1, 4, and 12–16. Some scholars question whether there is any tradition to work with here and challenge the amnesty scene that leads to Barabbas' release, stressing how much blame is placed on the Jews.[718] This reading is too one-sided. Rome is portrayed as unjust in releasing someone the ruler senses is innocent of a capital crime. It is said Pilate was too ruthless to show this much respect to the Jews (Philo, *Embassy to Gaius* 38.299–305, esp. 301, 303, 305; Josephus, *Ant* 18.60–62; *War* 2.169–74 – taking money from the sacred treasury), but by this point in his rule he had faltered in his relationships with Jews, as Philo (see the previous discussion) and Josephus (Ant 18. 55–59) noted in the famous shields incident(s),[719] and likely had been told by Tiberius to be more careful with them. Releasing Jesus could have been a subtle swipe at these leaders (Mark 15:10 and sarcasm of 15:12), but in the end he accepted their

717   A. N. Sherwin-White, *Roman Society and Roman Law in the New Testament* (Oxford: Oxford University Press, 1963), 12–23. That Pilate had a role in Jesus' death is attested to by Tacitus, *Annals* 15.44, and with the collaboration of Jewish leaders according to Josephus, *Ant* 18.63–64.

718   Hooker, *Mark*, 366–67, raises the objections noted in this paragraph.

719   It is discussed whether these are two distinct events or two versions of the same incident; Evans, *Mark* 8:27–16:20, 477.

advice and avoided trouble with those who helped him with the Jewish population.[720]

After taking consultation to wrap up their own investigation of Jesus early that morning,[721] the leadership takes Jesus to Pilate with a plan to ask for his death (v 1). They hand him over to the prefect, using the verb so common in Mark (*paradidōmi*; Mark 9:31; 10:33, 14:10, 11, 18, 21, 41–44). They had translated the religious charge into a political one, Jesus was claiming to be a king Rome had not appointed; in short, sedition. Pilate, who was prefect of Judea from 26–36 CE, had three key responsibilities there: to keep the peace, collect taxes, and look after Caesar's interests there, enforcing his presence with power.[722] Whatever the leaders said to him led him to ask Jesus if he was the king of the Jews (v 2). This topic dominates the chapter (Mark 15:9, 12, 18, 26, 32). Jesus' response is, "You say."[723] The force is likely both ironic and with the idea "but not quite in the sense you have asked it." Ironically, Jesus had worked hard not to be seen as a political Messiah in the sense that his disciples had originally hoped and some in the public at times had expected.[724] Now he is on trial for being that figure. He realizes the promise, but not in the way of power that Pilate's question suggests. John 18:36–37 points to the difference.

The leaders press their case against Jesus (v 3). Mark gives no details. Luke 23:2 has three charges against Jesus: subverting the nation, forbidding the payment of taxes to Caesar, and claiming that he is a king. Mark seems to be aware of this last claim. Matthew runs parallel to Mark. John 18:33 also has Pilate ask about being king of the Jews.

Pilate is surprised that Jesus gives no real reply, especially given how many charges they have leveled against him. Pilate asks the question, fully

---

[720] Witherington, *Mark*, 390.

[721] For this understanding to prepare for the common morning Roman proceedings, Witherington, *Mark*, 388–89, and Lane, *Mark*, 545. Witherington points out the public impact of having Rome act as the most public and shameful way to remove Jesus. The locale of this examination is either the Antonia Fortress where Romans troops stayed or Herod's palace where visiting Roman rulers resided on visits (Josephus, *War* 2.301; Philo, *Embassy to Gaius* 38.299–301).

[722] For a detailed look at Pilate, see Helen Bond, *Pontius Pilate in History and Interpretation* (Cambridge: Cambridge University Press, 1998), and for a full survey of issues tied to the trial and crucifixion, Robert Webb, "The Roman Examination and Crucifixion of Jesus," in Bock and Webb, *Key Events*, 669–773.

[723] On the grammar, BDF §441; Matt 26:25, 64; 27:11; Luke 22:70; 23:3; John 18:37; Lane, *Mark*, 551.

[724] Lane, *Mark*, 550–51.

expecting Jesus to give a reply as the interrogative *ouk* indicates (**v 4**). Pilate is thinking like a Roman, as Jesus' silence and a failure to reply could lead to a presumption of guilt, by suggesting there is no answer.[725] This remark about how much he was being charged suggests more than Jesus' claimed kingship was raised against him. Jesus still offers no rebuttal, leaving Pilate amazed (**v 5**). Mark again evokes Isa 53:7 about being silent like a lamb, as in Mark 14:60.

Now the custom of releasing a prisoner at feast time is noted (**v 6**). It has been called the *privilegium paschale*. We have no outside record of this practice in Judea, since outside of Josephus and Philo we have next to nothing on Pilate outside the Gospels. Though some doubt it for lack of corroboration elsewhere, there would be no value in noting a custom, seemingly deeply rooted in the telling of the trial scene story, that people knew did not exist. This is especially the case if this were a custom done especially for Jews and Mark writes to a largely Gentile audience. Why note it at all? In fact, it would be counterproductive to create a scene that those familiar with the event knew never took place. Its mention exists in two tradition streams (Mark and John), pointing to multiple attestation. A similar act of amnesty is attested from a governor in Egypt from 85 CE.[726] All of this makes it more likely than not.

The crowd seeks out Pilate to exercise his custom (**v 8**). He starts with Jesus, identified as king of the Jews (**v 9**). In verse 12, he notes that some of them call him the king of the Jews. So we are dealing with a claim in Pilate's view. The text says he said this about Jesus because he knew Jesus was handed over because of envy (**v 10**). Pilate is using his custom as a time to play a little with the leaders. Pilate seems to take the claim as less than serious at one level, since Jesus has no power or army. Pilate's willingness

---

[725] A. N. Sherwin-White, *Roman Society and Roman Law in the New Testament* (Oxford: Oxford University Press, 1963), 25–26. Evans, *Mark 8:27–16:20*, 479, argues Jesus was acting in a manner the Greco-Roman ethical tradition would have respected (Plutarch, *Moralia* 498D–E).

[726] Lane, *Mark*, 552–53. Marcus, *Mark 8–16*, 1028, argues for the plausibility of an occasional Roman response to a Jewish request for amnesty at this feast that celebrated release from prison. Evans, *Mark 8:27–16:20*, 680, notes that *m Pesah* 8:6 may point to the custom, as it allows a Passover lamb to be slaughtered for one out of prison. Collins, *Mark*, 714–15, argues that Mark added the story, challenging the evidence others raise. She never explains how, in an account that purports to be historical *and* apologetic, an invented story would have helped the cause when people knew what the history was. This is not about literature written long after the fact. See E. Bammel, "The Trial before Pilate," in *Jesus and the Politics of His Day*, ed. E. Bammel and C. F. D. Moule (Cambridge: Cambridge University Press, 1984), 427–28.

to use this title reflects the fact that he sees little threatening about Jesus, even given his popularity with some people.[727]

Now the chief priests had stirred up the crowd to call for the release of Barabbas (v 22). There is some question about whether Pilate would release such a prisoner and accept such a specific request.[728] The situation, with the active involvement of the leadership versus a popular teacher, is not a normal one. This could have caused Pilate to be more careful. The verb *anaseiō* means to shake up, but in this context it is to stir up a crowd (Luke 23:5; BDAG, 71).[729] Marcus sees this crowd as being made up of locals who had rejected Jesus.[730]

Mark had already described Barabbas as one imprisoned for murder during an insurrection (v 7; *stasis*; BDAG, 940; Jdt 7:15; 2 Macc 4:30; 14:6). Ironically, his name means "son of the father," but Mark makes nothing of that. Barabbas is in jail for sedition, the very charge Jesus is facing. He is described as having been arrested with a group that committed murder. We do not know about the specific incident being referenced here. Did it involve one of the earlier shield incidents? Perhaps it was an otherwise unattested public disturbance in what was known to be a turbulent region. Mark is not clear about whether Barabbas was a murderer himself or was simply an accomplice with a reputation (Matt 27:16). Regardless, he was a man associated with violence.

Pilate asks, "What is to be done with the one 'you call' [yet another tweak] king of the Jews?" (v 12). Again, questions have been raised

---

[727] This detail also explains why Collins's challenge, *Mark*, 720, to the historicity of the scene by rejecting Pilate's use of the title for Jesus is not decisive. She argues that Pilate's authority would be threatened if the people recognized Jesus as their king. The point is true if the prospect of widespread popularity was real, but Pilate feels no real threat. The Jewish leaders are against Jesus, and the teacher shows no real means in Pilate's view to challenge mighty Rome.

[728] Hooker, *Mark*, 368–69. Despite her objections, she goes on to argue that the event is probably grounded in some historical incident, the details of which are beyond us. Others prefer to see a better connection between the incident and its reporting. Part of the objection is whether Pilate would release a murderer; however, the text does not explicitly say Barabbas murdered, but rather that he was in a group that did (*hoitines* n v 7 is plural); Evans, *Mark 8:27–16:20*, 481; contra Edwards, *Mark*, 460, who calls Barabbas a murderer. She also calls the connection between Barabbas' release and Jesus' fate implausible, but that is not so if Pilate was trying to push the crowd to make a choice to release Jesus because Pilate sensed his innocence. The move is potentially politically astute. He only did the people's will in this difficult case. The fact that it failed caused Pilate simply to follow the counsel of those leaders he worked with in this area. Such twists are not unusual in politics.

[729] Cranfield, *Mark*, 450.

[730] Marcus, *Mark 8–16*, 1030.

regarding whether Pilate would have actually done this.[731] However, Pilate is gaining a sense of the crowd and the populace's wishes here while dealing with a figure he sees as insignificant, aside from the current public stir. If he gives Jesus over to death or any punishment with the leaders and the crowd's support, he has the protection of public affirmation from the very people he has sometimes gotten into trouble with for what he has done in the past. The act is a reflection of a shrewd politician.[732] Of course, for Mark, what emerges as a result of the crowd's cries for Barabbas is a substitution of one worthy of the crime being set free with Jesus dying in his place, a picture of what the cross means (Rom 5:8; 1 Pet 3:18).[733]

The crowd responds to Pilate's query about what to do with Jesus with cries that he be crucified (**v 13**). Pilate, seemingly surprised, asks why and wants to know what he has done wrong (**v 14**). He is seeking assurance of public support and that sentencing Jesus will not result in public chaos. The crowd does not answer the question but continues to call for Jesus' death. Pilate's ambivalence is answered by the crowd's insistence.

Pilate decides to satisfy the crowd's request (**v 15**). This does soften the Roman involvement in the death and makes it clear that the movement Jesus started was not really seen as criminal, but it does not let Rome completely off the hook. To execute someone you sense is innocent is not a flattering portrait of justice.

Pilate releases Barabbas and, flogging Jesus, has him sent to the soldiers to be crucified. Flogging (*flagellum*) was a particular painful exercise involving whips loaded with either wooden, metal, bone chips, or even hooks (Josephus, *War* 3.306, 308; 5:449; Philo, *Flaccus* 72; Dio Chrysostom, *Discourses* 4.67). Such whippings were predominately given to those of slave status.[734] The purpose was to cause bleeding that was designed to speed up death on the cross as well as to inflict pain. Pilate was doing his job of keeping the peace in his view (Luke 23:2; John 19:12). Crucifixion was seen as the cruelest form of execution that a Roman citizen could not be subject to experiencing (Valerius Maximus 2.7.12; Tacitus *Histories* 2.72;

---

[731] Collins, *Mark*, 720. To see, as she does, the crowd as a metaphor for choices about the Jewish War in 66–70 CE is simply farfetched. Lane, *Mark*, 556, calls this a tactical blunder, but it is more like testing the populace to see how emotional any decision will be. It is shrewd versus incompetent.

[732] Edwards, *Mark*, 463, raises the possibility that the departure of the more anti-Semitic Sejanus in Rome led to a shift in Roman policy toward Jews, with more sensitivity to them; also D. Flusser, *Jesus* (Jerusalem: Magnes, 2001), 160–62.

[733] Edwards, *Mark*, 461.

[734] Collins, *Mark*, 721, n. 102.

4.11; Juvenal, *Satires* 14.77–78).[735] Domitian was horrified by it (Suetonius, *Domitian* 11). Quintilian (*Declamationes* 274) noted that it was located in the most public locales so that most people could see it.

With Barabbas free and Jesus headed to the cross, the substitution is complete. Rome has issued a death decree and a verdict of guilty. Jesus dies as a claimed "king of the Jews" (Mark 15:26). It is a regal and messianic association that leads to his death.

15:16–41 Jesus Is Crucified amid Cosmic Signs That Lead to a Centurion's Confession

15:16 The soldiers led him into the palace court, which is the praetorium, and called together the whole cohort.

15:17 They dressed him in a purple cloak and weaving a crown of thorns, they placed it on him.

15:18 They began to salute him: "Hail. King of the Jews."

15:19 And they struck him on the head with a staff and spit on him and kneeling down they paid homage to him.

15:20 When they had finished mocking him, they stripped him of the purple cloak and dressed him with his own clothes. And they led him away that they might crucify him.

15:21 And they impressed a passerby to carry his cross, Simon of Cyrene, who was coming in from the country, the father of Alexander and Rufus.

15:22 They brought Jesus to a place called Golgotha, which is translated "place of the skull."

15:23 They gave him wine mixed with myrrh, but he did not take it.

15:24 Then they crucified him and *divided his clothes casting lots* for them, to decide what each would take.

15:25 It was nine o'clock in the morning when they crucified him.

15:26 The inscription of the charge against him being written, "the king of the Jews."

15:27 And they crucified two outlaws with him, one on his right and one on his left.

15:29 Those who passed by defamed him, shaking their heads and saying, "Aha, you can destroy the temple and rebuild it in three days,

15:30 save yourself and come down from the cross."

---

[735] M. Hengel, *Crucifixion in the Ancient Word and the Folly of the Message of the Cross* (Philadelphia: Fortress, 1977).

15:31 Likewise also the chief priests with the scribes were mocking to one another and saying, "He saved others, but he cannot save himself.

15:32 Let the Christ, the king of Israel, come down from the cross now, that we may see and believe." Those who were crucified with him mocked him.

15:33 Now when it was noon, darkness came over the whole earth until three in the afternoon.

15:34 Around three o'clock Jesus cried out, "*Eloi, Eloi, lema sabachthani?*" which means, "*My God, my God, why have you forsaken me?*"

15:35 And some of the bystanders hearing it said, "Look, he calls for Elijah."

15:36 Someone, running, filled a sponge with sour wine and gave it to him to drink, saying, "Let us see if Elijah will come to take him down."

15:37 But Jesus cried out with a loud voice and breathed his last.

15:38 And the temple curtain was torn in two, from top to bottom.

15:39 Now when the centurion, who stood in front of him saw how he died, he said, "Truly this man was God's son."

15:40 There were also women, watching from a distance, among them were Mary Magdalene and Mary the mother of James the younger and of Joses, and Salome.

15:41 When he was in Galilee, they had followed him and given him support. Many other women who had come with him to Jerusalem were there too.

The crucifixion scene includes mocking and then a description of Jesus' death. As he entrusts himself to God, the creation reacts and a centurion is moved to recognize Jesus. The parallels are Matthew 27:27–56, Luke 23:11, 26, 32–39, 44–49; and John 19:2–3, 17–24, 28–30.[736] This mocking is located in different spots in the Gospels, coming before a sentence and after the flogging in John 19:1–3 and associated with Herod's soldiers in the midst of a series of examinations Luke gives in 23:11.

When Jesus is placed in the hands of the soldiers at the palace court, he is mocked (vv 16–17). We are likely at Herod's palace and a large courtyard area where a large number of soldiers could gather. The location is often associated with the Jaffa Gate area of today and the Citadel. A cohort (*speira*) could refer to 600 men or to a maniple of 200, although Josephus could speak of cohorts of 1,000 (BDAG, 936; *War* 3.67).[737] These were mostly non-Jewish soldiers from Syro-Palestine.[738]

---

[736] The gaps in the verses of the parallels reflect scenes unique to those Gospels.
[737] Witherington, *Mark*, 392.
[738] Marcus, *Mark 8–16*, 1039.

They dressed him in a purple cloak to mock his kingship (Jdg 8:26; Esth 8:15; 1 Macc 8:14; 10:20; 11:58; Plutarch, *Tiberius Gracchus* 14.2; Cicero, *Scaurus* 45; Suetonius, *Tiberius* 17.2; Josephus, *Ant* 17.197). They made a crown of thorns, to mirror an emperor's laurel wreath, and placed it on his head. They cried out in mock honor, "Hail, king of the Jews," in imitation of greetings to Caesar (v 18; Suetonius, *Claudias* 21.6 with its famous refrain, "Hail, Emperor, we who are about to die salute you"; also Josephus, *Ant* 10:211). They beat him on the head with some type of reed or staff that pictures a scepter and spit on him (v 19). Finally, they bowed down in mock worship. These soldiers also saw no threat in Jesus and made sport of what was taking place. Such things were not unusual for this kind of a setting where shame was the point for the one sentenced to die.[739]

Completing their fun and efforts to shame Jesus, they get him ready for crucifixion (v 20). The word for mock here can appear in contexts where someone is being treated cruelly (*empaizō*; 2 Macc 7:7, 10). They remove the purple cloak and dress him in his own clothes. Then they depart to the crucifixion site. John 19:17 had Jesus carry the cross, at least for a time.[740] Mark lacks any such detail. Jesus is apparently too weak to carry the cross so they impress into service a man coming in from the countryside to carry the cross (v 21). His name is Simon of Cyrene. His family apparently was known to the audience, as Mark describes him as the father of Alexander and Rufus. It may be that Rufus is the same figure who became a leader in Rome (Rom 16:13), but there is really no way to know. He would have been carrying the cross beam. The main pole would have already been at the site. The shape was with a T, †, or an X. There was a place left to display the charge, which favors a † shape.

Jesus arrives at Golgotha, a location whose name means "place of the skull" (v 22). This site has traditionally been associated with the present location of the Church of the Holy Sepulchre, some 300 meters from Herod's palace.[741] It meets the requirement of execution outside the city walls of the time (Lev 24:14; Num 15:35–36; 1 Kings 21:13).[742] The Romans built a pagan shrine on this site in the second century, pointing to its sacred

---

[739] Evans, *Mark 8:27–16:20*, 488, notes incidents in Philo, *Flaccus* 6.36–39 – involving a street person, Carabas, mocked as king, Dio Cassius 64.20–21, and Eleazar in 4 Macc 6:1–30.
[740] John generally avoids any indications of weakness for Jesus.
[741] France, *Mark*, 642. Collins, *Mark*, 740, shows the likelihood the church was outside the wall.
[742] Witherington, *Mark*, 394.

character and implicitly claiming Roman victory over the God represented by the sacred locale.

Jesus is offered wine mixed with myrrh, but he refuses to take it (**v 23**). Such an offer is not unusual (Prov 31:6; Pliny, *Natural History* 14.15, 92–93), and is often seen as an act of mercy. This is not certain. It is soldiers who offer the wine, making mercy an unlikely motive. It may continue the mocking.[743] They place him on the cross (**v 24**). If a find made in 1968 at Giv'at ha-Mivtar is any guide, his feet were nailed together at the heels.[744] This made breathing difficult. Death would eventually come either from a loss of blood or from being unable to breathe. John 20:27 also suggests nailing, but another option would have been to use ropes.

As he hangs on the cross, the soldiers divide his clothes and cast die for who gets what. It is unclear whether Jesus was crucified in the nude or left with an undergarment out of sensitivity to Jewish concerns (Jub. 3:30–31; *m Sanh* 6:3). The language of dividing clothes reflects Ps 22:18. Jesus is portrayed as a righteous sufferer. Those executed like this had no property rights (Tacitus, *Annals* 6.29).

It was the third hour, or 9:00 AM, when he was crucified (**v 25**). John 19:14 mentions that it was about the sixth hour when Jesus was presented to the crowd. Does Mark start with the whipping and mocking in giving the time and see the entire suffering as part of the event?[745] He does divide the day into three-hour segments (Mark 15:33–34 – sixth and ninth hours). The inscription, known as the *titulus*, listed the charge: "the king of the Jews" (**v 26**).[746] The *titulus* is not only descriptive, but also ironic, because those who crucified Jesus for this reason rejected the claim. John 19:20 has the charge noted in three languages. The parallels all have slight variation, but all mention king of the Jews (Matt 27:37 – "this is Jesus, king of the Jews"; Luke 23:38 – "this is the king of the Jews"; John 19:19 – "Jesus the Nazarene the king of the Jews"). This shows the kind of variation and gist

---

743 So Evans, *Mark 8:27–16:20*, 501, who speaks of "fine" wine offered to the alleged king.

744 This is one of the more famous archeological finds dealing with the background to Jesus' death. On this find, Joe Zias and James Charlesworth, "CRUCIFIXION: Archaeology, Jesus and the Dead Sea Scrolls," in *Jesus and the Dead Sea Scrolls*, ed. James Charlesworth (New York: Doubleday, 1993), 279–80.

745 Lane, *Mark*, 567, claims this verse is a later gloss, but there is no solid evidence for this. It is better to see Mark as referring to all of these Roman events as when the crucifixion started. Stein, *Mark*, 712–13, suggests that if the real hour were between the third and sixth hours, estimates of time could go in either direction, given that the three-hour increments for time were most common.

746 E. Bammel, "The *Titulus*," in *Jesus and the Politics of His Day*, ed. E. Bammel and C. F. D. Moule (Cambridge: Cambridge University Press, 1984), 353–64.

common in passing on tradition. The description "king of the Jews" is of Roman origin and not a Christian creation. It is the way Herod was described by Josephus (*Ant* 14.280; 15.409; *War* 1.282–85). Christians preferred Messiah or Son of God, possibly because "king" said too little.[747] Matt 27:37 has it placed above Jesus' head. Jesus is executed for sedition, claiming to be a king Rome did not appoint. This has messianic implications. It shows that the attachment of messianism to Jesus was not a post-Easter phenomenon as some claim.[748] Jesus was not executed merely for being a prophetic figure, but for claiming to be the answer to a promise from God beyond the empire.

Jesus is crucified with two outlaws or, more likely, insurrectionists, one on his right and the other to his left (**v 27**).[749] They probably were much like Barabbas (*lēstas* – Mark 14:48; 15:7; John 18:40).

Mark describes in succession three sets of taunters. First, Jesus was mocked by observers, who wagged their heads and slandered him as he died (**v 29**). The text speaks of blasphemy, which is slander (*blasphēmeō* – BDAG, 178; Mark 2:7; 3:28–29). Jesus had been charged with blasphemy by the leadership in Mark 14:64, so the use of the verb is ironic. The real blasphemy for Mark is in slandering Jesus. By wagging their heads, Ps 22:7 is invoked (on wagging heads as a sign of derision – Ps 109:25; Lam 2:15; Jer 18:16). The allusion points to Jesus as a righteous sufferer. Some recall the false claim to destroy the temple and rebuild it in three days (Mark 14:58). They see the alleged claim as an empty one. They call on him to save himself and come down from the cross (**v 30**). Implicit is the idea that one who claims to be king and deliver people on God's behalf cannot suffer crucifixion. Ironically, for Mark, saving is exactly what Jesus was doing, just not himself but others (Mark 10:45 – a ransom for many). As for disqualification, that depends on whether God vindicates him or not.

Second, the chief priests and scribes mocked him (**v 31**).[750] A second term (*empaizō*) is used here (BDAG, 323). It means to ridicule or make fun

---

[747] Evans, *Mark 8:27–16:20*, 503–504, has the discussion defending the historicity of this detail. He notes that having the charge accompany the victim is described by Suetonius, *Caligula* 32.2, and *Domitian* 10:1 ad Dio Cassius 54.3.6–7 and 73.16.5.

[748] Correctly, Witherington, *Mark*, 396.

[749] Lane, *Mark*, 568. Mark 15:28 is not likely to have been original in Mark. It reads, "And the Scripture was fulfilled that said, 'He was counted among those who were rebels.'" It is basically a Byzantine reading, with Alexandrian and Western texts (א, A, B, C, D) lacking it. It likely is a harmonization with Luke 22:37 that cites Isa 53:12.

[750] Collins, *Mark*, 749–51, is skeptical about much of this taunting, especially by the chief priests, claiming that they would have avoided such a sordid scene. However, if they pushed for this result, their attendance to see the result of their efforts, and to make a

of someone. They also claimed that he saved others, alluding to his miraculous work, but cannot save himself. So come down, King of Israel, so
they may see and believe was their taunt (v 32). The attitude is like Wis 2:18,
where God will help the righteous one who is God's son by providing rescue
from one's opponents. Wis 2:17 asks for visual proof that God is at work.[751]
The allusion to seeing may recall Jesus' remark about their seeing the Son of
Man seated at God's right hand and riding the clouds (Mark 14:62). Jesus
was predicting a vindication with this remark, even if they sentenced him.
The lack of response when Jesus is vindicated shows this current taunt was
nothing more than sarcasm. The vindication by resurrection is God's
answer in support of a claim like that made in the Wis 2 text.

Third, even those crucified with him abused him as he was dying. Yet a
third term appears here (*oneidizō* – BDAG, 710, revile). The array of verbs
means that all disrespected him in every way. Mark does not have any
indication of one of the thieves coming to faith as in Luke 23:40–43.
Matthew and John say nothing about any abuse from those crucified
with Jesus. In Mark, Jesus suffers with everyone around him mocking
him. Edwards calls it a "chorus of scorn."[752] For Mark, they are all missing
what God is doing.

Mark has run through a fairly summarized version of the events that
took place from the morning to the afternoon. The presence of cosmic
signs and the end causes him to slow down. At noon darkness fell over the
area for three hours (v 33). Creation reflects an apocalyptic darkness
pointing to judgment (Exod 10:21–22; Deut 28:29; Isa 13:10; Joel 2:10;
Amos 8:9–10).[753] Philo (*Providence* 2.50) spoke of such darkness as

---

[751] point that this is what happens to people who make such claims and to those who
critique how the leaders run things, would not have been at all unexpected. The
skepticism about such taunting and the amount of Markan creation she sees is excessive.
Edwards, *Mark*, 473–74.
[752] Edwards, *Mark*, 473.
[753] One should not press the language too much. It points to a reaction in the heavens
that was atypical of this time of day. The *Gospel of Peter* 5:15 speaks of darkness on all
of Judea. Marcus, *Mark 8–16*, 1054, observes that this is not a description of some
natural phenomenon like a solar eclipse, which was not possible at a full moon, or a
wind storm of some type. Against this is the suggestion of Colin Humphreys and
W. G. Waddington, "The Jewish Calendar, A Lunar Eclipse and the Date of Christ's
Crucifixion," *Tyndale Bulletin* 43 (1992): 331–51, that a lunar eclipse is the point, while
arguing for a date of April 3, 33, as the date for this event. Humphreys and
Waddington have to explain Luke 23:45 and its seeming mention of a solar eclipse
to make their claim. The debate may press the language too much. Luke's reference
may not be to an eclipse but simply to a very dark day.

indicating the death of a king or the destruction of a city.[754] Ancients paid attention to such signs.

At 3:00, Jesus cried out to God, invoking Ps 22:1 in its Aramaic form, asking why God had forsaken him, which Mark interprets into Greek for his audience (**v 34**). It is the only saying Mark has from the cross. The shepherd is struck (Zech 13:7 in Mark 14:27). Mark cites the words of Ps 22 and translates them to point to this scene's importance, but the earlier allusion to Zechariah in Mark 14:27 points to its significance. In the abandonment, Jesus senses the pain of what he is enduring. Collins points out that this is not the noble quiet death of a Socrates, Eleazar of 2 Macc 6:30 and chapter 7, or the later portrayal of Polycarp in the account of his martyrdom (chaps. 4, 15–16).[755] Mark does invoke a psalm that ends with a note of trust in God (Ps 22:22–31) and expects vindication, but what he highlights in the citation is the sense of distance Jesus is experiencing. This explains why Jesus was so concerned at Gethsemane. The moment was terrifying. Cranfield says it this way: "the cry [is] to be understood in the light of 14:36, 2 Cor. 5:21, Gal. 3:13. The burden of the world's sin, his complete self-identification with sinners, involved not merely a felt, but a real, abandonment by his Father. It is in the cry of dereliction that the full horror of man's sin stands revealed."[756] The depth of the disruption shows the reality of the experience.

Those hearing Jesus' cry thought that Jesus had called for Elijah to deliver him (**v 35**). This makes the listeners with this response likely to have been Jews, given that Jesus had spoken a Semitic language and Elijah was a Jewish hope.[757] Elijah was held to be a protector of the innocent tied to the eschaton (Sir 48:10). The reaction of the heavens may have led to attention being drawn to Elijah along with Jesus' utterance.

Someone offers him sour wine on a stick (**v 36**). We are not told whether it was a solider or bystander. This was wine vinegar, a favorite beverage of the lower ranks of society (BDAG, 715; Plutarch, *Cato Major* 1.7 – what one drank for a raging thirst). Ps 69:21, another righteous sufferer psalm, is evoked. The offer comes with an additional prospect – might Elijah come

---

[754] Lane, *Mark*, 571. Other examples are in Diogenes Laertius 4.64 – moon darkens at death of Carneades; Plutarch, *Caesar* 69.3–5; Virgil, *Georgics* 1.463–68 – sun hid its face at Caesar's death; Evans, *Mark 8:27–16:20*, 506. Collins, *Mark*, 752, adds Romance of Alexander 3.33.5 for similar phenomena.

[755] Collins, *Mark*, 754.

[756] Cranfield, *Mark*, 548.

[757] Cranfield, *Mark*, 459.

to rescue him?[758] John 19:30 seems to have him take this offer. Was it an effort to refresh him and prolong his life? It is hard to know whether the act was sympathetic or another example of mockery. The latter is especially possible given how negative most of the crowd has been in Mark.[759] Then Jesus cries out a final time and takes his final breath (**v 37**).

The temple curtain is ripped in two from top to bottom as Jesus dies (**v 38**). Mark describes yet another response from creation, alongside the darkness. Matthew 27:51–53 adds a reference to an earthquake. This curtain could be the one tied to the Holy Place (Exod 26:37) or the one leading into the Holy of Holies (Exod 26:31). The term used (*to katapetasma*) is used in the LXX of the veil before the Holy of Holies (Exod 26:31–37), yet the outer veil would be a more public event, being the more visible veil.[760] So it is not clear which is meant. These curtains were at least 55 cubits high, or 81 feet tall.[761] The symbolic meaning of the act is debated. Was it to signal the temple's destruction?[762] Or was it a sign that access to God had been opened up as the heavens split (Mark 1:10), since the curtain prevented entrance to some?[763] Or might it be both?[764] It is unlikely the sign was strictly negative. Jesus' act has both positive and negative results, so a sign going both ways is more likely. The temple is opened so that this holy place is judged and left empty, but the Spirit is now free to traverse the earth. The event is uncorroborated, but there is a curious later tradition in Judaism that during the last forty years before the Temple's demise, the sanctuary doors would open by themselves (*b. Yoma* 39b).

The frantic sequence of events marks the final moments of Jesus' death. Mockers have spoken, and now creation speaks. One is supposed to hear the groaning that represents. The passage asks what kind of deliverer

---

[758] On the syntax with the verb *aphete*, BDAG, 157, 5b. It renders into "Let us leave it and see," so "Let us see."

[759] Marcus, *Mark 8–16*, 1056; Collins, *Mark*, 755–56, adds that Elijah is already tied to John the Baptist by Mark. One can add that for Mark, Jesus' vindication is God's business. So an appeal to Elijah is seen as misguided at best and sarcastic at the worst.

[760] Evans, *Mark 8:27–16:20*, 509. Hooker, *Mark*, 377, notes Josephus uses the same word to compare both veils (*Ant* 8.75).

[761] France, *Mark*, 656.

[762] As France, *Mark*, 657, Evans, *Mark 8:27–16:20*, 509, and some of the Fathers (Tertullian *Against Marcion* 4.42) argue; see Lane, *Mark*, 575.

[763] John Nolland, *Luke*, 1157–58, discussing the parallel.

[764] See my own discussion in *Luke 9:51–24:53*, 1861; Hooker, *Mark*, 377–78, cites Heb 9:11–12, 24–28, and 10:19–20 as evidence of a positive image and notes a story of the temple doors opening on their own as a comparison (Josephus, *War*, 6.293; also *War* 5.212 and 219 use it of both). She notes that the next verse in Mark 15:39 points to doors opened to Gentiles (Eph 2:14).

would be hanging and dying on a cross. The answer is one whose actions cause creation to shudder, one through whom God is working out his plan. Lane remarks, "The meaning of his death becomes clear only from the perspective of the triumph of resurrection which marked his vindication and demonstrated that death had no claim on him."[765] Jesus does not come down from the cross to escape sin and death. He is taken up from it to continue in the sacrificial task he had undertaken.

A centurion, seeing the cosmic sign of darkness and having heard the cries of pain, reads the signs he sees (**v 39**).[766] Seeing how Jesus died, he declares, "Truly this man was God's Son." He senses that Jesus has died as an innocent. It is the first such confession by a person in Mark. Luke 23:43 has the confession that Jesus was innocent/righteous, making the same point.[767] This is the climactic confession of the crucifixion and of the book. It matches the titles in 1:1 (and 1:11). This soldier, neutral or even initially hostile in his view of Jesus, saw all that transpired and recognized Jesus' unique relationship to God. Jesus was not merely king of the Jews; he had some special connection to God. If Jesus is innocent, that has implications for his claims.

The soldier was probably the centurion in charge of the execution. Mark uses a Latin loan word to describe the solider (*kēnturiōn*, meaning "centurion"; BDAG, 540). In contrast to all the mockery by the Jewish leaders and others, this Gentile saw what was going on. Apparently the final words, the darkness, and Jesus' shout were what convinced him that they had killed one who was what he claimed to be. For Jesus to be strong enough to shout at the end of a crucifixion was unusual. How much the centurion actually understood of what he confessed is debated, as he likely would not have had the background to know much more than that Jesus was a divinely enabled, commissioned King.[768] Still, his confession was more than a contradiction to the death sentence Jesus had received. Jesus was innocent and a king. The fuller meaning of the title "Son of God" was clear to Mark's readers (1:1, 11; 3:11; 5:7; 9:7; 12:6; 13:32; 14:61–62). At the end of

---

[765] Lane, *Mark*, 574.

[766] Hooker, *Mark*, 378, reads the text as claiming the centurion is only responding to how Jesus died and as excluding the signs, making a contrast to Matt 27:54. However, how Jesus died includes all that came with the death; Collins, *Mark*, 765, " a response to one or more omens." He would not have seen a torn curtain from where he was in Jerusalem. The combination of Jesus on the cross and darkness is what is in view, so, correctly, France, *Mark*, 658.

[767] Edwards, *Mark*, 479.

[768] Evans, *Mark 8:27–16:20*, 510.

everything, a Gentile is the person who is most spiritually sensitive to what is taking place. Mark wants his readers to appreciate what the centurion sees. The one executed was seen by one of his executioners as executing the will of God.

Among those watching from a distance were three female disciples: Mary Magdalene (Luke 8:2), Mary the mother of James the younger and Joses, and Salome (**v 40**). Salome may be the mother of the sons of Zebedee (Matt 27:56). We know nothing else about the other Mary tied to James and Joses, but she apparently was known to Mark's audience and could have been the wife of Clopas (John 19:25) or James, the son of Alphaeus (Mark 3:18). A problem in identifying the person is how common the name Mary was. She is not Mary, the mother of Jesus, because if it were her, she likely would not be described this way.

The note about the women is made with a sense that they were among the witnesses to some of what took place. These women had followed Jesus in Galilee and had supported him in the ministry (**v 41**). They were faithful witnesses. In a culture where women were undervalued, this note is significant.[769] The remark here is like Luke 8:1–3 that also discusses support for Jesus by women, but Mark has delayed mention of women who are praised until this last week (the woman who anoints Jesus in Mark 14:3–9, these women, and those who go to the tomb).[770] The remark also notes that these women were not alone. Other unspecified women who had come with him to Jerusalem were among them. So, Jesus is crucified, suffering abandonment, garnering a reaction from creation, and a confession from a solider, with the events witnessed from a distance by female disciples.

15:42–47 Jesus Is Buried by Joseph of Arimathea in a Tomb Two Women Observed

> **15:42** Now it was already evening, since it was the day of preparation, which is the day before the Sabbath.
>
> **15:43** Joseph of Arimathea, a highly regarded member of the council, who also himself was looking forward to the kingdom of God, went to Pilate and asked for the body of Jesus.
>
> **15:44** Pilate was surprised that he already was dead and he called the centurion and asked him if he had been dead for some time.

---

[769] In fact, women were rarely taken to be legal witnesses (Josephus, *Ant.* 4.219; *m Roš HaŠ.* 1:8; *m Šebu. 4:1*), so this detail is quite historical. It would not have been invented.

[770] France, *Mark*, 661–62.

15:45 When Pilate was informed by the centurion, he gave the body to Joseph.

15:46 After Joseph bought a linen cloth and took down the body, he wrapped it in the linen and placed it in a tomb cut out of rock. And he rolled a stone across the entrance of the tomb.

15:47 Mary Magdalene and Mary the mother of Joses saw where it was buried.

This scene summarizes Jesus' burial. It is noted in all four Gospels. The parallels are Matt 27:57–61, Luke 23:50–56, and John 19:38–42.

It was the day before the Sabbath when Jesus died, a Friday (v 42). Evening had come on what is called the day of preparation. Since nothing gets done on the Sabbath, and burials usually took place on the day of the death; any burial had to take place quickly. This was true even of the burial of criminals (Deut 21:23). Joseph of Arimathea had acted on Jesus' behalf (v 43). He is named in all four Gospels (Matt 27:57; Luke 23:51; John 19:38). Arimathea is probably Ramathaim, some 20 miles northwest from Jerusalem (Josephus, *Ant* 13.127). He was a highly regarded man of the council. He was one who looked forward to the kingdom of God, indicating he was open to Jesus if not a follower. Matt 27:57 and John 19:38 call him a disciple. Luke 23:51 said he did not agree with the council's decision.

He went to Pilate to ask for Jesus' body. It is part of Jewish tradition that a criminal not be buried in a family tomb (*m Sanh* 6:5). Mark says that he was bold or had courage (*tolmēsas*) in making the request (BDAG, 1010). To speak up for the executed man was a risk. In addition, in Roman law someone executed had no rights. The magistrate controlled the burial (Tacitus, *Annals* 6.29). Normally bodies were left to rot or tossed aside to be eaten by predatory birds (Horace, *Epistles* 1, 16, 48; Petronias, *Satura* 111).[771] Sometimes family members did get the body (Plutarch, *Antonius* 2; Cicero, *Philippian Orations* II.vii.17; Philo, *Flaccus* 10.83). Joseph hoped to bury Jesus. Jewish piety held that bodies should be treated with respect and viewed burial as an act of respect (2 Sam. 21:12–14; Tob 1:17–19; 2:3–7; 12:12–13; Sir 7:33; 38:16; Josephus, *War* 3.377 – Jews even bury our enemies).[772] Joseph shows common Jewish pious respect for Jesus, but his motive appears to have been more than just that.

---

[771] Lane, *Mark*, 578.
[772] Lane, *Mark*, 578.

Pilate expressed surprise that Jesus was already dead (**v 44**). Such execution could take several hours or even more than a day.[773] So he asked the centurion if Jesus had been dead for some time.[774] Did the centurion accompany Joseph when he made his request? Had Joseph started with him? Is this the same centurion who had just confessed Jesus in verse 39? It looks as though that is possible in Mark's understanding. The centurion told Pilate Jesus was dead, and so the prefect gave Jesus' body to Joseph (**v 45**). Literally the text says that Pilate gifted or bestowed (*dōreomai*) the body to Joseph (BDAG, 266). It was in his care to do with what he wished.

So Joseph bought a long linen (*sindoni*) cloth (BDAG, 924), wrapped the body in it, and placed it in a tomb hewn from rock that had a large stone covering the entrance, a family tomb usually of fairly wealthy vintage (**v 46**).[775] Matt 27:60 says that it was his own new tomb. It is debated whether someone from Arimathea would have had a tomb in Jerusalem, but it cannot be known whether this council member now lived in Jerusalem, explaining why his tomb was new, or whether he, like other pious Jews, had wished to be buried in Jerusalem.[776] If later Mishnaic practice is a guide, the tomb had to be 50 cubits, or about 75 feet, from the city wall (*m B. Bat* 2:9).[777] Normal financial exchange did not take place on a feast day, so this would have been arranged to be paid later (*m Shab* 23:1).[778] This kind of arrangement may also have applied to the women buying spices in Mark 16:1. Sometimes special circumstances allowed for exceptions. Everything was done quickly to complete the task before the Sabbath arrived.[779]

---

[773] Hengel, *Crucifixion*, 29–31.

[774] There is a textual problem here with the alternative reading (B, D, W) asking if Jesus was already dead, a simpler reading. The harder reading is more likely here – Jesus had been dead for a time (so ℵ, A, C, L).

[775] If one goes just by the King David Hotel in Jerusalem, one can see an example of such a tomb from Herod's family. After a year, the bones would have been moved to an ossuary (a bone box) and could have been shifted to a family tomb. This practice ceased after the first century.

[776] Evans, *Mark 8:27–16:20*, 520, notes the debate; France, *Mark*, 669.

[777] Edwards, *Mark*, 489–90.

[778] Hooker, *Mark*, 381.

[779] There is some discussion of whether the burial is done in a way that pictures dishonor, whether it reflects haste, or whether Mark has simply summarized and not mentioned all the details. Collins, *Mark*, 779, opts for haste. Evans, *Mark 8:27–16:20*, 520, argues for a dishonorable burial. I prefer the third option. Things were done quickly and Jesus' burial in a non-family tomb is a matter of shame, but it also is likely Mark has summarized and not noted every possible detail; France, *Mark*, 668, cites *m Shab* 23:5 as evidence that the

Common *loculus* tombs were 2 by 2 by 6 feet, or they could be a vault of 6 by 9 feet (*m B. Bat* 6:8).[780] The covering stone for such a tomb could be 5 or 6 feet in diameter, be rectangular or circular, and weigh 500 to 3,000 pounds.[781] It was set in a groove but still was difficult to move without multiple people present to help. Joseph put the body in the tomb and rolled the stone to cover the entrance. The reality of the move suggests that Joseph did not do all of this alone, but had servants, at least, to help him.[782] John 19:39–40 has Joseph and Nicodemus anoint the body with spices, but Mark makes no mention of this. No mention is made of the other criminals, as they are of no concern to Mark.[783]

Mary Magdalene and Mary the mother of Joses saw where the body was placed (**v 47**). Two witnesses verified that Jesus was quite dead and very buried. Scripture notes the use of women as witnesses, a status they often lacked in the custom of the culture.

16:1–8 The Angelic Announcement of a Raised Jesus Leaves Three Women Speechless and Fearing as They Are Told to Tell the Disciples to Meet Jesus in Galilee

16:1 And when the Sabbath was over, Mary Magdalene, Mary the mother of James, and Salome bought aromatic spices so they might go and anoint him.

16:2 And very early on the first day of the week, after sunrise, they came to the tomb.

16:3 And they were asking each other, "Who will roll away the stone for us from the entrance to the tomb?"

16:4 And looking up, they saw that the stone, which was very large, had been rolled away.

16:5 And coming into the tomb, they saw a young man dressed in a white robe sitting on the right side and they were alarmed.

---

washing of a body by a pious Jew, if not an anointing, was likely to have taken place. Later accounts serve to supplement those features. The idea that Jesus was left to rot is less than persuasive, not just because of Jewish sensibilities to the uncleanness of dying bodies left overnight, but also because if such an end were well known, the kerygma about an empty tomb never could have gotten off the ground in Jerusalem to gain credibility for the message that was preached early on.

[780] Marcus, *Mark 8–16*, 1071–72; Edwards, *Mark*, 490.
[781] Evans, *Mark 8:27–16:20*, 535; Marcus, *Mark 8–16*, 1072.
[782] Lane, *Mark*, 580.
[783] Speculation based on their absence simply ignores that Mark is summarizing here, not giving an exhaustive account.

16:6 But he said to them, "Do not be alarmed. You are looking for Jesus the Nazarene, who was crucified. He is raised. He is not here. Look, there is the place where they laid him.

16:7 But go and tell his disciples and Peter that he is going ahead of you into Galilee. You will see him there, just as he told you."

16:8 And going out, they ran from the tomb, for trembling and amazement had seized them. And they said nothing to anyone, for they were afraid.

The account of the empty tomb leads to the declaration of resurrection and the reaction to it. The parallels to this part of the Markan account are Matt 28:1–8, Luke 24:1–11, and John 20:1, 11–12. Resurrection for a Jew involves a physical dimension, whether expressed in body terms or in a glorified form like the angels (Dan 12:2 – awake from the dust of the earth; 2 Macc 7:10–11 – prospective martyr expects to get his physical body back; *1 En* 39:4–7; 104:2–6 – like angels; 1 Cor 15:1–58 – on analogy with Jesus, physical and glorified).[784] The issue of historicity in a resurrection is a major worldview challenge for many. How this scene is evaluated is directly related to that worldview question. Those for whom resurrection is impossible or unlikely will by default relegate these accounts into a non-real category when evaluating them as genuine events. Those open to divine activity in the world will take a different tack and remain open to the historical possibilities.[785]

It is important to note that how a Jewish movement came to teach and preach an executed messianic claimant is a dilemma that a non-resurrection approach to the passage has trouble answering. There was no teaching or expectation of a dead Messiah, much less one who would

---

[784] Collins, *Mark*, 781–94, has a full excursus on Jewish and Greco-Roman views of resurrection. She places Mark 16 in line with Jewish expectations of a raised physical but transformed body. She claims this is a distinct view from Paul, but this seems exaggerated. If the Transfiguration is any guide in Mark 9:1–8, then Mark's view echoes that of Paul, as Jesus appears with a glorified body in a preview of what is to come.

[785] There is a complex question of how to treat resurrection claims and historicity as well. Is history even capable of rendering such an evaluation? Robert Webb, "The Historical Enterprise and Historical Jesus Research," in Bock and Webb, *Key Events*, 9–93, esp. 39–54, takes a close look at the philosophical and historiographical issues tied up in this discussion. He discusses three models: Ontological Naturalistic History, which views resurrection as impossible; Methodological Naturalistic History, which says history can make no judgment for such a claim, even though such an event could be real; and Critical Theistic History, which is open to saying that such events are historical. Webb opts for the second camp. I prefer the third.

rise from the dead.[786] So the creation of this category is an anomaly. The resort to some type of a shared psychological experience of a living Jesus has much to overcome in terms of getting to such a community consensus. It is more likely that an original defining event triggered the new categories of teaching, preaching, and hope. This is the one event all four Gospels cover in their resurrection accounts.

Interestingly, and counterculturally, it is rooted in the testimony of women. The church never would have created such a scenario to carry their core resurrection claims. Selling a difficult idea (resurrection) through the testimony of people (women) who do not count culturally as witnesses was not a plan designed in some budding church leaders' conference room to turn around a discouraged community.[787] The women are in the account because they were in the event.

When the Sabbath day had passed, Mary Magdalene, Mary the mother of James, and Salome, the women of Mark 15:40, buy aromatic spices to anoint the body and pay honor to the dead Jesus (v 1; 2 Chron 16:14; *m Shab* 23:5). This would have been Saturday evening. Whether they are doing something they thought had not been done or are simply acting to honor

---

[786] M. Hengel, *Studies in Early Christology* (Edinburgh: T & T Clark 1995), 12–14, points vividly to a twofold problem if Jesus did not place himself in a messianic category: (1) there was no analogy for a resurrected Messiah, so (2) exaltation does not generate messiahship. It had to be there beforehand and was not invented to make Jesus into something he had not raised himself. In fact, Hengel (14) goes on to say that such a scenario is not believable: "if the eleven disciples with Peter at their head, on the basis of appearances so difficult for us to comprehend, and completely unprompted, reached the view that Jesus was Son of Man exalted to God, knowing in reality he had been merely a simple proclaimer of the imminent kingdom of God, a rabbi and a prophet knowing nothing at all of eschatological offices, dignities and titles, did they not completely falsify the pure (and so unmythologically modern sounding) intention of their master?" In other words, the resurrection does not establish a messiahship where no impetus for its existence previously existed. Nor can messiahship explain why we discuss resurrection. As Witherington, *Mark*, 411, says "nothing less than an appearance of Jesus could serve to reform the scattered and frightened disciples, either the women or the men. This is to say, nothing less than an eschatological act of God, a miracle, founded or refounded the community of Jesus." For a full study of resurrection in the Greco-Roman and Jewish context, N. T. Wright, *The Resurrection of the Son of God* (Minneapolis: Fortress, 2003), esp. 210–11, 372–74, 685–718. He emphasizes how a resurrected figure functioning within history and dividing it before a general resurrection at the end of time is a doctrinal innovation/mutation and that the empty tomb and meetings together form the only sufficient cause of the community's teaching on resurrection. For discussion of resurrection, empty tomb, and historicity issues, G. Osborne, "Jesus' Empty Tomb and His Appearance in Jerusalem," in Bock and Webb, *Key Events*, 775–823.

[787] On women not being witnesses, see *m Sheb* 1:8 – "an oath of testimony applies to men not women" and *m Rosh Hash* 1:8 – "any evidence a woman is not eligible to bring."

Jesus in their own way in light of an act like Mark 14:3–9 is not said. They clearly expect him to be dead and there, as they go to lay "another wreath" on the tomb.[788] This kind of activity for the dead was allowed on days like the Sabbath and likely for feast days (*m Shab* 23:5). The spices dealt with the stench of a dead corpse. For Mark, Jesus' body had already been anointed (Mark 14:3–9), but the women simply go to the tomb to honor Jesus in their own way.

Early in the morning, after the sun rose on Sunday, they went to the tomb (**v 2**). The double temporal reference fits Mark's habit of repeating himself (Mark 1:32–34; 14:12). Jesus is raised on the third day, counting inclusively (Mark 8:31–32). Their one concern was how they would get the stone rolled away (**v 3**). Everything changes when they arrive at the tomb and find their concern about the stone has already been addressed.[789]

On their arrival, they saw the very large stone rolled back (**v 4**). Most stones on ancient tombs were rectangular in shape, but those of the wealthy could be rounded.[790] Mark does not reveal a shape here, but the idea of rolling more likely points to a rounded stone. Mark gives no detail as to how this took place, giving yet more evidence of how summarizing an account he is giving. Matt 28:2 speaks of an angel doing the work with an accompanying earthquake.

On entering the tomb to investigate, they saw a young man dressed in a white robe sitting on the right side (**v 5**).[791] They were astounded and alarmed to see him. They had no expectation of what they were seeing. The robe suggests an angel, given the parallel tradition of the other Synoptics. In Judaism, angels were described as young men (2 Macc 3:26, 33; 10:29–31; 11: 8–12; Josephus, *Ant* 5.277), and so also in the OT (Gen 18:2, 16, 22; 19:1; Jdg 13:6).[792] The picture of white also echoes the glorified bodies of Mark 9:3 and Rev 7:9, 13 and 10:1 of angels (OT and Judaism: Dan 7:9; 1 En 62:15–16; 87:2). This is not likely to be a human who beat the women to the tomb, as there is no such figure in the listing of male witnesses to resurrection in 1 Cor 15:3–8. In other witness scenes

---

[788] So Witherington, *Mark*, 413.

[789] Three details in Matthew's account in 27:62–66 and 28:2–4 have no role in Mark. He makes no mention of an earthquake in the rolling way of the stone or of an angel's role in that event. Nor does Mark mention the prospect of guards being present at the tomb.

[790] A. Kloner, "Did a Rolling Stone Close Jesus' Tomb?" *BAR* 25.5 (1999): 22–29, 76.

[791] The idea that this is a rehabilitation of the naked young man of Mark 14 is unlikely, if one sees an angel here as opposed to a human. If the parallels to the empty tomb point to the same figure, then an angel is meant.

[792] France, *Mark*, 679; Marcus, *Mark 8–16*, 1080, who notes Acts 1:9–11 in the NT.

in the Gospel, those participants are named. This is a figure who knows what has taken place and announces it to show heaven's perspective on the events.

The surprise visitor addresses them, telling them not to be alarmed (v 6). He knows they are looking for Jesus the Nazarene, who was crucified, but he is raised. The passive verb looks to God doing the raising. So Jesus is not to be found. There is no body to anoint. If they look at the place in the tomb where his body was left, it is empty. The same Jesus who was buried now is raised. There is continuity between the historical earthly Jesus and the raised, vindicated Jesus.[793] In all the Gospels, the women are the first witnesses of the proclamation of the new movement delivered from heaven. This is not a vision, but a concrete event.

So they are to go and tell the disciples, including Peter, who had denied him, that Jesus has gone ahead of them into Galilee (v 7). There they will see him, just as he told them in Mark 14:28. Matt 28:16–20 has an appearance there, as does John 21. The plan and the program are at work. The vindication Jesus had predicted before the Jewish leaders had taken place. Even though the disciples had fled and abandoned Jesus, and even denied him, they have their calling renewed by Jesus in yet another act of forgiveness.

There is a tension between these Galilean appearances and the command in Luke 24:49 to remain in Jerusalem. Some see these as contradictory; however, it is important to recall that these disciples had come to Jerusalem as pilgrims to observe a feast for a week, not intending to stay. A call to launch a mission from Jerusalem would have required a trip back home to regather in Jerusalem. So Luke's "remain" in Jerusalem should not be overpressed to say more than it means. The mission will go out from Jerusalem. It will be the headquarters of the initial movement. Instruction also came in Galilee as well. Each author made choices in terms of which setting to highlight. John 20–21 had appearances in both locations.

The women ran from the tomb (v 8). They were shaking and astonished, as is common in such an encounter with a transcendent being or with abnormal power (Mark 1:21–22). Mark notes that they said nothing to anyone, for they were afraid.[794] But this is understatement. It portrays the declaration as initially shocking as a revelation from beyond, leaving

---

[793] Witherington, *Mark*, 414.
[794] The Gospel ends oddly with a *gar*. On how rare this is, though possible, Collins, *Mark*, 797–99; K. Iverson, "A Further Word on Final Γάρ (Mark 16:8)," *CBQ* (2006): 79–94.

one speechless, even seemingly disobedient, but that cannot be the end of the story. The only way anyone knows the account of what took place is if they talked. So they eventually had to have overcome their fear. It is here our current copies of Mark end, leaving readers a choice. Do they fear or move on to faith, as the women clearly did by telling their story? If the Gospel ended here, then Mark leaves the end of the story open with a note of the wonder about the event.[795] It fits other scenes where fear leads people either to walk away from God or to take a step of faith (Mark 4:40–41; 5:15–20, 34–36).[796] The question becomes what you, the reader, will do with the empty tomb and what it shows about Jesus.

A Note on Other Endings and the Conclusion of Mark

The nature of Mark's ending is a matter for discussion. It seems so abrupt to have ended here. Two famous longer endings exist: a single verse ending, and a much more extensive ending that is familiar because it was present in most older English translations as well as many manuscripts.

In fact, five endings to Mark have been preserved:

(1) The Gospel could end at 16:8, per the evidence of ℵ, B, 304, syr^s, cop^{sa}, (one MS) arm, geo (two MSS), Hesychius, Eusebius, and MSS according to Eusebius, Jerome, and Severus.

(2) The "shorter ending" of Mark 16:9 per the evidence of it^k. It reads, "They reported briefly to those around Peter all they had been commanded. After these things Jesus himself sent out through them, from the east to the west, the holy and imperishable preaching of eternal salvation. Amen."

(3) The "longer ending" of Mark 16:9–20, per the evidence of A, C, D, 037, 038, f^{33}, the Byzantine tradition, Irenaeus, Augustine, and MSS according to Eusebius, Jerome, and Severus.[797]

The longer text of 16:9–20 looks mostly like a summary of the ends of the other Gospels. It has an appearance to Mary Magdalene, who, when she

---

[795] Collins, *Mark*, 801.
[796] Lane, *Mark*, 591–92.
[797] Collins, *Mark*, 804–806, discusses how these manuscripts display this ending in some detail. J. A. Kelhoffer, *Miracle and Mission: The Authentication of Missionaries and Their Message in the Longer Ending of Mark* (Tübingen: Mohr/Siebeck, 2000), 48–156, as a full analysis of this longer ending. Eusebius, Jerome, and Severus are aware of the issue because of the difference in the manuscripts.

tells the story, is not believed (vv 9–11). This echoes John 20:11–18 and Luke 24:11.

Jesus appears to two as they travel to the country, and when they return, they are not believed (vv 12–13). This looks like an allusion to the Emmaus road (Luke 24:13–35), but with a different end.

Appearing to the eleven, he rebukes them for their lack of faith and gives them a commission to go into the world and preach the Gospel to every creature. He notes that signs will accompany their message (vv 14–18). This echoes Luke 24:38–41 and/or John 20:19, 26. The commission is a variation on Matthew's commission in Matt 28:19–20. The remarks on salvation are like John 3:18 and 36. The mention of tongues points to Acts 2:4, 10:46, whereas serpents and poison look like Acts 28:3–5. The laying on of hands for the sick parallels Acts 9:17 and 28:8.

Then Jesus is taken up into heaven to sit at God's right hand (v 19). This is an allusion to Acts 1:9–11 and the Peter's speech context at Acts 2:32–36.

The disciples go out and proclaim the gospel everywhere while the Lord works through them and confirms the word through signs (v 20). How this ending is to be evaluated is discussed later.[798]

(4) There is an alternate longer ending with an addition after 16:14 ("And they excused themselves, saying, 'This age of lawlessness and unbelief is under Satan, who does not allow the truth and power of God to prevail over the unclean things of the spirits. Therefore reveal your righteousness now' – thus they spoke to Christ. And Christ replied to them, 'The term of years of Satan's power has been fulfilled, but other terrible things draw near. And for those who have sinned I was handed over to death, that they may return to the truth and sin no more, that they may inherit the spiritual and imperishable glory of righteousness that is in heaven' "; see the NRSV[mg] and the NLT[mg]), per the evidence of W and MSS according to Jerome.

(5) Including both the shorter ending and the traditional longer ending is also possible, per the evidence of L, 044, 083, 099, 274[mg], 579, syr[h (mg)], cop (MSS), and cop[bo] (MSS).

There are basically three options: (1) one of the longer endings is original, (2) the current end is original, or (3) we have lost Mark's original ending

---

[798] Evans, *Mark 8:27–16:20*, 546–47, shows how influential Luke-Acts is on this ending, esp. Luke 24.

and it was lost very early on in the circulation of the Gospel, with none of the other extant alternate readings being that ending.

The manuscript evidence suggests that 16:8 is the original ending of Mark, given that the two earliest extant MSS (א and B) end there.[799] However, there are even more indications of this being the end of the Gospel, at least at the point of the Gospel's early circulation. Certain church fathers, such as Clement and Origen, did not know of the longer ending, whereas Eusebius, Jerome, and Severus noted its absence in most of the Gr. MSS they knew. It is also lacking in the Eusebian canons on the Gospels from the third century. Victor of Antioch in circa 500 CE noted that most copies of Mark in his time lacked the longer ending.[800] This is important evidence for its non-originality, for if it existed, there is no good explanation for their not using it.[801] Finally, Edwards observes how many new words we have in these short final additions: in the one-verse shorter ending, we have none, and in the longer ending, we have eighteen.[802] He also notes that some of the syntax is unlike the rest of the Gospel. So the hard, external evidence we have is for the ending at Mark 16:8. The ending can make sense in light of themes in Mark, as the exposition noted, and in light of the gospel tradition as a whole. It is not required that a gospel have an appearance at the end.

However, many find the ending at 16:8 so abrupt that they suggest that the original ending of Mark has been lost or that this ending was not Mark's original intention.[803] Even if 16:8 did not originally conclude this Gospel, there still is no clear support for a longer ending other than these factors: (1) the stylistic oddity of *gar* (for) ending the book,[804] and (2) the post-resurrection appearances of Jesus in Matthew and Luke, suggesting an

---

799   Lane, *Mark*, 591–92.
800   Marcus, *Mark 8–16*, 1089.
801   France, *Mark*, 685–87.
802   Edwards, *Mark*, 498–99. On syntax and words, the form of *parēngelmena*, *hieron* as an adjective, and the following syntactical constructions: *meta tauta*, *Kyrios Iēsous*, *meta to lalēsai*, *tois met' autou genomenois*. This ending is old, however: *Epistula Apostolorum* 9–10 (c. 145), perhaps Justin Martyr (*Apol* 1.45; c. 155), Tatian's *Diatessaron* (c. 170), and Irenaeus (*Adv Haer* 3.9–12; c. 180); Hengel *Studies in Mark*, 71, 167–69. This makes it likely that it existed by the early second century and gives it some value as to what some second-century believers claimed about the resurrection. Hengel ties it to the Papias and Ignatius period.
803   France, *Mark*, 684; Evans, *Mark 8:27–16:20*, 538–39.
804   There are examples of books ending with *gar*, but it is rare; P. W. van der Horst, "Can a Book End with a ΓΑΡ? A Note on Mark XVI.8," *JTS* 23 (1972): 121–24; S. L. Cox, *A History and Critique of Scholarship concerning the Markan Endings* (Lewiston, NY: Mellen, 1993), 223–27. Cox says he has more than a thousand examples.

appearance in the original Mark. The former is not a decisive objection, and the latter is a subjective judgment.

Several arguments for another, now lost, longer ending exist. These arguments are presented in more detail with assessment because many scholars do hold that the original ending has been lost.[805]

First, there is the claim that the fulfilment of the resurrection is not well accounted for by the Mark 16:8 ending. But the statement "he is risen" is in the account (Mark 16:6), so it is hard to make much of this argument.

Second, Matt 28:8 and 10, Luke 24:9–11, and John 20:1, 11–18 all report the women telling the disciples about the empty tomb, indicating a tradition that reported the women speaking about what took place. This observation is correct; the question is only whether Mark, being likely the first evangelist to write, took this path. We have examples of Gospel writers telling us things with unique detail that one sees that the other Gospels cover at least in general. However, in a world full of editorial choices, it is hard to know what to make of a "he must have had this event" argument. Sometimes a writer goes a different direction. The other factor at play in this final scene is that a belief in resurrection and awareness of this larger tradition is likely in the communities to which Mark wrote. So how much does he have to say once he reports on the fact of the empty tomb, the resurrection, and its announcement? Do any of the additional scenes really add to what is affirmed here, namely, that he is raised? Finally, Mark has previewed what is to come in the Transfiguration appearance of Mark 9:1–8. There we see Jesus in a glorified state, so his Gospel is not without an indication of what resurrection meant for Jesus.

Third, the existence of the shorter and longer endings point to copyist dissatisfaction with Mark's ending at 16:8. This is correct, but could well be influenced by the rest of the Gospel tradition that did have appearances, making this argument a variation of the last one. So the claim tied to this argument – that we are seeing ancients react to Mark's abrupt and finding it inadequate – is also probably influenced by the comparison to other Gospel endings, thus coloring the judgment about how short Mark's ending is.

---

[805] Stein, *Mark*, 733–37, and France, *Mark*, 670–74, 683–84, who notes Mark may never have finished it, which raises the question of why it was sent out then. France is certainly correct that the decision here is a matter of a decision rooted in "literary and theological taste" and that "how else Mark might have intended to finish the book, and of why the text as we have it has no such ending, is speculative" (673). Also holding to this view are Edwards, *Mark*, 501–504, Evans, *Mark 8:27–16:20*, 538–39, Witherington, *Mark*, 416–18, and esp. Gundry, *Mark*, 1009–12.

Fourth, the appearances were an integral part of early church preaching (1 Cor. 15:5–8; Acts 1:3–11, 22; 2:32; 3:15; 10:41; 13:31). It makes it hard to think Mark would omit them. This is argument two repeated, only now with considerations from Acts and the epistles added. What this shows is that the shorter reading is the harder text. Is it too hard? That is the real question. The judgment call tied with this question is why opinion is so divided on it.

Fifth, some claim the explanations given for why Mark 16:8 ends as it does would not have been convincing to first-century readers and reflect a more modern kind of reading.[806] It is hard to know whether we know the ancient mind this well. The fact that some manuscripts survived without an addition show that, for some, this was seen and accepted as the ending. The existence of several longer versions strongly suggests that they are later additions to the abrupt ending of 16:8 or to an earlier version that had a lost, but likely shorter version of a longer ending. That the traditional longer version (16:9–20) contains mostly a combination of the other Gospels' endings also suggests its secondary character, as does its distinct vocabulary. There are numerous points of contact with the other Gospels – three with Luke, two with Matthew, two with John, and five with Acts. A response does not stop there. In fact, there has been study of open endings at a literary level in ancient materials. Jodi Lee Magness's *Marking the End: Sense and Absence in the Gospel of Mark* has surveyed ancient literature to show that open endings are not a merely modern phenomenon.[807] To note but two biblical examples, we have how Acts ends with reference to the future of Israel (Acts 28:30-31) and the end of the Prodigal Son (what did the older brother do? Luke 15:25–32). Magness speaks of fear and silence in Mark, and I have dealt with the themes of fear, faith, and choice in Mark 5:15 (the town chose fear by asking Jesus to leave), 4:41 (fear leading the disciples to ponder who Jesus is), 5:36 (Jairus is told not to fear but to believe), and 6:19–20 (Herod hesitates to act against John out of fear).[808] So these themes are present in the reading of the Gospel.

---

[806] France, *Mark*, 671–72.

[807] J. Lee Magness, *Marking the End: Sense and Absence in the Gospel of Mark* (Eugene, OR: Wipf and Stock, 2002).

[808] D. L. Bock, "The Ending of Mark: A Response to the Essays," in *Perspective on the Ending of Mark: 4 Views*, ed. David A. Black (Nashville: Broadman and Holman, 2008), 124–41. I am responding to four views where Dan Wallace defends a Mark 16:8 ending, Maurice Robinson opts for the long ending, J. K. Elliott opts for a lost ending, and David Black argues for a Markan supplement. The essay has much to say about method in approaching this issue.

Sixth, a Gospel with a bold start in Mark 1:1 would not end with negative responses of fear and fright.[809] The result is intolerable, with no need to be so stealthy about resurrection. This is actually a variation of the previous argument about such an ending being unsatisfying. A part of this argument says that Mark ends with the focus on the disciples, not Jesus, but that is less than a sensitive literary reading of this final scene.[810] Jesus' absence drives the unit, and Jesus' prediction in Mark 14:62 about what his vindication means allows the message of the resurrection to come through.

Seventh, there is debate on a book's ending with *gar*. Two examples seem present: Plotinus, *Ennead* 5.5 and Plato, *Protagoras* 328c. The debate is about whether these works count as books. It is clear to everyone in the debate that such an ending is rare. This point is well taken.

Eighth, the theme of a Galilean meeting in Mark 14:28 and 16:7 looks for fulfilment. This is actually a finer form of arguments 2 through 4. The claim is that this event is the only one not fulfilled in Mark. That is not correct. The prophecies about the end are not fulfilled. The case could be modified to say that, of the events that have taken place, this one alone stands unfulfilled. That claim depends in part on whether Mark was written before or after 70 CE. In addition, the existence of tradition in the church about the appearances, which surely Mark's audience had access to, means they may well have been aware of such appearance accounts, making telling that story unnecessary.

Ninth, there are points about fear that do not fit a conclusion on that point. Most Markan pericopes start rather than end on fear (Mark 5:33, 36; 6:20, 50; 9:6; 10:32; 11:32). Only 10 percent of Markan pericopes end with a *gar* (six out of sixty-six uses).[811] These observations are correct and do point to some evidence that something followed, but the question is whether this argument is persuasive enough.

So, we either have a Gospel that ended with an open ending for reader reflection at Mark 16:8,[812] or we have lost an original ending that we have not recovered. Either option is possible, but the short ending as the original is slightly preferred. On this conclusion, one should not be at all dogmatic. If a longer ending did exist, it likely would have noted an appearance in

---

[809] For Edwards, *Mark*, 501, this is the key argument.

[810] This is a response to Stein's claim, *Mark*, 737, that a short ending is too focused on the disciples.

[811] Gundry, *Mark*, 1009–12, makes these points as part of his more complete argument.

[812] With Lane, *Mark*, 591–92; Collins, *Mark*, 799; Marcus, *Mark 8–16*, 1091–96; Hooker, *Mark*, 391–94.

Galilee, and its loss must have taken place extremely early for it to have been so totally lost. That Mark did not finish his Gospel is less than likely. Had that been the case, it is more likely an ending would have been supplied as it was sent out for circulation.[813] That an original longer ending was lost also is less than likely for a work that probably would have circulated in various early copies as a key Gospel. Also to be noted is that Matthew and Luke follow Mark's passion and resurrection narrative closely and then diverge from each other afterward, pointing to an absence of anything in Mark holding them together.[814] All of this suggests that Mark 16:8 is the likely ending of the Gospel, with readers left to ponder that the tomb is empty and that the resurrection stands declared by an angel. Mark closes with the question: will one believe the cosmic act of heaven in vindicating Jesus?

---

[813]   Marcus, *Mark*, 1091. He also discusses (pp. 1091–92) and rejects the theory that the end of the manuscript was quickly lost or mutilated.

[814]   Lane, *Mark*, 601; Marcus, *Mark 8–16*, 1089.

Scripture Index

Hosea
  2, 150
  6:6, 29, 148, 222, 312
  9:10, 291
  9:16–17, 291
  11:1, 116, 228
  13:13, 324
  13:16, 327
Joel
  2:10, 328, 370
  2:28–32, 113
  2:31, 328
  3:13, 181
  3:15, 328
Amos
  1:13, 327
  2:6, 276
  3:7, 301
  4:2, 122
  5:11–12, 276
  5:21–24, 222
  8:9, 328
  8:9–10, 370
  8:9–14, 151
  9:5, 328
  9:11, 313
Jonah
  1:1–16, 184
  1:4, 184
  1:6, 185
  1:14, 185
  1:16, 186
  3:9, 185
  3:9–10, 111
Micah
  1:4, 328
  3:12, 321
  4:9–10, 324
  6:6–8, 222, 312
  7:1, 291
  7:6, 325
Nahum
  1:5, 328
  3:18, 212
Habakkuk
  1:14–17, 122
  3:6, 328
Haggai 2:6, 323
Zechariah
  1:6, 301

2:6, 329
2:10, 329
3:8, 181, 313
6:12, 181, 313, 354
7:5, 149
8:6, 276
8:19, 149
9–14, 243, 296
9:9, 288,
10:2, 212, 344
13:2, 127
13:7, 343, 350, 371
14:1–9, 287
14:3–4, 322
14:4, 322, 323, 345
Malachi
  2:13–16, 266
  3:1, 110, 207, 241, 252
  3:2–3, 249
  3:3–10, 293
  3:5, 273, 315
  4:5–6, 207, 241, 249, 252
Matthew
  1:20, 314
  3:7–9, 114
  3:7–10, 299
  3:11, 113
  3:17, 117
  4:1, 117
  4:17, 119
  4:24, 140
  5:13, 261
  5:15, 180
  5:17, 148
  5:26, 317
  5:32, 269,
  6:10, 332
  6:12, 297
  6:19–21, 274
  6:24–25, 179
  7:2, 180,
  7:6, 228
  7:21–23, 245
  8, 229
  8–12, 139
  8:3, 136
  8:5–10, 227
  8:5–13, 125, 140
  8:6, 140
  8:11, 213, 343

Subject Index